Educational Assessment of Students

EIGHTH EDITION

Educational Assessment of Students

Susan M. Brookhart
Professor Emerita, Duquesne University

Anthony J. Nitko
Professor Emeritus, University of Pittsburgh

330 Hudson Street, NY NY 10013

Director and Publisher: Kevin M. Davis
Content Producer: Janelle Rogers
Media Producer: Lauren Carlson
Portfolio Management Assistant: Casey Coriell
Executive Field Marketing Manager: Krista Clark
Executive Product Marketing Manager: Christopher Barry
Procurement Specialist: Carol Melville
Full Service Project Management: Katie Ostler, Cenveo® Publisher Services
Cover Designer: Cenveo® Publisher Services
Cover Image: Paradoxe/offset.com
Composition: Cenveo® Publisher Services
Printer/Binder: LSC Communications
Cover Printer: LSC Communications
Text Font: 11/13 Palatino LT Pro

Library of Congress Cataloging-in-Publication Data is on file with the Library of Congress.

ISBN-10:   0-13-480707-3
ISBN-13: 978-0-13-480707-2

About the Authors

Susan M. Brookhart is an independent consultant in educational assessment and Professor Emerita and former Chairperson of the Department of Educational Foundations and Leadership in the School of Education at Duquesne University. She has served on several state assessment technical advisory committees. Previous to her higher education experience, she taught both elementary and middle school. Her research interests include the role of both formative and summative classroom assessment in student motivation and achievement, the connection between classroom assessment and large-scale assessment, and grading.

Professor Brookhart was the 2007–2009 editor of *Educational Measurement: Issues and Practice*. She has served as the education columnist for *National Forum*, the journal of Phi Kappa Phi. She is a past president of the American Educational Research Association's Special Interest Group on Classroom Assessment. She was named the 2014 Jason Millman Scholar by the Consortium for Research on Educational Assessment and Teaching Effectiveness (CREATE) and is the recipient of the 2015 Samuel J. Messick Memorial Lecture Award from ETS/TOEFL.

In all, Professor Brookhart is author or coauthor of 18 books and over 70 articles and book chapters on classroom assessment, teacher professional development, and evaluation. With Anthony J. Nitko, she is the coauthor of *Assessment and Grading in Classrooms*. With the late Norman E. Gronlund, she is the coauthor of *Gronlund's Writing Instructional Objectives* (8th ed.). Some of the journals in which her research has appeared are *Applied Measurement in Education*, *Assessment in Education: Principles, Policy, & Practice*, *Educational Measurement: Issues and Practice*, *Journal of Educational Measurement*, *Journal of Educational Research*, *Oxford Review of Education*, *Review of Educational Research*, and *Teachers College Record*. She also serves on the editorial boards of *Applied Measurement in Education*, *Assessment in Education: Principles, Policy, & Practice*, *Educational Assessment*, and *Teachers College Record*.

Professor Brookhart's assessment books for practitioners include *How to Give Effective Feedback to Your Students*, *Formative Classroom Walkthroughs: How Principals and Teachers Collaborate to Raise Student Achievement* (with Connie M. Moss), *How to Assess Higher-Order Thinking Skills in Your Classroom*, *How to Use Grading to Support Learning*, *Learning Targets: Helping Students Aim for Understanding in Today's Lesson* (with Connie M. Moss), and *How to Create and Use Rubrics for Formative Assessment and Grading*.

Anthony J. Nitko is a private consultant in educational measurement and Professor Emeritus and former Chairperson of the Department of Psychology in Education at the University of Pittsburgh. His research interests include curriculum-based criterion-referenced testing, integrating testing and instruction, classroom assessment, and the assessment of knowledge and higher-order thinking skills.

Professor Nitko is author of the chapter "Designing Tests That Are Integrated with

Instruction" in the Third Edition of *Educational Measurement* and coauthor (with Susan Brookhart) of *Assessment and Grading in Classrooms*. He coauthored (with Susan Brookhart) the chapter "Strategies for Constructing Assessments of Higher-Order Thinking Skills" (2011). He also coauthored (with C. M. Lindvall) *Measuring Pupil Achievement and Aptitude* (with T-C Hsu), *Pitt Educational Testing Aids* (PETA) (a package of computer programs for classroom teachers), and (with R. Glaser) the chapter "Measurement in Learning and Instruction" in the Second Edition of *Educational Measurement*.

Professor Nitko has been Editor of the journal *Educational Measurement: Issues and Practice*, and later served as the International News Editor of this journal. He was also Editor of d'News, the AERA Division D newsletter. Some of the journals in which his research has appeared include *American Educational Research Journal*, *Applied Measurement in Education*, *Assessment in Education:*

Principles, Policy, & Practice, Educational Evaluation and Policy Analysis, Educational Measurement: Issues and Practice, Educational Technology, Journal of Educational Measurement, and *Research in Developmental Disabilities*.

Professor Nitko is a member of several professional organizations, was elected as Fellow to the American Psychological Association, served on several committees of the American Educational Research Association, was elected Secretary of AERA Division D, served on committees of the National Council on Measurement in Education, and was elected to the Board of Directors and as President of the latter.

Professor Nitko received Fulbright awards to Malawi and to Barbados. He has served as a consultant to various government and private agencies in Bangladesh, Barbados, Botswana, Egypt, Ethiopia, Indonesia, Jamaica, Jordan, Liberia, Malawi, Maldives, Namibia, Oman, Saudi Arabia, Singapore, United States, Viet Nam, and Yemen.

Brief Contents

Contents

NOTE: Every effort has been made to provide accurate and current Internet information in this book. However, the Internet and information posted on it are constantly changing, so it is inevitable that some of the Internet addresses listed in this textbook will change.

Preface

As for the previous editions, the goal of *Educational Assessment of Students*, Eighth Edition, is to help teachers and those in training to teach to improve their skills through better assessment of students. It focuses directly on the professional practices of elementary and secondary schoolteachers. This edition features:

- A continued strong emphasis on classroom assessment, both formative and summative.
- Complete coverage of the basics as well as advanced topics and topics of contemporary interest.
- Practical advice and examples of how good and poor classroom assessments affect students' learning.
- A revised chapter on standardized testing to reflect recent changes in the assessment landscape.

Educational Assessment of Students is a core text written for a first course in educational testing and constructing classroom assessments, and it serves equally as the textbook for an undergraduate course or a first graduate course in educational assessment. No formal coursework in statistics or college mathematics is necessary to understand the text.

The book provides complete coverage of educational assessment, including developing plans that integrate teaching and assessment; using formative assessment strategies and providing effective feedback to students; crafting objective, performance, and portfolio assessments; evaluating students and discussing evaluations with parents; and interpreting state-mandated tests and standardized achievement tests.

It is important in a first course that students receive a balanced treatment of the topics. Because the book is a comprehensive treatment of traditional and alternative assessments, we give examples, discuss the pros and cons, and give guidance for crafting every assessment technique that we introduce. Research is cited that supports or refutes assessment and teaching practices.

The text prepares teachers and those in training to teach as professionals. We recognize that teachers' experiences and judgments are necessary for proper and valid use of educational assessment. We do not hesitate to point out teachers' and school administrators' erroneous judgments and assessment abuses, however, where good lessons can be learned from them.

NEW AND REVISED CONTENT

In preparing this edition, we made a special effort to make it easy for the reader to apply the material to classroom practice through improved explanations, improved practical examples and illustrations, checklists, and step-by-step, how-to instructions. As with previous editions, we have written the text from the viewpoint that assessment is part of good teaching practice that helps the teacher improve students' learning. Material new to the eighth edition includes:

1. Updated information that reflects the Elementary and Secondary Education Act of 2015 and the current assessment landscape.

2. A change in the order of chapters to put the chapter on higher-order thinking before the chapter on essay questions.

3. Up-to-date discussion of published achievement tests in Chapter 16.

4. Update of websites related to assessment, including a discussion of how to access information about state testing programs on the Internet, and update of references.

MyLab EDUCATION

One of the most visible changes in the new edition, also one of the most significant, is the expansion of the digital learning and assessment resources embedded in the etext and the inclusion of MyLab in the text. MyLab for Education is an online homework, tutorial, and assessment program designed to work with the text to engage learners and to improve learning. Within its structured environment, learners practice what they learn, test their understanding, and receive feedback to guide their learning and to ensure their mastery of key learning outcomes. The MyLab portion of the new edition of *Educational Assessment of Students* is designed to bring learners more directly into the world of K-12 classrooms and to help them see the very real impact that the assessment concepts covered in the book have on learners. The materials in MyLab Education with *Educational Assessment of Students* include three types of resources.

- **Application Exercises** allow readers to practice assessment tasks like writing different types of assessment items, clearly communicating learning targets to students, interpreting standardized assessment reports, and grading.

- **Video Examples** illustrate classroom assessment in action, helping students better understand course content.

- **Self-Check Quizzes** help students assess how well they have mastered chapter learning outcomes. The multiple-choice, automatically graded quizzes provide rationales for both correct and incorrect answers.

SPECIAL FEATURES

The following special features highlight the practicality of this text:

1. Examples of how to craft classroom assessments and what they typically look like.

2. Checklists with succinct tips for evaluating the quality of each type of assessment taught in the book.

3. Strategies for assessing higher-order thinking that serve as models and descriptions for developing problem-solving and critical-thinking assessments.

4. Key concepts that serve to introduce each chapter, coupled with online MyLab exercises and videos.

5. Important terms and concepts listed at the beginning of the chapter and defined in both the chapter's text and in a glossary.

6. End-of-chapter exercises that let students apply their learning to practical situations and an appendix with answers to even-numbered exercises.

7. Appendixes of statistical concepts with spreadsheet applications and tutorials for calculating reliability coefficients for instructors and students interested in a more quantitative approach than the text provides.

ACKNOWLEDGMENTS

A project of this magnitude requires the help of many persons. We are very much indebted to the reviewers whose critical reading contributed greatly to the technical accuracy, readability, and pedagogy of the eighth edition: Kathryn Anderson Alvestad, University of Maryland; Mary K. Boudreaux, University of Memphis; Kristin L. Koskey, The University of Akron; Connie M. Moss, Duquesne University. Special thanks go to Steve Ferrara, Measured Progress, and to Michael J. Young, Pearson Assessment, for helpful reviews and suggestions for improvement and updating.

We would also like to thank the reviewers for the second, third, fourth, fifth, sixth, and seventh editions: Peter W. Airasian, Boston College; Lawrence M. Aleamoni, University of Arizona; Kathryn Anderson Alvestad, University of Maryland, College Park; Carol E. Baker, University of Pittsburgh; W. L. Bashaw, University of Georgia; Gary Bingham, Georgia State University; Pamela Broadston, University of Arkansas at Little Rock; Deborah Brown, West Chester University; Marcia Burell, SUNY Oswego; Heidi Legg Burross, University of Arizona; Alice Corkill, University of Nevada at Las Vegas; Lee Doebler, University of Montevallo; Leonard S. Feldt, University of Iowa;

Terry Fogg, Minnesota State University; Betty E. Gridley, Ball State University; Gretchen Guiton, University of Southern California; Anthony E. Kelly, George Mason University; Jin-Ah Kim, Illinois State University; Thomas M. Haladyna, Arizona State University; Charles Hughes, Pennsylvania State University; Louise F. Jernigan, Eastern Michigan University; Suzanne Lane, University of Pittsburgh; Robert Lange, University of Central Florida; Robert W. Lissitz, University of Maryland; Nancy Martin, University of Texas–San Antonio; Craig Mertler, Bowling Green State University; William P. Moore, University of Kansas; Pamela A. Moss, University of Michigan; Robert Paugh, University of Central Florida; Susan E. Phillips, Michigan State University; Bruce Rogers, University of Northern Iowa; Marianne Robin Russo, Florida Atlantic University; John Shimkanin, California University of Pennsylvania; William M. Stallings, Georgia State University; Hoi K. Suen, Pennsylvania State University; James S. Terwilliger, University of Minnesota; Charles L. Thomas, George Mason University; Michael S. Trevisan, Washington State University; Anthony Truog, University of Wisconsin–Whitewater; Tary L. Wallace, University of South Florida, Sarasota-Manatee; Kinnard White, University of North Carolina; Richard Wolf, Teachers College, Columbia University; and David R. Young, State University of New York–Cortland.

We thank our students at the School of Education, University of Pittsburgh; the School of Education, Duquesne University; the College of Education, University of Arizona; the Curriculum Development and Evaluation Centre, Botswana Ministry of Education; teachers working with the Jamaica Ministry of Education; teachers and assessors at the Examination Development Center, Indonesia Ministry of Education and Culture; and trainers with the Integrated Language Project in Egypt, who used the second, third, and fourth editions. They provided insightful feedback and corrections of errors that have greatly improved the usefulness of the text. Francis Amedahe helped classify chapter learning targets and write test items for the third edition. Sarah Bonner contributed test items, practical examples for classroom activities, and many elements of the Instructor's Manual for the fourth edition. To all of these persons, and others we have failed to mention, we offer our most sincere thanks and appreciation.

We are grateful for permission to use checklists and examples that Anthony Nitko originally published with colleagues Harry Hsu and Maury Lindvall. Specifically, the checklists for evaluating the quality of a test blueprint (Chapter 6), multiple-choice items (Chapter 10), matching exercises (Chapter 10), and essay items (Chapter 12) and the example in Figure 6.4 originally appeared in A. J. Nitko and T-C. Hsu, *Teacher's Guide to Better Classroom Testing: A Judgmental Approach*, 1987, Pittsburgh, PA: Institute for Practice and Research in Education, School of Education, University of Pittsburgh. The examples in Figures 13.4, 17.4, and 17.12 originally appeared in C. M. Lindvall and A. J. Nitko, *Measuring Student Achievement and Aptitude* (Second Edition), 1975, New York: Harcourt Brace Jovanovich.

Special thanks to Veronica Nitko and Frank Brookhart, whose support and encouragement were invaluable throughout the work on this text and its previous editions.

Educational Assessment
of Students

CHAPTER

1

Classroom Decision Making and Using Assessment

KEY CONCEPTS

1. *Assessment, test, measurement,* and *evaluation* are different but related terms.
2. Different kinds of educational decisions require different types of assessment information. Classroom formative and summative assessments provide teachers and students with the information they need to improve learning. High-stakes assessments provide those in authority with the information they use to classify and sanction.

IMPORTANT TERMS

accountability testing

assessment

classification decisions

content standards

credentialing

diagnostic assessments

disaggregation of test results

evaluation

formative evaluation of schools, programs, or materials

formative assessment of students' achievement

high-stakes assessments (tests)

measurement

performance standards

placement decisions

selection decisions

sizing up

summative evaluation of schools, programs, or materials

summative assessment of students' achievement

test

WHAT IS ASSESSMENT?

Assessment is everywhere in schooling, sometimes hidden in plain sight. Consider this example:

Example

Meghan's educational assessment began in kindergarten with an interview and an observation. On registration day, Meghan and her mother came to school and were interviewed briefly. A teacher rated Meghan's cognitive and social-emotional skills. Her development was judged normal, and she attended kindergarten.

During the year, she had difficulty paying attention to the teacher and participating in group activities, although she was neither aggressive nor hostile. She was given a "readiness test" at the end of kindergarten and performed as an average child. Her teacher recommended that she continue on to first grade, but her parents balked: They didn't think she was ready.

They took her to a child guidance clinic and requested further psychological assessment. The clinical psychologist administered an individual intelligence test and a "projective test" in which Meghan was asked to tell a story about what was happening in each of a set of pictures. The psychologist interviewed her, her parents, and her teacher. The psychologist described her as normal, both in cognitive ability and in social-emotional development.

Her parents withdrew her from the school she was attending and placed her in another school to repeat kindergarten. Later, they reported that whereas her first experience was difficult for her, her second kindergarten year was a great success. In their view, a teacher who was particularly sensitive to Meghan's needs helped accelerate her cognitive development. By the end of the year, she had also become more confident and regularly participated in group activities.

This brief anecdote shows assessments being used early in life. Most of us recall more easily the assessments applied to us later in our lives, as older children and as adults. You may not even associate the term *assessment* with Meghan's interviews. Yet interviews are included in the broad definition of assessments.

The general public often uses the terms *assessment*, *test*, *measurement*, and *evaluation* interchangeably, but it is important for you to distinguish among them. This section explains the relationship among these terms (shown in Figure 1.1) and the way assessments inform educational decisions (Figure 1.2, see next section).

Assessment

Assessment is a broad term defined as a process for obtaining information for making decisions about students; curricula, programs, and schools; and educational policy. When we say we are "assessing a student's competence," for example, we mean we are collecting information to help us decide the degree to which the student has achieved intended learning outcomes. A large number of assessment techniques may be used to collect this information: formal and informal observations of a student; paper-and-pencil tests; performance assessment tasks and their associated rubrics, for example a student's performance on homework, lab work, research papers, projects, and during oral questioning; and analyses of a student's records. This book will help you decide which of these techniques are best for your particular teaching situations.

Guidelines for Selecting and Using Classroom Assessments

In order to focus your assessment activities on the information you need to make particular educational decisions in the classroom, you need to become competent in selecting and using assessments. These five guiding principles will help you select and use educational assessments meaningfully.

1. *Be clear about the learning objectives you want to assess.* Before you can assess a student, you must know the kind(s) of student knowledge, skill(s), and performance(s) about which you need information. The knowledge, skills, and performances you want students to learn are sometimes called learning goals or standards. The more clearly you are able to specify these learning goals, the better you will be able to select the appropriate assessment techniques. Most often, you will be working with state standards and local curriculum goals (see Chapter 2).

2. *Be sure that the assessment techniques you select match the learning goal.* For example, if the goal specifies that students will be able to write poetry, solve a mathematical problem, or design a scientific experiment, the assessments should require students to do these things. The assessment techniques selected should be as practical and efficient to use as possible, but practicality and efficiency should not be the overriding considerations.

FIGURE 1.1 **Relationship among the terms** *assessments, tests, measurement,* **and** *evaluation.*

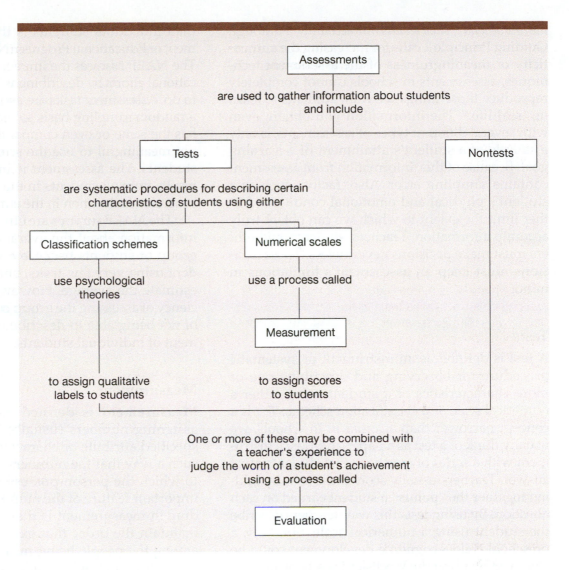

3. *Be sure that the selected assessment techniques serve the needs of the learners.*   Proper assessment tools are concrete examples for students of what they are expected to do with their learning. Assessment techniques should provide learners with opportunities for determining specifically what they have achieved and specifically what they must do to improve their performance. Therefore, you should select assessment methods that allow you to provide meaningful feedback to the learners. You should be able to tell students how closely they have approximated the learning goals. Good assessment is good instruction.

4. *Whenever possible, be sure to use multiple indicators of performance for each learning objective.*   One format of assessment (such as short-answer questions or matching exercises) provides an incomplete picture

of what a student has learned. Because one assessment format tends to emphasize only one aspect of a complex learning goal, it typically underrepresents that goal. Getting information about a student's achievement from several assessment modalities usually enhances the validity of your assessments. Matching exercises, for example, emphasize recall and recognition of factual information; essay questions emphasize organizing ideas and demonstrating writing skill under the pressure of time limits; and a monthlong project emphasizes freely using resources and research to more thoroughly analyze the topic. All three of these assessment techniques may be needed to ascertain the extent to which a student has achieved a given learning standard.

5. *Be sure that when you interpret—or help students interpret—the results of assessments, you take*

the limitations of such results into account. Although Guiding Principle 2 calls for increasing the authenticity or meaningfulness of the assessment techniques, assessments in schools cannot completely reproduce those things we want students to learn in "real life." The information you obtain, even with several different types of assessments, is only a sample of a student's attainment of a learning goal. Because of this, information from assessment contains sampling error. Also, factors such as a student's physical and emotional conditions further limit the extent to which we can obtain truly accurate information. Teachers, students, and others must make decisions nevertheless. Those decisions must keep an assessment's limitations in mind.

Tests

A **test** is defined as an instrument or systematic procedure for observing and describing one or more characteristics of a student using either a numerical scale or a classification scheme. *Test* is a concept narrower than *assessment*. In schools, we usually think of a test as a paper-and-pencil instrument with a series of questions that students must answer. Teachers usually score these tests by adding together the "points" a student earned on each question. By using tests this way, teachers describe the student using a numerical scale. Similarly, a preschool child's cognitive development could be observed by using the Wechsler Preschool and Primary Scale of Intelligence (see Chapter 19) and described as having a percentile rank of 50 (see Chapter 17). Not all tests use numerical scales. Others use systematic observation procedures to place students into categories.

Although it is natural to assume that tests are designed to provide information about an individual, this is not always true. States have testing programs designed to determine whether their *schools* have attained certain goals or standards. Although these tests are administered to individual students, a state uses the results to measure the effectiveness of a school. In such cases, individual names are not associated with scores when reporting to the government. The "score" for the school system (or for a specific school at a specific grade level) is usually the percentage of the school's students who meet or exceed that state's standards.

Another example of an assessment program designed to survey the educational system rather than individual students is the National Assessment of Educational Progress (NAEP) (nces.ed.gov). The NAEP assesses the impact of the nation's educational efforts by describing what students are able to do. Assessment tasks are assigned to students on a random sampling basis so that not every student has the same or even comparable tasks. Thus, it is not meaningful to use the scores with individual students. The assessment is intended to pool the results from all students in the sample to show the progress of education in the entire country.

The NAEP surveys are efficient ways to gather information about the average performance of a group of students because they assess each student using very few tasks, but pool the results to estimate the average. However, this gain in efficiency of assessing the group comes at the expense of not being able to describe validly the achievement of individual students.

Measurement

Measurement is defined as a procedure for assigning numbers (usually called scores) to a specified attribute or characteristic of a person in such a way that the numbers describe the degree to which the person possesses the attribute. An important feature of the number-assigning procedure in measurement is that the resulting scores maintain the order that exists in the real world among the people being measured. At the minimum, this principle would mean, for example, that if you are a better speller than we are, a test that measures our spelling abilities should result in your score (your measurement) being higher than ours.

For many of the characteristics measured in education and psychology, the number-assigning procedure is to count the correct answers or to sum points earned on a test. Alternatively, we may use a scale to rate the quality of a student's product (for example, an essay or a response to an open-ended mathematics task) or performance (how well the student carries out chemistry lab procedures). (See Chapter 13 for examples.) Most measurement specialists would probably agree that although a counting or rating procedure is crude, as a practical matter scores from assessments are useful when they are validated by using data from research (Kane, 2006).

Thus, an assessment may or may not provide measurements. If a procedure describes a student by qualitative labels or categories but not by numbers, the student is assessed, but not measured in the sense used here. *Assessment* is a broader term than *test* or *measurement* because not all types of assessments yield measurements.

Evaluation

Evaluation is defined as the process of making a value judgment about the worth of a student's product or performance. For example, you may judge a student's writing as exceptionally good for his grade placement. This evaluation may lead you to encourage the student to enter a national essay competition. To make this evaluation, you would first have to assess his writing ability. You may gather information by reviewing the student's journal, comparing his writing to that of other students and to known quality standards of writing, and so on. Such assessments provide information you may use to judge the quality or worth of the student's writing. Your judgment that the student's writing is of high quality would lead you to decide to encourage him to enter the competition. Evaluations are the bases for decisions about what course of action to follow.

Evaluation may or may not be based on measurements or test results. Among others, evaluations may be based on counting things, using checklists, or using rating scales. Clearly, evaluation does occur in the absence of tests, measurements, and other objective information. You can—and probably often do—evaluate students on the basis of assessments such as systematic observation and qualitative description, without measuring them. Even if objective information is available and used, evaluators must integrate it into their own experiences to come to decisions. So, degrees of subjectivity, inconsistency, and bias influence all evaluations. Testing and measurement, because they are more formal, standardized, and objective than other assessment techniques, reduce some of the inconsistency and subjectivity that influence evaluation. The general public, however, sometimes thinks that because numbers look objective they remove the element of judgment from evaluation; this is called the illusion of "mechanical objectivity" (Porter, 1995, p. 4).

Evaluation of Schools, Programs, or Materials
Not all evaluations are of individual students. You also can evaluate a textbook, a set of instructional materials, an instructional procedure, a curriculum, an educational program, or a school. Each of these things may be evaluated during development as well as after they are completely developed. The terms *formative* and *summative* evaluation are also used to distinguish the roles of evaluation during these two periods (Cronbach, 1963; Scriven, 1967). Historically, these terms arose first in the context of evaluation of schools or programs and were then applied to students. The convention has become that "formative and summative evaluation" refers to schools, programs, or materials, and "formative and summative assessment" refers to students. We will follow that convention.

Formative evaluation of schools, programs, or materials is judgment about quality or worth made during the design or development of instructional materials, instructional procedures, curricula, or educational programs. The evaluator uses these judgments to modify, form, or otherwise improve the school, program, or educational material. A teacher also engages in formative evaluation when revising lessons or learning materials based on information obtained from their previous use.

Summative evaluation of schools, programs, or materials is judgment about the quality or worth of schools, already-completed instructional materials, instructional procedures, curricula, or educational programs. Such evaluations tend to summarize strengths and weaknesses; they describe the extent to which a properly implemented program or procedure has attained its stated goals and objectives. Summative evaluations appraise the effectiveness of a particular educational product as well as under what conditions it is effective. Summative evaluations usually are directed less toward providing suggestions for improvement than are formative evaluations.

Evaluation of Students You may evaluate students for formative or summative purposes, as well. Classroom formative and summative assessments both should be based on the same intended learning outcomes. Figure 1.2 shows common uses for classroom assessment results. The uses are organized into two groups: formative and summative. One use of assessment, controlling students' behavior, is not listed in Figure 1.2 because it is a poor, and sometimes unethical, practice. Controlling students through assessments turns a process of information gathering into a process of threatening and punishing with negative consequences for learning and self-efficacy.

FIGURE 1.2 Examples of basic purposes for which classroom assessment results are used.

I. *Formative uses* help teachers monitor or guide student learning while it is still in progress. This table contains *teacher* uses of formative assessment information; see Chapter 7 for descriptions of *student* uses of formative assessment information.

    A. *Sizing-up uses* help a teacher form initial impressions of students' strengths, weaknesses, learning characteristics, and personalities at the beginning of the year or course.

    B. *Diagnosing individual students' learning needs* helps a teacher and the student identify what the student has learned and what still needs to be learned, decide how instruction needs to be differentiated, and decide what feedback each student needs about how to improve.

    C. *Diagnosing the group's learning needs* helps a teacher identify how the class as a whole has progressed in its learning, what might need to be reinforced or retaught, and when the group is ready to move on to new learning.

    D. *Using assessment procedures as teaching tools* is a way in which a teacher uses the assessment process as a teaching strategy. For example, a teacher may give practice tests or "mock exams" to help students understand the types of tasks used on the assessment, practice answering and recording answers in the desired way, or improve the speed at which they respond. In some cases, the performance assessed is identical or nearly identical to the desired learning objective so that "practicing the assessment" is akin to teaching the intended knowledge or skill.

    E. *Communicating achievement expectations* to students helps teachers clarify for students exactly what they are expected to be able to perform when their learning is complete. This communication may be done by showing the actual assessment tasks or by reviewing the various levels or degrees of performance of previous students on specific assessment tasks so that current students may be clear about the level of learning expected of them.

    F. *Providing specific feedback* gives students information about how to improve. It is only effective if teachers also give students opportunities to use the feedback.

    G. *Promoting students' self-assessment* helps students monitor their own learning, set goals, and take action to meet them.

    H. *Planning instructional uses* helps a teacher design and implement appropriate learning and instruction activities, decide what content to include or emphasize, and organize and manage the classroom as a learning environment.

II. *Summative uses* help a teacher evaluate student learning after teaching one or more units of a course of study.

    A. *Assigning grades for report cards* is a way in which a teacher records evaluations of each student's learning progress to communicate evaluations to students, their parents, and responsible educational authorities.

    B. *Placing students into remedial and advanced courses* is a way in which a teacher attempts to adapt instruction to individuals' needs when teaching is group based. Students who do poorly in the teacher's class may be placed into remedial classes that provide either alternate or supplemental instruction that is more suitable for the students' current level of educational development. Similarly, students whose educational development in the subject is above that of the rest of the class may be placed into a higher level or more enriched class.

    C. *Evaluating one's own teaching* requires a teacher to review the learning that students have been able to demonstrate after the lessons are complete, identify which lessons were successful with which students, and formulate modifications in teaching strategies that will lead to improved student performance the next time the lessons are taught.

Formative assessment of students' achievement means judging the quality of a student's achievement while the student is still in the process of learning. We make formative assessments of students to guide their next learning steps. When you ask questions in class to see whether students understand the lesson, for example, you are obtaining information to formatively evaluate their learning. You can then adjust your lesson if students do not understand. Students participate in formative assessment as well, interpreting information about their own performances to adjust their learning strategies (Moss & Brookhart, 2009); see Chapter 7 for more information about students' use of formative assessment information. High-quality formative assessment and feedback to students increase student learning (Hattie & Timperley, 2007). In general, formative assessments are less formal than summative assessments. We recommend that you record the results of these assessments to help your memory; however, you do not use them to report official letter grades or achievement progress. Some computer programs are designed to record teacher formative assessment observations (e.g., LSI Tracker, www.learningsciences.com/lsitracker/).

Typically, you use the most informal assessments for sizing-up purposes. **Sizing up** means to form a general impression of a student's strengths, weaknesses, learning characteristics, and personality at the beginning of a course or at the start of the year. The following example illustrates how a teacher pulled together various informally obtained pieces of information to size up Saleene, a fifth-grade student:

Saleene (a fifth grader) walks into class each day with a worried and tired look on her face. Praising her work, or even the smallest positive action, will crack a smile on her cheeks, though the impact is brief. She is inattentive, even during the exercises we do step by step. Saleene has a hearing disability that makes it hard for her to follow directions and classroom discussions. She is shy, but sometimes will ask for help. But before she gives herself a chance, she will put her head down on her desk and close her eyes. Her self-esteem is low. I am concerned that she will be this way all year. (Airasian, 2001, p. 38)

You can see that this teacher used information about Saleene's cognitive, affective, and psychomotor traits to help form a general strategy for how to teach her.

Other formative decisions also require quality information. These include diagnosing individual students' learning needs (for all students, not just those in special education), communicating achievement expectations, using assessment in instruction, diagnosing the group's learning needs, providing feedback, promoting student self-assessment, and planning instruction (see Chapters 7 and 8). These decisions require valid information from carefully planned assessment.

Summative assessment of students' achievement means judging the quality or worth of a student's achievement after the instructional process is completed. Giving letter grades on report cards is one example of reporting your summative evaluation of a student's achievement (see Chapter 15). Parents and school authorities interpret those grades as the progress students have made toward achieving the curriculum's learning goals. Summative uses of assessment also help you evaluate your own teaching after you finish teaching one or more units. Placement and evaluation decisions are also summative uses for assessment results. Because of the finality of summative assessment, you should prepare to keep records of students' results on summative assessments and ensure the validity of each result for supporting the decisions based on them. Most schools and districts use grading software for this purpose (e.g., PowerSchool, powerschool.com) and you will be required to learn and use the system that is in place in your district.

MyLab Education **Self-Check 1.1**

MyLab Education **Application Exercise 1.1:**
Testing Fit for Purpose

ASSESSMENT AND CLASSROOM DECISIONS

We began this chapter with Meghan's story. Her story illustrates that assessment results can contribute to a decision, but everyone concerned may not interpret the results in the same way. Although Meghan's parents may have been right to have her repeat kindergarten, there is no way of knowing what would have happened had she gone straight to first grade, because she didn't.

Decisions involve using different kinds of information. Sometimes test scores play a major role; at other times, less formal assessments play a more dominant role. In Meghan's case, both informal (teachers' observations, interviews) and formal (readiness test, intelligence test, projective test) assessments were administered.

Making good classroom decisions requires more than good intentions or previous experience. Good decisions, such as what to teach, how to teach it, and how to evaluate students' achievement, are based on high-quality information. Successful teachers obtain information about their students from high-quality assessments.

Similarly, assessment involves more than testing and grading students. Assessment involves gathering and using information to improve your teaching and your students' learning. Whether you use teacher-made assessment procedures, assessments from your district's curriculum materials, or state and standardized assessments, you need to be able to explain the results correctly to students, parents, other teachers, and school administrators. Further, as you develop professionally, you may have the opportunity to participate in local and state committees concerned with assessment issues. The media emphasize assessment as a major concern and consider it a newsworthy issue. It is likely to remain so for much of your professional career. This book discusses a variety of educational decisions that depend on assessments, especially in the classroom.

ASSESSMENT AND EDUCATIONAL DECISIONS ABOUT STUDENTS

Assessment provides information for decisions about students; schools, curricula, and programs; and educational policy. This section discusses several types of educational decisions made about students. It puts assessment into a broader context to give you a better idea of the purposes for which assessments are used (see Figure 1.3).

FIGURE 1.3   Examples of types of educational decisions for which assessments may be used.

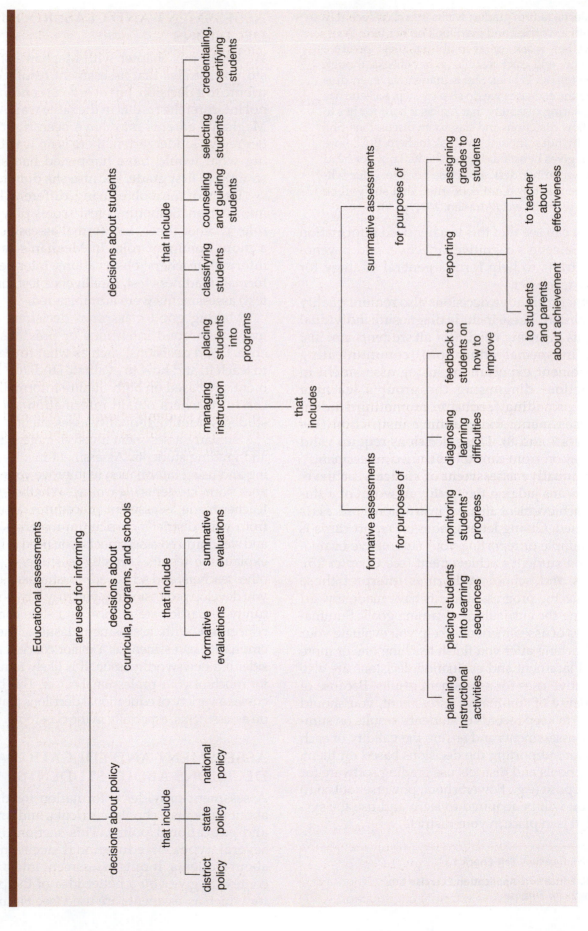

Understanding the features of different types of decisions will help you evaluate various assessment techniques that you may be considering. There is no simple answer to the question, "Is this a good assessment procedure?" An assessment procedure may serve some types of decisions very well, others not so well. Understanding the different types of decisions discussed in this section will also help you explain to parents why you used various assessments with their children. Finally, although you may not be required to make all of these types of student decisions yourself, by the time your students have completed their education they will have experienced virtually all of them.

Instructional Decisions

Teachers make decisions about students at the rate of one every 2 to 3 minutes (Shavelson & Stern, 1981). That's about 20 decisions every class period! Sound teaching decisions require sound information. Sound assessment procedures gather sound information. Researchers estimate that teachers may spend from one third to one half of their time in assessment-related activities (Stiggins, Conklin, & Associates, 1992).

To help you think about the many decisions a teacher must make, we have organized a set of questions teachers must answer before, during, and after teaching. Examples of assessment methods that may give you useful information for making the decisions are listed after each question.

Decisions Before Beginning Teaching

1. *What content do I need to cover during the next day, week, month, marking period, and so on?* Possible assessment methods: Review state standards, the curriculum, the syllabus, and the textbook; examine copies of the standardized tests my students will need to pass.

2. *What student abilities (cultural background factors, interests, skills, etc.) do I need to take into account as I plan my teaching activities?* Possible assessment methods: Informal observation of students during class discussions; conversations with students and students' previous teachers; studying students' permanent records to see their scholastic aptitude test results, past grades, and standardized test results; reviewing the Individualized Education Plan (IEP) or 504 Plan for students with identified disabilities; knowledge of the student's personal family circumstances.

3. *What materials are appropriate for me to use with this group of students?* Possible assessment methods: Class discussions in which students' motivations, interests, beliefs, and experiences with learning topics can be observed; results from short pretests; study of the students' permanent records to learn previous teachers' evaluations and the students' standardized achievement test results.

4. *With what learning activities will my students and I need to be engaged as I teach the lesson (unit, course)?* Possible assessment methods: Review the types of activities used previously; knowledge of typical student learning progressions in this area; analysis of the sequence of the learning activities students will follow; review of students' interest and achievement when those activities were used previously.

5. *What learning objectives do I want my students to achieve as a result of my teaching?* Possible assessment methods: Review of statements of goals and learning objectives; review of test questions students should be able to answer; review of the things students should be able to do and of the thinking skills students should be able to demonstrate after learning.

6. *How should I organize and arrange the students in the class for the upcoming lessons and activities?* Possible assessment methods: Informal observation of students with special learning and social needs; recollection of students' behavior during previous learning activities; information about what classroom arrangements worked best in the past when students were pursuing similar learning goals.

Decisions During Teaching

1. *Is my lesson going well? Are students catching on (i.e., learning)?* Possible assessment methods: Observations of students during learning activities; student responses to questions; observations of students' interactions.

2. *What should I do to make this lesson (activity) work better?* Possible assessment methods: Diagnosis of the types of errors students made or misconceptions students have; identifying alternative ways to teach the material; identifying which students are not participating or are acting inappropriately.

3. *What feedback should I give each student about how well he or she is learning?*   Possible assessment methods: Informal observation and experience on the amount and type of feedback information different students require; information about how close each student has come to achieving the learning objective; students' homework and quiz results; interviews of students.

4. *Are my students ready to move to the next activity in the learning sequence?*   Possible assessment methods: Informal observation and checking of students' completed work and questioning students about their understanding; analysis of students' homework, quizzes, and test results; results of student self-assessment.

Decisions After a Teaching Segment

1. *How well are my students achieving the short- and long-term instructional objectives?*   Possible assessment methods: Classroom tests, projects, observations, interviews with students; analysis of standardized test results.

2. *What strengths and weaknesses will I report to each student and to his or her guardian or parent?*   Possible assessment methods: Observations of each student's classroom participation; review of each student's homework results; review of each student's standardized achievement and scholastic aptitude test results when they become available; review of information about a student's personal family circumstances.

3. *What grade should I give each student for the lesson or unit, marking period, or course?*   Possible assessment methods: Combining results from classroom assessments, quizzes, tests, class projects, papers, labs, etc.; observation about how well the student has attained intended learning goals.

4. *How effectively did I teach this material to the students?*   Possible assessment methods: Review of summaries of the class's performance on the important instructional objectives and on selected questions on standardized tests, and of how well the students liked the activities and lesson materials.

5. *How effective are the curriculum and materials I used?*   Possible assessment methods: Review of summaries of informal observations of students' interests and reactions to the learning activities and materials, of the class's achievement on classroom tests that match the curriculum, and of

several past classes' performance on selected areas of standardized tests.

These lists of questions and assessments are not exhaustive. These examples illustrate that your teaching decisions require you to use many different types of information. Further, they illustrate that the exact type of information you need varies greatly from one situation to the next. The following sections describe different kinds of instructional decisions.

Instructional Diagnosis and Remediation   Sometimes the instruction an individual student receives is not effective: Any student, not just those identified for special education, may need special remedial help or special instruction that relies on alternative methods or materials. Assessments that provide some of the information needed to make this type of decision are called **diagnostic assessments**. Diagnostic decisions center on the question, "What learning activities should I use to best adapt to this student's individual requirements and thereby maximize the student's opportunities to attain the chosen learning objective?" Diagnosis implies identifying both the appropriate content and the types of learning activities that will help a student attain the learning objective (Nitko, 1989).

Feedback to Students   Assessments can provide feedback to students about their learning. Feedback, however, is likely to improve learning only under certain conditions. Simply assessing students and reporting the results to them is not likely to affect their performance. Learners must review both correct and incorrect performance and, in addition, be able to correct their incorrect performance. Feedback must give specific guidance to students about what to do to improve. Teachers must make room in their instructional plans for students to use the feedback, typically by revising work or by additional studying. Therefore, teachers who give students only their grade on a paper or test are not providing enough feedback to help students improve.

Assessments can be used to provide feedback that helps learning, provided you integrate them into your instructional process. Feedback from classroom assessment procedures will not help your students learn if the students lack a command of the prerequisite learning and/or have comprehended little of the lesson prior to the assessment.

It is especially important that students correct their errors before you go on to new instruction. Additional discussion of feedback appears in Chapter 8.

Feedback to the Teacher   Assessments provide feedback to the teacher about how well students have learned and how well the teacher has taught. Of course, if students have failed to grasp important points, the teacher should reteach the material before proceeding to new material. Assessment results about the effectiveness of a teaching episode can also be a rich source of discussion in teacher professional learning communities if your school uses this method for teacher professional development.

Modeling Learning Expectations   Assessments serve as examples for students by showing them what you want them to learn. Assessments, as well as other assignments, should therefore *embody* the students' learning target (Shepard, 2006) so that students get an accurate and clear idea of what they are to learn. Students can compare their current performance with desired performance. You may teach students to identify the way(s) in which their current performance matches the expected performance and how to remedy any deficiencies. In this way, good assessment is good instruction. Also, as students evaluate their own performance, you may teach them the appropriate criteria for judging how well they are learning as well as what is important to learn.

Motivating Students   Assessments may also motivate students to study. Unfortunately, some teachers use this form of accountability as a weapon rather than as a constructive force. Teachers may hope that using an assessment as a possible threat will encourage their students to take studying seriously. Sometimes teachers use the "surprise quiz" or "pop quiz" in this manner to encourage more frequent studying and less cramming.

Studies have not justified use of assessments this way. Rather, assessments ought to be viewed in a more positive light: as tools for instruction and feedback to students. Positive motivation comes as students understand what they need to do to improve and realize they are capable of taking those steps. Also, teachers or parents who stress test performance as the sole or major criterion for school success may create undue test anxiety for students. As a result, students may perform less well in the long run.

Assigning Grades to Students   One of the most obvious reasons for giving classroom assessments is to help you assign grades to students. Periodically, teachers must officially record their evaluations of students' progress. The grades or symbols (A, B, C, etc.) that you report represent your summative evaluations or judgments about how well your students have achieved important learning goals. Use a mixture of assessment formats to provide the information you need to make these evaluations. Do not use test scores alone to justify your grades. Some teachers do this because assigning grades involves evaluative decisions, and judgments are often difficult to justify and explain. Tests, especially those of the objective variety, seem to reduce judgment and subjectivity, even though this is not necessarily true. A more complete discussion of grading, including suggestions for assigning grades, appears in Chapter 15.

Jennifer McDaniel, AP Calculus teacher
Clay County High School, Manchester, KY

MyLab Education

Video Example 1.1

This teachers and students on this video show how using both formative and summative assessment effectively hinges on making sure that students understand what they are trying to learn and know what resources are available for them to pursue those targets. Pay special attention to the students' descriptions of how learning targets and assessment information help them regulate their own learning.

Selection Decisions

Most people are familiar with **selection decisions**: An institution or organization decides that some persons are acceptable, whereas others are not; those who are unacceptable are rejected and are no longer the concern of the institution or organization. This feature—rejection and the elimination of those rejected from immediate institutional concern—is central to a selection decision. For example, college admissions are often selection decisions: Some candidates are admitted and others are not; those who are rejected are no longer the college's concern. (Some critics may argue that those rejected should still be of concern to society generally.)

When an institution uses an assessment procedure for selection, it is important to show that candidates' results on the assessments bear a significant relationship to success in the program or job for which the institution is selecting persons. If data do not show that these assessment results can distinguish effectively between those candidates likely to succeed and those unlikely to succeed, then these assessment procedures should be improved or eliminated. In fact, it may be illegal to continue to use assessment results that bear no relationship to success on the job (Equal Employment Opportunity Commission, Civil Service Commission, Department of Justice, Department of Labor, & Department of the Treasury, 1979; United States Supreme Court, 1971).

Selection decisions need not be perfect to be useful, however. Assessment results cannot be expected to have perfect validity for selection, or any other, decisions (see Chapter 3). Figure 1.4 illustrates the use of imperfect assessments in selection. Some applicants would have been successful had they been selected instead of rejected (false negative decisions); and some, even though they were accepted, turned out to be unsuccessful (false positive decisions). Assessments can be evaluated, then, in terms of the consequences of the decisions made when using them.

Placement Decisions

In **placement decisions**, persons are assigned to different levels of the same general type of instruction, education, or work; no one is rejected, but all remain within the institution to be assigned to some level. Students not enrolled in honors sections, for example, must be placed at other educational levels. Or, first-grade students with low scores on a reading readiness test cannot be sent home. They must be placed in appropriate educational settings and taught to read. You may recognize a decision as a placement decision by noting whether the institution must account for all candidates instead of sending some away, as in selection decisions.

Most decisions in schools are placement decisions. Educators who use the language of selection are often using the language incorrectly. On closer examination, they are speaking about placement decisions. For example, when an educator speaks of "screening" students for a gifted and talented program, the decisions are actually placement decisions because their ultimate purpose is to place

FIGURE 1.4 A simplified illustration of how a selection situation uses assessments and the consequences of those decisions. The assessments and the decision rules are evaluated in terms of their consequences.

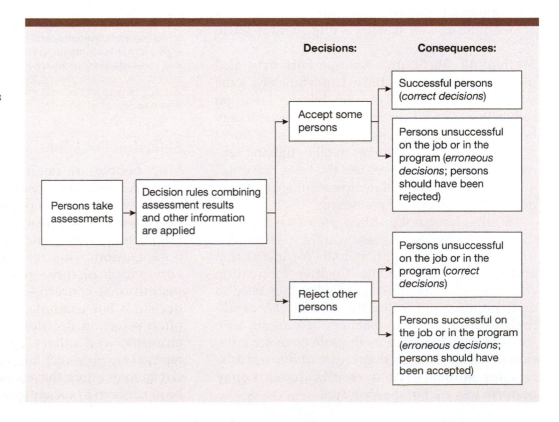

all students in appropriate educational programs. The schools are not free to teach some students and to reject the rest. If one instructional method is inappropriate for a particular student, then an appropriate alternative method needs to be found. In the end, all students are served.

Classification Decisions

Sometimes a decision results in a person being assigned to one of several different but unordered categories, jobs, or programs. These types of decisions are called **classification decisions**. For example, educational legislation concerning persons with disabilities has given a legal status to many labels for classifying children with disabilities and strongly encourages classifying them into one (or more) of a few designated categories. These categories are unordered (blindness is not higher or lower than deafness), so these are classification decisions rather than placement decisions.

You may consider *classification* as a more general term that subsumes *selection* and *placement* as special cases. *Classification* refers to cases in which the categories are essentially unordered, *placement* refers to cases in which the categories represent ordered levels of education without rejection, and *selection* refers to cases in which students are accepted or rejected. This book considers the three types of decisions separately.

Counseling and Guidance Decisions

Assessment results frequently assist students in exploring, choosing, and preparing for careers. A single assessment result is not used for making guidance and counseling decisions. Rather, a series of assessments is administered, including an interview, an interest inventory, various aptitude tests, a personality questionnaire, and an achievement battery. Information from these assessments, along with additional background information, is discussed with the student during a series of counseling sessions. This process facilitates a student's decision making and provides a beginning for exploring different careers. Exploring career options is likely to involve an ongoing and changing series of decisions that occur throughout a person's life.

Credentialing and Certification Decisions

Credentialing and certification decisions reflect whether a student has attained certain standards

of learning. Certification decisions may focus on whether a student has attained minimum competence or obtained a high standard, depending on the legal mandate. Certification and credentialing may be mandated by a state's legislation or may be voluntary. If a state law requires students to achieve certain standards of performance, most often students are administered an assessment procedure created at the state level. Those who meet the standards are awarded a credential (such as a high school diploma).

Assessment procedures for certification present special problems for validation. Individual students cannot reasonably be held accountable for instruction that the teacher failed to deliver or which was delivered poorly, even though, on the average, teaching was adequate. A critical point, therefore, is whether the quality of instruction corresponds to what the assessment procedure covers. The closer the correspondence, the fairer the certification is to the student. If students did not have the opportunity to learn how to perform the tasks that appear on the certification assessment procedure, either because a specific school lacked the necessary resources or a particular teacher failed to deliver appropriate instruction, the assessment-based certification process seems inherently unjust.

Data Driven Decision Making

The phrase "data driven decision making" means analyzing, interpreting, and using data in a manner that contributes to improved instruction and increased student learning (Boudett, City, & Murnane, 2005). The phrase is recently popular, but the concept behind it, using assessment information—of all kinds, not just test scores—to inform educational decisions, is not. This section has described types of decisions educators make and the assessment information on which they should be based, and these concepts have been around for decades. The contents of this book are intended to help you develop the skills of understanding, interpreting, and using assessment information—the "data" in "data driven decision making"—in your work. In a sense, then, this whole book is about data driven decision making. The discussion of pretesting and differentiating instruction in Chapter 6 is especially relevant for classroom instructional decision making. The discussion of appropriate uses of standardized tests in Chapter 16 is especially relevant for school- and program-level decision making.

However, most educational decisions benefit from considering multiple assessments at multiple levels, and we encourage you to use all the assessment concepts in this book as you make educational decisions.

HIGH-STAKES ASSESSMENT AND ACCOUNTABILITY

It may not come as a surprise to you that what you teach and how you teach it are not entirely under your control. Legally mandated external assessment programs place constraints on your teaching. You need to be aware of these as you plan your classroom instruction.

High-Stakes Testing

High-stakes assessments (tests) are used for decisions that result in serious consequences for school administrators, teachers, or students. Here are some examples:

Examples

High-Stakes Testing

Example 1. In a certain country, at the end of their secondary schooling, students must pass an examination for each subject they studied. The examinations cover the concepts and skills that are in the curriculum. Students are marked as A, B, C, D, and F for each examination. Students must get no Fs in order to be awarded the secondary school certificate. Persons without a secondary school certificate find it difficult to get a job in the country because employers see the certificate as indicating that candidates for a job have necessary minimum competencies. Students who fail may study on their own time and take the examination again, but they cannot repeat the schooling because there are only a limited number of places in secondary schools. Students must have As and Bs but no Ds or Fs to be considered for a place in one of the few universities.

Example 2. In a certain state, students must pass tests in English, writing, and mathematics before Grade 12; otherwise they cannot receive a high school diploma. They begin taking the test in Grade 10, and they may repeat the tests they failed once each year up to Grade 12. Students who do not pass all of the tests by the end of Grade 12 receive only an attendance certificate.

Example 3. In another state, students take annual state-mandated tests in reading and mathematics

from Grades 3 through 11. Students do not have to pass the tests, but each school is evaluated by how well its students do. If a school's students do not show a pattern of continued improvement on the tests, the state sanctions the school by dismissing the administrative staff and perhaps some of the teachers. It turns over the running of the school to a state-appointed team until the test scores show regular improvement.

In Example 1, the consequences of assessment are quite serious for individual students: If they fail to pass all subjects, they may not get a job because employers require a secondary school certificate; if they fail to do well on the examinations, they have no opportunity for attending a university. The stakes are high in Example 2, but not quite as high as in Example 1. Students can stay in school for several years, prepare for the tests, and retake the tests each year. In Example 3, there are high stakes for school administrators and teachers, but not for individual students. In fact, the tests may be low stakes for the students because there appear to be no consequences for their doing poorly on the tests.

Accountability Testing

Although the use of high-stakes testing in the United States can be traced back to Horace Mann in the 1850s, modern high-stakes testing in the United States grew out of school reform movements that developed during the 1980s. Educational reformers and state legislators wanted to ensure that virtually all students could meet educational standards set by the state and demanded by employers. Employers needed to increase productivity and to be competitive in world markets. They needed a better-educated workforce to handle the demands of rapidly increasing technology and greater intellectual skills needed in the workplace. State legislators considered testing to be one way of holding schools accountable for students learning the educational standards set by a state.

Assessment that is used to hold individual students or school officials responsible for ensuring that students meet state standards is called **accountability testing**. Usually accountability testing is accompanied by high-stakes consequences. A state's accountability testing may take several forms, as is shown by the examples above. A state may require both individual and school accountability, too. Check your state's education department website for its current regulations regarding individual and school accountability.

Federal Legislation

The Elementary and Secondary Education Act, which dates back to 1965 and President Lyndon Johnsons' War on Poverty, has had several major amendments. The most recent include the No Child Left Behind Act (NCLB, 2001) and the Every Student Succeeds Act (ESSA, 2015). NCLB is important to our discussion of high-stakes assessment because it required states to establish challenging content standards and performance standards (referred to as *achievement standards* in the NCLB literature) and to demonstrate by way of tests and other assessments how well students attained high levels of achievement on these standards. A state's failure to provide this demonstration resulted in loss of federal education funds authorized under NCLB. Assessment under NCLB was a school-level accountability tool.

ESSA requirements are set to go into effect in the 2017–2018 school year. States still have to submit accountability plans to the federal government, but states can select their own goals. Elementary schools need to use at least four indicators, three academic (state tests, English-language proficiency, and another academic indicator that could be a growth measure) and one additional indicator selected by the state. High schools use the same indicators plus graduation rate. States are required to intervene in the lowest-performing 5 percent of schools and schools with graduation rates of 67 percent or less (Editorial Projects in Education Research Center, 2016).

Standards-Based Proficiency Requirements **Content standards** describe the subject-matter facts, concepts, principles, and so on that students are expected to learn. **Performance standards** describe the things students can perform or do once the content standards are learned. (We discuss state standards and how to align your learning objectives to them in Chapter 2.) When students are assessed on a state's standards, they are classified into one of three categories for purposes of reporting to the federal government: basic, proficient, and advanced. A state may have more than three categories, but all must be aligned to these three. Under NCLB, the goal originally was for 100 percent of the students

in each school to reach the proficient level or higher on the state's content and performance standards by 2014. In addition, schools were to show *adequate yearly progress* (*AYP*) toward this goal or have sanctions imposed. Under ESSA, proficiency test results are one of several indicators.

High-Stakes Sanctions NCLB sanctions and corrective actions for schools that failed to make adequate yearly progress after 2 years were quite restrictive and entirely punitive; there were no official rewards for schools that did well. In addition, reaching 100% proficiency was a statistically unattainable goal, and, as 2014 approached, more and more schools failed to meet AYP goals. Beginning in 2011, the federal government allowed states to apply for waivers from some of the NCLB requirements—such as meeting original AYP goals—and sanctions. In order to qualify for a waiver, states had to address certain guidelines (U.S. Department of Education, 2012). In contrast, under ESSA, states will monitor school-based turnaround efforts for schools in the bottom 5 percent or with low graduation rates. In districts where subgroups of students are underperforming over time, the state and district must draw up a comprehensive improvement plan.

Disaggregation An important provision of NCLB that was continued in ESSA is that a state must report test summaries at the school level and must disaggregate the data. **Disaggregation of test results** means that the test results for the total population of students are separated in order to report on individual subgroups of students—such as students who are poor, who are members of minority groups, who have limited English proficiency, and who have disabilities—in addition to reporting on the total student population. The reason for this requirement is to ensure that states are accountable for all students learning the challenging state standards, including those in these subgroups. In some instances in the past, states reported only on the whole population of their students, thus masking the fact that some subgroups of students were not receiving quality education and were failing to meet the standards.

Assessment of Students with Disabilities Under NCLB and ESSA, all students must be assessed, including students with disabilities and students with limited English proficiency.

Ninety-five percent of students with disabilities must participate in the assessment. Students' disabilities may be used as a basis for accommodations to the assessment process when they are unable to participate under the standardized conditions set for the general student population. Further, alternative assessment methods must be found to assess those students who cannot participate even with accommodations. However, under ESSA only one percent of students can be given alternative tests (Editorial Projects in Education Research Center), even though about 13 percent of students receive special services (nces.ed .gov/programs/coe/indicator_cgg.asp).

Issues in the Current Accountability Climate

Whether NCLB assessment and accountability requirements have improved or hindered education is controversial, and as of this writing, the ESSA requirements had not taken effect. Advocates of strong accountability testing support the federal government's position that "No Child Left Behind is designed to change the culture of America's schools by closing the achievement gap, offering more flexibility, giving parents more options, and teaching students based on what works" (U.S. Department of Education, n.d.). Proponents view assessment as an objective way to ensure that all students demonstrate that learning has occurred. There is some evidence that Black-White and Hispanic-White achievement gaps have decreased since NCLB, although male-female gaps remain unchanged (Reardon, Greenberg, Kalogrides, Shores, & Valentino, 2012).

Critics point to the inevitable corruption of test scores when stakes are high, including the narrowing of the curriculum to easily tested objectives whenever the focus of the school is on improving scores on tests (e.g., Nichols & Berliner, 2008). Some have argued that the large-scale accountability tests are not instructionally sensitive, that is, they do not reflect students' actual classroom learning (Popham, 2005). Others point out that "for special education students and the schools that serve them, the requirements of two federal education laws and their implementing regulations, the Individuals with Disabilities Education Act (IDEA) and the No Child Left Behind Act (NCLB), are in conflict" (Phillips, 2005). Finally, as tests become more rigorous, pass rates will decline, at least initially. Some states have already raised passing scores on their state accountability

tests to get ready for the higher expectations for student achievement in the new Common Core assessments, and have seen such results (Ujifusa, 2012). They are working to inform the public about changes in their accountability systems.

MyLab Education Self-Check 1.2

MyLab Education Application Exercise 1.2:
Assessment and Classroom Decisions

ASSESSMENT LITERACY

Acquiring the knowledge and skills to assess students is widely discussed today under the term **assessment literacy.** Originally, Stiggins (1991) coined the term to refer to teachers' basic assessment knowledge and skill, and the disposition and practice of using those skills in their teaching, especially regarding assessment of student learning and achievement. More recently, scholars have realized that knowledge and skills alone are not sufficient to insure integrated use of high-quality assessment into teaching. Assessment knowledge and skill needs to be linked to teachers' educational philosophies and theories of action (DeLuca, 2012). For example, teachers who embrace student-centered formative assessment practices and use them regularly rely on a cognitive or socio-cognitive view of learning. Teachers who believe that teaching means transmitting information to students will not maintain student-centered assessment practices for long. Teacher assessment literacy in practice may be conceived as resting on a foundation of assessment knowledge and skills, integrated with a teacher's view of learning, and eventually constructing a teacher's identity as an assessor (Xu & Brown, 2016). In other words, the way a teacher understands and practices assessment ultimately helps define "who she is" as a teacher and assessor.

The American Federation of Teachers, the National Council on Measurement in Education, and the National Education Association published *Standards for Teacher Competence in Educational Assessment of Students* in 1990. These standards are somewhat dated now. Most importantly, they do not address formative assessment skills like being able to help students generate and use assessment information for their own learning. Appendix A presents a more recent synthesis of the various knowledge and skills that, taken together, comprise what today would be called assessment literacy for teachers. The aim of this book is to develop these understandings and skills in its readers. We will advocate for student-centered uses of these understandings, and we hope that after study of this material and work in your classroom with students, you ultimately develop an identity as a competent, confident assessor of student learning.

CONCLUSION

This chapter introduced you to basic assessment terms and concepts as well as basic types and purposes of educational decisions. It would not be exaggerating to say that appropriate assessment information should support everything teachers and administrators do in schools. The remainder of this book is devoted to developing the knowledge and skills you will need to accomplish that assessment well. In Chapter 2, we turn to defining instructional goals, which are the foundation on which formative and summative assessment, as well as instruction, must be based.

EXERCISES

1. Self-reflect on a specific lesson you have taught or would like to teach. Make a list of the decisions you made (or need to make) before, during, and after this lesson. Next to each decision, identify how you will obtain the information needed to make the decision. What criteria might you use to judge the quality of each piece of information?

2. Decide whether each of the following statements is true or false. Defend your answers.
   a. To make evaluations, one must use measurements.
   b. To measure an important educational attribute of a student, one must use a test.
   c. To evaluate a student, one must measure that student.
   d. To test a student, one must measure that student.
   e. Any piece of information a teacher obtains about a student is an assessment.
   f. To evaluate a student, one must assess that student.

3. Describe the accountability context in your state.
   a. Obtain a copy of your state's most recent accountability report, which should be available on your state's education department website. How does your state currently meet federal reporting requirements?
   b. What educational assessments does your state use in its accountability plan? What are their names, what standards/content areas do they assess, and what information about them is available on your state's education department website?
   c. Has your state endorsed the Common Core State Standards Initiative? Is your state a participant in the PARCC or Smarter Balanced assessment consortia? What is its role in the consortium (is it a governing or participating state)?

4. Classify each of these statements as reflecting a selection, classification, placement, career guidance, diagnostic/remediation, or certification decision. Defend your answers.
   a. After students begin kindergarten, they are given a battery of perceptual skills tests to decide which children should receive special perceptual skills training and which should remain in the "regular" program.
   b. A child study team decides whether each child who has been administered a series of screening tests should be included in a particular category of disability (students with hearing impairments, learning disabilities, etc.).
   c. After a school psychologist assesses a student, local education authorities assign the student to the resource room, where the teacher for students with learning disabilities gives the student special instruction each day.
   d. Each graduate of this department of education is required to take and pass the state's test before being allowed to teach in the schools.

5. Self-reflect on each of the teacher assessment knowledge and skills found in Appendix A. Under each standard, describe the kinds of competence you now have and those that you hope to have at the end of this course.

CHAPTER
2

Describing the Goals of Instruction

KEY CONCEPTS

1. Learning objectives focus instruction and assessment. Derive learning objectives from state standards.
2. Specific learning objectives should be student centered, performance centered, and content centered. Align both instruction *and* assessment to your learning objectives and the state standards from which they were derived.
3. Taxonomies of thinking skills help you get the most out of your learning goals and assessment tasks.

IMPORTANT TERMS

affective domain

alignment study

analysis, application, comprehension, evaluation, knowledge, synthesis

cognitive domain

conceptual knowledge, factual knowledge, procedural knowledge, and metacognitive knowledge

content centered

developmental learning objective

educational goals

general learning goal

learning objective

mastery learning objectives

performance centered

psychomotor domain

specific learning objectives

standards

student centered

taxonomies of instructional objectives

IMPORTANCE OF SPECIFYING LEARNING OUTCOMES

A **learning objective** specifies what you would like students to achieve when they have completed an instructional segment. The goal of teaching should involve more than "covering the material" and "keeping students actively engaged." The focus of your teaching should be on student achievement as well as on the learning process. So, your learning objectives should state what students ought to be able to do or value after you have taught them.

Some learning objectives are *cognitive*, meaning that they deal primarily with intellectual knowledge and thinking skills. For example, you may want students to read a claim made by a political figure and determine whether there is evidence available to support that claim. Other learning outcomes are *affective*, meaning that they deal with how students should feel or what they should value. For example, you may want students to value the right to vote in elections over other activities competing for their time. Still other learning objectives are *psychomotor*, meaning that they deal primarily with motor skills and physical perceptions. For example, you may want students to set up, focus, and use a microscope properly during a science investigation of pond water.

Deciding the specific objectives you expect students to achieve in their learning is one important step in the teaching process. Instruction may be thought of as involving three fundamental but interrelated activities:

1. Deciding what students are to learn.
2. Carrying out the actual instruction.
3. Evaluating the learning.

Activity 1 requires you to articulate in some way what you expect students to be able to do after you have taught them. Usually, you do this by specifying student-friendly learning targets or by providing several concrete examples of the tasks students should be able to do to demonstrate that the learning targets have been reached. Activity 1 informs you and the students about what is expected as a result of teaching and studying. Your understanding of the learning objectives guides your teaching and provides a criterion for deciding whether students have attained the desired change.

Activity 2 is the heart of the teaching process itself. Here you provide the conditions and activities for students to learn. These include formative assessment procedures like monitoring students' progress and giving them feedback on what they need to improve their achievement of their learning targets. See Chapters 7 and 8 for more information on formative assessment and feedback.

Activity 3, evaluating whether learning has occurred, is summative assessment. Through it you and your students come to know how well the learning objectives have been reached. The more clearly you specify the learning targets, the more directed your teaching efforts and your students' learning efforts will be.

These three fundamental activities are interactive rather than a straight one–two–three process. Setting clear learning objectives helps you plan your teaching efficiently, conduct your instruction—whether whole-class, differentiated by groups, or individualized—effectively, and assess student outcomes validly. Assessing and evaluating students using clearly specified learning objectives provides you with information about how to guide students' learning and how effective your instruction has been. This information, in turn, may be used to adjust your teaching, to plan the next instructional activities, or to better specify the instructional objectives. Setting clear learning objectives also helps you communicate them to others.

Before you can design procedures to evaluate students' learning, you should have clearly in mind the students' performances you want to evaluate. If you are not clear on which important learning outcomes you want to evaluate, it is hardly possible to make a valid assessment of those outcomes. Statements of specific learning objectives are important for the following four aspects of classroom assessment:

1. *The general planning for an assessment procedure* is made easier by knowing the specific outcomes you wish students to achieve.
2. *Selecting and creating assessment procedures* depend on your knowing which specific achievements you should assess.
3. *Evaluating an existing assessment procedure* is easier when you know the specific learning objectives.
4. *Properly judging the content relevance of an assessment procedure* requires you to know the specific achievements you should assess (see Chapter 3).

EDUCATIONAL GOALS, STATE STANDARDS, AND LEARNING OBJECTIVES

This section discusses several closely related concepts. You might find it helpful to refer to Figure 2.1 when studying them.

Educational Goals Versus Specific Learning Objectives

Schooling and other organized instruction help students attain **educational goals**. One of the many ways to define educational goals is that they "are those human activities which contribute to the functioning of a society (including the functioning of an individual in society), and which can be acquired through learning" (Gagné, Briggs, & Wager, 1988, p. 39).

Educational goals are stated in broad terms. They give direction and purpose to planning overall educational activities. Examples of statements of broad educational goals appear in reports prepared by state departments of education, local school systems, and associations such as the National Council of Teachers of Mathematics, the American Association for the Advancement of Science, and the Association of American Geographers. Here is one example of an educational goal:

FIGURE 2.1   Relationships among the concepts of standards, goals, and learning objectives.

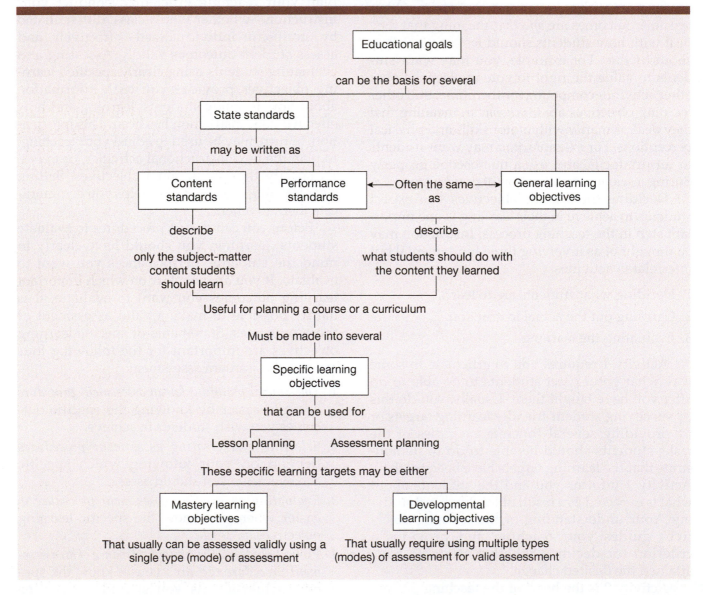

Example

Every student should acquire skills in using scientific measurement.

These types of broad goals are organized into subject-matter areas such as mathematics and history. The broad goals, as well as statements of subject-matter area and content-specific thinking processes, serve as a curriculum framework within which you and other educators can define specific learning objectives.

State Standards

State education agencies take the process further by publishing expected learning outcomes or *standards*, and your school is held accountable for students' achieving these particular standards. You can obtain a copy of your state's standards from your school principal, central administration office, or your state's education department website. We encourage you to locate your state's education department website and familiarize yourself with the standards in the content and grade level you intend to teach right now, before you read further. **Standards** are statements about what students are expected to learn. Some states call these statements *essential skills, learning expectations, learning outcomes, achievement expectations,* or other names.

Often there are two sets of achievement standards. *Content standards* are statements about the subject-matter facts, concepts, principles, and so on that students are expected to learn. For example, a standard for life science might be, "Students should know that the cell nucleus is where genetic information is located in plants and animals." *Performance standards* are statements about the things students can perform or do once the content standards are learned. For example, "Students can identify the cell nucleus in microscopic slides of various plant and animal cells."

State education departments prepare standards used in schools. Local school districts are required to teach students to achieve these standards and are held accountable for students achieving them through the state's assessment system. Professional organizations can prepare standards, too. These organizations try to influence what is taught by publicly promoting their own standards. Examples of professional

organizations with published standards are the National Academy of Sciences, National Council of Teachers of English, and National Council of Teachers of Mathematics. Most standards from professional organizations can be found on the organizations' websites.

The Common Core State Standards Initiative has prepared standards in English Language Arts and Literacy in History/Social Studies, Science, and Technical Subjects and in Mathematics. Released in June 2010, these standards were adopted by 45 states. Since that time, several states have withdrawn or are in the process of rewriting their standards, although at least 37 states remain with the Common Core initiative (Education Week, 2016). At the present time, two consortia of states are working on common state assessments and assessment systems that could take the place of individual state assessments in these content areas.

Common Core State Standards

Most states are using the Common Core State Standards (corestandards.org) in English/Language Arts and Mathematics as 85 percent or more of their state standards in these two areas. There are two main standards documents, which both have appendices.

The *Common Core State Standards for English Language Arts & Literacy in History/Social Studies, Science, and Technical Subjects* are organized by grade level under the categories of reading, writing, speaking, listening, and language (grammar and usage), in two levels (K through 5 and 6 through 12). In K through 5, standards for English Language Arts and for literacy in History/Social Studies, Science, and Technical Subjects are grouped together. In 6 through 12, the English Language Arts standards are described separately from the standards for literacy in History/Social Studies and Science/Technical Subjects.

Example

The Common Core "Reading Standards for Literature K5" include five areas, one of which is "Key Ideas and Details." Anchor Standard 1 in this area states: "Read closely to determine what the text says explicitly and to make logical inferences from it; cite specific textual evidence when writing or speaking to support conclusions drawn from the text." To support this anchor standard, a progression of learning is expected through the grade levels.

Kindergarten: With prompting and support, ask and answer questions about key details in a text.

Grade 1: Ask and answer questions about key details in a text.

Grade 2: Ask and answer such questions as who, what, where, when, why, and how to demonstrate understanding of key details in a text.

Grade 3: Ask and answer questions to demonstrate understanding of a text, referring explicitly to the text as the basis for the answers.

Grade 4: Refer to details and examples in a text when explaining what the text says explicitly and when drawing inferences from the text.

Grade 5: Quote accurately from a text when explaining what the text says explicitly and when drawing inferences from the text.

These standards are a bit different from most states' English Language Arts (ELA) standards. They emphasize reading and comprehending informational texts more than most states' prior ELA standards. The level of cognitive demand is also greater than most states' prior standards with much more emphasis on analysis (Porter, McMaken, Hwang, & Yang, 2011). The Common Core ELA Standards have three appendices. Appendix A presents research supporting key elements of the standards and a glossary of key terms. Appendix B presents sample reading texts and sample performance tasks and is very helpful for illustrating the standards for ELA teachers. Appendix C presents samples of student writing with annotations, again very helpful for illustrating the standards for ELA teachers.

The *Common Core State Standards for Mathematics* are organized by grade level from K through 8 and by topic for high school. K through 8 standards are in clusters. In Grades K through 5, clusters include counting and cardinality (K only), operations and algebraic thinking, number and operations in base 10, measurement and data, and geometry. In Grades 6 through 8, clusters include ratios and proportional relationships, the number system, expressions and equations, geometry, and statistics and probability. High school topics include number and quantity, algebra, functions, modeling, geometry, and statistics and probability. As for ELA, the Common Core mathematics

standards are a bit different from most states' previous mathematics standards. They emphasize number sense, operations, measurement, and basic algebra much more, and consumer applications, advanced algebra, and instructional technology much less (Porter et al., 2011).

Example

Common Core State Standard in Mathematics 4.NBT.1 (Grade 4, cluster Numbers and Operations in Base 10, Standard 1):

> Recognize that in a multi-digit whole number, a digit in one place represents ten times what it represents in the place to its right. *For example, recognize that $700 \div 70 = 10$ by applying concepts of place value and division.*

The Common Core State Standards (CCSS) in Mathematics also have standards for mathematical practices. These standards apply to both elementary and high school content standards. The mathematical practice standards are as follows (National Governors Association Center for Best Practices & Council of Chief State School Officers, 2010). Students:

1. Make sense of problems and persevere in solving them.
2. Reason abstractly and quantitatively.
3. Construct viable arguments and critique the reasoning of others.
4. Model with mathematics.
5. Use appropriate tools strategically.
6. Attend to precision.
7. Look for and make use of structure.
8. Look for and express regularity in repeated reasoning.

The Common Core mathematics standards have one appendix, *Designing High School Mathematics Courses Based on the Common Core State Standards.*

Currently, states use their own standards for subjects not covered by the Common Core State Standards. The Next Generation Science Standards for Today's Students and Tomorrow's Workforce have recently been prepared (http://nextgenscience.org/get-to-know). The National Council for the Social Studies has recently prepared the College, Career, and Civic

Life (C3) Framework for Social Studies State Standards: Guidance for Enhancing the Rigor of K–12 Civics, Economics, Geography, and History (http://www.socialstudies.org/c3).

Deriving Learning Goals and Instructional Objectives from State Standards

After officially adopting a state's standards, a school must make sure all students are taught and achieve those standards. Many districts use curriculum maps to specify how each of the learning goals in their curriculum are derived from standards. Different terms are sometimes used: "objectives," "standards," or even "learning targets." We reserve the term "learning targets" for a particular student-centered function in formative assessment (see Chapter 7), and therefore we do not use the term for statements that are written for teachers' planning purposes.

Generate a set of learning goals and objectives by analyzing the standards. Break standards into unit goals and, under each of those goals, observable and measurable specific learning objectives. The remainder of this section describes the concepts and skills you need to do this. The example below shows how specific learning objectives are developed from a state standard and compares statements of standards, general learning goals, and specific learning objectives for third-grade reading in one school district:

Example

State standard
- Communicate well in writing for a variety of purposes.

General learning goal
- Write for narrative, persuasive, imaginative, and expository purposes.

Specific learning objectives
- Explains the difference between narrative, persuasive, imaginative, and expository writing purposes.
- Applies prewriting skills and strategies to generate ideas, clarify purpose, and define audience before beginning to write.
- After receiving feedback on the first draft in the areas of ideas, organization, voice, word choice, and sentence fluency, uses the feedback to revise the draft.
- Reviews and revises the second draft for grammatical correctness and proper use of standard writing conventions.

General Learning Goals Versus Specific Learning Objectives

A **general learning goal** is a statement of an expected learning outcome that is derived from an educational goal or state standard. General learning goals are more specific than educational goals or standards and usually clear enough for general planning of a course. However, they need to be made more specific before they can become learning objectives that you can use when planning lessons. The following example of a general learning goal might be stated for a primary school science unit on measurement in the metric system:

Example

Acquire the skills needed to use common instruments to measure length, volume, and mass in metric units.

To teach and assess this general learning goal, you may need to break it down into two or more specific learning objectives. A **specific learning objective** is a clear statement about what students are to achieve at the end of a unit of instruction. Here are three examples of specific learning objectives that are derived from the preceding general learning goal:

Example

1. Measure the length of objects to the nearest tenth of a meter using a meter stick.
2. Measure the mass of objects to the nearest tenth of a kilogram using a simple beam balance and one set of weights.
3. Measure the volume of liquids to the nearest tenth of a liter using a graduated cylinder.

When learning objectives are made more specific, the achievement you are to teach and to assess becomes clear. But beware of overspecificity. Long lists of very narrow "bits" of behavior can fragment the subject to be taught.

The following examples show learning objectives that are too specific, along with a suggested revision:

Example

	The student is able to:
Too specific:	Estimate the number of beans in a jar.
Better:	Solve practical problems using calculations and estimation.
Rationale:	"Beans in a jar" is not the real objective of learning. Rather, it is but one of the many possible tasks that a student should complete to demonstrate achievement of estimation and calculation. The learning objective should describe this less specific achievement.

Example

	The student is able to:
Too specific:	Explain the meaning of the term *cold front*.
Better:	Explain the meaning of key weather terms.
Rationale:	"Cold front" is only one of several key weather terms that are included in a unit. Listing a separate learning objective for each term taught in the unit fragments the unit's focus on general weather terminology.

A second danger is that lists of specific objectives may become too long and be ignored. Identify a few of the most important learning objectives for each instructional unit and focus on these. Beware of a common mistake, which we sometimes call "overdoing it." Don't try to teach too many standards and/or too many unit goals and specific learning objectives at once. That will set you and your students up to fail.

> **MyLab Education** Self-Check 2.1
>
> **MyLab Education** Application Exercise 2.1:
> Deriving Learning Objectives from State Standards

EVALUATING THE LEARNING OBJECTIVES OF A COURSE OR UNIT

Prepare a complete list of the learning objectives for a unit before you teach it. A complete list is not necessarily long. You can use this checklist to evaluate your list of learning objectives:

Checklist

Checklist for Evaluating a List of Learning Objectives for a Course or Unit

1. Are all the learning objectives appropriate for students' educational level?
2. Is the list of learning objectives limited to only the important outcomes for the course or unit?
3. Are all the learning objectives consistent with your state's published learning standards?
4. Are all the learning objectives consistent with your local school's philosophy and general goals?
5. Can all the learning objectives be defended by currently accepted learning principles?
6. Can all the learning objectives be taught within the time limits of the course or unit?
7. Can all the learning objectives be taught with available teaching resources?

HOW TO WRITE SPECIFIC LEARNING OBJECTIVES

To be useful for classroom instruction and assessment (Gronlund & Brookhart, 2009) learning objectives must be:

1. **Student centered**: Objectives focus on the student.
2. **Performance centered**: Objectives are worded in terms of what a student can perform after the required learning experiences.
3. **Content centered**: Objectives state the specific content to which the student should apply the performance.

Student Centered

Because instruction focuses on changes in student performance, learning objectives should describe student performances. It is not unusual, however, for some teacher guides, curriculum frameworks, and other materials to contain statements that do not focus on the student. Consider this statement:

Example

Poor: Provide the opportunity for students to express their opinions in classroom discussions about why peace is so difficult to attain.

The problem with the preceding statement is that it is an activity statement *for teachers* rather than a learning objective for students. You may "provide the opportunity for students to express their opinions," yet each student may not express his or her opinion. Learning objectives need to be student centered if they are to be the basis for crafting assessment procedures. Thus, you should say:

Example

Better: A student will express and support his or her opinion in classroom discussions about why peace is so difficult to attain.

Student-centered learning objectives allow you to decide whether the students actually have achieved what you intended from the lesson.

Performance Centered

A learning objective should state a performance—that is, an observable activity. You can accomplish this kind of statement by including an action verb that specifies a student performance.

To help beginners write learning objectives that describe students' performances, Figure 2.2 lists further examples of various action verbs.

When verbs such as these are used in statements of learning objectives, the objectives will usually satisfy the second criterion of expressing observable student performance.

A balance is necessary between verbs that are too broad (and thus imply too many nonequivalent performances) and those that are too specific (and which are often just ways of marking answers). Consider this learning objective, which is stated too specifically:

Example

Poor: The student is able to put an X on the picture of the correct geometric shape (circle, triangle, rectangle, square, or ellipse) when the name of the shape is given.

The main intent of such an objective is to select or identify the correct shape, not just to make Xs. Any response that indicates the student has correctly identified the required shape is acceptable. Thus, the learning objective should be written as:

Example

Better: The student is able to identify a picture of a geometric shape (circle, triangle, rectangle, square, or ellipse) when the name of the shape is given.

FIGURE 2.2 Action verbs sometimes used in learning objectives.

Specific but acceptable verbs			
add, total	describe	match	rename
alphabetize	divide	measure	rephrase
choose	draw	multiply	select
complete, supply	explain	name	sort, classify
construct, make	identify	order, arrange	state
convert	label	pick out	subtract, take away
count	list	regroup	weigh
delete			

Too broad, unacceptable verbs			
apply	examine	interpret	respond
deduce	generate	observe	test
do	infer	perform	use

Too specific, essentially indicator verbs			
check	draw a line between	put a mark on	underline
circle	draw a ring around	put an X on	write the letter of
color the same as	put a box around	shade	write the number of

Toss-up verbs, requiring further clarification			
answer	contrast	differentiate	give
collect, synthesize	demonstrate	discriminate	locate
compare	determine	distinguish	predict

Figure 2.2 suggests some verbs that maintain this balance and illustrates other verbs that are too specific or too broad to make useful statements of learning objectives.

Content Oriented

A learning objective should indicate the content to which a student's performance is to apply. The following learning objective is poor because it lacks a reference to content:

Example

Poor: The student is able to write definitions of the important terms used in the text.

To modify this learning objective, you need to include a reference to a specific list of "important words" or in some other way describe them:

Example

Better: The student is able to write definitions of the terms listed in the "Important Terms" sections of Chapters 1 through 5 of the textbook.

If you do not refer to content in your learning objective, you will be uncertain whether an assessment task is valid for evaluating the student. For example, the assessment may require students to define words that, although in the text, may be unimportant. Without knowing the content, it is difficult for anyone to determine what, if anything, was learned.

Specific Learning Objectives as Mastery Statements

Assessment focuses on what you can see students doing. From this observation, you will infer whether they have attained the learning objectives. For example, a high school biology unit on living cells may have as a general learning goal that students should "learn the organizations and functions of cells." But what can the student do to demonstrate learning of this general goal? There may be several answers to this question, each phrased as a specific instructional objective and each describing what a student can do, as shown in the following example:

Example

1. The student can draw models of various types of cells and label their parts.

2. The student can list the parts of a cell and describe the structures included in each.

3. The student can explain the functions that different cells perform and how these functions are related to each other.

Statements of what students can do at the end of instruction may be called **mastery learning objectives**. They have also been called *specific learning outcomes* and *behavioral objectives*.

Mastery Learning Objectives Versus Developmental Learning Objectives

Some skills and abilities are more aptly stated at a somewhat higher level of abstraction than mastery learning objectives to communicate that they are continuously developed throughout life. Consider the following examples:

Examples

1. Combine information and ideas from several sources to reach conclusions and solve problems.

2. Analyze and make critical judgments about the viewpoints expressed in passages.

3. Use numerical concepts and measurements to describe real-world objects.

4. Interpret statistical data found in material from a variety of disciplines.

5. Write imaginative and creative stories.

6. Use examples from materials read to support your point of view.

7. Communicate your ideas using visual media such as drawings and figures.

Because of the lifelong nature of these objectives, they may be called *developmental objectives* (Gronlund & Brookhart, 2009) or **developmental learning objectives**.

At first glance, it might seem that all one needs to do is to insert a "can do" phrase in front of each of the preceding statements to transform them to mastery learning objectives. However, it is not that simple. First, each statement represents a broad domain of loosely related performances. Second, each statement represents skills or abilities typically thought of as developing continuously to higher levels rather than the all-or-none dichotomy implied by the mastery learning objectives.

The Problem of a Broad, Heterogeneous Domain Consider Developmental Learning

Objective 2 in the previous list. Now, think about questions you could ask students to assess how well they have achieved this learning objective. Your questions need to require students to analyze a reading passage and make inferences based on information in it. The example below shows three possible questions. These questions are passage-based items from the *National Assessment of Educational Progress* civics test. The numbers in the brackets are the percentage of twelfth-grade students who answered each question correctly.

Example

1. In what way does the article show one of the strengths of federalism? [32%] (2006-12C7, question 9)

2. In what fundamental way do the two quotes above show different understandings of the rights of citizens? [51%] (2006-12C7, question 3)

3. The events at Central High School in Little Rock showed that . . . [60%] (2006-12C5, question 17)

You can see that each question refers to a different passage with different viewpoints expressed. Further, the percentage of students answering one question is quite different from the percentage answering another. Studies of these types of questions show that those who answer one question right are not necessarily the same students who get another question right. We can conclude from this that Developmental Learning Objective 2 represents a broad domain of reading passages and that mastering one part of the domain does not mean mastering another. This is the case with developmental learning objectives like those listed previously.

The Issue of Continuous Development of Skill

The second concern, the continuous or developmental nature of these learning objectives, stems from the fact that even the simplest developmental objective is a matter of degree. Continuous development is possible throughout life. All we can reasonably expect to do for a particular course or unit of instruction is to identify a sample of specific learning outcomes that represent degrees of progress toward the objectives. The essential concern here is that the skills represented by these learning objectives are complex, the number of tasks that can be used to demonstrate learning is vast, and each represents goals to work toward continuously rather than to master completely (Gronlund & Brookhart, 2009).

Teaching and Assessing Developmental Learning Objectives One way to begin designing instruction and assessing progress toward developmental objectives is to list several specific learning outcomes for each objective. The outcomes should represent the *key* performances expected of a student at a particular grade level. This principle is illustrated in the following example, which clarifies a broad instructional objective in science by listing several specific learning outcomes that support it:

Example

Developmental learning objective:	Interprets and uses Boyle's law to explain phenomena and solve problems.

Specific learning outcomes clarifying this developmental objective:

1. States a definition of Boyle's law.
2. States the domain to which Boyle's law applies.
3. Describes the relationship between Boyle's law and Charles's law.
4. Uses Boyle's law to explain an observation in a lab experiment.
5. Appropriately analyzes a new (to the student) situation in terms of Boyle's law.
6. Solves a new problem or makes an appropriate choice for a course of action, taking into account the implications of Boyle's law.

Although this list of six specific outcomes might be made longer, the six would likely be considered adequate for describing what is meant by "interpreting and using Boyle's law" at the end of an introductory course in high school physics. Specific tasks could then be prepared for assessing achievement of the six specific outcomes. Some tasks might assess only one of these learning outcomes; others could require a student to use several of these outcomes in combination. A student's overall score could be interpreted as indicating the degree to which a student has acquired the ability to interpret and use Boyle's law, rather than as a "mastery/nonmastery" description.

ALIGNING ASSESSMENT TASKS WITH LEARNING OBJECTIVES

Chapters 6 through 14 discuss the details of creating high-quality assessments. Here we wish simply to point out that the basic purpose of any assessment is to determine the extent to which each student has achieved the stated learning objectives. Although this purpose sounds straightforward, it is not always an easy criterion to meet. The validity of your assessment results determines the quality of your evaluation. Validity has many aspects (see Chapter 3); here we discuss validity only in relation to matching assessment tasks to learning objectives.

Aligning Assessments to Mastery Learning Objectives

The specific tasks or procedures you use in an assessment should require the student to display the skill or knowledge stated in the learning objective. For instance, if the main intent of your learning objective is for a student to build an apparatus, write a poem, or perform a physical skill, your assessment procedure must give the student the opportunity to *perform*. Assessment procedures that require a student only to name the parts of an apparatus, to analyze an existing poem, or to describe the sequence of steps needed for performing a physical skill do not require the performance stated in these learning objectives. Therefore, they would be invalid for assessing them: They are not aligned to the learning objectives' main intents. A very basic requirement for the validity of classroom assessment procedures is that the assessment procedures should be aligned with the intentions of the specific learning objectives that you include in your assessment plan.

Aligning Assessments to Developmental Learning Objectives

As is often the case, developmental learning objectives define a broad domain of performance application. To ensure the validity of your classroom assessment, you may need to assess the same learning objective in several different ways. For example, you might assess writing achievement both by scoring several samples of students' written assignments and by using a grammar and usage test. The test provides the opportunity to assess grammar and usage that might not appear in the natural course of the student's writing, but that may well be part of the learning objective. Observing a student's natural writing habits permits you to infer how well the student is likely to use language in typical writing situations. Using both procedures increases how comprehensively you assess the student's writing ability and the validity of your evaluation.

Another reason for using more than one assessment procedure is to obtain more reliable results. Your subjective evaluation of a student's written essay on a topic might be supplemented by a test made up of more objectively scored items. Combining the less reliable information about the student's written work (that is, your subjective evaluation) with the more reliable information (the objectively scored test) yields a more reliable overall evaluation result. Reliability is discussed in more detail in Chapter 4.

Aligning Assessments to State Standards

Earlier in this chapter, we showed how you can derive your learning objectives from your state's standards. It is important that you maintain consistency by aligning your classroom assessments as well as the learning objectives with the state's standards. First, align your assessments with the learning objectives that you derive from the state's standards (in the manner we showed earlier). Second, ensure that your assessments match the span of content covered by the standards, the depth of thinking implied by the standards, the topical emphasis in the standards, and the same types of performances as are specified in the standards.

Creating Assessments That Require Students to Use Combinations of Learning Objectives

It is important to create learning and assessment situations that require students to use combinations of specific skills and knowledge to perform complex tasks and solve real-life problems. Figure 2.3 shows a beans-in-a-jar problem. In solving this problem, students are expected to use several specific skills and knowledge (listed at the upper right of the figure) to accurately estimate the number of beans in the jar. "Beans in a jar" is not the

FIGURE 2.3   An example of a complex assessment task.

BEANS IN A JAR
Applying rate and ratio

In the task for this benchmark, students were first shown a jar filled with beans and asked to estimate the number of beans. They were then asked to work out the number of beans more accurately using any of the following materials: a calculator, a balance scale and masses, a ruler, a graduated cylinder, and a transparent centimeter-squared grid. They were told they could count some but not all of the beans. If the students did not know how to proceed, the evaluators suggested they weigh a small handful of beans. The students were asked to keep an ongoing record of their solutions. After they had solved the problem, they were asked to describe the problem and their solutions.

Key objectives from the Ontario Ministry of Education and Toronto Board guidelines

- Apply ratio and rate in problem solving
- Consolidate conversions among commonly used metric units
- Collect and organize data
- Consolidate and apply operations with whole numbers and decimals with and without a calculator
- Apply estimation, rounding and reasonableness of results in calculations, in problem solving and in applications
- Develop facility in communication skills involving the use of the language and notation of mathematics
- Develop problem-solving abilities

Norm-referenced interpretations	Task score	Criterion-referenced interpretations
20% of the students scored 5 (80% scored lower than 5)	5	The student understands the problem and immediately begins to search for a strategy, perhaps experimenting with different methods and materials before proceeding. The student monitors the solution as it develops and may check and remeasure. The student uses the materials efficiently and accurately and keeps a good record of the data. All the calculations are performed accurately and a reasonable answer is produced. The student gives a clear explanation of the solution demonstrating sound reasoning with proportions. The student takes ownership of the task and enjoys its challenge.
19% of the students scored 4 (61% scored lower than 4)	4	The student may make some false starts and may be helped by the evaluator to get focused. The student may use some materials to no purpose or inaccurately, perhaps confusing volume and mass. The student reasons with proportions correctly. Although stuck at various points in the solution, the student perseveres and usually produces a reasonable answer. The student usually gives a clear explanation and enjoys the activity.
20% of the students attained 3 (41% scored lower than 3; the average score is 3.0)	3	There is some confusion in one or more aspects of the solution to the problem. The student may confuse units, make arithmetic errors, or perform incorrect operations. The student may have some idea of proportionality but is unable to use it correctly. The student does not use the materials to the best advantage. The student seeks assistance from the evaluator. Although not totally confident, the student may persevere in an attempt to arrive at an answer to the problem.
24% of the students attained 2 (17% scored lower than 2)	2	The student may make a start at solving the problem but is unable to complete a solution. The student may repeatedly switch methods and materials and be unable to find an effective strategy. There is considerable confusion with units and the interpretation of various measurements. The student usually guesses at the operations that should be performed with the data. The student lacks confidence and seeks a great deal of assistance from the evaluator.
17% of the students attained 1	1	The student may estimate the number of beans but gives no response or very limited response to working out the number more accurately.

Source: From John L. Clark (1992). The Toronto Board of Education's Benchmarks in Mathematics. *The Arithmetic Teacher: Mathematics Through the Middle Grades, 39* (6), pp. 51–55. Reprinted with permission from *The Arithmetic Teacher,* copyright 1992 by the National Council of Teachers of Mathematics. All rights reserved.

learning objective itself, of course. Rather, it is only one example of many possible tasks in which the learning objective is to apply a combination of proportional reasoning, estimation, measurement, and other skills to solve complex problems.

Notice that in this example, the most important outcomes teachers should assess are the processes and strategies students use to solve these problems. The criteria for these are listed under "criterion-referenced interpretations" in Figure 2.3. An assessment procedure that focuses exclusively on the degree of correctness of students' answers to tasks like this would be invalid because it misses assessing the processes that students use.

SOURCES FOR LOCATING LEARNING OBJECTIVES

You may find lists of learning objectives in instructional materials and teachers' manuals, local and state curriculum frameworks, the Common Core State Standards, state websites containing performance standards, reports of the National Assessment of Educational Progress, books on teaching methods, manuals accompanying tests (especially criterion-referenced tests), and reports from educational associations. More than likely you will have to adapt the learning objectives you find in these sources to your own situation. Nevertheless, these sources do provide a starting place: It is much easier to adapt and revise learning objectives statements than to write them without any assistance. Please remember that your learning objectives are for your (teacher) use in planning instruction and assessment. We take up the important skill of communicating student-friendly lesson-by-lesson learning targets to students, to guide their learning and formative assessment, in Chapter 7.

Finally, a learning objective often will cut across several lessons or subject areas. The objective of being able to use library and print resources to obtain information for a report, for example, is likely to be common to social studies, mathematics, and language arts curricula. The taxonomies in the next section were created so that each category would apply across several curricular areas.

MyLab Education Self-Check 2.2

MyLab Education Application Exercise 2.2:
Writing a Learning Objective

Crystal Thayer, Grade 4 teacher
Lewis County Schools, Tollesboro, KY

MyLab Education

Video Example 2.1

Focusing students on learning—as opposed to compliance—requires a classroom atmosphere where students feel free to say what they think. It also requires that both teachers and students understand the difference between what students are doing and what they are learning from doing it. This kind of classroom atmosphere supports a goal- or learning-driven model of instruction.

TAXONOMIES OF LEARNING OBJECTIVES

Simply writing learning objectives "off the top of your head" can be frustrating because a seemingly endless number of possible objectives exist. Further, you are likely to write first those objectives that have a very narrow focus, specify content topics, and represent lower level cognitive skills. A taxonomy can help you bring to mind the wide range of important learning objectives and thinking skills.

Taxonomies of instructional learning objectives are highly organized schemes for classifying learning objectives into various levels of complexity. Generally, educational learning objectives fall into one of three domains, although a complex performance may involve more than one of them.

1. **Cognitive domain**: Objectives focus on knowledge and abilities requiring memory, thinking, and reasoning processes.

2. **Affective domain**: Objectives focus on feelings, interests, attitudes, dispositions, and emotional states.

3. **Psychomotor domain**: Objectives focus on motor skills and perceptual processes.

Learning objectives within each domain may be classified by using a taxonomy for that domain. Because there is more than one way to define a classification scheme, several different taxonomies have been developed for sorting learning objectives in a given domain. Only two of these taxonomies for the cognitive domain are described here. Other cognitive domain taxonomies are summarized in Appendix D. Chapter 6 will discuss using taxonomies to develop an assessment plan. The other chapters in Part II discuss creating tasks to assess learning objectives at different taxonomy levels.

COGNITIVE DOMAIN TAXONOMIES

Taxonomies are not teaching hierarchies. Their only purpose is to classify various learning objectives and assessment tasks. For example, you should not teach "recall" first and "higher-order thinking" second. If you did that, younger and lower-achieving students would be doomed to spend all their time on drill. Use the taxonomy to help you explore each learning objective at several levels. A taxonomy gives you a tool to judge whether you have taught and assessed a wide enough range of thinking skills. Including a wide range of thinking skills in an assessment usually improves its validity.

It is also important to recognize that student performance on complex tasks involves using several thinking skills at the same time. It is possible, therefore, to classify a given learning objective or assessment task into more than one taxonomy category (Krathwohl, 2002). For most classroom purposes, classify each learning objective into the category that represents the thinking skill that is (a) most prominently used or (b) the main intent of the learning objective or assessment task. Then use the classification to decide if some important skills have received too little or too much attention in your teaching and assessment.

Bloom's Taxonomy

The *Taxonomy of Educational Objectives: The Classification of Educational Goals, Handbook I: Cognitive Domain* (Bloom, Englehart, Furst, Hill, & Krathwohl, 1956) had an enormous influence on how we think of educational goals and teaching practice. This taxonomy is a comprehensive outline of a range of cognitive abilities that you might teach, classified into six major headings arranged from simple to complex.

The six main headings of the original Bloom's taxonomy are Knowledge, Comprehension, Application, Analysis, Synthesis, and Evaluation.

1. **Knowledge** involves the recall of specifics and universals, the recall of methods and processes, or the recall of a pattern, structure, or setting. For measurement purposes, the recall situation involves little more than bringing to mind the appropriate material (p. 201).
2. **Comprehension** represents the lowest level of understanding. It refers to a type of understanding or apprehension such that the individual knows what is being communicated and can make use of the material or idea being communicated without necessarily relating it to other material or seeing its fullest implications (p. 204).
3. **Application** involves the use of abstractions in particular and concrete situations to solve new or novel problems. The abstractions may be in the form of general ideas, rules of procedure, or generalized methods. The abstractions may also be technical principles, ideas, and theories, which must be remembered and applied (p. 205).
4. **Analysis** involves the breakdown of a communication into its constituent elements or parts such that the relative hierarchy of ideas is made clear and/or the relations between the ideas expressed are made explicit. Such analyses are intended to clarify the communication, to indicate how the communication is organized and conveys its effects, and to identify its basis and arrangements (p. 205).
5. **Synthesis** involves the putting together of elements and parts so as to form a whole. This process involves working with pieces, parts, elements, and so on, arranging and combining them in such a way as to constitute a pattern or structure not clearly there before (p. 206).
6. **Evaluation** requires judgments about the value of material and methods for given purposes, quantitative and qualitative judgments about the extent to which materials and methods satisfy criteria, and the use of a standard of appraisal. The criteria may be determined by the student or supplied to him (p. 207).

Revised Bloom's Taxonomy

Relationship of the Revision to the Original
The original *Taxonomy of Educational Objectives* has been revised as *A Taxonomy for Learning, Teaching, and Assessing: A Revision of Bloom's Taxonomy of Educational Objectives* (Anderson et al., 2001). The revised taxonomy improves on the original by adding a two-dimensional framework into which you may classify learning objectives and assessment items. The two dimensions are the Knowledge Dimension and Cognitive Process Dimension.

The Cognitive Process Dimension is very much like the original Bloom's *taxonomy*. Its categories are Remember, Understand, Apply, Analyze, Evaluate, and Create. The cognitive processes of Synthesis and Evaluation from the old taxonomy have switched their order and become Evaluate and Create in the new taxonomy. This change makes sense, in that evaluation requires making a judgment after analyzing something against criteria while creating requires putting together something new. The definitions of the Cognitive Process Dimension categories remain like the original Bloom's taxonomy definitions presented above, with one exception: Knowledge.

Bloom's original Knowledge category has been divided into two parts: the Knowledge Dimension and the Cognitive Process category Remember. The Knowledge Dimension has four subcategories: **Factual Knowledge, Conceptual Knowledge, Procedural Knowledge, and Metacognitive Knowledge**. The Knowledge Dimension contains the type of content a learning objective refers to: factual knowledge, conceptual knowledge, procedural knowledge, or metacognitive knowledge.

The Taxonomy Table   A two-dimensional table is constructed to describe the location of a learning objective and its corresponding assessment on both dimensions simultaneously (see Figure 2.4). The figure shows 24 cells, each defined by one Knowledge and one Cognitive Process subcategory. Note that the subcategories of the Knowledge Dimension are lettered, whereas the subcategories of the Cognitive Process Dimension are numbered. As a shortcut, we can refer to a particular cell by its letter and number. Thus, a learning objective that requires students to remember some factual knowledge is placed in cell 1A.

Classifying Learning Objectives and Assessment Items   To help you ensure you write learning objectives at a variety of cognitive levels—as appropriate to the standard—Figure 2.5 suggests

FIGURE 2.4 Taxonomy table from the revised taxonomy..

Knowledge Dimension	Cognitive Process Dimension					
	1. Remember	2. Understand	3. Apply	4. Analyze	5. Evaluate	6. Create
A. Factual Knowledge						
B. Conceptual Knowledge						
C. Procedural Knowledge						
D. Metacognitive Knowledge						

Source: Anderson, Lorin W.; Krathwohl, David R.; Airasian, Peter W.; Cruikshank, Kathleen A.; Mayer, Richard E.; Pintrich Paul R.; Raths, James; Wittrock, Merlin C., *A Taxonomy for Learning, Teaching, and Assessing: A Revision of Bloom's Taxonomy of Educational Objectives, Complete Edition* 1st ed., © 2001, pp. 28, 46, 67–68. Reprinted and electronically reproduced by permission of Pearson Education, Inc., Upper Saddle River, New Jersey.

FIGURE 2.5 Action verbs to use when writing learning objectives.

Remember	Define, describe, explain, identify, label, list, match, name, outline, reproduce, select, state
Understand	Convert, describe, distinguish, estimate, extend, generalize, give examples, paraphrase, rewrite, summarize
Apply	Apply, change, classify (examples of a concept), compute, demonstrate, discover, modify, operate, predict, prepare, relate, show, solve, use
Analyze	Analyze, arrange, associate, compare, contrast, infer, organize, solve, support (a thesis)
Evaluate	Appraise, compare, conclude, contrast, criticize, evaluate, judge, justify, support (a judgment), verify
Create	Classify (infer the classification system), construct, create, extend, formulate, generate, synthesize

FIGURE 2.6 How different outcomes for science and social studies may be classified using the Anderson et al. revised taxonomy.

Anderson et al. Category	Science		Social Studies	
Remember	• Recall the names of parts of a flower	1A	• List known causes of the Civil War	1B
	• Identify and label the parts of insects	1A	• Recall general principles of migration of peoples of Africa	1B
	• List the steps in a process	1C		
Understand	• Explain the digestive processes in one's own words	2B	• Explain the meaning of technical concepts in one's own words	2B
			• Give examples of propaganda usage from current events	2B
Apply	• Use scientific principles to make a simple machine	3B,C	• Use specified principles to explain current events	3B,C
	• Find real examples of igneous rock and mineral formations	3B	• Carry out a survey and collect data from the field	3C
Analyze	• Show how scientific principles or concepts are applied in the design of a refrigerator	4B,C	• Identify the credible and noncredible claims of an advertisement for clothing	4B,C
			• Show the different component parts of a political speech	4B
Evaluate	• Use criteria or standards to evaluate the conclusions drawn from the research findings	5B,C	• Use a specific set of criteria to evaluate several political speeches	5B
Create	• Determine what the rule is that underlies the results obtained from several experiments or investigations	6B	• Show the similarities among several schools of social thought	6B
			• Develop plans for peace between two countries	6B,C

some action verbs you might use to write learning objectives at each level of the Cognitive Process Dimension. Please note that the list is suggestive, not exhaustive. In addition, remember that you need to consider the meaning of the whole learning objective, not just the verb, when you classify the cognitive level of a learning objective. Using one of these verbs does not guarantee a description of learning at a particular level.

Suppose you are teaching students to understand the elements that authors use when writing short stories. Suppose the short stories you select all concern people's personal problems and that the characters in these stories handle their personal problems inappropriately. The sample learning objectives and questions that follow may help you direct your assessment plans. Later chapters will detail how to design assessment tasks. At this point, we are studying only the range of thinking skills that should be taught and assessed. Also, remember that the examples are classified into the most appropriate cell(s) in the taxonomy and that they may also overlap into some of the other cells.

Example

Remember Factual Knowledge [1A]

Sample learning objective:	Recall the main characters in each of the short stories read and what they did.
Sample assessment items:	(1) List the names of all of the characters in "Witch's Forest." (2) In "Witch's Forest," what did Sally do when her mother refused to let her go into the forest?

Example

Understand Conceptual Knowledge [2B]

Sample learning objective:	Explain the main ideas and themes of the short stories that we read.
Sample assessment item:	Write using your own words what "Witch's Forest" was all about.

Example

Apply Conceptual Knowledge [3B]

Sample learning objective: Relate the personal problems of the characters in the short stories that we read to problems that real people face.

Sample assessment item: Are the problems Sally had with her mother in the story similar to the problems you or someone you know has with his or her mother? Explain why or why not.

Example

Analyze Procedural Knowledge [4C]

Sample learning objective: Identify the literary devices that authors use to convey their characters' feelings to the reader.

Sample assessment item: In "Witch's Forest," Sally was upset with her mother. In "Dog Long Gone," Billy was upset with his brother. What words and phrases did the authors of these two stories use to show how upset these characters were? Explain and give examples.

Example

Evaluate and Create Using Conceptual and Procedural Knowledge [5B, C; 6B, C]

Sample learning objectives: (1) Develop one's own set of three or four criteria for judging the quality of a short story. [6B, C]
(2) Use the three or four criteria to evaluate several new stories that were not read in class. [5B, C]

Sample assessment items: (1) So far we have read four short stories. What are three or four different traits that make a story high quality? Use these traits to develop three or four criteria that you could use to evaluate the quality of any short story.
(2) Read the two new short stories assigned to you. Use the criteria you developed to evaluate these two stories. Evaluate each story on every criterion. Summarize your findings.

Example

Create Using Conceptual and Procedural Knowledge [6B, C]

Sample learning objective: Describe, across all of the stories read, the general approach that the characters used to resolve their problems unsuccessfully.

Sample assessment item: So far we have read "Witch's Forest," "Dog Long Gone," "Simon's Top," and "Woman With No Manners." In every story, one character was not able to solve the personal problem he or she faced. What were the ways these characters tried to solve their problems? What do these unsuccessful ways to solve problems have in common? What would you have done differently that might have been more successful?

Figure 2.6 shows how learning objectives in science and social studies may be classified in the revised taxonomy. The value of such a taxonomy is that it calls your attention to the variety of abilities and skills toward which you can direct instruction and assessment.

Advantage of the Revised Taxonomy The advantage of the revised taxonomy is that it allows you to consider a broader range of learning objectives than the original one-dimensional taxonomy. If you classify your learning objectives, your assessment items, and your teaching activities into the Taxonomy Table shown in Figure 2.4, you can immediately see the types of knowledge and thinking on which your instructional unit focuses. Not every unit should have learning objectives and assessments in every one of the 24 cells, of course. But over the semester, your teaching should address and evaluate students' learning in all (or nearly all) of them.

Different Modes of Assessments for Different Taxonomy Levels

Learning objectives classified in the first three cognitive categories are more easily assessed with short-answer, true-false, multiple-choice, or matching test items. Learning objectives classified in the last three cognitive categories might be partially tested by such item formats, but their assessment usually requires a variety of other procedures such as essay questions, class projects, observing performance in labs, and portfolios. Learning objectives at more complex thinking levels require students to actually produce or create something, rather than simply to answer questions. Carefully reading the various subcategories of the taxonomy in Appendix D should make this more apparent.

Condensing the Taxonomy   Because it is sometimes difficult for teachers to classify learning objectives into all six cognitive categories, some schools have opted to use a shorter version of the Bloom taxonomy. For example, some have reduced it to three categories: Remember (or Knowledge), Understand (or Comprehension), and Higher-Order Thinking. The "Higher-Order Thinking" category collapses Apply, Analyze, Evaluate, and Create learning objectives into one group. Other schools formed three categories somewhat differently: Remember and Understand (Knowledge and Comprehension), Apply, and Higher-Order Thinking (including Analyze, Evaluate, and Create). The advantage of these condensations is that they eliminate the need for struggling with how to classify learning objectives into one of the top three categories of the taxonomy. A disadvantage of using a condensed version of the taxonomy is that teachers may stop trying to teach learning objectives in the Evaluate and Create categories because, after condensing, Apply and Analyze—generally easier skills to assess—will be in the same category as Evaluate and Create.

Webb's Depth of Knowledge Levels

As part of the No Child Left Behind legislation, states were required to show evidence that the state accountability tests are well matched with the state standards they are intended to measure. **Alignment studies** are conducted to document this match. Most alignment studies are concerned with both the content and the level of cognition represented in the test. One widely used method for conducting alignment studies was developed by Webb (1997). Expert review data are often sought to document whether the test items and standards match in content, whether they match in level of cognitive

challenge, and whether they match in relative emphasis or weight given to each standard. As part of this methodology, Webb developed a taxonomy called Depth of Knowledge (Webb, 1997; Webb, Herman, & Webb, 2007).

The Depth of Knowledge levels are four broad categories that can apply across different content areas. Their general descriptions are as follows (Webb, Herman, & Webb, 2007).

Level 1—Recall

- Recall a fact, definition, or simple procedure
- Apply a simple algorithm or formula (solve a one-step problem)
- Example verbs: identify, recall, recognize, use, and measure

Level 2—Skill/Concept

- Make a mental decision requiring more than rote action or recall
- Interpret information, read a graph, notice patterns
- Solve a two-step problem
- Example verbs: classify, organize, estimate, make observations, collect and display data, compare data

Level 3—Strategic Thinking

- Reason, plan, use evidence, make conjectures
- Explain one's thinking
- Perform tasks that have multiple ways to give good responses
- Example verbs: explain, plan, reason

Level 4—Extended Thinking

- Use complex reasoning, perform extended tasks over time
- Design and conduct experiments
- Draw conclusions or synthesize ideas across multiple texts
- Example verbs: design, make connections, synthesize

Appendix D presents more specific examples of work at each of the four levels in specific subject areas: English language arts, mathematics, science, and social studies.

Choosing a Taxonomy

We have discussed two different schemes for classifying cognitive learning objectives, Bloom's and Webb's. There are many more taxonomies that we have not discussed, some of which are in Appendix D of this book. Which one should you use? That depends on whether this is a personal decision for use in your classroom only or a more general decision about a taxonomy that will be used throughout your school system.

Checklist

Criteria for Selecting a Taxonomy of Cognitive Learning Objectives

1. *Completeness:* To what degree can your major learning objectives be classified within this taxonomy?

   Not at all   Somewhat   To a great extent

2. *Point of view:* To what extent can this taxonomy be used as a platform for explaining your teaching methods or your curriculum characteristics to others?

   Not at all   Somewhat   To a great extent

3. *Reform:* To what extent can this taxonomy help you evaluate your curriculum and learning objectives and revise as needed?

   Not at all   Somewhat   To a great extent

4. *Simplicity:* How easy is it for parents, teachers, and education officials to understand this taxonomy?

   Not at all   Somewhat   To a great extent

5. *Reporting:* How useful is this taxonomy in organizing reports on assessment results for individual students, educational officials, government officials, or the public?

   Not at all   Somewhat   To a great extent

To choose among the various taxonomies, apply the practical criteria in the checklist to judge each taxonomy or classification scheme you are considering. If the decision is a personal one for a single classroom, then not all criteria may apply.

> **MyLab Education Self-Check 2.3**
>
> **MyLab Education Application Exercise 2.3:** Classifying Learning Outcomes

CONCLUSION

Well-conceived learning objectives are the foundation for both instruction and assessment. They are also the means by which instruction and assessment are coordinated. Such coordination or alignment is the basis for valid classroom assessment. In Chapter 3, we consider the broader concept of validity for both classroom and large-scale assessment.

EXERCISES

1. Write three specific learning objectives for a lesson you plan to teach. Explain how each objective meets the three criteria: student centered, performance centered, and content centered.

2. Following are three learning objectives. Decide whether each is a mastery learning or a developmental learning objective. Explain your choices.
   a. The student is able to take the square root of any number using a handheld calculator.
   b. The student is able to determine whether the thesis of the argument is supported adequately.
   c. When given data, the student is able to construct a graph to describe the trend in the data.

3. Obtain a copy of the Common Core State Standards in either English/language arts or mathematics. Select one unit you are teaching or plan to teach in the future that is based on one or more of these standards. Explain what you would need to do to align your classroom learning objectives and student assessments with the standard(s) you selected. Summarize the results and report them to your class.

4. Decide whether each learning objective listed here belongs to the cognitive, affective, or psychomotor domain. Does the performance of each learning objective require some use of elements from domains other than the one into which you classified it? Which one(s)? Explain why. Does this mean you should reclassify that objective? Explain.
   a. The student is able to adjust a television to get the best color resolution.
   b. The student demonstrates knowledge of parliamentary law by conducting a meeting without violating parliamentary procedures.
   c. The student contributes to group maintenance when working with classmates on a science project.
   d. The student makes five baskets in 10 attempts on the basketball court while standing at the foul line.

CHAPTER
3

Validity of Assessment Results

KEY CONCEPTS

1. Validity is the soundness of your interpretations and uses of students' assessment results. For classroom assessment, the major validity concerns are (a) ensuring that the assessments truly match the learning objectives (as intended and as taught, in both content and process) and (b) ensuring that the consequences serve students and their learning.

2. For large-scale assessment, validity evidence can be of several types: content, thinking skills, internal structure, external structure, reliability, generalization, consequences, and practicality. A validity argument proceeds in three steps: describing intended purpose for the assessment scores, providing evidence that the assessment scores serve the intended purpose, and investigating intended and unintended consequences of using the assessment scores.

3. The correlation coefficient quantifies the degree of relationship between two scores. It is used in validity evidence whenever the relationship between two scores is of interest.

4. The validity of accommodations made when assessing students with disabilities depends on the purpose of the assessment.

IMPORTANT TERMS

argument-based approach to validation
accommodations
concurrent validity evidence
content relevance
content representativeness
correlation coefficient
curricular relevance
ethnic and gender stereotyping
expectancy table
external structure
four principles for validation
internal structure
interpretive argument
modifications
multiple-assessment strategy
negative correlation
objectivity
passage dependency
Pearson product-moment correlation coefficient
positive correlation
predictive validity evidence
scatter diagram (scattergram)
table of specifications
validity
validity argument
validity coefficient

GENERAL NATURE OF VALIDITY

In Chapter 1, we discussed guiding principles for selecting and using assessment. Applying those principles leads to meaningful assessment results. Meaningful assessment is one way to talk about validity. **Validity** is the soundness of your interpretations and uses of students' assessment results. To validate your interpretations and uses of students' assessment results, combine evidence from a variety of sources that demonstrate these interpretations and uses are appropriate and demonstrate that students experience no serious negative consequences when results are used as you intend.

The question "Are these assessment results valid?" has many different answers *depending on how the results are interpreted and used*. For example, suppose your school administers the ABC Reading Test and wishes to use the scores for one or more of the following purposes: to describe students' growth in reading comprehension; to place students into high, middle, and low reading groups; and to evaluate the school's reading program. The scores from this hypothetical test may have a high degree of validity for one of these purposes but may not for the others.

Thus, we may not say, "Is the ABC Reading Test valid?" except as an informal, shorthand way of speaking. Rather, we must ask more specific questions such as, "Is it valid to interpret the scores from the ABC Reading Test as measuring reading comprehension?" or "Is it valid to use ABC Reading Test scores to place students into reading groups?" and so on.

The scores from our hypothetical ABC Reading Test, for example, may be highly valid when used to evaluate the reading program in your school district because the items on it match the district's reading program objectives quite well. On the other hand, scores from the same test may have poor validity for evaluating your neighboring district's reading program because the items match that district's reading program objectives poorly.

Make judgments about the validity of interpretations or uses of assessment results only after studying and combining several types of validity evidence. As an example, before coming to a conclusion about the validity of a proposed interpretation or the use of the ABC Reading Test's scores, collect evidence about several relevant aspects of how well it samples the reading domain. Do the skills assessed represent "authentic" or appropriate reading? Are the scores unduly influenced by irrelevant factors such as the students' moods or their motivation to be tested? How closely do the tested skills match your school district's reading objectives? Are the scores reliable?

Validity is a judgment you make *after considering evidence from all relevant areas*. Until you have collected, reviewed, weighed, and combined all relevant evidence, your evaluation of the validity of the results is incomplete. In effect, validating specific interpretations and uses of assessment results requires making a convincing argument that the evidence supports them (Kane, 1992, 2006, 2013; Mislevy, 2016).

FOUR PRINCIPLES FOR VALIDATION

Four principles for validation will help you decide how valid your assessment results are (Messick, 1989b, 1994). Base your validity judgment on all four principles, not just on one of them.

1. The *interpretations* (or meanings) you give to your students' assessment results are valid only to the degree that you can point to evidence that supports their appropriateness.
2. The *uses* you may make of your assessment results are valid only to the degree to which you can point to evidence that supports their appropriateness.
3. The interpretations and uses of your assessment results are valid only when the *values* implied by them are appropriate.
4. The interpretations and uses you make of your assessment results are valid only when the *consequences* of these interpretations and uses are consistent with appropriate values.

These principles are explained in the following paragraphs.

Appropriate Interpretations

Consider, for example, a Lincoln School student, Hiram. Hiram has taken the ABC Reading Test each year, but his scores suddenly rose this year. How would you interpret the sudden increase in Hiram's score? Here are several possible interpretations: (a) his reading comprehension has improved, (b) his motivation to do well on reading comprehension tests has improved, and (c) his skill in answering multiple-choice reading comprehension test items has improved. These interpretations are not mutually exclusive. Hiram may have improved in one or more of these areas.

The Lincoln School staff may like to interpret Hiram's assessments to mean an improvement in his reading comprehension. Before they can claim that such an interpretation has some degree of validity, however, they need to offer evidence. First, they need to show that the ABC Reading Test measures reading comprehension in the way reading specialists define comprehension. Second, they need evidence to show that Hiram's increased test performance is due primarily to his improved reading, rather than simply a result of his increased motivation to do well on the test and his improved test-taking skills. Third, they need to use other evidence that exists in the school: Hiram's reading teacher and/or classroom teacher should compare his test performance with his classroom reading performance.

Appropriate Uses

We distinguish between *interpretations*—the meanings you assign to the scores—and *uses*—what actions you take based on the scores. What are some of the test uses that the Lincoln School staff might have in mind? They may want, for example, to (a) certify that Hiram is reading at an appropriate level for his grade; (b) diagnose or identify the types of reading comprehension problems Hiram may be experiencing; (c) place Hiram into a remedial, regular, or advanced reading group; and (d) continually monitor Hiram's growth in reading comprehension. The Lincoln School staff may wish to use Hiram's scores for more than one of these purposes. However, the validity of any of Lincoln School's uses of the ABC Reading Test scores depends on the evidence teachers and school officials can find to support each use. For example, what evidence can Lincoln School provide to demonstrate that students assigned to remedial reading groups based on their ABC Reading Test scores will learn to read better than if they were assigned to the regular reading classes? Evidence should be provided separately for each intended use of assessment results. For published standardized tests, much of this evidence may be available already in the test's technical manual, so a school may not need to do its own research. This is not always the case, however.

Notice that the Lincoln School examples used wording that implied a reading comprehension *interpretation* of the test results. This illustrates an important point about the assessment validation process: *To validate a particular usage of assessment results, you must also employ a validated interpretation or meaning of those results.* Thus, Lincoln School must first establish the degree to which the ABC Reading Test measures reading comprehension. If it cannot do this, the school would not be able to validate any further use of the test scores that are based on the assumption that the test measures reading comprehension.

Appropriate Values

The interpretations you give to and the uses you make of your students' assessment results arise from your educational and social values. What values were implied when Lincoln School's staff interpreted Hiram's ABC Reading Test scores as measuring reading comprehension and used them to describe and to plan his reading development?

First, the very choice of the ABC Reading Test implied that the staff valued the format and content of the test items. Suppose that the ABC Reading Test consists of several short passages (less than 500 words), each followed by several multiple-choice questions. Further, suppose the themes of the reading passages ignore (or are irrelevant to) African American, Hispanic, Native American, or other minority cultural experiences. Using and interpreting this test as a measure of reading comprehension implies the staff accepted that such cultural and ethnic experiences are unimportant in assessing a student's reading comprehension.

Second, using a multiple-choice format for assessing reading comprehension is also a value judgment: Should longer, more "authentic" reading passages and open-ended questions be used instead? Does the less expensive multiple-choice test have more value than the more costly authentic assessment?

Third, the staff's use of the test scores to assign students to different reading groups implies that they value homogeneous grouping for reading instruction. This choice also implies that the benefits received from being taught with others of similar reading ability outweigh the benefits received from being taught in a more mixed reading ability group.

Again, notice that the discussion of value judgments in the preceding paragraphs uses a reading comprehension interpretation of the test results *and* describes specific ways of using the scores. This example illustrates that you must consider proper interpretations, relevant uses, and appropriate values when asking how valid your assessment results are.

Appropriate Consequences

Whenever you interpret and use your students' assessment results, intended and unintended consequences result: Every action you take has a consequence. You must consider these consequences when judging whether you are using the assessment results validly. What are the intended and unintended consequences for Lincoln School? Lincoln School's intended consequence for placing children with low ABC Reading Test scores into remedial reading groups was to improve these children's reading ability as rapidly as possible. As the students' reading comprehension improves, the staff believes, so will their other schoolwork and their self-esteem.

But suppose something unintended and unvalued happens instead. Suppose the remedial reading students quickly come to see themselves as incompetent, and their self-esteem declines. Suppose, too, that out of frustration their teachers begin drilling them on material the students do not understand, instead of building on what they already know. Suppose that eventually the students never leave the remedial reading track. In the face of these unintended and negative consequences, would Lincoln School's use of the ABC Reading Test scores to form remedial groups still be highly valid? Even if the test measured reading comprehension, when such negative consequences occur, its continued use would be devastating to some children. Interpretations and uses of assessment results must have positively valued consequences (and avoid negatively valued consequences) to have a high degree of validity.

This example uses a reading comprehension interpretation of the test results, describes a specific use of the results (placement into remedial reading groups), and incorporates a positively valued intention (improved student reading and self-esteem). The example also shows, however, that positively valued consequences may not result for all students. You must consider appropriate interpretations, appropriate uses, appropriate values, *and* appropriate consequences when asking how valid your assessment results are.

VALIDITY OF TEACHER-MADE CLASSROOM ASSESSMENT RESULTS

Validity criteria apply to inferences made from all types of classroom assessments, including brief assignments, long-term assignments, and quizzes. As you read this section, keep a common classroom assessment example in mind, for instance a test at the end of a unit or a major project for the unit. Several criteria may be used to improve the validity of using your assessment results for grading students. These criteria are summarized in Figure 3.1, which organizes them into several categories discussed in this section.

Content Representativeness and Relevance

The validity of your classroom assessment results depends very much on how well your assessment samples your learning objectives (see Chapter 2). To create valid assessments, you must (a) clearly identify the important learning objectives and (b) be sure they are well sampled by the assessment procedure.

The learning objectives you teach and assess should fit into the appropriate context of your school district, your state standards, and the discipline you are teaching. The tasks included on your assessment should reflect the important content and thinking skills outcomes specified in your school's and state's standards. Review each assessment task to ensure that, from the content perspective, it is relevant, important, stated accurately, has an accurate key or scoring rubric, and represents something that is meaningful to learn. Focus on the following questions:

1. *Does my assessment procedure emphasize what I have taught?*   Students have a right to expect to be evaluated on what you have emphasized in class. If you have spent a lot of time on one area of the material, the assessment should feature that area prominently. This intended emphasis may not happen if you uncritically use the tests that come with the curriculum materials or the textbook. Often, the items on these tests are of poor quality, emphasize low-level thinking skills (Center for the Study of Testing, Evaluation, and Educational Policy, 1992), or emphasize different content than was emphasized during teaching. We recall a tragic anecdote in this regard. A teacher used one of these tests without carefully reviewing it. The day of the test, the teacher

FIGURE 3.1 **Criteria for improving the validity of scores from classroom assessments used for assigning grades to students.**

Category	Criteria to be attained. Your assessment should:
Content representativeness and relevance	1. Emphasize what you taught
	2. Represent school's stated curricular content
	3. Represent current thinking about the subject
	4. Contain content worth learning
Thinking processes and skills represented	5. Require students to integrate and use several thinking skills
	6. Represent thinking processes and skills stated in school's curriculum
	7. Contain tasks that cannot be completed without using intended thinking skills
	8. Allow enough time for students to use complex skills and processes
Consistency with other classroom assessments	9. Yield pattern of results consistent with your other assessments of the class
	10. Contain individual tasks (items) that are not too easy or too difficult
Reliability and objectivity	11. Use a systematic procedure for every student to assign quality ratings or marks
	12. Provide each student with several opportunities to demonstrate competence for each learning objective assessed
Fairness to different types of students	13. Contain tasks that are interpreted appropriately by students with different backgrounds
	14. Accommodate students with disabilities or learning difficulties, if necessary
	15. Be free of ethnic, racial, and gender bias
Economy, efficiency, practicality, instructional features	16. Require a reasonable amount of time for you to construct and use
	17. Represent appropriate use of students' class time
	18. Represent appropriate use of your class time
Multiple assessment usage	19. Be used in conjunction with other assessment results for important decisions
Positive consequences for learning	20. Result in both you and the students getting information that benefits student learning
	21. Avoid inappropriate impediments to learning

discovered that 10 of the 40 items covered material that she had not taught. In desperation, the teacher used the first 15 minutes of testing time to try to teach these concepts and then gave the test. Of course, this assessment not only lacked validity but also produced student frustration and disastrous results. This case is an example, too, of unethical use of a test on the part of the teacher.

2. *Do my assessment tasks and scoring schemes accurately represent the outcomes specified in my school's and state's curriculum framework?*   Assessments that you use in grading and in the formative assessments that precede grading should reflect the learning objectives that the school district and state identify as important. Students' grades will be recorded and eventually will be interpreted by persons who have seen the curriculum but who are not familiar with what you taught in the classroom. They will expect the grades to reflect the district's learning objectives and the state's standards. Because grades are based on your assessments, your assessments should reflect these learning outcomes.

3. *Are my assessment tasks in line with the current thinking about what should be taught and how it should be assessed?* Educators, philosophers, curriculum theorists, researchers, and others are constantly redefining what is worth learning. Professional teachers keep abreast of these developments and implement them in their teaching and assessment practices.

4. *Is the content in my assessment important and worth learning?* Content included in your assessment should be of great value or significance to a student's further learning or life skills. The curriculum and content you teach contain many specifics. Be certain that the assessed content relates directly, rather than tangentially, to important student learning objectives.

Most worthwhile learning involves students' applying combinations of skills and content rather than using isolated skills or memorizing bits of content. Teaching and assessment, therefore, should also require students to apply several aspects of such knowledge, skills, and processes in combination.

Thinking Processes and Skills Represented

Closely related to content representativeness and relevance is whether your assessment method permits you to evaluate students on a sufficiently wide range of thinking skills and processes. Assessment instruments that cover broad areas of learning—a unit, marking period, or semester—should comprehensively assess different types of thinking skills. We stressed using taxonomies in Chapter 2 because of the importance of this comprehensiveness. A taxonomy is used along with a content outline to write an assessment blueprint. This blueprint helps you ensure that your assessment covers the important thinking skills and content. Such comprehensiveness can be accomplished only by consciously planning for it. Chapter 6 discusses how to develop assessment plans, and Figure 6.5 shows an example of a test blueprint.

The following questions will help you judge the validity of your classroom assessment in relation to thinking skills and processes:

5. *Do the tasks on my assessment instrument require students to use important thinking skills and processes?* Every classroom assessment procedure should require students to use a mixture of thinking skills and processes. The issue here, however, is the degree to which your assessment mirrors the important thinking skills used in the discipline and the state standards you are teaching. For example, a mathematics assessment should help you assess whether a student uses good mathematics thinking when solving problems, not only whether the student can obtain the right answer. Assessment in social studies should help you assess how students think critically and apply the material to their daily lives, rather than simply assessing whether they can "compare and contrast" or "list the factors that caused. ..." Assessment tasks should at least simulate real-life applications at levels appropriate for the students you teach. They should require students to use combinations of several skills and knowledge whenever possible.

6. *Does my assessment instrument represent the kinds of thinking skills that my school's curriculum framework and state's standards view as important?* Local curricula and state standards often include certain types of higher-order critical thinking and performances as goals of instruction (see Chapter 11). Your lesson's learning objectives should be aligned with these curricula and standards, your teaching should foster the kind of thinking in the objectives, and your assessments should likewise reflect the level of thinking specified in the objectives.

7. *During the assessment, do students actually use the types of thinking I expect them to use?* If you are going to interpret students' assessment as reflecting complex thinking skills, then you should be sure that students are actually using them when completing the assessment. Check this by observing the strategies your students appear to use during the assessment. You may interview a few students, asking them to "think aloud" as they solve assessment tasks. You may also review the tasks on your assessment. Poorly constructed test items will give clues to the correct answers and lower the chances that students will need to use the important thinking skills you want them to use. Similarly, ambiguously worded questions confuse students, interfering with their use of important strategies, and lower the validity of their scores.

8. *Do I allow enough time for students to demonstrate the type of thinking I am trying to assess?* Complex thinking, meaningful problem solving, and creative applications require considerable time

for most students to demonstrate. A 40- to 50-minute classroom period is usually too short to permit valid assessment of such thinking. You may need to assess students over a longer period for the results to be validly interpreted as reflecting these types of learning outcomes. In other words, you may need to give a test over a longer time or assess some learning objectives using projects or portfolios.

Consistency with Other Classroom Assessments

Over the course of the unit, marking period, or semester, you will have observed the individuals in your class many times. You will have collected much information that is relevant to evaluating each student's attainments. The results of a student's assessment for grading should be consistent with the student's pattern of performance on instructional activities and formative assessments throughout the period. Some students may perform better or worse than you expect, of course, and you should try to determine why. However, the pattern of assessment results for the entire class should not surprise you. If it is a surprise, there may be a validity problem with your assessment procedure. Evaluate this possibility by focusing on these questions:

9. *Is the pattern of results in the class consistent with what I expected based on my other assessments of them?* If the pattern for the class is quite different from what you were expecting, review your assessment procedure in relation to Questions 1 through 8. For example, perhaps the emphasis of your test did not match the emphasis of your teaching. Perhaps it did not match the content emphasis of the other assessments on which you based your expectations. If these reasons explain the discrepancy, you may not be able to interpret the assessment results as mastery or use them for validly grading the students.

10. *Do I make the assessment tasks too difficult or too easy for my students?* When assessment tasks are too difficult or too easy, the results will not be consistent with your other student observations. All students will attain nearly the same result, and you will be unable to distinguish the degrees to which students have achieved your objectives. This lack of variation in scores may lower the validity of the results. Also, assessments that are too difficult frustrate students, making them feel as if their study time was wasted. Such a situation is a negative consequence and does not encourage students' best performances. Assessment tasks should be challenging, of course, but not so difficult that only one or two students in the class can perform well on them.

Reliability and Objectivity

Reliability refers to the consistency of assessment results. Reliability is the subject of a separate chapter (Chapter 4) but is necessary for valid assessment results. If your students' scores on your assessments are so inconsistent as to be essentially random numbers, your assessments cannot be valid. Inconsistencies that lower the validity of your classroom assessment scores are caused by such factors as using too short a test, failing to use proper scoring rubrics, and succumbing to your own day-to-day fluctuations in judgment. Chapter 4 will address these factors in more detail.

Objectivity is the degree to which two or more qualified evaluators will agree on what quality rating or score to assign a student's performance. Objectivity is not an all-or-nothing characteristic, of course. It is a matter of degree: All assessment results are more or less objective.

This fact does not mean that the more subjective assessment procedures should be eliminated. As a professional and expert teacher, your judgments are extremely valuable and important to students. What students seek is consistency and fairness in your professional judgment. When evaluating your classroom assessment procedures, keep focused on these questions:

11. *Do I use a scoring guide for obtaining quality ratings or scores from students' performance on the assessment?* Such a guide may be a scoring key, a scoring rubric, or a rating scale with each rating level clearly defined. Apply your scoring guide in the same manner to the work of every student you are assessing. Your scoring guide should be clear enough that a qualified teaching colleague could use it and obtain the same results as you do.

12. *Is my assessment instrument long enough to be a representative sample of the types of learning outcomes I am assessing?* Your assessment should contain several opportunities for students to demonstrate their knowledge and skill for each

learning objective. If practical constraints do not allow for a more complete assessment in one class period, consider using another class period, a take-home assessment, or a combination of results from several assessments administered over the marking period.

Fairness to Different Types of Students

Your assessment procedures should be fair to students from all ethnic and socioeconomic backgrounds, as well as students with disabilities who are mainstreamed in your class. For example, a deaf student may understand the concepts you have taught but not be able to express that understanding on your written or oral assessment. Deaf students' general vocabulary and verbal skills usually lag behind that of their hearing peers, even though their content knowledge may be on par. In such cases, a more valid assessment of a student's understanding may be obtained through a special assessment with a lower verbal load (e.g., simplifying or explaining the nontechnical or nonsubject-specific vocabulary) or through an alternative communication mode (e.g., using a signed language). Chapter 5 discusses assessment accommodation strategies; the last section of this chapter discusses important validity issues concerning accommodation strategies.

Similarly, your assessment should not contain material that is subtly or blatantly offensive to any subgroup of students or that perpetuates **ethnic and gender stereotyping**. For example, you would be perpetuating stereotypes if your assessment materials depict (in words or pictures) only majority race members or males as leaders, technically trained, professional, and so on, or minority race(s) or females only as followers, unskilled, or technically backward (Camilli, 2006). As you evaluate your classroom assessment procedure for fairness, focus on the following questions:

13. *Do I word the problems or tasks on my assessment so that students with different ethnic and socioeconomic backgrounds will interpret them in appropriate ways?* "Appropriate interpretation" of assessment tasks does not mean that everyone has identical interpretations. There may be several appropriate ways to interpret the same task. Good classroom assessments will permit you to evaluate the richness in diversity of your students' thinking. You may wish to interview a few

students to understand how they interpreted the tasks you set. You should also check whether all students understood the assessment directions and the scoring rules. If students do not understand your directions, they may respond inappropriately through no fault of their own. If this happens, the assessment results will not be valid for purposes of grading.

14. *Do I modify the wording or the administrative conditions of the assessment tasks to accommodate students with disabilities or special learning problems?* The basic interpretation you wish to make is whether the students have achieved the learning objectives you are assessing. If the way that you organize your assessment materials inhibits students' ability to communicate their understanding, your assessment results are less valid. Some teachers may balk at the idea of assessment accommodations. They may claim that such adaptations for a few students make the assessment unstandardized and unfair to the majority of students. But fairness is not a matter of a vote for how to obtain information in which the majority wins. Valid assessment results give us a clear picture of what each student is capable of doing in relation to the learning objectives. A key principle is to modify elements that are not part of the learning objective (e.g., the reading level of questions is not relevant to many learning objectives in social studies, but it is in reading).

15. *Do the pictures, stories, verbal statements, or other aspects of my assessment procedure perpetuate racial, ethnic, or gender stereotypes?* Assessments need not be free of any reference to race, ethnicity, or gender. Instead, eliminate stereotypes and balance the references among various groups to represent a diversity of peoples and views.

Economy, Efficiency, Practicality, Instructional Features

Assessment activities should not consume all of your time. Practical questions about feasibility also inform validity judgments, because assessment information needs to be useful and usable.

16. *Is the assessment relatively easy for me to construct and not too cumbersome to use to evaluate students?* There is a tension between how easy it is to create assessment tasks and how easy it is to obtain quality ratings or scores. It is simpler to develop essay questions, for example, than to

develop complex problem-solving performance tasks or good multiple-choice items. Once developed, however, multiple-choice items are easier to score and may be reused for next year's class. Problem-solving performance tasks set in real-life settings are difficult to construct properly. However, they let you assess more completely whether students can use what they learned than do either the typical teacher-crafted multiple-choice items or short-answer questions.

17. *Would the time needed to use this assessment be better spent directly teaching my students instead?* Balance assessment time with other uses of students' class time. Some procedures, such as interviews and individual observations of students' performance, require a long time to complete. Also, while interviewing or observing one student, you need to keep the remainder of the class meaningfully engaged in learning. Group tests, on the other hand, are more efficient because you administer them to all the students at the same time. Depending on what information you need, you will sometimes opt for more efficient group tests and sometimes for more time-consuming methods.

18. *Does my assessment represent the best use of my time?* Essay tests, term papers, projects, and lengthy written works generally require much student time to complete and much teacher time to grade and evaluate. When using these procedures, you must decide whether they are a wise investment of your time. However, grading time and student-learning time need not be entirely separate. For example, you may be able to evaluate a term paper or a project in a student conference. If you can do this in a nonthreatening way, "talking through" the reasons for your evaluation with the student, the student will have a chance to understand the quality of work you are expecting. This opportunity may also let the student ask questions, clarify the criteria you are using, contribute to the evaluation itself, and otherwise improve her grasp of the learning objectives. Such rich interaction is often not possible with multiple-choice testing, which usually yields only one score.

Multiple-Assessment Usage

19. *Do I use one assessment result in conjunction with other assessment results?* No one assessment technique will produce perfectly valid results for a given purpose. A **multiple-assessment strategy** combines the results from several different types of assessments (such as homework, class performance, quizzes, projects, and tests) to improve the validity of your decisions about a student's attainments. Weighing one assessment outcome too heavily in relation to others (like making the student's semester grade depend almost exclusively on his end-of-semester test performance) results in lowered validity. Evaluate the validity of inferences made from multiple assessments with evidence of how the multiple assessments, taken together, represent the learning objectives you wish to assess.

Positive Consequences for Learning

20. *Do my assessments result in both the students' and my getting information that helps students learn?* The major intended positive consequence of classroom assessment is classroom learning. If this is not the result, your assessment is not functioning validly.

21. *Do my assessments avoid inappropriate negative consequences?* Inappropriate negative consequences vary widely. One example is a test that results in students drawing inaccurate conclusions about what knowledge and skill means in a particular domain, as when a middle school algebra test results in students concluding that knowledge of algebra is rote application of formulas. Another inappropriate negative consequence would be a student inaccurately concluding that she "isn't smart" in a particular domain as the result of taking an inappropriately difficult test— or concluding that she is a whiz as the result of taking an inappropriately easy test.

MyLab Education Self-Check 3.1

MyLab Education Application Exercise 3.1: Validity of Classroom Grading Practices

---

VALIDITY OF LARGE-SCALE ASSESSMENT RESULTS

Large-scale assessments are external, *extra-classroom assessments* that include district- and state-mandated assessments, standardized achievement and aptitude tests, attitude inventories, and individually administered intelligence tests, to name only a few. These and other assessment methods are described in Part III of this book.

In this section, we discuss the types of evidence required to support the valid interpretation and use of their results. Understanding these kinds of validity evidence will help you to locate the proper information to evaluate and select an assessment instrument.

Construct an Argument for Validity, Supported by Evidence

At least eight types of evidence may be considered before you reach a decision about the validity of an assessment's results for a particular interpretation and use. The types of evidence do not carry the same weight, however, because assessment results are interpreted and used differently in different settings. Each setting requires a somewhat different emphasis on various types of evidence.

Figure 3.2 summarizes eight types of evidence that validity theorists (Cronbach, 1988, 1989; Kane, 2006, 2013; Linn, Baker, & Dunbar, 1991; Messick, 1989a, 1989b) have identified as important. In addition, the figure lists the typical questions each type of evidence addresses and the typical procedures used to gather the evidence.

You will notice the similarity between some of the types of evidence and questions in Figure 3.2 and the material presented in the previous section on validating the results of teacher-made assessments. All validation procedures amount to marshaling evidence in support of an intended interpretation or use. The purposes for using external assessments are usually different from those of classroom assessments, however. Therefore, the emphases and mixes of evidence used to judge validity differ also.

Much of this kind of evidence is available if you know what to look for. Presentations of validity arguments and evidence for state accountability tests should be available in the tests' technical reports. Sometimes these are available on state department of education websites. Other information about such tests, for example information about test development, administration and scoring, a description of the students who took the test, item analyses, score distributions, and reliability statistics will also be included in the technical reports. As an example, the technical reports for the Pennsylvania System of School Assessment (PSSA) are available at http://www.education.pa.gov/K-12/Assessment%20and%20Accountability/PSSA/Pages/PSSA-Technical-Reports.aspx#tab-1.

Other large-scale tests (see Chapters 16 and 19 for examples) should also have technical manuals that you can find on their websites or obtain from the test publisher. For most of the tests you will administer and use in your teaching career, you will not need to construct a validity argument, but rather you will need to be able to read and follow a validity argument that is provided with the test. You will need to know that the information we describe below should exist and seek it out. You will need to know why validity evidence is important and what it means.

Measurement specialists now recommend that validity be used as a unitary concept (American Educational Research Association et al., 2014; Kane, 2006; Messick, 1989b). This book follows this recommendation. Thus, you should think of the following as types of evidence that support an assessment's validity, not as different kinds of validity. The discussion throughout this chapter stresses that you must be prepared to review and combine several types of evidence before judging the validity of particular assessment results for a given purpose.

Kane (1992, 2001, 2002, 2006, 2013) suggests that you (a) state clearly what interpretations and uses you intend to make of the assessment results, (b) present a logically coherent argument to support your claim that the assessment results can be interpreted and used as you intend, and (c) support your logical argument by citing evidence for and against your intended interpretation(s) and use(s). This approach is called the **argument-based approach to validation** (Kane, 2006, p. 23).

1. An **interpretive argument** specifies the proposed interpretations and uses of test results by laying out the network of inferences and assumptions leading from the observed performances to the conclusions and decisions based on the performances.

2. The **validity argument** provides an evaluation of the interpretive argument.

Evidence to support your validity argument and refute potential counterarguments comes from the various categories described in Figure 3.2. The types of evidence you emphasize in your argument will depend on the assessment practice you want to validate. Kane (1992) gives the following example: Suppose that you want to validate using an algebra placement test to assign students either to a remedial algebra course or to

FIGURE 3.2 Summary of the different types of validity evidence for educational assessments.

Type of evidence	Examples of questions to be answered	Techniques often used to obtain answers
1. Content representativeness and relevance (called *content evidence*)	a. How well do the assessment tasks represent the domain of important content? b. How well do the assessment tasks represent the curriculum and state standards? c. How well do the assessment tasks reflect current thinking about what should be taught and assessed? d. Are the assessment tasks worthy of being learned?	Obtain a description of the curriculum and content to be learned. Check each assessment task to see if it matches important content and learning outcomes. Rate each assessment task for its relevance, importance, accuracy, and meaningfulness. The assessment procedure is viewed as a whole, and judgments are made about representativeness and relevance of the entire collection of tasks.
2. Types of thinking skills and processes required (called *substantive evidence*)	a. How much do the assessment tasks require students to use important thinking skills and processes? b. How well do the assessment tasks represent the types of thinking skills in important curriculum outcomes and state standards? c. Do students actually use intended thinking skills and processes to complete the assessment procedure?	Analyze the assessment procedure to reveal the types of cognitions required to perform the tasks successfully. Determine the relationship between the strategies students are taught to use and those they are required to use during the assessment. Students may be asked to "think aloud" while performing the assessment tasks and the resultant protocols analyzed to identify cognitions the students used. Judge the assessment procedure as a whole to decide whether desirable, representative, and relevant thinking skills and processes are being assessed.
3. Relationships among the assessment tasks or parts of the assessment (called *internal structure evidence*)	a. Do all the assessment tasks "work together" so that each task contributes positively toward assessing the quality of interest? b. If the different parts of the assessment procedure are supposed to provide unique information, do the results support this uniqueness? c. If the different parts of the assessment procedure are supposed to provide the same or similar information, do the results support this? d. Are the students' responses scored in a way that is consistent with the constructs and theory on which the assessment is based?	a. Evaluate correlations of task scores with total scores from the assessment to decide whether all tasks contribute positively. b. Score each part of the assessment separately; correlate these part scores and evaluate whether the pattern of relationships is as intended. c. Use logic, substantive knowledge, and experience to generate explanations for high and low performance on the assessment. Include competing hypotheses not consistent with intended interpretations. d. Conduct empirical studies, both experimental and correlational, to support or refute the hypotheses generated in (c) above.
4. Relationships of assessment results to the results of other variables (called *external structure evidence*)	a. Are the results of this assessment consistent with the results of other similar assessments for these students? How well does performance on this assessment procedure reflect the quality or trait that is measured by other tests? b. How well does performance on this assessment procedure predict current or future performance on other valued tasks or measures (criteria)? c. How well can the assessment results be used to select persons for jobs, schools, etc.? What is the magnitude of error? d. How well can the assessment results be used to assign pupils to different types of instruction? Is learning better when pupils are assigned this way?	a. Identify criterion tasks. Analyze their important characteristics. b. Compare scores from the assessment to scores on the criterion measure(s) to be predicted. c. Analyze various classification and prediction errors. d. Evaluate whether the results from this assessment converge with or diverge from results from other assessments in the way expected when the proposed interpretation of the students' performance is used (called *convergent and discriminant evidence*).

FIGURE 3.2 *(Continued)*

Type of evidence	Examples of questions to be answered	Techniques often used to obtain answers
5. Reliability over time, assessors, and content domain (called *reliability evidence*)	a. Will the same students obtain nearly the same results if the assessment procedure was applied on another occasion? What is the margin of error? b. If different persons administered, graded, or scored the assessment results, would the students' outcomes be the same? What is the margin of error? c. If a second, alternate form of the assessment procedure were to be developed, with similar content, would the students' results be very similar? What is the margin of error?	Conduct studies focusing on the consistency (reliability) of the assessment results. These studies are described in more detail in Chapter 4.
6. Generalization of interpretations over different types of people, under different conditions, or with special instruction/intervention (called *generalization evidence*)	a. Does the assessment procedure give significantly different results when it is used with students from different socioeconomic and ethnic backgrounds, but of the same ability? If so, is this fair or unbiased? b. Will students' results from the assessment procedure be altered drastically if they are given special incentives or motives? If so, should this change how the assessment results are interpreted? c. Will special intervention, changes in instructions, or special coaching significantly alter the results students obtain on the assessment? If so, should this change how the assessment results are interpreted?	a. Use logic, substantive knowledge, and experience to generate explanations (hypotheses) about how the interpretation of the assessment results might change when the procedure is applied to different types of people, under different conditions, or with special instruction (intervention). b. Conduct empirical studies, both experimental and correlational, to support or refute the hypotheses generated in (a) above.
7. Value of the intended and/or unintended consequences (called *consequential evidence*)	a. What do we expect to happen to the students if we interpret and use the assessment results in this particular way? To what degree do these expected consequences happen, and is that good? b. What side effects do we anticipate for students if we interpret and use the assessment results in this particular way? To what degree are these anticipated side effects occurring, and are they positive or negative? c. What unanticipated negative side effects occurred for students for whom we interpreted and used the assessment results in this particular way? Can these negative side effects be avoided by using other assessment procedures/techniques or by altering our interpretations?	a. Conduct studies to describe the intended outcomes of using the given assessment procedure and to determine the degree to which these outcomes are realized for all students. b. Conduct studies to determine whether anticipated or unanticipated side effects have resulted from interpreting and using the given assessment procedure in a certain way.
8. Cost, efficiency, practicality, instructional features (called *practicality evidence*)	a. Can the assessment procedure accommodate typical numbers of students? b. Is the assessment procedure easy for teachers to use? c. Can the assessment procedure give timely results to guide instruction? d. Do the assessment results meaningfully explain individual differences? e. Do the assessment results identify misunderstandings that need to be corrected? f. Would an alternative assessment procedure be more efficient?	Logical analyses, cost analyses, reviews by teachers, and field trial data are used to come to decisions about the factors of cost, efficiency, practicality, and usefulness of instructional features.

a calculus course. To validate this assessment practice, Kane points out that you need arguments supported by evidence that the following are reasonable:

1. You can appropriately assess students' success in the calculus course (i.e., a suitable criterion assessment procedure is available).

2. You can identify the algebra concepts and thinking skills that students will use frequently in the calculus course.

3. The algebra content and thinking skills assessed by the placement test match those frequently used in the calculus course.

4. The remedial course to which low-scoring students will be assigned will succeed in teaching students the algebra concepts and skills needed in the calculus course.

5. Scores on the placement test are reliable (i.e., students' scores are consistent across different samples of test items, different testing occasions, and different persons scoring the test).

6. It is not helpful for students with high ability in algebra to take the remedial algebra course (i.e., students who score high on the placement tests will not significantly improve their chances of success in calculus by first taking this particular remedial algebra course).

7. The placement test scores are not affected by systematic errors that would lower the validity of your interpretation that the placement test measures algebra knowledge and thinking skills.

Before we discuss the details of the eight types of evidence in Figure 3.2, you should note the following:

1. *The importance of each type of evidence changes as interpretations and uses of assessment results change.* All of the evidence types in Figure 3.2 apply to nearly every kind of assessment procedure. However, different interpretations and uses of assessment procedure results will require some types of evidence to be stronger than others. For example, the SAT is intended to predict first-year college grade point averages. Thus, a university or college should weigh more heavily the test's predictive powers and its potential for negative consequences, such as reducing the number of men it selects, than evidence that the test matches curriculum objectives and content, which should weigh less.

2. *Providing evidence is the responsibility of both the publisher and the user.* Publishers and other agencies that produce assessments are responsible for providing data that support the reliability, validity, and other technical aspects of assessment results. These responsibilities are described in the *Standards for Educational and Psychological Testing* (American Educational Research Association, American Psychological Association, & National Council on Measurement in Education, 2014). The responsibilities of persons who *use* assessment procedures produced by others are described in a number of resources such as the *Code of Fair Testing Practices in Education* (Joint Committee on Testing Practices, 2004), reproduced in Appendix B, and *Responsibilities of Users of Standardized Tests* (*RUST*; 3rd ed., Association for Assessment in Counseling and Education, 2003).

3. *Validity of assessment results is a primary concern even if you cannot afford to conduct validity studies.* Educators at different levels have differing amounts of resources and opportunities for gathering evidence about the validity of results. Teachers have the fewest opportunities and resources; school district administrators have more; and state-level educators even more. This fact does not relieve those with fewer resources (e.g., teachers) from the requirement of validating their interpretations and uses of assessment results. There is a professional obligation to raise issues about the validity of the assessments being used and to seek help in establishing their validity.

Content Representativeness and Relevance: Content Evidence

The idea of content representativeness and relevance applies to all sorts of assessments: achievement tests, aptitude tests, personality tests, student-teacher observation procedures, performance rating scales, and so on. This section focuses mostly on large-scale achievement tests.

Domain Definition As shown in Figure 3.2, this type of evidence comes from judging the content of the tasks or items on an instrument. Evidence of an assessment's **content representativeness** comes from judgments of informed persons that focus on whether the assessment tasks are a representative sample from a larger domain of performance. Any assessment is but a sample of the items that could be presented to students.

Because we cannot present every possible task to a student, we must sample from the domain in such a way that our sample represents the domain fairly. (Think of *re*-presenting the domain in a smaller version.) Evidence of an assessment's **content relevance** comes from judgments of informed persons that focus on how much of the test user's domain definition includes the assessment tasks.

One question that arises is whose definition of the domain is appropriate: the assessment developer's or the assessment user's? The ABC Reading Test, for example, may emphasize paragraph and sentence reading but may not separately measure word attack skills or vocabulary. School personnel selecting a reading test may view these latter areas as relevant to the definition of the reading domain. Here, the test developer and the test user disagree on the definition of the domain and, therefore, on what is or is not to be included in the assessment. Making separate judgments about how well the tasks on the assessment represent (a) the developer's domain and (b) the user's domain will clarify whether the evidence supports a school's intended use of the assessment procedure.

Table of Specifications   A test developer often defines the domain assessed in an accompanying manual or technical publication. Within the manual, a typical tool for defining the domain for standardized survey achievement tests is a **table of specifications**. This table contains the major content categories and skills that are assessed. It describes the percentage of tasks (items) for each content-skills combination. The percentage of tasks per combination is a rough measure of the weight that a combination contributes to the student's total score.

Curricular Relevance and Content Domains   An assessment method is relevant to a school's definition of the achievement domain to the extent that it matches the school's curriculum learning objectives. Evidence of an assessment's **curricular relevance** comes from judgments by informed persons of the degree of overlap between a curriculum and the items contained in the assessment instrument. Figure 3.3 may help clarify the distinction between matching the assessment to the developer's achievement domain and the

FIGURE 3.3   **A schematic illustration of the relationship between an assessment instrument, a developer's content domain, and the curriculum-specific domains of two schools. An assessment may match the developer's domain yet may lack curricular relevance for some schools.**

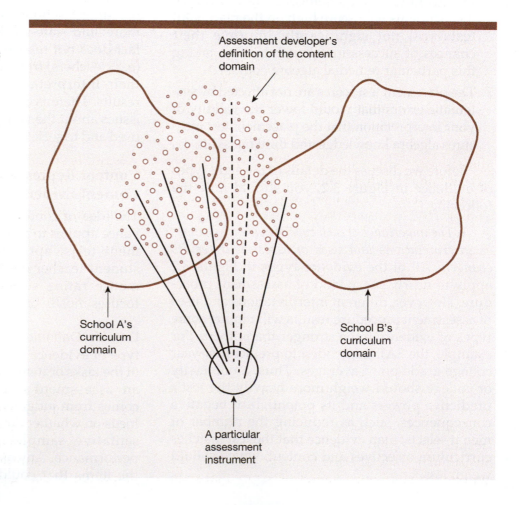

curricular relevance of the assessment. The developer's definition of achievement and the sample of tasks comprising a particular assessment are shown in the center of the figure. The assessment matches the developer's domain if the tasks on it adequately represent the developer's definition. (Both the solid and broken straight lines show these tasks.) The assessment's curricular relevance is based on how well the tasks on the instrument represent your school's curriculum framework. (In Figure 3.3, the solid straight lines show these tasks.) As the figure shows, the assessment illustrated has more curriculum relevance for School A than for School B: A considerable proportion of School A's curriculum is not assessed, however.

This is typical: A school's curriculum framework is usually much broader and richer than any single extra classroom assessment instrument. Thus, even though the assessment instrument illustrated has more curricular relevance for School A than for School B, that degree of relevance still may not be sufficient for the school to use the instrument.

Curricular relevance is more than a simple proportion of the content that matches the curriculum. The instrument must be reviewed as a whole to judge whether different content areas receive emphasis in keeping with the local curriculum's learning goals. The individual tasks on the assessment must also (a) reflect current thinking of subject-matter experts about what is important to teach and to assess, (b) accurately portray the subject matter, (c) be keyed correctly, and (d) contain meaningful and important content. In addition, the individual assessment tasks must be constructed well, so they actually do tap the intended domain.

Alignment of State Standards and Accountability Tests

One important issue for states and schools is the alignment of the assessments used for accountability and the educational standards states specify. In Chapter 2, we mentioned alignment studies, which are empirical studies involving the collection of ratings from trained judges and summaries of students' responses to test items that have the aim of describing, in the most objective ways possible, the degree to which the actual test items on a state's assessment instrument(s) are aligned to the educational content and performance standards set by that state.

These studies provide evidence that falls into the content and substantive categories of Figure 3.2.

In Chapter 2, we focused on the fact that alignment studies use a taxonomy to investigate the alignment of state standards and state tests with regard to thinking skills. Alignment studies investigate other issues of content representativeness and relevance, as well. At a minimum, such studies should provide information about how well their state's assessment(s) match the following:

1. *Content* span, ideas, and detail that are specified by their state's standards.
2. *Depth* of understanding, cognitive complexity, and ability to apply the knowledge described in the state's standards.
3. *Emphasis* of different topics and cognitive processes that are reflected in the state's standards.
4. *Performances* expected of the students as these are described by the state's standards.
5. *Implied applicability* of the state's standards to all students. (For example, does the assessment allow all students, regardless of disability or limited English proficiency, to display completely and fairly their achievement of the state's standards?) (La Marca, Redfield, Winter, Bailey, & Despriet, 2000).

Alignment studies often take into account several years of state assessments rather than only one year's testing. This practice is helpful because, as we have stated earlier, one test is but a sample of the possible domain of items that could be presented to students. Alignment over several years is sometimes a more appropriate criterion. Additional information about alignment of assessments with state standards may be found in Achieve (2004); Rabinowitz, Roeber, Schroeder, & Sheinker (2006); Council of Chief State School Officers (2006); and Porter and Smithson (2001).

Thinking Skills and Processes: Substantive Evidence

An assessment should be judged not only in terms of the content it covers but also in terms of the thinking processes and skills students must use to complete the tasks successfully. As for classroom assessments, large-scale achievement assessments should require students to use important thinking processes and skills as defined by the curriculum framework, by the state's standards, and by experts in the subject matter being assessed. Assessment instruments sometimes ask students to use combinations of skills and knowledge together to work on "real-life" applications.

Assessment developers should provide you with student-based data to support claims that the assessment tasks require students to use higher-order thinking processes and skills (Leighton & Gierl, 2007). This information should include (a) a detailed description of the processes and abilities that they claim to be assessing, (b) a clear demonstration of how each type of task or assessment exercise assesses each of these processes and skills, and (c) evidence from research studies showing that, when responding successfully, students use the thinking processes and skills that are claimed. The latter may take the form of small studies conducted in *cognitive labs*. Students are asked to "think aloud" as they work through the tasks on the instrument. Their thinking is organized into "protocols" and analyzed to reveal the types of thinking strategies students say they have used (Ericsson & Simon, 1999). Zucker, Sassman, and Case (2004) give an example of how one test publisher uses the cognitive lab approach to develop and validate a standardized test.

Studies should also demonstrate that students do not use inappropriate processes to solve the tasks. For example, suppose a multiple-choice mathematics test developer claims to be assessing students' higher-order, problem-solving ability. The developer should provide evidence that students do, in fact, use the intended higher-order abilities and not merely recall.

Relationships Among Parts of Assessment: Internal Structure Evidence

An assessment instrument should not be simply a collection of assessment tasks or test questions. Each task in the procedure should contribute positively to the total result. The **internal structure** of an assessment instrument is described by the interrelationships among the tasks and the relationship between the tasks and the total results. The internal and external structures of an assessment procedure are important in interpreting the assessment results as indicators of a person's standing on an educational or psychological construct. For example, a test may claim to have a unidimensional

internal structure that assesses only one student ability, such as arithmetic problem solving. The developer should provide evidence that each task on this assessment differentiates students along this single dimension, arithmetic problem solving. Often, however, assessment tasks measure more than one dimension. For example, solving an arithmetic problem may depend heavily on reading skill, vocabulary knowledge, computational speed, and general speed of working, as well as arithmetic problem solving. In this case, you may not validly interpret the results as reflecting only the students' arithmetic problem-solving ability.

On the other hand, some assessment instruments are deliberately crafted to assess two or more dimensions. For example, some scholastic aptitude tests provide measures of verbal ability, quantitative ability, and nonverbal ability. (See Chapter 19 for examples.) If so, then the technical manual should contain evidence that verbal, quantitative, and nonverbal test scores are meaningfully different. Evidence from research studies should demonstrate that, although students' scores on the three parts of the test might be moderately related (because they are aspects of a global or general scholastic aptitude), they are different enough to be interpreted as three different aspects of scholastic aptitude.

Test developers often use *correlation coefficients* as evidence to support the validity of these types of interpretations. These coefficients measure the degree of relationship between two or more sets of assessment scores. Correlation coefficients are explained later in this chapter.

Relationships of Results to Other Variables: External Structure Evidence

Evidence about the validity of assessment interpretation and use also comes from how well the assessment results correlate with other variables or criteria. For example, the SAT measures both verbal and mathematics abilities. Its validity depends in part on its internal structure—whether the verbal items in fact measure verbal ability, mathematics items measure mathematics ability, and the scores on the two parts of the test are meaningfully different. However, the primary use of the SAT is to provide information that helps admissions officers select applicants who are likely to succeed in college. The most important validity evidence must come, therefore, from studies that establish the correlation of the SAT test scores with an external variable, namely, grades in college. The **external structure** of an assessment is the pattern of relationships between assessment results (scores) and scores from variables external to the assessment.

The specific evidence you need depends on how you want to interpret and use the assessment results. If you want to use the assessment results to help select candidates for college, for example, then you need to establish that the assessment results are positively correlated with a college success criterion such as grade point average. Sometimes we want to validate that a new assessment measures the same ability as one that already exists. For example, we may want to validate that a multiple-choice and an oral assessment both measure reading comprehension. If they both measure the same ability, you would expect their scores to be positively correlated: Students with high scores on one should also have high scores on the other. If the scores on the two assessments differ significantly, it is likely that they measure different attributes. Additional research would be needed to establish which score, if any, measures reading comprehension. A researcher generates hypotheses and counterhypotheses about the relationships of assessment results to external criteria results from logical analysis, experience, previous research, and a theory about the nature of the traits or characteristics being assessed.

Notice from these two examples that some evidence helps predict future performance (such as success in college), and some evidence estimates the individual's current status on a variable. **Predictive validity evidence** refers to the extent to which individuals' *future performance* on a criterion can be predicted from their prior performance on an assessment instrument. For example, we could collect high school students' grade point averages, wait until they finish one year of college, collect their college grade point averages, and correlate high school grades with them. Prediction over time is the aim. **Concurrent validity evidence** refers to the extent to which individuals' *current status* on a criterion can be estimated from their current performance on an assessment instrument. For example, we can study students already in college, give them a special aptitude test, and collect their current grade point averages. The relationship between the grades and the test is

concurrent validity evidence because the two measures were collected at the same time. The distinction is important because the time interval between administering the assessment instrument and obtaining criterion results affects the strength of the relationship between the two results: Usually the longer the time interval between the two results, the lower the correlation between them.

To understand the external structure information that test developers usually offer, it is necessary to know a little bit about *correlation coefficients*. We turn to this necessary digression in the following paragraphs.

Correlation Coefficient

The **correlation coefficient** is a statistical index that quantifies the degree of relationship between the scores from one assessment and the scores from another. The index is reported on a scale of −1 to +1.

Students' Scores on Different Tests An example showing the relationship between the scores from several tests will help explain correlation. The example in Figure 3.4 shows the scores of 11 students on each of three tests. The students have been arranged in descending order according to their verbal aptitude scores (V). Look at the first two columns of scores and notice that the verbal scores and the reading scores (R) order the students in about the same way. This is not a perfect ordering, however. Notice, too, that the relationship between the verbal and arithmetic scores (A) is less strong: The order of the students is not as similar on these tests as it is on the verbal and reading tests.

Comparing Students' Rank Orders This correspondence is clearer when we transform each score to a rank, as in the last three columns of the example in Figure 3.4. The ranks of the students on verbal aptitude and reading, though not identical in every case, are quite close. The ranks of the students on verbal aptitude and arithmetic correspond less closely, but the ranks are still similar. There is more shifting in the students' ranks from verbal aptitude to arithmetic than there is from verbal aptitude to reading. Comparing students' rank orders on two assessments is one way of studying how correlated the results are.

FIGURE 3.4 Hypothetical scores for 11 pupils on a verbal aptitude test, a reading test, and an arithmetic test.

Pupil	Verbal score (V)	Reading score (R)	Arithmetic score (A)	Verbal rank order	Reading rank order	Arithmetic rank order
A	82	59	48	1	1	4
B	77	54	65	2	4	1
C	70	55	43	3	3	7
D	65	58	58	4	2	2
E	59	51	40	5	5	8.5
F	53	44	47	6	6	5
G	45	38	55	7	7	3
H	41	34	44	8	9	6
I	34	35	25	9	8	11
J	30	30	40	10	10	8.5
K	23	26	33	11	11	10

Scatter Diagrams Another way to study the correlation between the scores from assessments is graphically with a **scatter diagram** (sometimes called a **scattergram**). A scatter diagram is a graph on which the paired scores are plotted. The example in Figure 3.5 shows these plots for V vs. R and V vs. A. When completed, the graph shows the relationship between the paired scores for the entire group of 11 students.

You can obtain considerable insight into how the scores on two assessments are related by making a scatter diagram. In Figure 3.5(A), the plots lie along an almost straight line from the lower left of the graph to the upper right. In Figure 3.5(B), however, the plots do not come as close to a straight line. However, there is a trend in the graph from the lower left of the graph to the upper right.

The tendency for points of a scatter diagram to lie along a straight line is central to the concept of correlation. The higher the degree of correlation between two sets of scores, the closer the points come to lying along a straight line. As the degree of correlation lessens, the points tend to scatter away from this straight line. These points scatter in an elliptical shape: the narrower the elliptical pattern in the scattergram, the higher the degree of correlation; the less the degree of correlation, the wider these elliptical patterns of the scatter diagrams. When the two sets of scores

FIGURE 3.5 Scatter diagram of the verbal aptitude versus reading test scores and the verbal aptitude versus arithmetic test scores for the 11 pupils shown in Figure 3.4.

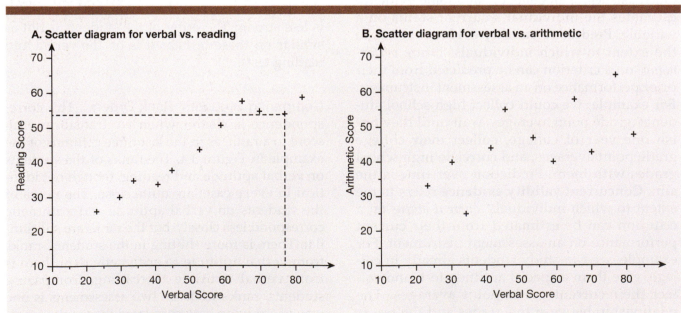

have no relationship, the pattern will widen until it is circular, rather than elliptical.

Pearson Product-Moment Correlation Coefficients

Visually comparing rank orders of scores and plotting scatter diagrams are two qualitative ways of studying the correlation between the scores. Most published assessment material uses a quantitative measure of correlation called the **Pearson product-moment correlation coefficient**, which is denoted by r. Of the many different types of correlation coefficients, r is most commonly used in validity studies. For sake of simplicity, we shall refer to r as the *correlation coefficient* in this text.

A correlation coefficient has a possible range of values from −1.00 through 0.00 to +1.00. A correlation of 0.00 means that the two sets of scores are unrelated: Students' scores on one assessment cannot be predicted from their scores on the other assessment. In **positive correlations**, high scores on one assessment are associated with high scores on another. In **negative correlations**, high scores on one assessment are associated with low scores on another. A perfect positive relationship would have a correlation coefficient of +1.00. A perfect negative relationship would have a correlation coefficient of −1.00. In either case, a student's score on one assessment can perfectly predict his score on the other assessment.

Numerical Values of the Correlation Coefficients for Scores in Figure 3.4

What are the numerical values of the correlation coefficients for the scores in the example in Figure 3.4? We do not consider calculations in this chapter. Rather, we focus on conceptual understanding. You may wish to calculate the correlation coefficients on your own, however. If so, use the procedure shown in Appendix F. If you applied the procedure described in Appendix F, you would find that the correlation between the verbal and reading test scores is 0.97 and between the verbal and arithmetic scores is 0.71. You can see that these correlation coefficients are consistent with the impression you had when you compared the rank orders of the scores in the table and studied the scatter diagrams. The number 0.97 reflects a high positive relationship (it is close to 1.00), whereas 0.71 indicates a weaker relationship.

Degrees of Relationship

It is helpful in understanding correlation coefficients to relate them to scatter diagrams. Figure 3.6 shows the scatter diagrams and corresponding correlation coefficients for paired scores that have different degrees of relationships. Each dot represents a pair of scores for a person. The scatter diagrams are arranged to illustrate that positive and negative correlation coefficients having the same absolute numerical value (i.e., the number without the algebraic sign) represent the same strength or degree of relationship.

Compare Scatter Diagrams A and E, for example. Both show perfect correlation, but Diagram A shows a perfect positive correlation, whereas Diagram E shows a perfect negative correlation. The *strength* of the relationship is identical in both cases, but the *direction* of the relationship differs. The negative sign on the correlation coefficient shows that the direction of the relationship is negative. Because the correlation is perfect in both cases, knowing a person's score on one assessment would allow us to predict exactly the score the person obtained on the second assessment: Perfect correlation means perfect prediction.

Perfect correlations are seldom found in practical work with educational and psychological assessment scores. There are many reasons for this, such as the assessments containing random errors of measurement, the units of measurement being unequal, the distributions of the scores not having identical shapes, and the two assessment results not being related in a simple, linear manner.

Other degrees of relationship are shown in Figure 3.6. In B and F, the correlations are −0.90 and +0.90, respectively. Correlations of this magnitude indicate that the assessment results are highly related. Again, the degree of relationship is the same in B and F, but the directions of the relationships are opposite. In both cases, the plotted points in the scatter diagram tend to fall along straight lines, even though they do not fall exactly on the lines as they do in A and E. Although perfect prediction of scores on one assessment from scores on another is not possible when the correlation is −.90 or +.90, reasonably accurate predictions are possible.

Comparing B with F and C with G, we see that as the correlation between the scores declines; a greater scatter occurs away from a straight line. With a correlation of +0.60 or −0.60, it is still possible to predict a person's score on Y from knowledge of the person's score on X, but such predictions would

FIGURE 3.6   Scatter diagrams for different degrees of correlation.

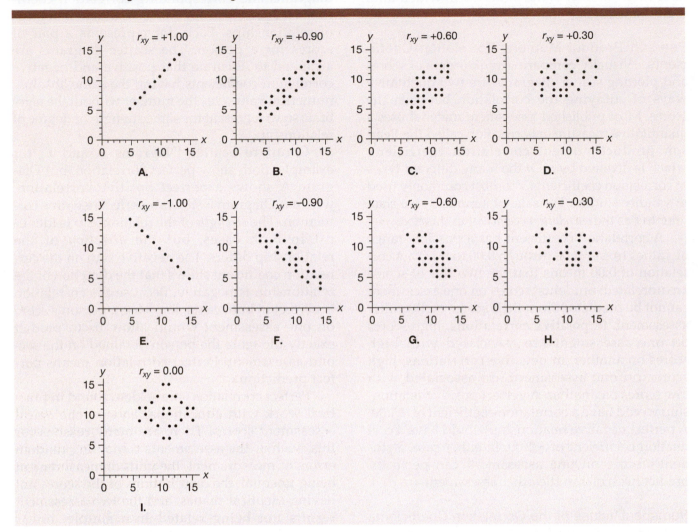

have to be made with broader margins of error than in the case when $r = -0.90$ or $r = +0.90$ In D and H, the correlations are $+0.30$ and -0.30, respectively, and the elliptical patterns are broader still.

Finally, scatter Diagram I illustrates a complete lack of correlation between two sets of scores. A person with a high score on Assessment X could have either a high, middle, or low score on Assessment Y. Thus, the scores are said to be unrelated or uncorrelated, and $r = 0.00$. Note the circular pattern of the points in the scatter diagram.

In practical work with assessments, correlations of exactly 0.00, −1.00, and −1.00 are rare. These particular numerical values, however, serve as benchmarks. Actual correlation coefficients take on meaning in the context of these limiting values.

Correlation and Causation   If the scores from two assessments correlate, it does not necessarily follow that the underlying traits are causally related. For example, there is a positive correlation between shoe sizes and reading comprehension grade-equivalent scores for a population of elementary school children. Children with larger feet read better: They are older and have had more reading instruction. The larger feet are in eighth grade and, relative to first and second graders, so are the better readers. A third variable, amount of reading instruction, not size of foot, is the most likely "cause" of the correlation between shoe size and reading scores. Of course, we wouldn't recommend a reading readiness program in which we stretched each child's feet. Yet some educators have erroneously recommended instructional procedures primarily on the basis of correlations rather than on demonstrations of their effectiveness.

Correlation Coefficients and Sample Sizes   The correlation coefficients reported in studies of

FIGURE 3.7 An example of how a change in only one pair of scores can alter the correlation coefficient. In this example, N = 25 pairs of scores.

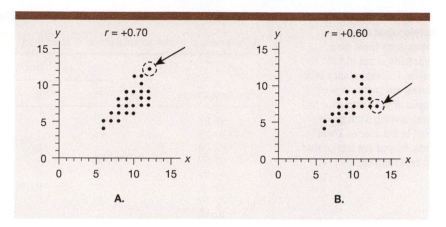

A.   B.

assessments and in test manuals are based on scores obtained from *samples of persons*, not on the scores of all persons in the population. A correlation computed from a sample only estimates the numerical value of the correlation in the complete population. You should have less confidence in the exact values of correlations computed from smaller samples than you would from correlations computed from larger samples. In small samples, even one pair of scores can affect the numerical value of the correlation coefficient substantially. The example in Figure 3.7 demonstrates this result. The correlation of 0.70 in Diagram A drops to 0.60 in Diagram B when the person with $X = 12$, $Y = 12$ is replaced by another person with $X = 13$, $Y = 7$, even though all the other scores remain the same.

Factors That Raise or Lower Correlation Coefficients Correlation coefficients appear in test manuals and research reports. When we encounter them, our first tendency is to interpret them as reporting the true relationship between the characteristics our instruments assess. In fact, the similarity of the characteristics being assessed is only one factor that affects the magnitude of the correlation coefficient reported. In general, higher correlations result when (a) the traits being assessed are alike, (b) the reliability of the scores on both assessments is high, (c) the range of scores on both assessments is large, (d) the shapes of the score distributions on the two assessments are alike, and (e) the time interval between administering the two assessments is short. Figure 3.8 summarizes these factors and gives an example of each. Often, more than one of these factors operates at the same time. Read reports of correlational validity evidence cautiously, keeping these factors in mind as possible explanations of the numerical correlation values you are interpreting.

FIGURE 3.8 Factors affecting the magnitude of correlation coefficients.

Factor	Effect on correlation coefficient	Example
Similarity of traits assessed	The more similar the traits, the higher the correlation.	Verbal aptitude and reading comprehension test scores will be more highly correlated than verbal aptitude and mathematics aptitude test scores.
Reliability of the scores	Less reliable scores correlate lower than more reliable scores.	Subjective rating of students' correct English usage from essay examinations correlates lower with reading comprehension test scores than do correct English usage scores from multiple-choice tests.
Range or spread of scores	The larger the range (spread) of scores, the higher the correlation is likely to be.	Algebra aptitude test scores will have a higher correlation with end-of-semester mathematics grades when all first-year high school students are included in the sample than when only those first-year students in honors mathematics are included.
Similarity of distribution	The more different the shapes of the distribution of scores on the two assessments, the lower the correlation.	Scores from an achievement test that is very difficult and scores from one that is very easy for a particular group of students will correlate less than if the two tests were moderately difficult for this group.
Time interval between assessment administrations	The shorter the time interval between assessment administrations, the higher the correlation is likely to be.	An algebra aptitude test is administered at the beginning of the school year. The correlation between its scores and mathematics grades at the end of the first semester will be higher than with mathematics grades of the same students after two years.

FIGURE 3.9   The development of an expectancy table for a hypothetical set of 100 pupils. The expectancy table shows the percentage of pupils at each predictor test level earning each grade level in the course. These percentages are interpreted as probabilities.

A. Frequency of grades for each predictor score level

| Predictor test score | Number of pupils receiving each grade | | | | | |
	F	D	C	B	A	Totals
80–89			1	3	1	5
70–79		1	4	5	2	12
60–69		3	5	6	1	15
50–59		4	8	5	1	18
40–49	1	5	8	4		18
30–39	1	6	5	3		15
20–29	2	5	4	1		12
10–19	1	2	1			4
0–9	1					1
Totals	**6**	**26**	**36**	**27**	**5**	**100**

B. Expectancy table made by converting frequencies into percentages

| Predictor test score | Percentage of pupils receiving each grade | | | | | |
	F	D	C	B	A	Totals
80–89			20	60	20	100
70–79		8	33	42	17	100
60–69		20	33	40	7	100
50–59		22	44	28	6	100
40–49	6	28	44	22		100
30–39	7	40	33	20		100
20–29	17	42	33	8		100
10–19	25	50	25			100
0–9	100					100

Validity Coefficients

The usual procedure when collecting predictive or concurrent validation evidence is to compute correlations between scores from the assessment instrument and criterion scores. Such a correlation is sometimes referred to as a **validity coefficient**, although, as you can easily see from Figure 3.2, no single number is appropriate to judge the validity of assessment results. In selection situations, however, high validity coefficients typically are strong evidence that the selection test is useful for selecting people who will be successful.[1] This is because high correlations are evidence that

predictions of success will be reasonably accurate (recall our discussion of Figure 3.6). Note that realistically you would expect neither a perfect (error-free) prediction nor a correlation of 1.00.

Expectancy Tables

Another way to display predictive validity data is to make an expectancy table. An **expectancy table** is a grid or two-way table that permits predictions about how likely it is for a person with a specific assessment result to attain each criterion score level. Figure 3.9 illustrates how an expectancy table is developed to indicate the probability that students at particular aptitude score levels will attain each letter grade in a course. Of course, expectancy tables can be developed to predict other criteria such as supervisors' ratings, amount of sales, success in clinical treatment, and other relevant criteria.

First, a table is constructed, such as in Figure 3.9(A), in which each cell contains the

---

[1] Note that you cannot judge from the correlation coefficient the likely size of the errors that may be made when the assessment results are used to predict criterion scores. For example, if you were predicting college grade point averages, the correlation would not tell you how many GPA units your prediction is likely to be in error. An index that can estimate the likely size of errors of prediction is called the *standard error of estimate*. Its equation is $SD_{est} = SD_y \sqrt{1-r^2}$

number of persons with a particular score who attained each course grade (criterion score level). For example, 15 students had aptitude test scores between 60 and 69. This number is shown in the right margin of the 60–69 row. Three of these 15 attained a course grade of D, five a grade of C, six a grade of B, and one a grade of A.

Second, each cell frequency in Figure 3.9(A) is divided by its corresponding row total, converted to a percentage, and put into an expectancy table such as Figure 3.9(B). These percentages may be interpreted as probabilities or chances out of 100 to answer such questions as the following: "At this school, what is the probability that a person with an aptitude test score of 65 will succeed in this course?" First, note that a person with a score of 65 is a member of the group whose scores are between 60 and 69. Second, if we define *succeed* to mean *a grade of C or better*, then 33% + 40% + 7% = 80% of the students with aptitude scores between 60 and 69 were successful. Since a person with an aptitude score of 65 is a member of this group, the answer to the question is as follows: "A person with an aptitude score of 65 has an 80% chance of being successful in this course."

Expectancy tables can help parents and students interpret assessment results, too. For example, suppose an expectancy table is made for a particular college showing how admissions test scores are related to first-year-student grade point averages. Persons reading the table can then interpret the admission test results in terms of a student's chances to obtain various grade point averages. Such interpretations of admissions test scores give more information than the typically reported scaled score or percentile rank (see Appendix F).

If you interpret assessment results using expectancy tables, you should observe common sense cautions. For example, assessment instruments used to predict success seldom, if ever, measure students' initiative, persistence, or motivation. Thus, they cannot predict with certainty what a *particular student* will do. Rather, the table represents the experience of other students in the past and can offer some guidance only. Therefore, never tell a student that the data in the table "prove" the student can (or cannot) be successful. You must explain that the data show the experience of other students similar to him or her.

The Criterion

Your judgment about whether the assessment developer has provided appropriate validity evidence depends in part on whether the assessment results have been correlated with relevant criteria. Obtaining suitable criterion measures to use in validating assessment results is so difficult that this has been dubbed the *criterion problem* (Thorndike, 1951).

Kinds of Criteria A variety of criteria are used to provide validity evidence. Personnel classification and selection research in government and industry use four general types: production (quantity and quality of goods, sales), personal data (accidents on the job, length of service, group membership, training course grades), samples of actual or simulated job performance, and judgments by others (checklists, supervisors' ratings). In education, criteria fall into three types: (1) achievement test scores; (2) ratings, grades, and other quantified judgments of teachers; and (3) career data. A common example is a reading readiness test given at the beginning of first grade. Scores are often validated by correlating them with scores from a reading achievement test (the criterion) administered at the end of first grade. Using grade point averages to validate scores from aptitude and admissions tests was mentioned already. Sometimes teachers' ratings of students' self-concept, sociability, and so on are used as criterion measures. Scores from vocational interest inventories are validated in part by relating them to career data. (See Chapter 19.)

Any single criterion measure is incomplete. Each represents partial attainment of the ultimate performance that an assessment procedure would like to predict. For this reason, the validation process for a test claiming to be useful in predicting performance should include several studies of how the test's scores relate to various criteria. You will need to review all of these studies before evaluating the predictive evidence for a test.

Judging the Worth of Criteria The criterion measures used in a validity study are themselves evaluated in four broad areas: (1) relevance to the long-term or ultimate real-life performance, (2) degree of reliability, (3) extent of bias against individuals or groups, and (4) practical problems of availability and convenience. Most often of interest in a predictive validity study are one or more ultimate real-life performances. But such ultimate criteria frequently do not occur until many years after the developer initially obtains the assessment results. In such cases, intermediate criteria are used. A developer must present a suitable rationale for using an intermediate criterion before you can accept the data as part of the predictive validity evidence.

Low Criterion Reliability Limits Validity If assessment results have low reliability (see Chapter 4), then they will have a lower correlation with other measures than if they had high reliability. Even if predictor instruments have good reliability, they will not be able to predict criterion scores that are unreliable.

Systematic Errors Systematic errors in criterion measurement may lead you to the wrong conclusion about the validity of an instrument's scores. For example, a validity study may correlate the test's scores with teachers' ratings of students. If these ratings favor boys over girls, or students with high verbal skills over those with lower verbal skills, the criterion measures themselves may be inappropriate. Systematic biases such as these introduce irrelevant factors into the validation process; in other words, they "contaminate" the criterion scores. Thus, before accepting correlation results as evidence for predictive validity, think carefully about the possibility that the scores on the criteria themselves may be biased or invalid.

Practical Considerations Ideally, scores from an instrument should be validated using data from ultimate real-life criteria. However, practical considerations limit the degree to which a developer can do this. Practicality should not be the sole driving force in a developer's decision to select criterion measures, however. Sometimes a developer could, with very little extra expense and effort, obtain criterion measures that are more appropriate than the ones used in a validation study.

Reliability over Time, Assessors, and Content Domains: Reliability Evidence

Reliability refers to the consistency of the assessment results over time, if and when they are repeated, across raters, or over different forms of the assessment (different content). For example, suppose the scores from the ABC Reading Test administered today correlated 0.00 with the scores from this same test administered next week. This correlation is evidence that the scores have no consistency over this period. You would question the validity of this test if students' scores had little or no consistency from one week to the next because you would believe that reading ability should be stable over a short period. If an assessment instrument produces inconsistent or unstable results, you can have little confidence in those results. Therefore, the reliability of an assessment's results limits its validity. This point is discussed in greater detail in Chapter 4.

Generalization of Interpretation over People, Conditions, or Special Instructions and Interventions: Generalization Evidence

This category of validation evidence addresses how broadly you may interpret and use assessment results. For example, does the ABC Reading Test measure the type of reading comprehension required of students in higher levels of schooling and in real life? Does it measure reading comprehension among non-White students in the same way that it measures White students? Is it appropriate to use the scores from this test for remedial reading groups of Spanish-speaking students? Do scores on the ABC Reading Test greatly depend on students' moods or motivations at the time the test is administered? If students receive special instruction on what strategies to use to answer the questions on this test (e.g., read the question first, then look for the answer in the text), will this greatly affect their scores?

Answers to questions such as these help us see the assessment results in a broader perspective. Usually, the answers show that our interpretations of assessment results cannot be simplistic. The validity of our interpretations and uses of the results are limited to certain conditions.

Consider the following illustration: Suppose the ABC Reading Test had the typical format—a passage of one or two paragraphs followed by several multiple-choice questions. The test directions call for the student to read each passage and to answer the questions that follow it by marking a separate answer sheet.

At first glance, it appears that the student needs to read and understand the questions. However, there are some other compelling hypotheses. If these factors alter the student's score, then you cannot interpret the test as a pure measure of reading comprehension or make decisions about students as if the scores depend on such a pure reading comprehension interpretation. It may be that the passage refers to a specific topic, theme, or experience about which some students may have a lot of prior knowledge. Prior knowledge or poor-quality test items may create passage independence (the student can answer the questions without reading the passage). **Passage dependency** describes the degree to which answers to questions depend on reading and comprehending the passage. Passage-independent items cannot be said to assess reading comprehension. Overly stringent time limits, poor test administration and/or unclear directions, student "testwiseness," and student skill at using answer sheets also may affect the test score in ways that do not reflect reading comprehension.

These factors, and others like them, stand as counterhypotheses to the intended interpretation of the scores as measures of reading comprehension. As you raise these questions, you should look in the publisher's manual and technical reports for research evidence concerning them. Not all evidence will be included in the publisher's materials, however, especially if it is unfavorable evidence. The *Mental Measurements Yearbooks* (see Chapter 18) contain reviews of tests and bibliographies of research in which particular tests have appeared. You may have to review research literature to obtain additional information.

Intended and Unintended Consequences: Consequential Evidence

As mentioned at the beginning of this chapter in connection with the four principles for validation, the meanings and uses you give to assessment results arise from your educational and social values. We discussed the consequences and pressures on school curricula when there is a mismatch between the a priori domain sampled by an assessment instrument and the curricular and instructional domains in a local school system.

There are also consequences and pressures associated with accountability assessment.

Most state assessment and accountability programs, for example, are intended to have the following positive consequences (Lane & Stone, 2002):

- Increase the educational efforts of students, teachers, and school administrators.
- Improve curriculum content and instructional strategies.
- Improve all students' learning.
- Improve teachers' professional development and a school's support for that development.
- Improve the focus and nature of how students are prepared for assessments.
- Increase the students', teachers', administrators', and public's awareness of the value of standards, criteria, and assessments to evaluate schools.

Evidence about how well these intended consequences are achieved becomes part of the case for the validating state assessment programs.

It is not enough, however, to collect evidence only about whether a program's intended consequences have been achieved. A state's assessment and accountability program validation effort should also look for evidence of negative, unintended consequences such as the following (Lane & Stone, 2002):

- A narrowing of the curriculum and classroom teaching to focus only on what is likely to be included in the state assessment, while ignoring the broader curriculum goals and purposes.
- Preparing students only to take tests without improving the quality of their achievement of the state's standards.
- Using unethical test preparation practices such as giving out the questions beforehand.
- Increasing achievement of only some students (e.g., students in schools that have high socioeconomic levels of parents) whereas the achievement of others (e.g., students in schools from lower socioeconomic levels of parents) remains low or decreases.
- An increase in inappropriate uses of assessment results such as transferring or punishing

teachers and principals whose students have low scores.

■ A decrease in some students' motivation to learn and achieve because of past poor performance on the assessments.

A validation program should look for evidence of negative, unintended consequences as well as evidence of achieving the positive, intended consequences of an assessment program.

Cost, Efficiency, Practicality, and Instructional Features: Practicality Evidence

Assessment results may be technically sound, but practical barriers may impede their proper (and therefore valid) use. For example, if an assessment procedure is too complex for teachers to use, they will not use it properly and it will yield results of low validity. The validity of an assessment instrument will improve if it is administered and interpreted properly. Some assessment instruments may be accompanied by computerized score reports that help teachers identify students who need special help. The availability of these and other auxiliary materials increases the likelihood that results will be used as intended.

Although assessment cost is not a major consideration for validity, it is a consideration nevertheless. Of concern here is determining which will be the most cost-effective option from among the various choices of similar assessment instruments. Which one will deliver the most valid results under the practical circumstances in a particular school setting? Will the cheapest alternative be the most valid alternative?

MyLab Education **Self-Check 3.2**

MyLab Education **Application Exercise 3.2:**
Evaluating Validity Evidence

MyLab Education **Self-Check 3.3**

MyLab Education **Application Exercise 3.3:**
Using Correlation to Evaluate Predictive Power

VALIDITY ISSUES WHEN ACCOMMODATING STUDENTS WITH DISABILITIES

In Chapter 1, we discussed accountability assessments and the fact that under NCLB all students

must be assessed, including students with disabilities. Students' disabilities may be used as a basis for accommodations to the assessment process for those students unable to participate in the assessment under the standardized conditions set for the general school population. Further, alternative assessment methods must be found to assess those students who cannot participate even with accommodations. Assessment **accommodations** are changes in either the conditions or materials of assessment that allow the achievement of students with disabilities to be evaluated in the same areas as other students, without changing the underlying achievement construct assessed. Assessment **modifications** are changes in either the conditions or materials of assessment that allow the achievement of students with disabilities, even though the underlying achievement construct may no longer be the same as it is for the assessment of other students.

Standardized test accommodations for students with physical disabilities are less controversial than accommodations for students with cognitive disabilities such as learning disabilities (Phillips, 1994). One concern is the validity of the test result interpretations: If a test was administered under accommodating conditions, do the scores mean the same thing as the scores for students who took the test under standard conditions?

Validity of Scores from Test Accommodations

The validity of interpretations depends on the type of test administered, the purpose of the testing, the type of accommodation, the type of disability the student has, and the nature of the interpretation itself. If the purpose of testing, for example, is to assess a student's knowledge and ability in a subject such as social studies or mathematics, then it may be appropriate for a student with a severe reading disability to have a reader (someone to read the test questions). In this case, the concepts, principles, and procedures of the subject are independent of the printed medium in which they are presented on the test. Thus, it is logical for you to assess a student's understanding of them through an appropriate accommodation.

If you can reasonably argue that reading is not part of the knowledge and ability being assessed, you could also argue that poor readers without learning disabilities should also have their mathematics and social studies tests read to them. Under this scenario, it would be considered fair, for example, to provide a reader for both students with learning disabilities and for poor readers, if they so desired.

On the other hand, a student with a severe reading disability (such as dyslexia) may be unable to complete the reading comprehension section of a standardized achievement test. If the purpose of testing were to assess a student's ability to read standard printed English, it would be invalid to provide a reader for the student on such a test.

However, suppose the student can read some material if given more time to answer. This accommodation violates the standardization conditions, thus invalidating the usual norm-referenced interpretations such as grade equivalents, percentile ranks, and standard scores. Nevertheless, by giving the student more time, you discovered what test material he or she could read when the time element is removed. Your interpretation of the results cannot ignore the accommodations, however; you would need to preface your norm-referenced interpretation with something like the following example:

Example

"Here is how Sally compares to other students. The other students took the test under standard conditions and with limited time. However, Sally took the test under nonstandard conditions and with no time limits because [give your rationale]."

This emphasizes a point we made earlier in this chapter: *Validity refers to your interpretations of the scores*.

How Should Accommodated Norm-Referenced Scores Be Reported? The issue of whether to report any norm-referenced information about a student's performance when the test administration violated the standardized testing conditions (e.g., failing to keep to the time limits) remains controversial. If a test's standardized administration conditions are violated, some would view the following as inappropriate: (a) reporting any type of norm-referencing information for the accommodated students and (b) including in school averages the results from the students who had accommodated

administrations of the test (Phillips, personal communication, 2001). Whether the individual results for students administered the test under accommodated conditions should be identified or flagged in records or reports also remains controversial (Sireci, 2005). Legal requirements, such as federal reporting requirements, state that the percentage of students achieving the proficient level or better on a state's standards needs to be reported, regardless of accommodations.

How Should Accommodated Criterion-Referenced Scores Be Reported? A criterion-referenced interpretation (e.g., an interpretation of the type of material read and types of questions answered) is often made for test results. However, speed of reading is also part of this interpretation for standardized achievement tests because of the limits imposed by the standardization conditions. Therefore, your criterion-referenced interpretation would need to be stated in a manner that reflects the nonstandard administration, such as in the following example:

Example

"These are the types of materials and questions Sally was able to read when she took the test under non-standard conditions and with no time limits."

It is sometimes possible to report two results: the student's performance under standard conditions and the student's performance under accommodated conditions.

Measurement Perspective on Accommodations and Modifications

From a strict measurement perspective, in which the validity of a testing program is a primary concern, the following questions might be considered:

1. Will changes in format or testing conditions change the skill being measured?

2. Will the scores received under standard conditions mean something different than scores received with the requested accommodation?

3. Would examinees who do not need accommodations benefit if they were nevertheless allowed the same accommodations?

4. Do examinees requesting or granted accommodations have any capacity for adjusting to standard test administration conditions?

5. Is the disability evidence or testing accommodation policy based on procedures with doubtful validity and reliability? (adapted from Phillips, 1994, p. 104).

Phillips argues that if you answer yes to any of these questions, a test accommodation is not appropriate because it would compromise the validity of the test results. She points out the potential conflict between providing maximum participation in society for persons with disabilities and maintaining test validity. Also, in the case of extended time, the most common test accommodation, there is some evidence that the accommodation does change the construct somewhat, but there is no reference point for deciding whether small changes are of practical importance (Lovett, 2010; Sireci, Scarpati, & Li, 2005).

Not all would agree with Phillips's conclusions. For example, even though modifications may change the skill assessed or the meaning of the scores (see Questions 1 and 2), such changes may be more, rather than less, valid. Phillips's argument assumes that administering the test under standard conditions is the criterion against which accommodations should be judged. It also assumes that the skill or ability assessed by the test under standard conditions is the relevant skill and ability to be assessed.

These assumptions may not be correct. For example, reading short passages and answering questions under timed standard conditions (the typical reading comprehension test) is not the ultimate learning goal, nor is it a direct assessment of "real-world" reading. Accommodations to the standard test conditions may change both the skill required and the meaning of the results in a more positive direction. This, in turn, may make the accommodated test results more like the ultimate learning goals in the real world—especially for students with certain disabilities.

In this chapter, we have limited our discussion of accommodations to validity concerns. This text includes more information on accommodations. Chapter 5 discusses legal and ethical considerations regarding accommodations, identifies the most common type of accommodations in state testing programs, and reviews studies of the use of accommodations in large-scale tests. Chapter 14 discusses the use of accommodations in classroom assessment and the assistance that technology can give. Chapter 18 examines a set of principles called universal design that large-scale test developers may apply to minimize the need for accommodations.

MyLab Education Self-Check 3.4

MyLab Education Application Exercise 3.4:
Using Accommodations and Modifications

CONCLUSION

The validity of classroom and large-scale assessment results depends on intended purposes and uses. This chapter has outlined the various types of evidence that should be considered in arguments that particular assessment results are valid for a particular purpose or use. We introduced the concept of reliability as a necessary but not sufficient condition for validity. Chapter 4 discusses reliability in more detail.

EXERCISES

1. Obtain a teacher-made classroom assessment instrument that has been used for assigning students' marks or letter grades. Using the criteria listed in Figure 3.1 and, if possible, an interview with the teacher, evaluate the validity of using the assessment results for grading students. Then briefly describe how valid this assessment is for this purpose and why. Finally, using the criteria in Figure 3.1, describe how you could improve the validity of this assessment instrument.

2. Assume that a new high school science aptitude test is being developed, and in the course of that development several procedures and techniques have been used to provide evidence for its validity. These procedures are listed in the following statements. For each statement, decide which type of evidence in Figure 3.2 is directly addressed. Explain why you made the choice you did.
   a. For a sample of 150 students in Grade 10, scores on the odd-numbered items were correlated with scores on the even-numbered items.
   b. Scores from 300 first-year students obtained from a September administration of the test

were correlated with scores of the same group obtained from a February administration.

c. Scores of 200 first-year students obtained from a September administration of the test were correlated with the general science course grades of these same students obtained from school records in January.

d. Scores of students who had taken one, two, three, and four science courses were compared to see if they differed on the average.

e. A section of the test manual describes seven aspects of science aptitude and the number of items measuring each aspect.

3. Obtain a teacher-made classroom assessment instrument (either of your own construction or from someone else). Identify the main or intended interpretations of student results from that assessment instrument. Analyze the assessment logically. Playing "devil's advocate," identify three counterinterpretations (i.e., possible alternative interpretations that raise questions about the validity of the intended interpretation). Then specify the kind(s) of evidence that could be collected to verify the intended interpretation and invalidate each of the three counterinterpretations. Attach the test to this exercise.

4. Each of the following statements is a question that an educator can ask about an assessment procedure. Using Figure 3.2, identify for each statement the type(s) of validity evidence that is (are) most important in answering the question directly. Then briefly explain your choice.

a. "Is this spelling test from a book publisher representative of the type of spelling patterns we teach our sixth graders?"

b. "Can scores on this reading test help me assign students to different instructional groups?"

c. "I'm using this performance assessment to select persons for a special training program. Are the results significantly influenced by the personality of the person administering the assessment?"

d. "Does this mathematics performance assessment really assess the mathematics ability of these students?"

e. "We now use a procedure to rate student teachers. Does this procedure permit a student teacher to be observed in the broad range of classroom situations likely to be encountered when teaching in this state?"

5. Read each statement and decide whether it is true or false. Then explain why you marked it the way you did.

a. A verbal reasoning test is given at the start of Grade 9. Scores on this test are correlated with English grades assigned in Grades 9 through 12. The correlations between the test scores and the Grade 12 marks will likely be the lowest of the four correlations.

b. A certain predictor test has perfect reliability (reliability coefficient = 1.00). This means that the predictor test is likely to have very high correlation with just about any criterion measure an investigator wants to use.

c. Another predictor test has zero reliability (reliability coefficient = 0.00). This means that the predictor test will likely correlate zero with just about any criterion measure the investigator wants to use.

Reliability of Assessment Results

KEY CONCEPTS

1. Reliability is the degree to which students' results remain consistent over replications of an assessment procedure. Reliability is a necessary but not sufficient piece of evidence to support the validity of test score interpretations and the quality of educational decisions based on them. For classroom assessment, major reliability concerns are (a) deciding what kind of consistency, dependability, or accuracy is important for a particular assessment and (b) ensuring and appraising evidence of that consistency/dependability/accuracy.

2. For large-scale assessment, reliability can be studied with quantitative measures of the consistency across times, items or tasks, forms, or raters. Types of reliability coefficients include test-retest, alternate forms, internal consistency, and scorer reliability.

3. Each observed score is composed of a true score and an error score. The standard error of measurement estimates the amount of error in scores and is used to interpret performance.

4. The more important the education decision, the higher the level of assessment reliability should be. Reliability can be improved by lengthening the assessment, using multiple sources of evidence, and by several other means.

IMPORTANT TERMS

decision consistency index

domain of achievement

error score

homogeneous tasks

inter-rater reliability

measurement error

obtained score

parallel forms

percentage of agreement

reliability

reliability coefficient

scorer reliability

speeded assessment

stability coefficient

standard error of measurement (*SEM*)

true score

types of reliability coefficients: alternate-form, coefficient alpha, delayed alternate-forms, KR20 and KR21, odd-even split-halves procedure, parallel forms, Spearman-Brown double length formula, split-halves, test-retest

uncertainty interval (confidence interval, score band)

underinterpreting versus overinterpreting score differences

GENERAL NATURE OF RELIABILITY

Suppose you asked students today to write an essay explaining the pros and cons of democratic elections. Suppose, further, that you repeated this same essay with the same students a month from now without any instruction in the meantime. If your marks of each student's essay responses are essentially the same on both occasions, we say that the results are consistent over this period. We say the results are reliable over a month's time.

Now suppose that you mark each student's essay tonight. Then tomorrow, without revealing the marks you assigned, you give the essays to a teaching colleague to mark. If the marks you assigned each student essentially agree with the marks independently assigned by your colleague, we would say that results are consistent or reliable with respect to different graders.

Now suppose you rephrased the essay question in a different but equivalent way and asked the students to write essays for both versions. If the qualities of each student's essays were essentially the same on the two versions of the task, we would say that the students' responses are consistent or reliable with respect to equivalent versions of the same task.

Reliability, then, is the degree to which students' results remain consistent over replications of an assessment procedure. That is, reliability is the degree to which students' assessment results are the same when (1) they complete the same task(s) on two or more different occasions, (2) two or more teachers mark their performance on the same task(s), or (3) they complete two or more different but equivalent tasks on the same or different occasions. Consistent scores over repeated assessment is the key to understanding reliability. As with validity, reliability refers to the students' assessment results or scores, not to the assessment instrument itself.

Consistency is an important concept to consider in deciding how much confidence to place in your students' assessment results. Later in this chapter, we describe this concept of consistency in more specific ways. This analysis will lead to various indices of the degree of reliability. First, however, we briefly discuss the relationship between reliability and validity.

Reliability Is Necessary but Not Sufficient for Validity

Validity, as we discussed in the last chapter, relates to the confidence we have in interpreting students' assessment results and in using them to make decisions. Interpretations and decisions are less valid when students' assessment results are inconsistent. *An assessment result's degree of reliability limits its degree of validity*.

Although high degrees of validity require high degrees of reliability, the reverse is not true. A highly reliable assessment does not guarantee that you can make highly valid interpretations or decisions. This is because reliability is only one of many validity criteria (see Figures 3.1 and 3.2). As an illustration, consider this example:

Example

Ms. Cortez teaches seventh-grade arithmetic. She creates a computation and problem-solving test to assess her students' ability to solve problems involving area and perimeter. Because this paper-and-pencil test has a moderately large number of items, Ms. Cortez can be confident that the resulting scores will be very reliable. Knowing that these scores are reliable, however, is not enough to conclude they are valid for a particular decision. Suppose Ms. Cortez wanted to use the scores to identify students for special help with area and perimeter, yet the problems on the test were all word problems that required reading skills as well as geometry skills. It is likely that some of the students identified by low scores on the test would be poor readers not necessarily in need of remedial work in area and perimeter.

An assessment's reliability affects the quality (validity) of decisions. Here is an example:

Example

Ms. Cortez decided that mastering 80 percent of the targeted domain of computations is passing. The test is only a sample from the domain, however. If the test scores were of low reliability, it is very likely that among all those students who actually mastered 80 percent or more of the targeted *domain*, some would have *test scores* below 80 percent. These students would be erroneously classified as failures. On the other hand, among the students who truly know slightly less than 80 percent of the targeted *domain*, some are very likely to *pass the test*. These students would be erroneously classified as having sufficient competence.

Inconsistencies like those that are of concern in this example are called *measurement errors*. Errors of measurement are always of concern to persons who need to make decisions about students.

CAUSES OF MEASUREMENT ERROR OR INCONSISTENCY

Reliability and **measurement error** are complementary ways of speaking about the same assessment phenomenon. The concept of reliability focuses on the consistency of assessment results; the concept of measurement error focuses on their inconsistencies. Inconsistencies have different causes. Not every cause, however, is equally important to your particular interpretation and use of assessment results.

Consider the following situation. Suppose all of the tasks that might be appropriate for assessing achievement for a particular set of learning objectives could be described. This description of possible tasks is called a **domain of achievement**. For example, the domain could be all the open-ended tasks that might be used to assess fifth-grade students' ability to solve mathematical problems involving proportions.

Now suppose you wish to determine the percentage of the domain a student knows. Rather than administering the entire domain, an impossible feat, you select from the domain a random sample of 10 tasks and administer them to the student. Clearly, the student's score on this assessment depends on which tasks happen to be included in the sample. A different sample of 10 tasks would be easier or harder than the first sample, resulting in a higher or lower score for the student. Suppose the student's results are 80 percent right on the first sample and 50 percent right on the second. Their inconsistency is a result of using a different content sample (or "form" of the assessment procedure).

Next consider this second situation: Suppose you administered the first sample of 10 tasks on Tuesday, which was a "bad day" for a student, and the student attained 40 percent right. Perhaps the student had an upsetting encounter on the playground before class, had eaten no breakfast, or had allergies acting up that made concentration difficult. For whatever reason, on Tuesday the student's performance was off. Suppose, now, that the same 10 tasks were administered on Friday. Perhaps Friday was a very good day, and the student performed much better than normal, attaining 70 percent. This type of inconsistency is a result of sampling on a different occasion. The identical content sample (i.e., the same 10 tasks) was administered on both Tuesday and Friday, so any source of the scoring inconsistency cannot be content sampling.

This description considers two of the factors influencing consistency of assessment performance: (1) the content or particular sample of tasks appearing on any form of the assessment and (2) the occasion on which the assessment is administered. It is also possible that both content and occasion may work together to influence assessment performance.

Interpreting assessment results a student obtained on a particular occasion with a particular sample of tasks has definite limitations. Assessment results must be reasonably consistent (perfect consistency is not possible) over different samples of content, tasks, and occasions; otherwise, we can have little confidence in them.

Assessment results may be consistent in some ways but not in others. For example, students' assessment results may not be consistent over repeated assessment on different samples of tasks administered on the same occasion, but may be very consistent over repeated assessment on the same sample of tasks over a month. Consider what type of repeated assessment is most appropriate to the way you want to use the results.

RELIABILITY OF CLASSROOM ASSESSMENTS

For classroom teachers, the key to reliability is understanding how to decide what sort of consistency is important for different assessment purposes (Parkes, 2007). You should be confident that your information is solid and trustworthy, not a fluke or random occurrence. Figure 4.1 organizes advice for producing reliable results according to type of assessment. For discussion, the figure is divided into assessments that are more often summative and those that are more often formative, but in reality, the line between the two is fluid. The designation of formative or summative depends on how you and students use the assessment.

FIGURE 4.1   Reliability concerns for classroom assessment.

Reliability for More Summative (Formal, Graded) Assessments		
Assessment	**Most important type of consistency, dependability, or accuracy**	**Your assessments should:**
All types	Consistency within student (not that they always do the same, but that they consistently try to show what they know)	■ Encourage students to perform their best ■ Match the assessment difficulty to the students' ability levels ■ Have scoring criteria that are available and well understood by students before they start the assignment
Objective tests (multiple-choice, true-false, matching, etc.)	Consistent performance from item to item	■ Have enough items ■ Allow enough time for students
Essays, papers, projects scored with rubrics	Accuracy of rater judgment Consistency across forms (prompts, assignments)	■ Have clear enough directions for students that all are likely to produce work you can score ■ Have a systematic procedure for scoring, including procedures to avoid rater errors ■ Use multiple markers when possible
Grades	Consistency among assignments Decision consistency	■ Use a sufficient number of different procedures to assess all important aspects of learning objective(s) ■ Combine results from several assessments ■ Differentiate among students
Makeup work	Consistency across occasion (and sometimes form)	■ If from absence, use a procedure (usually alternate forms and/or an honors system) to ensure equivalence ■ If from re-dos, performance should show consistency with the last (bad) performance except for changes due to learning progress
Reliability for More Formative (Informal, Ungraded, Practice) Assessments		
Assessment	**Most important type of consistency, dependability, or accuracy**	**Your assessments should:**
Oral questioning	Dependability of interpretation of answer(s); Accuracy of rater (teacher) judgment	■ Use a sufficient number of questions or observations ■ Allow enough time for students
Observations	Dependability of interpretation; Accuracy of rater (teacher) judgment	■ Interpret the answers or observed behavior with the most likely and reasonable explanation ■ Have a systematic procedure to ensure questioning or observing all students
Peer editing, group collaboration ratings, and other peer evaluation techniques	Accuracy of rater (peer) judgment	■ Have a systematic procedure for rating and instruct students in its use ■ Use student procedures that emphasize respect, judging the work not the person, and so on ■ Use several ratings for the same student and trim extremes if necessary
Self-assessment	Accuracy of rater (self) judgment	■ Have a systematic procedure for rating and instruct students in its use

All types of assessments should be dependable in the sense that they provide achievement information and represent what students know or can do, as opposed to representing resistance or lack of attention or motivation. Teachers need to maintain a classroom environment that encourages students to perform at their best.

As well, teachers should match the assessment difficulty to students' ability levels.

Students should not have to face an assessment hopelessly—and neither should they be expected to "skate" through questions that are too easy. Either extreme discourages true student engagement. Scoring criteria should be available and well understood by students *before* they start the assignment. Clear, well-understood criteria are more likely to be used in the same manner by all raters.

Objective Tests

For objective tests, students' performance should be consistent from item to item. Tests should have enough items that the consistency can show itself. For example, suppose you have only one question about a particular kind of math problem, and the student gets it right. How confident would you be in generalizing to say that he has "100 percent mastery" in this area? Would you be more confident if he got two items in this area correct? How many would it take before you were really comfortable saying, "Yes, he can do this"? Also, be sure to allow enough time for students to do the items. Performance should indicate achievement and not running out of time.

Essays, Papers, and Projects Scored with Rubrics

For tasks scored with partial credit—multipoint items, or tasks scored with rubrics or grades—the major reliability concern is accuracy of judgment. Often, one teacher (you) grades assignments, and there is no other rater with whom to compare, although once in a while it's a good thing to get another teacher to double-score as a check on your accuracy.

There are several ways to help make your judgment as accurate as possible. Ensure that your directions are clear enough, so all students are likely to produce work that you are able to score. If every student does something very different, it's hard to score accurately. Use systematic scoring procedures: clear rubrics or scoring guides. Score work without looking at the student's name. Score answers to one question, or one essay or assignment, before moving on to the next, so you are concentrating on one scoring scheme at a time. Use multiple markers when possible.

Grades

For report card (marking period) grades, consistency among assignments and decision consistency ("Would I make the same grading decision about this student again?") are important. Use a sufficient number of different procedures to assess all the important aspects of the learning objectives. Combine results from several assessments to arrive at a grade. Combining the results of several assessments increases the reliability of

a grade in the same way as having more items increases the reliability of one test score. The more observations, the more stability in judgment.

Use assessments that differentiate among students. If every student is an A, every student looks the same on the scale you're using, which is not likely to be the case. We are not advocating deliberately using assignments that are too hard in order to pass some students and fail others. Rather, make sure that you use assignments that distribute students along the assignments' scoring scales so that you get an accurate picture of their achievement. Then decide on the grades they should receive using procedures that are systematic and fair.

Makeup Work

For makeup work, the reliability concern is consistency across occasions and sometimes forms. If the student is making up work missed because of absence, use a procedure to ensure equivalence. The procedure could involve an honor system in which, for example, students know not to tell their absent friends what questions are on a test, or the procedure could be to use another form of the same test or assignment.

If the student is redoing work because of poor performance the first time, you should have confidence that any increase in work quality actually represents a reliable increase in learning. Changes in the work should be interpretable as changes in learning. For example, if a student neglected to follow certain directions or left something out of an assignment, realizes that fact, and receives permission to redo the work, the changes should reflect this realization. However, the revisions shouldn't sound like someone else wrote them or reflect a different approach or information that isn't consistent with that student's work as you know it.

Oral Questioning and Observations

Reliability concerns for oral questioning and for observations of students include the dependability of your interpretations and the accuracy of your judgment. Use a sufficient number of questions or observations. This point is easiest to illustrate in the negative. If you only ask a student one question about a chapter she read, how sure are you that you can interpret a correct answer to mean she read and understood the whole chapter? The number of questions or observations needed depends on the judgment to be made. If you see a kindergartner tie his shoes properly twice, you might conclude he knows how to tie his shoes. But you might want more than two observations to conclude that a student knows how to graph a linear function in algebra.

Allow enough time for students to answer oral questions or to do whatever you're observing. As with tests and assignments, oral or observed performance should indicate achievement and not lack of time. Interpret answers or observed behavior with the most likely and reasonable explanation (not the explanation you want to be true, or hope is true). Have a systematic procedure to ensure that you observe or call on all students. It's easy to call on students whose hands are waving wildly and ignore the rest. It's difficult to remember which students you called on from day to day. A class roster check sheet can help keep you organized. Alternatively, use a procedure that ensures you call on students randomly.

Peer Editing, Group Collaboration Ratings, and Other Peer Assessment Techniques

For peer assessment, the most important reliability concern is accuracy of judgment. Have a systematic procedure for rating and instruct students in its use. The clearer you make your directions or rubrics, the more likely students are to use them in the same way. Use student procedures that emphasize respect, judging the work and not the person, and so on. The aim is to have peers judge student achievement against criteria, not to give personal or social opinions.

Self-Assessment

For self-assessment, the most important reliability concern is accuracy of self-judgment. Have a systematic procedure for rating and instruct students in its use. Give them lots of opportunity to practice. You also need to create a classroom environment where it is safe for a student to describe his needs for improvement and where mistakes are interpreted as opportunities to learn and not cause for penalty.

MyLab Education **Self-Check 4.1**

MyLab Education **Application Exercise 4.1**:
Importance of Reliability

RELIABILITY OF LARGE-SCALE ASSESSMENTS

Quantifying the Consistency of Assessment Results

When an assessment yields quantitative scores or measurements of students, it is possible to quantify reliability and measurement error. Statistical methods can indicate the degree of reliability and the approximate size of the measurement error in the assessment results.

The advantage of using these indices is that they can provide guidance on the quality of your assessment results. A low reliability index means that the assessment results are not very consistent. As a result, the quality of your assessment information is poor. The decisions you make using poor-quality information will not be optimal.

The general strategy to obtain reliability coefficients is to administer the assessment to a group of students one or more times and obtain the scores. Then, one of two approaches is used to examine consistency. One approach is to correlate the scores from the two administrations. As discussed in Chapter 3, a correlation coefficient is an index of whether the relative standing of students in the group (as determined by their scores) differs from one assessment to the next. In the context of score consistency, this correlation is called a **reliability coefficient**. A second approach is to estimate the amount by which we can expect a student's score to change from one administration to the next. The index expressing this variation in score consistency is called the *standard error of measurement* (to be discussed later). Reliability coefficients are most useful when you are comparing assessment procedures that report students' scores on different scales. Standard errors of measurement are more useful than reliability coefficients when you are using a particular instrument and are concerned with interpreting students' scores.

Both reliability coefficients and standard errors of measurement are widely used in describing the quality of assessment methods, so you should understand the basic ideas behind them. Understanding these indices is essential for using assessment results responsibly, even if you do not calculate them yourself. We first discuss various types of reliability coefficients and then address the standard error of measurement. Our approach is conceptual and does not emphasize calculations. Appendix G shows how to calculate these indices.

Overview of Reliability Coefficients

This section discusses ways of estimating reliability coefficients. We discuss three categories of reliability coefficients: (1) those that focus on the consistency of student scores over time (occasions), (2) those that focus on consistency of scores from one sample of content to another (forms), and (3) those that focus on the consistency of marks or ratings of student responses (raters).

Figure 4.2 shows these three categories, lists each of the coefficients we discuss in each category, the major questions for which the coefficients provide answers, and the type of measurement error each addresses. As you

examine this figure and study this section, you will realize that the question "Are these scores reliable?" has many different answers depending on the types of measurement errors that concern you.

Estimating Reliability over Time

Suppose we ask questions such as the following: To what extent are scores on identical tasks likely to be different because they were administered on different occasions? Or, if a student teacher had been observed on a Monday, would the ratings agree with the ratings from observations made on Wednesday? Or if Dr. Adams rates a teacher on Monday and Dr. Meyers rates on Thursday, would the two ratings be likely to agree? Procedures for estimating reliability in situations like these are the subject of this section.

FIGURE 4.2   **Summary of reliability coefficients.**

Type of coefficient	Major question(s) answered	What is counted as measurement error or inconsistency
	I. Influence of occasions (or time)	
Test-retest	a. How are scores on the identical content sample affected by testing on another occasion? b. How stable are scores on this particular test form over time?	Time or occasion sampling
Alternate forms (with time interval)	a. How consistent are the test scores regardless of form used or occasion on which it is administered? b. How stable are scores on this trial over time (and content samples)?	Time or occasion sampling and content sampling
	II. Influence of forms (different content samples)	
Alternate forms (no time interval)	a. Are scores affected by sampling different content on the same occasion? b. Are two carefully matched test forms interchangeable (equivalent, parallel)?	Content sampling
Split-halves	a. Same as above. b. What is an estimate of the alternate-forms reliability coefficient?	Content sampling
Kuder-Richardson formulas 20 and 21, coefficient alpha	a. Same as above, except equivalence or parallelism of forms may not concern the investigator. b. How consistent are responses as a set? c. Are scores affected by content sampling on the same occasion?	Content sampling
	III. Influence of raters (different scorers)	
Scorer reliability	a. To what extent will the scores be different if different scorers (raters, judges) are used? b. To what extent is the test objective? c. Are the results from different scorers (observers, raters, judges) interchangeable?	Scorer sampling

Test-Retest Reliability The first reliability question in the preceding paragraph centers on the *stability of scores* on a fixed sample of assessment tasks over a specified time period. Studying data obtained from administering the identical tasks to a group of students on two separate occasions will answer this question. Because the same tasks (rather than equivalent tasks) are administered at two different times, the correlation between the scores on the two occasions is known as the **test-retest reliability coefficient**. Sometimes, it is also called a **stability coefficient**.

This paradigm is as follows:

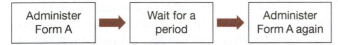

You may recall that a correlation of 0.00 represents no relationship between two sets of scores, and a correlation of 1.00 is a perfect positive relationship. Reliability coefficients have a range of 0.00 to 1.00. A completely unreliable (inconsistent) set of scores has a reliability coefficient of 0.00. A perfectly reliable set, containing no measurement errors, has a reliability coefficient of 1.00. If students were tested on two occasions, and if their scores were identical, they would be ranked identically on the two tests; thus, the test-retest coefficient would be 1.00. Test-retest coefficients of 1.00 rarely occur, however. Typically, test-retest coefficients for standardized achievement and aptitude tests are between 0.80 and 0.90 when the interval between testing is 3 to 6 months.

It is important when you interpret these test-retest coefficients to know (a) the length of time between the two administrations of the assessment and (b) the expected stability of the performance being measured. In general, the longer the interval between the repeated administrations, the lower the reliability. Further, the less stable the performance of students, the lower the reliability. For example, some performances of infants and young children are not consistent from one day to the next. You would expect the test-retest reliability of assessments of these performances to be low, too. On the other hand, traits such as older students' general scholastic aptitude tend to remain stable over a semester or a year. Test-retest reliability of assessments of this trait usually will be relatively high over a longer period, and assessments of general scholastic aptitude tend to be useful in predicting future performance over these periods. The validity of assessment results as predictors of future performance lessens when the results lack stability.

Alternate-Forms Reliability (with Time Interval) Another procedure for estimating reliability is to administer one form of an assessment on one occasion and an **alternate form** on another occasion. This permits both content and occasion to vary. The correlation between the scores on the two occasions is influenced by differences in both content and in occasion. This paradigm is depicted as follows:

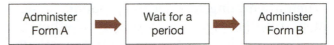

This correlation is known as the **delayed alternate-forms reliability coefficient** or the *delayed equivalent-forms reliability coefficient*. The two forms are built to the same content specifications (i.e., same blueprint) and level of difficulty, but they contain different questions or tasks. When this paradigm is applied, the reliability coefficient reflects both the equivalence of the assessment techniques and the stability of students' performance.

The comments about the time interval for the test-retest reliability coefficient also apply to the delayed alternate-forms coefficient. Because a new sample of tasks is administered (Form B), this process eliminates the effects of students' remembering specific assessment questions. It does not eliminate general practice effects, however.

Delayed alternate-forms reliability is important when you want to generalize your interpretation of assessment results over both occasions and content samples. You may ask, for example, "How well does this test assess the ability to solve mathematics problems, regardless of test form used or occasion on which I administer the test?" Many interpretations of assessment results can use this framework. For example, in estimating a student teacher's "teaching ability," a supervisor may want to focus on the consistency of ratings obtained on different occasions and from different raters. Rarely is teaching ability defined in terms of only a single occasion (e.g., many supervisors' ratings on Tuesday, October 5) or a specific supervisor's ratings over several occasions (e.g., Mr. Washington's ratings of teachers throughout the year).

The *meaning of occasions* needs to be carefully specified when interpreting delayed alternate-forms reliability coefficients. For instance, if children are observed while learning a subject they happen to enjoy very much or with an exceptionally enthralling teacher, their attentiveness may fluctuate little from day to day. But relatively large fluctuations in attentiveness might occur within the same day as students move from mathematics instruction to language arts to gym.

Estimating Reliability on a Single Occasion

Alternate-Forms Reliability (No Time Interval)

When attempting to interpret students' assessment results, you may wonder whether the results would have been different with a different sample of assessment tasks. If so, your primary concern is the consistency of two sets of results (one set from each of two comparable forms) obtained on the same occasion.

One way to provide the type of reliability information this question implies is to administer two forms of an assessment to the same group of students on the same (or nearly the same) occasion and to correlate the scores. This correlation is known as the **alternate-forms reliability coefficient** or the *equivalent-forms reliability coefficient*. This coefficient is most often used with standardized tests that have two interchangeable forms. Look for alternate-forms reliability coefficients in the publisher's test manual whenever you intend to use two or more forms of a test.

For an alternate-forms reliability coefficient, only inconsistencies due to fluctuations in content samples are counted as measurement error. Other factors such as practice effects, fatigue, and boredom—all of which may occur on this one occasion—are considered part of the students' true scores.

Two forms of an assessment that are made up of tasks carefully matched to the same blueprint are called **parallel forms**. In this case, the correlation of the scores from the two forms is referred to as a parallel-forms reliability coefficient. Ideally, scores from parallel forms of a test should (a) have equal observed score means and standard deviations, (b) measure students with equal accuracy (i.e., have equal standard errors of measurement), (c) correlate equally with other measurements, and (d) measure the same attribute in precisely the same way. If the two forms of the assessment meet

these criteria, it wouldn't matter to the student which form he or she takes: They are interchangeable. Alternate forms that are "built" simply by drawing random samples of tasks from the same domain are not strictly parallel because chance will determine the composition of each form.

Any systematic score differences from one form to another are especially important when an individual's scores are to be interpreted on their own merits rather than on the basis of the individual's relative standing in a group. Here is an example:

Example

A test is used to certify teachers. It has a passing score. Candidates with test scores above the passing score are certified; those below the passing score are not. It doesn't matter how one candidate's scores on the test compare to others; it only matters whether the candidate's score is above the passing mark. If different candidates take different forms of the certification test, they expect the forms to be equivalent.

Note that in this example, candidates are not well served when the different forms of such a certification test lack equivalence. If one form is more difficult than an alternate form, more candidates than necessary are failed. A less difficult alternate form has the opposite consequence: Many candidates are certified who may not be qualified. A correlation coefficient of the scores from the two forms won't reveal such consequences because the coefficient reflects only rank order rather than the exact values of the scores.

Parallel Forms Do Not Always Exist   Although in principle several parallel forms of an assessment might exist, in practice many assessments have no parallel form. Further, assessments that do have parallel forms seldom have more than two or three forms. When any of the following occurs, a developer usually does not create a parallel form of the assessment (Thorndike, 1951):

1. *The assessment procedure will be used only once with each student.* Repeated testing for practical decisions is not anticipated.

2. *The very act of taking the assessment may change the student.* For example, if tasks are crafted to assess the strategies students use to solve unfamiliar problems, completing the assessment tasks themselves may result in the student

becoming more familiar with the different types of problems and better at the strategies for solving them.

3. *Only one way exists to assess the ability of interest.*

4. *It is too costly to build a parallel form of the assessment.*

In situations such as the preceding, methods other than alternate-forms reliability are used to evaluate the extent to which content sampling affects observed scores. We discuss two such methods in this section: split-halves and Kuder-Richardson. Both estimate reliability from a single administration of an assessment.

Split-Halves Reliability Coefficients The first way that alternate-forms reliability may be estimated from a single form of an assessment is by a method known as the split-halves procedure. In applying the **split-halves procedure**, the entire test is administered once to the students. Then the test's items are organized into two equivalent halves. Each half (called a *split*) is considered to be a separate (albeit smaller) sample of tasks. For purposes of analysis, every student receives a score for each half of the test. These half-test scores form the basis for estimating the extent of error due to content sampling for the full-length assessment. There are many possible split-halves procedures (Feldt & Brennan, 1989; Haertel, 2006). We discuss only one here: the **Spearman-Brown double length formula** (Brown, 1910; Spearman, 1910). Appendix G provides a computing guide for the Spearman-Brown formula as well as for another split-half method, the Rulon (1939) method.

Spearman-Brown Double Length Formula The **Spearman-Brown double length formula** (sometimes called the *Spearman-Brown prophecy formula*) is an estimate of the parallel-forms correlation. Students receive scores on each half of the test. Their scores on the halves are correlated. Because this correlation reflects the correspondence of two sets of scores from only half the test rather than the full-length assessment, this correlation is adjusted or "stepped up" to estimate the reliability of the whole test. The Spearman-Brown formula is simple to use:

Whole test reliability

$$= \frac{2 \times \text{correlation between half test scores}}{1 + \text{correlation between half test scores}} \quad \text{[Eq. 4.1]}$$

For example, assume that the correlation between the half-test scores is 0.60. The Spearman-Brown double length reliability estimate for the full-length test is:

$$\text{Whole test reliability} = \frac{2 \times 0.60}{1 + 0.60} = \frac{1.20}{1.60} = 0.75$$

The double length formula can be used to estimate a parallel form's reliability coefficient. To do so properly requires organizing the assessment's items into parallel halves, making the halves equivalent in terms of content coverage, difficulty level, and variability in essentially the same manner as when two parallel forms are constructed.

An assessment's items may be organized into halves in many ways (see Haertel, 2006, pp. 73–74), but not all prove satisfactory when applying split-halves procedures. The most commonly used procedure to organize the items is to let the odd-numbered items (1, 3, 5, 7, . . .) comprise one of the halves and the even-numbered (2, 4, 6, 8, . . .) comprise the other half. This is known as the **odd-even split-halves procedure**. Splitting the assessment and instrument into halves this way works fine as long as (a) the odd half and the even half can be considered parallel content samples, and (b) the assessment is not speeded. A **speeded assessment** is one for which there is not enough time for everyone to consider and attempt to answer each item. If an assessment is speeded, agreement among students' scores on the two halves is spuriously high. In general, a **split-halves procedure** should not be used with speeded or partially speeded assessments unless precautions are taken to administer and time each half separately. The odd-even split-halves procedure is inappropriate when groups of items are linked together, such as when a cluster of items requires answers based on the same reading selection (or on the same data table, figure, graph, etc.) or when items are grouped in homogeneous clusters in a matching exercise.

Kuder-Richardson Reliability Coefficients A second way to obtain a reliability estimate from a single form of the test is by using one of the Kuder and Richardson (1937) procedures. The two discussed here, **Kuder-Richardson formula 20 (KR20)** and **Kuder-Richardson formula 21 (KR21)**, are used when test items are scored dichotomously (0 or 1). The names of these procedures derive from the numbering scheme Kuder and Richardson used to identify the formulas in their 1937 paper.

The Kuder-Richardson formula 20, like the split-half formula, estimates reliability from a single administration of a test. Unlike the split-half procedure, however, KR20 does not require splitting the test in half. Instead, it uses data on the proportion of persons answering each item correctly and the standard deviation of the total scores. The Kuder-Richardson formula 21 procedure is a simpler version of KR20: It uses only the mean and standard deviation of the total scores. Appendix G illustrates the computation of these reliability estimates. The KR20 formula is most often used in published reports of standardized tests and is often provided as output in computer programs that analyze classroom test data.

Kuder-Richardson formulas 20 and 21 are used when the test contains only dichotomously scored items. Not all assessments contain only items scored that way. Some assessments contain a mixture of item types. In these cases, a more general version of KR20 is used. This reliability estimate is known as **coefficient alpha** (Cronbach, 1951). Appendix G shows an example of how to calculate this coefficient as well. Because coefficient alpha is a more general version of KR20, it can be used with items scored either 0 or 1 or on a more continuous scale (e.g., 0, 1, 2, 3, and 4). Rating scales and rubrics, for example, use a more continuous scale.

The split-half and Kuder-Richardson procedures assume that the consistency with which students respond from one assessment task to the next is a good foundation to estimate the reliability coefficient for the total scores. This focus on task-to-task consistency within an assessment has led to these coefficients being called *internal consistency reliability estimates*.

These three procedures are sensitive to the homogeneity of the tasks as well as to their specific content. **Homogeneous tasks** all measure the same trait or attribute. An assessment procedure in which different tasks measure different traits is said to contain *heterogeneous tasks*. If assessment tasks are homogeneous, the KR20 and coefficient alpha procedures will give nearly the same results as the split-halves procedure. When the assessment tasks are heterogeneous, results from the KR20 and coefficient alpha procedures are lower

than the split-halves procedure. For this reason, KR20 and coefficient alpha are often called *lower bound estimates of reliability*.

It should be noted that KR20 and coefficient alpha are equal to the average of all possible split-half reliability coefficients that could be computed for the assessment procedure in question (see Cronbach, 1951). "All possible split-halves" means not just the odd-even split but also all different splits that could divide a test into halves.

The length of the test, as well as its homogeneity, influences the numerical values of KR20 and coefficient alpha. Longer tests will tend to have higher values of KR20 or coefficient alpha, even though they may be heterogeneous. The KR20, KR21, and alpha coefficients are influenced by speed in the same manner as split-halves coefficients. They should not be used with speeded or partially speeded tests.

The KR20 and coefficient alpha procedures are usually not appropriate to use when a test is composed of items organized in clusters (e.g., several different types of reading passage, each with several items that are based on the respective reading passage) or containing a mixture of assessment formats (e.g., a combination of multiple-choice, short-answer, and performance assessments). For tests comprised of such heterogeneous exercise formats, where the various sections are not strictly parallel but are *congeneric* (meaning students' scores on the parts are related, but may have different means and variances), a stratified coefficient alpha may be used. See Haertel (2006) for an explanation of stratified alpha and other more advanced resources on reliability.

Finally, as you may notice in Figure 4.2, KR20, KR21, coefficient alpha, and the split-halves methods do not consider sampling of occasions or sampling of raters as sources of measurement error. To estimate the degree of inconsistency attributed to students' day-to-day fluctuations in performance, you must use test-retest or delayed alternate-forms coefficients. To estimate the degree of inconsistency attributed to persons who rate or mark an assessment, you must use inter-rater reliability coefficients (see the next section). If KR20 or coefficient alpha are used inappropriately to describe assessment reliability for these other types of inconsistency questions, they will overestimate the assessment reliability (Brennan, 2001) and could lead you to believe the assessment results are more consistent than they really are.

Estimating Inter-Rater Reliability

Yet another source of measurement error arises from the persons (or machines) who score students' work. Here concern focuses on questions such as the following: (a) To what extent would a student obtain the same score if a different teacher had scored the paper or rated the performance? (b) To what extent might the assessment procedure be said to be objective? and (c) Are the results obtained from different scorers (observers, raters, judges) interchangeable? Inter-rater reliability is especially important for essay questions, open-ended questions, performance assessments, and portfolio assessments.

Correlating Raters' Scores   The most straightforward way to estimate this type of reliability is to have two persons score each student's paper or rate each student's performance. The two scores for each student—one score from each scorer—are then correlated. This correlation coefficient is called **scorer reliability** or **inter-rater reliability**. It is an index of the scorers' consistency in marking the same students. In this case, *consistency* is defined as similarity of students' rank ordering by the two teachers or judges. The group of four students' ratings in Figure 4.3 illustrates this point in an admittedly exaggerated situation.

The ratings in this illustration don't "agree" in the absolute sense. Agreement in the absolute sense happens when two scorers assign identical scores or ratings to each student. But they do agree perfectly in the relative sense because the rankings are in perfect agreement: The correlation coefficient of 1.00 reflects this.

Percentage Agreement   The extent to which the identical assignment of scores occurs is sometimes expressed as a **percentage of agreement**, which is defined as an index of the consistency of decisions made by two independent judges. If scorers always agree in their assignment of scores, there is 100 percent agreement; if they never agree, the percentage of agreement is zero; partial agreement is expressed as a percentage falling between these two values.

Percentage of agreement is quite a different concept than a reliability coefficient based on a correlation coefficient: In general, the numerical values of the two will differ. The choice between a percentage of agreement index and a correlation index of inter-rater reliability depends on whether a student's absolute (actual) or relative (rank order) score level is important for a particular interpretation and use. Suppose that in Figure 4.3 a rating of five or better was needed to "pass." If the scores of Rater A were used, then everyone "failed," but if the scores of Rater B were used, everyone passed. For interpretations of pass and fail, the actual score level is important. A serious source of error (in this example) is the particular scorer or rater employed: The raters do not seem to agree on the scores that rate the students. Only the percentage of agreement will show this. Suppose, on the other hand, that only the rank order of the scores is important, such as when you want to know who in the class is the best, next best, and so on. In this case, the two observers agree perfectly on who the "best" and the "next best" are. In other words, they agree perfectly on their ranking or relative level of accomplishment. The correlation inter-rater reliability coefficient shows this.

MyLab Education   Self-Check 4.2

MyLab Education   Application Exercise 4.2:
Evaluating Reliability Estimates

FIGURE 4.3   **Ratings and rank order of four students.**

Students	Ratings from:		Ratings converted to ranks	
	Rater A	**Rater B**	**Rank from A**	**Rank from B**
Tony	4	8	1	1
Marya	3	7	2	2
Bobby	2	6	3	3
Meghan	1	5	4	4
Mean	2.5	6.5	$r_{AB} = 1.00$	
SD	1.12	1.12		

OBTAINED SCORES, TRUE SCORES, AND ERROR SCORES

In the preceding sections, we often referred to students' scores. In this section, we dig more deeply into the idea that students' assessment results are reported as scores. The scores students receive when you assess them are called **obtained scores**. Obtained scores include ratings from open-ended tasks such as essays, number-right scores from multiple-choice or short-answer tests, and standard scores or grade-equivalent scores from norm-referenced standardized tests. Think of each student's obtained score as containing some measurement error. This means that the obtained score is really composed of two parts: a true score and an error score. The sum of these two scores equals the obtained score. Whenever we assess a student, we really want to know the student's true score. However, we are always "stuck" with the obtained score because the true score is not available to us. The obtained scores from our assessments are only *estimates* of the students' true status. Because obtained scores contain errors, we must learn to live with measurement errors—and to be cautious in our interpretation of obtained scores.

If you could quantify the amount of error in a student's obtained score, you would have the **error score**. Often the error score is referred to as measurement error. The **true score** is the remaining portion of the observed score and contains no measurement error. In other words, if we subtract the error score from the student's obtained score, the result is the student's true score.

As an illustration, suppose you had two students, Suzanne and Georgia. Assume that you gave them the same problem-solving test and that both students scored 52. The score, 52, is their obtained score, the only score you see. You might be tempted to use these results to conclude that Suzanne and Georgia have the same problem-solving ability. However, the obtained score, 52, contains measurement error that needs to be acknowledged.

Let us further assume that Suzanne's true score is 50 and that Georgia's true score is 53. If you could create a problem-solving test that resulted in scores without measurement error, you would see that Georgia has somewhat more ability than Suzanne. Unfortunately, creating such a perfect test is impossible. Consequently, both students ended up getting identical obtained scores of 52.

How much measurement error is in their obtained scores? In our example, Georgia's true score is 53. Thus, her error score is $52 - 53 = -1$. Suzanne's true score, on the other hand, is 50, so her error score is $52 - 50 = +2$. This illustrates that errors of measurement may be either positive (e.g., $+2$) or negative (e.g., -1).

Although we illustrated two students having different true scores but the same obtained score, other possibilities exist. Two students may have the *same true score*, but as a result of measurement errors, they may receive *different obtained scores*. The point is that you need to treat an observed test score as an imperfect piece of information. How can you improve assessment to get a better estimate of a person's true score? To estimate a student's true score better, you need to include more than one test in your overall evaluation.

A student's true score for a particular assessment procedure is defined as the hypothetical average (mean) of the observed scores the student would obtain if repeatedly assessed under the same conditions (Lord & Novick, 1968). Because a true score is an average, it is constant from one administration of an assessment procedure to the next. (Different students will have different true scores, however.) For each separate administration of the assessment procedure, a student's error score is different. On any one occasion the student's error score may be either positive, negative, or zero. These measurement errors result in the student's obtained scores being higher or lower than the student's true score. One consequence of these measurement errors is that scores obtained from any two administrations of an assessment procedure do not rank students in identical order.

STANDARD ERROR OF MEASUREMENT
Defining the Standard Error of Measurement

Because no procedure assesses with perfect consistency, your score interpretations are improved if you take into account the likely size of measurement errors. One way to describe the inconsistency of assessment scores is to assess a student repeatedly and note how much scores vary. This process can only be done hypothetically, however. If you could assess a student many times (without changing the student's ability with respect to the trait you are assessing), you would obtain a collection of the student's obtained scores. Some scores would be higher than others, but most would cluster around an average (mean) value. This average is the true score. The standard deviation or spread of this distribution is the **standard error of measurement (SEM)**. The *SEM* estimates the likely difference of students' obtained scores from their true scores.

In practice, you cannot repeatedly reassess students without changing them, so the standard error of measurement is not calculated by actually reassessing students. Instead, it is estimated using the following equation.

$$SEM = SD_x \sqrt{1 - \text{reliability coefficient}} \quad \text{[Eq. 4.2]}$$

where SD_x is the standard deviation of the obtained scores of the assessment. (See Appendix F for a description of standard deviation.)

The *SEM* is an estimate of the standard deviation of the errors of measurement. For example, if SD_x equals 10 and the reliability coefficient equals 0.84, then

$$SEM = 10\sqrt{1-.84} = 10\sqrt{.16} = 10(.4) = 4$$

The standard error of measurement helps us understand the size of measurement error for a particular assessment procedure. One interpretation is that the numerical value of *SEM* estimates the amount by which a student's observed scores are likely to deviate from her true score. Thus, in the preceding example, *SEM* = 4.0 means that a student's obtained scores are likely to be about four points above or below her true score. Because of this likely deviation from the true score, you must interpret the obtained score as only an estimate of the student's true score.

Another interpretation of *SEM* uses a normal distribution. It is assumed that the hypothetical distribution of obtained scores, resulting from repeatedly assessing a student, is normal in form. (See Chapter 17 for a discussion of normal distributions.) The mean of this distribution is the student's true score, whereas the standard deviation is the standard error of measurement. Using the relationship between standard deviation and percent of cases under a normal curve from Chapter 17, it can be said that 68 percent of the time the student's obtained scores will be within a distance of 1 *SEM* from the true score.

FIGURE 4.4 A hypothetical normal distribution of scores resulting from repeated assessment of one student whose "true" score is 52.

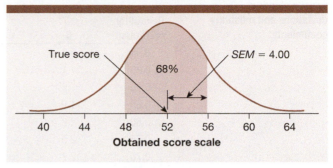

This meaning of the *SEM* is illustrated in Figure 4.4 for a hypothetical student with a true score of 52 and *SEM* of 4.0. Following the normal curve interpretation, one third (32%) of the time that a student is retested, her obtained scores will be outside the bounds shown at the bottom of the shaded area in Figure 4.4: They will be greater than 56 (52 + 4) about one sixth (16%) of the time and less than 48 (52 − 4) about one sixth of the time.

Reliability Coefficients and *SEMs*

If the standard error of measurement became smaller, observed scores would cluster more closely around the true score because two thirds of the time they are within ± 1 *SEM* of the true score. This illustrates graphically what we mean by consistency: If the observed assessment scores tend to be very near a student's true score, the scores are consistent. More consistency means smaller measurement errors.

The size of the standard error of measurement, however, depends on both the reliability coefficient and the standard deviation of the obtained scores. In the preceding example, if SD_x = 5 instead of 10, then *SEM* = 2.0. Thus, while the reliability remained at 0.84, *SEM* became smaller when SD_x is smaller. This smaller *SEM* illustrates that the standard deviation of the scores should be taken into account when interpreting the consistency of assessment results.

Because different assessment procedures have different units of measurement as well as different standard deviations, it is usually true that the only way to compare the consistency of the scores from two different assessment methods is by looking at their reliability coefficients. A *SEM* calculated for students' raw scores would have radically different numerical value than the *SEM*

FIGURE 4.5 Standard error of measurement for various standard deviations and reliability coefficients.

Reliability coefficient	Standard deviation					
	5	10	15	20	25	30
0.98	0.7	1.4	2.1	2.8	3.5	4.2
0.95	1.1	2.2	3.4	4.5	5.6	6.7
0.90	1.6	3.2	4.7	6.2	7.9	9.5
0.85	1.9	3.9	5.8	7.7	9.7	11.6
0.80	2.2	4.5	6.7	8.9	11.1	13.4
0.75	2.5	5.0	7.5	10.0	12.5	15.0
0.70	2.7	5.5	8.2	11.0	13.7	16.4
0.65	3.0	5.9	8.9	11.8	14.8	17.7
0.60	3.2	6.3	9.5	12.6	15.8	19.0
0.50	3.5	7.1	10.6	14.1	17.7	21.2
0.20	4.5	8.9	13.4	17.9	22.4	26.8
0.10	4.7	9.5	14.2	19.0	23.7	28.5

calculated for the same students after these same raw scores are converted into grade-equivalent scores on the same test.

The relationship between the SD_x, the reliability coefficient, and the SEM is shown in Figure 4.5. When the reliability coefficient is fixed, SEM becomes larger as SD_x increases. When the SD_x is fixed, SEM becomes smaller as the reliability coefficient becomes larger. If a test manual does not report SEM, Figure 4.5 can provide a rough estimate once the SD_x and the reliability coefficient are known.

Finally, remember that the type of reliability coefficient you use in the SEM formula is important. Each reliability coefficient estimates the reliability for different types of measurement error (see column three of Figure 4.2). This means that the SEM will estimate the likely size of the same type of measurement error as the reliability coefficient used in the formula.

Using the *SEM* to Set Score Bands

An obtained score is likely to be near, but not exactly equal to, the student's true score. You can use the SEM to help express how students' true scores can differ from their obtained scores. To accomplish this result, you add to and subtract the value of the SEM from each student's obtained score, thus forming the boundaries of an **uncertainty interval (score band) or confidence interval** for scores. This kind of uncertainty interval has a 68 percent chance of containing the student's true score. You can use this method to help

you interpret a student's score on one test, a student's score on two tests, or two different students' scores on the same test.

The examples that follow show how to accomplish this result. In all the examples, we will use grade-equivalent scores from a hypothetical standardized achievement test that has a reliability coefficient of 0.84 and a standard deviation of 1.0 (on the grade-equivalent scale). For this test, the SEM would then be equal to 0.4. It would be quite likely that, upon retesting, a student's score would shift up or down the scale 4 grade-equivalent months (0.4).

Uncertainty Interval for One Student's Score   To show the uncertainty interval for a student, you would add +0.4 to the student's obtained score to compute the upper limit of the uncertainty interval and subtract 0.4 from the student's obtained score to find the lower limit of the band. Any number between the upper and the lower limits of the interval could be the student's true score.

Example

Suppose Harry's obtained grade-equivalent score in science is 7.8. After making the uncertainty interval, our interpretation is that Harry's true grade-equivalent score is probably between 7.4 and 8.2.

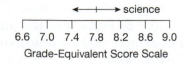

Using *SEM* to Interpret the Difference Between Two Scores When a student takes a battery of achievement tests, the student usually has two or more scores, one for each subject. These scores may not be identical. We can set an uncertainty interval around each of these scores. If the intervals for two scores overlap, it is likely that the student's true scores are not meaningfully different. If the intervals overlap, the observed-score differences for the student could have come about 68 percent of the time simply by measurement error.

Example

Harry's obtained grade-equivalent score in science is 7.8, whereas in mathematics it is 7.4. Do these facts mean he is stronger in science than in math? No. The uncertainty interval for science is 7.4 to 8.2; for math it is 7.0 to 7.8. Because the uncertainty intervals overlap, it is likely that his true scores on the two tests are not meaningfully different.

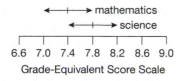

Grade-Equivalent Score Scale

Using *SEM* to Interpret the Difference Between Two Students' Scores Sometimes you want to see if one student is stronger than another student in a subject by comparing their scores on the same achievement test. The students' obtained scores may be different, but because the scores contain measurement error, are the students' true scores different? To answer this question, form an uncertainty interval around each student's score. Then, see if the intervals overlap. No overlap means that the students' true scores are probably meaningfully different. If the intervals do overlap, there may be no meaningful differences in the two students' true scores because differences of the size observed could arise simply by errors of measurement 68 percent of the time.

Example

In reading, Sally's obtained grade-equivalent score was 8.2 whereas Jane's was 7.0. The uncertainty interval for Sally is 7.8 to 8.6; for Jane it is 6.6 to 7.4.

Does this mean Sally is a stronger reader than Jane? Yes, because the intervals do not overlap.

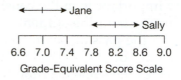

Grade-Equivalent Score Scale

Be cautious about **overinterpreting score differences** in scores by acting as if small differences in scores have an important meaning. You should not be so conservative, however, as to ignore meaningful score differences and consequently err by **underinterpreting score differences**. Perhaps a more widespread problem than overinterpreting scores is a "do-nothing pattern": failing to interpret score changes or ups and downs of profiles because of overdemanding criteria of 68 percent, 90 percent, or 95 percent uncertainty intervals. To avoid wasting valuable information, corroborate the information obtained from one assessment with information from other sources that you already have (such as classroom performance), thereby reducing the probability of overinterpretation errors.

Interpreting the Difference Between School-Level Scores The uncertainty interval (or confidence interval) interpretations in the sections above apply to scores for individual students. The same principle of interpreting uncertainty intervals is applied when interpreting the difference between school-level scores (for example, whether the average for School A and the average for School B are truly different). While the construction of confidence intervals for aggregated scores is beyond the scope of this text, we thought it important to let you know that it could be done and at the same time caution you that it requires more than just the *SEM* to do it.

MyLab Education **Self-Check 4.3**

MyLab Education **Application Exercise 4.3:**
Using Standard Error of Measurement to Interpret Test Scores

RELIABILITY OF MASTERY AND PASS-FAIL DECISIONS

We have been discussing consistency of students' scores. This consistency is of concern no matter what type of assessment method you are using.

There are certain classroom situations, however, when the consistency of the exact score a student receives is less important than the consistency of the decision made about the student. For example, you may set the passing score on a mastery test as 80 percent correct. A student who gets 85 percent receives the same decision (i.e., pass), as does the student who gets 92 percent. Similarly, two students with 50 percent and 65 percent, respectively, both fail.

In this type of assessment interpretation, it makes more sense to speak of *decision consistency* than of score consistency. A **decision consistency index** describes how consistent the classification decisions are rather than how consistent the scores are. For example, suppose you crafted two equivalent forms of a mastery test. Such indexes answer the question, "Would both tests classify the same students as masters and nonmasters?"

Error of Classification

Figure 4.6 illustrates how measurement error may cause an assessment to mask a student's true mastery status. Whenever a student's true status is not revealed by the assessment results, a decision error or error of misclassification occurs.

Several factors influence how often decision errors occur when assessing mastery.

1. *The assessment tool may contain tasks that have weak validity for assessing the type of mastery you have in mind.* This problem may happen, for example, in achievement tests that report student proficiency based on narrowly defined performance on items that do not truly represent the domain.

2. *Longer assessment methods usually lead to more accurate mastery decisions.* Judging mastery from a short test (e.g., fewer than 10 response-choice items) or from one project or one performance activity usually raises decision errors to unacceptably high levels. Use several different pieces of assessment information before finalizing a mastery decision about a student.

3. *Low inter-rater reliability is associated with high rates of mastery decision errors.* More reliable assessments generally lead to more accurate mastery decisions.

4. *The passing score you set for deciding mastery affects the rate of decision errors.* In general, setting the passing score very high (90% or 95%) or very low (20% or 30%) will increase errors of classification.

5. *Students whose true mastery status is very close to the passing score you set are the ones who are most likely to be misclassified.* For example, if you set the passing score at 80 percent, students whose true mastery status is in the range of 70 percent to 90 percent will have higher rates of erroneous classification than students outside this range. When students' assessment results are close to the passing score, you should use information from other sources (such as performance in class, homework, project performance) in addition to the main assessment before making a final mastery decision.

Percentage Agreement

A quantitative index of decision consistency can be calculated by administering two **parallel forms** of a mastery test to the same group of students and studying whether students are consistently

FIGURE 4.6   Relationship between a student's true mastery status and possible errors of classification when drawing conclusions from assessment results.

		True status of a student with respect to the degree of domain proficiency	
		Master	**Nonmaster**
Conclusion the teacher drew about the student from the assessment results	The assessment results are interpreted as mastery	*There is no misclassification:* Both the student's true status and the conclusion the teacher drew from the assessment results agree.	*An error of classification:* The student is a nonmaster, but the teacher concluded that the assessment results showed mastery.
	The assessment results are interpreted as nonmastery	*An error of classification:* Student is a master, but the teacher concluded that the assessment results showed nonmastery.	*There is no misclassification:* Both the student's true status and the conclusion the teacher drew from the assessment results agree.

classified as masters or nonmasters. Two indices may be calculated: percentage of agreement (P_A) and kappa coefficient (κ) (Cohen, 1960). Here we show the calculation of P_A. Appendix G shows an example of calculating kappa coefficient.

As stated earlier, the percentage of agreement is an index of the consistency of decisions made by two independent judges: It is the percentage of students for whom the two judges reached the same decision. The percentage of agreement is calculated by the following formula when the assessments classify students into two categories (e.g., "mastery" and "nonmastery"):

$$P_A = \begin{bmatrix} \text{Percentage consistent} \\ \text{mastery decisions} \end{bmatrix}$$
$$+ \begin{bmatrix} \text{Percentage consistent} \\ \text{nonmastery decisions} \end{bmatrix} \quad \text{[Eq. 4.3]}$$

Example

Two forms of an assessment, A and B, were administered to a group of 25 students, and the mastery criterion on each form was 80 percent. Figure 4.7 summarizes how consistently the two assessment results classified these students. Eleven students were classified as masters by both forms, nine as nonmasters by both forms, and the others as masters by one and nonmasters by the other. For this example, the percent of agreement is calculated as follows:

$$P_A = \frac{11}{25} + \frac{9}{25} = \frac{20}{25} = 0.80$$

The percentage agreement, $P_A = 0.80$ in this example, is the "total proportion of consistent classification that occurs for whatever reason on the two tests" (Subkoviak, 1980, p. 152).

As described by Equation 4.3 and as illustrated here, percentage agreement requires administering two forms of the assessment to the same group of students. Instead of using two forms, you may also use a test-retest paradigm or two independent judges of mastery. The latter may be especially important whenever you are using assessments that are not paper-and-pencil tests, such as judging whether a student's product or project meets minimum standards.

The percentage agreement need not be limited to the simple, two-category case illustrated here: More than two categories could be used for classifying students. Formulas for computing decision consistency and accuracy for such situations may be found in Lee, Hanson, and Brennan (2002). You may also estimate percentage agreement from only one administration of the assessment (see Huynh, 1976; Subkoviak, 1976).

FACTORS AFFECTING RELIABILITY AND *SEM* AND HOW TO IMPROVE RELIABILITY

You should keep a number of factors in mind when interpreting reliability and *SEM* information, especially when comparing such information from two or more assessment procedures.

Perfect reliability is indicated by a coefficient of 1.00. This value is virtually unattainable in practice, however, because most assessment results have some degree of inconsistency in every population of students. Different types of assessment instruments have different levels of reliability. Standardized multiple-choice achievement tests typically have reliability coefficients in the 0.85 to 0.95 range. Open-ended paper-and-pencil assessments are typically in the 0.65 to 0.80 range. Portfolio scoring may have reliability in the 0.40 to 0.60 range.

A general rule for estimating how close a reliability coefficient should be to 1.00 for a single assessment instrument is as follows: *The more important and the less reversible is the decision about an individual based on the assessment instrument, the higher the reliability should be.* Decisions such as whether a

FIGURE 4.7 Hypothetical example of how 25 students were classified using the scores from two forms of a mastery test.

		Results from Form A		
		Mastery	**Nonmastery**	**Marginal totals**
Results from Form B	**Mastery**	11	4	15
	Nonmastery	1	9	10
	Marginal totals	12	13	25

person is awarded a diploma, admitted to a higher educational program, put into a special education classroom, and given a job are examples of high-stakes decisions which, if erroneous, would have serious consequences for that individual. *The results of a single assessment instrument should not be used alone to make high-stakes decisions. High-reliability coefficients, equal to 0.90 or higher, should be demanded for each instrument used for such decisions.* (Another reason for using more than one instrument in these situations is that they require high validity, as well as high reliability. A single assessment instrument seldom has sufficient validity to be used alone.)

What can be done to improve the reliability of assessment results? Figure 4.8 gives nine suggestions. These suggestions are based on factors known to influence reliability and standard error of measurement.

1. *Longer assessment procedures are more reliable than shorter procedures.* The greater the number of items, judges, occasions of observation, and so on, that enter into formulation of a score, the more reliable that score will be. The general Spearman-Brown formula shows the relation between lengthening an assessment by adding similar tasks and the reliability of the resultant assessment procedure. Appendix G shows a computational example.

2. *The numerical value computed for a reliability coefficient will fluctuate from one sample to another.* The reliability coefficients reported in a test manual are based on samples of students. These numerical values will fluctuate from one sample to the next. Any one published number is only an estimate of what the reliability coefficient would be if the entire population of students were tested. Sampling fluctuations are greater for small samples drawn from the population than from large samples.

3. *The narrower the range of a group's ability, the lower the reliability coefficient tends to be.* Many educators use assessment results to make decisions about students with similar abilities, grade levels, and ages. It is much easier, however, to distinguish individual differences in ability when students vary widely from one another. Look in test manuals for reliability coefficients calculated on data from students whose abilities are as close together as those with whom you must deal. Put less stock in a published high-reliability coefficient that was derived by pooling samples from groups with wide ranges of ability or from groups spanning many age levels. This process is especially important when you will be using the assessment to evaluate students whose abilities are close.

4. *Students at different achievement levels may be assessed with different degrees of accuracy.* The *SEM*, being a single number for an entire test, represents only an average amount of score inconsistency. The consistency of results, however, varies with the achievement level. The *SEM* may be larger in the middle of the score range than at the extremes. If so, very high- and very low-scoring students are assessed with somewhat more consistency than are middle-range students. The technical manual of a published test should tell you which achievement levels are more consistently assessed.

5. *The longer the interval between testing, the lower test-retest and alternate-forms reliability coefficients will tend to be.* If the same assessment is

FIGURE 4.8 How to improve the reliability of assessment results.

1. *Lengthen the assessment procedure.* Whenever practical, give more time, use more questions, more observations, and so on.
2. *Broaden the scope of the procedure.* Use procedures that assess all of the essential and important aspects of the largest learning performance.
3. *Improve objectivity.* Use a systematic, more formal procedure for scoring student performance (e.g., a scoring schema or rubric).
4. *Use multiple markers.* Whenever possible, have more than one qualified person score each student's essay, term paper, performance, portfolio, or open-ended assessment task. Average the results or confer to reconcile differences.
5. *Combine results from several assessments.* When making important educational decisions, use a combination of the results from several different assessment methods rather than a single assessment result.
6. *Provide sufficient time to students.* Within practical limits, be sure that every student has enough time to complete the assessment procedure.
7. *Teach students how to perform their best.* Provide practice and training to students on how to "put their best foot forward," strategies to use, and so on, before using an assessment method.
8. *Match the assessment difficulty to students' ability levels.* Be sure the assessment procedure contains tasks that are not too easy or too difficult for the students. Tailor the assessment to each student's ability level, if possible.
9. *Differentiate among students.* Select assessment tasks that do a good job of differentiating the best students from the least able students.

administered twice, the students' scores will be more similar when the time between the administrations is short than when it is long.

6. *More objectively scored assessment results are more reliable.* Objectivity is the degree to which two qualified observers assign the same scores to the same student performances. We called this inter-rater reliability. As with multiple-choice and true-false questions, alternative assessment methods should be marked as objectively as possible. Increasing objectivity increases reliability, and this consistency will have a positive effect on the validity.

7. *Different methods of estimating reliability will not give the same result.* The reliability coefficients differ because they include different sources of error, as described in Figure 4.2. Be careful to use the proper coefficient in your interpretation of assessments. Using the improper reliability coefficient will mean incorrectly describing an assessment's quality.

MyLab Education Self-Check 4.4

MyLab Education Application Exercise 4.4:
Improving the Reliability of Classroom Tests

CONCLUSION

Reliability is the consistency of measurement over relevant dimensions (time, raters, content sampling) that affect our confidence in the accuracy and dependability of results. Reliability is an important consideration for both classroom and large-scale assessment, although different methods are emphasized for each. Measurement error is a complementary concept to reliability. The size of the standard error of measurement can be useful for interpreting performance ranges and identifying true differences in performance. Having completed our introduction to the measurement quality concepts of validity (Chapter 3) and reliability (Chapter 4), we turn in Chapter 5 to professional responsibilities, ethical behavior, and legal requirements in educational assessment.

EXERCISES

1. Which type(s) of reliability coefficient(s), if any, would be a major source of information needed to answer each of the following questions?
   a. A teacher wonders whether her student Meghan's test score could be a result of her having an off day.
   b. An eighth-grade teacher wonders whether the students' aptitude test scores will predict their success in ninth grade.
   c. A tenth-grade English teacher wonders whether the grades he assigns to his students' essays are equivalent to the grades his colleague would assign them.
   d. A twelfth-grade physics teacher wonders whether her final exam this year is equivalent to her final exam last year.
   e. An eighth-grade English teacher has students create portfolios of their work over the semester.

Using the portfolios, she classifies the students into three groups: excellent, satisfactory, and unsatisfactory. The teacher wonders whether her classification of students can be made with fewer errors.

2. The correlation between students' scores on the odd and even items of a test is 0.40. The teacher claims that the students would attain the same scores if he used an equivalent test. Is the teacher's claim justifiable? Support your conclusion using an appropriate reliability coefficient.

3. A test-retest reliability coefficient is 0.75 and the test standard deviation is 15. By how many points can we expect individual students' test scores to differ when we test them on two different occasions? (Use Figure 4.5 to help you.)

4. The examples on page 81 illustrate the use of the *SEM* to form confidence bands for students to help us interpret their scores. Suppose that for the students in the figure, the *SEM* equals 0.2 instead of 0.4. How, if at all, would the interpretations of each of the three illustrations in the examples change?

5. For each of the following types of assessment procedures, explain which cause(s) of measurement error is (are) of most concern and why:
   a. Student essays in social studies exams
   b. Science projects
   c. Grades on art projects
   d. True-false tests in science
   e. Portfolios in English courses
   f. Mathematics homework problems
   g. A teacher's marks for students' daily participation in class
   h. A paper-and-pencil test for a unit in social studies consisting of multiple-choice, matching, and short-answer questions

CHAPTER
5

Professional Responsibilities, Ethical Behavior, and Legal Requirements in Educational Assessments

KEY CONCEPTS

1. Areas of teachers' professional assessment responsibility include creating, choosing, administering, and scoring assessments, as well as interpreting and communicating assessment results. Ethical and professional responsibility issues also surround test security, access to student data for research purposes, purging and correcting students' records, confidentiality of students' achievement records, and informed consent.

2. Students have assessment rights, including access to information, under the U.S. Constitution and federal legislation.

3. Steps can be taken to process students' requests for accommodations and make testing accommodation programs legally defensible.

4. Test or assessment bias can mean several different things. Issues of test fairness apply to both classroom and extraclassroom assessments.

IMPORTANT TERMS

bias (assessment or test)
bias as content/experience differential
bias as differential validity
bias as mean differences
bias as misinterpretation of scores
bias as the statistical model
bias as the wrong criterion
bias stemming from testing conditions
Classroom Assessment Standards
Code of Fair Testing Practices in Education (Revised)
Code of Professional Responsibilities in Educational Measurement (CPR)
confidentiality
construct
differential item functioning (DIF)
due process
facial bias
fair assessment or test
gender stereotype
individualized education program (IEP)
informed consent
mandated tests
privacy
professional responsibility
psychometric issues
race stereotype
role stereotypes
standardized tests
test-takers' rights

A TEACHER'S PROFESSIONAL RESPONSIBILITIES IN ASSESSMENT

Responsibility to Use Quality Information to Make Decisions

In your classroom, you control how you gather and use information to improve your students' learning. Along with this independence comes **professional responsibility** for gathering and using information appropriately, according to professional standards of practice and ethical principles of behavior. You make hundreds of decisions as you teach. Formal and informal assessment tools help you gather useful information for making decisions about your students. Each decision you make will have positive or negative consequences for your students.

The consequences differ in their degree of seriousness for the students. Serious consequences of decisions occur when students benefit or lose something very valuable and cannot easily recover from an incorrect initial decision. Sometimes, these are called *high-stakes decisions*. For example, your decision to give a student a low final grade in chemistry may lower the student's chances of being admitted as a chemistry major at a particular college. Less serious consequences occur when students benefit or lose something less valuable and can easily recover from an incorrect initial decision. Sometimes, these are called *low-stakes decisions*. For example, you may decide to reteach a particular chemistry concept to a student, but as you are reteaching, you discover that the student already understands the concept. It is easy for you to readjust your teaching, and the student can easily recover from your incorrect initial decision. When the consequences of a decision are serious, you have an added responsibility to use the best available information in your decision-making process.

One way to improve your educational decisions is to use high-quality assessment information: information that is highly valid and highly reliable for the decisions at hand. Of course, using high-quality information does not guarantee that your decisions will be correct. However, if you base a decision on poor-quality or erroneous information, you are very likely to make an incorrect decision. This mistake may be harmful to a student. If you cause harm to your students, either deliberately or through negligence, your actions are unprofessional and unethical, and they may even be illegal.

Professional associations often develop codes of ethical behavior for their members. These codes provide guidance on how to act responsibly. Codes of ethics commonly cover such areas as the professional's role in society, conflicts of interest, and communication with clients and the public. Figure 5.1 lists some of the codes that contain statements of professional responsibility when using assessments.

Much of the information in this chapter is adapted from the principles described in the National Council on Measurement in Education's (NCME) **Code of Professional Responsibilities in Educational Measurement (*CPR*)**. A copy of the *CPR* is reproduced in Appendix C. The focus in this chapter is on ethical, professional, and legal responsibilities of classroom teacher assessment. The *CPR*, however, offers guidance to a wide range of educational professionals who are involved in assessment activities, including the following: teachers; school and district administrators; professional support staff (supervisors, counselors, school psychologists, etc.); technical, legislative, and policy staff members of research, evaluation, and assessment organizations; test preparation service providers; faculty members and administrators at colleges and universities; and professionals in business who implement educational programs (NCME, 1995).

The *CPR* assumes that an informed user of educational assessments will behave in accordance with other assessment-related professional standards. These include the **Code of Fair Testing Practices in Education (Revised)** (Joint Committee on Testing Practices, 2004), the **Classroom Assessment Standards** (Joint Committee on Testing Practices, 2015), and the *Standards for Educational and Psychological Testing* (American Educational Research Association [AERA] et al., 2014). The *Code of Fair Testing Practices in Education (Revised)* is reproduced in this book as Appendix B. The AERA *Standards* are discussed in Chapter 18 but are not reproduced in this book.

General principles of professional behavior require that you do the following:

1. protect the safety, health, and welfare of all examinees;

2. be knowledgeable about, and behave in compliance with, state and federal laws relevant to the conduct of professional activities;

FIGURE 5.1   Professional association codes of professional responsibilities related to using educational assessments.

American Association for Supervision and Administration, National Association of Elemetary School Principals, National Association of Secondary School Principals, National Council on Measurement in Education. (1997). *Competency standards in student assessment for educational administrators.* Available from buros.org

American Educational Research Association, American Psychological Association, & National Council on Measurement in Education. (2014). *Standards for educational and psychological testing.* Washington, DC: American Educational Research Association.

American Educational Research Association. (2011). *Code of ethics.* Washington, DC: Author. Available from aera.net

American Federation of Teachers, National Council on Measurement in Education, & National Education Association. (1990). *Standards for teacher competence in educational assessment of students.* Washington, DC: National Council on Measurement in Education. Available from buros.org

American Psychological Association. (2010). *Ethical principles of psychologists and code of conduct.* Washington, DC: Author. Available from apa.org.

American Psychological Association. (1998). *Rights and responsibilities of test takers.* Washington, DC: Author. Available from apa.org

American Counseling Association. (2005). *ACA code of ethics.* Alexandria, VA: Author. Available from counseling.org

Joint Advisory Committee. (1993). *Principles for fair student assessment practices for education in Canada.* Edmonton, Alberta: Author, Centre for Research in Applied Measurement and Evaluation, University of Alberta. Available from education.ualberta.ca

Joint Committee on Standards for Educational Evaluation. (2009). *Personnel evaluation standards* (2nd ed.). Thousand Oaks, CA: Sage. Summary available from jcsee.org

Joint Committee on Standards for Educational Evaluation. (2011). *The program evaluation standards: A guide for evaluators and evaluation users* (3rd ed.). Thousand Oaks, CA: Sage. Summary available from jcsee.org

Joint Committee on Standards for Educational Evaluation. (2015). *The classroom assessment standards for preK-12 teachers.* Kindle Direct Press.

Joint Committee on Testing Practices. (2004). *Code of fair testing practices in education (revised).* Washington, DC: Science Directorate, American Psychological Association. Available from apa.org

National Council on Measurement in Education (NCME). (1995). *Code of professional responsibilities in educational measurement (CPR).* Washington, DC: Author. Available from ncme.org

3. maintain and improve [your] . . . professional competence in educational assessment;

4. provide assessment services only in areas of [your] . . . competence and experience, affording full disclosure of [your] professional qualifications;

5. promote the understanding of sound assessment practices in education;

6. adhere to the highest standards of conduct and promote professionally responsible conduct with educational institutions and agencies that provide educational services; and

7. perform all professional responsibilities with honesty, integrity, due care, and fairness. (NCME, 1995, p. 2)

SIX CATEGORIES OF RESPONSIBILITY FOR TEACHERS

Your teaching involves six categories of assessment-related activities. Each has its own specific professional and ethical concerns:

1. When *creating assessments,* you are responsible for ensuring they are of high quality.

2. When *choosing assessments* or selecting assessments that others have developed, you are responsible for making sure they are appropriate for your intended use.

3. When *administering assessments,* you are responsible for ensuring that your administration process is fair to all students and will produce interpretable results.

4. When *scoring assessment results,* you are responsible for evaluating the responses accurately and reporting the results to students in a timely manner.

5. When *interpreting and using assessment results,* you are responsible for ensuring that your interpretations are as valid as possible, are used to promote positive student outcomes, and are used to minimize negative student outcomes.

6. When *communicating assessment results,* you are responsible for providing complete, useful, and correct information about students' performance that will promote positive student outcomes and minimize negative student outcomes.

The next sections discuss teachers' professional responsibilities in each of these six areas. Our discussion is based on the *CPR* and other sources.

Responsibilities When Creating Assessments

General Responsibilities

If no appropriate assessment is available, you must create one. In this case, your professional responsibilities focus on producing an assessment that provides results that (a) are as valid as possible for the interpretations and use you intend to make of them and (b) are as reliable as needed for the seriousness of the consequences of the decisions you will make. *Validity* refers to how you interpret and use the results (see Chapter 3).

Example

Suppose a state's standards require schools to teach how well a student is able to solve real-life problems using mathematics principles and generalizations. Thus, a teacher's responsibility is not only to teach but also to create assessment tasks that require students to engage in real-life problem-solving thinking and activities.

Reliability refers to how consistent the assessment results are (see Chapter 4). Consider the following example:

Example

A teacher is deciding what grade to give a student for the term. The teacher should collect enough evidence to be sure she has a consistent picture of the student's achievement. Therefore, the teacher would be acting irresponsibly if the teacher based the term-grade decision on only a few test questions or a brief performance assessment.

You may increase the reliability of the information you use by combining the results from several assessments of the same learning outcomes: quizzes, classroom performance, projects, and tests. This "triangulation" of results gives you a more reliable, hence more valid, picture of student achievement. Thus, it demonstrates a more responsible assessment strategy on your part.

Specific Responsibilities

In addition to this general responsibility to craft valid and reliable assessment procedures, teachers have more specific responsibilities. As a teacher, you have a professional responsibility to do the following:

1. *Apply sound principles* of assessment planning, assessment design, task development, item writing, rubric development, and assessment marking to each formal assessment you use.

2. *Create assessment procedures* that are free from characteristics irrelevant to assessing the learning outcome. Assessment procedures should be free of gender, ethnic, race, social class, and religious bias and stereotypes.

3. *Accommodate in appropriate ways* students in your class with disabilities or special needs.

4. *Obtain permission* necessary to use copyrighted material in assessments you develop.

5. *Present the assessment results in a way that encourages* students and others to interpret them properly.

6. *Ensure that assessment materials do not contain errors* and inaccuracies in the content, instructions, and scoring key (or rubrics). If you discover errors after administering an assessment, correct them as soon as possible and rescore responses. Test questions containing errors should not be counted in the total score. You may need to readminister the assessment if rescoring cannot correct the error and if the decision it depends on is a serious one.

Responsibilities When Choosing Assessments

Choosing Assessments for Classroom Use

Although you will often have to create your own assessments, you will no doubt also use assessments developed by others. Many times these will be assessments that accompany published learning materials: quizzes and tests in the teacher's edition of the book, separate tests and performance tasks sold to accompany instructional units, specimen items and tasks on the Internet and in teachers' magazines and journals, and so on. Your main professional obligations in using these assessments are the same as those you apply when creating your own: Their results must (a) be valid for your intended interpretation and use and (b) have a degree of reliability appropriate to the importance of the decision(s) you will make using the results. In addition, many of the six specific responsibilities listed in the last section also apply to assessments you obtain from other sources.

In some ways, fulfilling your professional responsibilities when using others' assessment tools is more difficult than when you design your own. Others' assessment tasks may not match the content, emphasis, vocabulary, or methods you used in teaching. When you consider using published assessments, check them for assessment quality and for a match with your teaching. Adapt and improve a classroom assessment instead of using it "straight out of the box" if it does not.

The fact that an assessment is published does not guarantee the accuracy of its content or its quality as an assessment tool. Many commercially available assessment tasks are not prepared or reviewed by professional assessment task developers. Many were not prepared personally by the author(s) of the curriculum materials or textbooks, but by others such as subcontractors of the publishing company or students of the authors. Evaluate published assessments carefully before you use them.

Serving on Assessment Selection Committees
More experienced teachers sometimes serve on committees at the district or state level to review and select published assessments. Local education authorities should include teachers on assessment selection panels. The *CPR* states that persons providing such service have a special responsibility "to make sure that the assessments are appropriate for their intended use" (NCME, 1995, p. 5).

If you review the 10 specific professional responsibilities in Section 3 of the *CPR* (Appendix C), you will see that those engaged in assessment selection activities must have considerable knowledge of both the subject matter to be assessed and the technical principles of educational assessment. Chapters 16 and 18 of this book are devoted to procedures for evaluating published achievement tests. The *Code of Fair Testing Practices in Education* (*Revised*) (Appendix B) contains additional principles and responsibilities for those who select and use published tests.

In addition, the *CPR* specifies that selectors of assessment procedures have a professional responsibility to consider an assessment procedure's potential for fulfilling its intended purposes and its potential misuses and misinterpretations. As discussed in Chapter 3, this process relates to the question of validity. If you intend to be involved in evaluating and selecting assessment tools as you fulfill your professional role outside the confines of your classroom, you should read widely to keep current about educational assessment in states and districts beyond your own. One source for learning

about how other districts and states are using and misusing assessments is the news publication *Education Week*.

Responsibilities When Administering Assessments

Give Students Sufficient Information
Usually, classroom assessments are meant to be opportunities for students to demonstrate their maximum performance. For students to perform at their maximum, they need basic information about the assessment, including (a) when it will be given, (b) the conditions under which they are expected to perform, (c) the content and abilities that will be assessed, (d) what the assessment will emphasize, (e) the standard or level of performance expected, (f) how the assessment performance will be scored, and (g) the effect the results of this assessment will have on any decisions (e.g., grades) you will make from the results. Providing this information to students is a professional responsibility.

Conduct the Administration Professionally
A special concern in administering classroom assessments is the assessment environment you establish. Rushing students unnecessarily or making the assessment tasks too long for the available time creates unfair conditions if the goal is to have the student demonstrate maximum performance. Similarly, if you make students nervous by standing near them or chatting to them as they try to perform the assessment, you create unfair conditions. Sometimes a teacher will be rude, short, or gruff to a student who asks an honest question about the assessment tasks (especially when the teacher did not create the task or its directions carefully and as a result created some ambiguity). Your professional responsibility is to provide "reasonable opportunities for individuals to ask questions about the assessment procedures or directions prior to and at appropriate times during administration" (NCME, 1995, p. 6).

Accommodate Students with Disabilities
It is not unusual to have students with disabilities in your class. You have a professional and possibly legal responsibility to make reasonable accommodations to assess them properly, even if you are a regular education teacher and have not majored in special education. *Assessment accommodations* are changes in either the conditions or materials

of assessment that allow the achievement of students with disabilities to be evaluated in the same areas as nondisabled students. Distinguish accommodations from *assessment modifications*, which are changes in either the conditions or materials of assessment that allow the achievement of students with disabilities to be evaluated but which may change the **construct**—the specific achievement outcome assessed.

Accommodations are intended to make the assessment of students with disabilities more fair and more valid by "leveling the field" for all students. Learning and assessment should not be impeded by the student's disability. Accommodations may be grouped into five types (National Center on Educational Outcomes, 2011):

1. *Presentation* (e.g., repeat directions, read aloud, large print, Braille)

2. *Equipment and material* (e.g., calculator, amplification equipment, manipulatives)

3. *Response* (e.g., mark answers in book, scribe records response, point)

4. *Timing/Scheduling* (e.g., extended time, frequent breaks)

5. *Setting* (e.g., study carrel, student's home, separate room)

As a general rule, the accommodations necessary for a classroom learning environment would be appropriate accommodations for administering a classroom assessment. The classroom learning environment accommodations are described in a student's **individualized education program** (IEP), and teachers have a legal responsibility to implement those accommodations. Each student's IEP is developed by a child study team from the school and is approved by a student's parents. It specifies learning goals, appropriate teaching methods, and classroom accommodations for the student. Often assessment conditions and accommodations are also specified. It is important to recognize that you should not introduce accommodations for the first time during an assessment (National Center on Educational Outcomes, 2011). They should be incorporated into the teaching and learning process.

Treat each student as an individual rather than as a stereotype of a disability category. For example, not all blind students can read Braille, and not all deaf students understand a signed language. The severity of students' disabilities varies widely, students' cognitive abilities vary widely, and many students have multiple disabilities. In addition, students may need accommodation for some domains of learning but not for others. The needs for accommodation found in their IEPs may not adequately describe the learning outcomes (domains) for which students need assessment accommodations. Thus, you should not rely on IEPs alone to determine the type of assessment accommodation a student needs. However, if an accommodation is stated in the IEP, there is a legal mandate to provide it.

Your school's administrators and the school's special-service professionals share professional responsibility in this area. Nevertheless, as the person most in touch with the students on a daily basis, you have a special obligation to identify reasonable accommodations for classroom assessment activities and to seek the help of the appropriate school personnel.

Students with disabilities are often very aware of what accommodations they may or may not need to be assessed in your class. Whenever possible, consult with the students themselves before you impose an assessment accommodation on them. Remember, however, that sometimes a student or a parent may believe that an accommodation will lead to a higher score. Getting higher scores is not the point. Rather, valid scores are the primary consideration. An accommodation should increase the validity of the scores, so they reflect students' true achievements. The scores after accommodation may not be higher, yet may be more valid.

Standardized and Mandated Tests

Mandated tests are tests required by school district policy or state law. **Standardized tests** are developed by professional agencies and use the same test materials and same administration procedures for all students. Your professional responsibilities in this area are similar to those you have in administering your own assessments with additional responsibilities related to (a) fully informing students and parents about the testing and how the results will be used, (b) carefully following the administration instructions in the test manual, (c) maintaining security, and (d) maintaining testing conditions appropriate for maximum performance. These and other responsibilities are described in Section 4 of the *CPR* in Appendix C. Chapter 16 describes how to administer standardized tests in more detail.

The same accommodations you make in your classroom assessments might not be appropriate for standardized and state-mandated tests. This fact is especially true if a student's score is to be interpreted using national norms. However, as a general rule, accommodations that students get for classroom assessment (typically based on their IEPs) should be similar to the accommodations students receive for large-scale tests. Follow the test administration instructions from your school's test director and the state's guidelines. Since the passage of the NCLB Act, a state's accountability assessment program specifies what accommodations are permitted and the criteria students must meet in order for those accommodations to be permitted. Visit the National Center on Educational Outcomes Website (https://nceo.info/) to see the latest requirements of each state.

Figure 5.2 describes the assessment accommodations listed in the most recently available National Center on Educational Outcomes reports (Lazarus et al., 2014; NCEO, 2011) as being allowed or allowed in certain circumstances during state testing by more than half the states (more than 25 of 50). There are many other possible accommodations in each category, some of which may be approved for use with your state test, and many others of which may be useful in conjunction with a student's IEP for classroom assessment. If your school does not have facilities or services for accommodating students, they may be available through your state or county itinerant service provider, a community agency that specializes in assisting persons with disabilities, or the office of services for students with disabilities at a local college or university.

Research on the effectiveness of these accommodations is beginning to be available, and the results are mixed, probably because a wide variety of accommodations are administered in different ways and to students with different characteristics. A standard approach for studies investigating the effectiveness of an accommodation is to test the hypothesis that the accommodation will improve the results for students with disabilities and will make no difference in the results for nondisabled students. This is called the *interaction hypothesis* (Sireci, Scarpati, & Li, 2005). A somewhat less stringent hypothesis is that the accommodation will improve the results for all students but will improve the results for students with disabilities more than for nondisabled students, sometimes called the *differential boost*

FIGURE 5.2 Types of accommodations allowed or allowed in certain circumstances by at least half of the states for state testing of students with disabilities.

Category	Assessment accommodations
Presentation Accommodations	Large print Braille Read aloud directions Read aloud questions Sign interpret directions Sign interpret questions Repeat/Reread/Clarify Speech to text
Equipment/Material Accommodations	Magnification equipment Amplification equipment Light/acoustics Calculator (at least in certain circumstances) Templates Noise buffer Adaptive/special furniture Abacus Assistive technology Dictionary/glossary
Response Accommodations	Proctor/human scribe Computer or machine Write in test booklets Communication device Brailler Speech device Word prediction software policies split (some allow, some do not)
Scheduling/Timing Accommodations	Extended time With breaks Time beneficial to student
Setting Accommodations	Individual Small group Carrel Separate room Seat location/proximity

Source: Christiansen, L. L., Braam, M., Scullin, S., & Thurlow, M. L. (2011). *2009 state policies on assessment participation and accommodation for students with disabilities* (Synthesis Report 83). Minneapolis: University of Minnesota, National Center on Educational Outcomes.
Lazarus, S. S., Kincaid, A., Thurlow, M. L., Rieke, R. L. & Dominguez, L. M. (2014). *2013 state policies for selected response accommodations on statewide assessments* (Synthesis Report 93). Minneapolis, MN: University of Minnesota, National Center on Educational Outcomes.

hypothesis (Fuchs & Fuchs, 1999). Both Lovett (2010) and Sireci, Scarpati, and Li (2005) found that extended time testing accommodations helped all students, but helped students with disabilities more. Gregg and Nelson (2012) reviewed studies of the effect of extended time testing accommodations specifically in the context of adolescents transitioning from high school, taking high school graduation tests and postsecondary entrance examinations, found only two studies that provided evidence for the differential boost hypothesis, and called for more research on this point. They did find evidence that nondisabled students without extra time still outperform students with disabilities with extra time.

Testing accommodations have also been studied for English language learners (ELLs), and the reported effects at this point are mixed. Kieffer, Lesaux, Rivera, and Francis (2009) reviewed studies of various accommodations for ELLs in large-scale assessments: simplified English, English dictionaries and glossaries, bilingual dictionaries and glossaries, native language version of assessments, dual language test booklets, dual language questions for English passages, and extra time. In their study, only English dictionaries or glossaries had an effect (although a small one) on closing the gap between ELL and non-ELL scores. Li and Suen (2012) did a meta-analysis of a larger group of studies and found that, overall, accommodations had a small but significant positive effect on achievement for ELLs. In their meta-analysis, type of accommodation did not matter but level of English proficiency did: Accommodations had larger effects for students with low English proficiency. Pennock-Roman and Rivera (2011) found that Spanish language version of tests had a large effect, for students with low English language proficiency. For students with medium to high English language proficiency, simplified English was the more effective accommodation. In addition, they found that English dictionaries and glossaries were effective. Pop-up computer glossaries were effective even without time accommodations, but paper-and-pencil versions required extra time as well to be effective.

Legally Defensible Assessment Accommodation Policies

Issues of accommodation are controversial. Educational authorities are urged to seek the advice of their legal counselors and of advocates of persons with disabilities as they draw up accommodation policies. Authorities should keep in mind, however, that because of the large differences in students' abilities among (and within) disability categories, consulting a wide range of advocacy groups is important for identifying appropriate policies and practices. For example, the reasonable accommodations required for students with intellectual disabilities are likely to be quite inappropriate for students with hearing losses who have no cognitive disabilities. You should be aware, too, that although the law may require "reasonable accommodations," exactly what that means is unclear. The teacher, the school officials, and the student (or parents) will need to base accommodations on reasonableness and validity, not on a parent's negotiating skill.

The following suggestions to improve the legal defensibility of accommodations are adapted from Phillips (1994), who is both an assessment specialist and a lawyer. Phillips's suggestions are for a state or school district program. Her suggestions help make the process more legally defensible. You are urged to consult the reference before attempting to implement these suggestions.

1. Prepare a written set of instructions for how a student (and/or parent) should request an assessment accommodation. Protect students' due-process rights by making sure students and parents are aware of these instructions.

2. Prepare a standard form for requesting accommodations, and describe clearly how to return the form and what the deadline is.

3. Require students (and/or parents) requesting accommodations to document their disability. Require:
   a. Verification of the qualifications and disability-related experience of the professional who is describing the disability.
   b. A letter signed by the qualified professional specifying the type(s) of accommodations required.
   c. Information the professional provided you regarding test results and the procedures used to make the diagnosis.
   d. Verification that the professional conducted an in-person evaluation within the past 12 months.
   e. Additional documentation for questionable cases, including documenting the professional's qualifications and requesting student's medical records.

4. Determine if the student's IEP requires a particular accommodation.

5. If you will flag the scores resulting from the accommodated assessment, notify the

students and/or the parents of this in writing. Require them to sign statements that they have been notified.

6. Designate a single professional staff member to review and act on all requests. Call in a qualified consultant to handle borderline cases.

7. Develop general guidelines for how to accommodate persons with similar disability patterns, but act only on an individual, case-by-case basis. You will want to treat similarly situated persons consistently, but because there are so many individual differences within a category, you need to work with students directly.

8. Designate a professional staff member to collect data that can be used to assess the validity of various accommodations for different types of students. Use this validity data to refine policies and procedures.

9. If you deny an accommodation request, provide for a speedy review of the case. Be sure all information and documentation are available to the reviewer(s) and that the reviewer(s) is (are) qualified to evaluate the decision.

10. Develop a formal appeal procedure and a process for the student whose accommodation is denied. Require the student, parent, or guardian to make a written request to appeal. Allow for new evidence and for representation by legal counsel.

11. Students who are protected by the Individuals with Disabilities Education Act of 1991, Section 504 of the Rehabilitation Act of 1973, and the Americans with Disabilities Act of 1990 probably cannot be asked to pay for additional services and accommodations.

12. Institutionalize or legalize your accommodation policies, so they can be sustained as personnel changes occur over the years. Do not depend on the goodwill of one person to implement the policies.

The preceding suggestions are designed to protect educational authorities and assessment organizations from legal action while ensuring due process for students with disabilities. These suggestions appear to place a heavy responsibility on students and their legal guardians for documenting disabilities and justifying needed accommodations. These suggestions also appear

to be set in an adversarial context, rather than a conciliatory or cooperative context.

In your classroom, you need not be as formal as these guidelines. However, be sure to use assessment modifications in a legally appropriate way. If parents challenge your assessment and student evaluation practices, you will then be able to defend your practices.

Responsibilities When Scoring Assessments

Your Own Classroom Assessments
Your professional obligations are as follows:

1. *Score student responses accurately* by using the appropriate tools such as scoring keys, scoring rubrics, checklists, or rating scales.

2. *Score students fairly* by removing from the scoring process anything that would cause unfair results. Examples include using objective items and a scoring key when appropriate, having students place their names on the back of their essay examinations, so you are not influenced by the name, scoring all student responses to one question before moving on to another, scoring performance tasks with a scoring rubric, periodically rescoring a sample of student responses as a check against your initial scoring, and having a colleague rescore a sample or all of your papers. Suggestions for designing scoring schemes for improving the fairness of scoring essay and performance assessments are given in Chapter 13.

3. *Provide students with feedback that helps them improve their learning.* Your professional responsibility goes beyond simply giving students the score they earned on the assessment. You have a responsibility to describe strengths and weaknesses to students and make suggestions for improvement. Students should have the opportunity to learn from the assessment (see Chapter 8).

4. *Explain to students the rationale for the correct answers and for the scoring rubrics you use.* Explaining how you arrived at the score and what standards and criteria you used helps teach students what is important to learn. This explanation clarifies the learning objective and teaches students the standards they are expected to meet. When possible, give students scoring rubrics ahead of time to use in doing an assignment or studying for a test.

5. *Give students the opportunity to review their evaluations individually.* Students have a right to know how their responses were marked and evaluated. They have a right to be assured that scoring was done accurately and fairly. You have the professional responsibility to go over your evaluation of a student's response with a student who requests it.

6. *Correct errors in scoring and make necessary adjustments as quickly as possible.* Because you are human, you will make scoring errors, even if you use multiple-choice tests and a scoring key. Don't be threatened by a request from a student or a parent to rescore an assessment. Should you discover scoring errors (even if no one else discovers them), correct these errors and readjust the scores accordingly. This review should be done in a timely manner.

7. *Score and return results in a timely manner.* Timely return of results helps a student more effectively monitor progress and adjust study strategies.

Standardized and Mandated Tests Occasionally, you may be asked to score standardized tests or other tests mandated by your school district or state. In such cases, you have a responsibility to follow the scoring procedures given in the test manual or in other materials and ensure your scoring is accurate. Read test materials beforehand and be sure that you understand how to apply the scoring guidelines. Teachers frequently make mistakes in applying scoring keys to multiple-choice items and when looking up norm-referenced scores (e.g., percentile ranks or grade equivalents) in the tables accompanying the test materials. A common error is to use the norm tables for the wrong time of year (e.g., referring to the fall norms table when the test was administered in the spring).

Sometimes teachers are required to score open-ended tasks, performance tasks, and portfolios for mandated state assessment programs. Districts or states requiring teachers to do this have the obligation to provide high-quality scoring rubrics and to train teachers to use them with high degrees of consistency. As a teacher, your responsibility is to learn how to use the rubrics and to apply them fairly and consistently. Finally, it should go without saying that you have a professional responsibility to score and report scores honestly.

Responsibilities When Interpreting and Using Assessment Results

Results from Your Own Assessments Your professional obligations in this area are as follows:

1. *Interpret students' performance on an assessment in light of the learning objectives you taught and emphasized.* Students should be held accountable for the content and skills they had an opportunity to learn.

2. *Interpret students' performance on one assessment by considering the results from other assessments.* No single assessment procedure is comprehensive enough to cover every important learning goal. Allow students multiple opportunities and modes to express their abilities with respect to the curriculum learning goals.

3. *Interpret a student's performance by realizing the limitations of the assessment procedure you used.* Not only does a single assessment procedure lack comprehensiveness but also it is not perfectly reliable. A student's score would likely change if you gave an assessment again tomorrow or next week or if you used slightly different questions or content. If someone else marked the responses, the grader may come up with different marks. Consider these limitations as you interpret and use assessment results. For example, do not base a grade completely on one test performance. Consider rescoring after an honest query about how you marked a paper.

4. *Help students and parents properly interpret the assessment results.* Help students and parents understand the proper uses and limitations of tests and other assessments. Place the results of all assessments into their proper interpretive context.

5. *Help students and parents understand the consequences of improperly interpreting your classroom assessment results.* Some parents make too much of a test score or the result of a single assessment. Others do not see the pattern of success or failure that develops over time. Help them understand the negative consequences of their misguided interpretations (e.g., discouraging a student's further learning) and the positive consequences of a correct interpretation (a steady improvement over the course of the marking period).

6. *Interpret student performance as a way of evaluating their attainment of learning goals rather than as a weapon for punishing or controlling students' behavior.* Although upcoming assessments may motivate students, they are poor weapons for controlling student behavior. It is irresponsible to threaten students with tests or try to manipulate them through some assessment procedure.

7. *Keep classroom assessment results confidential and protect students' rights of privacy.* Don't post students' names and assessment results on the classroom wall or reveal your students' results to other teachers who have no right to know them. Sometimes a parent will ask how a neighbor's child performed in relation to the parent's own child. Do not honor this request.

Standardized and Mandated Test Results

Because external tests do not exactly match curricular learning goals and your teaching emphasis, they often are misinterpreted by students, parents, and the public, who are unaware of the impact of school factors on the test results. Further, the test results are often reported as norm-referenced scores (e.g., percentile ranks, grade equivalents), many of which are not easy to interpret properly. School administrators and/or state education authorities are responsible for properly interpreting the results and for seeing to it that improper interpretations are avoided or at least minimized. Section 6 of the *CPR* (Appendix C) lists these responsibilities. Many of them apply to the classroom teacher as well.

Because standardized test results are often sent home through the teacher, teachers are often the first people parents contact when they have questions. For you to fulfill the professional responsibilities listed in Section 6 of the *CPR*, you need to understand reliability, validity, norm-referencing, criterion-referencing, and standardized tests. Chapter 3, 4, 16, 17, 18, and 19 are devoted to these topics and will help you fulfill your responsibilities in this area.

Responsibilities When Communicating Assessment Results

You are responsible for developing proper means of communicating correct interpretations of assessment results to students, parents, and school authorities. Determine the level of

understanding of the students, parents, or school officials and tailor your communication to that level. You may need to teach a parent the meaning of certain types of scores or assessment concepts. Check to make sure parents understand the meaning of educational measurement terms you use (e.g., *percentiles*, *T-scores*, *reliability*, *validity*).

You are also responsible for establishing and following a regular communication schedule to report student progress to parents. Your school may have a policy to communicate progress to parents when grades are sent home. These policies usually specify minimum communication patterns. You may need more frequent communication. However, don't overdo it: Daily progress reports may be inappropriate for students beyond preschool.

MyLab Education **Self-Check 5.1**

MyLab Education **Application Exercise 5.1:**
Teacher Professional Responsibilities in Grading

STUDENTS' RIGHTS AND RESPONSBILITIES AS TEST-TAKERS

Students' Rights Your school district and state department of education will have assessment and school-record policies and procedures covering students' and parents' rights. There are two main issues: participation and accommodation (Salvia & Ysseldyke, 2004). Participation in assessment means that students with disabilities have the right, and sometimes the obligation, to be assessed, including taking part in accountability assessment programs. In the past, students with disabilities were often excluded from taking accountability tests because officials believed including them would lower the test averages. This lowering, it was believed, would have impact on funding and the public image of a district or a school. Excluding students with disabilities resulted in a lack of data that would show whether a school was serving them well.

Federal laws now cover matters of participation and accommodation that apply to school districts and states receiving federal funds. These include the Fifth and Fourteenth Amendments to the U.S. Constitution, Section 504 of the Rehabilitation Act of 1973 (Public Law 93–112), the Family Educational Rights and Privacy Act of 1974 (FERPA; Public Law 93–380), the Education of All Handicapped Children Act of 1975 (Public Law 94–142), the Education of the Handicapped Act Amendment of 1986 (Public Law 99–457), the Individuals with Disabilities

Education Act Amendments of 1990 (IDEA; Public Law 101–476), the Rehabilitation Act of 1973 (Public Law 93–112), and the Americans with Disabilities Act of 1990 (ADA; Public Law 101–336), 1997 Amendments to the Individuals with Disabilities Education Act (Public Law 105–17), the No Child Left Behind Act of 2001 (NCLB; Public Law 107–110), and the Individuals with Disabilities Education Improvement Act of 2004 (Public Law 108–446). Figure 5.3 summarizes some of the student and parental rights under the laws.

Whether or not there is a legal requirement to do so, professional ethics suggest that some principles underlying the rights summarized in Figure 5.3 apply to classroom assessment practices. Check with the superintendent of your school district for information on your state's requirements regarding student and family rights. Your school should also have its own written policy on (a) maintenance and release of assessment results, (b) release of nonconfidential information, (c) nondiscrimination, and (d) representational consent information.

In addition to legal requirements, professional organizations have statements of test-takers' rights. The *CPR*, for example, suggests several areas for which test-takers (e.g., students) have rights. The Test-Takers' Rights Working Group of the Joint Committee on Testing Practices (1999) has prepared **test-takers' rights** statements. The Joint Committee on Testing Practices, whose subcommittee prepared this "bill of rights for test-takers," consisted of representatives from the American Educational Research Association, the American Psychological Association, the National

FIGURE 5.3 Some student and parent testing and school records rights mandated by federal legislation. (Not all of these are absolute rights under the cited legislation. Some exceptions may be granted by the courts.)

I. The Family Educational Rights and Privacy Act of 1974
   A. Right to inspect records
      1. Right to see all of a child's test records that are part of the child's official school record.
      2. Right to have test results explained.
      3. Written requests to see test results must be honored in 45 days.
      4. If a child is over 18, only the child has the right to the record.
   B. Right to privacy: Rights here limit access to the official school records (including test scores) to those who have legitimate educational needs.
   Additional Information: ed.gov

II. The Individuals with Disabilities Education Improvement Act of 2004 (IDEIA) and the Rehabilitation Act of 1973
   A. Right to parent involvement
      1. The first time a child is considered for special education placement, the parents must be given written notice in their native language, and their permission must be obtained to test the child.
      2. Right to challenge the accuracy of test scores used to plan the child's program.
      3. Right to file a written request to have the child tested by other than the school staff.
      4. Right to request a hearing if not satisfied with the school's decision as to what are the best services for the child.
   B. Right to fairness in testing[a,b]
      1. Right of the child to be tested in the language spoken at home.
      2. Tests given for placement cannot discriminate on the basis of race, sex, or socioeconomic status. The tests cannot be culturally biased.
      3. Right to be tested with a test that meets special needs (e.g., in Braille, orally, etc.).
      4. No single test score can be used to make special education decisions. Right to be tested in several different ways.
   Additional Information: gpo.gov; ed.gov

III. The Americans with Disabilities Act of 1990 (ADA)[b]
   A. Right to accommodated testing
      1. Right of a qualified person with disabilities to be tested in a way that he or she can understand what is being asked and in a way that he or she can respond.
      2. The test administrator is expected to provide all the necessary test locations, services, aids, or accommodations at no extra charge to the examinee.
   Additional Information: Office of Special Education and Rehabilitation Services, ed.gov.

Notes: (a) It may be argued in court that limited English proficiency is not a student disability. Rather, it is a temporary condition that can be overcome by instruction and study. It may be reasonable to treat English language limitations separately from disability issues (Phillips, personal communication, 2001).

(b) As interpreted by the courts, IDEIA and ADA require "reasonable accommodations" to adjust extraneous factors affecting test outcomes, and not modifications that alter the skills and abilities tested.

Council on Measurement in Education, the American Counseling Association, the American Speech-Language-Hearing Association, the National Association of School Psychologists, and the National Association of Test Directors.

A test-taker has the right to the following: (a) be informed of the rights and responsibilities of a test-taker; (b) be treated with respect and courtesy regardless of personal characteristics and orientations; (c) be tested with tests that are appropriate for the purpose for which they are to be used and that have been developed to meet professional standards; (d) receive an explanation prior to being tested about the purpose for testing, who will receive the test results, and what the plans are for using the results; (e) be told what accommodations are available and then be tested with appropriate accommodations; (f) be informed in advance about when the test will be administered, when the examinee will receive the results, and the cost of testing; (g) have the test administered and interpreted by appropriately trained persons who follow professional codes of responsibility; (h) be told the consequences of not taking a test, not completing a test, or canceling the scores on a test already taken; (i) be given an explanation of the results of testing in easily understood language and in a timely manner; (j) have test results kept confidential within the limits of law; and (k) be able to present his or her concerns about the testing process or results and have those concerns reviewed seriously.

Students' Responsibilities

Students as well as teachers have responsibilities in an assessment situation. Students are responsible for studying and preparing for tests and examinations in their classes. The same Test-Takers' Rights Working Group that prepared the test-takers' rights has prepared a list of test-takers' responsibilities. These include the responsibility to do the following: (a) attend to explanations of one's rights and responsibilities as a test-taker; (b) be respectful and courteous toward others during testing; (c) ask questions and clarify before the testing when uncertain about the purpose of testing, the manner in which it will be administered, what one will be expected to do, and how the results will be reported and used; (d) attend to instructions that are presented in writing or orally; (e) inform the examiner in advance of what accommodations or modifications are needed; (f) inform the examiner in advance of any current illness that may affect one's performance; (g) inform the examiner if one had difficulty understanding the language of the test; (h) learn the date, time, and place of the test; (i) pay for the test if necessary; (j) arrive on time, with the requisite materials, and prepared to begin the test; (k) follow the examiner's instructions; (l) respond and behave honestly during the examination; (m) understand the consequences of not taking the test and be prepared to accept those consequences if one chooses not to take it; (n) tell the appropriate persons if one believes that the testing conditions adversely affected one's performance; (o) find out about the confidentiality of the results; and (p) present any concerns one has about the testing process or the results to the appropriate persons in a timely manner.

Students who cheat are dishonest and behave unethically. Plagiarism in the form of copying homework or purchasing papers for projects and other take-home assignments is unethical. Parents, teachers, school administrators, and students should work together to address cheating and other forms of intellectual dishonesty. School policies and due-process procedures for handling dishonesty should be written and taught to students before enforcing them.

Danielle, High school student
Manchester, KY

MyLab Education

Video Example 5.1

These high school students discuss their responsibilities as learners. They affirm their responsibility to use formative assessment information to help themselves learn and to assist with the learning of others.

SECRECY, ACCESS, PRIVACY, CONFIDENTIALITY, AND THE TEACHER

Secrecy and Access

Secrecy and test security have been the hallmarks of the testing industry since the late 1920s and early 1930s, when large-scale abuse of testing abounded. Withholding test information—either about the items on the test or the exact score(s) a student attained—often was justified on the grounds that access to assessment results would do more harm than good. For example:

- A student might attempt to memorize only specific answers ("a" or "b") rather than focusing on mastery of the general skills the test was designed to measure; this behavior would distort the measurement of knowledge and ability.

- Tests that measure highly sensitive and personal characteristics may require a high degree of professional training to interpret the scores; examinees lacking this training might cause themselves harm by misinterpreting the results.

- Releasing test items might result in their being used by unqualified examiners who would misinterpret scores, causing examinees harm.

- Releasing copies of old forms of a test might require the test developer to spend unreasonable sums of money to develop new forms, assuming that new forms of the test could, in fact, be developed.

In recent years, however, the public has become aware that *some test abuses have resulted from such secrecy*. For example:

- Professionals themselves vary in qualifications and have, in fact, misinterpreted tests or abused results.

- Decisions made about educational placement, ostensibly on the basis of valid and objective test results, have later been discovered to be biased, misinterpreted, or otherwise invalid.

- Errors in scoring that could not be detected occurred because those having the greatest stake in their accuracy—the students and parents—could not scrutinize the tests.

- Although some tests were declared publicly to assess learned skills and abilities, examinees were unable to check their content to decide whether their preparation had been adequate or whether they should seek special remediation or training.

- Although professionals may have interpreted assessment results properly, records were often open to other persons, who used the results either unprofessionally or in a manner unauthorized by and detrimental to the examinee.

Problems such as these spawned a renewed public interest in the ethics of secrecy and the right of students and parents to know. A number of state and federal laws as well as court decisions have arisen, mandating greater access for students and parents to assessment results and toward greater participation in the assessment-based, decision-making process.

Figure 5.3 lists some of these access and participation rights under federal legislation. Your own school district should have written policies regarding students' and families' rights regarding access to records and assessment results.

Purging and Correcting School Records

Another issue is purging records—deleting outdated files and other student records and correcting erroneous information. Certainly, if you give an incorrect grade, you should correct the affected student's record. Computerized databases are relatively easy to update, and you have a professional responsibility to correct mistakes in the records. Information such as your anecdotal records should be purged when it is no longer necessary, usually within a year or two. Some schools have policies for systematic purging of student records. Others may depend on a student's parents to come in and periodically review the records for unnecessary, damaging, or erroneous information.

Privacy, Confidentiality, and the Teacher

Privacy and **confidentiality** affect you in several ways. In the classroom itself, for example, teachers sometimes keep charts or post students' progress. Other teachers have students mark each other's papers and call out the marks for reporting. Such public displays may or may not be in the form of grades. These practices raise the question of whether the evaluations should be confidential. The ethical nature of confidentiality may or may not be covered by existing laws. For example, the Supreme Court ruled that peer marking and calling out peers' marks to the teacher was not forbidden by the Family Educational Rights and Privacy Act (FERPA), even though the parents objected to the teacher's practice, because that act referred only to official school records (*Owasso Independent School District No. I0011 v. Falvo*, 2002).

Another example is the practice of keeping scores, grades, and anecdotal comments in a student's official school records. Ethical questions arise about who has authorized access to these files. Teachers and certain other persons have legitimate rights to obtain necessary information from them to help teach a given student. Many schools have forms or other means to keep records of who has used a student's records and for what purposes. Usually a student's test scores and other records cannot be transferred to another institution without that student's (or parents') written authorization. Unlike the informal peer-grading situation cited in the preceding paragraph, the FERPA covers official school records.

Wagging tongues in teachers' lounges are still another way confidentiality can be violated. It is your professional responsibility not to use the teachers' lounge as a place to spread confidential information about students.

Access to Student Data for Research Purposes

Usually, obtaining assessment results for research purposes is not considered a violation of privacy provided the student remains anonymous. The U.S. Department of Health and Human Services issues regulations protecting the welfare of human subjects in research projects. Although you are not a researcher, you should be sensitive to ethical principles of privacy and confidentiality because you may need to collect data to use on your research projects for graduate courses and degrees, and you may have to protect the rights of students under your care when others (within and outside the school) request student information.

Informed Consent

Privacy is not violated if persons give consent to others to obtain and use personal information. Without going into a detailed ethical analysis of the matter, we shall state that there are at least four levels of consent: informed consent, presumed consent, implied consent, and proxy consent. **Informed consent** is obtained directly from a student and presumes that the student, in giving that consent, has received and understands the following information (USDHHS, 2005): (a) the exact nature and extent to which personal information will remain anonymous, (b) to what extent participation is voluntary rather than required, (c) who (or what agency) is requesting the information and for what purpose, and (d) what will happen to the information after it is collected (including whether and/or when it will be destroyed).

Obviously, few young students will be able to understand the implications of all of this information, so their consent may not be truly informed. Often consent must come from a *proxy*, such as a parent or a school official. The extent to which school officials can grant permission for

collecting and using pupil information will depend, among other things, on the degree to which such consent is *presumed* or *implied* by the fact that students are entrusted to their care. This is sometimes referred to as *representational consent*.

> **MyLab Education Self-Check 5.2**
>
> **MyLab Education Application Exercise 5.2:** Students' Rights and Educational Measurement

TESTING CHALLENGED IN COURT

Plaintiffs seeking legal redress for real and/or perceived violations of rights may challenge testing programs in the courts. Notable among legal issues are race or gender discrimination, a test's contribution toward segregation in schools and other disparate impact issues, unfairness of particular tests, and the violation of due process—such as failure to give sufficient notice for a test or failure to give opportunities for hearings and appeals. Educational testing practices that have resulted in court cases include testing programs designed to control graduation, teacher certification tests designed to control who can teach in a state, and college admissions testing.

Court cases sometimes involve class-action suits in which the plaintiffs represent an entire group of persons, and the judgments handed down by the court apply to all members of the group. This was true, for example, in the *Debra P. v. Turlington* (1979, 1981) case, which challenged Florida's minimum-competency graduation test. The court recognized the following classes: "(a)... all present and future twelfth grade public school students in the State of Florida who have failed or who hereafter fail the SSAT-II [i.e., the State Student Assessment, Part II]. (b)...all present and future twelfth grade African-American public school students in the State of Florida who have failed or who hereafter fail the SSAT-II. (c)...all present and future twelfth grade African-American public school students in Hillsborough County, Florida who have failed or who hereafter fail the SSAT-II" (Fisher, 1980, p. 7).

Psychometric Issues Presented in Court

Some issues raised in court focus on the technical aspects of testing. We refer to these as **psychometric issues**. The following aspects of testing have been questioned in courts in connection with high-stakes testing such as graduation tests (Langenfeld & Crocker, 1994). They appear, however, to apply to many court cases involving other tests.

1. *Test security.* Plaintiffs and special interest groups may want to know the content of the test, sometimes before the test is used. Related to this issue are matters of test security, applicable state and federal "sunshine" laws, and "truth-in-testing" legislation.

2. *AERA, APA, and NCME Standards.* The *AERA, APA, and NCME Standards* (2014) were mentioned earlier in this chapter. The *Uniform Guidelines on Employee Selection and Procedures* (Equal Employment Opportunity Commission [EEOC], Civil Service Commission, Department of Labor, & Department of Justice, 1978) are used also when adverse impact is an issue. These guidelines may not strictly apply to student testing and to teacher certification. The EEOC guidelines apply only to employment testing. Student testing is covered under the Fourteenth Amendment of the U.S. Constitution. Some legal opinion holds that a state that requires licensing is not doing so as an employer. Although not a legal document, the *Standards* do represent a consensus of professional opinion and values as to what constitutes good test development practices. Plaintiffs sometimes use these *Standards* as a basis for arguing against the quality or use of a particular test or testing program.

3. *Reliability.* (See Chapter 4.) Plaintiffs may challenge either the magnitude of a test's reliability data or the appropriateness of using particular techniques for ascertaining reliability.

4. *Validity and opportunity to learn.* (See Chapter 3.) With educational tests designed to certify achievement of standards, the relationship of content on the test to content taught in the classroom is likely to be challenged. (This is sometimes called *curriculum relevance* or *curricular validity.*)

5. *Test development procedures.* Every stage of test development may be challenged in a particular case: the test plan; the qualifications of the item writers; the correspondence between items and objectives; the readability level; the correct and alternative options to multiple-choice items; the tryout and field procedures; the correctness of the scanning and reporting; and steps taken to reduce or minimize culture, race, gender, and/or regional bias.

6. *Passing scores.* Several methods for setting passing scores exist, all of which plaintiffs may attack. Such attacks may not succeed if a large group, legally empowered to do so, sets the passing score by following acceptable standard-setting practices (see Cizek, 2001).

7. *Mechanical issues.* Plaintiffs can criticize mechanical aspects of the test, such as the quality of instructions and directions for administering, the ink color, the print size, and other physical features of the test.

8. *Accommodations for persons with disabilities.* Plaintiffs with mental or physical disabilities can challenge a test if appropriate accommodations are denied. Accommodations include access to the testing room as well as accommodations such as those listed in Figure 5.2.

9. *Testing using English.* Plaintiffs may challenge a test if it is not in the first language of the student, especially if the student has had only a limited opportunity to learn English.

Nonpsychometric Issues Presented in Court

Nonpsychometric issues that are the basis for legal redress in the use of tests include the following:

1. *Legal authority.* Plaintiffs may challenge a test or testing program on whether the program has been legally authorized or whether individuals making the decisions about testing have the legal authority to do so.

2. *Segregation in the schools.* Here the challenge can be that the tests are biased against the lower-scoring group and/or that they reflect and perpetuate past segregation in the schools, which lowered the quality of education. Thus, the plaintiffs should not be denied access or certification based on test results. (Test bias is discussed later in this chapter.)

3. *Equal protection.* If tests are used for sanctions and rewards, the distribution should allow schools with high percentages of minorities or poor students the same opportunity to

achieve these rewards as schools with low numbers of minorities or poor students (Parkes & Stevens, 2003).

4. *Property interests in a diploma.* Substantive changes in graduation requirements require appropriate notice to the student. In a landmark case (*Debra P. v. Turlington*, 1984) concerning the Florida minimum-competency graduation test, the court held that "a diploma is a property right subject to the Fourteenth Amendment protections" (Phillips, 1994, p. 108).

5. *Due process.* This could be either substantive or procedural **due process**. *Substantive due process* concerns the appropriateness of the requirement (e.g., passing the teacher-certification test) and the purpose (e.g., maintaining high-quality teaching). *Procedural due process* focuses on how fairly the examinee was treated. Fairness includes notifying the examinee in advance of the requirement, test date, and so forth; giving opportunity for hearings and appeals; and making sure that the hearing is conducted fairly. One recent due-process case, *GI Forum v. Texas Education Agency* (2000), was decided in the U.S. District Court. It centered on whether the use of the *Texas Assessment of Academic Skills* as a graduation requirement adversely affected Texas minority students and violated their due-process rights of the law under the U.S. Constitution. The court upheld the use of the test for such purposes.

A court decision depends on the particular circumstances surrounding a given case, the evidence brought to bear in the case, and the opinion of the judge and jury involved.

MyLab Education Self-Check 5.3

MyLab Education Application Exercise 5.3:
Deciding on Accommodations in the Classroom

BIAS IN EDUCATIONAL ASSESSMENT
Definitions of Bias

One of the concerns surrounding the suitability of assessments for various decisions is whether a particular assessment is biased against particular groups. It is not always clear exactly what "biased assessment" means, because many definitions of

assessment or **test bias** exist in the media and the professional literature (Camilli, 2006). Sometimes persons who discuss bias have more than one type of bias in mind, although they may not distinguish between types.

Assessment Bias as Mean Differences

Many use the **bias as mean differences** approach. According to this approach, an assessment is biased against a particular group when the average (mean) score of that group falls short of the average score of another group. (The mean is explained in Appendix F.) Most assessment specialists would *not* subscribe to this definition of bias because average differences in groups' performances could represent real differences in the level of their attainment, rather than an artificial difference. Bias implies "unfair" or "unjust." Thus, *differences as differences* may not represent bias.

Although differences in groups' means do not necessarily indicate a biased assessment procedure, one should still try to explain why the groups differ. Such differences may indicate that the groups have been treated unfairly (not given equal opportunity to acquire the abilities assessed), and thus they have developed different ability levels. However, such mean differences in groups may mean that the assessment procedure is biased, too. In other words, several factors can cause a mean difference between groups, including a biased assessment. Unfortunately, knowing only that such differences exist does not explain why they exist.

Assessment Bias as Differential Item Functioning (DIF)

Instead of studying average total score differences among groups, some assessment developers study differences at the individual test item or assessment task level. An individual test question may favor one group over another; but the assessment, as a whole, may not show any difference. The approach here involves looking at whether persons *of the same ability* performed differently on the item. For example, you would study how boys of low ability compared to girls of low ability, boys of average ability compared to girls of average ability, and boys of high ability compared to girls of high ability. If these comparisons show that students in the two groups who are of the same ability perform differently on a task, this factor may indicate that the task is biased. However, just as average total test scores do not necessarily confirm a test is biased, so, too, do such item differences not necessarily confirm item bias. In other words, test items may function differently in two groups, but there may be no discernible bias. Because these differences do not prove bias, assessment specialists refer to the differences as **differential item functioning (DIF)** rather than as item bias.

Assessment Bias as Misinterpretation of Scores

Bias as misinterpretation of scores can creep into the interpretations of assessment results when someone tries to make inappropriate inferences about students' performances that go beyond the content domain of the assessment (Willingham & Cole, 1997). It is one thing to say, for example, that a female has difficulty solving two-step arithmetic word problems that involve knowledge of male suburban experiences; it's another to interpret performance on the assessment as an indication that females have lower arithmetic reasoning skills than males. The latter interpretation goes beyond the content domain and demands more evidence to support a claim that the interpretation is unbiased.

Assessment Bias as Sexist and Racist Content: Facial Bias

Facial bias is the use of offensive stereotypes in the language and pictures that make up assessment tasks and materials. Ours has been a White, male-dominated, Anglo-centric culture. A goal is not to perpetuate this image through the use of language and pictures in assessment (and other) materials. You can judge the content of assessment tasks (and other material) according to whether they represent male or female, White or non-White, as well as whether the content depicts certain **role stereotypes**. Under the definition of bias described here, an assessment would be biased if its tasks perpetuated undesirable role stereotypes, **race stereotypes**, or **gender stereotypes**. This judgment about the offensive nature of assessment content can be called facial bias. Most large-scale tests use a panel of judges to

screen test items for offensive or stereotypical material. The goal is not to produce faceless, gender-free, ethnic-free assessment materials. Rather, it is to represent gender and ethnic groups in a balanced, inoffensive, and fair way in those materials.

Assessment Bias as Differential Validity

Predictive validity refers to evidence that describes the extent to which a test is able to estimate a person's probable standing on a second measure called a criterion (see Chapter 3). The criterion of interest in assessment bias is usually some measure of job or school success. Under the definition of **bias as differential validity**, an assessment would be biased if it predicted criterion scores better for one group of persons (e.g., Whites) than for another (e.g., African Americans). A "fair" or unbiased assessment would, according to this definition, predict criterion scores with equal accuracy for all groups assessed. There have been a number of empirical studies of differential bias, but the overall conclusion is that few tests exhibit this pattern of differential correlation with educational success criteria. That is, educational selection tests seem to predict educational success equally well (or equally poorly) for most groups.

Assessment Bias as Content and Experience Differential

The definition of **bias as content/experience differential** is that an assessment is biased if the content of the assessment tasks differs radically from a particular subgroup of students' life experiences *and* the assessment results are interpreted without taking such differences into proper consideration. Assumptions about mainstream cultural experiences can underlie even simple questions. For example, one of the authors was once a substitute teacher in an inner-city elementary school on what happened to be a day of standardized testing. Over lunch in the teachers' lounge, one of the second-grade teachers angrily registered her objection to one of the vocabulary items, a picture of a detached garage and a selection of four words, one of which was *garage*. The school's neighborhood was mostly early 1900s row houses. Many of the children in this neighborhood had never seen a garage, much less a detached one.

Cabrera and Cabrera (2008) offer the "Chorizo Test," a 25-question "intelligence" test intended to sensitize teacher-education students and others to the linguistic bias and cultural stereotyping (in this case, against Hispanics) that can occur in standardized tests, along with permission to photocopy this test for educational purposes. When students' experiences and an assessment's content differ radically, it is probably not possible to offer the same construct interpretation (e.g., general verbal ability) for one subgroup's performance as that offered for another subgroup whose experience and assessment content more nearly match.

Assessment Bias as the Statistical Model Used for Selection Decisions

When many applicants vie for a limited number of openings, some procedure will be used to narrow the field. Most persons in this culture would reject the lottery (random drawing) as a means of selection, because a random process is uncorrelated with the ability to succeed on the job or in school. Most people believe that selection decisions should be based on "merits." Combinations of various assessments provide information that ranks applicants in order of merit. Among the information-gathering tools are interviews and the application form itself, as well as a variety of performance assessments and paper-and-pencil tests. All assessments used for selection must show some positive relationship to job or school success. The problem arises when certain subgroups score consistently lower on one or more of the assessments used in the selection process and when the assessments have slightly different relationships with the measures of the success criterion. The **bias as the statistical model** definition focuses on whether the statistical procedure used for selection is fair to all persons, regardless of group membership.

Assessment Bias as the Wrong Criterion Measure

Selection tests are used to predict success on a second measure called a criterion. But the criterion measure itself may be biased, making the selection process biased, even if the test is unbiased. That is **bias as the wrong criterion**. For example, suppose a job did not require reading skills and that on-the-job performance is the relevant criterion. Suppose further that an employer used a paper-and-pencil test of job knowledge as a substitute or proxy criterion measure instead of using a measure of actual job performance. Because in this case the paper-and-pencil test would be interpreted erroneously as the "ability to do the job," it would be a biased assessment against those who could not read or who were poor paper-and-pencil test-takers but might well be able to perform the job. Some criteria represent traditional cultural values (e.g., supervisors' ratings, grade point average) and may be used as proxies to an ultimate criterion measure such as job performance. Persons able to perform well on the ultimate criterion may not necessarily perform well on these proxy measures.

Bias Stemming from the Atmosphere and Conditions of Assessment

Basic test-taking stresses, such as test anxiety, feeling unwelcome, or being tested by a member of the opposite gender or another race, can adversely affect the performance of some groups. Others have argued that it is unfair to students and teachers in schools in impoverished areas to use an officially mandated test that serves to reinforce aspirations and achievement goals that are more realistic for the dominant group than for disadvantaged students. These situations describe **bias stemming from testing conditions**.

Possible Future Directions of Test Fairness

As the preceding discussion suggests, there is no one definition of test bias or assessment fairness. One thread of commonality you can see from all of these approaches is that test bias and **assessment** or **test fairness** reflect test validity. A **fair assessment or test** is one that provides scores that (a) are interpreted and used appropriately for specific purposes, (b) do not have negative or adverse consequences as a result of the way they are interpreted or used, and (c) promote appropriate values. In the future, assessment developers will need to focus on four issues to make assessment instruments fairer (Cole & Zieky, 2001):

1. Reduce group difference by controlling early in the development process what constructs to assess, what formats to assess them with, and the specific questions to include.

2. Recognize that because any one assessment contains only a limited representation of the ultimate learning outcomes, a student's achievement may not be assessed well by a particular procedure.

3. Develop methods for identifying misuses of an assessment and how to deal with these misuses.

4. Develop procedures for accommodating individual students, recognizing that different methods of assessment may be required to assess the same achievement with different students.

> **MyLab Education** **Self-Check 5.4**
>
> **MyLab Education** **Application Exercise 5.4:**
> Avoiding Bias in Classroom Assessment

CONCLUSION

Students' and teachers' rights and responsibilities regarding assessment are about giving and receiving accurate, timely, and fair information and about respecting other students and teachers, tests, and test consequences. While these rights and responsibilities will probably not have surprised you, it was worth devoting a chapter to thinking about them before we turn to the details of understanding classroom (Part II) and large-scale (Part III) assessment.

EXERCISES

1. Each of these statements describes a situation in which a teacher creates an assessment procedure. Read each statement and decide whether a violation of professional responsibility has occurred. After deciding, write an explanation justifying your decision. Discuss your findings with other members of your class.

   a. Ms. Jones schedules a short quiz in social studies every Friday. She announces this at the beginning of the semester, and every student is aware that this will occur. She jots down the questions on Friday mornings before class and photocopies them to give out during class. She has never taken a course in assessment, nor has she ever read a book on how to improve assessments.

   b. Mr. Roberts teaches science. There is a deaf student in his class. When a test is scheduled, he gives a copy of the test a few days ahead of schedule to the student's sign language interpreter, who simplifies the language of the questions but keeps the technical or scientific terminology. When other students are sitting for the test, the deaf student is in another room being administered the test by the student's sign language interpreter, who signs the questions to the student.

2. Each of these statements describes a situation in which a teacher chooses or helps choose an assessment procedure the teacher did not develop. Read each statement and decide whether a violation of

professional responsibility has occurred. After deciding, write an explanation justifying your decision. Discuss your findings with other members of your class.

   a. Mr. Smith teaches biology. His teacher's guide comes with a printed multiple-choice test covering the materials in the chapter he just taught. He gives the test to the office secretary for duplication a few days ahead of schedule. On the day he is to give the test, he goes over it to make an answer key. He discovers that out of 30 items, 10 cover material he did not thoroughly teach. He gives the test anyway, reasoning that all the material was in the chapter, which he asked students to read. All 30 items count toward students' grades.

   b. Ms. Williams teaches history. The authors of the textbook used in her class provide multiple-choice unit tests. One of the students brings the test home after the results are returned. The student's father goes over it and notices that, for 5 of the 40 items, his son's answers are correct according to the information in the textbook but were marked wrong by Ms. Williams. He writes a note to Ms. Williams describing the situation and citing the textbook pages to support his claim. Ms. Williams writes back saying the test was written by the textbook authors and is published, so it would be absurd to question the items' correctness. She refuses to reconsider the items or rescore the papers.

3. Each of the following statements describes a situation in which a teacher administers an assessment. Read each statement and decide whether a violation of professional responsibility has occurred. After deciding, write an explanation justifying your decision. Discuss your findings with other members of your class.

   a. Mr. Gordon likes to give "pop," or surprise, quizzes to keep his students "on their toes." These quizzes count for 50 percent of the students' grades.

   b. Ms. Stravinski believed that the allotted time for the standardized test she was requested to give in reading was too brief. Consequently, she gave the students an extra 10 minutes. She did not report this to anyone.

4. Each of these statements describes a situation in which a teacher scores an assessment. Read each statement and decide whether a violation of professional responsibility has occurred. Write an explanation justifying your decision. Discuss your findings with other members of your class.

a. Ms. Appleton is an itinerant teacher for students with hearing impairments who assists with the education of mainstreamed students at Mountain View High School. Billy David is a senior deaf student to whom she administers a standardized achievement test battery using an appropriate signed language. She knows that Billy's results will be sent to postsecondary schools for deaf students, and that they will use the results as part of the admission decision. When scoring the test by hand, she noticed that Billy's scores were unexpectedly low. She reviewed the questions he missed and said to herself, "I know he really knows the answers to these." So, she changed his answers to about 25 percent of the questions to give him a higher score. She rationalized her actions by thinking, "He really is a good student, and if I simply sent in the scores he got he would not be given the chance I know he deserves."

b. Mr. Pennel gives essay questions and performance tasks as a major part of his assessment. He seldom bothers with developing scoring rubrics because he doesn't know how to do so and they take time to develop. He'd rather spend the time teaching.

c. Ms. Dingle marks the assessments of John and Robert. They both receive the same score, which is on the borderline between an A and a B. She gives John an A and Robert a B. The boys are friends and they compare papers, discovering the different grades for the same score. John goes to Mrs. Dingle and tells her that Robert deserves the A. Mrs. Dingle says, "John, everyone knows that you are an A student, whereas Robert is a B student. My grades just reflect this fact so I won't change his grade."

5. What definition(s) of assessment bias is(are) implied by each of the following statements? Justify your classification and share your findings with other members of your class.

a. "This performance assessment is biased because it requires doing work outside school, and the students from wealthier families have more resources to help them do it well."

b. "This performance task is biased because it requires females to be familiar with automobiles and airplanes, something they are unlikely to be in this community."

c. "This performance assessment is biased because, overall, students from African American families do better on it than students from white families."

d. "This assessment is biased because on Tasks 3 and 7 boys score higher than girls at every ability level."

e. "This assessment is biased because all the pictorial material shows white males in professional roles but females and minorities in passive and subservient roles."

f. "This portfolio assessment is biased because the male teacher favors boys' responses that agree with his positions on controversial matters."

CHAPTER
6

Planning for Integrating Assessment and Instruction

KEY CONCEPTS

1. Assessment planning for a marking period should be based on learning goals and an outline of the main instructional and assessment strategies you will use. Assessment planning for a unit of instruction should be based on learning goals and objectives and detail the instructional and assessment strategies you will use. Use a blueprint to plan individual summative assessments.

2. A wide range of assessment options are available: paper-and-pencil, performance, long-term assignment, and personal communication formats. Each has advantages and disadvantages. Differentiated instruction relies on accurate, timely assessment in order to be effective. Assessment for Response to Intervention (RTI) involves planning for screening and for progress monitoring.

IMPORTANT TERMS

best works portfolio

blueprint or table of specifications

differentiated instruction

equivalence

feedback to students

growth portfolio

informal assessment techniques

marking period

paper-and-pencil assessments

performance assessment

preinstruction unit assessment framework

process

product

progress monitoring

Response to Intervention (RTI)

task formats

unit of instruction

Plans for teaching are incomplete unless they contain plans for assessment. This chapter focuses on how to improve your assessment planning. Good assessment planning and good instructional planning are two sides of the same coin; do them together. Both begin with, and are based on, identifying your learning goals and objectives—the essential knowledge and skills you want students to learn. Assessing how your students use their knowledge and skills allows you to monitor and evaluate their progress and appropriately differentiate instruction. Teachers typically do not get an adequate background in classroom assessment (Campbell, 2013). Understanding classroom assessment principles and practices will place you in a much-needed professional vanguard.

What and how you assess communicates in a powerful way what you really value in your students' learning. For example, you may tell your students how important it is for them to be independent and critical thinkers, but if your assessments consist of only matching exercises based on facts from the textbook, students will know differently. On the other hand, if your assessments require students to integrate their knowledge and skills to solve "real-life" problems, they learn that you really do expect them to develop integrating and problem-solving abilities. When you carefully define assessment tasks, you clarify what you want students to learn. To teach effectively, you must clearly have in mind how students should demonstrate their achievement.

Learning to create your own assessment tasks increases your freedom to design lessons. Knowing how to assess students validly, especially in relation to higher-order thinking skills, means that you are no longer chained to the assessment procedures already prepared by textbook publishers and others. Therefore, you can use a wider variety of teaching strategies, and you will improve the validity of your interpretations and uses of assessment results. You will improve your appreciation of the strengths and limitations of each type of assessment procedure. You will be able to use multiple, complementary measures to get a clear picture of what your students know and can do.

ASSESSMENT PLANNING FOR A MARKING PERIOD

Keeping in mind that you need to plan for both formative and summative assessment, the next thing to consider is the period for the plan. You may plan for a year, a semester, a marking period, a unit, or a lesson. Your plans for larger/longer segments of your teaching will be less detailed than your plans for smaller/shorter segments.

Begin with plans for a year or a semester, setting out the general approaches and strategies you will use to teach and to assess. Starting with the standards for your grade level and content area, outline the topics you will teach, the general learning objectives your students will achieve, and the main strategies you will use to assess them. Planning for a year is often done collegially, at the district level, using curriculum maps that link curriculum goals to the Common Core State Standards or other state standards. Some curriculum maps include plans for assessments. If your district's curriculum maps do not include general plans for assessment, consider working with your colleagues toward that end.

Plans for a marking period usually apply to two or three units of instruction. A **marking period** is the number of weeks you must teach before you need to prepare a grade for each student's report card. In a typical academic year, a marking period consists of 9 weeks. A **unit of instruction** is a teaching sequence covering from 1 to 7 weeks of lessons, depending on the students and topics you are teaching. Instructional units organize the larger curriculum into manageable teaching, learning, and assessment sequences. Planning for several units at one time allows for sequencing the units and for keeping your teaching and assessment approaches consistent. It also allows you to describe your plans for formative and summative assessment.

Plans for a single unit will necessarily be more detailed. You will describe the specific content, concepts, procedures, terminology, and thinking skills your students will learn and use. You also describe your teaching activities and your students' learning activities. You identify the learning objectives and student learning targets for the lessons, the specific formative and summative assessments you will use, and when you will use them.

The shortest term for planning is for a single day or one lesson. As you teach, you will begin to reflect on what you have previously taught these students and how well your students have achieved the unit's learning objectives to date. This reflection is an opportunity for you to adjust your unit plan. Each day, you adjust your teaching as you gather new information about your students and your teaching.

This latter point illustrates that your teaching and assessment plans are not set in stone. They are guidelines for teaching and assessing. They are flexible and subject to change as new information about your students' achievements accumulates.

Example of How to Develop an Assessment Plan for a Marking Period

Assessment planning for a marking period should be based on learning goals and an outline of the main instructional and assessment strategies you will use. Suppose you are teaching middle school science. Suppose, further, that you are planning for a 9-week marking period focused on the sixth-grade science standard (Pennsylvania Standard 3.3.6.A4): Describe how water on earth cycles in different forms and in different locations, including underground and in the atmosphere. Perhaps you plan to teach two units: one on the water cycle and one on weather and weather systems, both of which are contained in anchor standards listed under this larger standard. For each unit, you would outline the major points of content you will cover, the general sequence and timing of the units, and, most important, the learning objectives your students will achieve from each unit.

On the teaching side, you will need to answer a variety of questions. What overall approach and teaching strategy will you adopt? The water cycle and weather units are related; how will you make that clear to students? What kinds of learning activities will you need to create and use (e.g., creating a demonstration of condensation, cloud simulation, building a diorama of the water cycle, drawing weather maps, measuring variables related to weather such as wind speed and precipitation, collecting and reading weather maps, or conducting a weather prediction activity)?

Part of your teaching plan must include student assessment. How will you evaluate students' achievement of the learning objectives? What are your general strategies for formative assessment? Perhaps you plan for some in-class activities and exercises that will allow you to evaluate how well students are progressing. These also allow you to give students appropriate feedback. Perhaps you plan exercises that allow students to evaluate whether they have mastered the basic concepts. Your thinking should include planning for how often you assess. At what points in the lessons will homework or quizzes be appropriate, for example?

To provide formative **feedback to students**, you will have to assess their work. Will students and/or their peers assess their performance as well? If so, students will need criteria and scoring rubrics. When you use oral questioning, what levels of the taxonomy will you emphasize most? How will you respond to intermediate steps toward larger projects (plans, outlines, drafts, etc.)?

In order for formative feedback to help students improve their learning, you will probably have to teach your students how to use this feedback and provide opportunities for them to do so. You may need to teach them how to review and evaluate their own work as they proceed through the lessons.

Your summative evaluation strategy also needs to be planned. You might use a paper-and-pencil test at the end of each unit. You might use a project for one unit and a performance activity for another. For example, students may collect weather data and use those data to predict the weather. For some other subjects, reports, independent investigations, or portfolios might prove useful for summative evaluation. You will want to build in formative assessment opportunities along the way for the larger projects.

Your plan must include the weighting of each component as part of a final grade: How much will the tests, projects, and so forth count toward the grade? Will each count equally, or will some weigh more heavily than others? To be fair, you will need to explain the weighting to students in advance.

Figure 6.1 shows an assessment plan that a hypothetical teacher created when teaching the two science units referred to in the preceding paragraphs. Your own plan may be handwritten or word processed and used as a working document as you teach. The main points are that by planning you have (a) decided ahead about when and how you will assess, (b) recorded this thinking so that you do not forget, and (c) followed a systematic plan to achieve your assessment goals.

FIGURE 6.1   A long-term plan for a marking period in which two elementary science units will be taught.

Unit 1. The Water Cycle	
General learning target:	Understanding what the water cycle is, how it works, and how it helps living things. Ability to explain the water cycle and apply it to real life.
Time frame:	It will take 2 weeks to complete.
Formative assessment:	(a) Three homework assignments (taken from Chapter 8) (b) Condensation demonstrations (Group activity; I will ask students to explain what they are doing, how it relates to the water cycle, and how it relates to real life.) (c) Short quiz on the basic concepts at the end of Week 1
Summative assessment:	Brief essay after condensation demonstration A written test at the end of the unit (short-answer and an essay)
Weights:	(a) Brief essay 20% (b) End-of-unit test 80%
Unit 2. Weather Systems and Predicting Weather	
General learning target:	Understanding basic weather patterns, their movements, and their influence on local climate. Ability to understand weather maps, weather forecasts; ability to collect weather data and use them to make simple predictions.
Time frame:	It will take 7 weeks to complete.
Formative assessment:	(a) Seven homework assignments (taken from Chapter 9 and my own) (b) Seatwork on drawing a simple weather map with symbols (I will circulate among students and ask questions to check their understanding.) (c) Correct use of simple instruments to gather weather-related data (I will have each student demonstrate each instrument's use and give them feedback when necessary.) (d) Collection of weather maps and forecasts (I will discuss with students what the maps and forecasts mean and be sure they understand them.) (e) Four quizzes on the major concepts and a performance activity (Week 1, Week 3, Week 4, and Week 5)
Summative assessment:	(a) Map drawing (I will provide weather information; students will draw corresponding maps independently. This will be Quiz 2.) (b) End-of-unit test (short-answer, matching, map identification, essay question) (c) Independent investigation (Collect weather data for 2 weeks and make daily 2 day weather predictions. I will structure this activity. It will be done toward the end of the unit.)
Weights:	(a) Independent investigation 40% (b) Map drawing 20% (c) End-of-unit test 40%
Marking Period Grade	
Unit 1 marks count 30% Unit 2 marks count 70%	

ASSESSMENT PLANNING FOR ONE UNIT OF INSTRUCTION

Assessment planning for a unit of instruction should be based on learning goals and objectives and detail the instructional and assessment strategies you will use. You should be able to explain why you need to use each assessment strategy, how the assessments are related to the learning objectives and the lessons, and what actions you

will take once you have information about the students' achievement.

Example of an Assessment Plan for One Unit

Figure 6.2 shows an example of an assessment plan for one of the science units in Figure 6.1. It shows the thinking a teacher might use when deciding what assessments to conduct. The

FIGURE 6.2 An assessment activity plan for one unit of instruction.

	Assessment techniques	Description of assessment purpose, activity, and follow-up action (use)

Assessment techniques	Description of assessment purpose, activity, and follow-up action (use)
Pretest	About a week before beginning this unit, I will give a very brief pretest to get a sense of students' attitudes, experiences, knowledge, and beliefs about weather. (See Figure 6.4.) *Action:* I will use this information to help me develop discussions in class, to develop lessons that overcome students' misconceptions and fears about the weather, and to build on what students already know.

(Left margin, top to bottom arrow: More Formative in Nature ... More Summative in Nature)

Lesson 1	Lesson 2	Lesson 3	Lesson 4	Lesson 5	Lesson 6	Lesson 7
Comprehending basic weather concepts	Distinguishing weather patterns and systems	Identifying local weather conditions and patterns	Using basic tools for measuring weather	Understanding and making weather maps	Collecting and recording local weather data	Using data to predict local weather

Assessment techniques	Description
Observation and oral questioning	In every lesson, I will observe students and ask questions during the lesson to assess how well they are responding to the material, how well they seem to understand the daily activities and assignments, and whether they have any misconceptions about the weather concepts we are studying. *Action:* I'll adjust my teaching if most of the class is having difficulty. If only a few are experiencing difficulty, I'll work with them individually, in small groups, or ask another student to teach the concept.
Homework	I will assign homework after every lesson. Homework activities will focus on observing and discovering real-world examples of the weather concepts we learn in class. Students will record their observations and write explanations of them using proper scientific language learned in the unit. *Action:* As I read students' homework responses, I will note for each student how accurately and fluently the student uses scientific language to discuss the weather. I will also evaluate their observational and recording skills. I will reteach those materials for which many students experience difficulty. If only a few are having difficulty, I will work with them individually.

Quizzes			
Quiz 1 (covers Lesson 1): Short-answer questions testing basic vocabulary *Action:* Students not mastering the basic concepts will be retaught.	**Quiz 2** (covers Lessons 2 and 3): Short-answer questions with some diagrams. Focuses on weather patterns: local, national, and international. *Action:* I will use this quiz to monitor students' understanding of weather patterns and systems. I'll reteach or move on, depending on the outcomes.	**Quiz 3** (covers Lesson 4): This will be a performance activity. I want to be sure each student can use with accuracy the weather-measuring tools and can record data properly. *Action:* I will correct errors on the spot.	**Quiz 4** (covers Lesson 5): I want students to read, interpret, and draw simple weather maps. I will give weather data to the students and ask them to draw an appropriate map using the weather data. I will also give maps already drawn and ask students to interpret them. *Action:* I will reteach if there are problems.

Assessment technique	Description
Independent investigation (performance assessment)	**Predicting the Weather** (begins after Lesson 4, and includes Lessons 5 and 6): This performance assessment will help me evaluate whether students can apply the concepts from the lessons to the real world. It will help me evaluate whether they can synthesize and use criteria to evaluate the data they collect. Students will collect and measure weather data, record it, and use it to predict the local weather for two days in advance. They will repeat the exercise every day for at least 2 weeks. They will work independently. They will prepare a report describing what they did and evaluating their investigation and its accuracy. *Action:* This is a type of summative evaluation. I will use the exercise to help me decide how well the students have learned the concepts and principles in this unit. I should have a pretty good idea whether students can apply what they learned in class.
End-of-unit test	**Unit Test** (covers all lessons): This will come at the end of all the lessons. It will be a paper-and-pencil test given in class. (I may give it over 2 days.) It will be comprehensive, covering most of the important learning targets in the unit.) *Action:* I will use the results of this test along with the results from the drawing and the independent investigation to assign a grade to the students for the unit. (Weights are given in Figure 6.1.)

important points are that you can explain when and why you are using different assessment methods, that you match the assessment methods with the learning objective(s) for which they are appropriate, and that you can state what teaching action you will take once the information is gathered. *Assessments are useless if you do not take action when you see the results.*

Observe how Figure 6.2 is organized. Notice that in this example seven lessons are planned. Directly below each lesson is a brief statement of the lesson's main learning objective. The various types or methods of assessment (pretest, observation, homework, quizzes, independent investigations, end-of-unit test) are listed in the far-left column. Notice that as you go down the column, the purposes of assessment become more summative and the assessment procedure becomes more formal. The statements written in the body of this figure describe the purpose, procedure, and action to be taken for each assessment to improve students' achievement based on the assessment results.

When the statements in Figure 6.2 are spread across the page, that means the assessment's purpose, procedure, and actions apply to all of the lessons. In the figure, observation, oral questioning, and homework are of this character. Statements that appear directly below one or two lessons mean that the assessment applies to only those one or two lessons. The quizzes, independent investigation, and end-of-unit test are of this character. Because the seven lessons are spread out in sequence over time, the plan shows that some assessments occur at different times throughout the unit.

PREASSESSMENT TO PLAN YOUR TEACHING

Notice in Figure 6.2 that the teacher gave a pretest about a week before teaching this unit. The pretest results were not used to grade students. Rather, they were used to help the teacher understand the students' attitudes, knowledge, beliefs, and experiences about the weather so that the teacher could better teach the unit.

Importance of Preinstructional Unit Assessment

When you plan instruction for a unit, you consider more than covering the material. In most subjects, students bring to the unit a complex combination of knowledge, experiences, skills, beliefs, and attitudes

that are especially related to the topics to be taught. If you understand your students' thinking before teaching them, you can build your instruction on it (Guskey & McTighe, 2016). The preassessment does not need to be a formal test. You may, for example, have a class discussion about some of the topics that you will be teaching in an upcoming unit. From this discussion, you can gauge how much the class already knows about the topics and what kinds of misconceptions they may have. Use this information to plan your teaching of the unit.

Often students' beliefs about a topic are contrary to what you will teach. Even after you present the information, students' beliefs may not change. If students do not believe what you are teaching, then they do not integrate new concepts into their existing ways of thinking, and they will be unable to apply that information in the future. For example, youngsters know that wearing sweaters keeps them warm. When teaching a science unit on insulating properties, you may teach that air has insulating properties. If you ask youngsters what happens to the temperature of a cold bottle of soft drink when you wrap it in a sweater, many may say it gets very warm. If you tell them it will stay cold, many will not believe you because they know sweaters keep them warm. Knowing this fact, your teaching will have to include activities that change students' beliefs by building on their prior experiences and knowledge. Your instruction will have to offer a real demonstration and comprehensive explanation—for example, why a sweater keeps the student warm *and* the soft drink cool—before that instruction can alter their beliefs.

A Framework for Constructing Instruments

A **preinstruction unit assessment framework** is a plan you use to help you assess cognitive and affective learning objectives for an upcoming unit. Preinstruction assessments should be relatively short, however, so focus your assessment on only a few core elements. Do a written assessment, so you can easily summarize the information and use it to make your planning decisions. You could also organize a class discussion around the results.

It is especially helpful if you adopt a set framework and use it to generate assessment questions for every unit you teach. This structure establishes a comprehensive and consistent approach to gathering and using information. The framework in Figure 6.3 is useful. Depending

FIGURE 6.3 Framework for crafting a written assessment of students' attitudes, knowledge, beliefs, and experiences about a topic.

Area assessed	Example question
Students' prior school experience with the topic	Have you ever studied the water cycle before? When?
Students' interest in the topic	How interesting is the water cycle to you?
Students' attitudes toward the topic	Can you give me a reason why studying the water cycle is important? [Or, arrange a 3-minute mock debate, with one student assigned to convince the class that the water cycle is important and the other assigned to convince the class that it is not.]
Connections students make between the topic and other fields of study	What other topics is the water cycle related to? Explain how you know.
Students' knowledge of vocabulary related to the topic	Tell us what you know about these words: evaporation, condensation, precipitation.
Students' personal connections with the topic	Has anyone ever experienced a flood or a drought?

on the subject you teach, you might modify or emphasize some of the categories.

Pretesting for Metacognition Skills

Some teachers have found it useful to pretest students' abilities to monitor and control their own thinking as they perform learning activities (Kolencik & Hillwig, 2011). If students are aware that learning one thing is more difficult than another, if they are able habitually to check statements before accepting them as facts, or if they are able habitually to plan their work before beginning it, they are using *metacognitive skills*. You may wish to assess these skills before teaching, so you will have a better idea of how well your students can monitor and control their thinking about the assignments you will make during the unit. You may wish to integrate teaching some of the metacognitive skills into the unit. Questionnaires are often used for this purpose.

Ken Mattingly, Middle school science teacher
Rockcastle County Public Schools, Mt. Vernon, KY

MyLab Education

Video Example 6.1

Formative assessment should inform educational decisions made by both students (decisions about the self-regulation of learning) and teachers (decisions about planning or modifying instruction). This video emphasizes how formative assessment informs students' decisions about studying during a unit. Teachers also discuss how formative assessment informs their instructional planning.

Emily Roberts, Kindergarten teacher
Jefferson City Public Schools, Jefferson City, MO

MyLab Education

Video Example 6.2

Formative assessment should inform educational decisions made by both students (decisions about the self-regulation of learning) and teachers (decisions about planning or modifying instruction). This video emphasizes how formative assessment informs students' decisions about studying during a unit. Teachers also discuss how formative assessment informs their instructional planning.

PLANNING FOR ONE SUMMATIVE ASSESSMENT

This section focuses on one assessment purpose: using assessment results to grade students. This is an important responsibility, and you should not base a report card grade on only one test. Chapter 15 will discuss strategies and techniques for assigning report card grades. In this section, however, our focus is narrower—*how to develop a plan* for one formal summative assessment that will be graded.

Organizing a Blueprint

Before creating a test, make a **blueprint** to describe both the content the assessment should cover and the performance expected of the student in relation to that content. Some authors call the blueprint a **table of specifications**. The blueprint serves as a basis for setting the number of assessment tasks and for ensuring that the assessment will have the desired emphasis and balance. Thus, the elements

FIGURE 6.4   Example of a blueprint for summative assessment of a science unit.

Content outline	Remember	Understand	Apply	Total

I. Basic Parts of Cell
  A. Nucleus
  B. Cytoplasm
  C. Cell membrane
	Names and tells functions of each part of cell
	
	3 points
		Labels parts of cell shown on a line drawing
		
		3 points
			Given photographs of actual plant and animal cells, labels the parts
			2 points
				8 points
				40%

II. Plant vs. Animal cells
  A. Similarities
  B. Differences
    1. cell wall vs. membrane
    2. food manufacture
		Describes the cell wall and cell membrane Explains differences between plant and animal cells
		
		2 points
				2 points 10%

III. Cell Membrane
  A. Living nature of
  B. Diffusion
  C. Substances diffused by cells
	Lists substances diffused and not diffused by cell membranes Gives definition of diffusion
	3 points
		Distinguishes between diffusion and osmosis
		1 point
				4 points
				20%

IV. Division of Cells
  A. Phases in division
  B. Chromosomes and DNA
  C. Plant vs. Animal cell division
	Gives definitions of division, chromosomes, and DNA, States differences between plant and animal cell division
	4 points
			Given the numbers of chromosomes in a cell before division, states the number in each cell after division
			2 points
				6 points
				30%

Total	10 points 50%	6 points 30%	4 points 20%	20 points 100%

of a complete test plan include (a) content topics to assess, (b) types of thinking skills to assess, (c) specific learning objectives to assess, and (d) emphasis (number of item or points) for each learning objective to be assessed. Figure 6.4 illustrates such a blueprint for a science unit on cells. Advanced planning for developing a summative classroom assessment allows you to view the assessment as a whole. Plus, it simplifies the task of writing the test: It is easier to do that when a blueprint tells you exactly what kind of tasks and items you need.

The row headings along the left margin list the major topics (the knowledge) the assessment will cover. You can use a more detailed outline if you wish. The column headings across the top list the first three major cognitive process classifications of the revised Bloom taxonomy. This test does not tap the "analyze, evaluate, or create" levels of thinking. You might use a project or other performance assessment to address those. You may use one of the other taxonomies, described in more detail in Appendix D, if you prefer. The purpose of formally laying out this two-way grid is not to promote exact or rigorous classification. Rather, it is a tool to help you recall the higher-order cognitive skills that need to be systematically taught and evaluated in the classroom. Sometimes, teachers merge categories (e.g., remember/understand, apply/analyze) to simplify planning and yet maintain the blueprint's purpose of accurately representing desired cognitive levels.

The body of the blueprint lists the specific learning objectives. It is possible to add a reference to a Common Core State Standard or other state standard here, as well. Both a content topic and a level of complexity of the taxonomic category thus doubly classify the learning objectives. In this example, most of the learning objectives are at the lower and middle levels of the taxonomy. For a different emphasis, you would use the blueprint to identify the cells in which to write other objectives to assess.

The numbers in the blueprint in Figure 6.4 describe the emphasis of the assessment, both in terms of percentage of the total number of tasks and in terms of the percentage of tasks within each row or content category. You decide how many tasks to include on an assessment after you consider (a) the importance of each learning objective, (b) type of tasks, (c) content to be assessed,

(d) what you emphasized in your teaching, and (e) amount of time available for assessment.

Summing across rows, you can see what portion of the test measures each content category. If the weight is not as intended, adjust the blueprint. Adjusting the blueprint *before* you write test items is much more efficient than editing a whole test after it is written. Summing down columns, you can see what portion of the test taps different cognitive levels, as well. Again, if the weight is not as intended, adjust the blueprint, allocating the points where they need to be to match your learning objectives. Then (and only then), write the test.

The kind of blueprint in this example works with an objective test, where each item is worth 1 point, as well as for tests with multipoint items (for example, essay questions or problems to solve). Three points from the blueprint could be three 1-point items, or one 3-point item, or any combination of items worth 3 points.

Students will expect the various numbers of points on the assessment to correspond to the amount of time devoted to the material in class and to the emphasis they perceive you have placed on that material. If the assessment you are planning does not meet this expectation, it seems fair to notify the students of this fact well in advance of administering it.

As you can see, an assessment blueprint is a concise way to explain what is important for students to learn. Therefore, blueprints are useful instructional tools, too, especially with students in middle and high school. When you begin a unit, you can share your assessment blueprints with your students. Review and discuss the blueprint thoroughly with the students to ensure they (a) have no misunderstandings, (b) understand the unit's emphasis, (c) understand what they will be held accountable for performing, and (d) see how the summative assessment factors into their overall grades. In Chapter 5, we discussed your professional responsibility to give students sufficient information when administering assessments. A blueprint is an excellent way to provide this information to middle and senior high school students. Older students may offer suggestions for changing the emphasis or manner of assessment, thus more fully engaging in their own learning and evaluation. Students can write test questions for each blueprint cell. Use them for a practice test.

You need not attempt to devise a formal plan for all units in one semester or year. If you develop a blueprint for a few units each year, after a few years most units will have blueprints. As the learning objectives change, you can update these blueprints with less work than originally required. Also, several teachers could draft blueprints for different units in a subject and exchange them. Even if a colleague's blueprint has to be modified to suit your particular teaching approach, you will likely save considerable time. When changes in the blueprints do occur, you should revise and redistribute the blueprints.

Accommodations to the Summative Assessment

Any changes you have made to the items on the test, conditions of administration, or student response modes in order to accommodate students with disabilities must give you assessment information that is valid. Review the discussion of accommodations in Chapter 5 and the list in Figure 5.2.

Make sure that your accommodations for students who have IEPs are consistent with these educational plans. For example, if you are using a modified set of learning objectives for a student, consistent with the IEP, then a modified blueprint should be used to ensure the test reflects those learning objectives. If a student's IEP specifies that test items should be read to her, then (unless the test is a reading test) you should plan the logistics (the reader, a quiet location, etc.) to allow this to happen. Appendix E describes technology-based accommodations that can help give students access to testing materials.

Plan for assessing English language learners (ELLs) in your class according to the state standards (including Common Core State Standards), curriculum goals, and lesson objectives you are expected to teach them. Select task types that are most likely to allow the ELLs to show what they know, and plan for multiple opportunities for assessment (Educational Testing Service, 2009). ELLs vary greatly as individuals, so beyond these general guidelines you will plan specifically for your ELL students in a similar way as you would plan for any of your students, making sure that the tasks you set do not compromise validity by requiring knowledge and skills that you are not planning to assess.

For example, in a social studies unit test, if reading ability is not the skill you plan to test, make sure your students can handle the reading requirements of the test or make an accommodation (reading aloud, using a dictionary). Using dictionaries or glossaries is the only accommodation shown to have an effect on assessing ELLs (Kieffer, Lesaux, Rivera, & Francis, 2009), but on a case-by-case basis other accommodations (see the list in Figure 5.2) may be useful. Some ELL programs allow test directions and/or content to be presented in the student's native language; the use of the student's first language depends on the philosophy of the ELL program at the school.

IMPROVING THE VALIDITY OF ASSESSMENT PLANS

A blueprint is an excellent way to ensure that many of the criteria for improving validity are met. The checklist summarizes the suggestions we have made for test blueprints.

Checklist

A checklist for evaluating the quality of a teacher's plan for a summative unit assessment

Revise your assessment plan if you answer no to one or more of the questions in the checklist.

1. Does your plan clarify the purpose(s) of the assessment and what you expect it to tell you about each student?

2. Does your plan indicate the main subject-matter topics and performances you want to assess?

3. Will your plan help you to judge whether the assessment tasks match the major content topics and learning objectives you have specified?

4. Have you clearly identified the elements of knowledge and performance that all students need to know?

5. Does your plan give the most important learning objectives the heaviest weights in the total score? Are the least important learning objectives given the least weight?

6. Do you know what kind(s) of assessment tasks should be used to assess each content-thinking skill combination? Are these tasks the best ways to assess the combination?

7. Have you estimated the amount of time students need to complete this assessment? Is this estimated time realistic?

8. Have you estimated the amount of time you will need to evaluate the students' responses?

Two important validity principles from Chapter 3 should guide your assessment plans. Keep these principles at the forefront of your thinking, whether planning for a single assessment or multiple assessments:

1. Assessment results are valid only for specific interpretations and uses, not for all interpretations or uses.

2. Because no single assessment method gives perfectly valid results, more than one method should be used to assess the same achievement.

Figure 6.5 summarizes the main criteria and ways to improve the validity of your classroom assessments, and we discuss them below.

Matching Assessment Tasks to Learning Objectives

Your assessment plans specify the important learning objectives to be taught and assessed. Your teaching is most effective when your lesson plans, teaching activities, assessments, and learning objectives are all aligned. All four should also be aligned with your state's curriculum framework and standards (see Chapter 2).

To be valid, assessment tasks and procedures must match the learning objectives. For example, if an objective calls for students to build a model, write a poem, collect data, or perform a physical skill, the students should be administered a performance assessment. If your assessment task requires students only to list the parts of a model, to analyze an existing poem, to summarize data already collected, or to describe the sequence of steps needed for performing the physical skill, it does not match these learning objectives. The validity of your classroom assessment results plummets when even *some* of the tasks do not match the stated learning objectives.

As an example, consider the ninth-grade social studies learning objective stated here and the three assessment tasks that follow it:

Example

Learning objective: Students will explain in their own words the meaning of the concept of *culture*.

Task 1. Name three things that are important to the *culture* of indigenous Americans.

Task 2. Give a short talk to the class comparing three different *cultures*. In your talk, make sure you describe the similarities and differences among the cultures you have chosen.

Task 3. Write a paragraph telling in your own words what is meant by the term *culture*.

FIGURE 6.5   Criteria and ways to improve the validity of your classroom assessments.

Criteria to use	Ways to evaluate your assessment plan
Do assessment tasks align with curriculum, standards, and instruction?	■ Be sure you clearly understand the main intent of the learning objective to be taught and assessed. ■ *Think:* What is the main intent of the learning objective? Does the assessment task require a student to do exactly as the main intent requires? ■ Analyze the assessment task to identify which part(s) may not match the learning objective(s). Eliminate or rewrite the nonmatching parts.
Do you assess only important learning outcomes?	■ Review the learning objectives taught and assessed; prioritize them from most to least important. Eliminate assessments matching low-priority learning objectives. ■ Be sure your state's standards or learning expectations are assessed by one or more of your assessments. ■ Create assessments that require students to demonstrate more than one high-priority learning objective through the same task.
Do you use appropriate multiple assessment formats?	■ Become skilled in creating many types of assessment formats. ■ Learn the strengths and limitations of each type of assessment format. ■ Analyze each learning objective. *Think:* What are several different ways I can assess this achievement? How can I use two or more ways? ■ Analyze the assessment tasks to identify which part(s) may not match the learning objective(s). Eliminate or rewrite the nonmatching parts. ■ Plan for assessing each important learning objective in two or more ways.
Are your assessments understandable?	■ Be sure each assessment procedure has clear directions to the student and that you have prepared students concerning each assessment. ■ Learn to craft assessments well, so they will satisfy the criteria and checklists contained in Chapters 8 through 13. ■ Learn to craft scoring rubrics well, so they will satisfy the criteria and checklists in Chapter 12.
Do you follow appropriate validity criteria?	■ Use the criteria described in Chapter 3.
Are your assessments of appropriate length?	■ Be sure all students who know the material can finish within the time limits. ■ Follow the suggestions for improving reliability given in Chapter 4.
Are your assessment results equivalent across years?	■ Use blueprints from previous years to guide you in crafting this year's assessment blueprints. ■ Make the difficulty and complexity of this year's assessment tasks equivalent to last year's tasks.
Are your assessment tasks of appropriate difficulty and complexity?	■ Be sure the conditions and tools for students to use during the assessment are appropriate for the learning objectives and the students' educational development. ■ Add appropriate accommodations for students with disabilities (see Figure 5.2).

Only Task 3 matches the stated learning objective. Consider Task 1: The performance required applies to a specific cultural situation rather than to the general concept of culture as intended by the learning objective. Task 1 should not be used for the assessment of this objective. The performances required in Task 2 are to "compare" and to "describe" ("giving a talk" is only the way the student has to indicate she is describing similarities and differences among the cultures). Although these are worthwhile activities, they seem to go beyond the more limited scope and main intent of the learning objective. Because this task fails to match the learning objective, it should not appear on the assessment either.

What should you do if you create or identify a "great" task that does not match the stated learning objective? You have only three choices: disregard the task, modify the task so it matches the learning objective, or modify the learning objective so it matches the task. Often, crafting an excellent assessment task helps further clarify a learning objective: We see the full meaning of the objective, which was not previously clear from its verbal statement. If this is the case, then you should modify the stated learning objective, so it more clearly expresses what you intend.

Be careful, however. If you have already communicated the assessment plan to students, you need to be sure that you do not "surprise" them with a more complex or difficult task than the type for which they are preparing themselves. Changing the rules in midstream is often unethical. Usually, it guarantees that you lose the respect of at least some students. Rather than completely discarding the task, you could either modify it to suit the stated learning objective or save it until the next time you teach the unit. At that time, you can more clearly specify the objective.

Using Appropriate Multiple Assessment Task Formats

Many varieties of assessments are available. One of the criteria we discussed in Chapter 3 (Figure 3.1) is to present students with multiple ways to demonstrate their competence. The validity of your assessment results usually improves, therefore, if you use several **task formats** (paper-and-pencil tests, performance assessments, and personal communication) to assess students. Try to use the combination of formats that *most directly assesses the intents* of the stated learning objectives. The next section describes many different format options.

Making Assessments Understandable to Students

As you plan and create your assessments, remember that you need to make clear to students how and when they will be assessed, what they will be required to do, and when and how they will be evaluated. A section in Chapter 14, "Preparing Students for Assessment," describes some of the information about your planned assessment that your students need to know. In addition, be sure the directions to students, the assessment tasks (e.g., your test questions), and the scoring rubrics (e.g., criteria for full marks) are understandable to all students. For example, according to Jakwerth, Stancavage, and Reed (1999), students who leave constructed-response questions unanswered on the National Assessment of Educational Progress may do so because they "couldn't figure out what the question was

asking" (p. 9), "didn't really get the question" (p. 9), "thought it would take too long" (p. 9), or "didn't realize [I] had to do both parts" (p. 10). You can avoid such problems by clearly writing and explaining your assessments to students and, in turn, being sure that students understand before they begin.

Satisfying Appropriate Validity Criteria

The main criteria for judging the quality of your assessment are validity criteria. In Chapter 3 (Figure 3.1), we discussed seven categories of validity criteria for classroom assessments: (1) content representativeness and relevance; (2) thinking processes and skills represented; (3) consistency with other assessments; (4) reliability and objectivity; (5) fairness to different types of students; (6) economy, efficiency, practicality, and instructional features; and (7) multiple assessment usage. We cannot overstate how critical these validity criteria are for effective assessment.

Satisfying Appropriate Reliability Criteria

In Chapter 4, we discussed reliability concerns for classroom assessment (see Figure 4.1). The length of your assessment is one of the factors affecting reliability. Length depends on three major factors: (1) the amount of time you have available for assessment, (2) the students' educational development, and (3) the level of reliability you wish the results to have. Longer assessments are more reliable than shorter assessments. Classroom assessments should be power assessments; that is, every student who has learned the material should have enough time to perform each task. Your experience with the subject matter and the students you teach will help you decide how long to make the assessment.

As practical guidelines, use the time suggestions in Figure 6.6 for students in middle and senior high school. In 40 minutes of assessment, for example, you can administer a test with a short essay and 15 to 20 complex multiple-choice items. Modify these time suggestions to suit your students as your experience deepens.

Remember, too, that students will be taking state-mandated and other standardized tests: These tests are typically 40 to 60 minutes in length, even for elementary students. Your classroom assessments, therefore, should give students the opportunity to practice taking longer

FIGURE 6.6   Time requirements for certain assessment tasks.

Type of task	Approximate time per task (item)
True-false items	20–30 seconds
Multiple-choice (factual)	40–60 seconds
One-word fill-in	40–60 seconds
Multiple-choice (complex)	70–90 seconds
Matching (5 stems/6 choices)	2–4 minutes
Short-answer	2–4 minutes
Multiple-choice (w/calculations)	2–5 minutes
Word problems (simple arithmetic)	5–10 minutes
Short essays	15–20 minutes
Data analyses/graphing	15–25 minutes
Drawing models/labeling	20–30 minutes
Extended essays	35–50 minutes

assessments. You do not want the mandated assessment to be the first long test students take each year.

Ensuring Equivalence

If the content of the units you are assessing has remained essentially the same since the last time you taught them, your summative assessment instruments on the two occasions should be equivalent. Building this semester's assessment instruments to last semester's blueprints increases the likelihood the two instruments will be equivalent, even if you use different questions. Blueprints will help ensure that both years' assessments cover the same content and thinking skills and emphasize the same knowledge and skills. Equivalent instruments are fairer to students. **Equivalence** means that students past and present are required to know and perform tasks of similar complexity and difficulty to earn the same grade. Of course, if you changed the content or learning objectives of the unit, the blueprints and the assessment should change as well. Also, if results of your past assessments were unsatisfactory, you should not perpetuate them from year to year.

MyLab Education Self-Check 6.1

MyLab Education Application Exercises 6.1: Effective Planning

WHAT RANGE OF ASSESSMENT OPTIONS IS AVAILABLE?

Whether you are assessing for summative or formative purposes, you have a wide range of options at your disposal. Which should you use? Before deciding, you need to know three things: (1) the learning objective students should achieve, (2) the purpose for which you want to use the assessment results, and (3) the advantages of an assessment technique for the specific purpose you have in mind. This section discusses the general advantages and disadvantages of the many assessment options available to you. The assessment you use should be the most appropriate for assessing the learning objectives you wish students to achieve. You should defend your choice(s) on the basis of the validity and reliability of the results.

The most commonly used types of classroom assessment procedures are listed in Figure 6.7 along with their advantages, their limitations, and brief suggestions for improved use. The techniques are grouped into two categories: formative assessment techniques and summative assessment techniques. Note, however, that it is not the technique that makes an assessment formative or summative, but rather how it is used (to support further learning or to summarize and report learning). Thus, the categories describe techniques that usually are used formatively or summatively, but the categorization is not definitive. See Chapter 7 for more information about formative assessment.

Formative Assessment Options

Formative assessments gather information to help improve students' achievement of learning objectives. This information guides and fine-tunes both your thinking and your students'. You use formative assessment information to plan your next teaching activities, to diagnose the causes of students' learning difficulties, and to give students information about how to improve. Students use formative assessment to make decisions about how to take the next steps to get closer to their goals for learning and to reach desired quality levels in their performance. In fact, assessment is not truly "formative" unless students actually use the information for improvement.

You gather formative information while you are still teaching the material and while students are

FIGURE 6.7 Advantages, limitations, and pitfalls of alternative types of classroom assessment techniques.

Assessment alternatives	Advantages for teachers	Disadvantages for teachers	Suggestions for improved use
		Formative assessment techniques	
1. Conversations and comments from other teachers	(a) Fast way to obtain certain types of back-ground information about a student. (b) Permit colleagues to share experiences with specific students in other learning contexts, thereby broadening the perspective about the learners. (c) Permit attainment of information about a student's family, siblings, or peer problems that may be affecting the student's learning.	(a) Tend to reinforce stereotypes and biases toward a family or social class. (b) Students' learning under another teacher or in another context may be quite unlike their learning in the current context. (c) Others' opinions are not objective, often based on incomplete information, personal life view, or personal theory of personality.	(a) Do not believe hearsay, rumors, biases of others. (b) Do not gossip or reveal private and confidential information about students. (c) Keep the conversation professional.
2. Casual conversations with students	(a) Provide relaxed, informal setting for obtain-ing information. (b) Students may reveal their attitudes and motivations toward learning that are not exhibited in class.	(a) A student's mind may not be focused on the learning objective being assessed. (b) Inadequate sampling of students' knowledge; too few students assessed. (c) Inefficient; students' conversation may be ir-relevant to assessing their achievement.	(a) Do not appear as an inquisitor, always probing students. (b) Be careful not to misperceive a student's attitude or a student's degree of understanding.
3. Questioning students during instruction	(a) Permits judgments about students' thinking and learning progress during the course of teaching; gives teachers immediate feedback. (b) Permits teachers to ask questions requir-ing higher-order thinking and elaborated responses. (c) Permits student-to-student interaction to be assessed. (d) Permits assessment of students' ability to discuss issues with others orally and in some depth.	(a) Some students cannot express themselves well in front of other students. (b) Requires education in how to ask proper ques-tions and to plan for asking specific types of questions during the lesson. (c) Information obtained tends to be only a small sample of the learning objectives and of the students in the class. (d) Some learning objectives cannot be assessed by spontaneous and short oral responses; they require longer time frames in which students are free to think, create, and respond. (e) Records of students' responses are kept only in the teacher's mind, which may be unreliable.	(a) Be sure to ask questions of students who are reticent or slow to respond. Avoid focusing on verbally aggressive "stars." (b) Wait 5–10 seconds for a student to respond before moving on to another. (c) Avoid limiting questions to those requiring facts or a definite correct answer, thereby narrowing the focus of the assess-ment inappropriately. (d) Do not punish students for failing to participate in class question sessions or inappropriately reward those verbally aggressive students who participate fully. (e) Remember that students' verbal and nonverbal behavior in class may not indicate their true attitudes/values.
4. Daily homework and seatwork	(a) Provide formative information about how learning is progressing. (b) Allow errors to be diagnosed and corrected. (c) Combine practice, reinforcement, and as-sessment.	(a) Tend to focus on narrow segments of learning rather than integrating large complexes of skills and knowledge. (b) Sample only a small variety of content and skills on any one assignment. (c) Assignment may not be complete or may be copied from others.	(a) This method assesses learning that is only in the formative stages. It is generally inappropriate to assign summative letter grades from the results. (b) Failure to complete homework or completing it late is no reason to punish students. Figure out the reason for the problem and address it. (c) Do not inappropriately attribute poor test performance to the student not doing the homework. (d) Do not overuse homework as a teaching strategy (e.g., using it as a primary teaching method).

5. Teacher-made quizzes and tests	(a) Although primarily useful for summative evaluation, they may permit diagnosis of errors and faulty thinking. (b) Provide for students' written expression of knowledge.	(a) Do not overemphasize lower-level thinking skills. (b) Use open-ended or constructed-response tasks to gain insight into a student's thinking processes and errors. (c) For better diagnosis of a student's thinking, use tasks that require students to apply and use their knowledge to "real-life" situations.
6. In-depth interviews of individual students	(a) Permit in-depth probing of students' understanding, thinking patterns, and problem-solving strategies. (b) Permit follow-up questions tailored to a student's responses and allow a student to elaborate answers. (c) Permit diagnosis of faulty thinking and errors in performances.	(a) Require a lot of time to complete. (b) Require keeping the rest of the class occupied while one student is being interviewed. (c) Require learning skills in effective educational achievement interviewing and diagnosis.
7. Growth portfolios	(a) Allow large segments of a student's learning experiences to be reviewed. (b) Allow monitoring a student's growth and progress. (c) Communicate to students that growth and progress are more important than test results. (d) Allow student to participate in selecting and evaluating material to include in the portfolio. (e) Can become a focus of teaching and learning.	(a) Require a long time to accumulate evidence of growth and progress. (b) Require special effort to teach students how to use appropriate and realistic self-assessment techniques. (c) Require high-level knowledge of the subject matter to diagnose and guide students. (d) Require the ability to recognize complex and subtle pattern of growth and progress in the subjects. (e) Results tend to be inconsistent from teacher to teacher.
8. Attitude and values questionnaires	(a) Assess affective characteristics of students. (b) Knowing student's attitudes and values in relation to a specific topic or subject matter may be useful in planning teaching. (c) May provide insights into students' motivations.	(a) Remember that the way questions are worded significantly affects how students respond. (b) Remember that attitude questionnaire responses may change drastically from one occasion or context to another. (c) Remember that your personal theory of personality or personal value system may lead to incorrect interpretations of students' responses.
		(a) The results are sensitive to the way questions are worded. Students may misinterpret, not understand, or react differently than the assessor intended. (b) Can be easily "faked" by older and testwise students.

(continued)

FIGURE 6.7 (Continued)

Assessment alternatives	Advantages for teachers	Disadvantages for teachers	Suggestions for improved use
		Summative assessment techniques	
1. Teacher-made tests and quizzes	(a) Can assess a wide range of content and cognitive skills. (b) Can be aligned with what was actually taught. (c) Use a variety of task formats. (d) Allow for assessment of written expression.	(a) Difficult to assess complex skills or ability to use combinations of skills. (b) Require time to create, edit, and produce good items. (c) Class period is often too short for a complete assessment. (d) Focus exclusively on cognitive outcomes.	(a) Do not overemphasize lower-level thinking skills. (b) Do not overuse short-answer and response-choice items. (c) Craft task requiring students to apply knowledge to "real life."
2. Task focusing on procedures and processes	(a) Allow assessments of nonverbal as well as verbal responses. (b) Allow students to integrate several simple skills and knowledge to perform a complex, realistic task. (c) Allow for group and cooperative performance and assessment. (d) Allow assessment of steps used to complete an assignment.	(a) Focus on a narrow range of content knowledge and cognitive skills. (b) Require a great deal of time to properly formulate, administer, and rate. (c) May have low inter-rater reliability unless scoring rubrics are used. (d) Students' performance quality is not easily generalized across different content and tasks. (e) Tasks that students perceive as uninteresting, boring, or irrelevant do not elicit the students' best efforts.	(a) Investigate carefully the reason for student's failure to complete the task successfully. (b) Use a scoring rubric to increase the reliability and validity of results. (c) Do not confuse the evaluation of the process a student uses with the need to evaluate the correctness of the answers. (d) Allow sufficient time for students to adequately demonstrate the performance.
3. Projects and tasks focusing on products	(a) Same as 2(a), (b), and (c). (b) Permit several equally valid processes to be used to produce the product or complete the project. (c) Allow assessment of the quality of the product. (d) Allow longer time than class period to complete the tasks.	(a) Same as 2(a), (b), (c), (d), and (e). (b) Students may have unauthorized help outside class to complete the product or project. (c) All students in the class must have the same opportunity to use all appropriate materials and tools in order for the assessment to be fair.	(a) Same as 2(a), (b), (c), and (d). (b) Give adequate instruction to students on the criteria that will be used to evaluate their work, the standards that will be applied, and how students can use these criteria and standards to monitor their own progress in completing the work. (c) Do not mistake the aesthetic appearance of the product for substance and thoughtfulness. (d) Do not punish tardiness in completing the project or product by lowering the student's grade.
4. Best works portfolios	(a) Allow large segments of a student's learning experience to be assessed. (b) May allow students to participate in the selection of the material to be included in the portfolio. (c) Allow either quantitative or qualitative assessment of the works in the portfolio. (d) Permit a much broader assessment of learning objectives than tests.	(a) Require waiting a long time before reporting assessment results. (b) Students must be taught how to select work to include as well as how to present it effectively. (c) Teachers must learn to use a scoring rubric that assesses a wide variety of pieces of work. (d) Inter-rater reliability is low from teacher to teacher. (e) Require high levels of subject-matter knowledge to evaluate students' work properly.	(a) Be very clear about the learning objectives to be assessed. (b) Teach a student to use appropriate criteria to choose the work to include. (c) Do not collect too much material to evaluate. (d) Coordinate portfolio development with other teachers. (e) Develop and use scoring rubrics to define standards and maintain consistency.

Type	Descriptions	Recommendations
5. Textbook-supplied tests and quizzes	(a) Allow for assessment of written expression. (b) Already prepared, save teachers' time. (c) Match the content and sequence of the textbook or curricular materials.	(a) Often do not assess complex skills or ability to use combinations of skills. (b) Often do not match the emphases and presentations in class. (c) Focus on cognitive skills. (d) Class period is often too short for a complete assessment.	(a) Be skeptical that the items were made by professionals and are of high quality. (b) Carefully edit or rewrite the item to match what you have taught. (c) Remember that you are personally responsible for using a poor-quality test. You must not appeal to the authority of the textbook.
6. Standardized achievement tests	(a) Assess a wide range of cognitive abilities and skills that cover a year's learning. (b) Assess content and skills common to many schools across the country. (c) Items developed and screened by professionals, resulting in only the best items being included. (d) Corroborate what teachers know about pupils; sometimes indicate unexpected results for specific students. (e) Provide norm-referenced information that permits evaluation of students' progress in relation to students nationwide. (f) Provide legitimate comparisons of a student's achievement in two or more curricular areas. (g) Provide growth scales so students' long-term educational development can be monitored. (h) Useful for curriculum evaluation.	(a) Focus exclusively on cognitive outcomes. (b) Often the emphasis on a particular test is different from the emphasis of a particular teacher. (c) Do not provide diagnostic information. (d) Results usually take too long to get back to teachers, so are not directly useful for instructional planning.	(a) Avoid narrowing your instruction to prepare students for these tests when administrators put pressure on teachers. (b) Do not use these tests to evaluate teachers. (c) Do not confuse the quality of the learning that did occur in the classroom with the results on standardized tests when interpreting them. (d) Educate parents about the tests, limited validity for assessing a student's learning potentials.

still learning it. As a result, these are often **informal assessment techniques**. That is, they occur spontaneously as you need information, and you rarely stop teaching to do the assessment. Figure 6.7 summarizes eight categories of formative assessment options. The eight categories fall into three groups.

Oral Assessment Techniques

You may gather information to improve students' learning without creating tests or other paper-and-pencil tasks. Conversations with teachers who have taught a student may give you insight into the student's background and which approaches have worked in the past. These conversations may also help as you size up the class at the beginning of the term. Conversations with students give you additional insight into their feelings, attitudes, interests, and motivations.

As you teach a lesson, you question students about the material. These questions should encourage students to think about the material and to reveal their understandings, including misconceptions. This process will help you guide your teaching. Avoid the "recitation" type of questioning in which you seek short answers to your questions. This style of questioning provides little insight into students' thinking and, therefore, provides little formative information. Avoid the tendency to ignore or ask only simple questions of the shy and less verbal students (Good & Brophy, 2002). Consider using whiteboards, letter cards, or hand signals for student responses, so you can survey all students' answers, not just a few, for each question.

A good way to plan your oral questioning is to use a thinking skills taxonomy. In every lesson, be sure you ask several questions from the higher-order thinking categories of the taxonomy. Below are examples of some questions a teacher might ask students who have been studying the short story as a literary form:

Example

Remember	"Who was the main character in the last story we read?"
Understand	"What were some of the personal problems that the characters in this story had to solve?"
Apply	"Are the characters' problems in any way similar to the problems you or someone you know have had? Tell us about that. Don't use real names if you will embarrass the person."
Analyze	"What literary devices, style of writing, or 'writing trick' did the author use to help the reader really understand how the characters were feeling? Explain how this was done."
Evaluate	"What are three or four criteria that we can apply to all of the stories, so we can compare and evaluate their literary quality?"
Create	"So far this semester, we have read eight short stories. In each one, a character (sometimes two characters) wasn't able to solve his or her problem satisfactorily—even though each character tried to do so. Why is that? What do they all have in common that resulted in failure to solve their problems? What general problem-solving approach did all of these characters use that resulted in their failure?"

Paper-and-Pencil Assessment Techniques

Each day you give students seatwork and homework. These **paper-and-pencil assessments** let students practice the learning objectives and perhaps extend their learning beyond the specific material you taught. You should review the results of seatwork and homework not just for correctness, but for what the work reveals about students' thinking. If a student is exhibiting a pattern of errors, the student may have a misconception or may be using a rule consistently, but inappropriately. Providing that specific information as feedback to students who need it is a powerful way of personalizing learning and helps students change.

You also periodically create and administer short quizzes and tests. These monitor the progress students are making toward achieving learning objectives. Tests and exams tend to be somewhat formal and are more useful for summative assessment than for formative assessment. However, if you use open-ended response items and carefully review students' responses for insights into their thinking, you will be able to derive some diagnostic information from these techniques.

Portfolios

Other formative evaluation techniques are somewhat more labor intensive than the ones we have discussed so far. A **growth portfolio** is a selected sequence of a student's work that demonstrates progress or development toward achieving the learning objective(s). By containing "not-so-good works," "improved works," and "best works," the growth portfolio shows progress and learning during the course.

Typically, both the teacher and the student decide what a portfolio should include. Further, students are usually asked to describe the work they included, why they selected it, what it demonstrates about their learning, and their affective reactions to the material and to their learning experiences. Because a portfolio is built up over time, it permits closer integration of assessments with instruction than with some of the other techniques. These attributes are considered advantages of portfolios over one-shot assessment techniques because of the richness of information they provide the teacher.

Growth portfolios are usually evaluated qualitatively, although rating scales are sometimes used. Evaluating the evidence qualitatively requires a significant amount of skill and knowledge about student learning and the subject matter. The following excerpt from an evaluation of the language arts portfolio of an eighth-grade student illustrates both the richness of the information in the portfolio and the deep level of teacher knowledge required to evaluate it:

Example

Our experience is that growth is often manifested in qualitative changes in the writing—changes in the complexity of the problems that students undertake, which may involve losing control over other features of the writing like organization or mechanics. Take Gretchen . . . who included two pieces of expository response to literature in her portfolio. In one sense, the second piece is not as strong as the first—it is not well organized or coherent—but it is a richer interpretation. Unlike the first piece, which simply compares two groups of characters from *Lord of the Flies* . . . the second piece, on *Animal Farm*, has a thematic framework about the role of scapegoats that is played out with evidence from Gretchen's own personal experience, from the novel, and from a definition of the term acquired from another resource. A comparison of Gretchen's revisions in the two pieces shows a newly developed awareness of the need for elaboration and for evidence on particular points. (Moss et al., 1992, p. 13)

Chapter 13 describes portfolio construction and use in more detail.

Interviews In addition to portfolios, you may conduct *interviews with individual students*. Interviews can give you additional insights into students' thinking and learning difficulties. These interviews are more effective if you organize them

around key concepts or specific problem-solving tasks. For example, you could work with the student to create a concept map of the relevant concepts in a unit and discuss with the student how he believes the concepts to be related to one another. Or, for example, many writing teachers use individual writing conferences with students based on drafts of written work. You may also administer a simple questionnaire to your class to gain insight into students' attitudes and values associated with the concepts you are about to teach. We saw a framework for this strategy in Figure 6.3.

Jennifer McDaniel, AP Calculus teacher
Clay County High School, Manchester, KY

MyLab Education

Video Example 6.3

Formative assessment should inform educational decisions made by both students (decisions about the self-regulation of learning) and teachers (decisions about planning or modifying instruction). This video emphasizes how formative assessment informs students' decisions about studying during a unit. Teachers also discuss how formative assessment informs their instructional planning.

Summative Assessment Options

Summative assessments help you formally evaluate students' achievement, so you can report to students, parents, and school officials. This evaluation results in a home report or a report card grade. Summative assessment techniques are usually more formal than formative assessment techniques. Keep in mind, however, that formative and summative are not always distinct. For example, after you teach a unit, you may give a summative unit test. However, you may find students who have not achieved the learning objectives. This discovery will usually require you to reteach the students or provide remedial instruction. Because you have used the summative assessment to guide your teaching, it has provided formative assessment information.

Figure 6.7 shows six categories of summative assessment options. We may separate these into two groups: teacher-made assessments and external (extra-classroom) assessments.

Teacher-Made Assessments We have already mentioned tests and quizzes. These paper-and-pencil techniques may include open-ended questions (such as essays and other constructed-response formats), multiple-choice, true-false, and matching exercises. Chapters 9 through 11 discuss how to craft these formats.

But paper-and-pencil techniques are limited primarily to verbal expressions of knowledge. Students must read and respond to the assessment materials using some type of written response, ranging from simple marks and single words to complex and elaborated essays. Students' abilities to carry out actual experiments, to carry out library research, or to build a model, for example, are not assessed directly with paper-and-pencil techniques. Further, it is usually difficult for teachers to craft paper-and-pencil tasks that require students to apply knowledge and skills from several areas to solve real-life or "authentic" problems. Chapter 12 suggests techniques that assess higher-order thinking skills.

Performance assessment techniques require students to physically carry out a complex, extended **process** (e.g., present an argument orally, play a musical piece, or climb a knotted rope) or produce an important **product** (e.g., write a poem, report on an experiment, or create a painting). The performances you assess should (a) be very close to the ultimate learning objectives, (b) require students to use combinations of many different abilities and skills, and (c) require students to perform under "realistic conditions" (especially requiring student self-pacing, self-motivation, and self-evaluation). Some performance assessments require paper-and-pencil as a medium for expression (e.g., writing a research paper or a short story), but the emphasis in these performances is on the complexity of the product, and students are allowed appropriate time limits. This distinguishes such performance assessments from the short answers, decontextualized math problems, or brief (one class period) essay tasks found on typical paper-and-pencil assessments.

Because some performance assessments so closely measure some learning objectives, they may be used as instructional tools. For example, you may instruct a student on presenting arguments orally and require the student to perform the task several times over the course of the term. You might repeat the teaching-performance combination several times until the student has learned the technique to the degree of expertise appropriate to the student's level of educational development.

Principal disadvantages are that a great deal of time is required to craft appropriate tasks, to prepare marking schemes or rating scales, to carry out the assessment itself, and to administer several tasks. The last point relates to the validity of interpreting students' results. Seldom can you generalize a student's performance on one task to performance on another. That is, how well a student performs depends on the specific content and task to which the performance is linked (Baker, 1992; Linn, 1994). A student may write a good poem about the people in her neighborhood, but an awful poem about the traffic in Los Angeles. How good is the student as a poet in such cases? Quality performance assessment requires a very clear vision of an important learning objective and a high level of skill to translate that vision into appropriate tasks and grading criteria.

Previously, we discussed the growth portfolio as a formative assessment tool. Portfolios may also be used for summative evaluation. The **best works portfolio** is a representative selection of a student's best products that provides evidence of the degree to which the student has achieved specified learning objectives. In an art course, the items might be the student's best works in drawing, painting, sculpture, craftwork, and, perhaps, a medium chosen by the student. In mathematics, the portfolio might include reports on mathematical investigations, examples of how the student applied mathematics to a real problem, writings about mathematics or mathematicians, and examples of how to use mathematics in social studies, English, and science. Best works portfolios focus on summative evaluation. To improve reliability of portfolio evaluations, you need a scoring rubric. Share the rubric with students and teach them how to select their best work in light of those rubrics. Chapter 13 presents more details on portfolio assessments.

External (Extra-Classroom) Assessments

Teachers often use two other techniques. One involves the *quizzes and tests supplied by textbook publishers*. These are convenient because you don't have to create them yourself, and they match the book you are using. The problem is that these assessment materials are often of *poor quality*: They may not match local learning objectives very well, they tend to focus on low-level thinking skills, and they can be poorly crafted. As we mentioned in Chapter 5, you have a professional responsibility to improve these assessment materials before using them.

Standardized Achievement Test Standardized tests also provide summative assessment information. Unlike textbook tests, these materials are usually quite well crafted and supported by research on the validity of the scores. The tests consist of a battery of subtests, each covering a different curriculum area. Because the same group of students (norm group) took all subtests, the publisher's percentile norms allow you to compare a student's development in two or more curricular areas; and the publisher's score scales allow you to monitor a student's growth over time. Your own or your school district's tests cannot provide these types of information. A standardized test battery does not match your curriculum or your teaching goals exactly. Therefore, use it to assess broad goals (e.g., reading comprehension) rather than the specific learning objectives in your classroom. You will learn more details about this assessment option by studying Chapters 16 through 19.

DIFFERENTIATING INSTRUCTION

Differentiated instruction refers to instructional practices that are altered to meet the needs, abilities, interests, and motivations of students. Characterized by clearly focused learning objectives, preassessment and responses, flexible grouping, appropriate student choice during instruction, and ongoing formative assessment, some would say differentiated instruction is simply good instruction—instruction that is responsive to students' needs in the context of the standard or content being taught.

Our point in mentioning differentiated instruction in this chapter is that assessment planning is required to support it. Differentiated instruction relies on accurate, timely assessment in order to be effective. Appropriate preassessment will help you find out about students' prior knowledge, readiness, and interests regarding the learning objective. Ongoing formative assessment will keep students engaged and in charge of regulating their thoughts and actions during instruction. Ongoing formative assessment will also help you make instructional decisions and help you decide when it's time for summative assessment.

In the example in Figure 6.2, assessment information most pertinent to differentiated instruction will be obtained from the pretest, observation and oral questioning, and homework—that is,

toward the more formative end of the planning spectrum. Results from quizzes and independent investigations will also help. Differentiated instruction does not mean you never do whole-group activities. It does mean that you constantly review assessment information to maximize the effectiveness of the particular grouping, instructional activity, or assignment you decide on for each student, in order to get students ready for both individualized and undifferentiated work (Wormeli, 2006). To support these purposes, all your assessments, but especially your formative assessments, must be deeply aligned with your learning goals, must be frequent, and must produce timely responses and instructional decisions. Differentiated instruction, in short, relies on high-quality assessment and valid educational decisions based on that assessment more intensely than undifferentiated instruction does. Assessment planning is crucial for this approach.

ASSESSMENT PLANNING FOR RESPONSE TO INTERVENTION

Based on a definition in the 1975 Education of All Handicapped Children Act, "underachievers" have historically been identified as students with IQ/achievement discrepancies: students whose classroom work does not reach the expectations for students of their ability. The 2004 Individuals with Disabilities Education and Improvement Act added a second definition by which such students could be identified: Students who do not progress in otherwise effective instruction are not responsive to that instruction (Fuchs & Fuchs, 2007; Klotz & Canter, 2006).

Response to Intervention (RTI) is therefore an initiative that many states are using not only to identify students in need of special assistance but also to provide tiers of assistance in order to minimize the number of students identified for special education services. A complete description of RTI is beyond the scope of this book, but we mention it here in the chapter on assessment planning because planning for and implementing RTI-related assessment is increasingly a part of teachers' work. The assessment principles you are learning in this book will help you with the assessment you do for RTI.

Assessment for RTI involves planning for screening and for progress monitoring. As students enter school in kindergarten, they are screened to see whether they are at risk for not responding to regular instruction, typically by assessing readiness for reading and mathematics. Students who are potentially at risk are identified for **progress monitoring**, which is regular, classroom-based assessment to examine how students are responding to instruction.

Students who do not make progress—who are not responsive to the primary instruction—are identified for a first tier of assistance, typically some type of tutoring. Again, progress monitoring charts their improvement (or not) on basic elements of classroom instruction (e.g., letter recognition, reading fluency, or math problem solving, depending on the student). A specified amount of increase in achievement on the classroom-based assessment identifies students who respond to this first-tier intervention. Students who do not make progress are further identified for a second tier of intervention, for example, more intensive tutoring. Progress monitoring continues, assessing the responsiveness of the student to the second tier of intervention. If students do not respond with increased achievement, then they are eligible for more comprehensive evaluation and potential third-tier intervention, for example, learning or behavioral disability certification and special education placement. Even then, progress monitoring continues.

The intent of such a system is that ongoing progress monitoring will help the intermediate interventions work. Many students, with additional assistance, can make progress and do not need the more acute intervention of special education placement. Progress monitoring is the means by which this is determined. Progress monitoring usually takes the form of what once was called curriculum-based measurement (CBM) or curriculum-based assessment (CBA) in the literature (Fuchs & Fuchs, 2007). These assessments are made up of tasks (like reading a passage) or items (like math problems) that are part of regular classroom instruction. Achievement is typically mapped by graphing scores, for example, number of words read correctly per minute or number of problems solved correctly in some fixed amount of time. Appropriate and responsive progress is typically defined as an increase in achievement (e.g., weekly) sufficient to reach the student's goal by some stated time or by comparing the slope of the line graphing achievement to a cutoff level specified in a research-based program (Fuchs & Fuchs, 2007; Klotz & Canter, 2006).

If your school or district uses RTI methods, you will be involved in planning, administering, record keeping, and decision making for progress monitoring. Your understanding of assessment planning and assessment quality principles will help you with this work.

MyLab Education Self-Check 6.2

MyLab Education Applicaton Exercise 6.2:
Analyzing a Classroom Assessment Episode

USING TECHNOLOGY AS AN AID IN ASSESSMENT

Technological applications are increasing quickly, for both local classroom and school assessment and for large-scale testing. In this section, we discuss using technology in assessment for local classroom and school assessment. Chapter 18 discusses technology use for large-scale assessment.

Schools encounter four challenges as they try to integrate technology into assessment (BECTA, 2010). First, using technology to integrate assessment into everyday learning is a challenge. We think of this as the "tool" issue. Technology should be a tool for learning, as pencils and composition books were in a former day, not the focus of learning itself except in special cases. Second, locating and acquiring high-quality assessment tools is a challenge. Third, making assessment information available online, for parents and others, holds many challenges, both in the technology itself and in interpreting and presenting assessment information in a comprehensible way to a diverse audience. Fourth, sharing assessment information appropriately, for example between schools, is a challenge.

As schools tool up with technology, they should first identify what type of assessment support is needed and then select a technology that suits that purpose. A common pattern is for schools first to look to technology to support routine assessment tasks, then to use technology to create new learning networks, and finally to develop collaborative technologies (BECTA, 2010).

Technology to Support Routine Assessment Tasks

Examples of routine assessment tasks for which the assistance of technology has been harnessed include databases of assessment tasks, analysis tools, and grading software. We will have more to say about grading software in Chapter 15. Software, hardware, and related products vary greatly not only in their quality, cost, and user-friendliness but also in how well they match your teaching and school's instructional goals. Some programs can be run right out of the box, whereas others require considerable training. We are not able to review the products here. You can visit the *T.H.E. Journal* website (thejournal.com) or websites of firms that produce assessment and item-analysis software (e.g., Assessment Systems Corporation at assess.com).

Databases of Assessment Tasks Vendors have created software that allows banking or storing test items in a computer file (i.e., both the item's text and graphics). The software then allows you to select items from the bank, assemble tests, and print them for duplication. Item banking software can also be purchased without the items, allowing local teachers to input their own items. Some item banking software permits tests to be administered via intranet or Internet. Other software products offer alignment of assessments with state standards and school curriculum objectives. There are also databases of performance tasks. Item banks are typically purchased as software, but performance tasks are also offered for sale individually via the Internet.

Document storage software can be useful in creating databases of past papers and other assignments, which can be supportive especially of formative assessment. Saving past copies of student work gives teachers a bank of exemplars to use with current students.

Analysis Tools In some schools, students' responses on special answer sheets can be scanned directly into a program that does item analyses (see Chapter 14). In other schools, the scanner creates a computer file, but you must use your own program to analyze the data. You can duplicate much of the analysis done by specialized programs using a standard spreadsheet program that comes with office suite programs. Assessment Systems Corporation has free software for analyzing classroom tests (limit 50 items and 50 examinees). It is called CITAS (Classic Item and Test Analysis Spreadsheet) and is available at assess.com.

Using Technology to Create New Learning and Assessment Networks

Assessment networking tools like e-Portfolio software allow for both the collection of assessment evidence and the provision of feedback. In some such software, students as well as teachers can comment on the work of others. Some portfolio software are essentially document storage and comment tools. Others allow integration with other technologies, for example, video and audio files. Many e-Portfolio platforms are web based, which makes moving, sharing, and updating software much easier.

Using Collaborative Technologies

As schools develop experience, expertise, and a comfort level with integrating technology into assessment, they move past using technology to support what formerly were paper-and-pencil functions and into the realm sometimes called "Web 2.0." This expression refers to websites that do more than just dispense information, but rather allow the user to interact with the information. Blogs and wikis are examples of such collaborative technologies. Wikis are websites that allow users to change the content. Blogs are online collection of discrete posts; a user can respond to someone else's post, but cannot change it. Blogs are primarily text based, but there are blogs for posting pictures, videos, and audio files as well.

The potential effect on assessment of Web 2.0 technologies is greatest in the area of assessing higher-order thinking, where assessment and feedback go beyond whether a student's knowledge is correct. As the chapters in this section have demonstrated, assessment tasks are designed to make student thinking visible. Blogs and wikis allow individuals and groups of students to demonstrate what they are thinking, how they respond to the thinking of others, and what new thinking—and sometimes new products, as well—results. There is also a great potential for integrating assessment with learning, as students monitor and change their own thinking as a result of participation.

Wiki software has six core functions (De Wever, Van Keer, Schellens, & Valke, 2011). The *editing* function allows users to change the content of the wiki page. The *links* function allows users to link to other pages, forming a network. The *history* function allows users to return to a previous version of a page and to compare two versions of the same page. The *recent changes* function gives users a summary of recent changes to a page. The *sandbox* function allows users to experiment with changes without ruining a page. The *search* function allows users to search the wiki page. All of these functions have assessment potential. The editing and links function are especially suited to assessing the jointly constructed knowledge and understanding produced by a group of students working on a wiki. The history and recent changes functions are especially suited to assessing students' collaborative group process.

However, this evidence is very complex. Some recent research with students in higher education working on wiki projects demonstrates that the complexity of the evidence emphasizes the importance of the regular assessment principles we have discussed in this chapter. De Wever and his colleagues (2011) studied the reliability of rubrics among university students' self- and peer-assessments of collaborative group processes within their own groups. They gave students a rubric to use for this purpose. Reliability of overall peer assessment was high. Reliability for each criterion was not high at first, but improved as students had more explanation of the rubric and more experience with using it. These findings are consistent with what one would find with any self- or peer-assessment tool.

Ng and Lai (2012), however, did not find assessment results for self- and peer-assessment of wiki pages to be consistent. Probably the reason for this inconsistency is that their students were assigned to write or adapt their own rubrics, and each group's rubric was different. Two of the groups' rubrics included a criterion for collaborative work, and three did not. Furthermore, the description of the groups' rubrics demonstrates that what the authors called "rubrics" were really rating scales, using numerical or evaluative scales ("excellent," "good," and so on) instead of performance-level descriptions. Inconsistency in criteria and scales without performance-level descriptions would be an issue for any kind of performance assessment, not just assessment in a wiki context.

It seems reasonable to conclude that for the most part, the same assessment principles apply for assessment using technology for collaborative learning as for assessment of learning completed without technology. What is different is the nature of what is assessed, which can be more complex on several dimensions than products or processes completed without technology. One difference between assessment of collaborative learning with technology and other assessment that may turn out to be very important is the availability of many layers of self- and peer-assessment that are supported by technology-based collaborative learning. As our understanding of how students give and receive such feedback in technology-based collaborative learning evolves, we predict that our understanding of the effects of feedback will increase.

Using Technology to Make Tests More Accessible to Students with Disabilities

Many nonessential elements of testing can be altered or enhanced with computer applications that make tests more accessible to students with disabilities. These changes can be as simple as enlarging the font on a test, using a word processing program. They can be as complex as using augmentative communications systems for students who cannot speak. Dictionaries, thesauruses, and grammar checkers can help students prepare written test answers. Technology can assist a teacher in calculating readability of the text in assessments. The Internet can be a source of images to help make test items readable.

Teacher judgment is required to decide what accommodations are appropriate for particular students and particular assessments. For example, enlarging the font on a reading test would probably not change the construct being measured; it would merely make it easier for the student to read the passages. Changing the readability level of the passages, however, would change the construct being measured.

Technological solutions to problems of accessibility are changing at a fast pace. Salend (2009) organized various currently available technology solutions according to the principles of universal design. See Appendix E for this helpful list. The term *universal design* refers to the concept of preparing assessments to maximize accessibility for all students. It is a term that began in the field of architecture and is more often discussed in terms of large-scale assessments. For this reason, we discuss universal design in more detail in Chapter 18. For present purposes, however, our point is that there are many ways to make classroom tests more accessible, and this accessibility has greatly expanded with the availability of computer applications.

CONCLUSION

This chapter has introduced basic classroom assessment planning. The most important planning principle is to base both assessment and instruction on learning objectives and a deep understanding of the essential knowledge and skills students need to achieve them. The planning principles in this chapter apply to both formative and summative assessment. Chapters 7 and 8 discuss diagnostic and formative assessment in more detail. This chapter has also introduced basic assessment formats. Chapters 9 through 13 show how to create assessments in each of these formats in turn.

EXERCISES

1. Visit a classroom (if you are not an in-service teacher) or use your own teaching experience to complete the following:
    a. Identify one or more specific examples of formative and summative classroom assessment.
    b. For each example, describe what assessment tools and information the teacher used to make that decision.
    c. Classify each tool or technique into one of the assessment-option categories shown in Figure 6.7.
2. Visit a classroom, or look around your own classroom, and list all the instructional resources that provide assessment or assessment-like tools.
    a. Classify each as true-false, multiple-choice, matching, essay, short-answer, completion, performance assessments, projects, portfolios, oral questioning strategies, observation strategies, or in-depth interviewing strategies.
    b. Which type(s) is (are) dominant?
    c. Tally the thinking skill levels each appears to assess. Which levels of thinking do the majority seem to assess?
    d. Judge the quality of each of these materials using the criteria in Figure 3.1.
3. Select a unit in your subject area for which you might craft a summative assessment instrument. Develop a complete blueprint for this assessment, using Figure 6.4 as a model. Describe the kinds of tasks you would include, and explain how you would decide whether the tasks matched the learning objectives. Estimate the amount of time it would take students to complete your assessment.
4. Develop an assessment plan for a unit of instruction in your area. Using Figure 6.2 as a model, list lessons and learning objectives, types of assessment, purpose(s) of assessment, and actions to take using assessment results. Share your results with your classmates.
5. Develop an assessment plan for a marking period or a semester in an area you teach. Using Figure 6.1 as a model, include the standard(s) you are teaching, the time frame for the units, the formative and summative assessment strategies, and the weighting of the assessments within units and across units (i.e., for the entire time periods). Share your results with your classmates.

7

Diagnostic and Formative Assessments

KEY CONCEPTS

1. Diagnostic assessment is conducted to identify what knowledge and skills a student has mastered and potential reasons for nonmastery. Six approaches to diagnostic assessment are each based on a different definition of a learning "deficit."

2. Formative assessment is a cycle: Students and teachers focus on a learning target, evaluate current student work against the target, act to move the work closer to the target, and repeat the process. Unlike diagnostic assessment, formative assessment seeks to identify both strengths and weaknesses and involves both students and teachers. Six formative assessment strategies include sharing learning targets and criteria for success, giving feedback, fostering student self-assessment and goal setting, asking effective questions, and helping students ask effective questions.

IMPORTANT TERMS

concept mapping
learning progression
passing score
student self-assessment
surface feature

Some authors consider diagnostic assessment and formative assessment as two separate practices, one that takes place before instruction and one during instruction. Our perspective is that the older term *diagnostic assessment* and the newer term *formative assessment* are getting at a similar idea. Diagnostic assessment puts the emphasis on the teacher understanding the status of student learning for the sake of planning instruction. Formative assessment puts the emphasis on the students, as well as teachers, understanding the status of learning, for the purpose of identifying next steps to take for improvement (Assessment Reform Group, 2002). Consequently, a timing distinction does not seem completely useful.

In this chapter, we present six approaches to diagnosing learning difficulties, which teachers will find useful for ferreting out problems in enough detail to address them specifically in lesson plans. Next, we present six formative assessment strategies that can be implemented during the course of instruction and involve students in decisions about their learning.

DIAGNOSTIC ASSESSMENT

Diagnostic assessment of learning difficulties serves two related purposes: (1) to identify which learning targets a student has not mastered and (2) to suggest possible causes or reasons why the student has not mastered the learning targets. The emphasis is on learning deficits, that is, remediation of what the student does not know. Different approaches to diagnosis provide different levels of detail about students' deficits in learning. They also differ in the degree to which they emphasize identifying the targets not mastered or possible reasons why. We discuss six approaches here. Figure 7.1 illustrates each of the first four approaches with a specific example and serves as a tool for comparing the approaches. The last two approaches, illustrated later, are more in line with cognitively oriented instructional psychology.

FIGURE 7.1   **Examples of how different approaches to diagnostic assessment interpret the same student's performance.**

Examples of items along with responses of a hypothetical student

(a)	(b)	(c)	(d)	(e)	(f)	(g)	(h)	(i)
17	15	43	337	654	43	63	562	667
−12	−13	−32	−226	−423	−25	−57	−453	−374
5	2	11	111	231	×22	×14	×111	×313

Total score for subtraction = 5/9 or 56%. Percentile rank = 18

Approach 1.   Profile of strengths and weaknesses
   The score on the subtraction subtest shown above is compared to the scores on other subtests such as addition, multiplication, division, etc. A profile of strengths and weaknesses in arithmetic is created for each student.

Example: The score of five correct has a percentile rank of 18 and is lower than other subtest scores.

Interpretation of the results: The student is weak in subtraction.

Approaches 2 and 3. Prerequisite hierarchy combined with mastery of specific objectives
   The items above may be derived from a hierarchy of prerequisite arithmetic skills and the mastery of each skill in the hierarchy is assessed.

Example:	*Hierarchy of Skills*	*Score*
	(4) Subtract 3-digit numbers requiring borrowing from either tens' or hundreds' place. [Items (h) and (i)]	$^0/_2$ or 0 %
	(3) Subtract 2-digit numbers with borrowing from tens' place. [Items (f) and (g)]	$^1/_2$ or 50 %
	(2) Subtract two 2-digit and two 3-digit numbers when borrowing is not needed. [Items (c), (d), and (e)]	$^3/_3$ or 100 %
	(1) Subtract 2-digit numbers when numbers are less than 20. [Items (a) and (b)]	$^2/_2$ or 100 %

Interpretation of the results: The student has mastered the prerequisite Objectives 1 and 2, but has not mastered Objectives 3 and 4. Instruction should begin with Objective 3.

Approach 4. Identifying Errors
   The subtraction item(s) that the student answered incorrectly are studied and the student's errors are identified.

Example: The student's responses to Items (f), (g), (h), and (i) are wrong. These are studied to identify the type(s) of errors the student made.

Interpretation of the results: The student is not renaming (regrouping) from tens' to units' place and from hundreds' to tens' place.

Approach 1: Profiling Content Strengths and Weaknesses

In this approach, a deficit is defined as a student's low standing, relative to peers, in a broad learning outcome area in a subject. For example, a student may have less ability in subtraction and division than in addition and multiplication compared to peers. A school subject—say, elementary arithmetic or elementary reading—is subdivided into areas, each of which is treated as a separate trait or ability. *KeyMath*™-3 *Diagnostic Assessment* (Connolly, 2007), for example, divides mathematics into three areas (basic concepts, operations, and applications) and 10 subareas (numeration, algebra, geometry, measurement, data analysis and probability, mental computation and estimation, addition and subtraction, multiplication and division, foundations of problem solving, applied problem solving) and assesses a student in each area. Results are reported as a profile of strengths and weaknesses over the 10 subareas. As is typical of tests in this category, strengths and weaknesses are interpreted in norm-referenced ways: A student with a "weakness" is significantly below the norm. Percentile ranks (discussed in Chapter 17) are the primary type of norm-referenced score used in this context.

Strengths   This approach to diagnostic assessment is most useful to give you a general idea about students' performance in subareas of a subject matter. It fits with the intentions many states have of making large-scale test data "formative."

Weaknesses   If the set of items that a test has to indicate performance on a particular standard contains only a handful of items or tasks, the subtest scores probably will be unreliable. As a result, the students' strengths and weaknesses may be exaggerated or masked by chance errors of measurement.

Note that this approach does not tell you about attainment of particular learning goals in the absolute sense; rather, it gives relative strengths and weaknesses within the group. Diagnosis with such tests provides you with only general information about where their problems lie. It is much like saying, "The treasure lies to the north." The information is helpful, but it leaves you with a lot of work to do before the treasure can be found.

A good educational diagnostician will use the initial test results to formulate hypotheses concerning students' difficulties. You confirm or reject these hypotheses by following up and gathering additional information. Thus, although the initial profile of strengths and weaknesses may be unreliable, the final diagnosis will be much more reliable.

Approach 2: Identifying Prerequisite Deficits

In this approach, a deficit is defined as a student's failure to have learned concepts and skills necessary to profit from instruction in a course or a unit. Select one learning objective the student must be able to perform. Analyze it to identify the prerequisites a student must learn in order to achieve it. For each prerequisite identified, repeat the same analysis, generating a hierarchy of prerequisite performances. Once you have created the hierarchy, assess each student with several items for each of the prerequisites identified. At a minimum, use four or five items per prerequisite in the hierarchy.

This backward analytic procedure identifies critical prior learning, the lack of which could cause students problems in subsequent learning. The difference between this approach and the previous one is that here you focus on whether each prerequisite was learned rather than on the pattern of profile strengths and weaknesses. Your interpretation of results is criterion-referenced rather than norm-referenced. Figure 7.2 shows an example of a learning hierarchy for computational subtraction.

Strengths   This approach very specifically identifies skills that students need to learn before they are ready to be taught new learning targets. A hierarchy suggests the sequence for teaching the prerequisites. Assessments of prerequisite knowledge and skills are most helpful when you know very little about the students, especially when you expect large differences in their mastery of the prerequisites. Once you know each student's command of the prerequisites, you can tailor your teaching to meet his or her needs.

Weaknesses   This approach is limited by the care and accuracy with which you analyze the learning requirements of your curriculum. If you do not identify the proper prerequisites, your assessment will lack validity. Further, in a continuous-progress curriculum, the distinction between prerequisites

FIGURE 7.2   Prerequisite hierarchy of a subtraction unit.

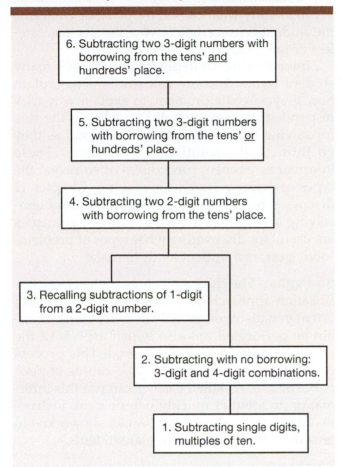

and "regular learning" is arbitrary, based more or less on instructional convenience.

The learning theory underlying this approach is a building-block approach, in which prerequisite performances build one on another to facilitate the learning of new targets. It is not clear that this building-block approach to learning is an appropriate teaching strategy for all subjects and for all students. Further, it does not provide information about *how* students understand or conceptualize their prerequisite knowledge.

Approach 3: Identifying Objectives Not Mastered

In this approach, a deficit is defined as a student's failure to master one or more end-of-instruction learning goals. Most so-called formative uses of state test data are in this category, for example, as results are used to group students as "below basic" on particular standards. Short tests assess each objective. The difference between this approach and the identifying prerequisite deficits

approach is that here you assess only the objectives that are the outcomes of the unit or the course, not the prerequisite objectives.

The diagnostic information you want to obtain from this approach is a list of learning objectives that students have and have not mastered. For each teaching unit, identify and write statements of the learning objectives that are the main outcomes of the unit or the course. For each learning objective, design four to eight test items. If possible, have another teacher review each item and rate how closely it matches the learning objectives. Revise the items as necessary to obtain a closer match. Assemble the items into a single assessment instrument if the list of learning objectives is relatively short (less than six). Otherwise, depending on the students' educational development, you may need to divide the assessment into two or more instruments. For ease of scoring, keep all the items that assess the same objective together in one assessment.

Set a "mastery" or passing score for each learning target. A frequently used **passing score** is 80 percent (or as near as you can come to this with the number of items you have for assessing a learning target). There is no educational justification for 80 percent, however. The important point is not the exact value of the passing score or passing percentage. Rather, it is the minimum level of knowledge a student needs to demonstrate with respect to each learning objective to benefit from further instruction. This amount may vary from one objective to the next. Use your own judgment, remembering that setting a standard too low or too high results in misclassifying students as masters or nonmasters.

Administer the assessment to the students, then separately score each learning objective. Prepare a class list and chart in which you can record the students' scores on each objective. This system lets you identify students with similar deficits. Students should receive remedial instruction on these objectives.

Strengths   Diagnostic assessments based on specific objectives are appealing because they (a) focus on specific and limited learning goals to teach, (b) communicate learning goals in an easy-to-understand form, and (c) focus your attention on students' observed performance. These features make assessment easier, instructional decision making simpler, and public accountability clearer.

Weaknesses Objectives-based diagnostic assessments are generally plagued with measurement error, primarily because the assessments tend to have too few items per objective. If you use a diagnostic assessment to decide whether a student has "mastered" an objective, evaluate its quality using an index such as percentage agreement, rather than a traditional reliability coefficient. Percentage agreement is discussed in Chapter 4. Consistency of classification (i.e., of mastery or nonmastery) is the main focus, rather than consistency of students' exact scores.

The objectives approach to diagnostic assessment has other serious limitations. The results give you little information about how to remediate the deficits you discover. As for identifying prerequisite deficits, this approach does not provide information about *how* students understand or conceptualize their knowledge. Further, a student's knowledge base is seen as a simple sum of previously learned specific behaviors.

Approach 4: Identifying Students' Errors

In this approach, a deficit is defined as the type(s) of errors a student makes. The goal is to identify student errors, rather than making a simple mastery-nonmastery decision about overall performance on a particular objective. Examples of errors are failure to regroup when "borrowing" in subtraction, improper pronunciation of vowels when reading, reversing *i* and *e* when spelling, and producing a sentence fragment when writing. Once you identify and classify a student's errors, you can attempt to provide instruction to remediate them.

Accurate error identification takes considerable experience and skill. Further, there may be more than one cause for an error. Consider the subtraction problems in Figure 7.1, for example. An inexperienced or unskilled teacher may not recognize the possible cause of the student's mistakes. Oftentimes, such teachers will say the student was "not careful" or "made careless errors." However, students' errors are rarely careless or random. Rather, *students' errors are often systematic*. Students may apply a rule or a procedure consistently in both appropriate and inappropriate situations. For instance, in Figure 7.1, the student appears to have consistently applied this rule: "Subtract the smaller digit from the larger digit." This rule works for problems (a) through (e), but does not work for problems (f) through (i). *It is important, therefore, that you consider every error a student makes as having some systematic cause.* Try to identify what caused the error, or what rule the student is using, before you dismiss it as careless or random.

Interviewing students helps uncover many student errors. You can ask students to explain how they solved a problem, to explain why they responded the way they did, to tell you the rule for solving the problem, or to talk aloud as they go through the solutions to problems. These informal assessment procedures often reveal the types of errors a student is making. Chapter 11 discusses higher-order thinking and problem-solving assessment. Those assessment strategies are useful for discovering what types of problem-solving errors a student tends to make.

Strengths The chief advantage of the error classification approach over the objectives approach is that you discover not only *that* an objective cannot be performed but also which aspects of the student's performance are flawed. This process narrows your search for possible causes of poor performance. A skilled teacher can use this information to identify quickly one or more instructional procedures that have previously worked to remediate the error with similar students.

Weaknesses Error classification procedures have some drawbacks. Students make many different kinds of errors, and frequently students demonstrate the same error for different reasons, so remedial instruction could be misdirected. Also, the amount of individual assessment and interpretation required seems prohibitive, given the amount of instructional time available. More serious, however, is the problem that if diagnosis only classifies errors, it still fails to identify the thinking processes a student has used to produce the errors. Just knowing the type of error (failing to borrow in subtraction) does not tell you the appropriate knowledge structures and cognitive processes a student needs to reach the desired outcome.

Approach 5: Identifying Student Knowledge Structures

In this approach, a deficit is defined as a student's inappropriate or incorrect mental organization of concepts and their interrelationships. A shortcoming of the diagnostic assessment approaches already mentioned is their strong ties to the **surface features** of subject-matter information and problem solving. Diagnosis should focus

FIGURE 7.3 **Hypothetical example of a student's concept map of rocks.**

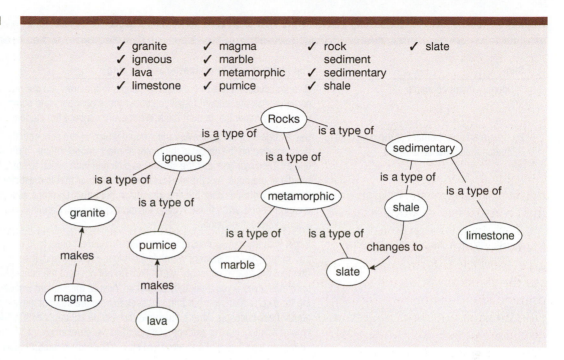

more on how students perceive the structure or organization of that content and how they process information and knowledge to solve problems using that content knowledge.

One example of preinstructional assessment is our Chapter 6 discussion of a cold drink and a sweater. If you ask younger students what will happen to the temperature of a bottle of cold soft drink when it is wrapped up in a wool sweater, many will say that the sweater will warm the drink. In their schemata, "sweater" is something that Mother tells you to put on to keep warm. Thus, even though you may explain things clearly, they do not believe that a sweater has insulating properties that will keep a cold drink cold. You must relate the new concepts to students' current schemata and help them reconstruct their knowledge structures, so they understand how keeping their bodies warm and keeping the soft drink cold are linked by the concept of insulation. To believe it, they need to understand the principles of insulation and how a sweater works as an insulator.

Several methods are used to assess students' knowledge structures. These methods share the common perspective that as individuals become more proficient, their knowledge becomes more interconnected, more deeply organized, and more accessible. Probably the one most commonly used in classrooms is **concept mapping**. A concept map is a graphic way to represent how a student understands the relationships among the major concepts in the subject. An example of how a

student might organize concepts related to a science unit on rocks is shown in Figure 7.3.

Notice that this concept map shows that the student has fairly well-organized knowledge of this unit's concepts. However, some important concept linkages are missing. For the most part, the student understands the concepts hierarchically (e.g., *granite* and *pumice* are included in the category called *igneous*, which is a type of *rock*). The student shows only one connection that is related to change or transformation of specific rocks or categories of rocks (*shale* changes to *slate*). The student can't fit into the map the concept *sediment* and so doesn't know that sediment can form *shale* or *limestone*. Other linkages are missing, too: Igneous rocks can weather and transform into sediment and sedimentary rocks; sedimentary rocks can form metamorphic rocks, which in turn can weather and return back to sedimentary rocks; and limestone can change into marble.

Suggestions for how to capture a student's concept map are given in Figure 7.4. For this task, the teacher shows a student the list of concepts at the top of Figure 7.3 and works with the student individually, following the procedure described in Figure 7.4, to create the concept map. As each concept is used in the map, it is crossed off the list.

As you can see from the example, using this approach to diagnosing requires individually assessing students, thoroughly knowing the subject so you can identify where a student has a missing link, and using considerable judgment when interpreting the resulting concept map. The

FIGURE 7.4   Suggestions for conducting a student interview to create a concept map useful for assessment.

Step	The focus of your interviewing and probing
1. Identify major concepts	Give the student a few of the major concepts in the area you are probing. You could put these on cards. Ask the student to tell you about these concepts and some of the other things about which they make the student think. Write every concept the student mentions in a list.
2. Create an arrangement of the concepts to match the student's thinking	Use a large sheet of paper. Ask the student which of the concepts (including the ones you initially showed on the cards) is the major or most important one. If the student does not identify one as the major one, ask the student to pick one with which to start. Write this concept in the middle of the page. Ask the student to select another that is most closely related to the one on the page. Write this near the one already on the page. Continue asking for the ones nearest to the central one. Write these around the central concept. Continue with the remaining concepts, asking where they belong.
3. Establish how the student relates the concepts to one another	Begin with the central concept, work with the nearest ones to it, one at a time, and take each pair in turn. Ask the student whether the two are related and, if so, why or how they are related. Connect the related concepts with a line. Do not connect the concepts the student says are unrelated, even if you think they should be. Assure the student frequently that you are not looking for a correct answer but that you seek to help the student explain how he or she is thinking about these concepts. After connecting the related concepts with a line, write on the line the type of relationship the student tells you (e.g., "is an example of," "is a," "causes," "is part of," "it makes it go," etc.). If a student just says, "They are related," probe further to understand what the relationship is.
4. Give feedback to the student and rearrange the map	Show the student the map so far. Talk about the arrangement. Give feedback to the student, explaining what the map tells you about the student's thinking, and ask if this is correct. Rearrange the map so that it better represents the student's thinking and understanding of the concepts. Talk about each concept and its relationships. Add new concepts if the student mentions them and determine how they are linked to the mapped concepts. Redraw the map if necessary.
5. Elaborate the map to show new concepts, linkages, and examples	Further discuss the rearranged map with the student. Ask the student to tell you more: What else does the student know about these concepts, what are some examples, why are the concepts related, etc.? Incorporate this new information into the map then add branches and expansions as necessary to depict the student's thinking.
6. Explore cross-linkages and complex relationships	Go over the map drawn to this point with the student. Ask the student about the pairs of concepts previously unconnected and about the connections of new concepts mentioned in Step 5. Ask the student if he or she thinks three or four concepts should be connected together and why. Record these complex relationships.
7. Give feedback to the student and rearrange to make the final map	Show the map to the student and discuss with the student what the map tells you about the student's thinking. Ask the student if this is accurate and rearrange the map to make it more accurately describe the student's organization of the concepts. Stop here if you have sufficient detail to understand the student's organization of the concepts. Otherwise, repeat Steps 5 and 6.

validity of your judgments improves if you corroborate your assessment of a student's "missing links" with other evidence about how the student understands the concepts, such as problem-solving tasks and the student's essays and class responses. Also, keep in mind that there may be more than one correct way to relate the information; more than one schema may be correct.

Strengths   This diagnostic approach focuses your attention on how a student thinks about the concepts and their interrelationships. It gives you some insight into how the student sees the concepts organized and, perhaps, how they might be related to other concepts and procedures a student has learned. These insights may help you explain why students are making errors, or why they are having difficulty solving problems.

Weaknesses   These procedures are experimental. We do not know the degree to which the results are valid, or whether different teachers would reach the same diagnosis for the same student. The way a student reacts to the teacher and the interviewing situation may drastically affect the results. Be cautious, therefore, when you interpret the results.

Approach 6: Identifying Competencies for Solving Word Problems

In this approach, a deficit is defined as a student's inability to perform one or more of the components necessary to solve a word problem. Solving word problems comprises a significant number of learning outcomes in social studies, mathematics, and science. A word problem is a short verbal account of a more or less realistic situation that requires students to use the given information to answer a question. Consider the following word problem:

Example

A bus is carrying 38 passengers. It stops at a bus stop, where 23 passengers get off the bus and 11 other passengers get on. How many passengers are on the bus as it pulls away from this bus stop?

To solve this problem, a student must mentally process it using knowledge from long-term memory in several ways (Mayer, Larkin, & Kadane, 1984):

1. *Translation*—The student must understand each statement in the problem. This kind of assessment requires a student to use factual and linguistic knowledge. To assess linguistic knowledge, focus your questions on the key terms and key phrases students must understand to translate the statement into a mental model of the problem.

Example

For example, in the preceding problem, a student must understand the concepts of *bus, carrying passengers, bus stop, get off the bus, get on the bus*, and *pulls away from this bus stop*. Linguistically, the student has to understand the meaning of the question, "How many passengers are on the bus as it pulls away from this bus stop?" Ask questions like: "What does 'pull away' mean in this sentence?"

2. *Understanding*—The student must form a mental representation or model of the problem. In other words, the student must use schematic knowledge to recognize how the problem fits into a general framework to identify the type of problem it is. (See Chapter 12 for a discussion of schemata.) To assess schematic knowledge, ask students questions to see if they know which rules or principles they must use to solve the problem.

Example

In the preceding problem, a student must recognize that this is an arithmetic problem involving only addition and subtraction. Ask: "What operations would you use to solve this problem?"

3. *Planning*—The student must form a strategy or plan for solving the problem. The student must use strategic knowledge. (See Chapter 11 for a discussion of assessing solution strategies.) To assess strategic knowledge, focus on the students' ability to identify the proper sequence of steps or the proper processes needed to reach the answer. For arithmetic word problems, teachers should determine whether students know which numbers to use, which operations to use with those numbers, and which order to use when applying those operations. You may wish to show students several sequences and ask which is the appropriate one for the given problem. All the numbers in the alternative solution strategies should relate to the word problem at hand.

Example

A student must recognize that to know how many passengers are on the bus as it leaves the bus stop, you must subtract from the 38 on the bus those 23 who got off at the stop and add to that remainder the 11 who got on at the stop. Arithmetically, the strategy is $(38 - 23) + 11$. (*Note:* Many problems may have more than one correct strategy.) Ask: "What number sentence would you write to solve this problem?"

4. *Execution*—The student must use an appropriate algorithm (procedure) and carry out the calculations or steps properly. The student must use algorithmic knowledge. To assess algorithmic knowledge, craft an item that presents the proper sequence and the proper numbers. The focus is on whether students can follow the algorithm without the context of the word problem. To avoid clueing the students as to the proper schema and strategy, present the algorithmic item after you have completed questioning for linguistic, schematic, and strategic knowledge.

Example

The student must be able to correctly arrive at 26 as the number of passengers on the bus as it leaves the bus stop. Ask students to calculate $(38 - 23) + 11 = $ ____ .

The diagnosis in this approach is to identify students who are unable to solve word problems and whether their deficits lie in linguistic and factual knowledge, schematic knowledge, strategic knowledge, and/or algorithmic knowledge. Your remedial instruction focuses on teaching students to use the type of knowledge in which they are deficient.

Strengths   This approach is most appropriate when you have word problems that are solved by applying a formula or a set of arithmetic operations in an algorithm. These include arithmetic word problems (such as money, time, rate, and cost), word problems in algebra, statistics word problems, social studies word problems involving mathematics, and science word problems. The framework you use to interpret the diagnosis (linguistic, schematic, strategic, and algorithmic knowledge) can be applied consistently across many categories of problems. The framework also suggests how you could remediate a student's deficits.

Weaknesses   This approach requires many items per knowledge category to ensure sufficient reliability. The procedure is time-consuming. Patterns you observe for one type of problem (e.g., money) may not emerge in other problem types (e.g., time). This fact makes diagnosis less valid if you try to generalize student deficits across problem types. The validity of the approach also depends heavily on how well you are able to identify key phrases, appropriate schemata, and appropriate strategies for solving the problems. If multiple strategies for problem solving are appropriate, you must be careful to allow students to express these and not confuse the diagnosis by discounting them.

> **MyLab Education** **Self-Check 7.1**
>
> **MyLab Education** **Application Exercise 7.1:**
> Interpreting Diagnostic Information

FORMATIVE ASSESSMENT

While the main purpose of diagnostic assessment is to support remediation of learning deficits, the main purpose of formative assessment is to support learning at all levels, improving on strengths as well as remediating weaknesses. In fact, another term for *formative assessment* is *assessment for learning*. And while the main emphasis in diagnostic assessment is to provide information for teacher planning, the main emphasis in formative assessment is to involve students in both generating and using assessment information.

Formative assessment cycles assessment information back into the learning process itself. Effective formative assessment is based on sharing learning goals with students and places a high value on appropriate teacher feedback and **student self-assessment**. Helping teachers develop effective formative assessment skills is the most cost-effective strategy for raising student achievement known today (Wiliam, 2007). This is because of its "double-barreled" nature, namely, that formative assessment addresses student cognitive and motivational needs at the same time.

When we say formative assessment is a cycle, we mean the following: Students and teachers focus on a learning target, evaluate current student work against the target, act to move the work closer to the target, and repeat the process. This three-step process is an oversimplification, but it is a useful pattern to keep in mind for teaching and assessment (Sadler, 1983, 1989; Hattie & Timperley, 2007). In fact, if you had to only learn one thing about teaching, you might choose this cycle. From a student's point of view, the cycle is as follows:

- What am I aiming for?
- How close am I now?
- What else do I have to do to get there?

Teachers can obtain formative assessment information by talking with students, observing them working, or looking at the work itself. Similarly, students can obtain formative assessment information by monitoring either their work processes or products. All formative assessment strategies are systematic ways of collecting evidence about work processes or products and using the resulting evidence to improve the work and further learning.

Emily Roberts, Kindergarten teacher
Jefferson City Public Schools, Jefferson City, MO

MyLab Education

Video Example 7.1

These elementary school teachers describe the differences in both student learning and teacher planning that come with implementing formative assessment. In this video, they use the term "assessment for learning." Notice how their comments show that the most powerful strategy, and the foundation for all other formative assessment strategies, is making sure students understand their learning target for every lesson.

These secondary school teachers describe how the formative learning cycle makes a huge difference in their instructional planning and their students' learning. Notice how they describe that formative assessment (assessment for learning) helps shift students' focus from getting a good grade to understanding and learning and improves student motivation to learn.

Figure 7.5 provides examples of formative assessments classified according to the types of learning targets and activities to which they are suited. Examples of how to use the results of these formative assessments are also given. If the assessment information is not used, it cannot be formative, because it cannot advance student learning.

Formative assessment is student-centered, but it starts with the teacher's vision. First, you need to have the learning outcomes clear in your own mind. This is not always as straightforward as it sounds. We once did an evaluation of a professional development program to teach middle school teachers how to assess reading. The middle school teachers had all been trained as English teachers, and their main areas of study had been literature and writing. Of course, they knew what "reading" was, but they didn't understand learning goals in reading well enough to help the students who reached middle school needing basic reading instruction. Without a detailed understanding of the outcomes themselves, what they did with poor readers in their classroom was just "make them read" more, and their assessments indicated the students were—no surprise—poor readers. The professional development program divided reading outcomes into five areas: oral fluency, comprehension, strategy use, higher-order thinking, and motivation. The idea was that the program could then offer assessment techniques for each of the five areas. According to teachers' evaluation interviews, the single best thing the program gave them was not the assessment techniques, but a clearer definition of what it meant to be a good reader. Students began to improve as their teachers became better able to show them what they needed to work on (fluency, comprehension, and so on).

Second, you have to communicate the target to students in ways that they understand. Typically, writing your objective on the board is not enough. Sometimes communicating your goals will involve showing students instead of telling them. For example, silent reading works better in elementary classrooms in which the teacher models silent reading, shares the books she reads, and talks about why she liked them than in classrooms in which the teacher uses silent reading time to catch up on paperwork.

Third, the students have to engage. If you have been successful at communicating a learning target, you will have also helped students see why it is important for them to expend effort to reach it. This can be because of interest ("this topic is cool!") or academic, for example, when students are convinced to learn to write term papers in high school, so they can do what is required in college. It can be because students want to be able to do something you or other adults can do, or something their older peers can do. Sometimes several of these motivations occur at the same time. For any given learning target, there will be a mixture of motivations in your class. For example, one student may be interested in a particular topic and another simply convinced that it is an important school target.

Formative assessment is not used for grading. Students need—and deserve—an opportunity to learn before they are graded on how well they have learned. Formative assessment is used before instruction, to find out where students are, and during instruction, to find out how they are progressing. Formative assessment can be used after instruction and summative assessment, but if it is, the students should have the opportunity to revise their work to reflect their new learning. Formative assessment is informational, not judgmental. Students are free to pay attention to figuring out how they are doing and what they need to work on without worrying about a grade. Make formative assessment a part of your teaching. Plan your instruction in ways that provide opportunities for individual students to make formative decisions about their own learning.

Student self-assessment fosters both achievement and motivation. The effects of good formative assessment on achievement have been reported to be as much as 0.40 to 0.70 standard deviations—the equivalent of moving from the 50th percentile to the 65th or 75th percentile on a

FIGURE 7.5   Examples of formative assessment.

Type of learning target	Formative assessment techniques	Use of results
Learning targets involving concepts	Students reflect on previous learning, attitude, and interest	Extending class discussion Selecting appropriate and interesting class activities Identifying and correcting misconceptions Building on previous knowledge (using no more review than is necessary)
Writing (e.g., descriptive, narrative, persuasive, or expository paragraph)	Peer editing Self-assessment and teacher conference	Revising Future writing Reflecting on why the revision is better than the first draft
Learning math tables, spelling words, and other "facts"	Students predict what study strategies (e.g., flash cards) will work best for them and keep track of what works for them quiz by quiz Students record what they "know" and "don't know," gradually moving the "don'ts" into the "know" category as they progress	Students adjust own study strategies Students see exactly what they know and don't know, and they have control over moving their own knowledge
Science or social studies content from textbooks	Students summarize reading in their own words, meet with a peer, and discuss how their summaries are alike/different Students make lists of vocabulary or concepts they feel they understand and those they find difficult	Extending class discussion Focus studying for unit test
Learning targets involving seatwork	Students have a "teacher alert" on their desks, turned to the happy face or the green light when they're understanding and the sad face or red light when they need teacher help	Individual assistance in a "just in time" fashion, focused on the student-perceived source of difficulty
Learning targets involving classwork	Instead of questioning individual students, all students "vote" their answer, so you can scan the class for understanding Younger children can answer yes-no questions as a group by standing ("Stand up if you think that a soda wrapped in a sweater will get warm.") Older students can use answer cards for multiple choice questions, use electronic answer pads, or write one-minute responses on 3 × 5 cards	Adjust pacing of class instruction Adjust content of class instruction Extending class discussion Identifying and correcting misconceptions Building on previous knowledge (using no more review than is necessary) Understanding where all or most of the class is, not just a few students who have been called on
Learning targets involving projects or assignments graded with rubrics	Students look at examples of previous students' work across a range of quality levels and discuss what makes the work of that quality Students "translate" the rubrics into their own words to make them "kid-friendly" evaluation tools Peer assessment of drafts or partial products Self-assessment and teacher conference	Improved understanding of the qualities of good work Revising and finishing the project or assignment Reflecting on the qualities of one's own work for use in future work
Learning targets involving skills (e.g., reading aloud, using the library or computer, writing)	Students set and record a goal and work toward it Teacher suggests a goal, shares with students Observe students in the process of working (e.g., using a microscope) as well as the finished assignment	Students either realize goal (and set another) or can state how far they have come and what they still need to work on Adjust instruction at the individual or group level, as needed

standardized test (Black & William, 1998b)—or may be somewhat lower, around 0.25 (Kingston & Nash, 2011). These effects exist at all levels—primary, intermediate, and secondary—and are especially noticeable among lower achievers, although there is wide variation by content area. For example, a recent meta-analysis of studies of formative assessment and writing (Graham, Hebert, & Harris, 2015) concluded: "We found that feedback to students about writing from adults, peers, self, and computers statistically enhanced writing quality, yielding average effect sizes of 0.87, 0.58, 0.62, and 0.38, respectively" (p. 523).

There are many reasons for the effectiveness of formative assessment, mostly based in constructivist and socio-cognitive theories of learning (Penuel & Shepard, 2016).

- Formative assessment helps teachers and students identify what students can do with help and what they can do independently.

- Participating in formative assessment is active learning, keeping students on task and focused on learning goals.

- Formative assessment, especially peer and self-evaluation, helps students with the social construction of knowledge.

- Formative assessment allows students to receive feedback on precisely the points they need in order to improve. It shows them what to do next to get better.

Motivational benefits of formative assessment are a little more complicated. Different students respond differently to the various aspects of the formative assessment process. Students who can size up their work, figure out how close they are to their goal, and plan what they need to do to improve are, in fact, learning as they do those things. Carrying out their plans for improvement not only makes their work better but also helps them feel in control, and that practice is motivating. This process, called self-regulation, has been found to be a characteristic of successful, motivated learners (Zimmerman & Schunk, 2011).

Below, we present six strategies for formative assessment as well as examples under each: sharing learning targets and criteria for success, feedback that feeds forward, student goal setting, student self-assessment, asking effective questions, and helping students ask effective questions (Moss & Brookhart, 2009). Other authors organize the same formative assessment concepts and processes into different numbers of strategies. Wiliam (2010, p. 31) lists five strategies: "clarifying, sharing, and understanding learning intentions and criteria for success; engineering effective classroom discussions, questions, and tasks that elicit evidence of learning; providing feedback that moves learners forward; activating students as instructional resources for one another; and activating students as the owners of their own learning." We know a professional developer in formative assessment who uses seven strategies. The number of strategies is not the important thing; the strategies are not theories, but simply ways of organizing teachers' formative assessment practices. The main point is having a workable repertoire of strategies that accomplish the formative assessment purpose: to

have both students and teachers generate and use assessment information to advance learning.

Strategy 1: Sharing Learning Targets and Criteria for Success

"Learning target" is a term that is often used loosely to mean student-friendly phrasing of any intended learning outcome, goal, or objective. While this definition is true in a general sense, we have found that a much more specific use of the word "learning target" is most useful for formative assessment (Moss & Brookhart, 2012), namely, the learning target for one lesson.

A *learning target* for one lesson describes the intended lesson-sized learning outcome and the nature of the evidence that will determine mastery of that outcome, from a student's point of view. It is closely linked to the *performance of understanding*, the learning activity for the lesson that will accomplish three things: show the student what the learning target means, develop the student's capabilities at that learning outcome, and provide evidence of where the student is in relation to that learning outcome. It is also closely linked to the *criteria for success* that students and their teachers will look for as evidence of learning. A complete and effective lesson-level learning target has all three: a statement of the target, a performance of understanding—something the students will do, make, say, or write—and success criteria for examining the quality of learning demonstrated in that performance. Of course, a series of daily lesson learning targets must function together to lead the student to the larger learning goals. But student learning happens one lesson at a time, which is the reason for focusing learning targets at the lesson level.

To design a learning target, identify the essential content knowledge and skills, including reasoning skills, which you intend to teach in the lesson. Make sure the intended knowledge and skills are derived from, and help lead students to, both your curriculum goals and one or more state standards or Common Core State Standards in the content area and grade level you teach. Design the performance of understanding—what the students are going to do, make, say, or write during the lesson.

Then, state the learning target. Using language from the point of view of a student who has not yet mastered the target, describe what students should be aiming to *learn* as they work on their performance of understanding and how they will know how well they are doing. Often, teachers begin learning targets with "I can" or "We are learning to."

Example

Learning Targets for One Lesson

- I can use exclamation marks.
- I can explain where and why the French settled in North America.
- We are learning to write a hypothesis that can be tested in an experiment.

To properly communicate a target, you need to share the criteria for good work. Otherwise, you and the students have no way to evaluate how close their work comes to being "good." You can do this by sharing criteria, for example, by giving students a copy of the scoring rubrics you will use to evaluate their final work. You can also show some examples of good work. Or, show some examples over a range of quality levels and let the students figure out what is "good" about the good work.

For some important assignments that you plan to use other years, ask some students if you can save a copy of their work to use in future classes. Most will be delighted. We know one teacher in Nebraska who saved "good example" copies of science notebooks each year to use with future students. She found that the quality level rose each year. Succeeding classes were able to grasp and meet, and then improve on, the standards of achievement shown in the notebooks.

Stephanie Harmon, High school science teacher
Rockcastle County Public Schools, Mt. Vernon, KY

MyLab Education

Video Example 7.3

In this video, a high school science teacher describes how her students "dissect" their learning targets to help them understand what it is they are trying to learn.

Strategy 2: Feedback That Feeds Forward

Armed with appropriate feedback, students should have what they need to improve. For mastery learning targets, this process is more short-term and immediate. (Practice today; find out what you need to work on; do better tomorrow.) For developmental learning targets like becoming

a good writer, the process is longer. Students can take into account feedback on today's writing, but also on previous writing, when they write tomorrow. Feedback is such an important element of formative assessment that we devote a whole chapter (Chapter 8) to it.

Strategy 3: Student Goal Setting

As a formative assessment strategy, student goal setting refers to the goal the *student* is trying to learn or achieve, as opposed to a curricular or unit goal. Students will work more productively and learn more intentionally if they themselves are focused on something specific that they understand is important to learn. As you teach students to set realistic, achievable goals, you are also teaching them the skills they need to be self-regulated learners.

Teach students to set goals that are neither too hard nor too easy but "just right"—the Goldilocks principle. Teach students to set goals that are not too specific ("I will learn the names of three different types of clouds"), nor too long-term ("I will learn how to predict the weather"), but again, just right. Then have students select the strategies they will use to reach the goal, use those strategies, and use assessment information to monitor their progress. Give students feedback along the way.

Examples

Student Goals and Strategies

- This week I read 52 words a minute. Next week I want to read 58 words a minute and have better expression. I will practice reading out loud to my parents for 10 minutes every night.
- I always approach my science work by trying to memorize facts. For this next unit, on Oceans, I am going to try to get better at explaining the *reasons* for the things we know about oceans. I will do this by asking "why" each time I learn a new term or concept and see how many of the reasons I can find out. At the end of the unit, I will see how many of my new concepts I can explain.

Notice that the goal-setting examples and strategies discussed here are all content-based. It is a misconception to think of goal setting as a free-standing "study skill." Students' learning goals are specific to the content area they are in, and the kinds of goals students set will differ a bit by subject. Notice also that the goal-setting examples here describe something students want to learn. It is not productive to set goals in terms of a score (e.g., "I want to get an A" or "I want to get a 95"). This is not student goal setting in the formative assessment sense. The reason is that the evidence needed in this case does not carry any message about where the student is with regard to a learning target and where the student should go next. Knowing I "sound like a robot" when I read helps me decide on a learning strategy ("try to sound more like a person reading a book to someone"). Conversely, knowing that I have scored at the B level doesn't give me any information on what to do to get an A.

Strategy 4: Student Self-Assessment

Sometimes, student goal setting arises out of episodes of student self-assessment. Students should have the opportunity to assess their own learning. Teach students effective self-assessment techniques; for many students, they don't come naturally. Most students will not automatically reflect on their own work in the manner that you intend. For example, if you ask a student, "What did you learn?" without providing any guidance on what to do, many will copy the title of the assignment: "I learned two-digit subtraction," or "I learned how a bill becomes a law." Offer opportunities for students to apply criteria to their own work in progress, discuss their work with peers, and reflect on their work after its completion.

Many self-assessment activities involve putting student or teacher observations on paper where they are easy to see and then discuss. For example, some teachers routinely use reflection sheets. Or, some have students indicate by red light/green light or happy/sad faces on their work whether they are certain or uncertain about their understanding. It is easier to see and interpret a red light than to try to guess from students' expressions that they don't understand.

MyLab Education

Video Example 7.4

Revisiting and reflecting upon the learning target for the day's lesson can help students debrief at the end of a lesson and get a sense of where they are in their learning. This video provides a third grade example.

Rubrics with clear performance-level descriptions can be helpful for student self-assessment. Even with good rubrics, however, students need instruction and practice in comparing their own work with the description in the rubric. Students can work together to compare their work to the learning targets. Teachers should provide a "safe" atmosphere for this, where criticism is seen as constructive and part of the learning process. That is an important lesson in itself.

There are some developmental differences in student use of self-assessment. Younger children may focus on neatness and other surface characteristics of work when they first do self-evaluation (Higgins, Harris, & Kuehn, 1994). With instruction and practice, children can learn to focus on the learning target (Ross, Rolheiser, & Hogaboam-Gray, 2002).

Narrowing the gap between the student performance and a learning goal may not be a smooth process. Depending on the scope of the learning goal, you may need additional rounds of the formative assessment process for that goal. For example, students may write a series of essays in high school, each one benefiting from preceding teacher feedback and self-evaluations. No matter the scope of the accomplishment, students should be able to see their work getting closer to the goal and should understand what specific feedback, insights, and learning strategies they used that helped them close the gap. This is an empowering cycle.

We saw an especially striking contrast of the benefits of teaching self-assessment in two first-grade classrooms in a school district in Pennsylvania. All students wrote reflection sheets to include in portfolios. One of the two first-grade teachers saw that her students had just filled in blanks on the reflection sheet, for example, writing "Adding 5s" in the blank after "What did you learn?" because that was the title of the assignment sheet. She asked her students follow-up questions to stimulate further thinking (questions like "What did you learn to do when you add 5s?") and gradually got more reflective answers (such as "You get 5 or 0 in the ones place" or "I learned I [already] know it"). The other first-grade teacher just passed out the reflection sheets like worksheets, because the evaluation required it. Most of her students stayed in the "copying" phase. The difference between these classes was quite apparent to those of us who got to see both.

Here is an example of both student self-assessment and goal setting. The graph in the first panel of Figure 7.6 spanned the whole 10-week project. The reflection sheet in the second panel of Figure 7.6 was for just one of the weeks—in this example, the second week—of the project. Notice that this self-assessment and goal setting changed what might have been a rote memory task, memorizing multiplication facts, and enhanced it. Students used analytical and metacognitive skills as they monitored and adjusted their own work.

Example

Student Self-Assessment and Goal Setting

The "minute math" project was part of third graders' learning the multiplication facts from one to 10. Students took a timed, 5-minute test of 100 facts every

Friday. Then, they predicted and graphed what they would score the next week, set a goal (besides the score; for example, to learn the eight and nine tables better), and selected strategies (e.g., use flash cards) to reach that goal. The next week, they took the timed test again and graphed their score, compared it with their predicted score and their goal, and set a new goal for the next week. Figure 7.6 shows one student's graph and a portion of her goal sheet for one week.

The goal the student set for her learning was "the nines and eights," by which she meant memorizing the facts for multiplying by eight and nine. This is a goal about *learning*, not scoring. The student's "scoring goal" is part of her plan of action.

FIGURE 7.6 **Example of student self-assessment and goal setting: Minute math.**

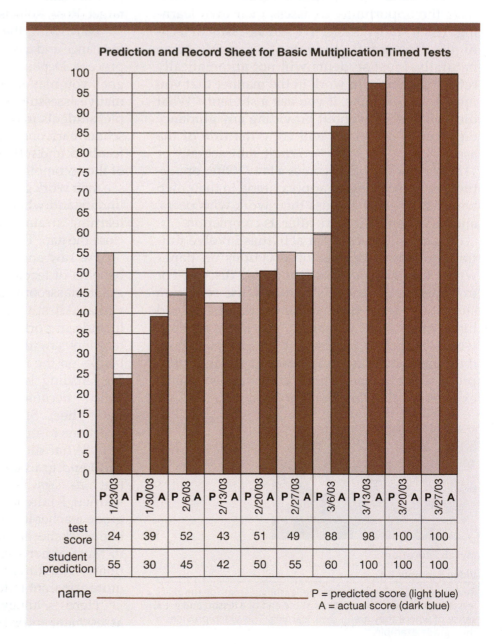

Prediction and Record Sheet for Basic Multiplication Timed Tests

	P 1/23/03 A	P 1/30/03 A	P 2/6/03 A	P 2/13/03 A	P 2/20/03 A	P 2/27/03 A	P 3/6/03 A	P 3/13/03 A	P 3/20/03 A	P 3/27/03 A
test score	24	39	52	43	51	49	88	98	100	100
student prediction	55	30	45	42	50	55	60	100	100	100

name _____

P = predicted score (light blue)
A = actual score (dark blue)

FIGURE 7.6   (*Continued*)

GPAR

Name_____   Date 1-30-03

GOAL-What do you want to learn?
____The nines and eights.____

LOCATION- Right now I can do __35__ facts in five minutes.
_____
_____

PLAN- My goal is to get __45__ / **100** facts on my next test. I need to improve in __3 days__
_____

ACTION- When will you begin?
Starting __Today__ I will use these study strategies to improve. (study flashcards, play multiplication games, study with parents, etc.)
____Singing songs and games.____

I will use these problem solving strategies to improve __by Monday__. (write a number sentence, use repeated addition, draw a picture, make a model, array)
____you bet i will improve____

RESULTS- Did you follow through with your plan? What happened? Did you see improvements?
_____
_____
_____

Note: GPAR means Goal, Plan, Act, Reflect
Source: Patricia Pozza. Used by permission.

Some of the students in this class had to be coached to write learning goals, not just scoring goals. This student had a plan, which was basically to enthusiastically endorse all of the strategies her teacher suggested. Over time, students like this one can be coached to focus their plans and strategies. Notice that in the short term, her strategies worked—her performance rose the next week—and in the long term, she achieved her general goal of learning all her multiplication facts.

Strategy 5: Asking Effective Questions

Asking effective questions is a formative assessment strategy because as students respond, student thinking becomes visible. Teachers and students have evidence of what students are understanding and what they are able to do with their knowledge.

Effective questioning requires attention to both content and process. As to the content of the questions, effective questions are open-ended; that is, they invite a range of responses as opposed to one correct answer or one set of correct answers. Asking thoughtful, open questions requires planning; you are not likely to come up with good ones "on the fly." Plan questions that ask students to think about the content under study and use it to solve a problem or suggest alternatives of some sort.

Examples

Open-Ended Questions That Elicit Student Thinking

■ What community organizations can you think of that help people work together?

■ What rule can you write that would help you decide whether something is a chemical change or a physical change?

■ Why do you think the main character didn't want to leave her home town?

Effective questioning also requires attention to the manner in which the questions are asked. When you ask students questions, make sure that everyone has a chance to be called on. Use a random calling method. Elementary school teachers often write each student's name on a popsicle stick, then draw randomly each time. This technique ensures that a good sample of students is selected, not just students who are volunteering—those students usually either know the answers or enjoy attention, or both. Other random calling methods use numbers, playing cards, and the like. If students know there is a realistic chance they will be called on, they will be more likely to think about the question. It isn't necessary to do random calling every single time you talk with students, of course, but it is necessary if you want to be able to interpret student responses as representative of the class, that is, when you are using questioning as a formative assessment strategy.

Once you ask a question, wait for the student to answer. Typically, teachers wait only a few seconds before moving on to another student. Questions that require thought take more time than that for students to answer. Finally, break out of the pattern of "Initiate-Respond-Evaluate," in which the teacher calls on a student, hears the response, and evaluates it, then calls on another student and repeats the process. Ask students to respond to each other, using question extenders like the examples below.

Examples

Question Extenders to Help Students Respond to and Extend the Ideas of Their Peers

■ Barry, what did you think of when you heard Tori's ideas?

■ Think about what Tori just said. What other information might we want to know to help us think about that?

■ Sarah, can you tell me if you *agree*, *disagree*, or *have something to add* to Tori's ideas?

In the process of drawing out student thinking, you will be generating evidence that both you and the students can use to assess their understanding and to identify next steps in learning.

Strategy 6: Helping Students Ask Effective Questions

Teacher talk is much more common in most classrooms than student talk. To manage their own learning, students have to learn to identify what questions they have and articulate them. They need to realize that learning means getting your questions answered. There are many ways to help students ask effective questions. Two of the most common are teaching students about different kinds of questions, so they can analyze their own questions and learn to ask better ones, and using question starters. All strategies to help students ask effective questions require that you give students practice at asking and answering their own questions.

To teach students about different kinds of questions, you need to develop a shared language. Even young children can learn the difference between "in the book" and "in my head" questions. These are the two main categories in the Question-Answer Relationships (QAR) scheme (Raphael & Au, 2005). "In the book questions" are literal questions whose answer can be found in the text, while "in my head" questions require inferences from the text or connections from one's own life and experiences. "In the book" questions can be further subdivided into "right there" and "think and search" questions, depending on whether the answer is in one location or must be compiled from several places in the text. "In my head" questions can be further subdivided into "author and me" questions that require inferences or connections to textual elements and "on my own" questions about students' backgrounds with topics or themes that do not require textual connections (for example, in a story about a dog, an "on my own" question might be, "Who can tell me about their dog?").

Some teachers teach students about open and closed questions. Open questions have the possibility of multiple good answers. Closed questions have one right answer or set of right answers. Students' responses to other students' open questions generate deeper evidence about student understanding that can go further in informing students' thinking about where they are going, what they already know, and what they should do next.

When students know about different kinds of questions, they can be coached to ask more open-ended questions that require thinking and give better evidence of their understanding than closed questions. Having a shared language to describe the questions helps in this process. Below is an example of using students' understanding of question types to ask effective questions and demonstrate their thinking

Example

Helping Students Ask Effective Questions

A high school social studies teacher taught his students about open and closed questions. Then, each time he assigned a textbook chapter for students to read, he did not assign the questions at the end of the chapter. Rather, he asked students to write five open and five closed questions about the text and answer them. He asked that students focus their questions on what they thought were the most important concepts, events, or people in the chapter (as opposed to questions about the first five facts in the chapter, for example). Students became more involved in the reading, were eager to find out what other students would say in answer to their questions, and in the process both students and teacher received evidence about students' understanding and application of concepts.

Some teachers we have known are very creative in their use of student questioning. One elementary teacher had students write six open-ended questions about a story they had read and write them on a paper pattern that, when cut out and folded, formed a cube (like a big dice). Students rolled their cubes and asked each other the questions that landed face-up. In this process, students shared their understanding of the story, and both the teacher and students got lots of evidence of what that understanding was. This same strategy could be used for understanding nonfiction texts, for example articles and chapters in science or social studies as well.

LEARNING PROGRESSIONS

Experience or study will teach you the common misconceptions your students are likely to have along the way as they learn a particular concept. Knowing these, you will be able to more meaningfully evaluate performance levels and suggest next steps. **Learning progressions** are developmental sequences that describe typical progress in understanding or skill in a particular domain (Gong, 2008; Heritage, 2008; Hess, 2007).

Formative assessment works best when it is used in the context of a continuum, a vertical "picture" of what it means to learn or progress in a domain. This concept is very different from the approach to learning goals and objectives taken by most state standards and most curriculum materials (Heritage, 2008). A learning progression maps student progress in *learning*, not in accomplishing the teaching- and activity-based "goals" that sometimes form the learning aims for lessons or units of instruction.

Different researchers have taken slightly different approaches to learning progressions. Forster and Masters (2004) used progress maps that described typical growth in an area of learning, which can be used by both classroom teachers and system evaluators to situate student learning on a continuum based in classroom instructional work. Wilson and Draney (2004) described a system of progress variables—specific understandings and skills at a level of detail appropriate for classroom—that could be aggregated to the more general descriptions required for judgment of achievement of a state standard or curriculum goal.

An example of a learning progression in reading and writing is found at the website for the New Zealand Ministry of Education (http://literacyprogressions.tki.org.nz/). Others have made more specific learning progress variables, for example, in understanding forces and motions (Wilson & Draney, 2004). Learning progressions have been developed more in some curriculum areas than in others.

A major insight for formative assessment that learning progressions have given us is to focus on the "big picture" of learning, viewing students' work as points along a developmental continuum. This process will help remove the blinders that can come with focusing too narrowly on students' successes or difficulties with a particular lesson activity, which is a real issue for classroom teachers whose instruction is, by definition, activity oriented.

Find a learning progression in your area, or construct a draft of one with colleagues, and see how mapping your students in this way helps you be more visionary in your selection of appropriate instruction and in giving appropriate feedback. Many teachers find, when trying to give feedback, that identifying what's wrong with a student's work and suggesting how to fix it comes much easier than identifying strengths in a student's work and suggesting how to build on them. Using a learning progression approach helps you see good work done in an assignment as more than an end of the road.

A COHERENT ASSESSMENT SYSTEM

Learning targets are the hub that connects

- assignments (which in embodying the learning targets serve to communicate them to students and to afford practice on them),
- teacher formative feedback and student self-assessment (which apprise the student of where he stands in relation to the learning targets and what he should do next),
- summative assessment (which evaluates the results of student efforts against the learning targets), and
- scoring criteria (which form the basis for teacher feedback and student self-assessment, and also can express the results of assessment in a symbol system designed to describe quality levels on the learning targets).

We have discussed the importance of assessments and scoring criteria matching learning targets, at both the content and cognitive levels, as a validity issue. The same principle of alignment holds for any classroom assignment, what we have called performances of understanding. Students will interpret what you ask them to "do" (their assignments) as what you want them to learn. Thus, all assignments, not just assessments, must embody the learning targets.

So, for example, if the learning target is for students to write descriptive paragraphs, the assignments should include practice writing descriptive paragraphs. Formative feedback on these should be based on your criteria for "good" descriptive paragraphs. Students should have the opportunity to use the feedback. Finally, they write a descriptive paragraph that is graded according to those same criteria.

Formative assessments give you information about how long to "form" and when to "sum."

When students' work gets close to the learning target, they are ready to demonstrate achievement on summative assessment. Students whose formative assessments show they don't need more practice, when classmates still do, can do enrichment work related to the learning target or use their time for some other work.

SYSTEMATIC RECORD KEEPING

Keep records of the important results of formative assessment, not for grading, but to keep yourself organized. For example, you should know what sort of feedback you have given, over time, to a student on a particular skill (e.g., writing). You can design your own class, individual, or group record-keeping sheets for specific purposes. You may wish to use a computer spreadsheet or database program. Or your school may choose to subscribe to a formative assessment system (e.g., LSI Tracker, http://www.learningsciences.com/lsitracker/) that stores learning targets and success criteria keyed to standards, record student achievement at the lesson level based on a variety of evidence, and produce summary reports for lessons, units, and students.

Keeping records will help ensure that you are systematic and have an opportunity to observe all students on all the behaviors or skills you have decided are important. You will be able to see for which students you have observed target behaviors or skills and make a point to observe the rest of them. Also, making notes will result in more complete and organized information than if you relied on your memory. Use patterns of observations to decide what each student needs, or what the group needs. If no natural opportunity to observe a skill presents itself, you may have to create one.

How many observations you want to see before you identify a pattern or draw conclusions will vary. For example, a kindergarten teacher might want to make sure she observes each child holding a pencil correctly at least five different times. A high school biology teacher might want to observe each student preparing a slide correctly at least twice.

MyLab Education **Self-Check 7.2**

MyLab Education **Application Exercises 7.2:**
(2 exercises) Analyzing Formative Assessment Episodes

CONCLUSION

This chapter has described diagnostic and formative assessment, both of which help inform teacher planning. Formative assessment should be directly helpful to students as well as teachers. It should help them decide about what and how to study, how to approach problems and other assignments, and how to develop learning strategies that work for them. In the next chapter, we focus on feedback, one of the most powerful formative assessment strategies.

EXERCISES

1. For a subject you teach or plan to teach, craft a diagnostic assessment procedure for Approaches 1, 2, 3, and 4. If there is time, try each approach with students who are experiencing learning difficulties. Revise your assessment procedure based on these student trials. Share the final versions of your assessment procedures with others in your course.

2. Each of these statements describes an instructional decision-making situation. Read each statement and decide the approach(es) to diagnostic assessment that may provide needed information.
   a. A teacher wonders whether Larissa missed several arithmetic story problems because she doesn't know her number facts.
   b. Trinh missed several addition computational problems involving mixed decimal fractions. His teacher wonders whether Trinh is counting the number of decimal places in each addend and using this count as the basis for placing the decimal point in the final answer.
   c. Lou missed several whole-number arithmetic problems involving carrying (regrouping). His teacher wonders whether Lou has not remembered to add his "carries" to the sum of the digits in the next column.
   d. Janet is a slow reader who frequently misses comprehension questions following a passage. Her teacher wonders whether Janet has reading reversals that cause her to misread some words in the passage.

3. For each of the following assessment activities, identify at least one formative use for the information the teacher will get from it. You may use Figure 7.5 to help you.

   a. Students set a "help" button on their desk to let the teacher know they're having trouble during math practice.
   b. Students get together in pairs to read and critique each others' reports on a planet.
   c. Students write new vocabulary words on flash cards and use a recipe box to file words into three categories: "know cold," "know most of the time," and "don't know."
   d. At the end of each social studies class, students write "one question I still have" on a 3 × 5 card and turn it in as their "ticket" out of class.

4. Identify the formative assessment strategy in use in each of the following assessment activities.
   a. An elementary math teacher shows her students a box and says, "You already know how to find the area of each of the sides of the box. Today we will learn to find how much space is available *inside* the box. That is called volume. You will know you can do it when you can find the volume of boxes of different sizes."
   b. Elementary students use a rubric for oral expression in reading. Each day for a week, they mark their level of oral expression, in their own judgment and as measured by the rubric, in order to get ready for a graded assessment on oral expression the following week.
   c. A high school civics teacher asks her class, "Who do you think is going to win the mayoral election?" She asks students to explain their reasoning and respond to their classmates' arguments. She listens to the student discussion and decides the students understand very well the effects of the media on elections and need some work on understanding the effects of local history and politics on elections.
   d. A high school science teacher has students design laboratory tests to compare the properties of water samples from different sources. He asks them to brainstorm a list of chemical and physical properties that they think might differ among the samples, turn them into questions (e.g., "How does the electrical connectivity of these samples compare?"), and then decide which ones they will test and what they expect to learn from doing it.

8

Providing Formative Feedback

KEY CONCEPTS

1. Formative feedback is information about a student's performance or understanding that is intended to improve learning. Feedback can come from many sources, including the teacher, peer, self, parent, books, and technology. Understanding the types and characteristics of feedback helps you develop a repertoire of feedback choices.

2. For feedback to feed learning forward, students need to have a clear understanding of their learning target and an immediate opportunity to use the feedback to make progress toward it. Differentiate feedback according to students' learning needs and language needs. Handle peer feedback as an instructional strategy to enhance learning for both peers—both the giver and receiver of feedback.

IMPORTANT TERMS

cognitive feedback

descriptive feedback

evaluative feedback

example prompts

outcome feedback

reminder prompts

scaffold prompts

Giving effective feedback is one of the most powerful and positive things a teacher can do for student learning. Hattie (2009) defined feedback as "information provided by an agent (e.g., teacher, peer, book, parent, or one's own experience) about aspects of one's performance or understanding" (p. 174). Hattie (2009) summarized 23 meta-analyses, in total representing 1,287 studies of studies of the effects of feedback, and found that the average effect size of feedback was 0.73, a strong effect analogous to moving from the 50th to the 77th percentile on a standardized test.

But the effects of feedback are not always positive. In one often-cited, classic meta-analysis of studies of feedback (Kluger & DeNisi, 1996), one third of the effects of feedback were negative, that is, feedback had a detrimental effect on performance. The feedback that is useful for learning is feedback that provides information to students that they can use to improve their task performance, select more productive strategies, and monitor their own learning (Hattie, 2009). Feedback that comes in the form of praise or punishment has relatively little effect on learning, primarily because it carries no information about the task at hand or the knowledge and skills required to complete it. The aim of this chapter is to describe various types and characteristics of feedback to enable you to choose feedback that will help students improve and avoid wasting your time with feedback that will not.

Feedback can come from many sources, including the teacher, peer, self, parent, books, and technology. Chapter 7 discussed student self-assessment as a formative assessment strategy. In this chapter, we focus on feedback from teachers, peers, and technology, that is, on feedback from sources external to the student.

TYPES AND CHARACTERISTICS OF FEEDBACK

Effective feedback is descriptive, specific, and contains information for improvement. The type of feedback you give should match the purpose you have for giving it. Understanding the types and characteristics of feedback helps you develop a repertoire of feedback choices.

Feedback Referencing Schemes

Feedback can vary according to the *kind of comparison* it makes.

- *Norm-referenced* feedback compares performance to other students. ("Your paragraph was the best in the class.")
- *Criterion-referenced* feedback compares performance to a standard and describes what students can or cannot do. ("You are particularly good at using a variety of descriptive adjectives.")
- *Self-referenced* feedback compares a student's performance to his own past performance or sometimes to expected performance. ("This paragraph is better than the last one you wrote.")

The best formative feedback for practice work is criterion-referenced or self-referenced feedback. Use criterion-referenced feedback for the work of most students in most situations. For students whose beliefs about their own capabilities are low, use self-referenced feedback to show them how they are improving.

Feedback Focus

Feedback can vary according to whether it describes *results* or *processes* underlying results.

- **Outcome feedback** is knowledge of results. ("You got a B on that paper.")
- **Cognitive feedback** describes the connections between aspects of the task or the process students used to do that task and the student's achievement. ("It doesn't seem like you used the study guide very much.")

Cognitive feedback helps students know what to do to improve. Outcome feedback only supports improvement if students can internally generate the cognitive feedback (Butler & Winne, 1995). For example, a student may get back a paragraph on which the teacher marked three comma faults and conclude on his own, "I should study comma use." However, many students need the scaffolding provided when the teacher explicitly provides cognitive feedback. Suggest a short-term learning goal (what to aim for next), and suggest specific strategies the student can use to get there.

Hattie (2009; Hattie & Timperley, 2007) described four levels of feedback, the first three of which form a progression. The first three levels help students focus on their work, the doing of their work, and their understanding of how they are doing their work. Level 1 is the *Task or Product Level*, subsuming comments about how well tasks are understood and performed. For example, "Your report presented a clear description of each planet, but only the names of their moons. Try to find some more information about the moons." Level 2 is the *Process Level*, subsuming comments about the process students used to do their work. For example, "I wonder what the report would look like if you organized each planet's section in the same way. That way readers could see the comparisons among planets more easily." Level 3 is the *Self-Regulation Level*, subsuming comments about students' understanding and monitoring of their own activities. For example, "You seem comfortable working with a large amount of information. Can you come up with some ideas about how to decide which information is more important, so you know what to emphasize?" Level 4 is the *Self Level*, subsuming personal comments and evaluative judgments. For example, "Smart boy!" This kind of feedback is not effective for learning and should not be used. In addition to being ineffective for learning, it can communicate to students that intelligence is a fixed trait and that students are pretty much stuck with their abilities (Dweck, 2000). Effective feedback, on the contrary, helps communicate to students that intelligence is malleable and that students become better learners with effort and persistence.

Feedback Function

Feedback can vary according to its *functional significance* (Ryan & Deci, 2000).

■ **Descriptive feedback** gives information about the work. ("You developed your main character with lots of thoughtful details.")
■ **Evaluative feedback** passes judgment on the work. (Giving an A or saying, "Good job!")

Students usually perceive descriptive feedback as informational in nature while they usually perceive evaluative feedback as controlling. Descriptive feedback is more useful for formative assessment than evaluative feedback, because it has the potential to give students information they can use to improve and, at the same time, suggest to them that they are the agents of their own learning—after all, they are the ones who choose and use the information. Check that the feedback you give students not only *is* descriptive but also that the descriptions are statements of how the work relates to criteria you have shared with students.

Tunstall and Gipps (1996) developed a two-dimensional typology for assessment feedback, based on observations and interviews of teachers and children in primary classrooms. (They also described feedback for socialization, for example about attitudes or participation in classroom routines, which is common in primary schools.) They classified assessment feedback according to whether it was descriptive or evaluative and also according to whether it was positive or negative. The descriptive and evaluative categories were further subdivided so that in all there were eight types of assessment feedback (Tunstall & Gipps, 1996, pp. 392–401). These are listed below, by category.

■ Evaluative feedback—passing judgment on students
  • Classroom and individual management
    ○ Rewarding (positive, e.g., stickers)
    ○ Punishing (negative, e.g., withholding recess)
  • Performance orientation
    ○ Approving (positive, e.g., check marks, "good girl")
    ○ Disapproving (negative, e.g., X, "you weren't listening")
■ Descriptive feedback
  • Mastery orientation
    ○ Specifying attainment (describing aspects of success, e.g., identifying criteria met)
    ○ Specifying improvement (describing aspects for correction, e.g., correcting, identifying criteria not met)
  • Learning orientation
    ○ Constructing achievement (working with the child to identify the learning processes in use and suggestions for extending the learning)
    ○ Constructing the way forward (working with the child to diagnose learning processes and suggest next steps toward meeting criteria)

Notice that what was *positive* and *negative* on the evaluative side becomes identifying the positive features of work and offering constructive criticism on the descriptive side. That is, effective formative feedback is descriptive and entirely positive in the sense of moving the student's work forward, even if errors or gaps are what is being identified.

Feedback Methods

Feedback can be delivered in many different ways. Teachers often ask for a recipe (for example, to always give written feedback or to always give immediate feedback), but unfortunately the best method for delivering feedback depends on the student, the teacher's relationship with the student, the content knowledge and skills in question, and the particular assignment or assessment. Here we will identify some ways that teacher feedback to students can vary and make recommendations based on reviews of the feedback literature (Brookhart, 2008a; Hattie & Timperley, 2007; Shute, 2008).

■ Feedback can be delivered with various kinds of *timing*. For knowledge of facts, for example memorizing addition facts, immediate feedback is best. Think of students checking their answers on the back of math flash cards. For more comprehensive skills and higher-order thinking tasks, consider delaying the feedback just a bit to allow the students to wrestle with their own ideas and also, potentially, to give you more evidence on which to base your feedback. But always deliver feedback when the student is still thinking of the work and still has an opportunity to use the feedback to improve the work. Students, for example, are likely to ignore feedback delivered after a final grade on a project.

■ Feedback can be delivered in various *amounts*, which has two aspects: how many points to comment on and how much to say about each point. Many times, feedback on schoolwork is too comprehensive. The teacher is thinking that she must comment on everything she sees that needs to be "fixed." This is a task-based, not a learning-focused, approach to feedback. Struggling students are often overwhelmed with the sheer volume of marks on the paper and cannot figure out what is important and what is not. And with a "fix it" feedback mentality, teachers often shortchange successful students, because there is little to "fix" and the teacher does not think to describe the strengths of the work in terms of where it is and where it should go next.

To decide how many points to comment on, ask yourself what are the one or two things the student needs to attend to next to take the next step toward mastery of the learning target he or she is striving for—or the next learning target in the progression, if the student has successfully mastered this one, or an interesting potential enhancement or enrichment of learning. Comment on that issue, and then give the student an opportunity to focus on it and demonstrate improvement.

Regarding how much to say about each point, that concern depends on the student's needs. Never give feedback that does the work *for* the student. For example, all of us have at one time or another received papers back from teachers that were basically copy-edited. Some students will need you only to point out something, and they will have all they need to improve their work. ("There are two comma faults in this paragraph—find them and fix them.") Some students will need more description and suggestions, and some students will need you to show them how to make improvements in their work.

Clarke (2003), like the other authors whose feedback classification schemes we have discussed, also recommends descriptive feedback that identifies what the student has accomplished, according to the learning criteria, and makes a suggestion for improvement. In order to help teachers realize they have choices about the way they make suggestions for improvement, she identified what she called three types of "improvement prompts" (Clarke, 2003, p. 83): reminder, scaffold, and example prompts.

Reminder prompts restate the learning target. They are useful for students who already have a grasp of the material, whose work needs fine-tuning. For example, "Remember we are learning to punctuate compound sentences" is all a student who basically understands how to do this would need to prompt him to go back over his work and find some compound sentences that were incorrectly punctuated.

Scaffold prompts give the student more support, when just restating the learning target isn't enough. Sometimes, scaffold prompts are in the form of detailed questions for the student. For example, "Can you find a word in that problem that suggests addition? Good. What two numbers should you add?" Other times, scaffold prompts walk the student through an aspect of the task that has proven to be a stumbling block.

Example prompts model the work that students need to do, inviting them to use one of the teacher's examples or create his own based on it. For example, a teacher might want a student to add more supporting details to a paragraph. She might suggest several things that, in her mind, support the point the student is trying to make and ask the student to select and write about one of her details or come up with one of his own in a similar manner.

Like selecting how many points to comment on, selecting how much detail to give a student on each point also requires judgment. Base your decisions about the amount of detail and support to give students on the principle of "less is more." Students who would understand what to do next with a simple reminder may not react well if you give them many suggestions and details, implying they are not capable of proceeding on their own. Students for whom the learning target is not clear will not be able to move forward if all they get is a simple reminder. Base your decisions about the amount of detail to give in your feedback on the student's needs, the content knowledge and skills to be learned, and the specific assignment or assessment.

■ Feedback can be delivered in several different *modes*. Feedback can be oral or written, or it can be delivered as a demonstration ("do it like this"). Written feedback can be delivered as comments at specific locations throughout the student's work, as a set of comments at the end, or both. Computer-delivered written feedback, for example using the "comments" function in a word processing program, likewise can be delivered at specific points in the work, as overall comments, or both.

Decisions about the mode of feedback delivery are often simply logical. For example, young children and poor readers need more oral feedback because they would not understand detailed written feedback. Give oral feedback as you monitor the processes students are using during in-class exercises; give written feedback for drafts of work on which you want the feedback to remain available to students as they revise their work. The best feedback comes in the form of a conversation with the student. While this process is not always possible, it allows you to check the student's understanding of your feedback and how he intends to use it, and it allows the student to ask questions.

■ Feedback can be addressed to different *audiences*—to individuals, small groups, or whole classes. Individual feedback is best when possible: It can be specific to the student's particular work and learning needs, and it can communicate that the teacher values the student's learning. Small and large group feedback is usually

oral and comes as part of a lesson or mini-lesson. ("It seems several of you are having trouble deciding how to begin solving this kind of equation. Let's go over again how to isolate the variable on one side of the equation, all by itself, and why that's important. I'll stop and ask someone to explain why we did each step.")

Using rubrics (see Chapter 13) permits a mixed method of group and individual feedback. Circle the rubric performance-level descriptions that characterize the student's work. In this way, every student gets general descriptive feedback from the performance level circled and general suggestions for what to do next from the performance descriptions just above it. With the general descriptions already taken care of, you can focus your individual comments on describing specific aspects of the student's work and specific suggestions for improvement.

Emily Roberts, Kindergarten teacher
Jefferson City Public Schools, Jefferson City, MO

MyLab Education

Video Example 8.1

This video shows a kindergarten teacher giving oral feedback to students as they are working. She is explicit about trying to understand student thinking. Her feedback is based on each student's next step in their journey toward a learning target.

Lisa Smith, Grade 3 teacher
Jefferson City Public Schools, Jefferson City, MO

MyLab Education

Video Example 8.2

This third grade teacher gives oral feedback to students by asking guided questions. Notice that the questions are designed to scaffold students' thinking. The teacher decides what questions to ask based on her observations of how students are thinking.

Feedback Word Choice

Verbal feedback, whether oral or written, also varies in other ways that any verbal communication can vary.

- Feedback varies in *clarity*. Students have to clearly understand what your feedback means if it is to be useful to them.

- Feedback varies in *specificity*. General statements are usually less helpful for improvement than specific descriptions and suggestions.

- Feedback varies in *person*. First-person ("I" statements) feedback works for some formative feedback (e.g., "I don't understand what you mean here"). Third-person feedback can help you describe the work, not the student (e.g., "This paragraph doesn't have supporting details" is better than "You didn't use supporting details"). Avoid second-person feedback. Saying "you" did this or that comes out sounding like finger wagging.

- Feedback varies in *tone*. Keep the tone supportive. We know, for example, of one teacher who wrote, "You think like a chicken!" That's not helpful.

Not all students will hear feedback in the way you intend. For example, some students who have low self-efficacy or who are fearful may hear feedback you intended to be descriptive as evaluative. They may simply hear in your description a judgment that their work is "no good." Observe how students hear and respond to your feedback and what they do as a result.

Effective Feedback

Generally, more descriptive feedback is better for formative assessment. If the description only affirms what is good, however, it may not help students improve in the future. A good plan for written feedback on a student's paper is to describe a couple of positive aspects of the work and one aspect that needs improvement.

Finally, keep in mind that as a major element of formative assessment, feedback should give information to *both* the teacher and the student. Effective feedback episodes help students learn what they are doing well and what they should do next, as we have shown. Less obvious, but equally important: Effective feedback episodes help *teachers* learn what their students are thinking, which helps teachers focus their feedback and next instructional moves. Some research has shown that teachers who are expert in formative assessment interpret student work in terms of how students are understanding concepts, while teachers who are not expert in formative assessment interpret student work in terms of how correct it is (e.g., 80% correct). When teachers

learn what students are thinking, they can focus their feedback and follow-up instruction directly on students' next, specific learning needs. When teachers evaluate correctness, the only feedback and follow-up they can do is to reteach topics in areas of low scores, without knowing what exactly to do differently to have better effects on learning (Hattie, 2009; Hattie & Timperley, 2007; Kroog, Ruiz-Primo, & Sands, 2014; Minstrell, Anderson, & Li, 2009).

The checklist summarizes the suggestions we have made to help your feedback be effective.

Checklist

A Checklist for Evaluating the Effectiveness of Feedback

1. Does the feedback describe the student's work, or the process the student used to do the work, against clear criteria?

2. Does the feedback arrive at a time when the student can use it?

3. Does the feedback contain the right amount of main points or ideas?

4. Is the feedback specific enough to support next steps but not so specific the work is done for the student?

5. Is the feedback positive in tone and intention?

6. Would the feedback be clear to the student?

7. Does the tone of the feedback imply the student is an active learner?

8. Does the feedback reflect something the teacher learned about the student's performance and the student's thinking?

9. Will the student receiving the feedback learn something from it?

MyLab Education Self-Check 8.1

MyLab Education Application Exercises 8.1:
Analyzing Feedback Episodes

HELPING STUDENTS USE FEEDBACK

Descriptive feedback with all the characteristics in the checklist can still be ineffective. Two time-sensitive issues are important. Before they receive feedback, students need to be aware of a learning target or larger learning aim in order to give the feedback a reference point. After they receive feedback, students need an immediate opportunity to use the feedback. Finally, feedback needs to be delivered in a safe environment where making mistakes is interpreted as an opportunity for learning.

The Role of Learning Targets in Feedback

Recall the formative assessment questions: What am I aiming for? How close am I now? What else do I have to do to get there? Descriptive feedback with suggestions for next steps helps the student answer the second and third questions—and can even help clarify the target itself. Without a clear understanding of what they are aiming for, students will have no reference point against which to process the feedback. In effect, using feedback would turn into an exercise in following directions, in doing what was suggested because the teacher suggested it instead of because students see how such moves would improve their own work. From a functional perspective, feedback information against a learning target can be perceived as *informational*, as students see its value for an aim of theirs. Feedback information without a learning target is more likely to be perceived as *controlling*, as it amounts to following additional directions from the teacher.

Immediate Opportunity to Use Feedback

Often teachers give feedback with the general intention that students will use it "next time" they do something similar. This is wishful thinking. In fact, specific descriptive feedback will fade to general evaluative impressions over time in students' memories. Students need opportunities to use specific feedback in the same formative learning cycle in which they are aiming for a specific learning target or goal (Brookhart, 2012; Fisher & Frey, 2009).

Thus, after feedback is given, and while students are still focused on both the task and the learning it represents, give students an opportunity to use the feedback. For writing or complex projects, this process means building in feedback opportunities along the way as students are working, not waiting until a final product is turned in, after which it is too late to revise, change course, or expand on strengths. For learning of facts and concepts, you should build in nongraded feedback opportunities (quizzes, classroom questions, games, computer practice sessions) so that students understand what they need to concentrate on, what misconceptions they may have, how new concepts are related, and so on, before a graded test.

The Feedback Environment

The formative assessment cycle requires that students receive feedback, process it as information to help them toward a learning goal they are seeking,

and use that information to improve their work and, ultimately, their understanding and skills in the domain under study. Teachers should create a classroom environment that communicates to the student that learning is possible for everyone and that mistakes and revisions are a natural part of the learning process. In evaluative classroom cultures, where attaining high grades is emphasized more than learning, it is not safe to make mistakes, because mistakes mean lost "points" and not opportunities for learning (Boekaerts, 2011).

Leighton, Chu, and Seitz (2012) reviewed research on instruction, learning, and assessment and proposed the *Learning Errors and Formative Feedback Model* (*LEAFF*) to describe the classroom and student dynamics that result in students either using feedback or ignoring it. They predicted that two things must happen for students to use feedback for improvement. First, the teacher must explicitly discuss the learning process and the value of feedback and provide relevant formative feedback to students that is patently useful to them. They contrast this process with "feckless feedback"—we love that term!—by which they mean ineffective, incompetent feedback that is not relevant to the intended learning or to the student's needs. Second, the students must have a mental model of the learning environment that understands it is for learning and feels emotionally safe. If students' comments in class are routinely evaluated as good or bad, if all work is graded immediately, or if students are often compared with each other, students will conclude that the name of the game in class is earning points or showing well, rather than learning. Having a genuine question or learning from a genuine mistake would be seen as showing weakness rather than trying to learn.

Melissa Vernon, Grade 1 teacher
Jefferson City Public Schools, Jefferson City, MO

MyLab Education

Video Example 8.3

These first graders are involved in both peer and self-assessment. Notice how the teacher teaches students to self-assess. She uses "Why" questions to teach students how to compare their writing to criteria contained in a writing scale. All students—not just first graders—need feedback on the quality of their self-assessment.

DIFFERENTIATING FEEDBACK

The effects of feedback depend not only on the information itself but also on the characteristics of the people who send (teacher) and receive (student) the message. Whether students hear feedback as informational or controlling depends in part on them. One student may listen to a helpful, clear description of how to improve a paper with gratitude, while another may hear the same feedback as just another confirmation of how stupid he is. Covington (1992) wrote that while no two children come to school with equal academic abilities and backgrounds, there is no reason that they should not all have access to equally motivational feedback. He called this "motivational equity."

Feedback for Successful Students

There is some evidence that good students use all information, including graded work, formatively (Brookhart, 2001). However, it is common for successful students to receive "good grades" as their only, or at least their major, feedback, because teachers feel there is nothing to say. The assignment is "perfect." The assumption behind such an approach to feedback for successful students is that achievement is about *scoring*, not *learning*. When you provide feedback to successful students that names and notices what they did well, according to the criteria you and the students are using, and gives them something to think about (not another assignment to do), you imply that learning never ends. Plus, you give the students evidence that you have thoughtfully considered their work, which is satisfying to them and contributes to a classroom atmosphere marked by caring about learning. Here is an example of feedback to a successful student.

Example

Feedback to a Successful Student

Third graders read an excerpt of informational text about the environment in general and about endangered species and then answered questions in writing. Their teacher wanted to know what they got out of the text, and she also wanted to know if they could answer comprehension questions with complete sentences and complete, relevant thoughts. One student's answers were complete and clear and showed a thorough understanding of the passage she had read. Her teacher wrote:

Nicely written! Your sentences are complete and they tell important things from the text. Thinking question: What would happen if we stopped hunting completely?

Notice that the teacher did not assign the student to do a report on hunting or write an essay about hunting, or anything like that, which the student might have perceived as "getting more work" as a result of doing well. Rather, the student was challenged to extend her thinking with an idea beyond what was in the text, but still relevant to the learning. This teacher did that with the use of what she called "thinking questions," a strategy she often used in feedback.

Successful students sometimes do need constructive criticism as well as suggestions for extending thinking. Providing suggestions for improvement to successful students is often well accomplished by a simple reminder prompt ("Remember we are working on constitutional rights") that will help the student focus his or her own thinking. Sometimes a simple scaffold prompt is all that is necessary ("Remember we are working on constitutional rights—which of the events in the scenario is related to a constitutional right?").

Feedback for Struggling Students

Struggling students often experience negative feelings after failure. These feelings get in the way of processing additional information about their learning. For them, the value of feedback is lost, overshadowed by the low grade. For unsuccessful and unmotivated students, you need to deal with negative feelings first, before providing other formative assessment information, in order to break the cycle of failure (Turner, Thorpe, & Meyer, 1998). One way to do that is to shift from criterion-referenced feedback—remember, describing student work against criteria is usually recommended—and focus on self-referenced feedback.

Self-referenced feedback compares a student's work with his or her own previous work, so it can be used in a positive manner whether the current work is better or worse than expected. For example, if a student wrote only two sentences in his paragraph today, you might say, "You wrote four sentences yesterday. Can you think of two more sentences that further explain these, like you did before?" And if a student's work has shown improvement, it is easy to make self-referenced feedback positive. For example, if a student wrote

FIGURE 8.1   Examples of good and poor feedback for a struggling student.

Writing prompt:
Imagine this situation. Your favorite book is missing from your school library. It might be a book that you like to read over and over again. Or it might be a book that your teacher or parent has read to you. Some of your friends also like to read this book. The school librarian is not sure she wants to buy the book again. Write a letter to convince your school librarian to buy the book again. In your letter, give lots of reasons why the book should be in your school library.

Example of poor feedback:
Corrected errors for the student, gave advice ("add more") the student probably couldn't follow.

> *Dear Librarian,* *what book?*
> I want you to buy this book again
> because it is a very funny book and
> it has mystereys in it. That's why
> I want you to buy it. *Add more.*
> *Sincerely,*

Example of more effective feedback:
Selected one next step to focus on (elaboration) and used example prompts to help the student. Did not comment on other errors (e.g., use of letter form, spelling) in order to focus the student on one priority improvement.

> I want you to by this book again
> because it is a very funny book and
> it has mystereys in it. That's why
> I want you to buy it,
> *These are two good reasons.*
> *Can you add the name of*
> *the book and explain why*
> *these reasons are important?*
> *For example, "I feel _____*
> *when I read funny stories"*
> *or "Mysteries are great*
> *because _____."*

Source of student work: National Assessment of Educational Progress released item, Grade 4, 2002, Block W21, Question #1. Available: nces.ed .gov/nationsreportcard/itmrlsx/

a paragraph with two sentences in it today, you might say, "I see two whole sentences with complete thoughts. And they both go together. There you have the beginning of a paragraph! You have come a long way since your last writing."

Struggling students, whose work is of low quality, often receive feedback that is entirely criticism and advice about what to "fix." These students need to hear their teachers name and notice what they did correctly, affirming the basis from which they will proceed to improve. Then, they need example prompts that will walk them through what to do next. For students whose work is very far off the mark, reteaching, not feedback, is recommended (Hattie & Timperley, 2007).

Figure 8.1 gives some examples of poor and exemplary feedback to a struggling student. Actually, for this student, the exemplary feedback might better be delivered orally, or partly orally, because of its length. Of course, we can't do that in a text-book, so we have presented it as written feedback.

We cannot say definitively what you should do in every case. For example, perhaps the student whose work is shown in Figure 8.1 would benefit more not by feedback, but by seeing some examples, receiving some additional instruction and reteaching, and trying again on a different assignment. However, the example in Figure 8.1 does show the type of feedback that is typically not useful and the type of feedback that, for many students, would be useful.

For struggling students, formative feedback should begin with statements of accomplishment and suggest small, doable steps for improvement. And even such careful efforts don't always work, as the following true story from one of the authors shows.

Kasim was a poster child for the cycle of failure. Fifteen years old and in my seventh-grade English class, he never completed any assignment. He would write a line or two of an exercise or assignment, and then simply stop. Most of his teachers—including myself, I'm ashamed to admit—worked on getting him to "behave" first and learn second, so the class was not disrupted for the other students. Kasim lived in a foster home, had been abused as a child, and had the scars to prove it.

One day, in response to a brief writing assignment, Kasim brought me a three-page story, printed in tiny, cramped letters. It was an autobiographical story about how he had been separated from his sister, did not know where she was, and missed her terribly. It had a strong voice, expressive vocabulary, and readable (if not perfect) mechanics. I was excited. He could write! (I really hadn't been too sure about that.) More than that, he had wanted to write. Perhaps I got too excited, but for whatever reason, when I tried to encourage him to talk about his story, he appeared embarrassed to have written it and shut down. That was the first and last complete piece he did in a whole year.

Kasim would be a grown man now. When I think of him, I hope he's alive, I hope he's not in jail, and I hope he has found his sister. I'm not sure what could have broken his failure cycle or changed his negative attitude toward school. If I had it to do all over again, especially knowing what I know now about students like Kasim, I would have done things differently. I would have given him short assignments with more opportunities for peer and teacher feedback and given him a whole lot more choice. Kasim's life was full of circumstances beyond his control and, with hindsight, that included my class.

Feedback for English Language Learners

The most important aspect of feedback to English language learners (ELLs) is whether they will be able to understand it (Hill & Flynn, 2006; Mo, 2007). Teachers usually give feedback in academic English, not conversational English. For example, the concept of "descriptive details" is an academic idea. The idea that there are steps to problem solving, that you define the problem, variables, and potential solution strategies, is an academic idea.

The more a teacher understands about the ELL's native language, the better. A student may use a word order or word choice that makes sense in his native language, thus representing some understanding. You may decide to use that "sensible but incorrect" response to help the student learn some English sentence structure. Or it might be more productive in the long run to focus on the substance of the content rather than the word order. For example, if the sentence was a response to a question about a science concept, did the student understand the concept and use it properly in his explanation?

Understanding steps in the development of ELLs' language proficiency level is helpful, so you can target your feedback to a level the student can understand. Mo (2007) suggested five areas you can observe that can help you gauge the communication proficiency of ELLs in your classroom:

- How well does the student understand classroom discussions? (Does the student understand classroom talk at all? Can s/he understand if speech is slow and includes repetition?)
- How well does the student speak? (Does the student hesitate or search for words? Does the student ever initiate a conversation?)
- How well does the student use academic English, especially academic vocabulary?
- How easy is it to understand what the student says?
- How well does the student use conventional grammar and sentence patterns? (p. 41)

Second language development proceeds in stages. Students are at first silent and receptive, understanding some words they are not comfortable speaking. Next steps include early language production and the emergence of speech to intermediate and advanced proficiency (Hill & Flynn, 2006; Reed & Railsback, 2003).

Your feedback should be consistent with the ELL instructional program or model you are using. Programs vary considerably in ways that affect how feedback is given, including the amount of native language use, the purpose of native language use—whether native language instruction is done for the purpose of transition to English or for further development in the native language itself, the amount of time allowed for the program, and the approach to teaching English used. If a program emphasizes all student transactions should be in English, then your feedback should be in English. If not, you can give some feedback in the student's native language or enlist another student in helping you do that, if either is possible in your classroom.

Feedback for ELL students should be conversational. This fact supports the student's English language development. Always check for understanding of the feedback; for example, you could ask the student what she is going to do next. Below are guidelines for giving feedback to ELLs, based on information provided in resources for mainstream teachers (Dalton, 1998; Hill & Flynn, 2006; Mo, 2007; Deussen, Autio, Miller, Lockwood, & Stewart, 2008).

Example

Giving Feedback to English Language Learners

1. Use oral feedback, and talk with the student (as opposed to giving an oral feedback monologue).
2. Allow sufficient time for students to review their work and respond.
3. Be descriptive. Focus on a concrete work product, especially on work done jointly or collaboratively with other students.
4. Make both criterion-referenced (compare student work to standards) and self-referenced (point out improvements) comments.
5. Use pictures, diagrams, gestures, and other nonverbal means of communication when possible.
6. Model correct English in your oral feedback.
7. Speak slowly. Repeat feedback. Use simple vocabulary and explain important words.
8. Model correct English by repeating students' words with correct pronunciation and usage, rather than correcting them (e.g., If a student says "She do that," say "She does that," rather than "'Do' should be 'does'").
9. Give individual feedback, not group or public feedback.
10. Respect students' cultural preferences when speaking (for example, whether or not to make eye contact, waiting to speak until spoken to).

PEER FEEDBACK

Students can evaluate their own or peers' work against criteria you provide, or criteria they deduce from examples, and offer feedback. Peer feedback, in theory, helps the giver of feedback learn as much as the receiver, because giving feedback is an exercise in identifying aspects of the learning target in the work of others. Just like using any other examples to clarify what is to be learned, peer feedback immerses the peer in a concrete example of what learning should look like. Some research suggests that for the improvement of one's work, self-evaluation leads more directly to improvement than peer evaluation (Sadler & Good, 2006).

We advocate using rubrics or some other structured listing of criteria as the basis for peer feedback. This structure should make it easier for students to focus on the criteria and the work, as opposed to them personally. It should also give students a shared language, the criteria names and performance-level descriptions in the rubric, to use in their discussion.

Peer feedback can be done in pairs or small groups. Pairs or groups should be formed with attention to student interest, ability, and/or compatibility, depending on the particular assignment. Prepare the students for peer feedback. First, make sure that the students understand the assignment on which they will be giving feedback and the rubrics they will use to do so. Have the students practice with anonymous examples to help them apply the criteria accurately. Second, make sure the students understand ground rules for good peer feedback. You can give students rules and have them explain or role play what they mean. Rules will differ by grade level, students, and content area.

Example

Ground Rules for Peer Editing

1. Read your peer's work carefully.
2. Talk about the work, not the person who did the work.
3. Use words from the rubrics to describe your peer's work.
4. Make suggestions for improvement.
5. Explain why you think your suggestions would help improve the work.

There should be ground rules for receiving peer feedback, as well. For example, the student who did the work should know that the peer's ideas may be well intentioned, but that he himself is responsible for deciding whether to take the peer's advice. That too should be understood as about the work, not the person—if I don't act on my peer's suggestion, it should be because I am not convinced the suggestion would help my work, not because of the person who gave the suggestion.

As for any skill, giving and receiving peer feedback should be explicitly taught. Give students opportunities to practice giving peer feedback. Give them feedback on their feedback, so they know how well they are doing it and what they can do to improve. Some teachers require students to turn in revised work with the peer feedback they received, and some teachers further require students to explain how their revised work is better or different because of the peer feedback.

MyLab Education

Video Example 8.4

Students need to be taught how to apply the criteria and performance level descriptions from rubrics to student work. In this lesson, high school science students are learning how to apply a rubric's performance level descriptions to the evidence of learning in strong and weak work samples.

FEEDBACK FROM TECHNOLOGY

Technology can assist in giving feedback in at least two ways. Teachers can use technological means to give feedback on regular assignments that students have submitted as paper or electronic documents, as the result of face-to-face or online instruction. In computer-based instruction, feedback is usually programmed into the instructional software, and the computer "gives" the feedback.

Technology-Assisted Feedback on Students' Work

If students submit work electronically, either via email or a class website, teachers can use the Comments function and/or the Track Changes function to make comments in a word-processed document and then return it to the student for review. This process is possible whether the class is a face-to-face class or an online class, and the general feedback principles summarized in the Checklist for Evaluating the Effectiveness of Feedback still apply. In the electronic comments, describe the work against criteria, selecting one or two points for improvement. Differentiate your feedback according to student needs, with different levels of scaffolding for more and less successful learners, but make at least one suggestion for improvement even for students whose work was excellent. Structure the opportunities for students to receive feedback before final, graded work is due so that students can use the feedback to improve while there is still time for that to make a difference.

There is evidence that the same feedback issues that apply in face-to-face classrooms apply for feedback given by instructors in online learning (Chetwynd & Dobbin, 2011). Providing descriptive feedback without grades attached and then structuring opportunities for students to use the feedback—not just hoping that they read it—is particularly important for online courses, where it is tempting to provide feedback on required assignments at the same time they are graded. Providing feedback that not only retrospectively critiques a particular assignment but also feeds forward (Chetwynd and Dobbin called this "future-altering" feedback) is an issue in online learning, just as for face-to-face learning.

One of the authors has given feedback to teachers participating in a professional development program who submitted assignments by email. The assignments were not word processing documents but rather scanned collections of student work and teacher reflections. In that case, I gave feedback via email, again using the same principles for effective feedback.

Written feedback is not the only way technology can assist in delivering feedback to students. Oral feedback has been explored, as well. In 2008, 38 faculty members at four institutions in the United Kingdom worked on an experimental project to give audio feedback to their over 1,200 students using MP3 files (Rotheram, 2009). The project was handled as a series of case studies with two hypotheses: (1) that using digital audio for feedback would save assessors' time and (2) provide richer feedback to students. On balance, the project did not save time, although it could in the long run save time for some. However, both students and faculty were enthusiastic about audio feedback. Students noted its personal nature and detail, and most faculty said they intended to continue using it after the funded project was over.

Feedback in Computer-Based Instruction

In instructional software, feedback can come from the computer program itself. Of course, human designers and instructors need to program the computer to give the feedback. The long history of feedback research, reported above and summarized in the Checklist for Evaluating the Effectiveness of Feedback, forms the starting point for many of the decisions made in design feedback for instructional software (Mory, 2004).

Since computerized instruction came into use, however, research has been done directly on the effects of various kinds of feedback that computers can provide. Almost all computer feedback provides knowledge of results (e.g., whether an answer was correct or incorrect); where computer programs differ is in the amount and type of elaboration (e.g., specific description about the answer or topic). Mason and Bruning (2001) identified eight types of computer feedback that have been tested in various studies.

- *No feedback*—typically used as a control condition (e.g., a total quiz score with no information about individual items)

- *Knowledge-of-response*—computer provides item-level correct/incorrect information

- *Answer-until-correct*—learner must stay on the same test item until it is correct

- *Knowledge-of-correct-response*—computer provides item-level correct/incorrect information and gives the correct answer

- *Topic-contingent*—computer provides item-level correct/incorrect information and routs the student back to learning material or to additional material

- *Response-contingent*—computer provides item-level correct/incorrect information and an explanation of why the incorrect answer is wrong and the correct answer is right

- *Bug-related*—computer provides item-level correct/incorrect information and information about specific errors (obtained from a "bug library" of common errors)

- *Attribute-isolation*—computer provides item-level correct/incorrect information and highlights important attributes of the concept being learned

As you can see, none of the elaborations described in these types of feedback provides students with specific information about what to do next. However, some of them give students enough information, so they can successfully navigate their own next steps. The research on elaborative feedback in computer-based instruction has been mixed; some studies have found it more effective than knowledge of the answers alone and some have not (Mason & Bruning, 2001). However, on balance, elaborated feedback has a stronger effect on learning than providing the correct answer, and that evidence is growing (Van der Kleij, Feskens, & Eggen, 2015). The effectiveness of elaborative feedback in computer-based instruction seems to depend on both the student and the task. Lower-ability students and recall-level tasks seem to benefit more from immediate, specific feedback (e.g., answer correct/incorrect); higher-ability students and higher-order thinking tasks may benefit more from feedback that requires them to more actively process information (e.g., links to resources) (Mason & Bruning, 2001). However, in general the trend is for more elaborative feedback to be more effective for learning, which is consistent with the findings for feedback generally, where specific description is better for learning than general feedback (Van der Kleij, Feskens, & Eggen, 2015).

MyLab Education Self-Check 8.2

MyLab Education Application Exercise 8.2: Analyzing and Improving a Feedback Episode

CONCLUSION

Chapters 7 and 8 have been about using assessment for formative purposes. We have devoted a whole chapter to feedback because of its importance in the formative assessment cycle. Feedback comes in many forms and from many sources, and not all of it is helpful. The goal of this chapter has been to encourage you to deliver constructive, descriptive feedback to students, in a safe and learning-oriented classroom atmosphere, and follow it with an immediate opportunity for students to use the feedback to improve.

In the next set of chapters (9 through 13), we discuss how to design and write test items, assessment tasks, and scoring schemes. As you read these chapters, remember that items or tasks themselves are not "formative" or "summative." The use of information—for further learning or for grading and other final decisions—determines that. You need high-quality information from well-designed assessment questions, items, and tasks for both uses.

EXERCISES

1. Think back over your own school experiences. Identify a teacher whose feedback was particularly helpful to you and from whom you think you learned a lot. Describe his or her feedback in terms of the types and characteristics of feedback you have learned, and then use this information to explain why this teacher's feedback was effective for you.

2. Identify the characteristics of each of the feedback examples below.
   a. "I never want to see such sloppy work again!"
   b. "Use a capital A for Anne's name."
   c. "It was so wonderful to read your insightful description of Captain Ahab; I feel you really understand his motives."
   d. "All your spelling words were correct, so you get an extra 5 minutes at the computer."

3. Obtain some student work with teacher feedback written on it from a class you work in or from a friend or family member. Talk with the student about the work, what the student was trying to learn, and what the student understood the feedback to mean. Using the concepts and terminology from this chapter, explain what you learned about feedback from your conversation with the student.

4. Identify the level of elaboration in the following feedback prompts: Is the comment a reminder, a scaffold, or an example prompt?
   a. "When you borrow from the tens column, cross out the 8 tens and consider it 7 tens and 10 ones. Like this (does problem). OK, now can you do the same thing on the next problem?"
   b. "Lamar, what do you use to start a sentence?"
   c. "Let's dig into this food chain a little more. First, if the grass disappeared from the prairie, what species would not have food to eat?"
   d. "We're focusing on the dramatic conflict here."

9

Fill-in-the-Blank and True-False Items

KEY CONCEPTS

1. Fill-in-the-blank items require a word, short phrase, number, or symbol response. As for all assessments, fill-in-the-blank tests should align with the content and performance requirements of your learning objectives.

2. A true-false item consists of a statement or a proposition that a student must judge and mark as either true or false. True-false items are very useful, because judging the truth of a proposition is important to thinking in any discipline. Most criticisms of true-false items are actually criticisms of poorly constructed true-false items.

IMPORTANT TERMS

fill-in-the-blank varieties: association

completion

question

partial credit

proposition

random guessing

scoring key

strip key

true-false varieties: correction

multiple true-false

right-wrong

true-false

yes-no

yes-no with explanation

verbal clues (specific determiners)

In this chapter, we discuss how to craft simple forms of items suitable for paper-and-pencil or computer-based quizzes and tests: fill-in-the-blank and true-false items. When referring specifically to these kinds of assessment tasks, we shall use the terms *item* and *test item*.

THREE FUNDAMENTAL PRINCIPLES FOR CRAFTING ASSESSMENTS

Any assessment should conform to three fundamental principles for crafting assessments:

1. Focus each assessment task entirely on important learning objectives (content and performance).
2. Craft each assessment task to elicit from students only the knowledge and performance that are relevant to the learning objectives you are assessing.
3. Ensure that each assessment task does not inhibit a student's ability to demonstrate attainment of the learning objectives you are assessing by drawing on other, nonessential knowledge or skills.

The first principle is a strong one. Limit assessment tasks to those that focus on only educationally important learning targets. Assessing whether students have learned trivial performances or minor points of content is a waste of time.

To apply the second principle, you need a clear idea of what the learning objective is. If a student has achieved the desired degree of learning, the student should complete the relevant assessment task correctly. If, on the other hand, a student has not achieved the desired degree of learning, the deficiency should also be apparent in the assessment results. Some poor assessment tasks elicit unwanted behaviors from students, such as bluffing, fear, wild guessing, craftiness, or testwise skills. Testwiseness is the ability to use assessment-taking strategies, clues from poorly written items, and experience in taking assessments to improve one's score beyond what one would otherwise attain from mastery of the subject matter itself (see Chapter 14). These extra, unwanted behaviors may lead you to an inaccurate evaluation. Many of the suggestions in the next several chapters are specific ways to help you apply the second principle.

The third principle recognizes that imprecise wording in a question, for example, may make an item so ambiguous that a student who has the knowledge may answer it wrong. Similarly, simple matters such as inappropriate vocabulary, poorly worded directions, or poorly drawn diagrams may lead an otherwise knowledgeable student to respond incorrectly. Even the format or arrangement of an item on the page can inhibit some students from responding correctly. The third principle is amplified and applied to each item format discussed in this and the subsequent chapters.

Not all assessment experts would agree that there are only three basic principles, but most are likely to agree that these three are the important and fundamental principles for constructing classroom assessment tasks. These three encompass most of the specific suggestions that assessment experts have made over the years except, perhaps, those practical suggestions for efficient scoring.

FILL-IN-THE-BLANK ITEMS

Varieties of Fill-in-the-Blank Formats

Fill-in-the-blank items require a word, short phrase, number, or symbol response. Acceptable responses are limited to one correct answer or, perhaps, slightly misspelled versions of the one correct answer. (Items that require composed short answers will be discussed in Chapter 12 with other written constructed reponse questions.) There are three types of fill-in-the-blank items: question, completion, and association. The **question variety** asks a direct question and the student answers. Here are two examples:

Examples

Question Variety of Fill-in-the-Blank Item

1. What is the capital city of Pennsylvania?   (Harrisburg)

2. How many microns make up one millimeter?   (1,000)

The **completion variety** presents a student with an incomplete sentence and requires the student to complete it. Here are two examples:

Examples

Completion Variety of Fill-in-the-Blank Item

1. The capital city of Pennsylvania is   (Harrisburg)

2. $4 + (6 \div 2) =$ (7)

The **association variety** consists of a list of terms or a picture for which students have to recall numbers, labels, symbols, or other terms. This type of question is also called the *identification* variety. Here are some examples:

Examples

Association Variety of Fill-in-the-Blank Item

On the blank next to the name of each chemical element, write the symbol used for it.

Element	Symbol
Barium	_____ (Ba)
Calcium	_____ (Ca)
Chlorine	_____ (Cl)
Potassium	_____ (K)
Zinc	_____ (Zn)

Usefulness of Fill-in-the-Blank Items

Abilities Assessed   Fill-in-the-blank items can assess students' performance of lower-order thinking skills such as recall and comprehension of information. The fill-in-the-blank format also can be used to assess higher-level abilities such as the following:

1. Ability to make simple interpretations of data and applications of rules (e.g., counting the number of syllables in a word, demonstrating knowledge of place value in a number system, identifying the parts of an organism or apparatus in a picture, applying the definition of an isosceles triangle).

2. Ability to solve numerical problems in science and mathematics.

3. Ability to manipulate mathematical symbols and balance mathematical and chemical equations.

Figure 9.1 lists a large number of examples of fill-in-the-blank items. As you will see in other chapters, multiple-choice and other objective items can also assess these abilities. The generic items from Figure 9.1 are for the sake of examples because they are not matched to specific learning objectives. An item used directly from this table is unlikely to assess what you have taught. Use these examples to help you craft items matched to your learning objectives.

Strengths and Shortcomings   The fill-in-the-blank format is popular because it is relatively easy to construct and can be scored objectively.

FIGURE 9.1   Examples of fill-in-the-blank items assessing different types of lower-order thinking skills.

	Examples of generic questions*	Examples of actual questions
Knowledge of terminology	What is a _____? What does _____ mean? Define the meaning of _____?	What is a geode?
Knowledge of specific facts	Who did _____? When did _____? Why did _____ happen? Name the causes of _____.	What is the title of the person who heads the executive branch of government?
Knowledge of conventions	What are _____ usually called? Where are _____ usually found? What is the proper way to _____? Who usually _____?	What are magnetic poles usually named?
Knowledge of trends and sequences	In what order does _____ happen? Name the stages in _____. After _____, what happens next? Over the last _____ years, what has happened to _____? List the causes of the _____.	Write the life cycle stages of the moth in their correct order. 1st _____ 2nd _____ 3rd _____ 4th _____
Knowledge of classifications and categories	To what group do _____ belong? In what category would you classify _____? Which _____ does not belong with the others? List the advantages and disadvantages of _____.	Mars, Earth, Jupiter, and Venus are all _____.

(Continued)

FIGURE 9.1 *(Continued)*

	Examples of generic questions*	Examples of actual questions
Knowledge of criteria	By what criteria would you judge _____? What standards should _____ meet? How do you know if _____ is of high quality?	What is the main criterion against which an organization such as Greenpeace would judge the voting record of a congressional representative?
Knowledge of methods, principles, techniques	How do you test for _____? When _____ increases, what happens to _____? What should you do to _____ to get the _____ effect?	Today the sun's rays are more oblique to Centerville than they were 4 months ago. How does Centerville's temperature today compare with its temperature 4 months ago?
Comprehension	Write _____ in your own words. Explain _____ in your own words. Draw a simple diagram to show _____.	What do these two lines from Shakespeare's Sonnet XV mean? "When I consider everything that grows, Holds in perfection but a little moment…"
Simple interpretations	Identify the _____ in the _____. How many _____ are shown below? Label _____. What is the _____ in _____?	In the blank, write the adjective in each phrase below. Phrase 1. A beautiful girl _____ 2. A mouse is a small rodent. _____ 3. John found the muddy river. _____
Solving numerical problems	(Problem statements or figures to calculate would be placed here.) Use the data above to find the _____.	Draw a graph to show John's activities between 2:00 P.M. and 2:45 P.M. ■ John left home at 2:00 P.M. ■ John ran from 2:00 P.M. to 2:15 P.M. ■ John walked from 2:15 P.M. to 2:30 P.M. ■ John sat from 2:30 P.M. to 2:45 P.M.
Manipulating symbols, equations	Balance these equations. Derive the formula for _____. Show that _____ equals _____. Factor the expressions below.	Balance this equation _____$Cu + H_2SO_4 =$ _____$CuSO_4 +$ _____$H_2O + SO_2$

*The "blanks" in the generic items are for you to fill in. The generic items are simply suggestions to help you generate your own items suitable for testing your students. Your items must match your learning objectives to be valid.

But fill-in-the-blank items are not free of subjectivity in scoring. You cannot anticipate all possible responses students will make. Therefore, you often have to make subjective judgments as to the correctness of what the students wrote. Spelling errors, grammatical errors, and legibility tend to complicate the scoring process further. For example, to the question "What is the name of the author of *Alice in Wonderland*?" students may respond Carroll Lewis, Louis Carroll, Charles Dodgson, Lutwidge Dodgson, or Lewis Carroll Dodgson. Which, if any, should be considered correct? Although subjective judgment is proper, it does slow down the scoring process. It also tends to lower the reliability of the obtained scores. When you use fill-in-the-blank items in online tests and quizzes, the online learning environment software will ask you to specify what you will accept as correct answers, and anything that is not an exact match with your specifications will be counted as incorrect.

An advantage of the fill-in-the-blank format is that it lowers the probability of getting the answer correct by random guessing. A student who guesses randomly on a true-false item has a 50–50 chance of guessing correctly; on a four-option multiple-choice item, the student has one chance in four of randomly guessing the correct answer. For most fill-in-the-blank items, however, the probability of randomly guessing the correct answer is zero. Fill-in-the-blank items do not prevent students from attempting to guess the answer—they only lower the probability of the students guessing correctly.

In principle, guessing can be distinguished from using one's partial knowledge to help formulate an answer. Partial knowledge is not likely to result in the (exact) correct answer in fill-in-the-blank items. Teachers, however, often give **partial credit** for responses judged to be partially correct. This practice is appropriate and can result in more reliable scores *if* you use a **scoring key** that shows the kinds of answers eligible for partial credit. Using such a scoring key makes your assignment of partial credit more consistent from student to student, thereby improving reliability.

Creating Fill-in-the-Blank Items

Fill-in-the-blank items are easy to construct with a few simple guidelines. The checklist summarizes these guidelines in the form of yes-no questions. Use this checklist to review items before you put them on your test. A no answer to any one question is sufficient reason for you to omit an item from tests until you correct the flaw. The guidelines are really applications of the three fundamental principles for crafting assessments. In the following paragraphs, we examine the checklist's guidelines in more detail.

Checklist

A Checklist for Evaluating the Quality of Fill-in-the-Blank Items

Ask these questions of every item you write. If you answer no to one or more questions, revise the item accordingly.

1. Does the item assess an important aspect of the unit's instructional targets?
2. Does the item match your assessment plan in terms of performance, emphasis, and number of points?
3. If possible, is the item written in question format?
4. Is the item worded clearly so that the correct answer is a brief phrase, single word, or single number?
5. Is the blank or answer space toward the end of the sentence?
6. Is the item paraphrased rather than a sentence copied from learning materials?
7. If the item is in the completion format, is the omitted word an important word rather than a trivial word?
8. Are there only one or two blanks?
9. Is the blank or answer space in this item (a) the same length as the blank in other items or (b) arranged in an appropriate column?
10. If appropriate, does the item (or the directions) tell the students the appropriate degree of detail, specificity, precision, or units you want the answer to have?
11. Does the item avoid grammatical (and other irrelevant) clues to the correct answer?

1–2. The first two guidelines concern the importance of what is assessed and how the item matches the test blueprint. Assess only important performance and content, and match tasks to your learning targets and the assessment plan. Even if you perform no other evaluation of your assessment, make it a habit to evaluate every test item using these two criteria.

3. The question format is the preferred format for a fill-in-the-blank item and is preferred over the completion format. Here's why: The completion format always implies a question. The student must read the incomplete sentence and mentally convert it to a question before answering. Therefore, the most straightforward thing to do is ask a direct question in the first place. Further, the meaning of the items is often clearer if you phrase them as questions instead of incomplete sentences. Consider how a completion item can be improved by converting it into a direct question:

Examples

Poor: The author of *Alice in Wonderland* was ____.

Better: What is the pen name of the author of *Alice in Wonderland*? (Lewis Carroll)

Because the first version is not written in a question format, many correct answers are possible, including "a story writer," "a mathematician," "an Englishman," and "buried in 1898." The second version phrases the statement as a question, focusing the item on the specific knowledge sought.

As with all such rules, this one does have exceptions. Occasionally, the question form of the item incorrectly suggests the need for a longer or more complex answer. In this case, the incomplete sentence serves better. Here is an example of how the question form of an item may imply a longer than necessary answer:

Examples

Poor:	Why are scoring guides recommended for use with essay tests?
Better:	The main reason for using a scoring guide with an essay test is to increase the (objectivity) of the scoring.

Although the first version in the example implies that the teacher wants a paragraph or more, the teacher really had a very simple response in mind. This miscommunication is corrected by the second, revised version of the item. Most of the time, the question format produces better items. Your first impulse, therefore, should be to write questions, not incomplete sentences.

4. *Word the items specifically and clearly.* Usually, fill-in-the-blank items require a single correct answer. You should word the question or incomplete sentence so this is clear to the student. Illustrations of how using the correct wording communicates that the teacher wants a single, specific answer include the following:

Examples

Poor:	Where is Pittsburgh, Pennsylvania, located? _____
Better:	Pittsburgh, Pennsylvania, is located at the confluence of what two rivers? (Allegheny and Monongahela)
Better:	What city is located at the confluence of the Allegheny and Monongahela rivers? (Pittsburgh, Pennsylvania)

Several answers to the first version are possible, depending on how specific you want the answer to be: "western Pennsylvania," "southwestern corner of Pennsylvania," "Ohio River," "Monongahela and Allegheny Rivers," and so on are all correct. If you want a specific answer, you must phrase the question in a focused and structured way. If you want to focus on the rivers, for example, the first rephrased version may be used. To focus on the city, use the second rephrased version.

Focusing the item is important because you want a certain answer. Some students who know the desired answer may not give it because they misinterpret the question. This misunderstanding is especially likely for students at the elementary levels who interpret questions literally. For example, in one classroom, fourth graders were

given a bar graph to interpret. The teacher then asked the poorly phrased question in the example below:

Example

Poor:	Was the population of Mexico greater in 1941 or 1951? _____

One hapless student examined the graph and responded "yes." We'll leave the revision of this item to you.

5. *Put the blank toward the end of the sentence.* This fifth guideline applies to completion items. If blanks are placed at the beginning or in the middle of the sentence, the student has to mentally rearrange the item as a question before responding to it. Even a knowledgeable student will have to read the item twice to answer it. The examples below show how to improve an item by putting the blank at the end:

Examples

Poor:	_____ is the name of the capital city of Illinois.
Better:	The name of the capital city of Illinois is (Springfield).

Teachers of elementary-level arithmetic recognize that the ability to solve missing addend problems (e.g., "5 + ____ = 12" or " ____ + 5 = 12") is quite difficult to learn. When blanks are not placed at the end of a sentence, the verbal item functions like these arithmetic problems. Unlike missing addend problems, however, putting blanks at the beginning of a sentence places an unintended barrier in the path of a youngster who has command of the relevant knowledge. Such barriers lower the validity of your assessments. Elementary students are sometimes observed stopping and puzzling at a blank without reading the entire item: They realize that they should write an answer there, but they lack the experience to read ahead and mentally rearrange the item as a question. If you rephrase the item as a direct question or place the blank at the end, these youngsters are able to display the knowledge they have acquired.

6. *Do not copy statements verbatim.* When you copy material, you encourage students' rote memorization rather than real comprehension and understanding. Further, textbook statements

used as test items are usually quoted out of context. This practice may lead to item ambiguity or to more than one correct answer. One suggestion is to think first of the answer and then make up a question to which that answer is the only correct response.

7. *A completion item should omit important words and not trivial words.*   Use the item to assess a student's knowledge of an important fact or concept. This means, for example, that you should not make the blanks the verbs in the statement. An exception, of course, would be a language usage item that focuses on the correct verb form.

8. *Limit blanks to one or two.*   With more than one or two blanks, a completion item usually becomes unintelligible or ambiguous so that several unintended answers could be considered correct. Consider the following example:

Examples

Poor:	____ and ____are two methods of purifying ____.
Better:	Two different methods of purifying water are (distillation) and (deionization).

9. *Keep all blanks the same length.*   Testwise students sometimes use the length of the blank as a clue to the answer. Avoid such unintended clues. When testing older students, you can save yourself considerable scoring time by using short blanks in the item and by placing spaces for students to record answers at the right or left margin of the paper or on a separate answer sheet. You can then lay a **strip key** with the correct answers along the edge of each student's paper and score papers quickly. Placing the items so that all blanks occur in a column accomplishes the same purpose.

10. *Specify the precision you expect in the answer.*   In a fill-in-the-blank test involving dates or numerical answers, be sure to specify the numerical units you expect the students to use, or how precise or accurate you want the answers to be. This clarifies the task. It also saves time for students who strive for a degree of precision beyond your intentions. This example illustrates how to state the degree of precision expected in the answers:

Examples

Poor:	If each letter to be mailed weighs 1 1/8 oz., how much will 10 letters weigh? ____
Better:	If each letter to be mailed weighs 1 1/8 oz., how much (to the nearest whole oz.) will 10 letters weigh? (11 oz.)

If there are more than one or two numerical items, you can describe the level of precision you expect in the general directions at the beginning of the set of questions, rather than adding words to each item.

11. *Avoid irrelevant clues.*   A test item is designed to assess a specific learning objective, but sometimes the wording provides an irrelevant clue. When this happens, a student may answer correctly without having achieved the objective. The verb in a sentence, for example, may unintentionally clue the student that the answer you want is plural or singular. An indefinite article may be a clue that the answer you want begins with a vowel. The next example shows the same item with and without clues:

Examples

Poor:	A specialist in urban planning is called an (urbanist).
Better:	A specialist in city planning is called a(n) (urbanist).

The poor version has two clues to the right answer: It uses *urban planning*, which clues *urbanist*, and it uses the indefinite article, *an*, which clues the student that the expected answer begins with a vowel sound. The better version corrects these flaws by substituting a synonym (*city planning*) and using *a(n)* for the indefinite article form.

MyLab Education **Self-Check 9.1**
MyLab Education **Application Exercise 9.1:**
Evaluating Fill-in-the-Blank Exercises

TRUE-FALSE ITEMS
Varieties of True-False Items

A true-false item consists of a statement or a **proposition** that a student must judge and mark as either true or false. There are at least six **true-false varieties**: true-false, yes-no, right-wrong, correction, multiple true-false, and yes-no with explanation. The true-false variety presents a proposition that a student judges true or false. Here is an example:

Example

The sum of all the angles in any four-sided closed figure equals 360 degrees.　　　　　　T　　F

The **yes-no** variety asks a direct question, to which a student answers yes or no. This is an example:

Example

Is it possible for a presidential candidate to become president of the United States without obtaining a majority of the votes cast on election day?
　　　　　　　　　　　　　　　　Yes　　No

The **right-wrong** variety presents a computation, equation, or language sentence that the student judges as correct or incorrect (right or wrong). Here are two examples:

Examples

Example assessing an arithmetic principle
　　　　　$5 + 3 \times 2 = 16$　　　　R　　W
Example assessing grammatical correctness
　　　　Did she know whom it was?　　C　　I

The **correction** variety requires a student to judge a proposition, as does the true-false variety, but the student is also required to correct any false statement to make it true. Here is an example along with the directions to the students:

Example

Read each statement below and decide if it is correct or incorrect. If it is incorrect, change the underlined word or phrase to make the statement correct.
　　The new student, who we met today, came from Greece.　　　　　　　　　　　　C　　I

The **multiple true-false** variety looks similar to a multiple-choice item. However, instead of selecting one option as correct, the student treats every option as a separate true-false statement. More than one choice may be true. Each choice is scored as a separate item. For example:

Example

Under the Bill of Rights, freedom of the press means that newspapers

1. have the right to print anything they wish without restrictions.　　T　　F
2. can be stopped from printing criticisms of the government.　　T　　F
3. have the right to attend any meeting of the executive branch of the federal government.　　T　　F

The **yes-no with explanation** variety asks a direct question and requires the student to respond yes or no. In addition, the student must explain why his or her choice is correct. Here are some examples:

Examples

A large urban school district polled 500 high school honors students and 500 regular high school students. Each student was asked whether he or she agreed with the statement: "Students should have more say in homework policies." These are the results:

Honors student, male　　Agree 12%　Disagree 35%
Honors student, female　Agree 3%　　Disagree 14%
Regular student, male　　Agree 48%　Disagree 12%
Regular student, female　Agree 28%　Disagree 7%

1. I assert that this poll proves that most students want more say in school homework policies. Am I correct?　Yes　　No
2. If you say no, explain why I am wrong: ____

Advantages and Criticisms of True-False Items

Teachers often use true-false items because (a) certain aspects of the subject matter readily lend themselves to verbal propositions that can be judged true or false, (b) they are relatively easy to write, (c) they can be scored easily and objectively, and (d) they can cover a wide range of content within a relatively short period. But some educators have severely criticized true-false items—*especially poorly constructed true-false items*. Among the more frequent criticisms are that poorly constructed true-false items assess only specific, frequently trivial facts, are ambiguously worded, are answered correctly by random guessing, and encourage students to study and accept only oversimplified statements of truth and factual details. If you follow the suggestions in this chapter for improving true-false items, you can avoid these criticisms.

Assess More Than Simple Recall

Well-written true-false items can assess a student's ability to identify the correctness or appropriateness of a variety of meaningful propositions, including the following (Ebel, 1972):

1. *Generalizations* in a subject area
2. *Comparisons* among concepts
3. *Causal or conditional propositions*
4. *Relationships* between two events, concepts, facts, or principles
5. *Explanations* for why events or phenomena occurred
6. *Instances or examples* of a concept or principle
7. *Evidential statements*
8. *Predictions* about phenomena or events
9. *Steps* in a procedure or process
10. *Computations* (or other kinds of results obtained from applying a procedure)
11. *Evaluations* of events or phenomena

Examples of items of each of these types are shown in Figure 9.2. Some of the key phrases used to construct items in each category appear as well. You may want to refer to Figure 9.2 from time to time to glean suggestions for writing true-false items. The final item should assess your intended thinking skill and learning objective. Using a key phrase from the figure does not guarantee that the item you craft will assess the thinking skill shown; check to make sure that it does.

Validity of the True-False Item Format

Ebel, perhaps more than any other measurement specialist, defended the use of well-written true-false items for classroom assessment. He offered the following argument for the validity of this format:

1. The essence of educational achievement is the command of useful verbal knowledge.
2. All verbal knowledge can be expressed in propositions.
3. A proposition is any sentence that can be said to be true or false.

4. The extent of a student's command of a particular area of knowledge is indicated by his success in judging the truth or falsity of propositions related to it. (Ebel, 1972, pp. 111–112)

Requiring students to identify the truth or falsity of propositions is not the only means of ascertaining their command of knowledge. Other ways of assessing command of knowledge are discussed further in the remaining chapters of this book.

Guessing on True-False Items

A common criticism of true-false tests is that they are subject to error because students can answer them with random guesses. It is well known that for a single true-false item, there is a 50–50 chance of answering the item correctly if true or false is selected at random, which means that persons guessing randomly can expect to get *on the average* one half of the true-false items correct. Several points, however, blunt this criticism (Ebel, 1972):

1. Blind (completely random) guessing is quite unlike informed guessing (guessing based on partial knowledge).
2. Well-motivated students tend to guess blindly on only a small percentage of the questions on a test.
3. It is very difficult to obtain a good score on a test by blind guessing alone.
4. If a given true-false test has a high reliability coefficient, that would be evidence that scores on that test are not seriously affected by blind guessing.

Random guessing, of the type that is assumed by the "50–50 chance" statement, is by definition random responding. Random guessing is sometimes called *blind guessing*. But most everyone's experience is that students rarely respond this way to test questions. Rather, students tend to use whatever partial knowledge they have about the subject of the questions and/or about the context in which the questions are embedded to make an informed guess. Such informed guessers have a higher than 50–50 chance of success on true-false items—but how much higher, we are unable to say. This fact means that scores from true-false items, as with other item types, are measures of partial knowledge when informed guessing

FIGURE 9.2   **Types of statements that could form the basis for your true-false items.**

Type of statement	Examples of introductory words or phrases	Examples of true-false items
Generalization	All . . . Most . . . Many . . .	All adverbs modify verbs. (F)
Comparative	The difference between . . . is . . . Both . . . and . . . require . . .	Both dependent and independent clauses contain subjects and verbs. (T)
Conditional	If . . . (then) . . . When . . .	When there is no coordinating conjunction between two independent clauses, they should be separated by a colon. (F)
Relational	The larger . . . The higher . . . The lower . . . Making . . . us likely to . . . Increasing . . . tends to . . . How much . . . depends on . . .	The amount of technical vocabulary you should include in an essay depends on your intended audience. (T)
Explanatory	The main reason for . . . The purpose of . . . One of the actors that adversely affect . . . Since . . . Although . . .	One of the factors affecting changes in rules governing English grammar and style is changes in how people use the language. (T)
Exemplary	An example of . . . One instance of . . .	The movie title *The Man Who Came to Dinner* contains a nonrestrictive clause. (F)
Evidential	Studies of . . . reveal . . .	Studies of contemporary literature show that some authors deliberately violate style and usage rules to create literary effects. (T)
Predictive	One could expect . . . Increasing . . . would result in . . .	Increasing the number of clauses in sentences usually increases the reading difficulty of a passage. (T)
Procedural	To find . . . one must . . . In order to . . . one must . . . One method of . . . is to . . . One essential step . . . is to . . . Use . . . of . . . The first step toward . . .	The first step toward composing a good essay is to write a rough draft. (F)
Computational	(Item includes numerical data and requires computation or estimation.)	There are two adjectives in the following sentence: "The quick brown fox jumped over the lazy dog." (F)
Evaluative	A good . . . It is better to . . . than . . . The best . . . is . . . The maximum . . . is . . . The easiest method of . . . is to . . . It is easy to demonstrate that . . . It is difficult to . . . It is possible to . . . It is reasonable to . . . It is necessary to . . . in order to . . . The major drawback to . . . is . . .	It is generally better to express complex ideas as two or more shorter sentences rather than one longer sentence. (T)

Note: To be valid, the items must match specific learning targets.

Source: Bloom, Benjamin S., *Taxonomy Of Educational Objectives Book 1/Cognitive Domain*, 1st Ed., ©1984, pp. 201–207. Adapted and electronically reproduced by permission of Pearson Education, Inc., Upper Saddle River, New Jersey.

FIGURE 9.3   Chances of a student obtaining various "good scores" by using only random guessing for all items on true-false tests of various lengths.

Number of T-F items on the test	Chances of getting the following percentage of T-F questions right:		
	60% or better	80% or better	100%
5	50 in 100	19 in 100	3 in 100
10	38 in 100	6 in 100	1 in 1,000
15	30 in 100	2 in 100	3 in 100,000
20	25 in 100	6 in 1,000	1 in 1,000,000
25	21 in 100	2 in 1,000	3 in 100,000,000

Note: Computations are based on binomial probability theory.

occurs. (Of course, persons who actually know the answer have a 100 percent chance of answering correctly!)

Although a student who is responding randomly on a single true-false item will have a 50–50 chance of being correct, the laws of chance indicate that the probability of getting a good score by random guessing on a test made up of many true-false items is quite small, especially for longer tests. This point is illustrated in Figure 9.3. Chances are only two in 100, for example, that a student who has guessed randomly on all the items on a 15-item test will get 80 percent or more of the items correct. If the test has 25 true-false questions and a student guesses randomly on all items, that student has only two chances in 1,000 of getting 80 percent or more items correct. Chances of a perfect (100% correct) paper are even smaller.

Suggestions for Getting Started

To write good true-false items, you must be able to identify propositions that (a) represent important ideas, (b) can be defended by competent critics as true or false, and (c) are not obviously correct to persons with general knowledge or good common sense who have not studied the subject. These propositions are then used as starting points to derive true-false items.

In this regard, Ebel (1972) suggested that you think of a segment of knowledge as being represented by a paragraph; the propositions are the main ideas of that paragraph. You can then use these main ideas as starting points for writing true-false items. Figure 9.2 offers suggestions on how to get started in phrasing true-false items from these propositions.

Frisbie and Becker (1990) offer these additional suggestions for getting started:

1. *Create pairs of items, one true and one false, related to the same idea, even though you will use only one.*   Creating pairs of items helps you check on a statement's ambiguity and whether you need to include qualifications in the wording. Frisbie and Becker suggest that your false item is not worth using if you can only write a true version of it by inserting the word *not.*

2. *If your statement asks students to make evaluative judgments ("The best...is...," "The most important...is...," etc.), try to rephrase it as a comparative statement ("Compared to..., A is better than...").*   The comparative statement allows you to put into the item itself the comparisons you want students to make. Usually, when you write "What is the best way to...", you raise in the mind of the student the question, "compared to what?" Thus, if you include your intended comparison in the statement itself, the inclusion clears up the ambiguity.

3. *Write false statements that reflect the actual misconceptions held by students who have not achieved the learning objectives.*   To do this properly, you have to know your students well and try to think about a proposition the way a misinformed or poorly prepared student thinks about it. As you teach, you may notice these misconceptions. Take notes, so you can recall them as you write items.

4. *You may wish to convert a multiple-choice item into two or more true-false items.*   The foils (or incorrect options) of a multiple-choice item may be used as a basis for writing false statements.

Suggestions for Improving True-False Items

Review and revise the first drafts of all your assessment tasks. Editing assessment tasks is an important step in the assessment development process. The checklist summarizes principles for improving the quality of true-false items. You should always use the checklist to review true-false items that come with your textbook and curriculum materials, because these true-false items are notorious for their poor quality. The principles implied by the checklist are explained and illustrated in the following section.

Checklist

A Checklist for Evaluating the Quality of True-False Items

Revise every item for which you answered no to one or more questions.

1. Does the item assess an important aspect of the unit's instructional targets?

2. Does the item match your assessment plan in terms of performance, emphasis, and number of points?

3. Does the item assess important ideas, knowledge, or understanding (rather than trivia, general knowledge, or common sense)?

4. Is the statement either definitely true or definitely false without adding further qualifications or conditions?

5. Is the statement paraphrased rather than copied verbatim from learning materials?

6. Are the word lengths of true statements about the same as those of false statements?

7. Did you avoid presenting items in a repetitive or easily learned pattern (e.g., TTFFTT, TFTFTF)?

8. Is the item free of verbal clues that give away the answer?

9. If the statement represents an opinion, have you stated the source of the opinion?

10. If the statement does not assess knowledge of the relationship between two ideas, does it focus on only one important idea?

1–2. The first items on the checklist cover the importance of what is assessed and its match to the test blueprint. As always, the first two criteria that your assessment tasks should meet are importance and match to your assessment plan. Eliminate every item failing to meet these two criteria.

3. Assess important ideas, rather than trivia, general knowledge, or common sense. Although this guideline applies to all assessment tasks, you need to be especially sensitive to this point when writing true-false items. It is easy to write items that assess trivial knowledge. Here are some examples of how to improve items, so they focus on more important ideas:

Examples

Poor:	George Washington had wooden teeth.	T	F
Better:	George Washington actively participated in the Constitutional Convention.	T	F

The poor item focuses on trivia rather than important information about Washington's role in the early days of the nation. The revised version at least asks a more significant fact about him.

4. Make sure the item is either definitely true or definitely false. A proposition should not be so general that a knowledgeable student can find exceptions that change the intended truth or falsity of the statement. Make sure the item is phrased in a way that makes it unambiguous to the *knowledgeable* student. (Items should, of course, appear ambiguous to the unprepared or unknowledgeable student.) A few suggestions for reducing item ambiguity include the following:

a. *Use short statements whenever possible.* Using short statements makes it easier to identify the idea you want the student to judge true or false. Complex, cumbersome statements make identifying the essential element in the item difficult even for knowledgeable students. If the information you want to describe in the statement is complex, use different sentences to separate the description from the statement students must judge true or false. Often, you can shorten a long, complex statement that contains extraneous material by simply editing it.

b. *Use exact language.* Frequently, quantitative terms can clarify an otherwise ambiguous statement. For example, instead of saying "approximately $5.00" or "approximately one half of," say "between $4.00 and $6.00" or "between 45% and 55%."

c. *Use positive statements and avoid double negatives,* many students find especially confusing. Here is an example of improving an item by avoiding negatives:

Examples

Poor:	The Monongahela River does not flow northward.	T	F
Better:	The Monongahela River flows southward.	T	F

If you must use a negative function word, be sure to <u>underline it</u> or use all capital letters, so students do NOT overlook it. Do not take a textbook sentence and make it false by adding a "not" to it. The practice of taking a textbook sentence and making it false by inserting negative function words (e.g., *not, neither, nor*) makes the item you write tricky for students.

5. *Avoid copying sentences verbatim.*   Students often find sentences copied from a text uninterpretable because they have been taken out of context. In addition, such statements are likely to communicate to students that the text's exact phrasing is important, rather than their own comprehension. This practice encourages students to engage in rote learning of textbook sentences. Recall from Figure 3.2 that one factor in the validity of your assessment is that it does not have such negative consequences.

Copying items from a text is more likely when a teacher is testing for knowledge of verbal concepts (including definitions) and statements of principles (rules). But testing for comprehension demands paraphrasing at the minimum, and enhancing a student's comprehension of concepts and principles seems to be a more important educational goal than encouraging a student to memorize textbook statements word-for-word.

6. *True and false statements should have approximately the same number of words.*   Teachers tend to make true statements more qualified and wordy than false statements. Testwise students can pick up on this irrelevant clue and get the item right without achieving the learning objective. Keep a watchful editorial eye and rewrite inappropriate statements.

7. *Don't present items in a repetitive or easily learned pattern*   (e.g., TFTFTF, TTFFTT, TFFTFF). Some teachers develop such patterns because they are easy to remember and thus make scoring

easier. But if it's easy for a teacher to remember, it will also be easy for testwise students to learn. Assessment results will then be invalid. You should also avoid a consistent practice of having many more true answers than false, or many more false answers than true. If students notice, for example, that you seldom use a false statement, they will (rightly) avoid choosing false when they are uncertain of the answer. Upper-grade students discover these patterns quickly when a teacher uses a lot of true-false items.

Not all educational assessment specialists agree on the proportion of true-to-false answers to include (Frisbie & Becker, 1990). Some specialists recommend having more false items than true ones, because false items have been shown to discriminate (distinguish between more and less knowledgeable students; see Chapter 14) better than true items (Barker & Ebel, 1981). *Discriminate* in this context means that false items tend to differentiate the most knowledgeable students from the least knowledgeable better than true items. Increased item discrimination improves the reliability of the total test scores.

8. *Do not use* **verbal clues** *(specific determiners) that give away the answer.*   A **specific determiner** is a word or phrase in a true-false or multiple-choice item that "overqualifies" a given statement and gives the student an unintended clue to the correct answer. Words such as *always, never,* and *every* tend to make propositions false. Words such as *often, usually,* and *frequently* tend to make propositions true. Testwise students will use these clues to respond correctly even though they do not have command of the requisite knowledge. Here is an example of a poor item using a specific determiner:

Example

Poor:	In a ground war, the army with more sophisticated weaponry always defeats its opponents.	T	F

9. *Attribute the opinion in a statement to an appropriate source.*   If your true-false item expresses an opinion, value, or attitude, attribute the statement to an appropriate source. You can use an introductory clause, such as "According to the text," "In the opinion of most specialists in this area," or "In Jones's view." This referencing reduces ambiguity in two ways: (a) it makes clear that the statement is not to be judged in general,

but rather in terms of the specific source, and (b) it makes clear that you are not asking for the student's personal opinion.

10. *Focus on one idea.* Have only one idea per item, unless the item is intended to assess knowledge of the relationship between two ideas. The following example shows how an item can be improved by focusing it on only one idea:

Examples

Poor:	The Monongahela River flows north to join the Allegheny River at Columbus, where they form the Ohio River.	T	F
Better:	The Monongahela River and the Allegheny River join to form the Ohio River.	T	F

In the poor item, a student may respond with the correct answer, F, for an inappropriate reason: The student may think (erroneously) that the Monongahela River does not flow north, may be unaware that the confluence of the rivers is at Pittsburgh, or may lack any knowledge about the three rivers. Thus, the student would get the item right without having the knowledge that getting the right answers implies. A separate statement for each idea may be necessary to identify precisely what the student knows.

Creating Multiple True-False Items

A multiple true-false item looks like a multiple-choice item in that it has a stem followed by several alternatives. Unlike when responding to a multiple-choice item, however, the student does not select the single correct or best answer; she responds true or false to every alternative. In turn, each alternative is scored correct or incorrect. Because of this, the item may be constructed to have several correct (true) alternatives instead of only one. The examples that follow illustrate this point.

Examples

**Which of the following were roles colonial women played in the American Revolution?

1. They served as officers in the army.		T	F
2. They followed soldiers in camps, cooking, and washing.		T	F
3. They kept the farms and shops running during the war.		T	F
4. They helped to run the colonial government.		T	F

**Which of these statements describes a necessary characteristic of cells?

1. They reproduce sexually.	Y	N
2. They make their own food.	Y	N
3. They move from place to place.	Y	N

Source: Adapted from NAEP released items: Grade 4, 2010, H3 #8; Grade 8, 2011, S11 #3

Format Notice three things about the format of the preceding examples. First, unlike multiple-choice items, the *options are numbered* consecutively, and asterisks set off the different clusters' stems. Second, you do not need to have a balance of true or false correct answers within one cluster. Some clusters, like the second one, may not have any true or any yes answers. Third, all of the statements within a cluster must relate to the same stem or question. Each statement within a cluster is treated as a separate true-false item. Thus, the example contains seven items, not two items.

Advantages This item format has several advantages: (a) Students can make two or three multiple true-false responses in the same time it takes them to answer one multiple-choice item; (b) a multiple true-false test created from multiple-choice items has a higher reliability than the original multiple-choice test; (c) multiple true-false items can assess the same abilities as straight multiple-choice items designed to assess parallel content; (d) students believe that multiple true-false items do a better job of assessing their knowledge than straight multiple-choice items; (e) students perceive multiple true-false items to be slightly harder than straight multiple-choice items; and (f) multiple true-false items may be easier to write than multiple-choice items because you are not limited to creating only one correct answer.

Limitations The multiple true-false item format shares many of the same limitations as multiple-choice items. These limitations are discussed in Chapter 10. Some research shows that standard multiple-choice items may be more appropriate than multiple true-false items for assessing higher-order thinking skills and when criterion-related validity evidence is important (Downing, Baranowski, Grosso, & Norcini, 1995).

MyLab Education **Self-Check 9.2**

MyLab Education **Application Exercise 9.2:** Evaluating True-False Items

CONCLUSION

In this chapter, we discussed how to write effective fill-in-the-blank and true-false test items. We summarized these item-writing principles in checklists. Some of these principles—assess an important aspect of the unit's instructional targets; match your assessment plan in terms of performance, emphasis, and number of points; and use clear, concise written expression—are principles for writing all types of test items, and some of the principles are unique to the item genre. We continue with two more item types, multiple-choice and matching, in Chapter 10.

EXERCISES

1. Write fill-in-the-blank items in your teaching area(s) that assess each of the lower-order thinking skills listed in Figure 9.1.
2. Each of the following fill-in-the-blank items contains one or more flaws. For each item, use the checklist for fill-in-the-blank items to identify the flaw(s), and rewrite the item, so it remedies the flaw(s) you identified but creates no new flaws.
   a. _____ is the substance that helps plants turn light energy to food.
   b. The Johnstown Flood occurred during _____.
   c. The _____ is the major reason why _____ and _____ exhibit _____.
   d. San Francisco was named after _____.
   e. A kilogram is equivalent to _____.
   f. Was the population greater in 1941 or 1951?
3. Obtain a teacher's edition of a textbook (or other curricular materials) that covers the material for the teaching unit you selected for Exercise 3 of Chapter 6.

Locate the completion and true-false items presented in the teacher's edition or textbook for this unit. Match those items to the learning objectives included in the assessment blueprint you crafted for Exercise 3. To what extent do these items match the learning objectives and the blueprint? What do your findings suggest about the way you should use the items the textbook gives you? About your need to craft items yourself? Prepare a short report and share your findings with others in this course.

4. Each of the following true-false items contains one or more flaws. For each item, use the checklist for true-false items to identify the flaw(s) and rewrite it, correcting the flaw(s) identified. Be sure your rewritten items do not exhibit new flaws.
   a. The two categories, plants and animals, are all that biologists need to classify every living thing.   T   F
   b. In the United States, it is warm in the winter.   T   F
   c. Editing assessment tasks is an important step in the assessment development process.   T   F
   d. The major problem in the world today is that too many people want more than their "fair share" of the Earth's resources.   T   F
   e. There were more teachers on strike in 1982 than in 1942, even though the employment rate was lower in 1942 than in 1982.   T   F
5. Write one true-false item in your teaching area(s) that assesses a student's use of each of the categories of propositions listed in Figure 9.2.

Multiple-Choice and Matching Exercises

KEY CONCEPTS

1. A multiple-choice item consists of one or more introductory sentences followed by a list of two or more suggested responses. The student must choose the correct answer. Follow item-writing guidelines to create high-quality, multiple-choice items. Alternative varieties of multiple-choice items include greater-less-same, best-answer, experiment-interpretation, and statement-and-comment items.

2. A matching exercise presents a student with three things: (1) directions for matching, (2) a list of premises, and (3) a list of responses. Follow item-writing guidelines to create high-quality matching exercises. Alternative varieties of matching exercises include masterlist and tabular formats.

IMPORTANT TERMS

"all of the above"

alternatives, choices, options

best-answer item

clueing, linking

context-dependent items, interpretive exercises, interpretive materials, linked items

correct-answervariety

decontextualized knowledge

direct assessment, indirect assessment

distractor rationale taxonomy

distractors, foils

experiment-interpretation items

filler alternatives, deadwood alternatives

greater-less-same items

homogeneous alternatives, heterogeneous alternatives

homogeneous premises and responses

incomplete stem

keyed alternative, key, keyed answer

masterlist variety, classification variety, keylist variety

matching exercise (basic)

multiple-choice item

"none of the above"

overlapping alternatives

perfect matching

plausible distractors, functional alternatives

premise list

response list

statement-and-comment items

stem

tabular (matrix) items

clang associations, grammatical clues

window dressing

MULTIPLE-CHOICE ITEMS

A **multiple-choice item** consists of one or more introductory sentences followed by a list of two or more suggested responses. The student must choose the correct answer from among the responses you list. The following example illustrates this format:

Example

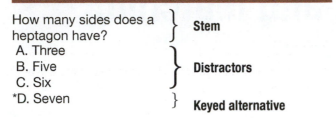

How many sides does a heptagon have? } **Stem**
A. Three
B. Five } **Distractors**
C. Six
*D. Seven } **Keyed alternative**

Note: Correct answers to multiple-choice items will be marked with an asterisk (*) in this book.

The **stem** is the part of the item that asks the question, sets the task a student must perform, or states the problem a student must solve. You write the stem so that a student understands what task to perform or what question to answer.

Teachers call the list of suggested responses by various names: **alternatives, choices,** and **options**. The alternatives should always be arranged in a meaningful way (logically, numerically, alphabetically, etc.).

The alternative that is the correct or best answer to the question or problem you pose is called the **keyed answer, keyed alternative,** or simply the **key.** The remaining incorrect alternatives are called **distractors or foils.** The purpose of the latter is to present plausible (but incorrect) answers to the question or solutions to the problem in the stem. These foils should be plausible only to students who do not have the level of knowledge or understanding required by your learning objective—those who haven't learned the material well enough. Conversely, the foils should not be plausible to students who have the degree of knowledge you desire.

In some cases, you may need to add information to make a question clearer or more authentic. You may wish to assess a learning objective, for example, that requires students to apply their knowledge to data in a table or a graph, to a situation described in a paragraph, to an object, or to an event simulated by a picture. If adding this kind of information makes the stem more than one or two sentences long, then the information is placed in a section that comes before the stem. This information is called **interpretive material,** and the items that refer to it are called **context-dependent items, interpretive exercises,** or **linked items** (the items are "linked" to the interpretive material). Figure 10.1 illustrates this assessment technique. The graph of

FIGURE 10.1   Item with interpretive material.

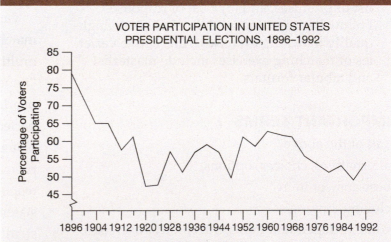

What does the graph show about voting behavior?

A. A majority of Americans never vote in presidential elections.

B. All eligible voters voted in the 1960 election.

C. Voter turnout generally declined from 1896 to 1988.

D. Fewer candidates have run for President since 1952.

Source: National Assessment of Educational Progress Released Item, 2010, Block C8, Question 10. Available: nces.ed.gov/nationsreportcard/itmrlsx/

voter participation is the interpretive material. We give more elaborate suggestions for context-dependent items in Chapter 11.

For paper-and-pencil tests and for most computer-based tests, the stems are numbered and the alternatives are lettered. For paper-and-pencil tests, students select an alternative by writing the letter or bubbling in a machine-readable answer sheet. For computer-based tests, students select an alternative by clicking on a radio button beside their choice. However, some computer-based tests use innovative multiple-choice format that allows students to select choices by clicking on active links right in the interpretive material. Here is an example.

Example

Read *The Dove and the Ant.* Then answer the question below.

An Ant, going to a river to drink, fell in, and <u>was carried along</u> in the stream. A Dove pitied her condition, and <u>threw into the river a small bough</u>, by means of which the Ant gained the shore. The Ant afterward, seeing a man with a fowling-piece <u>aiming at the Dove</u>, stung him in the foot sharply, and made him miss his aim, and so saved the Dove's life.

The moral of this tale is, "Sometimes your smallest friends are your biggest allies." Click on the phrase that gives the best evidence that the ant was the dove's ally.

[The underlined words are the choices. Students click on the one they wish to select.]

The National Association for the Education of Young Children and the National Association of Early Childhood Specialists in State Departments of Education (NAEYC, 2003) recommend that for children up through age eight assessment should be tied to children's daily activities, especially systematic observations of students' play (for preschoolers) and work (for kindergarten and first-grade students). For K–1 children, some paper-and-pencil methods may be used in addition to observations. Multiple-choice questions for young children may include pictures and are often assessments of their developing vocabulary. Here is an example.

Example

[Directions given orally: Circle the word that means the same as the picture.]

ball

bat

bed

baby

Mapping a Continuum of Proficiency

Think of a student as being located at some point along a continuum of learning for a given learning objective. You can construct a test item for students at a specific level of this learning continuum. The students who are at this level (or above it) should be able to answer the item correctly; others, lower on the continuum of learning, will not. Consider the following items:

Examples

---

1. In what year did the United States enter World War I?
   - A. 1776
   - B. 1812
   - *C. 1917
   - D. 1981
2. In what year did the United States enter World War I?
   - A. 1901
   - *B. 1917
   - C. 1941
   - D. 1950
3. In what year did the United States enter World War I?
   - A. 1913
   - B. 1915
   - C. 1916
   - *D. 1917

All three items ask the same question, but the specificity of knowledge that is required to answer that question increases from Item 1 to Item 3. In this example, you can easily see how *the alternatives operate to make the item easy or difficult*: The alternatives require the students to make finer distinctions among the dates. Some research supports the idea that similarity among the alternatives increases the difficulty of an item (Ascalon, Meyers, Davis, & Smits, 2007). Although the example uses dates, similarities can also be the result of using certain words or concepts. Of course, manipulating the alternatives is not the only way to create more difficult items.

For which level of knowledge should an item be written? There is no general rule, but keep in mind the type of students, the level of instruction, the purpose for which you will use the assessment results, and the level of knowledge your students need to attain at this point in their educational development. Also, consider the thinking levels your test will assess. In effect, you need to decide, at least roughly, what level of proficiency is sufficient for each important learning objective. Then construct test items that will allow you to distinguish students who lack sufficient proficiency from those who have acquired it. Or if you are trying to map students along a range of proficiencies (A, B, C, D, F, for example; or basic, proficient, advanced; etc.), you should include items along the range of the continuum so that each category of students will have some items that indicate the proficiency level.

The preceding description represents an idealized situation. Seldom will your real assessment tasks separate students this neatly. Some less knowledgeable students probably will answer some tasks correctly, and other, more knowledgeable students, will not. In general, though, keep in mind this principle:

> The basic purpose of an assessment task, whether or not it is a multiple-choice item, is to identify students who have attained a sufficient (or necessary) level of knowledge (skill, ability, or performance) of the learning objective being assessed.

Varieties of Multiple-Choice Items

Teachers and professional test developers use several varieties of multiple-choice items. Some of these are shown in Figure 10.2. Teachers usually find that the **correct-answer**, best-answer, incomplete-statement, and negative varieties in Figure 10.2 are the most useful. As you grow more skilled at evaluating students, you will find that you need to use several of these variations to obtain valid results. We will discuss some of these item varieties in this textbook. See Haladyna (2004) for details about other varieties.

Direct Versus Indirect Assessment

A multiple-choice test can be a **direct assessment** of certain abilities. Well-written multiple-choice items, especially those requiring the use of interpretive materials, can help directly assess a student's ability to discriminate and make correct choices; to comprehend concepts, principles, and generalizations; to make judgments about and choices among various courses of action; to infer and reason; to compute; to interpret new data or new information; and to apply information and knowledge in structured situations.

Multiple-choice items are only **indirect assessments** of other important educational outcomes, such as the ability to recall (as opposed to recognize) information under minimal prompting conditions, to articulate explanations and give examples, to produce and express unique or original ideas, to solve problems that are not well structured, to organize personal thoughts, to display thought processes or patterns of reasoning, to work in groups, and to construct or build things. These are important abilities. Many of them can be assessed directly with other paper-and-pencil formats such as extended written assignments. Others require alternative assessment techniques such as observing a student over an extended period working alone or in a group; interviewing a student; or assessing a student's performance, product, or creation. These latter techniques are discussed in Chapter 13.

Advantages and Criticisms of Multiple-Choice Items

Advantages   The following are advantages of multiple-choice items:

1. *The multiple-choice format can be used to assess a greater variety of learning objectives than other formats of response-choice items.* The various abilities were discussed in the preceding paragraphs.

2. *Multiple-choice items* (and other types of response-choice items) *do not require students to write out and elaborate their answers and thus minimize the opportunity for less knowledgeable students to "bluff" or "dress up" their answers.* Some consider this a disadvantage.

3. *Multiple-choice tests focus on reading and thinking.* They do not require students to use writing processes under examination conditions.

4. *Students have less chance to guess the correct answer to a multiple-choice item than a true-false item or a poorly constructed matching exercise.* The probability of a student blindly guessing the correct answer to a three-alternative item is 1/3, to a four-alternative item it is 1/4, and so on.

5. *The distractor a student chooses may give you diagnostic insight into difficulties the student is experiencing.* However, for distractors to work this way you must carefully craft them, so they are

FIGURE 10.2 Varieties of multiple-choice items.

A. *The correct-answer variety*

Who invented the sewing machine?
  A. Fulton
  *B. Howe
  C. Singer
  D. White
  E. Whitney

B. *The best-answer variety*

What was the basic purpose of the Marshall Plan?
  A. military defended western Europe
  *B. reestablish business and industry in western Europe
  C. settle United States' differences with Russia
  D. directly help the hungry and homeless in Europe

C. *The multiple-response variety*

What factors are principally responsible for the clotting of blood?

  A. contact of blood with a foreign substance
  *B. contact of blood with injured tissue
  C. oxidation of hemoglobin
  D. presence of unchanged prothrombin

D. *The incomplete-statement variety*

Millions of dollars of corn, oats, wheat, and rye are destroyed annually in the United States by

  A. mildews.
  B. molds.
  C. rusts.
  *D. smuts.

E. *The negative variety*

Which of these is NOT true of viruses?
  A. Viruses live only in plants and animals.
  B. Viruses reproduce themselves.
  *C. Viruses are composed of very large living cells.
  D. Viruses can cause diseases.

F. *The substitution variety*

Passage to be read

  Surely the forces of education should be fully utilized to acquaint youth with the real nature of the dangers to democracy, *for* no other place
                    1
  offers *as good or better opportunities than* the school
                    2
  for a *rational* consideration of the problems involved.
                    3

Items to be answered

1. *A. , for
   B. . For
   C. - for
   D. no punctuation needed

2. A. As good or better opportunities than
   B. as good opportunities or better than
   C. as good opportunities as or better than
   *D. better opportunities than

3. *A. rational
   B. radical
   C. reasonable
   D. realistic

G. *The incomplete-alternative variety*[a]

An apple that has a sharp, pungent, but not disagreeably sour or bitter, taste is said to be (4)

  A. p
  B. q
  *C. t
  D. v
  E. w

H. *The combined response variety*

In what order should these sentences be written in order to make a coherent paragraph?
  a. A sharp distinction must be drawn between table manners and sporting manners.
  b. This kind of handling of a spoon at the table, however, is likely to produce nothing more than an angry protest against squirting grapefruit juice about.
  c. Thus, for example, a fly ball caught by an outfielder in baseball or a completed pass in football is a subject for applause.
  d. Similarly, the dexterous handling of a spoon in golf to release a ball from a sand trap may win a championship match.
  e. But a biscuit or a muffin tossed and caught at table produces scorn and reproach.

  A. a, b, c, d, e
  *B. a, c, e, d, b
  C. a, e, c, d, b
  D. b, e, d, c, a

[a]The numeral in parentheses indicates the number of letters in the correct answer (which in this case is "tart"). Using this number rules out borderline correct answers.

attractive to students who make common errors or who hold common misconceptions. Note, too, that a single item is not a very reliable basis for a diagnosis. You will have to follow up to confirm your diagnosis.

Criticisms Multiple-choice items have been criticized on the following grounds. Most of these criticisms can apply to other types of assessments, as well.

1. *Students do not create or express their own ideas or solutions.* If you rely exclusively on multiple-choice testing, you will risk giving your students little or no opportunity to write about the topics in the subject they are learning.

2. *Poorly written multiple-choice items can be superficial, trivial, and limited to factual knowledge.* Of course, so can any poorly constructed assessment format. Gaining the knowledge and

skill to overcome this criticism is the reason you are taking this course!

3. *Because usually only one option of an item is keyed as correct, brighter students may be penalized for not choosing it.*   Brighter students may detect flaws in multiple-choice items due to ambiguities of wording, divergent viewpoints, or additional knowledge of the subject, whereas other students may not.

4. *Multiple-choice items tend to be based on "standardized," "vulgarized," or "approved" knowledge.*   The problems students solve on multiple-choice items tend to be very structured and closed. Creating the impression that all problems in a subject area have a single correct answer may encourage students to place too much faith in an authority figure's correctness or may misrepresent a subject area as having a fixed and limited knowledge base. Further, if you use multiple-choice tests that fail to use items linked to realistic interpretive materials, tests do not have a real-world context. This problem is referred to as **decontextualized knowledge**. As a result, your tests may not assess whether students can use what they have learned in a meaningful and authentic context.

5. *Exclusive use of multiple-choice testing for important or high-stakes assessments may shape education in undesirable ways.*   Those objecting to multiple-choice tests point out that the type of examination you use can shape the content and nature of instruction you deliver to students. If a high-stakes assessment's multiple-choice items focus on factual knowledge, teachers tend to use drill-and-practice techniques to prepare students for it. These strategies are less effective if the test contains multiple-choice items that assess using knowledge and applying higher-order thinking skills.

When Not to Use Multiple-Choice Items

Definite "Don'ts"   Test items must be aligned with the student achievements you want them to assess. You would not, for example, substitute multiple-choice questions on English mechanics and grammar for actual samples of writing when your learning objective calls for students to write. Nor would you use multiple-choice items when your main learning objective requires students to organize their own ideas, develop their own logical arguments, express their own thoughts and feelings, or otherwise demonstrate their self-expression abilities.

When You Have a Choice   At times, you have a choice between using fill-in-the-blank items for the entire test and using multiple-choice items for the entire test. On the surface, either format may seem appropriate. However, if most or all of the items in your test will assess students' simple recall, a fill-in-the-blank test is preferred when the following occurs:

1. Each of the items has only one correct answer and the correct answers are almost always a single word or number.

2. All of the items are computational problems calling for numerical answers.

3. Almost all of the items have only two possible plausible responses (e.g., yes vs. no, male vs. female, positive vs. negative).

4. The answer to each test item is short enough so that writing the answers doesn't take the student any longer than marking the answer to multiple-choice questions on an answer sheet.

When any one of these situations exists, it wil l be difficult for you to write good multiple-choice items requiring students to demonstrate the required degree of recollection and computation. Further, as in Situations 2 and 4, sometimes there is no advantage to the multiple-choice format over the more direct fill-in-the-blank format.

Exceptions   There are exceptions to these suggestions, of course. When you need to assess a large number of students over large areas of content, and when you have readily available machine scoring, multiple-choice items may be the only practical assessment. Or when you already have a test that includes lots of good multiple-choice items but only one or two of those items fit one of the four situations previously listed, it is more efficient to use the multiple-choice format for these items.

If your students will be administered a standardized achievement test (either by your school district or by the state), it will be to their advantage to have experience answering multiple-choice items. In fact, some educational measurement specialists argue that in such instances you would be remiss if you did not give

FIGURE 10.3 Suggestions for improving the quality of the stems of multiple-choice items.

To do

1. If possible, write as a direct question.
2. If an incomplete sentence is used, be sure
   a. it implies a direct question.
   b. the alternatives come at the end (rather than in the middle) of the sentence.
3. Control the wording so that vocabulary and sentence structure are at a relatively low and nontechnical level.
4. In items testing definitions, place the word or term in the stem and use definitions or descriptions as alternatives.

To avoid

1. Avoid extraneous, superfluous, and nonfunctioning words and phrases that are mere "window dressing."
2. Avoid (or use sparingly) negatively worded items.
3. Avoid phrasing the item so that the personal opinion of the examinee is an option.
4. Avoid textbook wording and "textbookish" or stereotyped phraseology.
5. Avoid "clueing" and "linking" items (i.e., having the correct answer to one item be clued or linked to the correctness of the answer to a previous item).

your students practice in taking multiple-choice tests. Therefore, you may wish to use multiple-choice items for at least some parts of your assessments to give students appropriate practice, even though one of the four situations exists.

Some writers advise against including multiple-choice items when the test will be used only once or when there are few students. It is easier to formulate fill-in-the-blank questions than to write good multiple-choice items, and scoring will not be time-consuming when there are few students. However, even when the number of students is small, if you plan to teach the same subject at the same level in subsequent years, it is usually worthwhile to develop a "pool" of multiple-choice items over time. You can then select items from this pool for future tests.

Classroom assessment generally benefits from a mixture of assessment formats. Create each task to best assess the respective learning objectives. The validity of your results, rather than your own convenience, should be your first priority.

Creating Basic Multiple-Choice Items

You will create useful multiple-choice items if you learn how to do five things: (1) focus items to assess specific learning objectives; (2) prepare the stem as a question or problem to be solved; (3) write a concise, correct alternative; (4) write distractors that are plausible; and (5) edit the item to remove irrelevant clues to the correct answer. First-draft multiple-choice items should not be put on a test until they are edited and polished. Editing items is a necessary step, even for the most experienced item writers. This section presents several item-writing guidelines for

improving items in this editorial stage. Our suggestions for crafting multiple-choice items are organized into three groups: suggestions for the stem, suggestions for the distractors, and suggestions for the correct alternative.

Crafting the Stem of the Item Suggestions for improving the quality of the stem portion of multiple-choice items are summarized in Figure 10.3 and discussed in more detail below.

Direct Question Asked or Implied After reading the stem, a student should understand the main intent of the item—what type of response you expect. The stem should ask a direct question or should clearly formulate a problem for the student to solve.

Incomplete sentences sometimes make good stems, but experience and research (Haladyna, Downing, & Rodriguez, 2002) indicate that item writers usually produce better items when they phrase the stem as a direct question. The reason is probably that when a teacher does not ask a direct question, the student must mentally rephrase the stem as a question appropriate to the alternatives presented. This process increases the cognitive complexity of the student's task, perhaps beyond what you may intend. When an incomplete sentence is used, a question is implied, of course. Older and brighter students are sometimes able to do this rephrasing without difficulty. However, many students may find that this extra process increases their difficulty in expressing what they know.

A simple way to check for this flaw is to cover the alternatives with your hand. Then, read the stem. On the basis of that stem alone, can you determine what is expected of the student? If not, the stem is incomplete, and you should rewrite it. The example that follows shows how an item is improved by rephrasing the incomplete stem as a question:

Example

Poor: Incomplete stem

1. W. E. B. Du Bois
   *A. actively pressed for complete political participation and full rights for African Americans.
   B. taught that the immediate need was for African Americans to raise their economic status by learning trades and crafts.
   C. emphasized helping African Americans through the National Urban League.
   D. founded the Association for the Study of Negro Life and History.

Better: Asks a question

2. Which of the following comes closest to expressing W. E. B. DuBois's ideas about priorities of activities of African Americans during the early twentieth century?
   A. African Americans should first improve their economic condition before becoming fully involved in politics.
   B. African Americans should postpone the fight for equal access to higher education until their majority acquire salable trade skills.
   C. African Americans should withdraw from white society to form a separate state in which they have complete political and economic control.
   *D. African Americans should become active, seeking out complete citizenship and full political participation immediately.

Question 1 is poor because the stem does not set a task or ask a question. (Cover the alternative. What task or problem does the stem set?) The student must read the entire item and infer that the teacher must be trying to find out something about W. E. B. DuBois's ideas. The student may very well know DuBois's ideas, but if the student makes the wrong inference about the teacher's intent, the student may answer the item incorrectly. Question 2 is better because the intent of the item is clear after the student reads the stem.

Put Alternatives at the End   This rule is similar to the rule for completion items to place the blank at the end of the incomplete sentence (Chapter 9). The

following example shows how an item is improved by listing alternatives at the end of the stem:

Examples

Poor: Options in the middle of the stem

1. Before the Civil War, the South's
   *A. emphasis on staple-crop production
   B. lack of suitable supply of raw materials
   C. short supply of personnel capable of operating the necessary machinery was one of the major reasons manufacturing developed more slowly than it did in the North.

Better: Options put at the end

2. Before the Civil War, why did manufacturing develop more slowly in the South than in the North?
   *A. The South emphasized staple-crop production.
   B. The South lacked a suitable supply of raw materials.
   C. The South had a short supply of people capable of operating the necessary machinery.

Control Vocabulary and Sentence Structure

When testing for subject-matter learning, make sure you phrase the item at a level suitable for the students. You don't want long sentences, difficult vocabulary, and unnecessarily complex sentence structures to interfere with students' ability to answer the item. This point is especially true for English language learners and for students with certain disabilities. For example, students with hearing disabilities frequently have relatively large language and vocabulary deficits. These students may very well have acquired the specific knowledge, concept, or principle you are assessing, but the way you phrase an item may interfere with their ability to demonstrate this knowledge. The example that follows illustrates how a simple information item can be complicated by uncontrolled language. The item is improved by making it more concise.

Examples

Poor: Unnecessary wordiness and complexity

1. Given the present-day utilization of the automobile in urban settings, which of the following represents an important contribution of Garrett A. Morgan's genius?
   A. automobile safety belts
   B. crosswalk markers
   *C. traffic lights
   D. vulcanized rubber tires

Better: More concise

2. Which of the following did Garrett A. Morgan invent?
   A. automobile safety belts
   B. crosswalk markers
   *C. traffic lights
   D. vulcanized rubber tires

Avoid "Window Dressing"   Item 1 in the preceding example demonstrates how extraneous wording can unnecessarily complicate an item. Less obvious is the use of words that tend to "dress up" a stem to make it sound as though it is testing something of practical importance. Often such **window dressing** creeps into an item when you are struggling to measure higher-level cognitive abilities, such as applications. Window dressing makes an item appear to measure applications when it does not. The next example shows how window dressing makes an item more difficult, less discriminating, less reliable, and less valid. The item is improved by eliminating the window dressing.

Examples

Poor: Window dressing

1. There are 10 preservice teachers in the Department of Education who recently registered for the college-sponsored weight loss program. At the beginning of the program each was weighed, and the 10 had a mean weight of 139.4 pounds. Suppose there were but three men in this group and that their mean weight was 180 pounds. What was the mean weight of the women at the beginning of the program?
   A. 115.0 pounds
   *B. 122.0 pounds
   C. 140.0 pounds
   D. 159.7 pounds

Better: More concise

2. Ten persons have a mean weight of 139.4 pounds. The mean weight of three of them is 180 pounds. What is the mean weight of the remaining seven persons?
   A. 115.0 pounds
   *B. 122.0 pounds
   C. 140.0 pounds
   D. 159.7 pounds

   Every word used in an item should have a purpose. Sometimes names, places, and other "facts" about a situation are necessary pieces of information: They can give the student the basis

for determining the correct answer. The following example shows an acceptable inclusion of facts in an item stem:

Example

A company owns a fleet of cars for which it pays all fuel expenses. Three readily available types of gasoline were tested to see which type was giving better mileage. The results are shown below in miles per gallon.

	Mean	Median
Type A	19.1	18.5
Type B	18.5	19.1
Type C	18.8	18.9

1. Assuming they all cost the same, which type of gasoline should the company use?
   *A. Type A
   B. Type B
   C. Type C

Avoid Negatively Worded Stems   Phrase items positively if possible. Negatively worded stems, such as "which of the following is not …," tend to confuse students, especially the younger or less careful ones. Even well-prepared students often overlook the *not* in an examination question. Positively worded items are easier for students than the corresponding negatively worded items (Haladyna et al., 2002). The following example shows how to improve an item by using positive wording:

Examples

Poor: Negatively phrased stem

1. Sometimes a teacher finds it necessary to use a mild form of punishment. When this occurs, which of the following should not happen?
   A. Children should not believe all of their behavior is bad.
   B. Children should understand the reason(s) why they are being punished.
   *C. Children should understand that the teacher, not them, controls when the punishment will end.

Better: Positively phrased stem

2. Sometimes a teacher finds it necessary to use a mild form of punishment. When this occurs, it is important that the children understand
   A. that it may be a long time before happy times return to the classroom.
   *B. the reason(s) why they are being punished.
   C. that the teacher, not the children, controls when their punishment will end.

If negatively phrased items must be used, use the negative word only in the stem or only in an option (not both) and either <u>underline</u> the negative word or place it in CAPITAL LETTERS.

Avoid Personal Opinions

Do not ask for students' personal opinions in the context of a multiple-choice test in which the students need to select one option as best or correct. Everyone is entitled to an opinion. If you ask for students' opinions in a multiple-choice item, every option could be correct. The following example illustrates this point:

Example

Poor: Makes the correct answer a matter of personal opinion

1. Which of the following men contributed most toward the improvement of the self-confidence of African Americans?
   A. W. E. B. DuBois
   B. Eugene K. Jones
   C. Booker T. Washington
   D. Carter G. Woodson

There is no single correct answer to the preceding question, because each man's contributions can be judged and evaluated in different ways. The question could form the basis for an extended-response essay or a term paper in which the students support their opinions with evidence and logical argument. In that case, do not grade the opinions or the positions taken. Rather, evaluate the way the students use the evidence to support their opinions.

Avoid Textbookish Wording

As with true-false items, when you copy sentences verbatim from the text, you end up with a poor item because (a) frequently, a sentence loses its meaning when you take it out of context, (b) you encourage rote memory of textbook material instead of comprehension, (c) you are likely to produce awkwardly worded items with implausible distractors, and (d) learners who have only a superficial understanding of the underlying concept or principle may obtain clues to the correct answer by simply recalling the textbook phrasing. Use a new, perhaps less familiar, wording of the stem and correct option to test a deeper comprehension of a concept or principle. Avoid textbookish phrasing.

The procedure we discussed in Chapter 9—stating main ideas of textbook passages in your own words and rephrasing these as questions—is a practical one for avoiding textbookish phrasing. Here is an example:

Examples

Poor: Uses textbookish phrasing

1. The annual incomes of five employees are $8,000, $8,000, $10,000, $11,000, and $25,000, respectively. Which index should be used to summarize the typical employee's income?
   A. mean
   *B. median
   C. mode

Better: Novel situation for students

A teacher keeps a record of how long it takes students to complete the 50-question final exam. The mean time was 46 minutes and the median time was 20 minutes. The teacher used this information to set the next exam's time at 20 minutes. The teacher reasoned that these data demonstrate that the typical student could complete the test in that time.

2. In all likelihood, this time limit is
   A. just about right.
   *B. too short.
   C. too long.

The first item is weak because most introductory statistics books associate the term *typical* with median and often use income examples to illustrate the application of the median. By knowing these superficial facts, the student can mark "B" without demonstrating an in-depth understanding of this statistical index. The better item, Question 2, assesses a different learning objective. It is better because it presents a novel situation and requires an application of the concept.

When testing older students, you may find it helpful to use stereotyped phraseology, certain "pat phrases," and verbal associations to make distractors plausible to students lacking the required degree of knowledge. These phrases may be put into the stem or into the distractors. Item 2, although it is a bit wordy and places a premium on reading, does just this. A student who interprets the correctness of using a particular statistical index only on the basis of the verbal association of *typical* with median will not answer the item correctly. Such a student will fail to notice that if the teacher set the time limit for the test at

20 minutes, only half of the class will have enough time to complete it, which is an inappropriate practice for a classroom test.

Create Independent Items With the possible exception of context-dependent items (see Chapter 11), each item should assess a distinct performance, and the correct answer to an item should not be clued by another item. Two flaws to avoid are linking and clueing. **Linking** means that the answer to one or more items depends on obtaining the correct answer to a previous item. Linked items frequently result in a double penalty for an incorrect answer, as when a computational result from one item is required to answer a subsequent item. **Clueing** means that a hint to the correct answer to one item is found in the contents of another item in the test. In the next example, Questions 1 and 2 illustrate linked items:

Examples

Preceding item

1. The perimeter of a rectangle is 350 centimeters. The length of the rectangle is 3 centimeters longer than the width. What is the width?
   A. 18.7 cm.
   *B. 86.0 cm.
   C. 89.0 cm.
   D. 116.7 cm.

Poor subsequent item: Linked to Item 1

2. What is the area of the rectangle described in Question 1?
   A. 1,050 sq. cm.
   B. 7,396 sq. cm.
   *C. 7,654 sq. cm.
   D. 8,188 sq. cm.

Better subsequent item: Independent of Item 1

3. The width of a rectangle is 4 centimeters and the length is 3 centimeters. What is the area?
   A. 9 sq. cm.
   *B. 12 sq. cm.
   C. 16 sq. cm.
   D. 17 sq. cm.

The "preceding item" is primarily computational. The poor subsequent item (Item 2) is linked to it. A student could make an incorrect computation in Item 1, obtaining 89.0, for example. Having already made a mistake in Item 1, the student also would get Item 2 wrong, because $89 \times (89 + 3) = 8,188$ is keyed as a wrong

answer. One solution to the problem is shown in the better subsequent item: You present a new numerical value for the student to use, which is independent of the preceding item. Thus, Item 3 is not linked to Item 1.

Of course, items may provide clues to other items even though they are not linked. Review all the items in your test to see if any item suggests an answer to other items.

Definitions Go in the Alternatives Teachers frequently assess whether students know the meaning of special terms or vocabulary words. Multiple-choice items are often used for this purpose. A common flaw, however, is to put the definition of the term in the stem and to use a list of words as alternatives. The flaw with this approach is that it increases the likelihood that students will get the answer correct by using only superficial knowledge of the definition being assessed. Students can obtain the correct answer by knowing only that the words in the definition seem similar to a word in the alternatives. To assess whether students have in-depth knowledge of a term, put the term in the stem and write various definitions in the alternatives. The item can be made easier or harder depending on how similar the alternatives are. The following example shows how to improve a definition item by putting the term in the stem and using different definitions as alternatives:

Examples

Poor: Definition in the stem

1. When measuring sound waves, the number of cycles per unit time is known as the
   A. amplitude.
   *B. frequency.
   C. speed.
   D. wavelength.

Better: Definitions in the alternatives

2. What is the *frequency* of a sound wave?
   *A. the number of cycles per unit time
   B. the magnitude of change within each phase
   C. the velocity of travel in air
   D. the distance over which the wave's shape repeats

Crafting Alternatives or Foils

The alternatives of a multiple-choice item present choices to the students. All of the choices must be

FIGURE 10.4   Suggestions for improving the alternatives of multiple-choice items.

To do	To avoid
1. In general, strive for creating three to five functional alternatives.	1. Avoid overlapping alternatives.
2. All alternatives should be homogeneous and appropriate to the stem.	2. Avoid making the alternatives a collection of true-false items.
3. Put repeated words and phrases in the stem.	3. Avoid using "not given," "none of the above," etc., as an alternative in *best-answer* type of items (use only with *correct-answer* variety).
4. Use consistent and correct punctuation in relation to the stem.	4. Avoid using "all of the above": limit its use to the *correct-answer* variety.
5. Arrange alternatives in a list format rather than in tandem.	5. Avoid using verbal clues in the alternatives.
6. Arrange alternatives in a logical or meaningful order.	6. Avoid using technical terms, unknown words or names, and "silly" terms or names as distractors.
7. All distractors should be grammatically correct with respect to the stem.	7. Avoid making it harder to eliminate a distractor than to choose the keyed alternative.

appropriate to the stem. If they are not, they may be confusing to knowledgeable students or may be easily eliminated by less knowledgeable ones. When all alternatives are appropriate to the stem, the item functions better as a complete unit. Suggestions for improving the quality of the alternatives are summarized in Figure 10.4 and discussed in more detail in the following text.

Plausible and Functional Alternatives   Many of the suggestions that follow will help you craft plausible distractors. **Plausible distractors** are incorrect alternatives that appear to be correct to students who have not mastered the assessed learning objective. To make distractors plausible, base them on errors students commonly make, such as computational errors, conceptual errors, or errors resulting from faulty common knowledge. In this way, your analysis of students' responses could help you identify their specific difficulties.

Figure 10.4 calls for using from three to five functional alternatives. A **functional alternative** serves the purpose for which it is written. A functional alternative used as a distractor attracts at least one of the students who do not have the degree of knowledge that you expect of all students. Also, an alternative that is the keyed answer is functional if all students who do have the degree of knowledge you expect select it.

For example, an item may have five alternatives. If even the most superficial learner easily eliminates two of the distractors, however, only the remaining three are seriously considered

plausible answers. In reality, then, the item has only three *functional* alternatives. For practical purposes, you may as well delete the two nonfunctional alternatives. Nonfunctional distractors are called **deadwood** or **filler alternatives**.

Teachers sometimes ask if each multiple-choice item should have the same number of alternatives and, if so, how many there should be. Assessment specialists have long recognized that there is no virtue in having the same number of alternatives for each item, especially for classroom assessment. Write as many functional distractors as is feasible (Haladyna, 2004). Only if you write functional alternatives is the item able to distinguish those who have the desired degree of knowledge from those who do not. Research suggests that having three functional alternatives is best, on balance (Rodriguez, 2005). The more alternatives you try to write, the harder it will be to make them functional. As a rule of thumb, strive to write three functional alternatives for most purposes, and use up to five functional alternatives if there is a justification for each (for example, if each distractor exemplifies a common kind of error). Don't waste your time trying to create the same number of alternatives for each item if by so doing you are creating nonfunctional fillers or deadwood. If a separate answer sheet is used for machine scoring, check the maximum spaces allowed per item and adjust the maximum number of alternatives accordingly.

Homogeneous Alternatives   Lack of homogeneity is a primary reason why distractors do not function. An item is said to have **homogeneous alternatives** when each alternative belongs to the same set of "things" *and* each alternative is appropriate to the question asked or problem posed by the stem. For example, if the stem asks students to identify the name of someone who invented a particular machine, then each alternative should be a name and each name should be an inventor to be appropriate to the stem.

An item has **heterogeneous alternatives** when one or more of its alternatives do not belong to the same set of things. The following example shows how to improve an item by making its alternatives homogeneous:

Examples

Poor: Heterogeneous alternatives that do not belong to the same category

1. What is the official state bird of Pennsylvania?
   A. mountain laurel
   B. Philadelphia
   *C. ruffed grouse
   D. Susquehanna River

Better: Homogeneous alternatives that belong to the same category

2. What is the official state bird of Pennsylvania?
   A. goldfinch
   B. robin
   *C. ruffed grouse
   D. wild turkey

You may also adjust the degree of homogeneity to control the difficulty of an item. The World War I items at the beginning of this chapter (p. 183) illustrated this point. Whether alternatives are perceived to be homogeneous by the students you are assessing depends on their level of educational development. Item 2 in the preceding example could be made more homogeneous (and more difficult) by using as alternatives the scientific names of several different species of grouse, for example. The World War I items illustrate this point, as well: The alternatives in Item 1 in that section may appear homogeneous to less knowledgeable, younger students, but they will likely appear to be quite heterogeneous alternatives to knowledgeable, older students.

Put Repeated Words in the Stem In general, it is better to put into the stem words or phrases that are repeated in each alternative. A more complete stem reduces the amount of reading required of

the students and makes the task clearer to the student. To accomplish this, you may find it necessary to rephrase the stem to focus it on the critical point of the learning objective. The next example shows how to improve an item by eliminating words that are repeated in each alternative:

Examples

Poor: Words repeated in each alternative

1. Which of the following is the best definition of *seismograph*?
   A. an apparatus for measuring sound waves
   B. an apparatus for measuring heat waves
   *C. an apparatus for measuring earthquake waves
   D. an apparatus for measuring ocean waves

Better: Stem is more focused and repeated words are incorporated into the stem

2. What type of waves does a *seismograph* measure?
   *A. earthquake waves
   B. heat waves
   C. ocean waves
   D. sound waves

Consistent, Correct Punctuation If the stem asks a direct question (i.e., it ends in a question mark), the options can be either (a) complete sentences; (b) single words, terms, names, or phrases; or (c) other incomplete sentences. Complete sentences begin with a capital letter and end with an appropriate punctuation mark; do not use a semicolon or other inappropriate terminal punctuation. If the options are single words or incomplete sentences, do not use terminal punctuation. However, use a consistent rule for capitalizing the initial word in each option: Throughout the test, either capitalize *all* initial words or capitalize *no* initial word (except a proper noun, of course).

An **incomplete stem** contains an incomplete sentence that the student must complete by choosing the correct alternative. In this case, choose alternatives to complete the sentence that would be plausible for students who have not mastered the learning objective. When writing this type of item, begin each alternative with a lowercase letter (unless an alternative's initial word is a proper noun) and end it with the appropriate terminal punctuation.

There are exceptions to these rules, of course, as when the purpose of an item is to assess knowledge of grammar rules. The next item illustrates this exception to the rule of using consistent punctuation:

Example

Choose the phrases that correctly complete the sentence.

1. Julia became very frightened and shouted,
   A. "Please save me."
   B. "Please save me?"
   *C. "Please save me!"

Arrangement of the Alternatives

Alternatives are less confusing and easier to read when they are arranged one below the other in list form rather than beside one another. Sometimes teachers place alternatives beside each other simply to save paper. This is a false economy, as you will confuse some students who do not know whether to read down or across and may mix up the letters in their responses.

Alternatives should be arranged in meaningful order, such as order of magnitude or size, degree to which they reflect a given quality, chronologically, or alphabetically. Such arrangements make locating the correct answer easier for the knowledgeable student, reduce reading and search time, and lessen the chance of careless errors. The next examples show acceptable arrangements of alternatives:

Examples

Alphabetical arrangement of alternatives

1. Which of the following is made from the shells of tiny animals?
   *A. chalk
   B. clay
   C. shale

Numerical arrangement of alternatives

2. A student's percentile rank is 4. What is the stanine corresponding to this percentile rank?
   A. 4
   B. 3
   C. 2
   *D. 1

Grammatically Correct Relationship to the Stem

Items that contain grammatical clues to the correct answer are easier and less reliable than items without such clues (Haladyna, 2004). Don't clue the correct answer or permit distractors to be eliminated on superficial bases. Examples of inappropriate **grammatical clues** include lack of subject-verb agreement, inappropriate indefinite article, and singular/plural confusion. Below are examples of improving items by eliminating grammatical clues to the correct answers:

Examples

Poor: The definite article "a" at the end of the stem and plural usage of "angles" in the alternatives clue the correct answer.

1. 90° angle is called a
   A. acute angle.
   B. obtuse angle.
   *C. right angle.

Better: Writing the stem as a direct question eliminates the grammatical clue.

2. What are 90° angles called?
   A. acute angles
   B. obtuse angles
   *C. right angles

Overlapping Alternatives

Each alternative should be distinct and not a logical subset of another alternative. Alternatives that include some or all of one another are called **overlapping alternatives**. If you write an item containing overlapping alternatives, you give the less knowledgeable, but testwise, student clues to the correct answer. Several examples of improving items written with overlapping alternatives follow:

Examples

Poor: All alternatives have essentially the same meaning.

1. Why is there a shortage of water in the lower basin of the Colorado River?
   A. The hot sun almost always shines.
   B. There is a wide, hot desert.
   C. The temperatures are very hot.
   *D. All of the above are reasons why.

Better: Each alternative has a distinct meaning.

2. Why is there a shortage of water in the lower basin of the Colorado River?
   *A. There is low rainfall and few tributaries at that region.
   B. The desert soaks up water quickly.
   C. A dam in the upper part made the lower part dry up.

In Item 1, Options A, B, and C essentially say the same thing: A testwise student, recognizing this overlap, would likely choose Option D even if the student knew nothing about the need for water in the lower Colorado River basin.

Avoid a Collection of True-False Alternatives A frequent cause of this type of flaw is that the teacher did not have in mind a clear problem or question when creating the item. Here is an example of improving an item by refocusing the collection of true-false alternatives:

Examples

Poor: Alternatives are an unfocused collection of true-false statements.

1. A *linear function* is
 *A. completely determined if we know two points.
  B. completely determined if we know one point.
  C. unrelated to the point-slope formula.
  D. the same as the y intercept.

Better: The stem focuses on a problem.

2. In which of the following situations would it be possible to write the *equation for a linear function*?
 *A. We know the line passes through the points (3,5) and (4,6).
  B. We know the slope is 1.
  C. We know the y intercept is (0,2).

In Item 1, it is difficult to identify any single question to which a student must respond. All options are related only by the fact that they could begin with the phrase, "A linear function is." Options B, C, and D, when used with that phrase, become false statements. This item is unfocused because it really embeds three ideas: how two points determine a line, the definition of the point-slope formula, and the definition of y intercept. Only one of these ideas should be selected and used as a basis for a revised item, as is done with Item 2. Or, rewrite the item as a multiple true-false item (see Chapter 9).

Avoid "None of the Above" Research on the phrase **"none of the above"** as an option in multiple-choice items indicates that it results in less reliable, more difficult items (Haladyna et al., 2002). Therefore, be very cautious when using this phrase as an option. This option should never be used with the best-answer variety (see the example given earlier in the chapter) of multiple-choice items. The very nature of a best-answer question requires that all of the options are to

some degree incorrect, but one of them is "best." It seems illogical to require students to choose "none of the above" under these conditions.

It does make sense, however, to use "none of the above" with some correct-answer questions, when students look for one option that is completely correct. In areas such as arithmetic, certain English mechanics, spelling, and the like, a single, completely correct answer can be definitely established and defended. Some assessment experts recommend using "none of the above" only when students are more likely to solve a problem first before looking at the options, as opposed to searching through the distractors before proceeding with the solution to the problem.

Two special problems associated with using "none of the above" are (1) students may not believe that this choice can be correct and, therefore, they do not think it is plausible; and (2) students who choose it may be given credit when their thinking is incorrect. To avoid the first problem, use "none of the above" as the correct answer to a few easy items near the beginning of the test. Students will then seriously consider "none of the above" as a possible correct answer for the remainder of the test. It may then be used as either a correct or incorrect answer later in the test. The second problem is handled by using "none of the above" as a *correct answer* in an item when the distractors encompass most of the wrong answers that can be expected (Item 1 below) or using it as a *distractor* for items in which most of the probable wrong answers cannot be incorporated into the distractors (Item 2).

Examples

Acceptable use of "none of the above": As a correct answer

1. What is the difference?
 106
 −21
  ?
 A. 81
 B. 89
 C. 101
 *D. None of the above

Acceptable use of "none of the above": As a plausible distractor

2. What is the sum?
 46
 47
 48
  ?
 *A. 141
 B. 161
 C. 171
 D. None of the above

More than likely, however, items such as 1 and 2 would be better as completion items than as multiple-choice items. If you used completion items, you would be able to check the students' wrong answers to determine why they responded incorrectly; then you could provide students with remediation.

Two final comments on this point: Avoid using "none of the above" as a filler to increase the number of distractors. Remember that distractors must be plausible. Second, as an option, "none of the above" is probably more confusing to younger students than to older ones.

Avoid "All of the Above"

Research on the use of "**all of the above**" is inconclusive (Haladyna et al., 2002). This option, if used at all, should be limited to correct-answer varieties of multiple-choice items. It cannot be used with best-answer varieties because "all of the options" cannot simultaneously be best. Two further difficulties arise: (1) Students who know that one option is correct may simply choose it and inadvertently go on to the next item without reviewing the remaining options, and (2) students who know that two out of four options are correct can choose "all of the above" without knowing the correctness of the third option. The first difficulty can be reduced to some extent by making the first choice in the list read "all of the following are correct." However, this wording can also confuse elementary and junior high students. Generally, the recommendation is to avoid using "all of the above." Rewrite items with multiple answers as two or more items and avoid these problems. Alternately, rewrite the item as a multiple true-false item (see Chapter 9).

Avoid Verbal Clues

Failure to follow this rule makes items easier and lowers the test reliability (Haladyna et al., 2002). Verbal clues include using overlapping alternatives, silly or absurd distractors, **clang associations** (i.e., soundalike words) or other associations between words in the stem and in the correct alternatives, repetition or resemblance between the correct alternative and the stem, and specific determiners. Verbal clues in the alternative frequently lead the less knowledgeable but verbally able student to the correct answer. An example follows:

Example

Poor: Answered by association of words in stem and in correct answer

Which government agency is most concerned with our nation's agricultural policies?
   *A. Department of Agriculture
   B. Department of Education
   C. Department of the Interior
   D. Department of Labor

The item above, for example, uses *agriculture* in both stem and alternative. This technique creates a "Who is buried in Grant's tomb?" type of question.

Specific determiners are words that overqualify a statement so that it is always true or always false. We saw how these operated with true-false items in Chapter 9; they can occur in multiple-choice items as well. Students can eliminate options that state something "always" or "never" happens, for example, without really thinking about their content.

Avoid Technical and Unfamiliar Wording

Teachers writing multiple-choice items sometimes use highly technical or unfamiliar words as distractors. This problem results in students needing more ability to reject the wrong answer than to choose the correct answer. Some studies indicate, however, that students view options containing unfamiliar technical words as less plausible, thereby making such alternatives nonfunctional.

Do Not Make a Distractor Too Plausible

Incorrect alternatives sometimes may be made so plausible that generally good students get the item wrong, whereas less able students respond correctly. (Such items are said to be *negatively discriminating*; see Chapter 14.) The good students' knowledge, though perhaps normally sufficient for selection of the correct answer when embedded in another context, may be insufficient for rejection of all the distractors in a particular item.

Example

In a high school civics class, students had been working on understanding the interrelatedness of economic, social, and political issues. On a test, they find this item.

1. An increase in the rate of inflation will result in a decrease in which of the following?

A. Federal and state income taxes
*B. The purchasing power of money
C. The level of prices
D. Interest rates

Several very good students chose option A instead of the correct answer, B. They knew the concept that purchasing power would decrease, but they continued to play out the repercussions as they had been doing in class. Politicians, they reasoned, would use reducing taxes as an election strategy, which would be very popular if voters found their money did not cover all their needs. Students who had been less thoughtful responded (as the item writer intended) with the simple definition of inflation.

Source of item: National Assessment of Educational Progress released item, Grade 12, 2006, block E1 question #6

Writing the Correct Alternative

You should word the correct alternative so that students *without* the requisite knowledge are *not clued* as to the correct answer and those students *with* the requisite knowledge *are able* to select the correct answer.

1. *In general, there should be only one correct or best answer to a multiple-choice item.* It is possible to write items that have more than one correct alternative. However, such items may not be as valid as you intend, especially with elementary and middle school students. Students may mark the first correct alternative they encounter and skip to the next item without considering all of the alternatives. Some beginning item writers attempt to compensate for this by using the combined response variety of multiple-choice items (see Figure 10.2) or by using "all of the above." This decision usually results in poorer-quality items.

2. *Be sure that competent authorities can agree that the answer keyed as correct (or best) is in fact correct (or best).* If you violate this rule, you may come into conflict with the more able student (or the student's parent). Further, if you insist there is only one correct answer when students also see another choice as equally logical and correct, students will likely see you as arbitrary and capricious. Have a knowledgeable colleague review the correctness of your keyed answers and the incorrectness of your distractors before you use them. The best way to do this is to have your colleague take your test without the correct answers marked. If the colleague chooses an answer that you did not key as correct, then there may be a problem with the correctness of your key.

3. *The correct alternative should be a grammatically correct response to the stem.* The knowledgeable student faces a conflict if the content of the keyed response is correct, but the grammar is incorrect.

4. *Check over the entire test to ensure that the correct alternatives do not follow an easily learned pattern.* Use the answer key you develop to tabulate the number of As, Bs, Cs, and so on that are keyed as correct. Sometimes teachers favor one or two positions (e.g., B and C) for the correct answers. Students will quickly catch on to this pattern, which lowers the validity of your assessment. Also, avoid repetitive, easily learned patterns, such as AABBCCDD or ABCDABCD.

5. *Avoid phrasing the correct alternative in a textbookish or stereotyped manner.* To assess comprehension and understanding, you must at least paraphrase textbook statements. Students quickly learn the idiosyncratic or stereotyped way in which you and the textbook phrase certain ideas. If your test items also reflect such idiosyncrasies, you will be encouraging students to select answers that "sound right" to them but that they do not necessarily understand. For more mature students, however, stereotyped phrases that have a "ring of truth" in the distractors may serve to distinguish those who have fully grasped the concept from those with only superficial knowledge. Use this tactic with senior high school and college students, but not with elementary and middle or junior high school students.

6. *The correct alternative should be of approximately the same overall length as the distractors.* Teachers sometimes make the correct option longer than the incorrect options by phrasing it in a more completely explained or more qualified manner. The testwise student can pick up on this and mark the longest or most complete answer without having the requisite knowledge. Research supports the generalization that if you violate this rule you will make the item easier (Haladyna et al., 2002). Don't be too scrupulous in counting words, however. If your correct answer is one or two words longer, don't worry about it.

7. *An advantage of a multiple-choice test is that it reduces the amount of time required for writing answers, thus allowing the assessment to cover more content.*   Don't defeat this purpose by requiring students to write out their answers. Have the students either mark (circle, check, etc.) the letter of the alternative they choose, write the letter on a blank next to the stem created for that purpose, or use a separate answer sheet. Separate answer sheets are not recommended for children below fourth or fifth grade. If your state has a testing program that uses separate answer sheets in the primary grades, however, use answer sheets with some of your classroom tests to give the children practice.

Encoding Meaning into Distractor Choices

Thus far we have discussed distractors that all serve the same purpose, namely, to appear plausible to those who do not know the correct answer. In scoring, all are equally "wrong." On a right-wrong, one/zero item scoring scale, choosing a distractor gets a student zero points. Several different programs of research have investigated encoding more meaning into distractors than simply "wrong."

It is possible to write distractors that help teachers identify what next steps a student should take. These can be based on cognitive developmental models of how children learn (Pellegrino, Chudowsky, & Glaser, 2001). So, for example, one of the distractors could represent what a student who is in the beginning stages of concept development would select, another distractor would represent what a student who has progressed to a second stage of concept development would select, and so on. In problem solving, distractors can be crafted to represent different kinds of mistakes. For example, for the problem $115 - 97 = ?$, one of the distractors might be 22, which is what a student who always subtracted the smaller number from the larger might select. Another distractor might be 28, which is what a student who knew how to borrow in the one's place, but not how to change the value in the ten's place, would select.

Pearson Assessment has developed a **distractor rationale taxonomy** (King, Gardner, Zucker, & Jorgensen, 2004) for multiple-choice items in reading and mathematics. These taxonomies describe types of errors in reading and mathematics, respectively, that correspond with different

levels of understanding. The advantage is that one distractor can be written for each level. A student whose incorrect answers are typically at a specific level can be given instruction targeted to that level of understanding. Figure 10.5 presents the distractor taxonomy for reading items and examples to illustrate its use.

A Checklist for Evaluating Multiple-Choice Items

Practicing the preceding rules will help you write better multiple-choice items. Some of the most useful rules are presented in the checklist. You can use this checklist to review the items you have written or those you have found in the quizzes and tests that come with your textbook or teaching materials. Revise every item that does not pass your checklist evaluation before you use it.

Checklist

A Checklist for Evaluating the Quality of Multiple-Choice Items

Ask these questions of every item you write. If you answer no to one or more questions, revise the item accordingly.

1. Does the item assess an important aspect of the unit's instructional objectives?
2. Does the item match your assessment plan in terms of performance, emphasis, and number of points?
3. Does the stem ask a direct question or set a specific problem?
4. Is the item based on a paraphrase rather than words lifted directly from a textbook?
5. Are the vocabulary and sentence structure at a relatively low and nontechnical level (except for content-related vocabulary)?
6. Is each alternative plausible so that a student who lacks knowledge of the correct answer cannot view it as absurd or silly?
7. If possible, is every incorrect alternative based on a common student error or misconception?
8. Is the correct answer to this item independent of the correct answers of other items?
9. Are all of the alternatives homogeneous and appropriate to the content of the stem?
10. Did you avoid using "all of the above" or "none of the above" as much as possible?
11. Is there only one correct or best answer to the item?

FIGURE 10.5   A distractor rationale taxonomy for reading items related to the main idea and vocabulary in context.

Level of understanding	Student error
LEVEL 1	Makes errors that reflect focus on decoding and retrieving facts or details that are not necessarily related to the text or item. Student invokes prior knowledge related to the general topic of the passage, but response is not text-based. These errors indicate that the student is grabbing bits and pieces of the text as he or she understands them, but the pieces are unrelated to the information required by the question being asked.
LEVEL 2	Makes errors that reflect initial understanding of facts or details in the text, but inability to relate them to each other or apply them to come to even a weak conclusion of inference. The student may be focusing on literal aspects of a text or on superficial connections to arrive at a response.
LEVEL 3	Makes errors that reflect analysis and interpretation, but conclusions or inferences arrived at are secondary or weaker than ones required for correct response. A distractor may be related to the correct response in meaning, but be too narrow or broad given the circumstances.
LEVEL 4	Correct response.

The examples are associated with a Grade 3 reading passage titled "Frogs and Toads."
The first example uses this taxonomy:

WHAT IS THE MAIN IDEA OF THE PASSAGE "FROGS AND TOADS"?

    A. Frogs and toads are cute. [Level 1: prior knowledge, not text-based]

    B. Toads have shorter legs than frogs have. [Level 2: text-based detail unrelated to main idea]

    C. Frogs are different than toads. [Level 3: only part of main idea]

    D. Frogs and toads share many differences and similarities. [Level 4: correct response]

The second example presents a traditional version of an item with the same stem, for contrast.

WHAT IS THE MAIN IDEA OF THE PASSAGE "FROGS AND TOADS"?

    A. Frogs live closer to water than toads.

    B. Frogs and toads are like cousins.

    C. Frogs are different than toads.

   *D. Frogs and toads share many differences and similarities.

All distractors are essentially Level 3: Each is related to the main idea but is not the best answer.

CREATING ALTERNATIVE VARIETIES OF MULTIPLE-CHOICE ITEMS

A number of multiple-choice item formats are rarely taught in traditional assessment courses, but they have considerable usefulness. The value of these item formats is fourfold. First, some of them will fit your learning goals much more closely than do typical true-false, matching, and multiple-choice formats, thus increasing the validity of your classroom assessments. Second, the formats are objectively scored. The more objective your scoring, the more likely you are to have reliable scores for evaluating your students. Third, because these tasks take students a relatively short time to complete, you can assess a wider range of content and learning goals by using one or more of these formats in addition to your traditional assessment formats. Fourth, these formats are relatively easy to create.

This section discusses four item formats: greater-less-same, best-answer, experiment-interpretation, and statement-and-comment (Gullicksen, 1986). After each format is illustrated, we discuss advantages and criticisms, then offer suggestions for improving the way you craft the items.

Greater-Less-Same Items

The **greater-less-same item** format consists of a pair of concepts, phrases, quantities, and so on that have a greater-than, same-as, or less-than relationship. The greater-less-same item format is

FIGURE 10.6   Examples of greater-less-same items.

Directions: The numbered items below contain pairs of statements. Compare the two members of each pair. If the thing described on the *left* is greater than the thing described on the right, circle the word "greater"; if the *left* is less than the right, circle "less"; and if the *left* and the right are essentially the same, circle "same."

1. Total area of Lake Erie	Greater Same (Less)	Total area of Lake Huron
2. Meaning of the prefix *mono-*	Greater (Same) Less	Meaning of the prefix *uni-*
3. Radius of Mars	Greater Same (Less)	Radius of Venus
4. Number of Christians in Africa	(Greater) Same Less	Number of Muslims in Africa
5. Atomic weight of Ca	(Greater) Same Less	Atomic weight of C
6. $\sqrt{3^2 + 7^2}$	Greater Same (Less)	$\sqrt{3^2} + \sqrt{7^2}$
7. First U.S. passenger railroad opened	Before Same time (After)	Erie Canal opened

used to assess qualitative, quantitative, or temporal relationships between two concepts. Several examples are shown in Figure 10.6.

The student's task is to identify the relationship between the concepts and record an answer. You may use before-during-after, more-same-less, heavier-same-lighter, or other ordered triads, depending on the context of the items. Also, instead of spelling out the words *greater*, *less*, *same*, you can use the letters *G*, *L*, and *S*, respectively. Using letters instead of words may be more appropriate for older students.

Begin to create items by first identifying the learning objectives you want to assess. This item format assesses objectives that include the ability to identify the relationships between two ideas, concepts, or situations. Make a list of concept pairs that are related; add to this list other paired relationships that your students can deduce from principles or criteria they have learned. Rephrase the members of each pair, so

they are clearly stated and fit the item format. When arranging the pairs, be sure that you do not have all the "greaters" on one side of the pair.

Write a set of directions for students that explains the basis on which they are to choose greater-same-less (before-during-after, etc.). Normally, *the set of items should refer to the same general topic.* In the examples in Figure 10.6, this is not the case, because we wanted to illustrate items from different subject areas. Therefore, the directions are too general. Your directions should be more focused on the set of items you are using and very clear. Notice, too, that Item 7 does not "fit" the directions.

The first time you use this format, you may need to give your students some sample items to help them understand what they are to do. Be sure the directions tell the students *which member* (i.e., *left* or *right member*) of the pairs in the set they are to use as a referent.

Organize all the items of this format into one section of your assessment. Put the directions and the sample item at the beginning of the set. The numbered items should follow. Be sure that the correct answers do not follow a set pattern (such as GSLGSL or GGLLSS). Review the set to be sure the items are concisely worded, the task is clear, and the relationships are not ambiguous.

The checklist that follows summarizes the suggestions in this section for judging the quality of greater-less-same items. Use the checklist to guide you in crafting this type of item format. Use it, too, to evaluate the item sets you have already crafted.

Checklist

A Checklist for Evaluating the Quality of Greater-Less-Same Items

Ask these questions of every item you write. If you answer no to one or more questions, revise the item accordingly.

1. Does each item in the greater-less-same set assess an important aspect of the unit's instructional objectives?

2. Does each item in the greater-less-same set match your assessment plan in terms of performance, emphasis, and number of points?

3. Do some of the items in the greater-less-same set require students to apply their knowledge and skill to new situations, examples, or events?

4. Do your directions clearly and completely explain the basis you intend students to use when judging "greater than," "less than," or "same as" for each pair of statements?

5. Do your directions state which pair member (left or right) is the referent?

6. Did you avoid using a pattern (GGSSLLGGSSLL, etc.) for the correct answers?

Advantages   The greater-less-same format is especially suited for assessing whether students understand the order of relationships between two concepts, events, or outcomes. These relationships include greater than versus less than, more of versus less of, before versus after, more correct versus less correct, more preferred versus less preferred, heavier versus lighter, and higher quality versus lesser quality. When you teach the relationships in class or when students learn the relationships from the textbook, this item assesses recall and recognition. However, this item format need not be limited to recall or remembering. You may teach a principle or a set of criteria and give several examples of its application in class. Then, when assessing the students, *present new examples*. A student can then apply the principle(s) or criteria you taught to *deduce the relationship* between the concept pairs. This process elevates the item, so it requires a higher level of thinking than remembering.

Criticisms   The criticisms of greater-less-same items are similar to those for matching and true-false items. That is, teachers often use them to assess rote association and disconnected bits of knowledge. Also, this format limits assessment to relationships among pairs of concepts. If you wish to assess a student's ability to order larger members of a set of events or facts, then use an item format that requires students to rank the members.

Best-Answer Items

Best-answer items are multiple-choice items for which every option is at least partly correct. The student's task is to select the best or most correct option. Here is an example of a best-answer item:

Example

Directions: The following question refers to the article below about the model United Nations General Assembly.
    Text of article:

MODEL U.N. Coming to Town

Local Students Represent the United States   (New York) Students from 15 countries from around the world will be arriving on Monday for a model session of the United Nations General Assembly. Each country will write a plan for the Assembly in one of four categories: Environment, Education, Culture, and Economic Development.

1. Which would be the best plan for the model United Nations General Assembly to improve the world environment?
    A. Feature different ethnic foods in the cafeteria next week.
    B. Plan a school lunch program in Chicago.
    C. Give food to refugees from war zones.
    *D. Study the effect of acid rain on crops.

Source: National Assessment of Educational Progress, released item: Civics, Grade 4, block 2006-4C3, no. 9. Available: nces. ed.gov/nationsreportcard/itmrls/

In this item format, each distractor contains partial misinterpretations or omissions. The keyed or best answer contains neither misinterpretations nor omissions. Only one option can be the "best." Therefore, you should never use "all of the above" or "none of the above" with this format. Neither can some combination of choices (such as "both A and C") be the keyed answer.

As always, first identify the learning outcomes you want to assess. Objectives that require students to choose among several partially correct alternatives may be assessed using this format. Before using this type of item, be sure you have taught your students to use criteria for selecting the best among several partially correct explanations, descriptions, and ideas. These are higher-order thinking skills (often called critical-thinking skills) in that students must use criteria (such as "completeness of response" and "no misinformation") to evaluate alternatives.

Begin by first drafting the question for the stem. Second, write several ways in which students' responses to that question are typically partially correct. These become the basis for writing distractors. You could also give your students several open-ended short-answer questions as homework. Then, select from among the students' responses those that represent excellent, good, and poor answers. Edited versions of these could be used as a basis for creating the options. (Do not use students' responses verbatim as alternatives. They may be poorly phrased or contain too many other errors to function well as partially correct distractors.)

Because the best-answer format is a multiple-choice format, follow the basic rules in the checklist for evaluating the quality of multiple-choice items. A typical flaw with best-answer items is that the best or keyed answer is the one with the longest wording because it contains the most complete information. Be sure the options have approximately equal numbers of words.

Use the following checklist for judging the quality of best-answer items. Use it, too, as an evaluation guide as you review and edit the items you have already created.

Checklist

A Checklist for Evaluating the Quality of Best-Answer Items

Ask these questions of every item you write. If you answer no to one or more questions, revise the item accordingly.

1. Does each best-answer item assess an important aspect of the unit's instructional objectives?

2. Does each best-answer item match your assessment plan in terms of performance, emphasis, and number of points?

3. Does each best-answer item require students to apply their knowledge and skill in some manner to new situations, examples, or events?

4. Do your directions clearly and completely explain the basis you intend students to use when judging "best"? Have your students been given practice in using the appropriate criteria for judging "best"?

5. Are all the options correct to some degree?

6. Is the keyed answer the only one that can be defended as "the best" by applying the criteria you specify in the directions?

7. Is each distractor based on an important misconception, misunderstanding, or way of being an incomplete answer? Did you avoid tricky or trivial ways of making a distractor partially correct or contain misinformation?

8. Are all of the options of equal length (within five words of each other)?

9. Did you avoid (a) having more than one "best" answer and (b) using "all of the above" or "none of the above"?

10. Did you apply all of the item-writing guidelines described in the multiple-choice checklist?

Advantages   Best-answer items assess students' ability to make relatively fine distinctions among the choices. They must comprehend the question and the criteria used to judge the "best" option. Thus, best-answer items assess relatively high-order verbal reasoning skills.

Criticisms   Best-answer items are difficult to write. You must know your subject and your students' faulty thinking patterns quite well. You need to create distractors that are partially correct, yet less defensible than the keyed answers, unlike typical multiple-choice items for which one option is the only correct one and the others are incorrect. Another criticism is that this format may be unsuitable for some students because their level of educational development is not high enough to make the fine distinctions necessary to select the best answer.

A third criticism is that different teachers may not teach consistently across sections of the same course. Thus, what is legitimately a best answer in one teacher's class might not be the best answer in another teacher's class. A fourth criticism is that "best" implies a set of criteria that students may not have been taught or may fail to understand. No answer is unequivocally best unless it is evaluated by applying these criteria. Your students must internalize criteria to apply them. Also, your own knowledge of the subject may be limited. As a result, what you consider the best answer may in fact not be best, because you do not understand other criteria by which the options may be evaluated. A fifth criticism is that a teacher may easily write a tricky item—that is, an item in which an option's correctness depends on a trivial fact, an idiosyncratic standard, or an easily overlooked word or phrase.

Experiment-Interpretation Items

The **experiment-interpretation item** consists of a description of an experiment followed by a multiple-choice item requiring students to recognize the best interpretation of the results from the experiment. Below are three examples. Items 1 and 2 are for a unit in general or physical science; Items 3 through 6 are for a social studies unit or a mathematics unit on statistical methods. We use the term *experiment* loosely in this section to mean any data-based research study, not only scientific or controlled studies. The experiment-interpretation item is similar to the best-answer format because very often the multiple-choice options will all have some degree of correctness, but only one is the best answer. A variation is to use a short-answer item along with or instead of the multiple-choice items (see example Items 3 through 6). For instance, you may ask a student to justify her choice on the multiple-choice item. Alternatively, you could use a short-answer question instead of the multiple-choice one.

Examples

Use the following information to answer Question 1.
  Billy and Jesse were walking through an empty lot near their home. Billy picked up a whitish rock. "Look," he said, "I found a limestone rock. I know it is a limestone rock because I found a rock last year that has the same color, and it was limestone."
  Jesse said, "Just because it looks the same it doesn't have to be the same."

1. Which of the following explanations best supports *Jesse's* point of view?

   A. During the year, the chemical properties of limestone probably changed.
   *B. Different minerals have very similar physical properties.
   C. One year is not long enough for the minerals in a rock to change their physical properties.

Use the following information to answer Question 2.
  Billy took the rock home and did an experiment with it. He put a piece of the rock in a clear glass and poured vinegar over it. The piece of rock bubbled and foamed. "There!" he said to Jesse, "That proves the rock is limestone."
  Jesse said, "No! You are wrong. You haven't proved it!"

2. Why was Jesse correct?
   A. Billy did the experiment only once. He needs to repeat the same type of experiment many times with different bits of the rock. If the mixture bubbles every time, that result will prove it.
   B. The experiment is correct, but Billy misinterpreted the results. Limestone does not bubble and foam in vinegar.
   *C. Billy should do many different kinds of experiments, not just vinegar tests, because many different kinds of substances bubble and foam in vinegar.
   D. Billy should not have used vinegar. He should have used distilled water. If the rock made the water warm, that would prove it is limestone.

Use the following information when answering Questions 3 to 6.
  For a social studies project, a class interviewed all the tenth-grade students. They asked how many hours per week students worked at after-school jobs. They also asked what their average grades were last term. They found that students with Fs and Ds worked eight to 10 hours per week, students with Cs and Bs worked 10 to 20 hours per week, and students with As worked eight to 10 hours per week.

Alternative Format A

Students choose from among teacher-provided interpretations but are required to write a justification of their choice.

3. Which of the following is the most valid interpretation of these findings?
   A. If you work 10 to 20 hours per week, you will only get Cs and Bs.
   B. Working after school is not related to your grades.
   *C. A student who works 10 to 20 hours per week is probably not an A student.
   D. The more hours a student works after school, the higher will be that student's grades.

4. Write a brief explanation of why your answer to Question 3 is the most valid interpretation of these findings.

_____

_____

_____

_____

Alternative Format B

Students supply their own interpretation and justify it in writing.

5. What is the most valid interpretation of the relationship the class found between the number of hours students worked and their grades?

_____

_____

_____

6. Write a brief explanation of why your interpretation of these findings is the most valid one.

_____

_____

_____

_____

The three variations (multiple-choice only, multiple-choice with short-answer, and short-answer only) in the social studies/mathematics example assess somewhat different abilities. Using multiple-choice only (Item 3) assesses a student's ability to evaluate each of *the interpretations you provide* and select the best one. Thus, you do not know a student's reasoning behind his selection. The multiple-choice with short-answer combination (Items 3 and 4) assesses a student's ability to explain or justify her choice from among the interpretations you provide as options, which helps you assess the reasoning behind students' choices. The short-answer *without the multiple-choice items* (Items 5 and 6) assess both a student's ability to interpret the experiment's results and his ability to explain his reasoning. In this latter format, there may be multiple correct responses to the constructed-response questions. As with other constructed-response items, you may want to give students partial credit if their response is not completely correct.

First, identify the learning objectives you want to assess. The experiment-interpretation assessment format is appropriate when a learning goal requires students to understand and interpret the results of empirical research. Before using this format for summative student evaluation, be sure you have taught and have given practice in interpreting the findings from empirical research studies.

Write the item to assess the student's ability to apply specific principles. In other words, you first identify the principles or rules you want students to apply then craft the item, so it requires students to use the principle in a new situation. For example, items in the preceding examples are crafted around the following principles:

- Different substances may share the same or similar physical properties such as color, texture, and solubility. [Item 1]

- Different substances may share the same or similar chemical properties, such as their reactivity with acids. [Item 2]

- Some patterns of relationships among variables are not strictly increasing or decreasing but are curvilinear. [Items 3 through 6]

After identifying the principle(s), create the item in such a way that it requires students to use or apply the principle(s). Usually, this means writing a description of the experiment or research study that results in findings that a student can then interpret using the principle(s). (See the interpretive text that immediately precedes Items 1, 2, 3/4, and 5/6 in the previous examples.)

Next, draft a stem that asks the student to interpret or explain the experimental findings you describe. You may then list several correct or partially correct interpretations. You may also list incorrect interpretations that result from incomplete or faulty reasoning. Avoid using distractors that are completely unrelated to the experiment you describe in the interpretive material or distractors that are "silly" or "tricky." For example, it would be inappropriate for you to use in Item 1 a distractor such as "Jesse knows that Billy is a liar."

As with the best-answer item format, distractors for this format should contain interpretations or explanations that contain your students' typical misconceptions. To determine these misinterpretations, you could assign several open-ended questions as homework and select from among the students' responses those that are excellent, good, and poor. Use these selections as a basis for creating multiple-choice options. The following checklist offers specific guidance for the experiment-interpretation item format.

Checklist

A Checklist for Evaluating the Quality of Experiment-Interpretation Items

Ask these questions of every item you write. If you answer no to one or more questions, revise the item accordingly.

1. Does each item assess an important aspect of the unit's instructional objectives?

2. Does each experiment-interpretation item match your assessment plan in terms of performance, emphasis, and number of points?

3. Does each item focus on requiring students to apply one or more important principles or criteria to new situations, examples, or events?

4. Have you given students opportunity to practice applying the appropriate criteria or principles for judging the "best" or "most valid" interpretation?

5. Did you describe an experiment or research study in concise but sufficient detail that a student can use the appropriate criteria or principles to interpret the results?

6. Is the keyed answer the only one that can be defended as the "best" or "most valid" interpretation?

7. Is each distractor based on an important misconception, misinterpretation, or misapplication of a criterion or principle? Did you avoid tricky or trivial ways of making a distractor partially correct or contain misinformation?

8. Did you avoid (a) having more than one "best" or "most valid" answer and (b) using "all of the above" or "none of the above"?

9. Did you apply all of the appropriate item-writing guidelines described in the multiple-choice checklist?

10. If you used short-answer items, did you apply all of the appropriate item-writing guidelines described in the short essay checklist (Chapter 12)?

Advantages   You may use the experiment-interpretation format to assess a student's ability to evaluate explanations, interpretations, and inferences from data. The multiple-choice-only version allows you to score the items more quickly and more objectively than the other versions. Because students are required only to select the correct answer, their response times are shorter. Therefore, you can use more items and cover more content within a shorter assessment period than with short-answer items.

If the experiments and findings you present in the items are new to the students, your items will assess your students' ability to apply principles and criteria from your subject area. Using experiments and data new to your students in assessment tasks requires you to teach students how to apply criteria and principles to a variety of situations, which moves your teaching away from teaching facts toward teaching students to actively apply their knowledge and skill.

If you require students to justify their multiple-choice answers, you will have some information about their reasoning processes. If you require a student both to supply his interpretation and to justify it, you can assess whether the student can generate and explain his own interpretations of experimental findings.

Criticisms   Like the best-answer item format, the experiment-interpretation format is not easy to write. You must know your subject matter and your students' thinking patterns well enough to create items that allow you to identify faulty thinking as well as correct answers. Faulty thinking must be reflected in your multiple-choice distractors; you must be able to create partially correct interpretations and incorrect interpretations that people typically make.

Use experiment-interpretation items to assess higher-order thinking. Do not use this format to assess whether a student can remember the "correct" interpretations of specific experimental results you taught. Using this format to assess remembering encourages students to look to the teacher or the text as the source of fixed knowledge. It discourages students from learning skills required to interpret the empirical results of experiments.

Statement-and-Comment Items

A **statement-and-comment item** presents a statement about some subject matter and requires the student either to write a comment about the statement or to select the most appropriate comment from among a list you provide. Here is an example of a statement-and-comment item:

Example

A. Multiple-Choice Version of a Statement-and-Comment Item

The Bundle of Sticks—Aesop An old man near the point of death summoned his sons around him to give them some parting advice. He ordered his servants to bring in a bundle of sticks, and said to his eldest son: "Break it." The son strained and strained, but with all his efforts was unable to break the bundle. The other sons also tried, but none of them was successful. "Untie the bundle," said the father, "and each of you take a stick." When they had done so, he called out to them: "Now, break," and each stick was easily broken. "You see my meaning," said their father.

Directions: The quote expresses the theme of Aesop's fable "The Bundle of Sticks." Choose the answer that best expresses how the theme applies to the fable.

1. "Union gives strength."
   A. The three sons all tried to break the bundle.
   *B. None of the sons could break the bundle of sticks.
   C. Each of the sons could break a single stick.

B. Short-Answer Version of a Statement-and-Comment Item

Directions: The quote expresses the theme of Aesop's fable "The Bundle of Sticks." Below the quote, explain how the theme applies to the fable.

2. "Union gives strength."

_____

_____

_____

_____

In the multiple-choice version, a student selects from among several alternate choices the best meaning of the quoted theme. The multiple-choice version is a special case of the best-answer item format. The alternatives should be phrased in language different from phrases learned in class. In the short-answer version, students must comment directly, writing their own interpretation of the quoted statement.

First, as always, identify the learning objectives you want to assess. This assessment format is appropriate when a learning target requires a student to comprehend statements and themes. Use different statements in the assessment than you used in class; otherwise, students can simply recall or repeat what was said in class discussion. If you give students the short-answer version as a homework exercise, you may use excellent, good, and poor student responses as a basis for creating the alternatives for the multiple-choice version. As with the best-answer variety, you usually cannot use students' responses verbatim as multiple-choice options; paraphrase them. Because the multiple-choice version of the statement-and-comment is a type of best-answer item, follow the guidelines suggested in the best-answer item checklist.

Advantages The statement-and-comment item format assesses a student's ability to evaluate interpretations of a given statement. The multiple-choice version assesses whether students can identify the best interpretation from among several. The open-ended version assesses students' ability to write their own interpretations about the meaning of the quoted statement.

Criticisms The statement-and-comment item format has limited applications. You must identify appropriate statements that students should interpret. Although there are many subjects for which such statements exist, the task itself represents a small range of learning objectives.

MyLab Education **Self-Check 10.1**

MyLab Education **Application Exercise 10.1:** Revising a Multiple-Choice Item

---

MATCHING EXERCISES

A **matching exercise** presents a student with three things: (1) directions for matching, (2) a **premise list**, and (3) a **response list**. The student's task is to match each premise with one of the responses, using as a basis for matching the criteria described in the directions. Figure 10.7 shows a matching exercise with its various parts labeled.

The sample exercise in Figure 10.7 requires simple matching based on associations that students must remember. You may create matching exercises, however, to assess students' comprehension of concepts and principles. Examples of these latter types appear later in the chapter.

In matching exercises, premises are listed in the left column and responses in the right column, or responses are listed vertically above the premises. Each premise is numbered because each is a separately scorable item. Matching exercises can have more responses than premises, more premises than responses, or an equal number of each. **Perfect matching** occurs when you have an equal number of premise statements and

FIGURE 10.7   Example of a matching exercise.

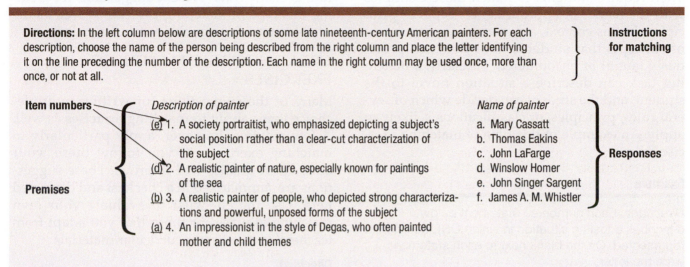

Directions: In the left column below are descriptions of some late nineteenth-century American painters. For each description, choose the name of the person being described from the right column and place the letter identifying it on the line preceding the number of the description. Each name in the right column may be used once, more than once, or not at all.

Instructions for matching

Item numbers

Premises

Description of painter

(e) 1. A society portraitist, who emphasized depicting a subject's social position rather than a clear-cut characterization of the subject

(d) 2. A realistic painter of nature, especially known for paintings of the sea

(b) 3. A realistic painter of people, who depicted strong characterizations and powerful, unposed forms of the subject

(a) 4. An impressionist in the style of Degas, who often painted mother and child themes

Name of painter

a. Mary Cassatt
b. Thomas Eakins
c. John LaFarge
d. Winslow Homer
e. John Singer Sargent
f. James A. M. Whistler

Responses

response statements. Most assessment specialists consider perfect matching to be undesirable because, if a student knows four of the five answers, the student automatically gets the fifth (last) choice correct, whether or not he knows the answer, which reduces the validity of the assessment results.

Matching exercises are very much like multiple-choice items. Each premise functions as a separate item. The elements in the list of responses function as alternatives. You could rewrite a matching exercise as a series of multiple-choice items: Each premise would then be a multiple-choice stem, but the same alternatives would be repeated for each of these stems, which leads to an important principle for crafting matching exercises: *Use matching exercises only when you have several multiple-choice items that require repeating the identical set of alternatives.*

Advantages and Criticisms of Matching Exercises

Advantages   A matching exercise can be a space-saving and objective way to assess a number of important learning objectives, such as your students' ability to identify associations or relationships between two sets of things. You can also develop matching exercises using pictorial materials to assess the students' abilities to match words and phrases with pictures of objects or with locations on maps and diagrams. Figure 10.8 gives examples of relationships that you may use as a basis for developing matching exercises.

Criticisms   Detractors criticize the matching exercise because students can use rote memorization to learn the elements in two lists and because teachers often use matching exercises only to assess such rote associations as names and dates. As a result, critics often see this assessment format as limited to the assessment of memorized factual information.

Thoughtful teachers, however, also use matching exercises to assess aspects of students' comprehension of concepts, principles, or schemes for classifying objects, ideas, or events. *If you want to assess students on these higher-level abilities, create exercises that present new examples or instances of the concept or principle to the students.*

FIGURE 10.8   Examples of different foundations for developing matching exercises.

Possible premise sets	Associated response sets
Accomplishments	Persons
Noted events	Dates
Definitions	Terms and phrases
Examples, applications	Rules, principles, and classifications
Concepts (ideas, operations, quantities, and qualities)	Symbols and signs
Titles of works	Authors and artists
Foreign words and phrases	English correspondence
Uses and functions	Parts and machines
Names of objects	Pictures of objects

Then require students to match these examples with the names of appropriate concepts or principles. In this context, *new examples* are instances of concepts that students have not been previously taught or encountered. Similarly, a matching task can describe a situation novel to the student, and the student can decide which of several rules, principles, or classifications is likely to apply. An example of this type of matching exercise follows:

Example

Directions: Each numbered statement below describes a testing situation in which ONE decision is represented. On the blank next to each statement, write the letter:

A. if the decision is primarily concerned with placement
B. if the decision is primarily concerned with selection
C. if the decision is primarily concerned with program improvement
D. if the decision is primarily concerned with theory development
E. if the decision is primarily concerned with motivating students

    (A)1. After children are admitted to kindergarten, they are given a screening test to determine which children should be given special training in perceptual skills.

    (A)2. At the end of the third grade, all students are given an extensive battery of reading tests, and reading profiles are developed for each child. On the basis of these profiles, some children are given a special reading program, whereas others continue on with the regular program.

    (B)3. High school seniors take a national scholastic aptitude test and send their scores to colleges they wish to attend. On the basis of these scores, colleges admit some students and do not admit others.

    (E)4. Students are informed about the learning targets their examination will cover and about how many points each examination question will be worth.

This exercise assesses a student's understanding of five concepts related to using tests for decision making. The placement of the response list above the premise list creates a type of matching exercise called the **masterlist variety**. It is also called the **classification** or **keylist variety**. Later

in this chapter, we present suggestions for creating this type of matching exercise as well as the double-matching exercise or tabular exercise.

CREATING BASIC MATCHING EXERCISES

Many of the suggestions for writing multiple-choice items apply to matching exercises as well. A few maxims, however, apply particularly to matching exercises. If you follow these, your assessment quality will improve. These suggestions are summarized in a checklist and discussed here. Use the checklist to evaluate your own matching exercises or those that you adapt from teachers' texts or other curricular materials.

Checklist

A Checklist for Evaluating the Quality of Matching Exercises

Ask these questions of every item you write. If you answer no to one or more questions, revise the item accordingly.

1. Does the exercise assess an important aspect of the unit's instructional objectives?
2. Does the exercise match your assessment plan in terms of performance, emphasis, and number of points?
3. Within this exercise, does every premise and response belong to the same category of things?
4. Do your directions clearly state the basis you intend students to use to complete the matching correctly?
5. Does every element in the response list function as a plausible alternative to every element in the premise list?
6. Are there fewer than 10 responses in this matching exercise?
7. Did you avoid "perfect matching"?
8. Are the longer statements in the premise list and the shorter statements (names, words, symbols, etc.) in the response list?
9. If possible, are the elements in the response list ordered in a meaningful way (logically, numerically, alphabetically, etc.)?
10. Are the premises numbered and the responses lettered?

1 and 2. *As always, your assessment tasks should meet the dual criteria of importance and fit with your assessment plan.* Eliminate every item that fails to meet these two criteria.

3. *Create homogeneous matching exercises.* Using **homogeneous premises and responses** means that the elements in the premise list and the elements in the response list together refer to the same category of things. For example, in the matching exercise in Figure 10.7, all premises and responses refer to late-nineteenth-century painters.

If the *entire* list of response choices is not plausible for *every* premise, the students' matching task may be trivial. As an example, consider the nonhomogeneous, poor-quality matching exercise shown here:

Example

Poor: Premises and response set are not homogeneous

<table>
<tr><td>(d) 1. Pennsylvania's official state flower</td><td>a. Ruffed grouse</td></tr>
<tr><td>(a) 2. Pennsylvania's official state bird</td><td>b. Pittsburgh</td></tr>
<tr><td>(b) 3. Major steel-producing city in the 1940s</td><td>c. 1,950,098</td></tr>
<tr><td>(c) 4. 1970 population of Philadelphia</td><td>d. Mountain laurel
e. Allegheny River</td></tr>
</table>

Not all of the responses in this example are plausible distractors for *each* premise. As a result, students can answer the items on the basis of general knowledge of a few of the associations and common sense, rather than on any special knowledge learned from the curriculum.

This matching exercise is poor for another, perhaps more important, reason: *The main focus of the exercise seems lost.* Even if you tried to improve it, your efforts would probably be self-defeating. You may attempt to make the exercise's responses more homogeneous, but this action may result in an exercise that does not assess the intended learning outcome. For example, you could make all the premises refer to different states and all the premises to different official state birds: The task would be to match the birds with the states. Your local curriculum, however, may only require students to identify their own state bird. Creating a homogeneous exercise, as in this example, may result in a test that does not match the curriculum and, therefore, cannot be used. Remember that the learning objectives determine the type of assessment.

Could anything be done to salvage this exercise? Remember the rule mentioned earlier in this chapter: You should reserve the matching exercise for situations when several multiple-choice items require the same set of responses. Returning to the example, note that each premise could be turned into a separate multiple-choice item, each with a different set of plausible options. Plausible options for a multiple-choice item on Pennsylvania's official state flower, for example, would include flowers native to the Pennsylvania region (e.g., daisies, roses, violets, etc.). Similarly, separate multiple-choice items could assess knowledge of the official state bird, names of cities, and size of cities.

Remember that the degree to which students perceive the exercise as homogeneous varies with their maturity and educational development. What may be a homogeneous exercise for primary schoolchildren may be less so for middle school youngsters and even less so for high schoolers. Consider, for example, the following matching exercise:

Example

Directions: Column A below lists important events in U.S. history. For each event, find in Column B the date it happened. Write the letter of the date on the blank to the left of each event. Each date in Column B may be used once, more than once, or not at all.

<table>
<tr><td>*Column A (events)*</td><td>*Column B (dates)*</td></tr>
<tr><td>(f) 1. United States entered World War I</td><td>a. 1492</td></tr>
<tr><td></td><td>b. 1607</td></tr>
<tr><td>(d) 2. Lincoln became president</td><td>c. 1776</td></tr>
<tr><td>(g) 3. Truman became president</td><td>d. 1861</td></tr>
<tr><td>(b) 4. Pilgrims landed at Cape Cod</td><td>e. 1880</td></tr>
<tr><td></td><td>f. 1917</td></tr>
<tr><td></td><td>g. 1945</td></tr>
</table>

The students' task is to match U.S. historical events with their dates. For younger, less experienced students, such a matching task would likely be difficult. It would appear homogeneous, however, because for these children all responses would be plausible options for each premise. High school students would find the task easier—even if they didn't know the exact dates—because they could use partial knowledge to organize the dates into early, middle, and recent history. For them, only Options f and g would be plausible for Item 1.

4. *Explain completely the intended basis for matching.* Make clear on what basis you want students to match the premises and the responses. The example below shows how to improve the directions by explaining the basis for the matching:

Example

Poor: Directions are incomplete

Match Column A with Column B. Write your answer on the blank to the left.

Better: Directions explain basis for matching

Column A lists parts of a plant cell. For each cell part, choose from Column B the main purpose of that cell part. Write the letter of that purpose on the blank to the left of the cell part.

Elementary students may need oral explanations and, perhaps, some practice with this format before you assess them. The masterlist variety of matching exercise usually requires more elaborate directions and may require special oral explanations even for high school students. Avoid long, involved written directions, however. These place an unnecessary premium on reading skill.

5. *All responses should function as plausible options for each premise.* Homogeneous premises and responses will minimize plausibility problems. Also, avoid using specific determiners and grammatical clues. For example, avoid beginning some premises or responses with *an* and others with *a,* having some plural whereas others are singular, stating some in the past tense whereas others are stated in the present or future tense. These clue the answer unnecessarily.

Avoid using incomplete sentences as premises, which makes it difficult to make all responses homogeneous and easier for students to respond correctly on the basis of superficial features such as grammatical clues or sentence structure. Here is an example of a poor matching exercise that comes about when incomplete sentences are used:

Example

Poor: Uses incomplete sentences

(c) 1. Matter in a liquid state has more energy

(e) 2. All solids can become gases

(d) 3. Changes in state are caused

(b) 4. Plasma is made up

    a. above its boiling point.

    b. of charged and uncharged atoms.

    c. than matter in a solid state.

    d. by heating or cooling.

    e. but some do not become liquids first.

6. *Use short lists of responses and premises.* For a single matching exercise, put no more than 5 to 10 elements in a response list. The reasons are that (a) longer lists make it difficult for you to develop homogeneous exercises, (b) longer matching exercises overload a test with one kind of performance, (c) longer lists require too much student searching time, and (d) students may attain a lower percentage of correct answers with longer matching exercises than with shorter exercises.

Shorter matching exercises make it easier to keep everything belonging to a single exercise on the same page. For some students, having to turn the page back and forth to answer the exercise may interfere with their ability to show you what they know. For these students, splitting an exercise between two pages increases the likelihood of carelessness, confusion, and short-term memory lapses. In short, a student's ability to answer a test item while flipping pages is not relevant to the learning objective you want to assess.

To fix an exercise that is too long, you can separate it into two or more shorter exercises, or you can use each response as a correct answer more than once. When you use this technique, alert students through either oral or written directions. One standard phrase you may use is as follows: "You may use each of the [names, dates, etc.] once, more than once, or not at all" (see the painters' example in Figure 10.7 at the beginning of this section).

7. *Avoid "perfect matching."* As we discussed previously, perfect matching is undesirable. It gives away at least one answer to the student who knows all but one of them. This student's final choice will be automatically correct because it is the only one left, thus lowering the validity of your assessment. Avoid perfect matching by including one or more responses that do not match any of the premises or by using a response as the correct answer for more than one premise.

8. *Use longer phrases in the premise list, shorter phrases in the response list.* Consider how a student approaches the matching exercise, first reading a premise, then searching through the response list for the correct answer, and rereading the response list for each premise. It is, therefore, more efficient and less time-consuming if students read the longer phrases only once. They can reread or scan the shorter phrases (words, symbols) as often as necessary.

9. *Arrange the response list in a logical order.* A student saves time if the response list is arranged in some meaningful order: Dates arranged chronologically, numbers in order of magnitude, words and names alphabetically, and qualitative phrases in a logical sequence. Such arrangements also may contribute to the clarity of the task, reduce student confusion, and lower incidence of student carelessness and oversight.

10. *Identify premises with numbers and responses with letters.* Remember, each premise is a separately scored item. Therefore, premises should carry numbers, which indicate their position in the sequence of items. For example, if the first 10 items are multiple-choice, and these are followed by a five-premise matching exercise, the five premises should be consecutively numbered 11 through 15.

CREATING ALTERNATIVE VARIETIES OF MATCHING EXERCISES

Two types of matching exercises—masterlist and tabular—may fit some of your learning objectives better than the more basic matching exercise. As with the alternative varieties of multiple-choice items we discussed previously, these matching formats are objectively scored, do not take students a long time to complete, and are often easier for you to craft than the basic matching format.

Masterlist (Keylist) Items

A masterlist (or keylist or classification) matching exercise has three parts: (1) directions to students, (2) the masterlist of options, and (3) a list or set of stems. To respond to a masterlist item set, a student reads each numbered stem and applies one of the options from the masterlist. Each stem is scored separately. Figure 10.9 shows a masterlist matching exercise for a tenth-grade civics course.

The content learning target for this masterlist exercise is the students' ability to relate constitutional *values and principles* to specific modern-day examples of actions or events. Therefore, in crafting this item you would ensure that each masterlist response choice (A, B, C, D) is a value or principle expressed by the U.S. Constitution, rather than a Preamble goal or some other aspect of the Constitution.

Notice that each numbered stem is a brief, realistic, and concrete example of an action or event that illustrates one of the four values in the masterlist. Because the learning objective calls for

FIGURE 10.9 Example of a masterlist matching exercise.

Directions: Read each numbered statement and decide which U.S. constitutional principle it illustrates. Mark your answer:

Directions — Explain the basis for using the masterlist.

A — if the action illustrates the principle of government by the **consent of the governed.**

B — if the action illustrates the principle of government in which the **majority rules.**

C — if the action illustrates the principle of government under a **federal system.**

D — if the action illustrates the principle of government with **limited governmental powers.**

Masterlist — This list of response choices is applied to each of the stems that follow it.

___ 1. A congressional representative voted for a tax bill that was unpopular in his state. In the next election he was not re-elected.

___ 2. A civil war was taking place in another country. The president of the United States began planning to help support the antigovernment forces but was warned by cabinet members that he could get in trouble if he attempted to send in the military without going through the proper channels. The president dropped his plans.

___ 3. A large number of people demonstrated for a ban on the use of nuclear weapons. Subsequently, a bill went to Congress asking for such a ban. However, the bill was defeated. The people continued to demonstrate but had to accept further possible use of nuclear weapons until there was a vote on another bill.

___ 4. A state in financial trouble decided to establish a system of taxes on goods imported into the state. The law was challenged and found to be in disagreement with a national law. The state had to seek other ways to raise money.

Stems — This list of stems presents situations, actions, or events that need to be classified into one of the categories in the masterlist.

FIGURE 10.10   **A masterlist item set that requires students to recognize proper interpretations of a graph.**

Use the graph below to help you answer Questions 1 through 5.

The graph shows that John left his home at 1:00 and arrived at his friend Bill's home at 1:45. The graph shows where John was in the community at different times.

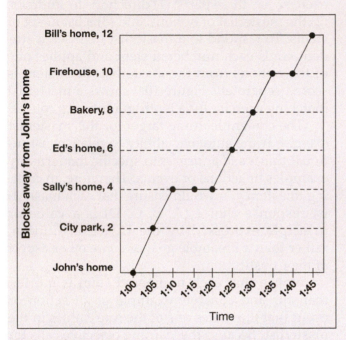

Directions: The numbered statements below tell what different students said about this graph. Read each statement and decide whether the information in the graph is consistent with a student's statement. Mark answer:

A — if the information in the graph **is consistent** with the statement.

B — if the information in the graph **contradicts** the statement.

C — if the information in the graph **neither contradicts nor is consistent** with the statement.

___ 1. John ran or walked very fast between his house and the city park.

___ 2. John stopped at Sally's home on his way to Bill's home.

___ 3. John stopped at Ed's home on his way to Bill's home.

___ 4. John stopped to buy something at the bakery before he got to Bill's home.

___ 5. John traveled faster after he passed by Sally's home than before he reached her home.

students to relate constitutional principles to concrete examples, each stem must be a concrete example. You would not use textbook abstractions or general descriptions. (For example, you would not word a stem in general language such as, "A law takes effect when the majority of Congress votes to approve it," because this statement describes a general principle rather than a concrete example.) Although the preceding exercise shows only four stems, you need not limit the stems to four. Use as many stems as are appropriate, as long as each stem is an example of one of the masterlist options. Further, although not the case in this example, each stem in a masterlist set may have more than one correct answer from the masterlist.

To create your masterlist item set, first identify the learning objective you want to assess. For example, this might be "the students' ability to recognize whether data support interpretations about what events occurred." Next write the masterlist of options on which you want to focus. For example, for the constitutional principles exercise given previously, you would list the four

constitutional principles; for the masterlist exercise in Figure 10.10, you would list *supportive*, *contradictory*, and *neither*. If you will use a table, graph, or other interpretive material, prepare it next.

Select one of the options from the masterlist and write as many stems for it as you can. For example, you might select "consent of the governed" as a principle and write four or five concrete examples that illustrate that principle in a real-world application. Continue selecting options and writing stems until you have several items for each option. Review the stems to be sure that they require students to apply their knowledge and skills to new real-world situations, examples, or events. Guided by your test blueprint, select the items that best fit with the point values and content and thinking skills required for your test.

Create the directions last. Be sure the directions clearly describe the basis on which the student is to solve the masterlist item set. For example, in the civics course exercise, the directions tell students they must read the examples in the statements and decide which constitutional principle each represents. In the graph interpretation example, the directions tell the student that the statements are interpretations of the graph and that the student must decide whether the graph supports or contradicts the interpretation. If your masterlist item set refers to interpretive material such as this, your directions should clearly describe the material and how students should use it.

After completing the preceding steps, polish your masterlist item set. Organize the interpretive material, if any, at the beginning of the set. Next, place the masterlist before the stems. *Assign letters to the masterlist response choices* that the students may use. If you will not use a machine-scorable answer sheet, your letters do not have to be *A*, *B*, *C*, *D*, or *E*. For example, in the civics course exercise, you could use *C* for "consent of the governed," *M* for "majority rules," and so on.

The stems are always numbered and follow the masterlist. If you are not using a separate answer sheet, put a blank *before* the stem number rather than at the end of the stem. You will score the papers much more quickly and accurately if the blank is before the number of the stem. Scramble the stems so that all the stems matching one masterlist option are not together, and make sure there is no discernible pattern to the answers (avoid ABCDABCD, etc.). If you have written too many stems, select the best ones, save the others for revision, and use them at a later date. Edit the stems to make them grammatically correct, clear, and concise. Limit each stem to 40 or fewer words. However, the stems and the other parts of the item set must provide enough information for the student to apply the rule or principle. For example, in the civics course exercise, Stem 2 would not have had sufficient information if it contained only these words:

1. A civil war was taking place in another country. The president of the United States began planning to help support the civil war.

More details are needed for students to figure out which principle the stem illustrates.

This checklist summarizes the suggestions in this section as a masterlist checklist. Use this checklist to guide you in creating and using masterlist item sets.

Checklist

A Checklist for Evaluating the Quality of Masterlist Exercises

Ask these questions of every item you write. If you answer no to one or more questions, revise the item accordingly.

1. Does the masterlist exercise assess an important aspect of the unit's instructional objectives?

2. Does the masterlist exercise match your assessment plan in terms of performance, emphasis, and number of points?

3. Does the masterlist exercise require the students to apply their knowledge and skill to new situations, examples, or events?

4. Did you provide enough information so that knowledgeable students are able to apply the knowledge and skill called for by the item?

5. Do your directions to the students clearly and completely explain the basis you intend them to use when applying masterlist response choices to the stems?

6. Within this masterlist exercise, does every stem and every response choice in the masterlist belong to the same category of things?

7. Does every response choice in the masterlist function as a plausible alternative for every stem?

8. Did you avoid "perfect matching"?

9. If possible, are the options in the masterlist ordered in a meaningful way (logically, numerically, alphabetically, etc.)?

10. Are the stems numbered and the masterlist response choices lettered?

Advantages   A masterlist item set is a variation of the matching exercise format, and it has many of the same advantages as that format. It is a space-saving and objective way to assess learning targets for which you want students to identify associations between two sets of things. However, it is best used to assess a student's *understanding of concepts.* The masterlist item also is an efficient way to assess a student's ability to (a) analyze a passage, table, or graph and (b) recognize an appropriate interpretation or conclusion drawn from this interpretative material.

To assess understanding, the examples you give students to classify or the material you give them to analyze cannot be the same examples you illustrated in class or that appeared in the textbook or assignments. If your examples are not "new to the students," then the masterlist item set becomes simply an alternate way to assess students' recall and recognition of verbal information. As with other matching exercises, you can use pictures, maps, symbols, or diagrams as stems.

Criticisms Because masterlist item sets are "cousins" to matching exercises, they share the same criticisms. Critics point out that teachers often limit using the format to assess rote associations such as names and dates, memorized lists of causes and effects, lists of symbols and definitions, and so on. As we described, use masterlist item sets to assess students' (a) comprehension of concepts, principles, or schemes for classifying objects, events, and ideas and (b) ability to analyze appropriate interpretations and conclusions.

Tabular (Matrix) Items

A **tabular (or matrix) item** format is a type of matching exercise in which elements from several lists of *responses* (e.g., presidents, political parties, famous firsts, and important events) are matched with elements from a common list of premises. The students' task is to select one or more elements from each response list and match the elements with one of the numbered premises. An example of a tabular item format is shown in Figure 10.11.

You can see that the example is a quadruple matching exercise: (a) match year and president, (b) match year and president's political party, (c) match year and famous first, and (d) match year and important event. One premise list and several response lists that

FIGURE 10.11 **A tabular or matrix item set.**

Directions: Match the names, political parties, famous firsts, and important events in the columns with the dates in the table below. Write the letter in the proper column in the table. You may use a letter once, more than once, or not at all in any cell in the table.

Presidents	Presidents' political parties	Famous firsts	Important event
A. Coolidge	K. Democrat	N. First airplane flight	U. Atomic bomb on Hiroshima
B. Eisenhower	L. Independent	O. First airplane flight across U.S.	V. Great Depression begins
C. Harding	M. Republican	P. First automobile trip across U.S.	W. NAACP founded
D. Hoover		Q. First telephone talk across U.S.	X. New Deal legislation passed
E. McKinley		R. First transatlantic solo flight	Y. North Pole reached
F. Roosevelt, F.D.		S. First U.S. satellite in space	Z. Panama Canal opened
G. Roosevelt, T.		T. First woman in cabinet	AA. Panama Canal Treaty signed
H. Taft			BB. Social Security Act passed
I. Truman			CC. United Nations founded
J. Wilson			DD. World War I ends
			EE. Korean Conflict begins

	Year	President	President's political party	Famous first	Important event	Score
1.	1901–1904					1. _____
2.	1905–1908					2. _____
3.	1909–1912					3. _____
4.	1913–1916					4. _____
5.	1917–1920					5. _____
6.	1921–1924					6. _____
7.	1925–1928					7. _____
8.	1929–1932					8. _____
9.	1933–1936					9. _____
10.	1937–1940					10. _____
11.	1941–1944					11. _____
12.	1945–1948					12. _____

correspond to it can be efficiently organized into a tabular or matrix item format. Notice that each premise is *numbered*. Thus, each premise is scored as a separate item.

First, as always, identify the learning objectives you wish to assess. Objectives for which students must cross-classify facts or examples, or for which they must identify several characteristics or properties of dates, events, or objects, are most suitable. Construct a list of premises. For instance, in the earlier example, the premises were the 4-year time spans defining a U.S. president's term of office. Next, create two or more lists of responses organized into homogeneous groups. Add to each list at least one *plausible* response that does not match any of the premises. This process will eliminate the perfect-matching flaw we discussed previously. For instance, in the earlier example, "Eisenhower," "Independent," "First U.S. satellite in space," and "Korean Conflict begins" do not match any of the premises (dates).

Create the table or matrix to correspond to your premise and response lists. Number the premises. Label the columns with the same headings you used for the response lists. For convenience, make a place to record scores at the right of the table, as is shown in the presidential term example.

Directions to students are created next. The directions should clearly tell the students what they are to match; the basis for that matching; how they should record their answers; and the fact that a response may be used once, more than once, or not at all.

Create the exercise in a layout modeled after the preceding example. Put the directions at the top and the lists of responses below the directions and above the table. The exercise is easier to understand with this arrangement than when the response lists follow the table. It is also easier for students to read and keep track of the responses if they appear first. Use letters to identify each response. There are fewer student clerical errors if the lettering continues consecutively across the lists as in the presidential term example. Finally, place the table and make places to record scores. A grid is easier for students to use and for you to score.

The checklist for tabular items summarizes the suggestions in this section. Use it as a guideline when creating the tabular item set and evaluating your item set when it is complete.

Checklist

A Checklist for Reviewing the Quality of Tabular (Matrix) Exercises

Ask these questions of every item you write. If you answer no to one or more questions, revise the item accordingly.

1. Does the tabular exercise assess an important aspect of the unit's instructional objectives?

2. Does the tabular exercise match your assessment plan in terms of performance, emphasis, and number of points?

3. Do your directions to students clearly explain (a) the basis you intend students to use when matching the responses to the premises, (b) how to mark their answers, and (c) that a response choice may be used once, more than once, or not at all?

4. Do the response choices within each response list all belong to the same category of things?

5. Does every response choice function as a plausible alternative to every premise?

6. Did you avoid "perfect matching"?

7. If possible, are the response choices ordered in a meaningful way (logically, numerically, alphabetically, etc.)?

8. Are the premises numbered and the response choices lettered?

9. On the test page, are the directions placed first, the response choices second, and the table third?

10. If possible, is the entire exercise printed on one page rather than split between two pages?

Scoring Scoring is a special concern with the tabular or matrix item format. Two options for scoring are available:

1. *You may score each numbered row as completely correct or incorrect* (score each row as a one [completely correct] or a zero [one or more elements are incorrect]).

2. *You may score each row according to how many elements are correctly placed in its cells* (score each cell in the row as a one [correct] or a zero [incorrect]).

Of these two options, we prefer the second: It gives partial credit and yields more reliable scores.

Special problems may arise when (a) the correct answer requires placing more than one response in a cell, but a student enters *fewer or more responses* than should be entered; and (b) the correct answer is a blank, but a student enters *some response(s)* in that cell. In the presidential term example, for instance, both Roosevelt and Truman were president in the span 1945–1948: Roosevelt died in office while Truman was the vice president. A student may place an E, an H, or both into the corresponding cell in the "President" column. How should this cell be scored? The correct answer is "E and H," so clearly this should be given full credit or 2 points (1 point for each). Students who mark only E or only H could be given partial credit (1 point), or they could be given no credit (0 points). Giving partial credit would seem to be the fairest thing to do.

Suppose, however, a student responded with both C and H. Option C is clearly incorrect, but Option H is correct yet incomplete. We recommend giving partial credit (1 point) for the correct portion and not subtracting points for the incorrect Option C. You could make a note to the student that Option C is incorrectly placed, however.

One way a clever student may attempt to "beat the system" is to put the letter of every response option in every cell of the table. Because the correct option(s) would always be included in a cell (along with all the other incorrect options), the student would get 100 percent if our suggestions for scoring were followed. What should you do if this happens? We suggest that you return the test paper to the student (without penalty) and ask the student to enter in the table cells only those few choices the student believes are correct.

Advantages The tabular or matrix item is a useful way to assess whether students can pull together facts and ideas into an organized format such as a table. It is easy to create for assessing recall of verbal information, such as facts, dates, generalizations, terminology, and characteristics of theories. It is also very efficient when you have one list of premises and many different lists of responses. You may recall that when writing a *basic* matching item, the responses within a list should be homogeneous; that is, all should belong to the same category. When you are writing a basic matching exercise and find the response list becoming heterogeneous, you may wish to reorganize the exercise into a tabular item set.

Criticisms Although it may be possible to create tabular item sets that assess complex or higher-order thinking skills, it is difficult to do so. Most teachers find this format most useful for assessing recall and recognition of verbal information. Because the format is easy to construct, some teachers overuse it (or its cousin, basic matching) and are therefore subject to criticism of focusing on facts rather than problem-solving, critical-thinking, or other higher-order cognitive skills. Also, scoring the set is problematic.

> **MyLab Education** **Self-Check 10.2**
>
> **MyLab Education** **Application Exercise 10.2:** Evaluating a Matching Exercise

CONCLUSION

This chapter has discussed writing multiple-choice items and matching exercises. With the fill-in-the-blank and true-false items discussed in Chapter 9, these formats comprise the common selected response, objectively scored items types used in paper-and-pencil tests. In Chapter 12, we turn to the essay question, a constructed-response format. Before we do that, however, Chapter 11 discusses assessing higher-order thinking, problem solving, and critical thinking, which is particularly suited to constructed-response formats.

EXERCISES

1. For the subject you teach, or one with which you are most familiar, construct one flawless multiple-choice item to assess each of the following abilities. Before writing each item, write a specific learning objective that the item will assess. After writing the items, use the checklist for multiple-choice items to evaluate and revise your items. Share your items with the other members of your class.
   a. Ability to discriminate two verbal concepts
   b. Ability to comprehend a principle or rule

c. Ability to select an appropriate course of action

d. Ability to interpret new data or new information

2. For the subject you teach, obtain curricular material that has multiple-choice items for teachers and students to use. Select from this material 10 items that would be appropriate for a unit you might teach. Evaluate each item using the multiple-choice checklist. Identify the flaw(s) in each item, and then revise the item to correct the flaw(s) without adding other flaws. Discuss your findings with the class.

3. For the subject you teach, obtain curricular material that has matching exercises for teachers and students to use. Select two exercises that would be appropriate for a unit you might teach. Evaluate each exercise using the matching exercise checklist. Identify the flaw(s) in each exercise and then revise the exercises to correct the flaw(s) without adding other flaws. Discuss your findings with the class.

4. Evaluate the matching exercise below using the matching exercise checklist. Prepare a list of the flaws found. For each flaw listed, explain why it is a flaw in this exercise. After completing your analysis, revise the exercise so it has no flaws. Share your findings with your class.

Instructions: Match the two columns.

A	B
1. chlorophyll	A. Green plants contain this substance
2. igneous	B. Type of rock formed when melted rock hardens
3. photosynthesis	C. A substance made up of both hydrogen and oxygen
4. water	D. Process by which green plants produce their food

5. Choose two different kinds of relationships from the following list and craft matching exercises for the subject you teach: accomplishments of persons, dates of noted events, definitions of terms, examples of applications of principles or rules, symbols for concepts, authors or artists and their specific works, English equivalents of foreign phrases, functions of specific parts of a mechanism, or names of pictured objects. Develop matching exercises for each of the two you chose. Evaluate and revise your exercises using the matching exercise checklist to eliminate all flaws. Present your matching exercises to your class.

Higher-Order Thinking, Problem Solving, and Critical Thinking

KEY CONCEPTS

1. To assess higher-order thinking, use tasks that require students to use knowledge or skill in novel situations. Context-dependent items sets are useful for this purpose.

2. A concept is a class or category of similar things. Four strategies for assessing understanding of concrete concepts and four strategies for assessing understanding of defined concepts are presented. A principle is a rule that relates two or more concepts. Four strategies for assessing comprehension and use of rule-governed thinking are presented. Reading skills involve thinking, too. Three strategies for assessing reading skills are presented.

3. Problem solving refers to the kind of thinking required when reaching a goal is not automatic and students must use one or more higher-order thinking processes to do it. Seventeen strategies for assessing problem solving are presented.

4. Critical thinking is reasonable and reflective thinking focused on deciding what to believe or do. Thirteen strategies for assessing critical thinking are presented. Use checklists or rating scales to assess dispositions toward critical thinking.

IMPORTANT TERMS

checklist

closed-response task

cloze reading exercise

concept

concrete concept

context-dependent item sets

critical thinking

defined concept

dispositions toward critical thinking

heuristic

IDEAL problem solver

ill-structured problems

MAZE item type

novel material

open-response task

principle

principle-governed thinking

problem

rating scale

relational concepts

schema (schemata)

well-structured problems

ASSESSING HIGHER-ORDER THINKING

Higher-order thinking skills are "skills that enhance the construction of deeper, conceptually-driven understanding" (Schraw & Robinson, 2011, p. 2) among students in all disciplines. Always a hallmark of a quality education, higher-order thinking has taken on new urgency with the publication and adoption of the Common Core State Standards (NGA & CCSSO, 2010) and with the press in all disciplines for students to develop flexible, life-long learning and thinking skills to enable them to function well in a quickly changing, information-based world (Partnership for 21st Century Skills, 2009).

A basic rule for assessment of higher-order thinking skills is to use tasks that require use of knowledge and skill in new or novel situations. If you only assess students' ability to recall what is in the textbook or what you say, you will not know whether they understand or can apply the reasons, explanations, and interpretations. In short, you must use **novel materials** to assess higher-order thinking. One way to do that is to use context-dependent item sets.

Context-Dependent Item Sets

Context-dependent item sets consist of introductory material followed by several items. Students must think about and use the information in the introductory material to answer the questions, solve the problems, or otherwise complete the assessment tasks. Context-dependent item sets are sometimes called interpretive exercises. The introductory material may be extracts from reading materials, pictures, graphs, drawings, paragraphs, poems, formulas, tables of numbers, lists of words or symbols, specimens, maps, films, and sound recordings. Here is one example:

Example

Pat set up four different jars with a burning candle in each jar. He put the lids on jars 1, 2, and 3 as shown in the picture below.

1. The candle in jar 1 burned for 2 minutes after the lid was put on. The candle in jar 2 burned for 8 minutes. About how long did the candle in jar 3 burn after the lid was put on?
   A. 1 minute
   *B. 4 minutes
   C. 8 minutes
   D. 10 minutes

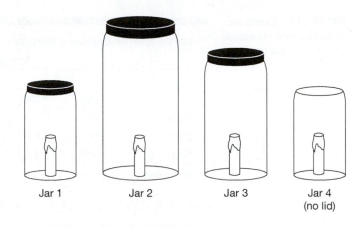

Jar 1   Jar 2   Jar 3   Jar 4 (no lid)

2. Pat did not put a lid on jar 4. The candle in jar 4 burned for a very long time. Tell why this candle kept burning so much longer than the other candles.

   _____
   _____
   _____
   _____
   _____

Source: National Assessment of Educational Progress released item Science Grade: 4, Block: 2005-4S12 No.: 3–4.

In this example, the interpretive material is a diagram of a science demonstration. This extract "simulates" a classroom laboratory exercise and thus presents a concrete, realistic example. A student must analyze or process the material in this example to answer the questions. The example shows a multiple-choice item and a short constructed-response item. Context-dependent item sets may be used, however, with any type of item format.

Ability to Use Reference Materials

Assessing the ability to use reference materials, maps, graphs, and tables also lends itself to using context-dependent item sets, whether you are assessing the ability to use both general reference materials or special subject-matter-specific materials. Reference-using skills you may teach and assess include alphabetizing, using tables of contents and indexes, using encyclopedias, using dictionaries, using general reference materials (calendars, maps and globes, textbooks, periodical indexes, atlases, and so on), using library services, and using the Internet and computer-based CDs. Skills in using these media should also be taught and assessed.

In this assessment area, interpretive materials might include a section of an index, a section

FIGURE 11.1   Examples of items written to assess graph and table reading skills.

Use the table below to answer Questions 1 and 2.

Average Temperature and Rainfall at Windy Hill Town

	2008		2009		2010		2011	
	Temp	Rain	Temp	Rain	Temp	Rain	Temp	Rain
September	64°	0.1 in	63°	0.2 in	66°	0.0 in	64°	0.3 in
October	72°	0.4 in	71°	0.5 in	74°	0.4 in	71°	0.6 in
November	77°	0.9 in	75°	1.0 in	78°	0.8 in	76°	0.7 in
December	81°	2.0 in	80°	2.7 in	85°	1.5 in	80°	2.1 in

Example of assessing the ability to locate and compare information from a table

1. When did the highest average rainfall occur?
   A. November of 2008
   B. November of 2009
   *C. December of 2009
   D. December of 2011

Example of assessing the ability to draw inferences based on trends and other information in a table

2. Which of the following events was most likely to have occurred between September and December of 2010?
   A. The roads were covered with ice and snow.
   *B. The town's water reserves were very low.
   C. The river flowing through the town overflowed its banks.

---

of a table of contents, a part of an atlas, a picture of a computer screen, and the like. You may have to rewrite or modify these materials before they are suitable for use in assessment, because (a) they contain material irrelevant or extraneous to assessing the objective at hand, (b) they are too long, or (c) the extract is out of context and is therefore not clear to students. You may need to obtain written permission to reproduce copyrighted materials. You may, of course, use entire volumes or take students to the library for the assessment. To do so, you will need sufficient materials (or computers) for all students, as well as sufficient uninterrupted time to administer this type of performance assessment.

Graphs and Tables

Much information is condensed in tables and graphs. Graph and table reading abilities are important to further learning in many areas, both in and out of school. Examples of some of the graph and table reading abilities that you can teach and assess include comprehending the topic on which a table or graph gives information, recognizing what is shown by each part of a graph or table, reading amounts, comparing two or more values, and interpreting relationships, trends, and other main points from the graph or table.

Item 1 of Figure 11.1 requires a student to read the table and locate the information in a cell and to compare several values read from the table to determine which is largest. Item 2 requires a student to make an inference concerning the likelihood of an event based on understanding the trends and facts presented.

Here is an example of how you could use a graph and multiple-choice items to assess capabilities to draw inference based on the displayed rates or trends, underlying relationships, and facts:

Example

Use the Information Below to Answer Questions 1 and 2

Before the exercise period began, the teacher divided the class into two groups. Group 1 was to walk around the track two times. Group 2 was to run around the track one time. All students took their pulses both before and after going around the track. The average pulse for each group is shown in the graph below.

Example of an item to assess the ability to draw an inference from a graph

1. According to the graph, which type of exercise made students' hearts beat faster?
   *A. Running
   B. Walking
   C. Neither—they had the same result with either walking or running

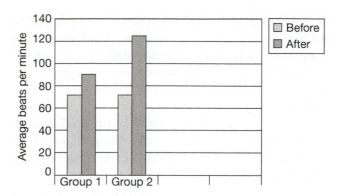

Example of an item assessing the ability to interpret trends underlying a graph

2. What would be the heartbeats about 1 hour after the exercise period when all the students are reading in the library?
   *A. About 70 for both groups
   B. About 70 for the group that walked twice around and about 130 for the group that ran once around
   C. About 90 for the group that walked twice around and about 130 for the group that ran once around
   D. Lower than 60 for both groups

Maps

Context-dependent items sets are useful for assessing map-reading ability, as well. Specific map-reading abilities include orienting maps and determining direction, locating and/or describing places on maps and globes, determining distances, tracing routes of travel, and interpreting time zones, landscapes, features, and the like. Below is an example of an item that assesses map-reading ability.

Example

(Population density map of the United States goes here)

1. A megalopolis is defined as a "supercity" made up of large cities with highly populated areas between them. Look at a population density map of the United States. Which pair of cities is part of a megalopolis?
   A. Denver and Salt Lake City
   B. Oklahoma City and Dallas
   *C. Boston and New York City
   D. Kansas City and St. Louis

Source: National Assessment of Educational Progress, released items, Grade 4 Geography, Block: 2001-4G7, No.: 3.

Advantages and Disadvantages of Context-Dependent Items

Advantages A context-dependent item set has these advantages: (a) It provides an opportunity to assess students on materials that are relatively close to the real-world contexts; (b) it provides, through the introductory material, the same context for all students; (c) its introductory material lessens the burden of memorizing and may moderate the effects of prior experience with the specific content; and (d) frequently, it is the only means to test certain intellectual abilities.

Disadvantages Some disadvantages of a context-dependent item set are (a) the set may be difficult to construct, (b) you must carefully create the introductory material to assess higher-order thinking skills, (c) a student's performance on one context-dependent item set may not generalize well to performance on another similar set, (d) the set often requires students to use additional abilities (such as reading comprehension and writing skills) that may go beyond the major focus of the assessment tasks, and (e) you may need special facilities (such as a scanner and/or drawing skill and equipment) to produce them that are not readily available.

Layout

The way context-dependent material is arranged on the pages of a test booklet is important because a poor arrangement may cause students to misread or misinterpret the item set. A side heading and directions should point students to the introductory material and to the particular tasks based on it. The introductory material is placed in the center of the page with items below it.

Keep the introductory material and all items that refer to it on the same page, if possible. Otherwise, students will be distracted as they flip pages back and forth while completing the assessment. Students with poor short-term attention and memory may lose their place or make careless errors.

> **MyLab Education** **Self-Check 11.1**
>
> **MyLab Education** **Application Exercise 11.1:**
> Interpreting a Context-Dependent Item

CONCEPT LEARNING

What Are Concepts?

A **concept** is a class or category of similar things (objects, people, events, or relations). Many of the things you teach are concepts. Students' understanding of concepts forms the basis for their higher-order learning. When we speak of the concept *red*, for example, we refer to a category of objects with a similar color. A student is said to have learned the concept *red* if the student (a) can identify examples or instances of red things (red tricycle, red book, red lipstick, etc.) *and* (b) does not refer to things that are not red (green tricycle, purple book, pink lipstick, etc.) as red. Concepts are ideas or abstractions: Only specific examples of a concept exist in the world. The individual members of the concept category are called *instances*, *examples*, or *exemplars*.

A distinction can be made between concrete concepts and defined concepts. A **concrete concept** refers to a class, the members of which have in common one or more physical, tangible qualities that can be heard, seen, tasted, felt, or smelled. Examples of concrete concepts include *large*, *triangle*, *green*, *house*, and *dog*. A **defined concept** refers to a class for which members can be defined in the same way by attributes that are not tangible. Defined concepts frequently involve relationships among other concepts and are sometimes called abstract or **relational concepts**. Defined concepts are usually learned by definitions. Examples of defined concepts include *diagonal*, *beside*, *friendliness*, *uncle*, and *mother*. Some concepts are learned initially as concrete concepts and later as defined concepts.

Understanding a concept goes beyond simply identifying examples of it. Concepts are related to each other and linked together in complex ways through schemata or networks. A **schema** is the way knowledge is represented in our minds through networks of connected concepts, information, rules, problem-solving strategies, and conditions for actions. For example, Woolfolk (2005) points out that we know counterfeit money is not real, even though it fits the *money* concept prototype and examples. We know it is counterfeit money because we link our concept of money to other concepts, such as the concepts of authority to print, crime, forgery, and so on. You need to help students connect concepts to their existing networks and schemata of knowledge before they can fully understand these concepts.

Strategies for Assessing Concrete Concept Learning

Figure 11.2 presents four commonly used strategies that can be used to assess whether a student has learned a concrete concept. These include students (1) naming the concept from examples, (2) discriminating examples from nonexamples, (3) producing their own examples, and (4) using the concept in performance assessment.

FIGURE 11.2 Strategies for assessing concrete concept learning.

Strategy for assessing concrete concept learning	Example
1. *Have students name the concept after seeing exemplars.*	1. What are the shapes in this group called? 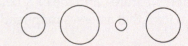 [Answer: Circles]
2. *Have students discriminate concept exemplars from nonexemplars.*	2. Which of these shapes are circles? 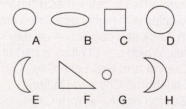 [Answer: A, D, G]
3. *Have students produce their own exemplars when given the concept name.*	3. Draw three circles. Be sure each is different from the others.
4. *Use performance assessment to assess concept understanding at a deeper level.*	4. *The teacher explains the task orally.* Draw a picture of a street or neighborhood that includes buildings, people, and cars. Do not use any circles or squares in your drawing. Then, explain why it was difficult to draw this picture without circles or squares.

Give the Name   Strategy 1 is usually an unsatisfactory way to assess concept learning. Students may learn the concept and perhaps can use it without learning the proper name of the concept. The give-the-name assessment strategy does not require students to discriminate the exemplars from nonexemplars, so you do not know whether the students have overgeneralized the concept. For example, students may think all shapes with round edges are circles. Finally, this assessment strategy does not require students to use or apply their understanding of the concept.

Discriminate Exemplars from Nonexemplars   Strategy 2 requires students to discriminate circles from other shapes. This assessment strategy is preferred over that of Strategy 1 because it does not require students to produce the concept name to complete the task and allows you to control the assessment situation. You need to control (a) the degree to which the exemplars and nonexemplars are familiar to students, (b) how typical the exemplars are of the concept, (c) the number and type of discriminations between exemplars and nonexemplars, and (d) the total number of exemplars you present. To use this strategy, present at least two exemplars for students to identify; otherwise, you do not know whether the students have undergeneralized the concept. Undergeneralizing means that the students think only one example is the same as the whole concept (e.g., thinking that the circle you showed in class on the board is the only circle). As with Strategy 1, this strategy does not require students to use or apply their understanding of a concept. Thus, it does not permit you to assess students' deeper understanding of it.

Ken Mattingly, Middle school science teacher
Rockcastle County Public Schools, Mt. Vernon, KY

MyLab Education

Video Example 11.1

Middle school science students are using models of strong and weak work to understand levels of performance described on a rubric. In effect, they are developing concepts for the criteria and performance levels. Listen to the students describe their growing understanding of these concepts as they describe the work they are reviewing.

Produce New Exemplars   Strategy 3 requires students to think up examples and you to judge the correctness of the examples. You also know whether the students' examples were explicitly taught, in which case you are assessing only remembering. This strategy may be useful for assessing simple concepts (such as circle), but it is not preferred for more complex concept assessment.

Performance Assessment for Deeper Understanding   None of the first three strategies assess students' deeper understanding of a concept. Students show their deeper understanding when they are able to (a) use the concept to solve problems; (b) relate the concept to other concepts, principles (rules), and generalizations they have learned; and (c) use the concept to learn new material. To assess students' deeper understanding, you must create assessments that are more complex and require more application of the concept than was illustrated by the previous items.

The example for Strategy 4 in Figure 11.2 shows a *performance task*, meaning that students have to do something with their knowledge. This assessment can be used to evaluate the following learning:

I. Content objectives (in combination)
   A. Identifies circles and squares
   B. Discriminates circles and squares from other shapes
   C. Understands the importance of shapes in the world

II. Complex thinking objective (problem solving)
   A. Identifies things that keep you from solving a problem

The assessment in this example takes a relatively long time to administer. The main performance involves the students creating a drawing of the neighborhood that includes buildings, cars, and people but that does not use circles and squares. This drawing presents a problem to be solved: How can you depict buildings, cars, and people, yet not use circles and squares? This is a difficult problem for a first grader because circles and squares are basic shapes comprising much of the students' experience. Students must distinguish among circles, squares, and other shapes to solve the problem. Notice, too, that the assessment requires you to do more than collect the drawings. You must interview or have a conference with

FIGURE 11.3   Scoring rubrics for the circle and squares drawing problem.

Identifies and discriminates circles and squares

3 Identifies circles and squares with little or no prompting.
2 Sometimes confuses circles and squares with ellipses or other curves; sometimes confuses squares with rectangles or other shapes.
1 Demonstrates severe misunderstanding of circles and/or squares.

Understands importance of circles and squares as the basic shapes comprising objects in the world

3 Demonstrates a thorough understanding of how circles and squares are the basic shapes that make up most objects in the world.
2 Displays an incomplete understanding of how circles and squares are used in the world and has some notable misconceptions about their use.
1 Does not understand how circles and squares are used in the world.

Understands that not being able to use circles and squares is an obstacle to depicting real-world objects accurately

3 Accurately identifies the most important obstacles or constraints imposed by not being able to use circles and squares in drawings of objects.
2 Identifies some constraints or obstacles about not using circles and squares that are accurate but also includes some that are inaccurate or irrelevant to the drawing problem.
1 Does not identify the most significant constraints or obstacles imposed by not being able to use circles and squares to solve the drawing problem.

each student using the drawing to prompt or draw out from the student information about how well the learning objectives have been attained.

Figure 11.3 gives an example of rubrics you could use to evaluate students. All learning objectives are represented in the scoring rubrics. However, you do not treat each rubric as a separate test item. You assess this task overall, rather than piece by piece, using a combination of activities including reviewing a student's drawing, conferencing with a student, and prompting a discussion of the mathematical content to obtain lots of information about the student's achievement. Only then do you evaluate how well the student has learned each objective.

An advantage of using Strategy 4 for assessing concepts through complex performance tasks is that students use the concepts in realistic situations. These situations activate students' cognitive frameworks and schemata. They require students to link the concepts to many other concepts as they complete the task. If you focus on a student's way(s) of using the target concepts while he or she engages in problem solving, you assess whether the student understands the concepts beyond simply naming and identifying them.

Strategies for Assessing Defined Concept Learning

Figure 11.4 presents four strategies that can help you assess students' learning of abstract or defined concepts. Of the four strategies, Strategy 1, requiring students to produce a definition, and Strategy 2, requiring students to produce new

exemplars of the concept, are the weaker strategies and may not be suitable for younger students. Strategy 3, requiring students to discriminate exemplars from nonexemplars, and Strategy 4, requiring students to identify components and demonstrate relationships, are the stronger strategies. Their main advantage is that they require students to recognize new exemplars, ensuring that they do not respond with rote memorization of definitions. The performance (drawing and labeling) aspect of Item 5 (Strategy 4) has the additional advantage of not depending solely on highly developed verbal skills.

Crystal Thayer, Grade 4 teacher
Lewis County Schools, Tollesboro, KY

MyLab Education

Video Example 11.2

This fourth grade teacher explains how she set up learning stations and assessments to address students' partial understandings and misconceptions.

ASSESSING WHETHER STUDENTS' THINKING USES RULES

Another important area of learning is rule-governed or principle-governed thinking. A **principle** is a rule that relates two or more concepts. Students learn abstract principles in later elementary and high school. Following are some examples:

FIGURE 11.4 Strategies for assessing defined concept learning.

Strategy for assessing defined concept learning	Example
1. *Have students produce a definition.*	1. Define a *prejudiced act* in your own words.
2. *Have students produce examples.*	2. Tell what is meant by *lonesome*.
3. *Have students discriminate exemplars from nonexemplars.*	3. Describe two examples of *acts of prejudice* that were not discussed in class or in the text but which you witnessed or experienced during the past few weeks.
4. *Have students identify components and demonstrate relationships.*	4. Which statement *most nearly* describes the concept of *lonesome?*

4. Which statement *most nearly* describes the concept of *lonesome?*
   A Ten-year-old Meghan decides to play alone today with her dollhouse, even though her friends asked her to play with them.
   B Each morning Professor Cory closes her office door to be by herself to write up her research reports.
   *C Each lunch period 15-year-old Marya stands by herself, not speaking to anyone in the crowded school cafeteria.
   D Clarisse, a cloistered nun, speaks to no one and spends many hours alone while praying.

(Picture of earth with person on it omitted to save space)

5. In the picture above, draw lines and an angle (or angles) to show the location of the zenith in relation to the person. Label the angle(s) and the zenith.

Example

Abstract principles learned in high school

- Experimental studies allow conclusions regarding functional relations while correlational studies allow only statements of co-occurrence.
- People tend to migrate to, and find success in, physical environments closely resembling those from which they came.
- The status of a group in a society is positively related to the priorities of that society.
- The rate of increase in law enforcement officials is negatively related to the stability of the society.

We say students use **principle-governed thinking** when they can apply a principle or rule appropriately in a variety of "new" situations. Assess students' understanding of a principle by asking them to apply it to a new situation rather than by simply mimicking something they heard in class.

Strategies for Assessing Comprehension of Rules and Principles

Most principles operate under certain conditions and not under others. Further, when the conditions exist and when a principle does operate, this dynamic leads to certain consequences and not to others (Figure 11.5), which suggests four basic strategies for creating tasks to assess students' comprehension of principles.

These tasks are difficult, especially for younger, inexperienced learners who are not well read. Further, students' performance on such tasks may be difficult to interpret. Here are some of the questions you have to answer about the students' responses to evaluate them properly:

- Are the students' examples new, or were they presented in the class or in the assigned materials?
- Why can't students give good examples?
- If students cannot write an explanation, do they understand the principle?
- Is there weak knowledge of the specific content to which you have asked the principle to be applied?

These item types require students to recall the principle without prompting and articulate it. Students unable to do these two things will not answer correctly. Further, there may be more than one correct explanation for the phenomena stated in your example, which occurs often when the

FIGURE 11.5 Strategies
for assessing rule-
governed thinking.

Strategy for assessing rule-governed thinking	Example
1. *Have students produce or identify consequences.*	1. Suppose the federal government increased the prime lending rate by one-half percent tomorrow. What would you expect to happen?
2. *Have students produce the consequences and explain why.*	2. Suppose hard economic times forced many cattle ranchers from the high plains of the United States to leave the country. Name two or more geographical locations in the world you would expect them to move. Explain your choices.
3. *Have students produce an explanation only.*	3. In the 2004 presidential election between George W. Bush and John Kerry, voter turnout was high. Why do you think this was the case? In your explanation, apply what you know about voter turnout to the 2004 current events context.
4. *Have students draw a conclusion based on application of a principle.*	4. A farmer planted a cornfield then divided it into two halves. Both halves were planted with the same amount of the same kind of corn and received the same amount of water and sunlight. The farmer tossed a coin to decide which half would receive a new fertilizer and which half would be fertilized with the same product as usual. Corn yield on the half-field with the new fertilizer was 25% more than for the other half-field. What can the farmer conclude?

"truth" of the principle or its applicability to all situations is open to question.

Because the items implementing Strategies 1 through 4 are highly verbal, they are likely to require a good level of reading comprehension. Students with poor reading skills who actually understand the principle may miss the item. You may try reading the item situations to poor readers to see if they will respond better. You also may be able to simplify the reading level.

MyLab Education **Self-Check 11.2**

MyLab Education **Application Exercise 11.2:**
Assessing Understanding of a Concept

PROBLEM SOLVING

The Nature of Problem Solving

Students incur a **problem** when they want to reach a specific outcome or goal but do not automatically recognize the proper path or solution to use to reach it. The problem to solve is how to reach the desired goal. When students cannot automatically recognize the proper way to reach the desired goal, they must use one or more higher-order thinking processes. These thinking processes are called *problem solving*. If the procedure for attaining a goal is so well known to students that they can complete the task without having to reason, they do not have to use problem-solving skills. Older students have a name for these kinds of tasks: They call them "no-brainers." They recognize that there is no problem to solve if you do not have to think about the proper solution.

This intuitive concept, no-brainer, should be a useful clue when you craft tasks to assess problem-solving ability. If the tasks require students simply to repeat a procedure you taught them in a situation that is more or less identical to the one you used in class, you have created a no-brainer task, and not a problem-solving task. To apply problem-solving skills, students need a task that is somehow different or new to them. The task need not be new to the world, just new to the students.

Well-Structured and Ill-Structured Problems Most of the problem tasks in teachers' editions of textbooks and in the end-of-chapter exercises in student texts are a few notches above no-brainers. They present tasks that are clearly laid out: All the information students need is given, the situations are very much the same as you have taught in class, and there is usually one correct answer that students can reach by applying a procedure you taught. These are known as **well-structured problems** (Davidson & Sternberg, 2003). Well-structured problems serve a useful purpose in giving students opportunities to rehearse the procedures or algorithms you taught.

However, well-structured problems are unlike the real-life or authentic problems students will eventually have to face. Most authentic problems are **ill-structured problems**. For ill-structured problems, students must (a) organize the information to understand it; (b) clarify the problem itself; (c) obtain all the information needed, which may not be immediately available; and (d) recognize that there may be several equally correct answers. A problem with a single correct answer is called a **closed-response task**; a problem with multiple correct answers is called an **open-response task**.

General Versus Subject-Specific Problem Solving

Controversies still exist among cognitive scientists, psychologists, and educators concerning whether we should teach students problem-solving strategies that are general or specific to each curriculum area—strategies specific, for example, to mathematics, history, or art. Strategies for solving curriculum-specific problems are less applicable across different subjects but more powerful within the specific curriculum; the general approach applies somewhat to every curriculum area but has limited power within any specific curriculum.

It appears that people actually use both general and specific strategies (Ericsson, 2003). Persons working in an area who have a great deal of knowledge and expertise apply well-known problem-solving strategies to solve problems specific to their area. However, if they work outside their area of expertise, the specific strategies no longer apply: They resort, then, to more general problem-solving strategies. However, as they develop expertise in an initially unfamiliar area, the general strategies are dropped in favor of more area-specific strategies.

Heuristics for Solving Problems

Knowledge-based problem-solving methods within a particular domain provide much better solution strategies than the general methods suggested in this section. Nevertheless, when students do not have a

knowledge-based strategy, a heuristic should be tried. A **heuristic** is a general problem-solving strategy that may help solve a given problem. The following is a list of 10 problem-solving heuristics:

1. Try to see the whole picture; do not focus only on details.
2. Withhold your judgment; do not rush to a solution too quickly.
3. Create a model for a problem using pictures, sketches, diagrams, graphs, equations, or symbols.
4. If one way of modeling or representing the problem does not work, try another way.
5. State the problem as a question; change the question if the original does not suggest a solution.
6. Be flexible: Look for unconventional or new ways to use the available tools; see the conventional in new ways; try responding to the situation from a different angle or point of view; think divergently.
7. Try working backward by starting with the goal and going backward to find the solution strategy.
8. Keep track of your partial solutions, so you can come back to them and resume where you left off.
9. Use analogical thinking: Ask, "What is this problem like? Where have I seen something similar to this?"
10. Talk about and through a problem; keep talking about it until a solution suggests itself.

The IDEAL Problem Solver

General problem-solving skills may be organized into a five-stage process that Bransford and Stein (1984) call the **IDEAL problem solver**:

I Identify the problem

D Define and represent the problem

E Explore possible strategies

A Act on the strategies

L Look back and evaluate the effects of your activities

The IDEAL method is an easily remembered way to think about the general stages of the problem-solving cycle (Pretz, Naples, & Sternberg, 2003).

Strategies for Assessing Problem-Solving Skills

If you evaluate only whether an answer is correct or incorrect, you are likely to miss the opportunity to evaluate students' thinking skills in general and problem-solving skills in particular. Assessing students' problem-solving skills requires set tasks that allow you to systematically evaluate students' thinking about problem solving. You need to craft different types of tasks to assess the different aspects of problem solving. Figure 11.6 shows assessment strategies grouped according to the IDEAL problem solver categories. The strategies suggest the general layout or structure of the tasks. You should apply them specifically to your own teaching area.

FIGURE 11.6   Strategies for assessing problem solving.

Problem-solving category	Strategy	Description
Identifying and recognizing problems	1. Identify the problem	Present a scenario or problem description. Ask students to identify the problem to be solved.
Defining and representing problems	2. Pose questions[1]	Present a statement that contains the problem and ask students to pose the question(s), using the language and concepts of the subject you are teaching, that need(s) to be answered to solve the problem.
	3. Demonstrate linguistic understanding	Present several problems students should be able to solve and underline the key phrases and common vocabulary they need to know to comprehend the context of the problem. Ask students to explain in their own words the meaning of these linguistic features of the problem.
	4. Identify irrelevancies	Present interpretive materials and a problem statement and ask students to identify all of the irrelevant information. Be sure the interpretive material contains information that is both relevant and irrelevant to the problem solution.
	5. Sort problem cards	Present a collection of two or more examples of each of several different types of problem statements and ask students to (a) sort the problems into categories or groups of their own choosing and (b) explain why the problems they put into a group belong together. Put each problem statement on a separate card, but do not specify the type of problem it is. Focus your assessment on whether students are attending to only the wording or other surface features of the problem or, more appropriately, to the deeper features of the problem. For example, students should group all problems that can be solved using the same mathematical principle, the same scientific law, etc., even though the problems are worded quite differently or are applied to different content.
	6. Identify assumptions	State a problem and ask students to state (a) a tentative solution and (b) what assumptions about the current and future problem situation they have made in reaching their solution.
	7. Describe multiple strategies	State a problem and ask students to (a) solve the problem in two or more ways and (b) show their solutions using pictures, diagrams, or graphs.
	8. Model the problem	State a problem and ask students to draw a diagram or picture showing the problem situation. Assess how the students represent the problem rather than on whether the problem is correctly solved. Drawings of time problems in mathematics, for example, should depict time lines, not scales.
	9. Identify obstacles	Present a difficult problem to solve, perhaps one missing a key piece of information, and ask students to explain (a) why it is difficult to complete the task, (b) what the obstacle(s) are, and/or (c) what additional information they need to overcome the obstacle(s). Assess whether students can identify the obstacle to solving the problem.
Exploring possible solution strategies	10. Justify solutions	Present a problem statement along with two or more possible solutions to the problem and ask students to (a) select one solution they believe is correct and (b) justify why it is correct.

FIGURE 11.6 (*Continued*)

Problem-solving category	Strategy	Description
	11. Justify strategies used	State a problem and two or more strategies for solving it, and ask students to explain why both strategies are correct. Be certain both strategies yield the correct solution. In writing an item you might, for example, state that these were different ways that two fictional students solved the problem.
	12. Integrate data	Present several types of interpretive material (story, cartoon, graph, data table) and a statement of a problem that requires using information from two or more of the interpretive material types. Then ask students to (a) solve the problem and (b) explain the procedure they used to reach a solution. The problem solution must require using information from two or more of the interpretive materials.
	13. Produce alternate strategies	Present a problem statement and ask students to state two or more alternative solutions to the problem. An alternative approach is to present, along with the problem statement, one strategy that solves the problem, and require students to show you another way the problem could be solved.
	14. Use analogies	Present a problem statement and a correct solution strategy, and ask students to (a) describe other problems that could (by analogy) be solved by using this same solution strategy and (b) explain why the solution to the problem they generated is like the solution to the problem you gave them. Assess the analogical relationship of the students' solution strategy to the solution strategy you gave them.
	15. Solve backward	Present a complex problem situation or a complex (multistep) task to complete, and ask students to work backward from the desired outcome to develop a plan or a strategy for completing the task or solving the problem. For example, ask students to develop the steps and time frame needed to complete a library research paper. Assess how well students use backward solution strategies.
Acting on and looking back on problem–solution strategies	16. Evaluate the quality of a solution	State a problem and ask students to evaluate several different strategies for solving the problem. Ask students to produce several different solutions, or provide several solutions and ask them to evaluate those provided. If you provide solutions to evaluate, be certain to vary their correctness and quality so that students can display their ability to evaluate. (For example, some may be more efficient, some may have negative consequences, and some may not work at all.) Ask students to determine the best strategy, explain why some strategies work better than others, and why some do not work at all. Assess the students' ability to justify the hierarchical ordering of the strategies' quality.
	17. Systematically evaluate strategies	Use the same types of tasks as in Strategy 16, but assess the extent to which students follow systematic procedures to evaluate each of the solution strategies you proposed.

[1]*Strategies 2, 7, 10, 11, and 12 were adapted from junior high school mathematics performance assessments described by Lane, Parke, and Moskal (1992). We stripped their definitions of mathematical content to suggest the general structure of the strategy.*

MyLab Education Self-Check 11.3

MyLab Education Application Exercise 11.3:
Analyzing an Assessment of Problem-Solving

CRITICAL THINKING

Curriculum frameworks frequently state that developing students' abilities for critical thinking is an important educational goal. What is critical thinking? In this chapter, we shall adopt the following definition: "**Critical thinking** is a process, the goal of which is to make reasonable decisions about what to believe and what to do" (Ennis, 1996, p. xvii). This definition implies the following five attributes (Norris & Ennis, 1989):

1. *Reasonable thinking*—using good reasons

2. *Reflective thinking*—being conscious of looking for and using good reasons

3. *Focused thinking*—thinking for a particular purpose or goal

4. *Deciding what to believe or do*—evaluating both statements (what to believe) and actions (what to do)

5. *Abilities and dispositions*—both cognitive skills (abilities) and tendency to use the abilities (dispositions)

Critical-thinking abilities are specific cognitive skills that are used when a student exhibits critical-thinking behavior. Here are some of the abilities typically considered in discussions of critical thinking that could be assessed (Ennis, 1985). They are grouped into five areas.

Elementary clarification

1. *Focus on a question*—Students can critically review an action, a verbal statement, a piece of discourse, a scientific or political argument, or even a cartoon to determine its main point(s) or the essence of the argument. Subskills include (a) formulating or identifying the question or issue being posed, (b) formulating or selecting the proper criteria to use in evaluating the material presented, and (c) keeping the issue and its proper context in mind.

2. *Analyze arguments*—Students can analyze the *details* of the arguments presented in verbal statements, discussions, scientific or political reports, cartoons, and so on. Subskills include (a) identifying the conclusions in a statement; (b) identifying the stated and unstated reasons behind an argument; (c) seeing similarities and differences among two or more arguments; (d) finding, pointing out, and ignoring (when appropriate) irrelevancies appearing in an argument; (e) representing the logic or structure of an argument; and (f) summarizing an argument.

3. *Ask and answer questions that clarify and challenge*—Students can do two things: (a) ask appropriate questions of someone who is presenting an argument and (b) answer critical questions appropriately when making an argument themselves.

Basic support

4. *Judge the credibility of a source*—Students can evaluate the quality of the source of the evidence someone uses in supporting a position, including (a) the expertise of the person giving the evidence, (b) whether the person giving the evidence has a conflict of interest, (c) whether different sources of evidence agree, (d) whether the source of evidence has a reputation for being accurate and correct, (e) whether the evidence was obtained by established procedures that give it validity, and (f) whether there are good reasons for using the evidence under the given circumstances. Each discipline will have specific rules of evidence, as well.

5. *Make and judge observations*—Students can evaluate the quality of information obtained from eyewitness or direct observation of an event, phenomenon, or person. Among the standards or criteria students should be able to use when making these judgments are whether (a) an observer reports with minimal dependence on others' observations, (b) the time between the event and the report by the observer is short, (c) an observer is not reporting hearsay, (d) an observer keeps records of the observation, (e) the observations reported are corroborated by others, (f) an observer had good access to the event or person, (g) an observer records the observations properly, and (h) an observer is a credible source.

Inference

6. *Make and evaluate deductions*—Students can think logically when they analyze statements and conclusions. Subskills include (a) using the logic of class inclusion (what elements or members should be logically included in a class or category); (b) using conditional logic (if-then reasoning); and (c) properly interpreting statements using logical terms (negatives; double negatives; necessary vs. sufficient conditions) and using and understanding words such as *if, or, some, not, both*).

7. *Make and evaluate inductions*—Students can draw reasonable conclusions by generalizing from given information or identifying the best explanation for a set of observations. Subskills include (a) identifying and using typical features or patterns in the data to make inferences; (b) using appropriate techniques to make inferences from sample data; (c) using patterns and trends shown in tables and graphs to make inferences; (d) being alert for alternative explanations of the data; and (e) recognizing the impact of data that conflicts with an explanation, hypothesis, or conclusion.

8. *Make and evaluate value judgments*—Students can identify when inferences have been

made on the basis of values, what these values are, and when to use their own values to make inferences. Subskills of this ability include (a) gathering and using appropriate background information before judging; (b) identifying the consequences of the inferences that could be drawn and weighing the consequences before drawing conclusions; (c) identifying alternative actions and their value; and (d) balancing alternatives, weighing consequences, and deciding rationally.

Advanced clarification

9. *Define terms and judge definitions*—Students can analyze the meanings and definitions of the terms used in the course of arguments, statements, and events to evaluate them critically. Subskills include (a) knowing the various forms that definitions may take; (b) judging the appropriateness of the use of a given form of definition in a given context for a given term; (c) judging the appropriateness for a given context of different stances (for functions) in making a definition, such as reporting a meaning, stipulating a meaning, and promoting a program; and (d) judging the correctness or appropriateness of the content of the definition itself (see Ennis, 1996, Chapters 12 and 13).

10. *Identify assumptions*—Students can identify assumptions that are part of someone's reasoning about what to believe or to do. In this case, we use the term *assumption* to mean an unstated basis for someone's reasoning. Be careful not to confuse this with the common usage that an assumption is a tentatively held conclusion or that an assumption is a dubious conclusion.

Strategies and tactics

11. *Decide on an action*—Students who can decide on an action are essentially good problem solvers. Subskills are those we discussed earlier in this chapter on problem solving: defining problems, formulating and evaluating solutions, viewing the total problem and taking action, and evaluating the action taken. The assessment strategies for this ability are the same as those you would use in assessing problem-solving skills.

12. *Interact with others*—Students can identify, be aware of, and judge the appropriateness of rhetorical devices to persuade, explain, or argue.

Among the rhetorical devices students should be able to identify are (a) argumentative verbal tactics (appeal to authority, straw man, etc.) and (b) presentation of a logical case.

Source: From *Evaluating Critical Thinking* (p. 14), by S. P. Norris and R. H. Ennis, 1989, Pacific Grove, CA: Critical Thinking Books and Software. Reprinted by permission.

Strategies for Assessing Critical-Thinking Abilities

The ultimate goal of education in critical thinking is to enable students to use these abilities spontaneously in school and in their lives after school. For example, students would be expected to spontaneously clarify the main point of an argument that someone was stating unclearly by asking the person, "What is your main point?" or "Can I say that your main point is _____?"

For the most part, critical-thinking abilities are best taught and assessed in some context. We present here the *strategies* you could use when crafting tasks assessing critical thinking in a content area. Some of these are illustrated with sample items. Practice applying these strategies to the subject(s) you teach.

The strategies shown in Figure 11.7 are organized around the headings used in the preceding list of critical-thinking abilities. Use these alone or in selective combinations that fit real-life circumstances. Give students instruction and practice in deciding on the appropriate analyses, deciding when to use combinations of critical-thinking skills in different circumstances, and applying principles and criteria. Make the situations realistic. Performance tasks, discussed in Chapter 13, offer assessment opportunities for doing this.

Strategies for Assessing Dispositions Toward Critical Thinking

Dispositions toward critical thinking are habits of mind or tendencies to use appropriate critical-thinking behaviors often. Students who are disposed toward critical thinking:

1. seek a statement of the thesis or question;
2. seek reasons;
3. try to be well informed;
4. use credible sources and mention them;
5. take into account the total situation;
6. keep their thinking relevant to the main point;

FIGURE 11.7   Strategies for assessing critical thinking.

Critical thinking category	Strategy	Description
Elementary clarification	1. Focus on a question	**Give students** ■ Statement of a problem ■ Political address ■ Statement of a government policy ■ Experiment and results **Ask students** ■ What is the main issue/problem? ■ What criteria should you use to evaluate the quality, goodness, or truth of the argument or conclusions?
	2. Analyze arguments	**Give students** ■ Description of a situation *and* ■ One or two arguments **Ask students** ■ What conclusions did the arguer draw? ■ What evidence is presented that appears to be intended to support the conclusion(s)? ■ What evidence is presented that appears to be intended to contradict a conclusion (although not the arguer's conclusion(s))? ■ What are the unstated assumptions that the arguer intended to use? ■ What are the unstated assumptions that need to hold for the argument(s) to be valid? ■ What part(s) of the statement is irrelevant to the argument(s)? ■ Outline the logical structure of the argument(s). ■ Summarize the main parts of the argument(s).
	3. Ask clarifying questions	**Give students** ■ Description of a situation *and* ■ An argument **Ask students** ■ What question(s) would you ask of the speaker or author? ■ Why would you ask these things?
Basic support of an argument	4. Judge the credibility of a source	**Give students** ■ Texts of arguments ■ Advertisements ■ Experiments and interpretations **Ask students** ■ Which parts, if any, of the material are credible, and why? ■ Which parts of the material are not credible, and why?
	5. Judge observation reports	**Give students** ■ Description of the context for the observation *and* ■ Report(s) of the observation(s) *and* ■ Background of the observer or reporter **Ask students** ■ Can you trust or believe the report of _____? ■ Which parts of the material are not credible, and which are not? Why?

Inferences	6. Judge deductions by
	  a. comparing different conclusions
	  b. judging the truth of a conclusion
		(a) **Give students**
		■ A statement that students are to assume is true *and*
		■ Alternatives consisting of one logically correct conclusion and two or more logically incorrect conclusions
		Ask students
		■ Which conclusion is logically appropriate?

FIGURE 11.7 (*Continued*)

Critical thinking category	Strategy	Description
	7. Judge inductions	(b) Give students ■ A statement that students are to assume is true *and* ■ An alternative consisting of one possibly correct conclusion Ask students ■ Must this conclusion follow? (a) *For response-choice items*, give students ■ Situation statement *and* ■ Information (data) *and* ■ Possible conclusions drawn from the information Ask students ■ Judge the conclusion as supported or contradicted (or neither) by the data *or* ■ Select the conclusion that best explains the data ■ Select plausible alternative hypotheses or explanations ■ Identify conflicting evidence (b) *For constructed-response items,* give students ■ Situation statement *and* ■ Information (data) Ask students ■ What conclusions are logically appropriate? ■ Draw the proper conclusion, if any, from the data *and* ■ Explain whether and why the conclusion is correct or incorrect
	8. Make judgments about values	Give students ■ Description of a situation *and* ■ Problem statement *and* ■ Possible solutions to the problem Ask students ■ What solutions are logically appropriate? ■ What are the positive and negative consequences of each solution? ■ Which is the most valuable solution, and why?
Advanced clarification	9. Judge definitions	Give students ■ Situation statement *and* ■ Argument or discourse Ask students ■ Analyze the way the speaker uses key terms to affect the listener ■ Explain whether and how the definitions of the key terms are used in the argument to convince the listener ■ In the selection, identify any shifts of meaning of the key term ____. What effect does the shift have? Why did the speaker shift meanings?
	10. Identify implicit assumptions	Give students ■ An argument or explanation with some of its bases not included *and* ■ One option that is the correct implicit assumption *and* ■ Two or more options that are not the implicit assumption *and* that are not conclusions Ask students ■ Which option is probably assumed?
Strategies and Tactics	11. Decide on an action	[This is essentially problem solving. Use the strategies for assessing problem solving in Figure 11.6.]

(Continued)

FIGURE 11.7   *(Continued)*

Critical thinking category	Strategy	Description
	12. Interact with others, including being sensitive to the feelings, level of knowledge, and sophistication of others.	Use performance assessment (e.g., a debate) and a scoring scheme, most likely a rubric or rating scale.
	13. Identify rhetorical mechanisms and tactics	Give students ■ Persuasive writing, a speech, an advertisement ■ A video clip of a speech or advertisement Ask students ■ What deceptive or misleading statements or strategies are used? Explain. ■ Which of the following types of deceptive or misleading statements or strategies are used, if any (followed by choices like straw man, circularity, hearsay, glittering generality, etc., as appropriate)?

Source: Outline is from *Evaluating Critical Thinking* (Table 1.2, p. 14), by Stephen P. Norris and Robert H. Ennis, 1989, Pacific Grove, CA: Critical Thinking Co. Reprinted by permission.

7. keep in mind the original or most basic concern;

8. look for alternatives;

9. are open-minded and
   a. seriously consider points of view other than their own;
   b. reason from starting points with which they disagree without letting the disagreement interfere with their reasoning;
   c. withhold judgment when the evidence and reasons are insufficient;

10. take a position and change a position when the evidence and reasons are sufficient to do so;

11. seek as much precision as the subject permits;

12. deal in an orderly manner with the parts of a complex whole;

13. employ their critical thinking abilities;

14. are sensitive to the feelings, level of knowledge, and degree of sophistication of others.

Source: From *Evaluating Critical Thinking* (p. 12), by S. P. Norris and R. H. Ennis, 1989, Pacific Grove, CA: Critical Thinking Books and Software. Reprinted by permission.

Although you can assess students' use of a critical-thinking ability or skill on one occasion, *assessment of students' dispositions requires you to focus on their long-term habits.* Your assessment should report how frequently over a marking period, term, or year students use critical thinking in the curriculum subject matter. Assess dispositions using either a checklist or a rating scale.

Checklists   A **checklist** is a tool that contains a list of behaviors. You observe students over a period of time and make a checkmark (✓) next to the behavior you have observed. You then have a record of which disposition behaviors students have exhibited. The more behaviors you checked, the greater the students' dispositions toward critical thinking. Chapter 13 gives specific suggestions for crafting these types of assessment devices. An example checklist that could be used to assess a student's critical-thinking dispositions is shown in Figure 11.8. It employs a slightly amended list of specific critical-thinking dispositions relevant to the U.S. history unit in which it was used.

This checklist helps you keep track of a student's critical-thinking actions over the course of a unit. You can see from the checklist that the student exhibited a number of dispositions frequently (e.g., "2. Looks for explanations and reasons," "6. Open-minded") and others not very frequently (e.g., "5. Looks for alternatives"). You can use this information to help the student develop his critical thinking, for example by helping him to develop the habit of always looking for alternatives.

Rating Scales   A simple **rating scale** is a device to record your judgments of the quality level of a

FIGURE 11.8 Example of a checklist to assess a student's use of critical-thinking dispositions throughout a teaching unit.

Individual Student's Critical-Thinking Disposition Record

Student's name: Class period: Dates:

Subject/unit: U.S. History/Unit III. Beginning a Government, 1780–1800

Critical-thinking dispositions	Class discussion of the Articles of the Confederation	Essay discussing arguments for and against ratification of the Constitution	Scrapbook collecting and analyzing events reported in the news-paper using concepts from the Constitution	Teams debate the issue, "Have political parties made the United States government better?"	Essay evaluating Washington as president
1. Seeks statements of the main point or question	✓	—	✓	✓	NA
2. Looks for explanations and reasons	✓	✓	✓	✓	✓
3. Uses and cites credible sources	—	✓	—	✓	—
4. Keeps to the main and relevant point(s)	—	—	NA	✓	✓
5. Looks for alternatives	—	—	NA	—	NA
6. Open-minded	✓	✓	✓	NA	—
7. Takes and changes a position on an issue with good reason(s)	✓	✓	NA	✓	—
8. Seeks to be accurate and precise in statements and work	NA	—	✓	✓	—
9. Sensitive to the feelings, levels of knowledge of others	✓	NA	NA		NA

student's dispositions toward each critical-thinking behavior. A rating scale usually has a line with points on it that range from poor quality to excellent quality. Usually, four or five quality points are further defined by describing what the behavior looks like at each point. These descriptions are called *anchors*. Figure 11.9 is an example of some of the dispositions toward critical thinking that a teacher might observe as a student completes an assignment. While this tool is laid out as a rating scale, its anchor descriptions are detailed enough that it really functions as a rubric. (See Chapter 13 for a description of the difference between rating scales and rubrics.)

In this example, each item's scale shows the degree to which a student is disposed toward using a particular critical-thinking habit. The numerical ratings on the scale are anchored by descriptions of specific and observable behaviors.

Over time, you can observe the student with respect to these habits. Then, at the end of the period, you use the rating scale to assess the student's disposition on each habit.

Finally, if students are to learn to be disposed toward using critical thinking in their daily activities, you should teach students critical-thinking skills. Assess both critical-thinking skills and dispositions continuously throughout the term or year.

MyLab Education Self-Check 11.4

MyLab Education Application Exercise 11.4: Assessing Critical-Thinking Skills

READING SKILLS

Reading skills involve thinking, too. Three strategies for assessing reading skills are presented.

FIGURE 11.9   Sample rating scale assessing the quality of some of a student's dispositions toward critical thinking that a teacher might observe as the student completes an assignment.

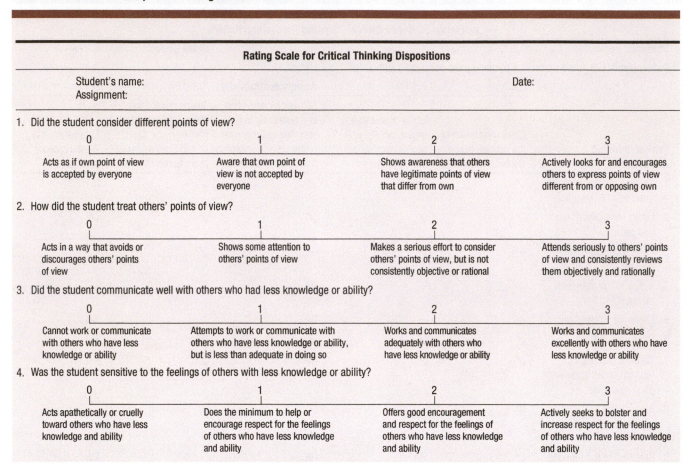

Rating Scale for Critical Thinking Dispositions

Student's name: Date:
Assignment:

1. Did the student consider different points of view?

0	1	2	3
Acts as if own point of view is accepted by everyone	Aware that own point of view is not accepted by everyone	Shows awareness that others have legitimate points of view that differ from own	Actively looks for and encourages others to express points of view different from or opposing own

2. How did the student treat others' points of view?

0	1	2	3
Acts in a way that avoids or discourages others' points of view	Shows some attention to others' points of view	Makes a serious effort to consider others' points of view, but is not consistently objective or rational	Attends seriously to others' points of view and consistently reviews them objectively and rationally

3. Did the student communicate well with others who had less knowledge or ability?

0	1	2	3
Cannot work or communicate with others who have less knowledge or ability	Attempts to work or communicate with others who have less knowledge or ability, but is less than adequate in doing so	Works and communicates adequately with others who have less knowledge or ability	Works and communicates excellently with others who have less knowledge or ability

4. Was the student sensitive to the feelings of others with less knowledge or ability?

0	1	2	3
Acts apathetically or cruelly toward others who have less knowledge and ability	Does the minimum to help or encourage respect for the feelings of others who have less knowledge and ability	Offers good encouragement and respect for the feelings of others who have less knowledge and ability	Actively seeks to bolster and increase respect for the feelings of others who have less knowledge and ability

Traditional Procedure   Having students read material in a subject area and answer questions based on that material is a desirable way to assess reading skills. To develop such assessments, select the reading materials carefully to represent the kind of material students should be able to read. Rewrite the reading material if needed so that the interpretive questions can be answered primarily on the basis of the material alone. Finally, phrase the questions in a way that does not require a student to have more background or special information than you deem appropriate for the level of students and subject matter at hand. Follow these steps:

1. *Locate a promising passage.*   Examine sources (texts, periodicals, reference works, specialized books, as well as collections and anthologies) until you find a passage for which you can write several interpretive items.

2. *Write initial test items.*   Write as many items for the passage as you can. Try to exploit all of the possibilities for interpretation of the passage that fit your original assessment plan.

3. *Rewrite the passage.*   After you have a tentative set of items, rewrite the passage to eliminate unessential material that does not contribute to the items you have written.

4. *Consider rewriting some of the items.*   Changes in the passage may require revising or eliminating some of the items you already wrote. The goal of Steps 3 and 4 is to produce a condensed and efficient passage and item set.

5. *Repeat Steps 3 and 4 as often as necessary,*   until you are satisfied that you have an efficient set of items.

Most commercial survey achievement tests contain reading comprehension subtests. Consult these for examples of using passages to assess reading comprehension.

Authentic Reading Assessment   If you are most interested in reading comprehension, rather than the students' ability to interpret subject-matter materials, the preceding type of condensation may be undesirable, especially if part of what you want to assess is the ability to read naturally occurring materials and the capacity to distinguish between relevant and extraneous material. Critics of standardized reading comprehension tests argue that the passages and questions created by the traditional 5-step procedure are too artificial. The critics would rather use materials that students need to read in the real world or in further schooling. They claim that students exposed to traditional reading comprehension tests come to believe that reading (a) consists of short passages, (b) requires answering questions whose answers are known by the authorities that set them, and (c) has little to do with interpreting the written word (Murphy, 1998).

Passages are considered authentic if they are drawn from the primary sources of a discipline, age-appropriate books and magazines, newspapers, and textbooks students may encounter. In addition, authentic reading tasks may require students to read longer passages than typically appear on traditional reading comprehension tests. They may also require students to read from several sources to compare points of view or obtain reliable and complete information. For example, a student may read four different accounts of an event or of a procedure and then answer questions about the event or procedure, or about comparisons among the different accounts read.

Alternatively, you may want to combine reading, writing, and subject-matter exercises, such as conducting science experiments. For instance, students can individually read several pieces and answer questions about them. Then you can organize students into groups to discuss the pieces they read and to share their insights interpreting them. Next, students can individually write essays or set up experiments to extend or synthesize the material they have read and discussed. The purpose of the intermediate discussion is to offer all students the opportunity to clarify points, obtain information they may have missed through their reading, and "level the playing field" somewhat before the writing phase of the assessment begins.

Longer and more authentic reading tasks use more of your class time for assessment than does the traditional method. An assessment that requires reading several original texts and writing essays after a class discussion may take several class periods to complete. You need to balance your assessment time against your teaching time before deciding which assessment strategy to use. You could try some combination of both. You could use more authentic assessment methods on some occasions and more efficient assessment methods on others. Compare students' performance and the type of information you obtain under the different approaches, which may give you some insight into the validity of the assessment results from each method.

The MAZE Item Type   Reading comprehension can be assessed through a multiple-choice variety of the **cloze reading exercise** known as the **MAZE item type**. The basic idea is to find an appropriate passage and embed a multiple-choice question in the passage that students can answer only if they comprehend the meaning of the surrounding passage. To better understand this procedure, consider the following multiple-choice item, which requires students to select the word that best completes the sentence, "The baby _____."

Example

MAZE multiple-choice item before it is embedded in text

1. The baby _____.
   A. cried
   B. laughed
   C. slept
   D. walked

Notice that all options correctly complete this sentence when it is read outside the context of a reading passage. Now, consider the same item when it is embedded in a brief passage as shown in Item 2 below:

Example

MAZE multiple-choice item after it is embedded in text

2. Mother and her six-month-old baby played for a long time. The baby _____. He enjoyed being tickled under the arms.
   A. cried
   *B. laughed
   C. slept
   D. walked

Option B is correct because of the context in which the item is embedded. Item 2 shows a simple paragraph of a few short sentences; this technique also can, and should, be applied to longer and more complex prose passages.

MAZE items appear to have a considerable advantage over the usual cloze exercises, in which only the blank appears and students must fill in the missing word. They (a) assess whether students can construct meaning from the passages, (b) are objectively scored, (c) do not result in a student filling in blanks with words that leave you wondering whether a student understands the passage, and (d) do not require students to have a great deal of outside knowledge for you to assess their ability to read.

The following suggestions for formulating MAZE test items are based on those used for the *Degrees of Reading Power* (Dreyfus, 2002) test.

1. *Design the items so that a student needs to read and understand the passage to answer correctly.*

As in the preceding example, when an item is considered in isolation, each option should make the sentence grammatically and semantically correct. However, once the item is embedded in the text, only one option should be correct.

2. *The passage should contain all the content information a student needs to answer the item correctly.* For the item to assess reading ability, a student should not have to depend on recall of special experiences to find the correct answer, which usually means the passages must be written specifically for the test.

3. *All of the items' options should be common words.* All students should recognize and understand the meaning of each option. It should be possible to conclude that when a student misses an item, the fault lies with the student's inability to comprehend the reading passage rather than the student's lack of knowledge about the meaning of the words in the item.

CONCLUSION

We have discussed strategies for assessing four aspects of higher-order thinking skills—concept learning, rule-governed or principled thinking, problem solving, and critical thinking—and reading comprehension. These categories overlap. Our separate presentation of each aspect was crafted to explain assessment strategies, not to imply there are separate "kinds" of thinking. However, we believe this tool-kit-style list of assessment strategies will come in quite handy. In the next chapter, we turn to performance assessments. These, too, can be used to assess higher-order thinking. They also assess students' abilities to create and construct products.

EXERCISES

1. Identify a principle or rule in a subject you teach or plan to teach. Then complete these tasks:
   a. State the subject and the grade level.
   b. State the principle and give its name.
   c. Describe in general terms the conditions under which it is appropriate to use the principle to solve a problem or explain a phenomenon.
   d. Using general terms, describe the most likely kinds of faulty inferences made or conclusions drawn by students who misinterpret or misapply the principle.
   e. Prepare one multiple-choice item to assess a student's ability to identify an appropriate conclusion to be made when applying this rule. Use the information in your answer to the previous question as a basis for formulating distractors. Use the checklist for judging the quality of multiple-choice items to improve your item.
   f. Prepare a constructed-response item to assess a student's ability to produce examples of conclusions after applying the principle. This item should assess the same principle that you used for constructing the multiple-choice item just written.
   g. Administer both of these items, one at a time, to a student at the appropriate grade level. Administer the constructed-response item first, then remove it from the student before administering the multiple-choice item.
   h. Compare the results you obtained. What were the similarities and differences in the quality of information you received? Which task is more valid? Why?
   i. Share your results with others in this class. How do your results compare with theirs? Were there differences with respect to subject matter and grade level assessed? What conclusions can the class draw from its collective experience?

2. For the subject you teach or plan to teach, develop a notebook with well-designed tasks that assess different problem-solving abilities. Organize your tasks according to the categories of the IDEAL problem solver. Structure your notebook as follows:
   a. Create one assessment task using each of the 17 assessment strategies for problem-solving assessment presented in Figure 11.6.
   b. Type one assessment task per page. Label the task with the subject, teaching unit, student grade level, assessment strategy, and category of the IDEAL problem solver the task assesses.
   c. On a separate page, craft a scoring rubric for the task and write a sample ideal response.
   d. Self-assess your work. Be sure that the content of each task and the scoring rubric are accurate and that the tasks are well crafted.
   e. Share your notebook with the other participants in this course.

3. Select a subject and grade level you teach or plan to teach, for which critical thinking is an important learning outcome. Then, complete the following tasks:
   a. Identify and briefly describe (in general terms) one or more teaching units in which critical-thinking abilities can be taught and practiced.
   b. On a large sheet of paper, create a table in which each row heading is one of the 13 critical-thinking abilities listed in Figure 11.7.
   c. Label the columns with the teaching and learning activities in the unit(s) that lend themselves to teaching and practicing critical-thinking abilities.
   d. For each cell in the body of the table, briefly describe how a student would demonstrate that he or she was engaging in the corresponding critical-thinking ability. Not every cell will be filled, because not every ability can be demonstrated with every activity you list. However, in the table as a whole, all abilities should be demonstrated at least once. If they are not, then add a unit or an activity to your table.
   e. Present your table to the others in this course. Discuss your activities and demonstrations. Revise your table on the basis of the discussion. Then share it with the other class members.

4. For the same subject and grade level you identified in Exercise 3, develop a notebook containing samples of tasks assessing each of the critical-thinking abilities listed in Figure 11.7. Structure your notebook around the 13 abilities as follows:
   a. Craft one assessment task using each of the critical-thinking assessment strategies described in this chapter.
   b. Type one assessment task per page. Label the task with the subject, teaching unit, student grade level, assessment strategy, and critical-thinking ability the task assesses.
   c. On a separate page, craft a scoring rubric or scoring guide for the task and write a sample ideal response.
   d. Review your work carefully. Be sure the content of each task and scoring rubric is accurate. Be sure the tasks are well crafted.
   e. Share your notebook with the other members of this course.

5. For a subject and grade level you teach or plan to teach, identify a graph and a table (chart) the students should be able to use:
   a. Craft a context-dependent item set for the graph assessing the students' ability to use it beyond simply reading values from it. Craft at least two tasks for the set. Review the items using the appropriate checklists from Chapters 8 and 9. Attach a completed checklist for each item.
   b. Share your context-dependent item sets with the other members of this course.

Essay Assessment Tasks

KEY CONCEPTS

1. Essay test items ask students to compose their responses and are scored with a judgment of the quality of those responses. Restricted-response essay items limit both the content of students' answers and the form of their written responses; extended-response essay items require students to express their own ideas and to organize their answers. Good essay questions ask students to use the higher-order thinking skills specified in their learning outcomes. Follow item-writing guidelines to create high-quality essay questions that assess subject-matter learning.

2. Score essays with rubrics or rating scales. For summative (graded) assessment, require all students to answer the same essay questions. Give feedback related to the intended learning outcomes.

IMPORTANT TERMS

carryover effect

expository writing

extended-response essay items

halo effect

imaginative writing

independent scoring of essays

narrative writing

optional essay questions

persuasive writing

prewriting activities

prompt

rater drift

restricted-response essay items

scoring reliability

Six + 1 Traits® of Writing

SOAP

writing process

writing traits (writing dimensions)

FORMATS FOR ESSAY ITEMS

Essay formats are usually classified into two groups: restricted-response items and extended-response items. Both types are useful tools, but for different purposes.

Restricted-Response Varieties

Restricted-response essay items restrict or limit both the content of students' answers and the form of their written responses, which is done by the way you phrase a restricted-response task. Restricted-response items should require students to apply their skills to solve new problems or to analyze novel situations by including interpretive material with the assessment. Interpretive material could be, for example, a paragraph or two describing a particular problem or social situation, an extract from a literary work, or a description of a scientific experiment or finding. Essay (and response-choice) items based on this kind of material are called interpretive exercises or context-dependent tasks. Interpretive exercises ask students to read, listen to, analyze, or otherwise interpret the accompanying material and then to complete one or more items based on it. The following examples illustrate restricted-response items and, by way of contrast, an extended-response item that requires students to analyze a particular poem in various ways. The items are intended for a high school literature course.

Example

Interpretive Material

On First Looking into Chapman's Homer

Much have I travell'd in the realms of gold,
And many goodly states and kingdoms seen;
Round many western islands have I been
Which bards in fealty to Apollo hold.
Oft of one wide expanse have I been told
That deep-brow'd Homer ruled as his demesne;
Yet did I never breathe its pure serene
Till I heard Chapman speak out loud and bold:
Then felt I like some watcher of the skies
When a new planet swims into his ken;
Or like stout Cortez when with eagle eyes
He star'd at the Pacific—and all his men
Look'd at each other with a wild surmise—
Silent, upon a peak in Darien.
—John Keats

Restricted-response questions

1. What is the poet's attitude toward literature as is apparent in lines 1 to 8? What words in these lines make that attitude apparent?
2. Summarize the mood described in lines 9 to 14.
3. What is the relationship between the attitude described in lines 1 to 8 and the mood established in lines 9 to 14?

Extended-response questions

1. Describe the way in which the structure of the poem reinforces the speaker's mood as it is presented in lines 9 to 14. In your essay, show how the attitude in the first part of the poem is related to the mood at the end of the poem.

Source: From "Evaluation of Learning in Literature," by A. C. Purves, in *Handbook on Formative and Summative Evaluation of Student Learning* (pp. 736, 755–756), by B. S. Bloom, J. T. Hastings, and G. F. Madaus (Eds.), 1971, New York: McGraw-Hill.

Often restricted-response items are limited to only certain aspects or components of very complex learning. The restricted-response items above, written at the "Analyze" cognitive level of the revised Bloom's taxonomy, ask a few of the many (perhaps 15 or 20) questions that a teacher might write to assess students' ability to analyze the mood of a poem. The extended-response item, by contrast, attempts to elicit from the student a rather complete and integrated analysis of the poem.

The advantage of restricted-response essay questions is that this format narrows the focus of assessment to a specific and well-defined performance, making it more likely that your students will interpret each question the way you intended. You are in a better position to assess the quality of student answers when a question is focused, and all students interpret it in the same way. When you are clear about what makes up high-quality answers, your scoring reliability improves and therefore the scores' validity improves as well.

Multiple-choice interpretive exercises assess many abilities more reliably than restricted-response essays. This point is illustrated in Figure 12.1. You can assess a student's ability to recall factual information better through completion, true-false, multiple-choice, and matching items than through essay items.

Extended-Response Varieties

Extended-response essay items require students to write essays in which they are free to express

FIGURE 12.1 Examples of varieties of learning outcomes that can be assessed using objective interpretive exercises and essay items.

Type of test item	Examples of complex learning outcomes that can be measured

Objective interpretive exercises	Ability to—
	    identify cause-effect relationships
	    identify the application of principles
	    identify logical arguments
	    identify the relevance of evidence
	    identify tenable hypotheses
	    identify valid conclusions
	    identify implicit assumptions
	    identify valid conclusions
	    identify the adequacy of procedures
	    (and similar outcomes based on the pupil's ability to *select* the answer)

Restricted-response essay questions	Ability to—
	    explain cause-effect relationships
	    apply principles
	    present and support relevant arguments
	    state tenable hypotheses
	    draw valid conclusions
	    state necessary assumptions
	    describe the limitations of data
	    explain methods and procedures
	    identify and explain obstacles to solving a problem
	    (and similar outcomes based on the pupil's ability to *supply* the answer)

Extended-response essay questions	Ability to—
	    produce, organize, and express ideas
	    integrate learning in different areas
	    make and explain connections among multiple texts
	    create original forms (e.g., designing an experiment)
	    pose, justify, and solve original problems
	    evaluate the worth of ideas or the usefulness of principles

and organize their own ideas and the interrelationships among their ideas. There are multiple ways to write a good answer. A student is free to choose the way to respond, and only a skilled teacher who is informed on the subject can judge the degrees of quality of a student's response. The two broad uses for the extended-response essay format are to assess students' (a) general writing ability and (b) subject-matter knowledge. This chapter discusses both of these essay purposes.

Writing Assessment   If your intention is to assess only writing ability, your essay must present the students with a prompt. A **prompt** is a brief statement that suggests a topic to write about, provides general guidance to the students, motivates the students to write, and elicits the students' best performance. You evaluate your students' performance by using a scoring rubric that defines various characteristics or qualities of writing.

Example

Extended-Response Imaginative Prompt

Pretend you are one of the characters in a fairy tale and have just been granted three wishes. What would your first wish be? Write the wish, and then write a story about what happens to you when the wish is granted.

In this example, the prompt stimulates the student to write in an imaginative way. The student is asked to use expressive writing ability to play an imaginative role and write a fantasy narrative. Later in this chapter, we will discuss criteria for evaluating students' writing.

Subject-Matter Knowledge Assessment   If the primary purpose of your assessment is to evaluate students' knowledge, understanding, and reasoning in a subject, then a different kind of prompt and essay structure is needed. Here is an example in the subject of social studies:

Example

Extended-Response Subject-Matter Essay Prompt

On June 28, 1914, a Serbian nationalist assassinated Archduke Francis Ferdinand, the heir to the Austro-Hungarian throne, in Sarajevo, Bosnia. Describe the political climate that caused this spark to escalate into a war between the Allied Powers and the Central Powers. Your description should explain how these political factors are related to at least two of the more general principles we have studied (e.g., power vacuum) and how those principles operated in what turned out to be the start of World War I.

In this example, the prompt set the task for the students by describing the general purpose of the essay the students are expected to develop. Students' responses are evaluated primarily using subject-matter criteria—how well students understand the political factors, how those factors fit with and exemplify political theory, and so forth. The essay is designed to assess students' competence in reasoning and applying knowledge in the subject of social studies.

Advantages   Some of your learning objectives center around the students' ability to organize ideas, develop a logical argument, discuss evaluations of certain positions or data, communicate thoughts and feelings, or demonstrate original thinking. The restricted-response essay format does not lend itself to assessing these types of learning objectives. Students need opportunities for more extended responses to demonstrate such skills and abilities. The extended-response essay is also suited to assessing learning objectives that require students to use a combination of skills such as interpreting material, solving a problem, and explaining the problem and its solution coherently.

Disadvantages   One disadvantage of an extended-response essay is poor **scoring reliability**. It is difficult to score an extended-response reliably. A common problem is that, without special training, different teachers will award different marks to the same essays. When the grades for the same responses are inconsistent from one teacher to the next, the validity of the assessment results is lowered. Another common problem with teachers' grading of essays is that they evaluate different students' essays using different

criteria. For example, a teacher may attend mainly to the quality of ideas in Johnny's paper, to the neatness and grammatical elegance of Sally's, and to the poor spelling in Harry's. As a result of student-to-student inconsistency, the assessment results are less valid.

A second disadvantage is that scoring essays is often time-consuming, especially if you want to give feedback to students so they can improve their learning. The time is well spent if essays are the best ways to assess important learning objectives, if performing them is a meaningful student activity, and if the students benefit from your feedback on the quality of their responses. Teachers' scoring quality may deteriorate if they must score large numbers of essays. Use essays when they are the most valid form of assessment for a learning objective and are worth the time they take to score well.

A scoring rubric should improve the reliability (consistency), hence the validity, of scoring essays. Using a scoring rubric also reduces scoring time. Chapter 13 gives suggestions for crafting scoring rubrics.

USEFULNESS OF ESSAY ASSESSMENTS

Abilities and Skills Assessed by Essay Items

The preceding paragraphs and Figure 12.1 described some of the abilities and skills that essays let students demonstrate. Notice that multiple-choice items can measure some of these same abilities. What is perhaps unique about the essay format is that it offers students the opportunity to display their abilities to write about, to organize, to express, and to explain interrelationships among ideas. You may assess memory, recall, and comprehension more easily with fill-in-the-blank and response-choice items. Select an assessment format that will assess exactly the learning objective you want students to achieve.

You may find it helpful to study different ways of phrasing questions, which will allow you to craft items that encourage students to use higher-level cognitive processes and skills. Figure 12.2 shows some examples of ways to phrase essay questions so they assess different learning objectives. Writing essay questions in such a manner will allow you to assess higher-order thinking skills. Notice that many of the questions use interpretive materials that are new or novel for the

FIGURE 12.2 How to phrase essay questions to assess content area learning objectives.

1. *Concept understanding:* Identifying examples, producing examples
   - Read the newspaper articles attached. Which events illustrate the concept of *political compromise*?
   - Explain in your own words the meaning of *prejudice*. Give an example of prejudice from your own experience.

2. *Concept understanding:* Classifying examples
   - Read the five mathematics word problems attached. Sort these problems into two groups. Explain why the problems in each group are similar and belong together. Explain how the two groups differ.
   - Study the pictures of the 10 paintings that are attached. Organize these paintings into two or more groups according to their style. Explain the reasons behind your grouping.

3. *Analysis*
   - Look at the family photo attached. Describe the mood or feeling in the photo as well as the body language of the people. Use metaphors or similes to make these descriptions.
   - Read the attached newspaper article. Which statements are opinions? Explain why you think so.

4. *Comparison*
   - Compare Artist A's use of color in her paintings with Artist B's use of color in his mask. How are they similar and different? What moods do the colors convey in each piece?
   - Read the attached statements of Senator A and Senator B. In what ways are their points of view similar? Explain the reasons for your conclusions.

5. *Using principles and rules:* Inference, prediction
   - Read the situation above about the Basarwa, a cultural group we did not study. Based on what we did study about cultural groups, what would you predict would happen to the Basarwa

in the next 20 years? Explain the principles you used to make your predictions.
   - Suppose the government of South Africa ordered all of the white citrus farmers to leave the country. Where would you expect them to go? Explain the principles you used to make these predictions.

6. *Inferences:* Deductions, predictions, generalizations
   - Compare the information in Table A with the information in Figure A. What conclusions do you draw about how successful rice farming will be in the region to which the data apply? Explain the reasons for your conclusions.
   - Read the attached statements from a scientist, senator, and newspaper editor about the consequences of continuing to use gasoline-powered automobile engines. What generalization can you make about the continued use of these engines in developed countries?
   - Study the data in the table above. What would you expect to happen to our exports of wheat over the next 5 years? Explain the assumptions you made for your predictions to be valid.

7. *Evaluation*
   - Above are the criteria we use to judge how well an author has used "voice" in writing. Attached is a short piece of writing by a student in a nearby school. Use the criteria to evaluate the writer's use of voice. Explain why good voice is or is not used by this writer. Use examples from the piece to illustrate your evaluation.
   - Use your daily log and records of your plant's growth to explain the present state of your plant. Explain why your plant is better or worse than your classmates' plants. What could you have done differently? What effect would that have had on your plant's present state?

students. Also notice that most of the questions ask the students to give reasons or explain their choices. Without asking for such explanations or reasons, you will not be assessing the higher-order thinking processes the students use.

Influence on Studying Strategies

You may use assessment to motivate students to study. It seems reasonable that the type of performances you expect from students on tests will influence their methods of study. Some research indicates that when students know that essay questions will be asked, they tend to focus on learning broad concepts and on articulating interrelationships, contrasting, comparing, and so on; those preparing for response-choice questions focus on recalling facts, details, and specific ideas

(Struyven, Dochy, & Janssens, 2005). But despite reporting that they prepare differently for different types of assessments, students do not necessarily *perform* differently on the different forms.

When a state department of education uses essay questions on its accountability tests, that method motivates teachers to require students to write more, and they report that students' writing skills improve (Evaluation Center, 1995). Outside observers report, however, that although students write more, they do not necessarily write better (Viadero, 1995).

Because both essay and response-choice formats can call for knowledge of specific facts, and both can call for application of complex reasoning skills, the questions' format may not be the key issue in how students plan their study strategies. The kinds of study strategies your students use in preparing for your assessments are more likely to reflect the type of thinking skills your assessment tasks require rather than the format (essay or not essay) of the tasks. If two different assessment formats require students to use the same kind of thinking skills, the formats ought to require the same types of study strategies. If your "essays" are really a regurgitation of facts, students' study strategies will focus on remembering and recalling facts, and you will not realize the advantages of essays and other open-ended response formats in your classroom.

The Common Core State Standards expect students to learn to write about ideas in History/Social Studies, Science, and technical subjects as well as English/Language Arts. Give students opportunities to learn how to write about the subject you teach. Assign students a significant number of writing tasks, so they can learn to write in your subject area and do not limit writing tasks to examinations. Use writing tasks in practice assignments, give feedback, and give students opportunities to use the feedback. Then, in the examination, give no or limited feedback. Focus your feedback efforts on formative learning opportunities, not on summative assessments when it is too late for students to use the feedback productively.

Various written assignments such as short compositions and longer term papers can help your students achieve these writing-oriented goals, which often means relying less on the questions and homework assignments that are in the back of the students' textbook chapters and more on your own assignments. Keep in mind that assessment results are more valid if you use multiple assessment formats. Your summative assessments should include both essay and response-choice items, so they cover a proper range of learning objectives.

Depth and Breadth of Content Sampling

Answering essay questions takes a long time and limits the breadth of content about which the student can write. If your students can answer one or two response-choice items in 1 minute, then they can answer 30 to 60 response-choice items in a half hour. Sixty items can cover a very broad area of content and at least parts of many instructional objectives. In the same 30 minutes, these same students can probably answer only one or two essay questions. Thus, you can assess in-depth learning of a narrower topic using one essay or broad, less in-depth, general coverage using many objective items. To improve the content coverage of their assessment, many teachers use both essay and objective test items.

To overcome the shortcoming of an essay's limited content sampling, use a series of compositions that students can write over a longer period. You can accumulate these in portfolios. Several out-of-class essays written over a marking period may better assess a particular learning objective than a single essay written during a brief examination period. In addition, asking students to write under the time pressure of an examination may not be the best method to assess their maximum ability.

Influence of Scoring Criteria and Exemplars

Use well-defined criteria to evaluate students' essay responses. Students should be taught the criteria as part of their regular instruction. Because local school districts and state educational authorities have recognized the importance of developing these criteria, teachers may be engaged in professional development activities to help define these criteria and to improve their application to students' responses. Much of this effort is focused on defining criteria or rubrics that are used with performance assessment, of which essay assessment can be considered a part.

Collaboration with other teachers helps teachers craft criteria and select examples of work at different quality levels that clarify the meaning of statements of state standards and of learning objectives in the curriculum. In addition, much work is going on currently to develop criteria for use with the Common Core State Standards. Use the principles you learn in this book to evaluate the quality of any commercially prepared criteria before you use them. Sharing quality criteria and exemplars with students will better integrate your assessment and instruction. Students learn what the characteristics of quality performance are and, through examples, learn what quality performance looks like.

CONSTRUCTING ESSAYS ASSESSING SUBJECT-MATTER LEARNING

The checklist that follows summarizes suggestions for improving essay items. As with previous checklists, an answer of no to any one of the checklist questions is sufficient reason not to use that essay item until you correct the flaw. The suggestions are discussed later in the chapter. First, we will look at a poorly written essay item and apply the checklist to it, which will give you an idea of how the item should be improved.

Checklist

A Checklist for Evaluating the Quality of Essays Assessing Subject-Matter Learning

Ask these questions of every item you write. If you answer no to one or more questions, revise the item accordingly.

1. Does the essay assess an important aspect of the unit's instructional objectives?

2. Does the essay match your assessment plan in terms of performance, emphasis, and number of points?

3. Does the essay require students to apply their knowledge to a new or novel situation?

4. When viewed in relation to other items on the test, does this item contribute to covering the range of content and thinking skills specified in your assessment plan?

5. Is the prompt focused? Does it define a task with specific directions, rather than leave the assignment so broad that virtually any response can satisfy the question?

6. Is the task defined by the prompt within the level of complexity that is appropriate for the educational maturity of the students?

7. Is the student required to demonstrate more than recall of facts, definitions, lists, ideas, generalizations, etc.?

8. Is the prompt worded in a way that leads all students to interpret the assignment in the way you intended?

9. Does the wording of the prompt make clear to students all of the following:
   a. Magnitude or length of the required writing?
   b. Purpose for which they are writing?
   c. Amount of time to be devoted to answering this item?
   d. Basis on which their answers will be evaluated?

10. If the essay prompt asks students to state and support their opinions on controversial matters, does the wording make it clear that the students' assessment will be based on the logic and evidence supporting their arguments, rather than on the actual position taken or opinion stated?

Case Study of a Poorly Written Essay Item

Before we discuss the suggestions in the checklist in detail, let's study a poorly worded essay question and use the checklist to evaluate it. This exercise should help you understand how to evaluate your own essay questions and will make the checklist explanations more meaningful to you.

The Poor Item Suppose a teacher wanted to assess the following tenth-grade U.S. history learning objective:

Example

Tenth-Grade Learning Objective to Be Assessed

Analyze reasons for success of the Colonials during the American War of Independence and explain what alternative actions the British or the Colonials could have taken to alter the outcomes.

The teacher wrote the following essay question to assess this learning objective. Overall, the teacher's essay item does not assess the objective very well.

Example

A Poorly Crafted Essay Item

Analyze the defeat of the British by the Colonials by listing the four factors discussed in class that led to the defeat.

Evaluation Using the Checklist Here is a point-by-point analysis using the checklist. The numbers refer to the point in the checklist:

Example

1. Yes, the factors contributing to the success of the Colonials are important to the learning outcome of this unit.

2. No, the learning objective calls for students to analyze reasons for success and explain alternative possibilities. The item requires neither analysis nor explanation.

3. No, the item requires only listing (recalling) information presented during the class.

4. Yes, this item, in relation to other items (not shown), contributes to the breadth of coverage the teacher had in mind for the unit.

5. Yes, what the student is to do (i.e., list) is clearly stated.

6. No, the learning objective implies that the students should be capable of more than the item requires. (The task set by the item, "listing from memory," is within the capability of the students, but it is below the appropriate level of complexity as specified by the objective.)

7. No, the item requires only recalling verbal information.

8. Questionable; some students may be confused by the word *analyze* but most will probably make a *list*.

9. a. Yes, the item says students should list four reasons.

   b. Perhaps the purpose is simply to repeat what was taught in class, but the purpose isn't stated.

   c. No, a time limit is not stated.

   d. No, but simply being right or wrong seems to be the implied basis for evaluation.

10. Not applicable; no opinion asked.

The Revised Item   After using the checklist, the teacher rethought the item in relation to the learning objective and what he had taught. The teacher revised the item to make it more in line with the objective. Here is the revised item:

Example

An Improved Essay Task

A. List four of the factors that led to the Colonial victory over the British in the War of Independence. (4 points)

B. For every factor you list, write a short explanation of how that factor helped the Colonists defeat the British. (4 points)

C. Choose one of these factors that in your opinion the British could have changed or overcome. Explain what actions the British could have taken to change or overcome this factor. (4 points)

D. What probably would have happened in the war if the British had taken the actions you stated? Why do you think this would have happened? (8 points)

Grading: Parts A and B will be marked on how correct your answers are. Parts C and D will be marked on how well you support your opinion, but not on what position you take.

Time limit: 40 minutes.

The revised item is more complex and more difficult than the original, but it comes closer to assessing the learning objective. Notice that the revised item is expanded to include recalling information, explaining the recalled information, and using higher-level skills. These higher-level skills require students to explain why they hold logically deduced opinions and to describe probable consequences of actions. The teacher's basis for grading is specified, as is a time limit. Because the class period at this school is 50 minutes long, this essay will probably be the only assessment that the teacher could do that day. To cover other aspects of the unit, the teacher would need additional assessments, including quizzes, homework, class discussions, and an objective test over the unit's content.

Discussion of the Checklist

1 and 2. *Importance of what is assessed and correspondence to the assessment plan.* We have stressed that each of your assessment tasks, no matter what their format, must focus on important learning objectives and must match your assessment plan. Learning objectives that require essays may be difficult for you to state because the intended learning outcome may be complex and abstract. Further, when assessing these complex learning objectives, you may need to use more than one type of assessment tasks. For example, you may want a student to demonstrate the ability to analyze critically and evaluate passages expressing different points of view about the equality of men and women. This complex learning objective will require assessing the student using several different tasks before you conclude the student has attained it.

Focus on the type of response you wish the student to make. You could, for example, write a specimen answer—an outline of the major points you want the students to make. Or you could state the way(s) you expect the student to approach the problem in an essay question. Then refine the essay question to clarify what you wish the student to do.

3. *Essential knowledge applied to new situations.* The essay question format has the potential of assessing a student's command of higher cognitive processes and skills. The best way to do this is to require a student to apply thinking skills to new or novel problems and situations. If a student is asked to write only information recalled from the textbook or class discussion, you are assessing only lower cognitive processes. You can

better assess recall of information by using fill-in-the-blank and response-choice formats.

4. *Covering the range of content and thinking skills.* As you read in Chapter 6, your assessment plan should cover your learning objectives' full range of content and thinking skills. Your plan plays a key role in guiding your assessment activities. That plan should include using essay questions for complex thinking, and it should balance the available assessment time against the range of coverage you have planned.

5. *Focus questions; clarify limits and purposes.* Phrase each question to focus attention on the issues or points on which you want the students to write. Students will assume the question, as phrased, is exactly what you want them to answer. If they interpret your question in many different ways, it will be impossible to evaluate their responses. Consider the extended-response example about analyzing a Keats poem. An unfocused version of this item might read: "Write an essay analyzing the poem." It is unlikely that such an unfocused item would result in an analysis of the poem's "mood," which is what the teacher had in mind. If an item is not focused, you will find it impossible to distinguish those students who can perform the learning outcome—but misinterpreted your question—from those who simply cannot apply the skills you taught.

Sometimes, if you find it difficult to state the nature of the task itself clearly, specifying the manner and criteria by which you will evaluate students' responses may increase clarity. For example, sometimes a teacher will give students an extract from a newspaper expressing a point of view and want students to evaluate the extracted statement by applying the strategies and criteria taught in class. However, a poorly stated question may simply say, "Do you agree or disagree with this article's position?" There's no telling what kind of responses students would make: Their responses would likely range from a simple yes or no to long-winded polemical entanglements. Focus the item more by specifying which aspects of the extract the students should address and support.

Focusing the question and specifying limits of the intended response do not mean providing information that gives away the answer. If you want the essay to assess the ability to organize a written argument or identify the central issue in a "fuzzy problem," for example, you should not

provide students with a particular organization in the question. However, you should tell students that the way they choose to organize the answer is important and that you will evaluate the essay on how well it is organized.

An important practical suggestion here is to have a colleague or friend review the questions and, if possible, to try the item with a few students. You can then revise the questions if necessary. Following such steps greatly improves the quality of essay questions.

6. *Complexity should be appropriate to educational level.* Because answering an essay requires students to read, think, and write, you must be sure that the item is appropriate to your students' level of educational development. Avoid the use of complicated sentence structures and phrasings for elementary students. Avoid phrases that are indirect or that add unnecessary reading to the question. Do not, however, oversimplify essays for more advanced students. Essays should challenge students to do their best thinking and use their best writing skills. Because essays require writing, your students must have the level of writing proficiency needed to answer the question. If students do not have sufficient writing skill to express their knowledge on your essay question, you should consider using another means of assessment.

7. *Require more than recall of verbal information.* Use fill-in-the-blank, true-false, matching, and multiple-choice formats to assess simple recall of verbal information. These formats are better for assessing such recall because they sample more of a student's verbal information store in a fixed time than essays do. Using fill-in and response-choice items increases the content coverage and the validity of the results for assessing recall. Use essays to assess higher-order thinking, including the ability to express one's own ideas, to compare, and explain reasons.

8. *Make the intention of the essay clear.* Make sure your essay question communicates clearly to the students the framework in which they are to respond: the issues their essays are to address, the amount of justification or evidence they are expected to bring to bear in their responses, and the level of detail you expect in their responses.

9. *Clarify response length, purpose, time limits, and evaluation criteria.* You should tell students (a) the approximate length you expect their response to be, (b) the purpose for which they are writing, (c) the

goal toward which their essay should aim, and (d) the audience for whom they should target their responses. If you impose time limits, you should clearly announce these to your students. If more than one answer can be correct, your students should know this. If you will evaluate spelling, grammar, and usage, tell students before they respond.

10. *Clarify how students' opinions will be evaluated.* Often an essay will require students to state and support their opinions on controversial or nonroutine matters. These essays provide excellent opportunities to assess students' abilities to analyze, evaluate, and create. In such items, you should make clear that students' answers will be evaluated on the logic shown in their answers and how well they use evidence to support their positions. You should reassure them that the opinions or positions they state will not be marked right or wrong per se.

OPTIONAL QUESTIONS

When the purpose for assessment is summative evaluation, you should require all students to answer the same questions (Hogan & Murphy, 2007). Some teachers believe that offering students **optional essay questions** (a choice of questions) is fairer because it permits students to "put their best foot forward." Research doesn't bear out this belief, however. Some students will choose to answer questions on which they do less well (Wainer & Thissen, 1994). Further, the topics on which questions are based vary in familiarity and difficulty for the students. We have already mentioned how difficult it is to generalize from one essay to the next. In addition, teachers marking essays frequently change their ratings based on their own perceptions of the nature and difficulty of topics. It is extremely difficult, often impossible, to compare tests equitably when students have taken different items (Wang, Wainer, & Thissen, 1995). If all the questions asked on an assessment represent important learning outcomes, then it seems logical and fair to hold all students accountable for answering all of them.

Perhaps the story would be different if general writing ability were being assessed, rather than subject-matter competence. You could argue that students may demonstrate general writing ability by writing on any one of a number of topics. If you follow this practice, you should score essays on each topic separately, rather than mixing topics together.

Focusing on one topic at a time will reduce the topic-to-topic differences that tend to raise or lower your rating of an essay quite apart from its merits. As we pointed out earlier in this chapter, however, the topic and the prompt of the essay questions are important determinants of how well a student performs. A student can write well about some topics and poorly about others. You might, for example, write a better essay on the frustrations of a teacher than on the frustrations of a professional golfer, simply because you know more about one area than the other. Similarly, the topics students choose or are assigned do affect their ability to answer appropriately. Even if you are assessing general writing ability, interpret cautiously students' responses to different topics and prompts. The most important thing for you to do is to use multiple topics and assess students over a period of time, rather than base your evaluation on a single essay.

> MyLab Education **Self-Check 12.1**
>
> MyLab Education **Application Exercise 12.1:** Analyzing Essay Questions

CONSTRUCTING PROMPTS FOR ASSESSING WRITING ACHIEVEMENT

Assessing students' writing achievement requires special attention to both writing prompts and scoring rubrics. We discuss writing prompts in this section and scoring rubrics for writing assessment in the next section.

Some school district or state assessment programs have adopted very specific writing instruction and assessment frameworks. We cannot discuss all of these in this book. Follow your school's or state's mandated program. You can adapt the guidelines in this book to your local situation.

General Suggestions for Integrating Writing Assessment and Instruction

Focus on the Characteristics of Good Writing For classroom purposes, teaching and evaluating students' writing should concentrate on characteristics or qualities of good writing, especially those that students can be taught to improve. Sometimes these writing qualities are called **writing traits** or **writing dimensions**. Teaching and assessing writing need to be highly integrated because to improve students need to know in some detail (a) what dimensions of their writing need improving and (b) how to make these improvements. Information from assessment should allow you to give students specific feedback that guides their writing improvement.

Educators differ as to what constitutes good student writing. State standards and school district guidelines will differ in the number and type of traits that define good writing. Many schools and states have adopted or adapted some or all of the **Six + 1 Traits**® **of Writing** developed by Education Northwest (educationnorthwest.org). These are as follows:

Example

1. Ideas
2. Organization
3. Voice
4. Word choice
5. Sentence fluency
6. Conventions
7. [Presentation—used when producing a final, published version is important]

Organize your assessment *and* teaching around the writing traits you adopt to help students understand what constitutes good writing. Using the traits as a framework for feedback avoids giving feedback that is too general to be helpful (for example, "You need to improve your writing").

Teach Students What Good Writing Is Students need to learn that good writing has certain qualities and that these traits or qualities are the criteria by which most writing can be evaluated. Students learn that your feedback on how well they have put these traits to work in their writing helps them improve. When the trait framework is made clear to students, you and they will have a shared vision of what good writing is. If this vision is shared across teachers and grades, then students will come to internalize the traits and use them to improve their daily writing. For instruction, focus on one trait at a time, and use formative assessment with plenty of feedback.

Part of writing instruction is to teach students that there is an orderly process for developing a piece of writing. All too often, students have the mistaken idea that they should write a final piece at one sitting. The **writing process** presented in Figure 12.3 is adapted from suggestions

FIGURE 12.3 How the writing traits may be integrated into a writing process.

1. *Prewriting activities*—Before writing, a writer clarifies the purpose for writing, begins to organize thoughts, brainstorms, and tries out new ideas. The writer discusses the ideas with others, decides the format and approach to writing, and determines the primary audience. A plan for the piece develops. The teacher may wish to schedule a content conference (Darden, 2000) to help students focus the ideas and content for the piece.

2. *Draft the piece*—The writer works up a preliminary draft of the piece to reflect the prewriting ideas. Ideas and plans change as the draft develops. The purpose for the writing is further clarified (even changed). The draft begins to take shape as ideas and content start to come together. The preliminary organization of the piece emerges so that a beginning, middle, and end appear. The draft is considered a work in progress, not the final piece.

3. *Obtain feedback for improving the draft*—Based on assessment, the writer gets feedback from the teacher, peers, or others. The assessment is used to make the feedback specific to the traits that have been adopted to define good writing (e.g., ideas, organization, choice of words, use of sentence variety). The teacher may wish to schedule a drafting conference (Darden, 2000) with the student to give some of the feedback.

4. *Revise the piece*—The writer uses specific feedback from the assessment to improve the piece in each of the trait areas. For example, as a result of specific feedback, the writer may incorporate more colorful or more exciting words into a story.

5. *Repeat Steps 3 and 4 if necessary*—The writer may not have implemented the suggestions from the feedback properly, or the writer may not understand the feedback and may need more instruction. Writing is not strictly a linear process; it may require many iterations. Student writers must learn that completing the assignment and turning it in is not a final step. The teacher may wish to schedule a process conference (Darden, 2000) with the student to discuss the choices the student made and suggest how to proceed with the revision.

6. *Edit*—The writer edits the revised piece by checking for correct English mechanics: specific points of spelling, grammar, punctuation, etc. English mechanics is one of the traits of good writing. The teacher may evaluate the written piece for how well the student has implemented mechanics. Note that English mechanics are assessed late in the writing process because the pedagogy is to have the student concentrate first on ideas, organization, word choice, etc., as the piece is being developed.

7. *Finalize and make the piece presentable*—The writer puts the piece into final form for presentation to the teacher with attention to handwriting or word processing, margins, and the like. Attention to appearance is left to the very end, after the piece is revised and polished.

Source: Based on the authors' interpretations of the ideas and suggestions developed at Education Northwest. Endorsement by Education Northwest should not be inferred.

developed by Education Northwest. The writing process begins with **prewriting activities** and continues with drafting, assessment, and feedback, until a final piece is produced.

Define Standards or Levels of Achievement for Each Writing Trait
For assessment-based feedback to be meaningful, you must use standards that clearly identify the student's achievement level on each trait. You can think of achievement as developing along a continuum from very poor achievement at one end to very high-level attainment at the other. The points along this continuum need to be defined, so you can pinpoint the students' current level of achievement. Once a student's current level is known, the continuum's definitions of more advanced levels help you guide the student to achieving that next level.

If your state or school has also adopted a particular framework for writing traits, it probably has also adopted the definitions of different levels of achievement for each of these traits. You will need to use these, rather than craft your own, because students will be expected to write according to them. These descriptions are usually in the form of scoring rubrics or scoring guides. Figure 12.4 illustrates Nebraska's analytic writing rubric for Grade 8. Nebraska also has writing rubrics for Grades 4 and 11.

Rubrics and trait definitions should apply across different types of writing. Students will be working with different genres or types of writing, as well as writing for different audiences. Because students are novice writers, it is likely to be confusing if each genre and purpose has very different criteria or traits. Pedagogically, it is better if the same few traits are applied to many different types of writing. If you and the students evaluate all writing using these same traits (ideas and content, organization, word choice, and so on), students will learn them more quickly and internalize the traits' meanings. As a result, students will more easily apply the traits to all their writing.

Crafting Writing Prompts
Students should learn to write for different purposes, for different audiences, and in different genres. To stimulate students to do these three things, you need to build into your writing prompts rhetorical clues that elicit the kind of writing that you have in mind. The prompts you write should include statements containing the following elements (Albertson, 1998):

1. *Subject*—inform the students whom or what the piece is supposed to be about.
2. *Occasion*—inform the students about the occasion or situation that requires the piece to be written.
3. *Audience*—inform the students of the intended audience for the piece.
4. *Purpose*—inform the students what the writing purpose is supposed to be: Is it to inform or narrate? to be imaginative? to be persuasive? (Sometimes the acronym **SOAP** is used for the four preceding elements.)
5. *Writer's role*—inform the students what role they are to play while writing (e.g., a friend, a student, a parent, etc.).
6. *Form*—inform the students if you expect the piece to take a certain form such as a poem, letter, paragraph, essay, and so on.

The following example shows how to improve a writing prompt by adding these rhetorical clues:

Example

Poor: No SOAP—Writing prompt does not provide suggestions for the subject, occasion, audience, or purpose of the piece.
Write a letter telling about an event.
Better: SOAP is built into the prompt.
Recall something important that you saw or that happened to you recently. It could be that you saw an accident, a crime, a good deed someone did. Maybe something funny happened to you recently.

Write a letter to a friend to describe what you saw or what happened to you, just the way it happened. Describe the event clearly, so your friend who was not there can tell exactly what it was like and how you felt about it.

Writing Prompts for Different Genres
Students should learn to write for different audiences and different purposes. The writing prompts you provide guide them in writing the specific type of piece you have in mind. Typically, classroom writing takes one of four forms: narrative, imaginative, expository, and persuasive.

Narrative writing describes something that really happened, usually a personal experience of

FIGURE 12.4   Nebraska Department of Education Scoring Guide for Descriptive Writing—Analytic—Grade 8.

	1	2	3	4
IDEAS/ CONTENT 35%	The picture of what is being described is unclear. Content has many digressions from the topic. Sensory details are lacking.	The picture of what is being described is limited. Content has some digressions from the topic. Sensory details are limited or unrelated.	The picture of what is being described is clear. Content is generally focused on the topic. Sensory details are adequate and related.	The picture of what is being described is clear and vivid. Content is well-focused on the topic. Sensory details are numerous and relevant.
ORGANIZATION 25%	Structural development of an introduction, body, and conclusion is lacking. Pacing is awkward. Transitions are missing or connections are unclear. Paragraphing is ineffective or missing.	Structural development of an introduction, body, and conclusion is limited. Pacing is somewhat inconsistent. Transitions are repetitious or weak. Paragraphing is irregular.	Structural development of an introduction, body, and conclusion is functional. Pacing is generally controlled. Transitions are functional. Paragraphing is generally successful.	Structural development of an introduction, body, and conclusion is effective. Pacing is well controlled. Transitions effectively show how ideas connect. Paragraphing is sound.
VOICE/WORD CHOICE 20%	Wording is inexpressive and lifeless, conveying little sense of the writer. Voice inappropriate for the purpose and audience. Language is neither specific, precise, nor varied. Few, if any, vivid words or phrases are used.	Wording is occasionally expressive, conveying a limited sense of the writer. Voice is sometimes inappropriate for the purpose and audience. Language is occasionally specific, precise, and varied. Some vivid words and phrases are used.	Wording is generally expressive, conveying a sense of the writer. Voice is generally appropriate for the purpose and audience. Language is generally specific, precise, and varied. Adequate vivid words and phrases are used.	Wording is expressive and engaging, conveying a strong sense of the writer throughout. Voice is well suited for the purpose and audience throughout. Language is specific, precise, and varied throughout. Numerous vivid words and phrases used effectively.
SENTENCE FLUENCY/ CONVENTIONS 20%	Sentences seldom vary in length or structure. Phrasing sounds awkward and unnatural. Fragments or run-ons confuse the reader. Grammar, usage, punctuation, and spelling errors throughout distract the reader.	Sentences occasionally vary in length or structure. Phrasing occasionally sounds unnatural. Fragments or run-ons sometimes confuse the reader. Grammar, usage, punctuation, and spelling errors may distract the reader.	Sentences generally vary in length or structure. Phrasing generally sounds natural. Fragments and run-ons, if present, do not confuse the reader. Grammar, usage, punctuation, and spelling are usually correct and errors do not distract the reader.	Sentences vary in length and structure throughout. Phrasing consistently sounds natural and conveys meaning. Fragments and run-ons, if present, are intended for stylistic effect. Grammar, usage, punctuation, and spelling are consistently correct and may be manipulated for stylistic effect.

Source: Nebraska State Department of Education, Statewide Assessment. Used by permission.

a student. Following is an example of a prompt that elicits narrative writing from students:

Example

Narrative Prompt

Think of one HAPPY thing that happened to you in the past. Maybe it was something that happened at home or at school or someplace else.

Write an essay that tells what happened. Be sure to give specific details that explain why this was a happy thing, so your classmates understand your feelings.

Imaginative writing describes something that did not, often could not, happen. Students use imagination and creativity to tell a story. Here is an example:

Example

Imaginative Prompt

Suppose that one day you woke up and found that you were a FISH. What would your life be like? What would happen to you?

Write a story that we can put into our class magazine that tells what happens to you when you are a fish. Be sure to give specific details about what your life as a fish is like.

Expository writing gives an explanation and information. Students are asked to give details, clarify things, and explain things. Here is an example:

Example

Expository Prompt

Animals change a lot when they grow. Think about ONE ANIMAL that you know a lot about.

Write an essay that explains how this animal changes as it grows. Be sure to explain very carefully and clearly so that your classmates reading your explanation can understand.

Students often use expository writing when answering subject-matter essay questions.

Persuasive writing convinces the reader of the writer's point of view. The writer may want the reader to accept his or her idea or to take some actions that the writer supports. Here is an example:

Example

Persuasive Prompt

Suppose students in this school had 30 minutes of free time each week. The school principal wants your suggestions about ONE THING students should do with this free time. What is the one thing you would suggest?

Write an essay to the school principal that would CONVINCE the principal that he should use your idea. Explain why your idea about using the free time is the best possible and should be followed. Give reasons to support your position.

Additional Suggestions for Writing Prompts

There are some special considerations when preparing classroom assessments that evaluate

students' ability to write. Albertson (1998) offers the following suggestions:

Do not prepare prompts that

- demand specialized knowledge on the part of students.
- ask students to write narratives about experiences that they may not have because of cultural or social background.
- ask for students' opinions about personal values, religious beliefs, or sensitive or controversial matters that parents would object to.
- encourage complaints and criticisms about the school, students' parents, or persons in the community.

Do prepare prompts that

- refer to specific situations rather than abstract situations.
- will be interesting to students.
- will be interesting to you when you evaluate students' writing.
- are in the realm of the students' experiences.

SCORING ESSAY ASSESSMENTS

Essay test questions should be scored with scoring scales that fit the point values planned in the test blueprint (see Chapter 6). Rubrics or rating scales should be used for this purpose. Chapter 13 gives specific details about how to write and apply scoring rubrics. Briefly, rubrics can be categorized in two ways: according to how many scales are used (*analytic* rubrics use several scales; *holistic* rubrics use one) and according to whether the rubrics are *task-specific* or *general* rubrics.

You may want to go to Chapter 13 now and read the section on rubrics. As an example to have in mind as you read the practical suggestions for scoring essays (below), Figure 12.5 shows two sets of task-specific scoring rubrics for the Keats poem on page 241.

Rubrics have many positive features. Probably the most important is that the descriptions of the qualities of work in general rubrics define what "good work" is and help students conceptualize the kind of performance they are aiming for. The writing trait rubrics shown earlier provide an excellent example. Thus, rubrics are a powerful instructional tool as well as an assessment tool.

FIGURE 12.5 Example of task-specific scoring rubrics.

The second essay question about our Keats poem read, "Summarize the mood described in lines 9 to 14." First, you must know what a good answer would say. That means you have to understand the poem very well yourself. Chapman did the first good English translations of Homer's *Iliad* and *Odyssey* (which, of course, were written in Greek). At that time (early 1600s), therefore, a whole body of classic literature became available to English-speaking people. This poem is about a reader who reads these works for the first time. He likens literature to a wonderful land ("realms of gold"; lines 1 to 8) and explains that coming across these works of Homer was like discovering a new land. He uses two images: the image of an astronomer discovering a new planet (lines 9 and 10) and the image of the explorer Cortez discovering the Pacific Ocean (lines 11–14).

Suppose you decided, then, that good student essays would identify these images and conclude that the mood was one of discovery, with its attendant feelings of surprise and delight. You also wanted good essays to be well organized for readers and written according to standard English grammar and usage conventions. These three dimensions (content, organization, and grammar/usage) are your criteria. You might use the following set of rubrics. Note that the content rubric ("description of mood") is task-specific. You could not share this rubric with the students before they wrote their essays because that would analyze the poem for them. Also note that the weights for the content rubric are doubled, making the ideas worth half (6 points) and the writing worth half (6 points).

EXAMPLE OF ANALYTIC SCORING RUBRICS FOR ESSAY QUESTION #2 (PAGE 219)

3 criteria, 12 points possible

Description of Mood (Discovery)

6 Identifies both astronomer and explorer images as discovery images and gives clear explanation

4 Identifies mood but explanation absent or unclear

2 Mood not identified or incorrectly identified

Organization

3 Thesis is clearly stated in topic sentence; how details support thesis is explicitly stated

2 Topic sentence includes thesis; supporting details are present

1 No topic/thesis sentence and/or no supporting details

Grammar/Usage

3 No errors or minor ones that do not impede reading

2 Some errors in grammar or usage, but meaning is clear

1 So many errors that meaning is unclear

Use analytic scoring (above) if feedback on different aspects of performance is required (for example, so a student knows what to work on to improve). Use holistic scoring (below) if one overall judgment is required (for example, on a final exam whose results a student might not see). Notice, however, that the holistic rubrics use the same criteria: content, organization, and grammar/usage. Assign the grade or score whose description most closely matches the student's essay.

EXAMPLE OF HOLISTIC SCORING RUBRICS FOR ESSAY QUESTION #2 (PAGE 241)

A Mood of discovery is clearly identified; support for this is derived from images of astronomer and explorer; writing is clear and well organized.

B Mood of discovery is identified; support is implied but not made explicit in discussion of images of astronomer and explorer; writing is clear and organized.

C Mood of discovery is identified; one of the images is described; organization is minimal; writing needs editing.

D Mood is not clearly identified or is incorrectly identified; writing is neither clear nor well organized.

F Essay is not about mood and/or so many errors in grammar and usage make meaning impossible to interpret.

Notice that your standards of achievement are embodied in these scoring levels. It would be possible to have "harder" or "easier" rubrics, for example, where the D in this scale might be an F in another.

Suggestions for Scoring Essay Test Questions

Principles for scoring essays are summarized in Figure 12.6. We discuss them below.

Use a Scoring Guide
Scoring rubrics and model answers were illustrated in the previous example. The point of using these tools is to improve the consistency of your scoring so that you apply the same standards from paper to paper. If your state has adopted general writing rubrics, use them.

Score One Question at a Time
If there is more than one essay question, score all students on the first question before moving on. Then score all answers to the next question. This method improves the uniformity with which you apply scoring standards to each student. It also makes you more familiar with the scoring guide for a given question, and you are less likely to be distracted by responses to other questions. Finally, using this method helps reduce carryover error discussed below. You can reduce carryover errors further by reshuffling the papers after scoring each question.

Score Subject-Matter Correctness Separately from Other Factors
When marking subject-matter essays, factors other than an answer's

FIGURE 12.6 Summary of principles for scoring responses to subject-matter essay items.

1. Prepare some type of scoring guide (e.g., an outline, a rubric, an "ideal" answer, or "specimen" responses from past administrations).
2. Grade all responses to one question before moving on to the next question.
3. Periodically rescore previously scored papers.
4. Score penmanship, general neatness, spelling, use of prescribed format, and English mechanics separately from subject-matter correctness.
5. Score papers without knowing the name of the pupil writing the response.
6. Provide pupils with feedback on the strengths and weaknesses of their responses.
7. When the grading decision is crucial, have two or more readers score the essays independently.

content often affect your evaluation. Among such factors are spelling, handwriting, neatness, and language usage. To avoid blending your judgment of the quality of the ideas or substantive content of a student's answer with these other factors, score the other factors separately—perhaps by using a rating scale (see Chapter 13).

Scoring separately for quality of ideas, correctness of content, and other factors also gives you the freedom to weight each factor appropriately in calculating the grade. For example, you can weight spelling zero or more heavily, depending on the state policy, school policy, or your classroom practice. You still report the results on the zero-weighted factor (e.g., spelling) to the student; you just don't make it part of the grade. But if a factor is to receive a weight of zero, why bother marking and reporting it separately? Two reasons: to allow more complete feedback to students and to allow you to separate your judgment from the substance of the essays, letting you better assess the content learning target.

Score Essays Anonymously

Scoring is more valid when you do not know the name of the student who wrote the response. Anonymous scoring of essays prevents the halo error described below. Further, if students know that you score papers anonymously, they are likely to perceive the grading process as fair. One suggestion for maintaining anonymity is to have students write their names on the back of the answer sheet or exam booklet. Other, more elaborate methods, such as using student numbers or other codes, are also effective.

Give Students Feedback

An important reason for using essays is the opportunity they give you to assess students' expressive abilities and thought

processes. For essay questions on graded tests, briefly note strengths and weaknesses in these areas for each student and explain how you arrived at the score you assigned. For essay questions in student practice work (class assignments or homework), use more detailed feedback and provide an opportunity for students to use that feedback to revise the essay or write another, similar essay. Use the suggestions for formative feedback from Chapter 8 to help the essay assessment provide an opportunity for further student learning.

Another suggestion for giving feedback on essays is to hold student conferences—that is, meet with each student individually to review answers and comments. A brief conference of 5 to 10 minutes with each student is more personal and can provide clearer guidance to the student than written comments in the paper's margin. A short, direct conference with each student may also save you hours of writing copious notes and commentary to clarify a point for the student.

Independent Scoring

The quirks of individual teachers do affect essay scores. The suggestions in Figure 12.6 help reduce the impact of your idiosyncrasies, but they do not entirely eliminate them. When important decisions rest on the scores from essays, more than one reader is necessary. Realistically, however, even though everyday grading decisions are important, it is unlikely that you will find the time or consistent cooperation of colleagues to carry out **independent scoring of essays**. Nevertheless, such a practice would improve the consistency of your scoring.

Scoring Reliability

The essay format often has very low inter-rater reliability. You can make a deliberate effort to overcome some of the negative factors that lower the reliability of essay scoring, as we discuss below. Attending to these factors will reduce the measurement errors in your evaluations of students' work. You can also improve the inter-rater reliability of essay scores by using scoring rubrics.

Inconsistent Standards

Grades assigned to a student's response may vary widely from one reader to the next, both because of the readers' inconsistencies and because of their differences in grading standards. Further, the same reader may mark the same essay differently from one day to the next. The lack of consistent standards in evaluating essays was a major justification for turning to true-false and multiple-choice assessments in education in the early 1900s. A way to overcome this consistency is to have all teachers use the same scoring rubrics.

Rater Drift

Even if scoring criteria are well defined, raters tend either not to pay attention to criteria over time or to interpret them differently as time passes. This tendency to change the way scoring criteria are applied over time occurs slowly and is called **rater drift**. Periodically, stop and determine whether you are applying the scoring standards the same way to later-scored papers as you did to earlier-scored papers.

Changes in the Topic and Prompt

Another factor that causes your assessment results to be inconsistent is the topic (subject) of the essay. A student's scores may vary widely, even when marked by the same reader, because of the topic, prompt, or questions (Sudweeks, Reeve, & Bradshaw, 2004). If you base your evaluation of a student on one essay question, you will not be able to make general statements about this student's performance on different topics. If your statements about a student are limited to only the one essay a student wrote, the validity of your overall evaluation (e.g., grades) is lowered, which is a strong reason for basing a student's marking period grade on multiple assessments collected over the entire marking period according to an assessment plan (see Chapter 6).

Halo Effect

The **halo effect** error occurs when your judgments of one characteristic of a person reflect your judgments of other characteristics or your general impression of that person. Thus, you may tend to grade a particular essay more leniently for a student you admire because you know in your heart that the student has command of the objective or topic. The halo effect works the other way, too: You may give a lower grade to a particular essay by a student because you know in your heart that he or she is not a "good student." One way to correct this flaw is to mark essays only after concealing the students' names.

Carryover Effect

A **carryover effect** error occurs when your judgment of a student's response to Question 1 affects your judgment of the student's response to Question 2. For example, a student may have a brilliant answer to Question 1 but a mediocre answer to Question 2. The carryover effect occurs when you score Question 2 more highly than it deserves after marking Question 1: You mark Question 2 more favorably because you "carried over" your favorable impression from Question 1. Therefore, score Question 1 for all students first, then go back and score Question 2 for all, and so on. Unless you do, the scores you assign to adjacent questions will likely be more similar regardless of the quality of the students' answers than scores on nonadjacent questions.

MyLab Education Self-Check 12.2

MyLab Education Application Exercise 12.2: Analyzing a Scoring Scheme for an Essay Question

---

WRITING ASSESSMENT AND TECHNOLOGY

The revolution in digital technology has made two major differences in the assessment of writing (Neal, 2011). Neal labels these "writing assessments as technologies" and "writing assessments with technologies." By the former, he means that incorporating the use of technology into writing itself is creating a new kind of expression, which draws on conventional writing skills but also includes new ones. In other words, the nature of the literacy itself is broadened. By the latter, he means using technological means to assist in assessing writing. The most obvious example of using technology in this way is machine-scoring of student writing. These changes began in the context of large-scale assessment, where the resources to develop technology were greater than in the classroom. As the digital age progresses, however, these changes are making their way into the classroom, especially changes in the types of writing tasks students do as a result of the availability of technology.

Changes in Writing Because of Technology

Writing assessments and assignments are no longer confined to handwritten, paper-based essays or themes. In most classrooms, students routinely include pictures acquired and printed as digital files in content-area reports. Student oral presentations are frequently accompanied by presentation slides, which can incorporate pictures, audio, and video. Multimedia assignments, which may or may not be uploaded to school or classroom intranet or Internet sites, are becoming more common. For example, students may be asked to develop autobiographies as multimedia assignments.

Many conventional writing skills are still important in creating these expanded digital "essays": ideas, content, voice, organization, style, and mechanics, for example. But there are other skills, as well, that are just now being identified and organized. Frey, Fisher, and Gonzalez (2010), for example, point out that the conventional "book report" assignment can give way to an assignment to write a review to post on amazon.com. This addition updates the task and makes it more relevant to twenty-first century literacy—but it also changes the nature of the writing task. Audience, especially, changes, from the teacher or teacher and classmates to a large, anonymous public. As the nature of the tasks change, the skills required to complete them and the criteria needed to assess them change, as well.

Both Neal (2011) in regard to writing in higher education and Frey and her colleagues (2010) in regard to K-12 education share the perspective that writing assessments are tools themselves, for gathering information about students' skills. As fascinated as we are at the moment with the technology itself, ultimately the written expression is more important. As people become more at ease with multimedia, hypertext, wikis, blogs, and the rest—some of which is yet to be invented—they will settle more into the background, as pens or typewriters did in a former age. At the present time, however, because the technologies are relatively new, it can be very difficult to separate use of the media from the ideas and content in students' writing or presenting.

Automated Essay Scoring

Long before questions arose about the nature of literacy in a digital age, researchers began experimenting with automating some of the chores associated with conventional writing assessment. Word processing or entering text into a text box, for example, renders student writing digital and searchable and removes any effects of handwriting on readability or comprehension. It is common now in many classrooms as well as for many large-scale assessments to require writing samples that are digital.

Automated essay scoring began even before students had routine access to word processors or computers. Ellis Page developed Project Essay Grader (PEG) in 1966, and it is still one of the most widely used automated essay scoring systems (Dikli, 2006). Other widely used systems include Intelligent Essay Assessor (IEA), E-rater (developed by Educational Testing Service), IntelliMetric, and Bayesian Essay Test Scoring System (BETSY). Each of these computer-based scoring systems uses a slightly different process, which in turn focuses on slightly different aspects of the texts. Each requires a set of "training" papers for a particular set of essays, between 100 and 1000, depending on the program. Therefore, their use is at present limited to large-scale assessment or very large courses.

Dikli (2006) presents a very readable description of these five automated essay scoring systems and discusses their advantages and disadvantages. The advantages of automated scoring include efficiency, immediate scoring and feedback, and practicality—allowing for more large-scale assessment of writing than would be possible if human scoring were required. Disadvantages include a focus on the final written product, as opposed to the writing process; the fact that most automated scoring systems are for the English language; and a debate over whether the construct of "good writing" is the same for a computer, however well programmed, and a human scorer.

Studies of the reliability and validity of automated essay scores typically use designs in which essays are scored by both the automated scoring system and human raters. Researchers are still investigating the precise nature of the relationship between automated and human scoring, and evidence is accumulating about the ways these two approaches to scoring are alike and different (McCurry, 2010). However, for large-scale applications, automated scoring can reliably reproduce human scores; automated scores correlate highly with humans' scores and produce score distributions with similar means and standard deviations (Bridgeman, Trapani, & Attali, 2012). Several familiar examination programs, including the Graduate Management Admissions Test (GMAT), the Test of English as a Foreign Language (TOEFL), and the Graduate Record Examination (GRE), use both human and automated scoring.

Technologies and their applications are changing rapidly. Perhaps more important for assessment, human expectations for and comfort with technology applications are changing rapidly as well. In the assessment of writing in particular, technology has already had an impact. Assessments associated with the Common Core State Standards (see Chapter 16) are expected to incorporate assessment technology in unprecedented ways.

CONCLUSION

Essay questions are an important tool for tapping higher-order thinking. Carefully worded and well-scored essay questions can be a window into students' thinking and reasoning with content in any discipline. The importance of this can hardly be overstated. After all, when we call someone an "educated person," what we really mean is that he or she can think.

EXERCISES

1. For each subject you teach (or plan to teach), identify different types of material that can accompany context-dependent items.
   a. For each type, state the educational level of the students for which it is intended.
   b. For each thinking-skill category in the examples given in Figure 12.2, write at least one essay item based on the material you identified. Use the examples as models for phrasing your essay prompts.
2. Each of the two essay items that follow has one or more flaws. Using the checklist for improving the quality of essay items, identify the flaw(s), then rewrite each item to eliminate the flaw(s). Check your rewritten essay item to be sure you have not added another flaw.
   a. Item A: State the two examples of prejudices we discussed in class.
   b. Item B: Evaluate the effect of air pollution on the quality of life in the western part of this state.
3. For each essay item you wrote in Exercise 1(b), apply the checklist for improving the quality of essay items. Revise any item for which you answered no to a checklist question. Exchange your items with one or more of the students in this course. Review each other's essay items using the checklist. Discuss with your classmates the reasons for assigning a no to an item. Discuss how to improve each item.

4. Following are four restricted-response essay questions that together constitute a science unit test. After each question is the keyed answer provided by the teacher and Jane Smith's answer. You are to do two things: First, decide the maximum marks (points) of each question. (The entire test has a maximum score of 50 points, so you need to distribute these among the four questions according to what you believe is appropriate.) Second, evaluate Jane Smith's answers against the answer key and award her points according to her answers' degree of correctness.

   Question 1 *What is the shape of a quartz crystal?*
      Answer key: Hexagonal
      Maximum marks: _____
      Jane's answer: "Six-sided hectogon."
      Jane's score: _____

   Question 2 *What is a saturated solution?*
      Answer key: A solution that contains as much dissolved substance as it can for a particular temperature.
      Maximum marks: _____
      Jane's answer: "Large crystals contain a great deal of substance that has been formed. This process of forming crystals is called crystallization. It occurs both in the laboratory and in nature."
      Jane's score: _____

   Question 3 *Write a paragraph describing how you can grow very large crystals.*
      Answer key: Any answer that says size of crystal is directly related to the rate of crystallization.
      Maximum marks: _____
      Jane's answer: "Large crystals contain a great deal of substance that has been formed. This process of forming crystals is called crystallization.

It occurs both in the laboratory and in nature."

Jane's score: _____

Question 4 *Name three major categories of rocks.*

Answer key: Igneous, sedimentary, and metamorphic

Maximum marks: _____

Jane's answer: "The three kinds are fire-formed, settled, and those that have changed their form."

Jane's score: _____

5. This exercise should be done during your class.

   a. Compare the maximum marks you assigned to each question in Exercise 4 with those assigned by other persons in this course. (Put the distributions of maximum marks on the board.) For which questions is there more agreement? For which is there less agreement?

   b. Discuss during class the reasons for agreement and disagreement. Make a list of the factors that seem to affect the maximum value that your classmates assign to each question.

   c. Suggest ways of reducing the variability among persons assigning maximum values to questions. Make sure the suggestions are specific to these four questions.

   d. Compare the scores you gave Jane on each question with the scores given by others in this course. On which items is there more agreement? On which is there less agreement?

   e. During class discuss the reasons for an agreement and disagreement in marking. Make a list of the factors that seem to affect the scores assigned to Jane for each question.

   f. Are the questions on which there is more agreement in scoring Jane's responses the same questions on which there is more agreement for maximum marks? Explain.

Performance and Portfolio Assessments

KEY CONCEPTS

1. A performance assessment (a) requires students to create a product, demonstrate a process, or both and (b) uses clearly defined criteria to evaluate the qualities of student work. Types of performance tasks range from structured, on-demand tasks to longer-term projects and portfolios. Advantages of performance assessment stem from its ability to assess complex learning outcomes. Disadvantages of performance assessment stem from the difficulties arising from that complexity.

2. To create a performance assessment, first be clear about the performance you want to assess. The second step in creating a performance assessment is to design the task to elicit the desired performance. The third step in creating a performance assessment is to design a scoring scheme that reflects the performance criteria. The scoring scheme may be one of several types of rubrics, a checklist, or a rating scale.

3. For purposes of assessment, a portfolio is a limited collection of a student's work used either to present the student's best work(s) or to demonstrate the student's educational growth over a given period of time.

IMPORTANT TERMS

adaptive assessment task
alternate solution strategies
alternative assessment
authentic assessment
behavior checklist
central tendency error
exemplars
graphic rating scale
halo effect
leniency error
logical error
numerical rating scale
on-demand task
performance task
personal bias
portfolio
procedure checklist
product checklist
reliability decay
rubrics (analytic, general, holistic, task-specific)
scaffolding
self-evaluation checklist
severity error
simulation
standardized patient format

PERFORMANCE ASSESSMENT

A performance assessment (a) requires students to create a product or demonstrate a process, or both, and (b) uses clearly defined criteria to evaluate the qualities of student work. A performance assessment requires students to do something with their knowledge, such as make something (build a bookshelf), produce a report (report on a group project that surveyed parents' attitudes), or demonstrate a process (show how to measure mass on a laboratory scale). Here are three examples.

Examples

Performance Assessment

- A kindergarten teacher asks each student to count to 100 by 10s.
- A fifth-grade teacher asks her students to listen carefully to a poem she reads them and stand up each time they hear a *simile*.
- A high school biology teacher asks students, working in pairs, to record each other's blood pressure, pulse, and respiration rate. Then, they run the length of a football field and repeat the measurements. They present their measurements in a table and write an explanation of the patterns they notice in the data.

A performance assessment must have two components: the performance task itself and a clear rubric for scoring. The task and rubric should be based on stated learning objectives. Classroom instructional activities that lack this scoring rubric component do not qualify as performance assessments. In practice, this line can become blurred; as good teachers observe students working, they sometimes do have criteria in mind and use their observations for formative purposes. For valid information from summative, graded performance assessments, both task and criteria are necessary.

The Performance Task A **performance task** is an assessment activity that requires students to demonstrate their achievement by producing an extended written or spoken answer, by engaging in group or individual activities, or by creating a specific product. A performance task typically requires direct demonstration of students' achievement of a learning objective. Do not use performance assessment to assess simple recall or comprehension objectives. Use performance tasks to assess learning objectives that require students to apply their knowledge and skills as they perform something. A good rule of thumb to remember is that simple learning objectives require simple assessment formats; complex learning objectives require complex assessment (Arter, 1998).

Performance assessment is sometimes called **alternative assessment** or **authentic assessment**. These terms are not interchangeable, however. The "alternative" in *alternative assessment* usually means in opposition to standardized achievement tests and to multiple-choice (true-false, matching, completion) item formats. The "authentic" in *authentic assessment* usually means presenting students with tasks that are directly meaningful to their education instead of indirectly meaningful. For example, reading several long works and using them to compare and contrast different social viewpoints is directly meaningful because it is the kind of thoughtful reading educated citizens do. Reading short paragraphs and answering questions about the "main idea" or about what the characters in the passage did, on the other hand, is indirectly meaningful because it is only one fragment or component of the ultimate learning objective of realistic reading. "Realistic" and "meaningful" are terms educators writing about authentic assessment often use. They beg some questions: "Realistic in which context?" and "Meaningful for whom?" And of course, there are degrees of authenticity; it is not an all-or-nothing concept.

Be sure that what your performance assessment requires students to do matches your learning objectives—in both content and thinking—and that your scoring **rubrics** evaluate those same learning objectives. For example, if the learning objective says that students must weigh chemicals on the laboratory scale, the performance task must require actual weighing, not an essay on how to use the scale. In addition, the scoring rubric must assess how well students weigh the chemicals and not simply specify that chemicals were weighed.

Rules for Scoring Use a coherent set of rules to assess the quality of student performance: The rules guide your judgments and ensure that you apply your judgments consistently. The rules may be in the form of rubrics, a rating scale, or a checklist.

Rubrics are coherent sets of criteria for students' work that include descriptions of levels of

FIGURE 13.1   Common types of performance assessment techniques.

Type of performance assessment	Description	Typical methods used for this type
Structured, on-demand tasks for individual students, groups, or both	The teacher decides what and when materials should be used, specifies the instructions for performance, describes the kinds of outcomes toward which students should work, tells the students they are being assessed, and gives students opportunities to prepare themselves for the assessment.	■ Paper-and-pencil tasks ■ Tasks requiring equipment and resources beyond paper-and-pencil tasks ■ Demonstrations
Naturally occurring or typical performance tasks	Observe students in natural settings: in typical classroom settings, on the playground, or at home. In natural settings you have to wait for the opportunity to arise for a particular student to perform the particular activity you would like to assess. The activity may not occur while you are observing.	
Longer-term projects for individual students, groups, or both	You can combine group and individual projects. Groups of students can work on a long-term project together; after the group activities are completed, individuals can prepare their own reports. The combination approach is useful when a project is complex and requires collaboration to complete in a reasonable time frame, yet the learning objectives require individual abilities.	■ Long-term reports ■ Tasks requiring equipment and resources beyond paper-and-pencil tasks ■ Experiments ■ Oral presentations and dramatizations
Simulations	On-demand events that happen under controlled conditions intended to mimic naturally occurring events	■ Actors and "standard patients" ■ Computerized audio-visual simulations

performance quality on the criteria. A *rating scale* consists of numerals, such as 0 to 3, or 1 to 4, that reflect the quality levels of performance. Each numeral may correspond to a verbal label for the quality level it represents. A *checklist* is a list of characteristics of a performance that can be marked yes/no or present/absent.

Types of Performance Assessments

Many types of tasks fit the broad definition we adopted here. Figure 13.1 lists most of these.

Structured, On-Demand Tasks   For structured, **on-demand tasks** or exercises, the teacher specifies the task and materials for performance, describes the kinds of outcomes toward which students should work, tells the students they are being assessed, and gives students opportunities to prepare themselves for the assessment.

Paper-and-Pencil Tasks   We have already studied many types of *paper-and-pencil tasks*. In Chapters 11 and 12, we discussed constructed-response and essay items. These formats permit students not only to record their answers but also to give explanations, articulate their reasoning, and express their

own approaches toward solving a problem. Sometimes your main focus is on the written product itself, such as the stories, reports, or drawings students create. At other times, you may be more interested in the process students use, for example, when students record the steps they used to complete an experiment or explain how they solved a problem. Here are some examples.

Examples

Paper-and-Pencil Tasks

- Solve an arithmetic story problem and explain how you solved it.
- Study the following graph that shows how Sally uses her time. Then, write a story about a typical day in Sally's life using the information from the graph.

Tasks Requiring Other Equipment and Resources   In subjects such as mathematics, science, mechanical drawing, art, first aid and lifesaving, consumer science, and driver's education, important outcomes require students to do something with equipment and resources rather than write about how to do it. In some academic subjects, performing a non-paper-and-pencil task might be a better option than using a written response, even though either could be done.

For example, in elementary school general science, you would *directly assess* students' understanding and use of the metric system if you required them to measure objects, volume, mass, and so on. You use *indirect assessment* if you require students only to perform numerical conversions from one system or unit of measurement to another, or to answer questions based on pictures of measuring equipment. You could assess students' estimation skills, measuring skills, and systematic thinking skills, for example, all in one task by giving students a jar of beans and some simple tools. After giving students suitable directions, you can observe how they solve the problem of estimating the number of beans in the jar. Here are some other examples.

Examples

Tasks Requiring Additional Resources Beyond Paper and Pencil

- Build as many geometric shapes as possible from this set of four triangles.
- Talk on this telephone to ask about a job and to request a job application.

You may use non-paper-and-pencil tasks to present problems to be solved by a group, an individual, or some combination of group and individual work. In the latter case, the group may work cooperatively on the task; after the group solves the problem, individuals describe or write up what the group did and the solution to the problem. Non-paper-and-pencil tasks may also be open response, allowing for alternative correct performances, or closed response, allowing only one best or correct answer.

Demonstrations A *demonstration* is an on-demand performance in which a student shows he can use knowledge and skills to complete a well-defined, complex task. Demonstrations are not as long or as complex as projects. Demonstrations are usually closed-response tasks. Tasks comprising a demonstration are often well defined and the "right" or "best way" is often known to both the student and the evaluator. However, individual variations are permitted; style and manner of presentation often count

when a student presents a demonstration. The 4-H Clubs often use demonstrations: Boys and girls demonstrate their skills in a variety of agricultural and homemaking areas. Here are some examples.

Examples

Demonstrations

- Demonstrate the proper way to knead dough for bread.
- Demonstrate how to set up the microscope for viewing stained slides.
- Demonstrate how to climb a rope.
- Demonstrate how to search for information on the Internet.

For the most part, demonstrations focus on how well a student uses her skills, rather than on how well the student can explain her thinking or articulate the principles underlying a phenomenon. If you use a demonstration for assessment purposes, you should carefully identify the appropriate learning objective and use an appropriate scoring rubric.

Naturally Occurring or Typical Performance Tasks In opposition to structured, on-demand performances are naturally occurring tasks. *Naturally occurring performances* require you to observe and assess students in natural settings: in typical classroom settings, while on the playground, or while at home. In these settings, you are likely to see the way a student typically performs on a learning objective, such as cooperating with members of a group to achieve a goal. In natural settings, you do not tell students they are being assessed, nor do you control the situation in any way.

Examples

Naturally Occurring Performance

- Observe a student's way of dealing with conflicts on the playground.
- Collect all pieces that each student wrote in every subject and analyze them for grammatical, spelling, and syntactic errors to determine a student's typical language usage (at least in school assignments).
- Observe whether a student makes change correctly when running a refreshment stand at the school fair.

Although a naturally occurring setting may let you assess students' typical performance, this is not always the case. In natural settings, you often have to wait for the opportunity to arise for a particular student to perform the particular activity you would like to assess. The activity may not occur while you are observing. Waiting lowers the efficiency of this assessment mode. For example, collecting writing assignments is unlikely to provide you with all the information you need to determine your students' command of the mechanics of writing. Not all spelling patterns and forms of sentence structure students need to learn, for example, are likely to appear in every student's writings. Thus, you would have no way of thoroughly assessing students' use of sentence structures. Formal assessment of performance learning objectives usually requires a structured performance assessment.

Longer-Term Projects   Long-term projects can be designed for individual or group work. An *individual project* is a long-term activity that results in a student product: a model, a functional object, a substantial report, or a collection. Properly crafted projects require students to apply and integrate a wide range of abilities and knowledge as well as display creativity, originality, and some sense of aesthetics. When students write a library research paper, for example, they must apply the skills of locating and using reference materials and sources: outlining, organizing, and planning a report; communicating using written language, word processing, and presentation style; and demonstrating their understanding of the topic. A good project will engage students in critical thinking, creative thinking, and problem solving.

Examples

Long-Term Projects

- Using resources in the school library, write a research paper on why voter turnout is so low during primary elections.
- Build a small piece of furniture using the hand tools you learned to use during the semester.
- Plan, conduct, and report on an experiment to investigate the hypothesis that a brightly colored advertisement will be remembered longer than a dull one.

The usefulness of projects as performance assessment tasks depends on four conditions: (1) the project focuses on one or more important curriculum learning objectives, (2) each student does his or her own work, (3) each student has equal access to the resources needed to prepare an excellent final product and to achieve an excellent evaluation, and (4) you can control your own biases toward certain types of products and fairly evaluate other well-done projects. Middle- and upper-middle-class students with highly educated parents, for example, often have access to more resources than their less fortunate peers. You may tend to evaluate such students' projects more highly because they use these resources and produce very good-looking products. However, by so doing you may be biasing your evaluations toward certain social classes of students.

To design projects for assessment purposes, make sure they are explicitly linked to learning objectives, evaluate students only on criteria related to those objectives, use a scoring rubric with clear descriptions of performance at each level of quality, and make sure the weight of each criterion is commensurate with its importance in your instructional plans. Limit the resources students may use to complete the project if students vary widely in their ability to access resources.

Because projects usually span several weeks, you must plan to manage them. Present directions in writing, and require progress reports for longer projects, which are an excellent opportunity for formative assessment and feedback. Make sure students are making regular progress. Mentor students to help them overcome operational problems that may be beyond their control (e.g., a key person who students were to interview for the project has become ill and cannot see them) and to keep them focused on completing the project. Monitor the procedures and processes the students are using to ensure they will be able to address the learning objectives set for the project.

A *group project* requires two or more students to work together on a longer project. The major purpose of a group project *as an assessment technique* is to evaluate whether students can work together cooperatively and appropriately to create a high-quality product. The learning objectives for a group project depend on the subject

FIGURE 13.2   A group project in a U.S. history course for students in middle school or high school.

HISTORICAL INVESTIGATION TASK

In recent years controversy has arisen over the status of Christopher Columbus. Was he a hero or villain? As we study Columbus, we will read from a number of resources penned by different historians that will present their views of Columbus.

In cooperative groups, choose at least two resources that describe conflicting reports of events that took place upon Columbus's "discovery" of the New World and during its settlement. Discuss the contradictions you find and try to determine why the historians reported the events differently. Using the resources available, develop a clear explanation of the reasons for the contradictions or present a scenario that clears up the contradictions.

Your group will explain to the class why historians seem to report the same event differently. In addition, your group will offer to the class its ideas for resolving the contradictions. Your group's presentation to the class may be either a dramatization, a panel discussion, or a debate.

Your project will be due 3 weeks from today. Every Friday one member of your group will tell the class the progress you made on the project during the past week, any problems the group had in completing the assignment, and what the group plans to complete during the next week.

Each member of the group will be assessed on the learning objectives that follow. You will be provided rubrics for each of the learning objectives, so you may see more clearly what the assessment will be.

Social Studies Content Learning Objective

1. Your understanding that recorded history is influenced by the perspective of the historian.

2. Your understanding of the events surrounding Columbus's discovery and settlement of the New World.

Complex Thinking Learning Objectives: Historical Investigation

1. Your ability to identify and explain the confusion, uncertainty, or contradiction surrounding a past event.

2. Your ability to develop and defend a logical and plausible resolution to the confusion, uncertainty, or contradiction surrounding a past event.

Effective Communication Learning Objectives

1. Your ability to communicate for a variety of purposes.

2. Your ability to communicate in a variety of ways.

Collaboration Learning Objectives

1. Your ability to work with all of the students in your group to complete the project successfully.

2. Your ability to contribute good ideas and resources for presenting the findings to the class.

3. Your ability to do several different kinds of activities to help the group complete the project successfully.

Source: Adapted from *Assessing Student Outcomes: Performance Assessment Using the Dimensions of Learning Model* (p. 60), by R. J. Marzano, D. Pickering, and J. McTighe, 1993, Alexandria, VA: Association for Supervision and Curriculum Development. Adapted by permission of McREL, 4601 DTC Blvd. #500, Denver, CO 80237.

matter and the level of the students you are assessing. For example, group projects may focus on the following:

- *Action-oriented learning objectives* (creating a newsletter)
- *Student-interest-oriented learning objectives* (writing a paper on a topic they're interested in)
- *Subject-matter-oriented learning objectives* (understanding how rivers are formed)
- *Interdisciplinary learning objectives* (designing a wildlife refuge)

An example of a subject-oriented group project is shown in Figure 13.2.

Do not use "group grades" to assess student learning of content objectives in a group project. Group grades are often invalid and unreliable. For example, two students who reached the same

level of knowledge and skills but were in two different groups might receive different grades. In addition, group grades do not give individual students feedback on their learning, so they send students the message that getting done with the project and receiving a grade is more important than knowing what their next steps in learning should be. Finally, group grades create pressure for some students to compensate for other students, which defeats the purpose of cooperative learning.

We suggest five strategies to build appropriate opportunities for individual grades into group projects (Brookhart, 2013d). This list is not exhaustive. You may use any strategy that you can defend is a valid and reliable (see Chapters 3 and 4) way to assess individual students' achievement of the learning outcomes your group project was intended to teach and assess. The prompts or questions, and the criteria and scoring rubrics, for any of these strategies need to be based squarely on the learning outcomes you intended the project to assess.

1. *Student reflection.* Give students a specific prompt for a reflection on what they learned, and ask them to write. Make sure your prompt follows the guidelines for good essay prompts in Chapter 12.

2. *Oral questioning.* If your group project results in group oral presentations, you can use questioning to discover what each student has learned. This method works best when each group presents on a different topic (all related to the same learning outcomes); otherwise, students in later presentations can just repeat answers given by students in earlier presentations. Prepare questions ahead of time, and make sure they require higher-order thinking (see Chapter 11).

3. *Multi-step design.* For complex performance assessments, design the task so that it includes multiple assessment opportunities along the way. Use earlier assessment opportunities for formative feedback and later ones for summative assessment (grading). For example, at the end of the planning stage of a long-term group project, each student can write a paragraph describing what they are learning (again, with a specific prompt) and how that will contribute to the product the group is producing. You can give formative feedback on these paragraphs. After the project is over, students can revisit their paragraphs, describe how their thinking has changed, what they actually did learn, and how their contribution to the project helped them do that. Use a specific prompt and a scoring rubric for grading.

4. *Write your own question.* Some projects lend themselves to students' asking and answering their own questions. For example, in a design project assessing students' knowledge of area and perimeter, students can write a question that occurred to them during their project work that they needed to solve, and explain how they solved it.

5. *Post-project test.* The main purpose of some group projects is to teach students facts and concepts (for example, reports about people, places, or things). We would argue that they still should require higher-order thinking, and

not be simply "retelling" projects. For example, instead of asking groups of students to pick a planet and report on it, ask them to pick a planet, pretend they are in the first party of astronauts to visit the planet, and design or describe what they would need to take. Nevertheless, for projects where familiarity with facts and concepts is one of the main goals, the project itself is actually a learning activity. For the grade, give individual students a well-designed test, using the principles for test design you are learning in this book.

To assess students' *group learning skills,* develop scoring rubrics. Rubrics are discussed later in this chapter, but for the sake of an example here, Figure 13.3 displays a set of general scoring rubrics for assessing collaboration and cooperation during group tasks. These rubrics could be adapted to a specific project. Notice that these rubrics assume the criteria will be applied individually to each group member. Teachers can do that, but students can also self- or peer-assess using rubrics for group learning. The results should be discussion and feedback about the group's functioning, and decisions about changes that may need to be made, rather than a grade.

Sometimes you may want to assess the functioning of a learning group as a whole. In that case, as well, we recommend using rubrics with clearly stated criteria. We also recommend that the group uses the rubrics for discussion and that you give the group feedback, not a grade, regarding how well their group is functioning. That feedback, like all feedback, should include observations about what is going well and suggestions for improvement.

In a *combined group and individual project,* groups of students work on a long-term project together, and after the group activities are completed, individuals prepare their own reports without assistance from the other group members. The combination approach is useful when a project is complex and requires the collaborative talents of several students to complete in a reasonable time frame, yet the learning objective requires that individual students have the ability to prepare final reports, interpret results on their own, and so on. Research on cooperative learning indicates that students achieve most when the learning setting requires both group goals and individual accountability (Slavin, 1988). Assessment in this type of combined group and

FIGURE 13.3   General rubrics for assessing collaboration and cooperation as students work in groups.

Learning Objective A: Works toward the achievement of group goals.

4 Actively helps to identify group goals and works hard to meet them.

3 Communicates commitment to the group's goals and effectively carries out assigned roles.

2 Communicates commitment to the group's goals but does not carry out assigned roles.

1 Does not work toward group goals or actively works against them.

Learning Objective B: Demonstrates effective interpersonal skills.

4 Actively promotes effective group interaction and the expression of ideas and opinions in a way that is sensitive to the feelings and knowledge base of others.

3 Participates in group interaction with prompting. Expresses ideas and opinions in a way that is sensitive to the feelings and knowledge base of others.

2 Participates in group interaction without prompting or expresses ideas and opinions without considering the feelings and knowledge base of others.

1 Does not participate in group interaction, even with prompting, or expresses ideas and opinions in a way that is insensitive to the feelings and knowledge base of others.

Learning Objective C: Contributes to group maintenance.

4 Actively helps the group to identify changes or modifications necessary in the group process and works toward carrying out those changes.

3 Helps identify changes or modifications necessary in the group process and works toward carrying out those changes.

2 When prompted, helps identify changes or modifications necessary in the group process, or is only minimally involved in carrying out those changes.

1 Does not attempt to identify changes or modifications necessary in the group process, even when prompted, or refuses to work toward carrying out those changes.

Learning Objective D: Effectively performs a variety of roles within a group.

4 Effectively performs multiple roles within the group.

3 Effectively performs two roles within the group.

2 Makes an attempt to perform more than one role within the group but has little success with secondary roles.

1 Rejects opportunities or requests to perform more than one role in the group.

Source: Adapted from *Assessing Student Outcomes: Performance Assessment Using the Dimensions of Learning Model* (pp. 87–88), by R. J. Marzano, D. Pickering, and J. McTighe, 1993, Alexandria, VA: Association for Supervision and Curriculum Development. Adapted by permission of McREL, 4601 DTC Blvd. #500, Denver, CO 80237.

individual learning project requires assessing a group's joint success on the project as well as the degree to which individuals attained the learning objectives.

Experiments   An *experiment* or *investigation* is an on-demand performance in which a student plans, conducts, and interprets the results of an empirical research study. The study focuses on answering specific research questions or on investigating specific research hypotheses. As defined here, experiments or investigations include a wide range of research activities that occur in both natural and social science disciplines. They include field and survey research investigations as well as laboratory and control-group experiments and may be conducted as individual or as group activities.

Experiments let you assess whether students use proper inquiry skills and methods. You can also assess whether students have developed proper conceptual frameworks and theoretical, discipline-based explanations of the phenomena they have investigated. To assess these latter aspects, focus on the quality of students' frames of reference, their mental representations of the problem they are studying, how well they plan or design the research, the quality of the questions or hypotheses they can specify, and the quality of explanations they offer for why the data relationships exist.

Oral Presentations and Dramatizations   *Oral presentations* permit students to verbalize their knowledge and use their oral skills in the form of interviews, speeches, or oral presentations.

FIGURE 13.4   Example of a simple rating scale for assessing the quality of a student's oral presentation.

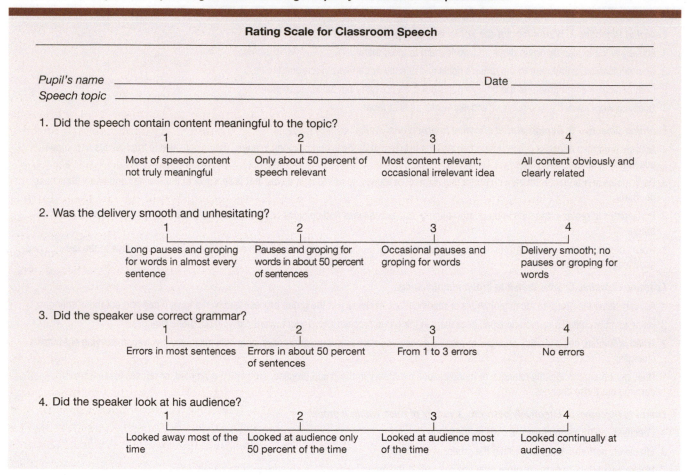

In language and language-arts curricula, many learning objectives focus on communication skills in addition to content. Fluency of speaking a foreign language is an important learning objective in some curricula. Another area in which oral presentations are especially useful is in speaking to a group. Figure 13.4 shows a simple scale for assessing the delivery of a classroom speech.

Debates are a special type of oral performance. A *debate* pits one student against another to argue issues logically in a formal exchange of views. Assessment focuses on the logical and persuasive quality of the argument and the rebuttals. Other *forensic activities* include poetry reading and oratories. *Dramatizations* combine oral, elocution, and movement skills. Students may express their understanding of fictional characters or historical persons, for example, by acting a role showing ideological positions and personal characteristics of these persons. For debates and other oral presentations that assess content knowledge

as well as oral skills, it is usually a good idea to have separate rubrics for content and for oral presentation.

Simulations Simulations are on-demand events that happen under controlled conditions and attempt to mimic naturally occurring events. For example, students can use anatomy simulation software to diagnose pathology in certain organs of the body and then describe conventional treatments. When the performance to be evaluated is the ability to interact with another person, an actor may be trained to play the role of the other person. Originally, the **standardized patient format** was used to assess the clinical skills of medical candidates and practicing doctors. An actor is trained to display the symptoms of a particular disorder. Each medical candidate meets and interviews this standardized patient to diagnose the illness and to prescribe treatment. A panel of evaluators observes this interaction and assesses the candidate.

Computerized Simulations With rapid advances in technology and software, multimedia simulations have become more realistic and complex. They have also become more common. The National Assessment of Educational Progress (NAEP) uses them, and the two consortia planning assessments of the Common Core State Standards plan to use them, as well. Assessment using computerized simulation can be composed of several parts asking for different kinds of student responses. For several different examples of simulation assessments in science at Grades 4, 8, and 12, visit the NAEP Questions Tool site (nces.ed. gov/) and select "Interactive Items." Here we describe one of them.

This computerized task is called "Here Comes the Sun." It is a fourth-grade item assessing whether students can predict the path of the sun and number of daylight hours in order to determine the best location for tomato plants. It is intended to take students 20 minutes to complete. The first screen is a welcome screen. It includes a picture of a farm and this text setting up the problem (NAEP, 2009):

> Two farmers in different places in the United States want to grow tomato plants. Tomato plants need a lot of daylight. You will look at data showing the hours of daylight in the two places. Then you will decide which place is better for growing the tomato plants. First, you will make observations about the path of the Sun as it seems to move across the sky. Click "NEXT" to start your observations.

The second screen is an explanation screen, with both text and diagrams, explaining how to read an interactive diagram that traces the path of the sun from sunrise to sunset over a point on the earth. One of the diagrams moves, and students can press "play," "pause," and "reset" until they think they understand how to read the sun simulation.

The third screen explains that students will play a sun simulation that includes a time readout (e.g., 4:20) and observe the path of the sun on January 1 and July 1. The simulation is button-driven. Students are to record sunrise and sunset on both dates and compare the days. They have control of the simulation with "play," "backward," "forward," and "reset" buttons. The third screen simply describes the task and shows students what the simulation looks like. Once students are sure they understand what they are

to do, they click "next" and are presented with a fourth screen, where the buttons activate the simulation, so they can practice. When they are ready to begin recording their data, they go to the fifth screen, where there are boxes in which they can record the times of sunrise and sunset on January 1. Then, they go to a sixth screen to record the times of sunrise and sunset on July 1. The sun's path simulation is available on each of these screens, and students use it to answer the questions. All of these recordings constitute Question 1 of the assessment.

A seventh screen presents students with a multiple-choice question with introductory material, an interpretive exercise of the sort we discussed in Chapter 11. The introductory material shows the data recordings of a hypothetical student, in table form, and asks students to select the observation that best interprets those data (Question 2).

An eighth screen presents a sun's path simulator that includes, for the first time, grid lines to show the height of the sun, as well as the timer that students have seen before. A multiple-choice question asks students to predict on which day the sun will be lowest in the sky at noon (Question 3). The ninth screen presents a live version of the sun's path simulator with two open-response boxes where students can type in text, labeled "difference 1" and "difference 2." Students are asked to describe two differences they observe about the sun's path on January 1 and July 1 (Question 4).

The tenth screen is another interpretive exercise. A bar graph constructed by a hypothetical student, displaying the amount (in hours and minutes) of sunlight on the first of each month over the course of a year, with the bar for October 1 missing, is presented on the left. On the right, students have to estimate how many hours of daylight probably occurred on October 1, based on the graph, recorded in one open-response box, and explain their reasoning in a second open-response box (Question 5).

The eleventh screen presents a final interpretive exercise (Question 6) with sunrise/sunset and amount of daylight information over the growing season. There are two tables, one for Place X and one for Place Y, which are labeled on outline maps of the United States. A multiple-choice question asks students to choose the place in which they would expect tomato plants to grow the most during the growing season.

An open-response box asks students to write an explanation for the answer they selected and use data from the tables to explain their reasoning.

For NAEP purposes, this assessment was scored as six separate questions, most with multiple score points. Question 1, assessing accurate recording of sunrise and sunset in winter and summer, allowed multiple answers within a range for each of the four recordings, allowed for partially correct answers, and used a scoring guide to combine all four results. Questions 2 and 3 were multiple-choice questions scored right or wrong. Questions 4, 5, and 6 rated student answers as complete, partial, or unsatisfactory/incorrect.

Computerized Adaptive Scenarios

If a computerized performance assessment presents a situation or scenario that is reasonably structured with a limited number of possible actions, an **adaptive assessment task** can be built whereby a student's response to one situation will determine what the next presentation will be. For example, the media present a scenario to the student and ask a question or call for a decision. The student responds, and the presentation continues in a way that depends on the response. In this way each student receives a somewhat different scenario, depending on the individual choices of action.

Advantages and Criticisms of Performance Assessments

Advantages of Performance Assessment

Performance assessments have several advantages over other assessments (Hambleton & Murphy, 1992; Rudner & Boston, 1994):

1. *Performance tasks clarify the meaning of complex learning objectives.* Authentic performance tasks can closely match complex learning objectives. When you present them to students and share them with parents, you make the learning goals clear through actual example.

2. *Performance tasks assess the ability "to do."* An important school outcome is the ability to use knowledge and skill to solve problems and lead a useful life, rather than simply to answer questions about doing.

3. *Performance assessment is consistent with modern learning theory.* Constructivist learning theory emphasizes that students should use their previous knowledge to build new knowledge structures, be actively involved in exploration and inquiry through tasklike activities, and construct meaning for themselves from educational experience. Most performance assessments engage students and actively involve them in complex tasks.

4. *Performance tasks require integration of knowledge, skills, and abilities.* Complex performance tasks, especially those that span longer periods, usually require students to use many different skills and abilities.

5. *Performance assessments may be linked more closely with teaching activities.* When your teaching requires students to be actively involved in inquiry and performance activities, performance assessments are a meaningful component.

6. *Performance tasks broaden the approach to student assessment.* Introducing performance assessment along with traditional objective formats broadens the types of learning objectives you assess and offers students a variety of ways of expressing their learning, which increases the validity of your student evaluations.

7. *Performance tasks let teachers assess the processes students use as well as the products they produce.* Many performance tasks offer you the opportunity to watch the way a student goes about solving a problem or completing a task. Appropriate scoring rubrics help you collect information about the quality of the processes and strategies students use, as well as assess the quality of the finished product.

Disadvantages of Performance Assessments

Although performance assessments offer several advantages over traditional objective assessment procedures, they have some distinct disadvantages (Hambleton & Murphy, 1992; Miller & Seraphine, 1993; Rudner & Boston, 1994):

1. *High-quality performance assessments are difficult to create.* They need to match the outcome to be assessed but not add on other qualities (e.g., reading ability, dramatic skill, artistic flair) that are not part of the outcomes to be assessed. High-quality scoring rubrics are difficult to create, as well. They need to effectively capture all relevant characteristics, with descriptions that can be reliably used by students and teachers alike, yet allow for the multiplicity of ways students might accomplish open-ended performance tasks.

2. *Completing performance tasks takes students a lot of time.* Even short on-demand paper-and-pencil tasks take 10 to 20 minutes per task to complete. Most authentic tasks take days or weeks to complete, which means either administering fewer tasks (thereby reducing the reliability of the results) or reducing the amount of instructional time.

3. *Scoring performance task responses takes a lot of time.* The more complex the performance and the product, the more time you can expect to spend on scoring.

4. *Scores from performance tasks may have lower scorer reliability.* If two teachers use different frameworks, have different levels of competence, use a different scoring rubric, or use no scoring rubrics at all, they will mark the same student's performance or product quite differently. Inconsistent scoring is not only frustrating to students, it also lowers the reliability and validity of the assessment results.

5. *Students' performance on one task provides little information about their performance on other tasks.* A serious problem with performance assessments is that a student's performance on a task very much depends on his or her prior knowledge, the particular wording and phrasing of the task, the context in which it is administered, and the specific subject-matter content embedded in the task (Lane et al., 1992; Linn, 1993; Shavelson & Baxter, 1991). These variables result in low reliability from the content-sampling point of view. You may have to use six or seven performance tasks to reliably evaluate a student for a learning objective, which implies that a student should be able to perform several different tasks under varied conditions and in several contexts.

6. *Performance tasks do not assess all learning objectives well.* If a learning objective focuses on memorizing and recalling, then objective format items such as short-answer, multiple-choice, matching, and true-false are better assessment choices. If your learning objectives emphasize logical thinking, understanding concepts, or verbal reasoning, objective formats may still be a better choice than performance formats. They allow a much broader content to be assessed and can assess that broad coverage in less time. Further, objective formats are easier to score and the results from them are more reliable. A balanced assessment approach is recommended.

7. *Completing performance tasks may be discouraging to less able students.* Complex tasks that require students to sustain their interest and intensity over a long period may discourage less able students. They may have partial knowledge of the learning objective but may fail to complete the task because it does not allow them to use or express this partial knowledge effectively. Group projects may help by permitting peers to share the work, use each other's partial knowledge and differential skills, and motivate one another.

8. *Performance assessments may underrepresent the learning of some cultural groups.* Performance tasks will not wash away differences among cultural groups; in fact, they are likely to make such differences more apparent. Multiple assessment formats may improve this situation somewhat because they allow knowledge, skills, and ability to be expressed in different formats and media, thus allowing students with different backgrounds to express their achievement of the learning objectives in different ways.

9. *Performance assessments may be corruptible.* As you use performance assessments, you will teach your students how to do well on them. This amounts to coaching them how to perform (often called "teaching to the test"). If your coaching amounts to teaching all aspects of your state's standards and your school's curriculum framework's learning objectives, you are doing the right thing. However, if you focus primarily on only one aspect of the learning objectives (e.g., how to write answers to constructed-response social studies items), you will lower the validity of your results.

In Chapters 2 and 11, we said that students' use of higher-order thinking is best assessed when they face new or novel tasks. Coaching tends to reduce the novelty of the task or change it from an "application" task to a "following-the-solution-strategy-the-teacher-taught-me" task. These types of coaching reduce the validity of your results because they do not assess the main intent of learning objectives that want students to learn to solve new and ill-structured problems.

MyLab Education Self-Check 13.1

MyLab Education Application Exercise 13.1:
Using Performance Assessment to Assess Higher-Order Thinking

DESIGNING PERFORMANCE ASSESSMENTS

Use a systematic approach to creating performance tasks. First, be very clear about the performance you want to assess. Then, design both a task and scoring scheme that match the intended performance. A well-designed performance task gives students the opportunity to apply their learning to a new situation, not just repeat information from class or from a text. Design performance tasks to help students make connections between the skills and abilities they learned in separate subjects and between "schoolhouse" learning and real-world activities. Share your scoring rubrics with students to clarify the learning objectives for them. The more students understand the skills and abilities they should use, the better able they are to identify where they should focus their practice and study efforts. We explain the steps for designing performance assessment in more detail below.

Step One: Be Clear About the Performance to Assess

Identify Objectives to Be Assessed
You may decide that two or three learning objectives can be assessed by the same complex performance assessment. Some learning objectives may cut across curricula (e.g., effective communication). Select only those learning objectives that can and should be assessed by performance tasks. Make sure the performance assessment you design fits into your assessment plan, along with tests and other assessments for other learning objectives, and supports ultimate achievement of state standards and curricular goals. The result should be a balanced assessment of worthwhile learning objectives of both knowledge and skills.

Identify Criteria for Assessment
Once you have identified the learning objectives you will assess, identify the performance criteria that you will look for in students' work. Sometimes these are called achievement dimensions or traits (for example, as in the Six + 1 Trait® writing assessment rubrics). The criteria should reference all the important aspects of learning that you intended students to develop as they worked to achieve the objectives and should be directly related to the objectives. Some state standards include performance criteria. Samples of student work can help you further clarify criteria for assessment.

Define Quality Levels
Each criterion or achievement dimension you assess actually represents a continuum of educational growth. Different students will attain different levels of achievement on each dimension. Further, one student may perform with high competence on some criteria but with less competence on others. Thus, part of creating your performance task is to define an achievement scale for each criterion. You define this scale by spelling out the different degrees of achievement—from high to low—on each dimension. The descriptions you write to define this achievement continuum for each criterion are often called performance-level descriptions. This continuum forms the basis for scoring rubrics, which we discuss later in this chapter.

Decide Whether to Assess a Process, a Product, or Both
Focus your assessment on the *process* students use if you taught students to use a particular procedure for which you can specify steps and accurately assess the extent to which your students follow the accepted procedure(s). Focus your assessment on the process students use if most of the evidence about the students' achievement of the learning objective is found in the way the performance is carried out, and little or none of the evidence you need to evaluate the students is present in the product itself. Here are some examples:

Examples

Learning Objectives That Require Students to Demonstrate a Certain Process

1. Use a particular long-division algorithm.
2. Use the posted safety procedures when handling laboratory chemicals.

In some cases, the learning objective permits several correct processes. In a mathematics curriculum, for example, a learning objective may ask students to learn several different procedures for division rather than a single correct algorithm.

Focus your assessment on the *product* students produce if most or all of the evidence about their achievement of the learning objectives is found in the product itself, and little or none of the evidence you need to evaluate students is found in the procedures they use or the ways in which they perform. Focus your assessment on the product students produce if there are multiple good ways to produce a high-quality product, and the exact method or sequence of steps does not make much difference as long as the product is good. Here are two examples:

Examples

Learning Objectives That Require Students to Produce a Product

1. Write haiku poems based on everyday experience.
2. Prepare a research term paper on the causes of volcanic eruptions.

There may be several equally good methods for completing such tasks, but the focus is on the result or products.

Sometimes *both product and process* are of equal importance. For example:

Examples

Learning Objectives That Require Students to Produce a Product by Performing a Certain Process

1. Write a research term paper by following certain steps you outline.
2. Follow all the steps in a recipe for homemade pizza, prepare a tasty dish.

Step Two: Design the Performance Task

Only when you have a clear understanding of the achievement you want to assess should you design the task(s) that will assess it. As you create an assessment task, be sure that the task will be within the students' ability range, can be adapted as needed for students with disabilities in you class, and suits your class size and available resources. Ask yourself:

- What ranges of tasks do the learning objectives imply?
- Which parts of the tasks should be structured, and to what degree?
- Does each task require students to perform all the important elements implied by the learning objectives?

- Do the tasks allow me to assess the achievement dimensions I need to assess?
- What must I tell students about the task and its scoring to communicate to them what they need to perform?
- Will students with different ethnic and social backgrounds interpret my task appropriately?

Create Meaningful Tasks If possible, choose a situation or task that is likely to have personal meaning for most of your students, which lets students become personally involved in solving a problem or doing well on the task. Blend the familiar and the novel, so students will be challenged but not frustrated by the task. Choose situations or tasks that assess whether students can transfer their knowledge and skills from classroom activities and examples to similar but new (for them) formats.

Create a draft of your task with your learning objectives clearly in mind. Consider whether you want a group or individual task. Consider the content knowledge and skills required, and the kind of thinking (analysis or synthesis, for example) required to master the learning objective.

Trying out assessment tasks (whether performance or traditional paper-and-pencil) before using them is next to impossible for classroom teachers. You can, however, have your colleagues review and criticize your tasks before you use them. The next best thing to actual student tryouts can and should be done: After you use an assessment task, use the information you obtain about flaws in the task or in the rubrics to revise the task or rubric; then reuse the task and rubric next year with a new class of students.

Things to Control to Craft Valid Tasks Tasks assessing the same content learning objective can differ from one another. These differences make some tasks useful for assessing different types of lifelong learning objectives. Figure 13.5 shows five properties of a task that you must control to produce a well-designed task. Study your task's learning objective to decide how to control these properties to make your task more valid.

Time Needed to Complete the Work Some learning objectives can be assessed in a relatively short period of 15 to 40 minutes. For example, the

FIGURE 13.5   Properties of tasks that you can vary to better align students' performance with the requirements of the achievement dimensions and learning objectives.

Task property	Variations in the task requirements
Time to complete the task	*Short tasks* can be done in one class period or less.
	Long tasks require a month or more, and work may need to be done outside class.
Task structure provided	Structure may vary in:
	Problem definition: High structure means you carefully define the problem the students must solve. Low structure means students are free to select and define the problem.
	Scaffolding: High structure means students are given lots of guidance or directions in how to begin a solution and what materials to use. Low structure means students have little or no guidance and must decide for themselves.
	Alternate strategies: High structure means there are very few correct or appropriate pathways to get to the correct answer. Low structure means there are many correct or appropriate approaches to get an acceptable answer.
	Alternate solutions: High structure means there is a correct answer to the task. Low structure means there is no single correct answer to this task.
Participation of groups	The task may require:
	Individual work only throughout all phases of performance.
	Mixed individual and group work in which some of the performance occurs in groups and some is strictly individual effort.
	Group work only throughout all phases of performance.
Product and process focus	The task may require:
	Process assessment only in which the students' performance of the steps and procedures and not the outcome are observed and evaluated.
	Both process and product assessment in which both the steps and the concrete outcome (product) are evaluated.
	Product assessment only in which only the concrete product or outcome is evaluated.
Performance modality	The task may require:
	A single modality in which the performance is limited to one mode (e.g., oral, written, wood model, etc.).
	Multiple modality in which the performance must be done in several modes (e.g., do both a written and an oral report).

ability to work in groups, write an essay or an explanation, plot a graph, or carry out simple experiments can be assessed with short tasks. Many learning objectives and dimensions, however, necessitate that the students complete long tasks. For example, doing an opinion survey and writing it up, building a model town, and developing complex plans for community action require a month or more, and much of the work may need to be done outside class. Task time limits must match the intent of the learning objective and the achievement dimensions you are looking for.

Task Structure   You can **structure a task** in various ways, including the way you define the problem, scaffold the instructions, require alternate strategies, and require alternate solutions. At one extreme your task may *define a problem* for students to solve (structured); at the other extreme you may require the students themselves to iden-

tify what the problem is (unstructured or ill-defined). **Scaffolding** is the degree of support, guidance, and direction you provide the students when they set out to complete the task. You may suggest how to attack the problem, what books or material to use, and the general nature of the end product you require. These directions and guidance statements add structure to the task. Less scaffolding means less structure.

If your task can be performed or solved using only one or two procedures or strategies, it has fewer **alternate solution strategies** and is more structured in this respect. Unstructured alternatives mean that there are many equally correct pathways to the correct answer or to producing the correct product. A similar analysis applies to the solution or the product itself: A task is unstructured in this respect when it has many correct or *acceptable solutions or products*. Just how a task may vary in these elements is shown in the following example:

Example

Showing How Controlling Properties Can Change a Performance Task

More structure:
Using these Styrofoam balls and pipe cleaners, make models of a helium atom and a neon atom. In writing, compare and contrast these elements. Compare them according to their atomic number, structure, standard state, position in the periodic table, and common uses. Whenever possible, refer to your models to support your comparison. You may use your textbook, other books in the library, and the Internet for information.

Less structure:
Choose two elements. Make models or diagrams to represent an atom of each element you chose. In writing, tell why you chose these two elements. Then, compare and contrast your elements on as many aspects as you think are important, again explaining why the aspects are important. Whenever possible, refer to your models or diagrams to support your comparison. You may use your textbook, other books in the library, and the Internet for information.

Participation of Groups   If your learning objectives call for cooperative or collaborative learning (or using other group-based skills), set a task using, at least in part, group activities. As described above, be careful to assess collaborative learning skills and content learning objectives separately and at the right level—group assessment of collaboration and individual assessment of individual learning.

Product and Process   If you want to assess process, you need to do the assessing while the students are performing. You may take away a product, on the other hand, and evaluate it at your convenience. Further, you cannot assess cognitive processes (mental activities) directly, only indirectly through some intermediate or "partial" products. For example, you can ask students to tell you or to write what they were thinking about while they were doing the task, or you may ask them to record the early drafts they made and ideas they used.

Indirect assessments of students' mental activities and thinking processes depend on the students having abilities other than those required to complete the task. They depend, for example, on the accuracy of the students' memories, their skills in understanding the thinking processes they used, and their abilities to describe these thinking processes orally or in writing. Because you assess cognitive processes only indirectly, your inferences and judgments about how well students use them—that is, the validity of your evaluation of students' use of cognitive processes—might be weak. Other processes, such as group processes and behaviors that occur in a sequence of steps, are more directly assessed because you can observe them directly.

Response Mode   Some learning objectives specify that students should be able to communicate their knowledge in several ways, solve a problem using several methods, or express themselves in a variety of modalities. For example, students may be required to use written or oral reports, posters, presentation software, or brochures. Do not vary the performance modality just for the sake of variety; rather, let state standards, your curriculum, and learning objectives drive your choices. Also, use alternate modes to accommodate students with disabilities or cultural differences if the mainstream, single mode is not appropriate for them.

Make the Task Clear to Students   Present directions to students that include student-friendly learning target(s) based on your objective(s), the criteria by which you will evaluate performance, and the instructions for completing the task in language that students will understand. Clearly state the time limits and the conditions under which you want the task done. Be sure students understand how long a response you are expecting. Share with students the rubrics you will use to assess their performance.

When students misinterpret a task, you cannot validly interpret their assessment results in the same way as you do those students who interpreted the task correctly. Students from certain ethnic, linguistic, or gender groups may not interpret your wording as you expect them to (Lane et al., 1992).

Number of Tasks   As a general rule, the fewer the number of tasks, the fewer learning objectives you can assess, the lower the score reliability, and the lower the validity of your interpretations. The number of performance tasks to include in your assessment depends on several factors; however, some of these factors you cannot control. You need to resolve the following issues to decide on the appropriate number of tasks:

1. *Crucial decisions.* What decisions will you make on the basis of the results of your performance assessment? Higher-stakes decisions require more tasks than lower-stakes decisions.

2. *Scope of your assessment.* How much instruction are you covering with this assessment—a unit or only one lesson? How much content is covered in a unit? The broader the scope of your assessment, the more tasks you will need.

3. *Mixture of assessment formats.* If you mix objective formats with performance tasks, you will be able to cover more aspects of the learning objectives, balance your assessment, and broaden your assessment scope. In this case, you may need fewer performance tasks because your assessment scope will be broader than if you used performance tasks alone.

4. *Complexity of the learning objective.* A complex learning objective requires integration of many skills and abilities and the task may need to be performed over a long time. In this case, practicality limits the number of tasks of this type you may give. Because more time is devoted to one (or at most a few) such tasks, the information may be quite reliable, but the scope or span of your assessment may not be very broad, which could present a validity problem.

5. *Time needed to complete each task.* As a practical matter, you can administer only a few tasks during a typical class period. Estimate how much time one task will take students to complete, and divide this into the length of the class period to determine the maximum number of tasks possible.

6. *Time available for the total assessment.* The number of tasks may shrink or expand depending on the available time.

7. *Diagnostic detail needed.* If you need a lot of detail to diagnose a student's learning or conceptual problems, you need to craft tasks that provide this rich detail, which usually means fewer tasks, more detailed performance, and more detailed scoring of the responses.

8. *Available human resources.* If you have an aide or a parent to help you administer or score the assessments, this help may free up some time so that you can give a few more tasks.

Evaluate Your Performance Tasks Use this checklist to evaluate individual performance tasks.

Checklist

A Checklist for Evaluating the Quality of Performance Tasks

Ask these questions of every performance task you design. If you answer no to one or more questions, revise the task accordingly before administering it to students.

1. Does the task focus on an important aspect of the unit's learning objectives?

2. Does the task match your assessment plan in terms of performance, emphasis, and number of points (marks)?

3. Does the task actually require a student to *do* something (i.e., a performance) rather than requiring only writing about how to do it, or simply to recall or copy information?

4. Do you allow enough time, so all of your students can complete the task under your specified conditions?

5. *If this is an open-response task,* do your wording and directions make it clear to students that they may use a variety of approaches and strategies, that you will accept more than one answer as correct, and that they need to fully elaborate their response?

6. *If the task is intended to be authentic or realistic,* do you present a situation that your level of students will recognize as coming from the real world?

7. *If this task requires using resources and locating information outside the classroom,* will all of your students have fair and equal access to the expected resources?

8. Do your directions and other wording:
   a. define a task that is appropriate to the educational maturity of your students?
   b. lead all students, including those from diverse cultural and ethnic backgrounds, to interpret the task requirements in the way you intend?
   c. make clear the purpose or goal of the task?
   d. make clear the length or the degree of elaboration of the response that you expect?
   e. make clear the bases on which you will evaluate the responses to the task?

9. Are the drawings, graphs, diagrams, charts, manipulatives, and other task materials clearly drawn, properly constructed, appropriate to the intended performance, and in good working order?

10. If you have students with disabilities in your class, have you modified or adapted the task to accommodate their needs?

FIGURE 13.6 Scoring schemes for performance assessment.

Recording method	Description	Recommended use	Example of uses
Checklists	Criteria: A list of specific steps in a procedure or specific behaviors. Scale: A yes/no or present/absent decision for each item on the list.	Primarily useful if the behaviors are in a sequence or if all the subtasks that make up the complete performance can be listed.	Assessing students performing the steps in setting up a microscope properly. Assessing students properly completing all the steps necessary to change the oil in a car.
Rating scales	Criteria: Achievement dimensions to be observed in the performance. Scale: A range of levels for rating the degree to which the quality represented in the criterion was present in the work.	Useful if each criterion can be judged according to the level or the degree of quality rather than as simply being present or absent.	Rating students' paintings on composition, texture, theme, and technique. Rating students' problem solutions for the level of mathematical knowledge, strategy use, and mathematical communication.
Rubrics	Criteria: Achievement dimensions to be observed in the performance. Scale: A range of performance levels with descriptions of what good work looks like at each level (or at every other level).	Useful for classroom instruction and assessment. Rubrics place descriptions in the hands of students, who can use them to produce work and to monitor their own work. Teachers can use them to clarify learning objectives at the beginning of a lesson and to evaluate achievement at the end of a lesson.	Evaluating a term paper according to quality of thesis, accuracy and completeness of content supporting the thesis, and quality of written presentation.

Step Three: Designing Scoring Schemes

The scoring scheme design is part of the performance assessment because the scoring scheme must give attention to the appropriate criteria in order for the assessment results to be meaningful. For example, if you have a rich problem-solving task that allows many different routes to a solution and requires students to explain their reasoning, but the scoring scheme only allocates points to a correct answer, the assessment results (the score) do not in fact indicate much about students' problem solving.

Rubrics, checklists, and rating scales are the most common scoring schemes used with performance assessment. Figure 13.6 summarizes their characteristics. The following sections describe how to develop rubrics, checklists, and rating scales.

Rubrics

Rubrics are coherent sets of criteria for students' work that include descriptions of levels of performance quality on the criteria. They differ from rating scales in that rating scales have coherent sets of criteria, but the continuum of performance is indicated with ratings, not performance level descriptions. Rubrics not only improve scoring consistency, they also improve validity by clarifying the standards of achievement you will use to evaluate your students.

Criteria Base your criteria on the learning objectives assessed, not the directions or elements of the task used to assess them. For example, for a report on a famous person, the criteria would not be Cover, Text, Visuals, and References, but rather characteristics of the learning that the student's report should demonstrate, perhaps Selection of subject, Analysis of famous person's contribution to history, Support with appropriate historical facts and reasoning. The most difficult part of creating effective rubrics is avoiding the trap of making rubrics that provide evidence that students followed their directions instead of providing evidence of students' learning (Brookhart, 2013a).

This checklist provides criteria for evaluating the criteria (pun not intended!) you select for rubrics.

Checklist

A Checklist for Evaluating the Criteria in Rubrics

Ask these questions of every criterion you intend to assess. If you answer no to one or more questions, revise the criteria accordingly.

1. *Does each criterion represent a characteristic that should be evident in the work of a student who had attained the intended standard, curricular goal, or instructional goal or objective?* In other words, is the criterion appropriate? Are the criteria faithful to the way the task should be performed outside the assessment context?

2. *Does each criterion have a clear, agreed-upon meaning that both students and teachers understand?* Is the criterion definable?

3. *Does each criterion describe a quality in the performance that can be perceived (seen or heard, usually) by someone other than the person performing?* Is the criterion observable?

4. *Does each criterion identify a separate aspect of the learning outcomes the performance is intended to assess?* Is the criterion distinct enough to support a separate judgment?

5. *Do all the criteria as a set describe the whole of the learning outcomes the performance is intended to assess?* Is the criterion list complete?

6. *Does each criterion support description over a range of performance levels?* With these supporting descriptions, would the criteria be useful for pointing to the ways students can improve?

Performance-Level Descriptions   Once you have decided on criteria, think of them each as ranging along a continuum of performance. Decide how many levels of performance you are going to describe. Never have more levels than you can distinguish and describe observable differences in student work. If you have no reason to do otherwise, use the number of levels that you will eventually need to use for report cards, typically four or five. Usually, you can use between three and five categories, such as A, B, C, D, and F; distinguished, proficient, apprentice, and novice; or 4, 3, 2, and 1. If your school uses grades A through F, for example, then you need five categories. Using only three quality levels in a scoring rubric will make your student evaluations unnecessarily complicated.

The most important principle for writing performance level descriptions of the levels is that they are true descriptions, not judgments (e.g., "thorough treatment of the topic" not "excellent

treatment of the topic"). Use language that depicts what qualities you will observe in the work rather than the conclusions you will eventually draw for summative evaluation. For example, *describe* what constitutes an A performance, a B performance, and so on, do not simply characterize A as Excellent and B as Good. To help you use the descriptions more reliably, select *specimens* or **exemplars** that are good examples of each scoring category. You can then compare the current students' answers to the exemplars that define each quality level.

This checklist provides criteria for evaluating the performance level descriptions you write for rubrics.

Checklist

A Checklist for Evaluating the Performance-Level Descriptions in Rubrics

Ask these questions of every set of performance-level descriptions you write for a given criterion. If you answer no to one or more questions, revise the performance-level descriptions accordingly.

1. *Are the performance-level descriptions truly descriptive?* Do they describe performance in terms of what is observed in the work, rather than evaluative judgments?

2. *Are the performance-level descriptions clear?* Do both students and teachers understand their meaning?

3. *Taken as a whole, do the performance-level descriptions cover the whole range of performance?* Is performance described from one extreme of the continuum of quality to another for each criterion, even if you do not expect some of the levels to be used (e.g., the lowest level on some criteria)?

4. *Are the performance-level descriptions sufficiently distinct across the continuum that you could distinguish among levels of student work?* Are the descriptions different enough from level to level that you can categorize work unambiguously? Is it possible to match examples of work to performance descriptions at each level?

5. *Are the descriptions of performance centered at the appropriate level?* For example, if the levels are Advanced, Proficient, Nearing Proficient, and Novice, does the description of performance at the "Proficient" level match what is expected for proficiency for the standard and grade level?

6. *Are the descriptions of performance parallel from one level to another?* Do performance descriptions at each level of the continuum for a given criterion describe different quality levels for the same aspects of the work?

People use many different strategies for actually writing rubrics. Most of them fall into one of two categories. The "top-down" method is deductive, reasoning from the objectives to criteria and performance-level descriptions. The "bottom-up" method is inductive, reasoning from student work to criteria and performance-level descriptions. Either method can be done by the teacher alone or with students. The two methods for creating rubrics do not necessarily lead to the same end product, and they are not equivalent procedures.

Melissa Vernon, Grade 1 teacher
Jefferson City Public Schools, Jefferson City, MO

MyLab Education

Video Example 13.1

A first grade teacher shows how sharing examples of strong and weak work can help students get a clear idea of the criteria for performance assessment. The term "exemplars" is sometimes used for examples used in this way. Listen to how the teacher talks with her students and how their responses illustrate what they are thinking about the criteria.

Designing Scoring Rubrics: The Top-Down Approach

To use a top-down approach, follow these steps:

Step 1. Adapt or create a list of the criteria or achievement dimensions that describe the qualities you will be assessing in students' work. Use the checklist for evaluating criteria (above).

Step 2. Develop descriptions of what student performance would look like at each performance level of each dimension. Use the checklist for evaluating performance-level descriptions (above).

Step 3. Share the rubric with students. Illustrate each level of each dimension with exemplars if you can. Have students match exemplars to the rubric and explain what the performance-level descriptions mean to them to make sure the descriptions are understandable.

Step 4. Use the rubric to assess the performances of several students. If you have sample work, students can do this with you.

Step 5. Revise the rubric as necessary. A first draft may need fine-tuning to make sure that everyone understands and interprets the criteria and performance-level descriptions in the intended manner.

Designing Scoring Rubrics: The Bottom-Up Approach

With the bottom-up approach you begin with samples of students' work to identify both criteria and performance-level descriptions. Follow these steps:

Step 1. Obtain copies of about 10 to 12 students' actual responses to a performance item. Be sure the responses you select illustrate various levels of quality of the general achievement you are assessing (e.g., science understanding, letter writing, critical reasoning, etc.) so that you can see what qualities of the work vary.

Step 2. Read the responses and sort all of them into three groups: high-quality responses, medium-quality responses, and low-quality responses. Alternatively, you can ask students to do this sorting. For tasks with which they have some experience (e.g., writing), and for which they therefore have some basis to begin to judge quality, this assignment is a particularly powerful learning experience. The resulting bottom-up rubrics that students have helped create can be used for student self-evaluation and teacher-provided formative feedback.

Step 3. After sorting, write (or have students write) very specific reasons why each response is in a particular group. How are the students' responses in one group (e.g., high-quality group) different from the responses in each of the other groups? Be as specific as you can. For example, don't say they write better or have better ideas. Rather, say the students' sentences are more complex, or the students express unusual ideas in a very clear way. Write a specific and complete explanation on every student's response as to why it is placed into the group. Move a student's response into a different category if it turns out to fit better there.

Step 4. Look at your comments across all categories and identify (or have students identify) the emerging dimensions. In essence, you are creating your own criteria in this step of the process. For example, if the responses are for a mathematics task, you may see computation, complete explanations, logical approach, and good mathematical reasoning as the dimensions.

Step 5. Separately for each of the three quality levels of each achievement dimension you identified in Step 4, write (or have students write) a specific student-centered description of what the responses at that level are typically like. The descriptions become the scoring rubric for marking new responses.

MyLab Education

Video Example 13.2

A high school student describes how students in his class co-create criteria for performance assessments, using the "bottom-up" approach described in the text.

Types of Rubrics

Rubrics can be categorized according to whether they use one scale or several and according to whether the descriptions of work quality are general (i.e., can be applied to many different tasks) or specific to the particular task. Figure 13.7 describes these types of rubrics and the advantages and disadvantages of each.

General rubrics describe performance quality in general terms, so the scoring can be applied to many different tasks. **Task-specific rubrics** describe performance quality in terms that reference the specific assignment. Note that whether a rubric is analytic or holistic is independent of whether it is general or task-specific. Rubrics can be described on both factors.

FIGURE 13.7   Advantages and disadvantages of different types of rubrics.

Type of rubric	Definition	Advantages	Disadvantages
Holistic or Analytic: One or Several Judgments?			
Analytic	■ Each criterion (dimension, trait) is evaluated separately.	■ Gives diagnostic information to teacher ■ Gives formative feedback to students. ■ Easier to link to instruction than holistic rubrics. ■ Good for formative assessment; adaptable for summative assessment; if you need an overall score for grading, you can combine the scores.	■ Takes more time to score than holistic rubrics. ■ Takes more time to achieve inter-rater reliability than with holistic rubrics.
Holistic	■ All criteria (dimensions, traits) are evaluated simultaneously.	■ Scoring is faster than with analytic rubrics. ■ Requires less time to achieve inter-rater reliability. ■ Good for summative assessment.	■ Single overall score does not communicate information about what to do to improve. ■ Not good for formative assessment.
Description of Performance: General or Task-Specific?			
General	■ Description of work gives characteristics that apply to a whole family of tasks (e.g., writing, problem solving).	■ Can share with students, explicitly linking assessment and instruction. ■ Reuse same rubrics with several tasks or assignments. ■ Supports learning by helping students see "good work" as bigger than one task. ■ Support student self-evaluation. ■ Students can help construct generic rubrics.	■ Lower reliability at first than with task-specific rubrics. ■ Requires practice to apply well.
Task-specific	■ Description of work refers to the specific content of a particular task (e.g., gives an answer, specifies a conclusion).	■ Teachers sometimes say using these makes scoring "easier." ■ Requires less time to achieve inter-rater reliability.	■ Cannot share with students (would give away answers). ■ Need to write new rubrics for each task. ■ For open-ended tasks, good answers not listed in rubrics may be evaluated poorly.

Analytic Scoring Rubrics An **analytic scoring rubric** (also called *scoring key*, *point scale*, or *trait scale*) requires you to evaluate specific dimensions, traits, or elements of a student's response. List the major criteria of good work (sometimes called *dimensions* or *traits*) and prepare performance-level descriptions for each of these criteria. An example of an analytic, task-specific scoring rubric for a restricted-response essay was presented in Chapter 12. Examples of general **analytic rubrics** for evaluating collaboration and cooperation were presented in Figure 13.3. The scales may all be of equal weight, or you may decide one or more of the aspects of performance is worth more points.

Usually students' responses will match the scoring rubric to various degrees. Assigning a rubric level to particular student work is like a "choose the best answer" type of multiple-choice question. The score is the one whose description most closely matches a student's work. The top and bottom of a rubric scale are usually easier categories to decide than the middle. The more consistently you match student work to rubric levels, the more reliable the scoring process.

A clear advantage of the analytic scoring rubric is that it provides you and your students with much more detail about their strengths and weaknesses. If you use an analytic scoring rubric, take advantage of this added information to enhance your teaching and to give students guidance concerning what they need to do to improve, both in the individual feedback you give to students and in instructional planning. For example, you could identify which elements or parts of the entire class's answers are weakest and direct your reteaching to that aspect, and also give your students specific feedback about those parts of the answer on which they did well.

Holistic Scoring Rubrics A **holistic scoring rubric** (also called global, sorting, or rating) requires you to make a judgment about the overall quality of each student's response. Holistic scoring is appropriate for extended-response subject-matter essays or papers involving a student's abilities to synthesize and create when no single description of good work can be prespecified. It is also appropriate for final exams or projects where giving feedback to students is not a consideration. States that do large-scale assessment of either writing or subject-matter essay responses often

prefer holistic scoring. The large numbers of papers to be marked often precludes the detailed scoring required by analytic rubrics. An example of a holistic, task-specific scoring rubric for a restricted-response essay was presented in Chapter 12.

Holistic rubrics still need criteria for good work. The difference is that for analytic rubrics, descriptions of levels of performance on each criterion are considered separately. For holistic rubrics, levels of performance on all criteria are considered simultaneously. The description that best fits the student work identifies the score to be given. Holistic scoring rubrics are easier to use and take less time for scoring than analytic rubrics. They permit an overall evaluation, which allows the rater to report a general impression over all aspects of the performance. Note that holistic and analytic scoring rubrics probably assess a student's performance differently (Taylor, 1998).

General Rubrics **General rubrics** use descriptions of work that apply to a whole family or set of assignments. General rubrics for writing, math problem solving, science laboratory work, analyzing literature, and so on are important instructional as well as assessment tools. As students practice and perform many different learning objectives in a subject throughout the school year, their learning improves if they apply the same general evaluation framework to all of the same type of work in that subject. Some research evidence supports the idea that when students routinely use general, but analytic, rubrics in the classroom, their achievement improves (Coe, Hanita, Nishioka, & Smiley, 2011). The Nebraska writing assessment rubric in Figure 12.4 is an example of a general, analytic rubric. Because of the instructional and formative assessment advantages, general, analytic rubrics are the kind you should use whenever students are involved in the assessment process—which should be most of the time.

For example, the Project Report rubric in Figure 13.8 is a general, analytic rubric that can be used each time a project report is assigned for different projects. Students who use this rubric several times will begin to understand what it means to have good content in a report, good thinking and communication, good organization and mechanics, and a good oral presentation. Students

FIGURE 13.8 Example of general, analytic rubrics for a project report.

	Exceeds Expectations	Meets Expectations	Approaching Expectations	Not Yet
Content	Report shows a thorough understanding of the concept and/or issue in the thesis or research question: by relating the concept/issue to other issues, by offering new ideas, or by a deep and nuanced analysis.	Report shows a complete and correct understanding of the concept and/or issue in the thesis or research question.	Report shows partial mastery of the concept and/or issue in the thesis or research question.	Report shows serious misconceptions or lack of understanding of the concept and/or issue in the thesis or research question; OR, there is no credible research question.
Thinking and Communication	Report states and justifies a sound thesis or research question addressing a clear issue in a complex or multi-faceted manner. Report carries readers along as the content and argument explore the thesis or answer the question.	Report states and justifies a sound thesis or research question. Report clearly explores the thesis or answers the question.	Report states and explains a thesis or research question. Report explores the thesis or answers the question, with some irrelevancies or lapses in logic.	Report does not state a thesis or research question, OR states an irrelevant or illogical thesis or question. Report does not follow from the thesis or question.
Organization and Mechanics	Report is organized and easy to follow. An organizing scheme (e.g., by time, or geography, or by steps in a procedure or argument) is used to carry the reader along. Report is readable: few if any errors in grammar or usage.	Report is organized. An organizing scheme is followed, at least most of the time. Report is readable.	Report is somewhat disorganized. An organizing scheme is not present or is misused. Report is somewhat difficult to read and follow.	Report is disorganized. No organizing scheme is apparent. Report is difficult to read and follow.
Oral Presentation	Oral presentation communicates the thesis/research question and important content from the written report, in a manner that is easy to listen to and follow. Written work has been extended for the oral presentation (e.g., with appropriate visuals as teaching aids).	Oral presentation communicates the thesis/ research question and important content from the written report, in a manner that listeners can follow.	Oral presentation communicates some part of a thesis/research question and some content from the written report; listeners may have some difficulty following.	Oral presentation does not communicate a thesis/ research question or much content; often listeners cannot follow.

could use this rubric for planning and self-assessment as they work on their report, and teachers could base feedback of outlines, drafts, and other partial products on the expectations in this rubric. When the time came for the final report to be graded, the teacher might consider weighting the Content criterion, or the Content and the Thinking and Communication criteria, double.

The mathematics problem-solving rubric in Figure 13.9 is an example of a general, holistic rubric for middle school mathematics. It has been organized around three criteria: mathematical knowledge, strategic knowledge, and communication (Lane, 1992). This three-part organization helps define the specific descriptions for each performance level on the rubric.

Task-Specific Rubrics A task-specific scoring rubric is a scoring scale that describes student performance in a way that is specific to a particular task. Here is an example of a holistic, task-specific scoring rubric. Of course, since the rubric is task-specific, we need to present the task as well for the rubric to make sense.

Example

Task: Ben sees a sign on the door of the movie theater. It says: "No food or drinks may be brought in from the outside." Is this an example of a rule or a law? Fill in the oval of your answer below [rule/law] and tell your reasons for choosing the answer you did.

Holistic, task-specific scoring rubric

Complete— "Rule" is marked and response shows an understanding that (governments) legislatures make laws, while here the theater owner or manager simply decided not to allow food or drinks in the theater.

FIGURE 13.9   Example of a holistic general scoring rubric for mathematics problem-solving tasks.

Score level = 4

Mathematical knowledge

- Shows understanding of the problem's mathematical concepts and principles;
- Uses appropriate mathematical terminology and notations;
- Executes algorithms completely and correctly.

Strategic knowledge

- May use relevant outside information of a formal or informal nature;
- Identifies all the important elements of the problem and shows understanding of the relationships between them;
- Reflects an appropriate and systematic strategy for solving the problem;
- Gives clear evidence of a solution process, and solution process is complete and systematic.

Communication

- Gives a complete response with a clear, unambiguous explanation and/or description;
- May include an appropriate and complete diagram;
- Communicates effectively to the identified audience;
- Presents strong supporting arguments which are logically sound and complete;
- May include examples and counter examples.

Score level = 3

Mathematical knowledge

- Shows nearly complete understanding of the problem's mathematical concepts and principles;
- Uses nearly correct mathematical terminology and notations;
- Executes algorithms completely. Computations are generally correct but may contain minor errors.

Strategic knowledge

- May use relevant outside information of a formal or informal nature;
- Identifies the most important elements of the problems and shows general understanding of the relationships between them;
- Gives clear evidence of a solution process. Solution process is complete or nearly complete, and systematic.

Communication

- Gives a fairly complete response with reasonably clear explanations or descriptions;
- May include a nearly complete, appropriate diagram;
- Generally communicates effectively to the identified audience;
- Presents supporting arguments which are logically sound but may contain some minor gaps.

Score level = 2

Mathematical knowledge

- Shows understanding of the problem's mathematical concepts and principles;
- May contain serious computational errors.

Strategic knowledge

- Identifies some important elements of the problems but shows only limited understanding of the relationships between them;
- Gives some evidence of a solution process, but solution process may be incomplete or somewhat unsystematic.

Communication

- Makes significant progress towards completion of the problem, but the explanation or description may be somewhat ambiguous or unclear;
- May include a diagram which is flawed or unclear;
- Communication may be somewhat vague or difficult to interpret;
- Argumentation may be incomplete or may be based on a logically unsound premise.

Score level = 1

Mathematical knowledge

- Shows very limited understanding of the problem's mathematical concepts and principles;
- May misuse or fail to use mathematical terms;
- May make major computational errors.

Strategic knowledge

- May attempt to use irrelevant outside information;
- Fails to identify important elements or places too much emphasis on unimportant elements;
- May reflect an inappropriate strategy for solving the problem;
- Gives incomplete evidence of a solution process; solution process may be missing, difficult to identify, or completely unsystematic.

Communication

- Has some satisfactory elements but may fail to complete or may omit significant parts of the problem; explanation or description may be missing or difficult to follow;
- May include a diagram which incorrectly represents the problem situation, or diagram may be unclear and difficult to interpret.

Score level = 0

Mathematical knowledge

- Shows no understanding of the problem's mathematical concepts and principles.

Strategic knowledge

- May attempt to use irrelevant outside information;
- Fails to indicate which elements of the problem are appropriate;
- Copies part of the problem, but without attempting a solution.

Communication

- Communicates ineffectively; words do not reflect the problem;
- May include drawings which completely misrepresent the problem situation.

Source: From "The Conceptual Framework for the Development of a Mathematics Performance Assessment Instrument," by S. Lane, 1992, *Educational Measurement: Issues and Practice*, 12(2), p. 23. Copyright 1992 by the National Council on Measurement in Education. Reprinted by permission of Wiley-Blackwell.

Acceptable—"Rule" is marked and response explains that the rule is specific only to this theater, OR this is not the case at other theaters, OR that laws must be obeyed by everyone.

Partial—"Rule" is marked, but explanation is weak (e.g., "A law is more serious.") or not present.

Unacceptable—"Law" is marked.

Source: National Assessment of Educational Progress released item, Grade 4, 1998, Block C7 #2.

Task-specific rubrics make scoring somewhat easier and more reliable at first, but they have serious disadvantages that lead us to recommend you only use task-specific rubrics for special purposes. First, you need to write a new rubric for each task, which means even though scoring takes less time, overall using task-specific rubrics takes more time than using general rubrics. Second, you cannot give students task-specific rubrics to use in their work. They lose out on the consistency and instructional value of considering general qualities of good work over a variety of tasks. However, task-specific rubrics are very useful for some purposes. They make for reliable and efficient scoring of essay questions or show-the-work problems on exams, which is probably their best use.

Checklists

A checklist consists of a list of specific behaviors, characteristics, or activities and a place for marking whether each is present or absent. You may use a checklist for assessing procedures students use, products students produce, or behaviors students exhibit. Students may use checklists to evaluate their own performance.

A **procedure checklist** assesses whether students follow the appropriate steps in a process or procedure. For example, a checklist may assess whether students are able to use a microscope properly. The form represents both the presence or absence of each step and the sequence that a particular student used to perform the task. Sometimes the major flaw in a student's performance is the order in which he or she performs the steps. Recording the correct sequence and the student's sequence on the form will help you attend to this aspect of performance.

A **product checklist** focuses on the quality of the things students make. Products include drawings, constructed models, essays, and term papers. These checklists identify the parts or other properties a product is supposed to have. You then inspect each product, checking whether those properties are present.

A **behavior checklist** consists of a list of discrete behaviors related to a specific area of student performance. For example, you may wish to identify the particular difficulties a student is having in the phonological, semantic, and syntactic aspects of spoken language. The behavior checklist might have items such as "uses only simple sentence structure" or "responds without delay to questions."

Students use a **self-evaluation checklist** to review and evaluate their own work. For example, many primary teachers teach students to use checklists like the one in this example as they are learning to write sentences. Some early primary teachers use a version of this checklist with just capital letter, period, and complete thought as the items to check.

Example

___

My sentence

_____ starts with a capital letter.

_____ ends with a period, question mark, or exclamation mark.

_____ is a complete thought.

_____ has a subject (naming part).

_____ has a predicate (telling part).

Teachers who use learning-focused rubrics like the one in Figure 13.8 sometimes use student self-evaluation checklists to help students make sure they have followed all the directions, and their assignment is ready to turn in. It is important to note that self-evaluation of fulfilling the requirements for the assignment is preliminary and formative. If using the checklist reveals that requirements are not met, the student knows what else needs to be done. It is *not* used for the grade for the assignment; the learning-focused rubrics, which the student has also been using formatively, are used for the grade. This kind of self-evaluation checklist is simply an aid to help students ascertain whether they have followed all necessary directions.

For example, consider the case of a middle school class that did projects about recycling. Groups of students were allowed to design their own project and work on it together; then each student had to write his or her own report. One group interviewed school cafeteria workers and designed a project to cut down on waste in the kitchen and lunchroom. One group designed a brochure for citizens explaining what they could do to run a more environmentally friendly home, then met with the mayor of the town and planned how to distribute the brochure, and so on. All of the students had to prepare final reports for grading with the rubric in Figure 13.8. However, before they turned in their reports, they used a self-evaluation checklist to make sure they had followed the directions and the reports had all their required elements, as below. This checklist served to evaluate following directions while there was still time to improve the reports if necessary, and it also served to separate evaluating the requirements of the assignment (ungraded) from evaluating the achievement dimensions (the criteria in Figure 13.8, which were part of the grade).

Example

My project report has

_____ a cover with my name, the date, and the title of the report

_____ an introduction that explains what the project was about and why we did it

_____ a section that explains what we did

_____ a section that explains our results or what happened

_____ a description of an interview of at least one person

_____ information from at least five written sources (including at least two books and at least two Internet sites)

_____ at least four charts, tables, graphs, or pictures

_____ a total of at least eight pages

_____ a bibliography in MLA style

Students can check to make sure that their own assignments meet all the requirements, or peers can do this. Wiliam (2011, p. 141) calls the strategy of having a peer "sign off" on the completeness of a classmate's assignment a "preflight checklist."

How to Create Checklists To create checklists, analyze the procedure you are evaluating or specify the precise characteristics of the desired student product. To create a *product checklist*, as for any scoring scheme, refer to the learning objective(s) you are assessing. What qualities must be present or absent in order to give evidence that the students have achieved these goals? It will help to examine several students' products—especially those products that differ greatly in quality. This examination will help you identify the characteristics and flaws you want to include in your checklist.

To create the kind of product checklist students can use to check whether they have followed the requirements for an assignment, use the directions you gave students for the assignment in the first place. Express the directions as a list of required attributes for the finished assignment (e.g., is word processed, has at least three sources).

To create a *procedure checklist*, first observe and study students performing, so you can identify all the appropriate steps. List each specific step in the procedure you want students to follow. Add to the list specific errors that students commonly make, but avoid unwieldy lists. Order the correct steps and the errors in the approximate sequence in which they should occur. Note that if several equally correct procedures for accomplishing the learning objective are available, developing a checklist this way will not be useful.

Rating Scales

A rating scale assesses the *degree to which* students have attained the achievement dimensions in the performance task. They typically use a frequency scale (e.g., always, frequently, sometimes, never) or an intensity scale (e.g., a great deal, somewhat, not at all). Because rubrics provide performance-level descriptions for each degree of attainment, rubrics are generally preferred over rating scales for academic performances. The descriptions help the student figure out what to do next to improve.

Rating scales are particularly useful for evaluating work habits and learning skills. Frequency scales, especially, are well suited to this purpose. As more and more districts are using standards-based report cards and separating academic achievement from work habits and learning skills, such rating scales are growing in importance. On some report cards, work habits and learning skills go by other names, for example "citizenship." Here is an example of part of a work habits scale from a typical standards-based report card.

Example

These and other work habits items are listed with columns for each report period. The rating scale used is Consistently, Often, Sometimes, Never.

Works independently

Follows directions

Completes class work on time

Returns homework on time

Sometimes you will see rating scales that are intended to be rubrics for evaluating academic products, but instead of listing criteria they list parts of the assignment and a grade. Beware of these! Here is an example of a very poor rating scale that someone who has not read this book might think would be a good way to evaluate the project report from Figure 13.8. As you can see, this is a rating scale masquerading as a rubric and gives the student no more information than the traditional practice of writing a letter or number on the work.

Example

This is a POOR example. It is an evaluative rating scale, listing the parts of a project and a grade for each, instead of listing criteria related to the intended learning and descriptions of performance at each level.

Cover: The cover includes name, date, and project title.

Excellent   Good   Fair   Poor

Introduction: The introduction explains what the project was about and why we did it.

Excellent   Good   Fair   Poor

Project procedure: This section explains what we did for the project.

Excellent   Good   Fair   Poor

Results: This section explains what happened when we did our project.

Excellent   Good   Fair   Poor

Interview: There is a personal interview of an adult who helped us with the project.

Excellent   Good   Fair   Poor

Visuals: The report has at least four tables, charts, or graphs that relate to the project.

Excellent   Good   Fair   Poor

Bibliography: We used at least five written sources, including at least two books and Internet sites, and listed them in MLA style.

Excellent   Good   Fair   Poor

The solution to the problem of poor rating scales such as this one is to ask yourself, not "What were the students supposed to *do*?" but rather "What were the students supposed to *learn*?"

Types of Rating Scales Although there are many varieties of rating scales, two varieties—numerical rating scales and graphic rating scales—serve for most classroom purposes.

To use a **numerical rating scale**, you must mentally translate judgments of quality or degree of achievement into numbers. However, simply providing students with a numerical rating (e.g., "on a scale of 1 to 5") does not give students much information. You will increase objectivity and consistency in results from numerical rating scales if you provide a short verbal description of the quality level each number represents. Alternately, you can associate each numerical level with an example or actual specimen of the products you are rating. The *Thorndike Handwriting Scale*, illustrated in Figure 13.10, is an example of the latter. In fact, this classic numerical rating scale functions much like a modern rubric with the exemplars at each quality level taking the place of a verbal performance-level description.

Graphic rating scales use an unbroken line to represent the particular achievement dimension on which you rate a student's performance or product. Verbal labels describing levels of quality define different parts of the line. Figure 13.11 is an example of a simple graphic rating scale that a teacher might use to rate a student's attainment of cooperative learning objectives in a group project: another example of the usefulness of a frequency scale for indicating student accomplishment of behavioral and work habits–type goals. In Figure 13.11, the end points of the line are "anchored" by Never and Always; Seldom, Occasionally, and Frequently define intermediate levels of achievement.

On a graphic rating scale, you can check any point along the line, not just the defined points. Thus, the graphic rating scale does not force your rating into a discrete category or into being a whole number, as does the numerical rating method. In practice, a serious problem with the use of verbal labels such as *usually*, *seldom*, and *frequently* is that they are undefined; different raters do not agree on what they mean (Betts & Hartley, 2012). Defining the levels on the scale

FIGURE 13.10 Example of a scale (Thorndike's) for measuring handwriting. A series of handwriting specimens were scaled on a numerical "quality" scale. To use the scale a student's sample of writing is matched to the quality of one of the specimens and assigned the given numerical value. This figure shows only some of the specimens.

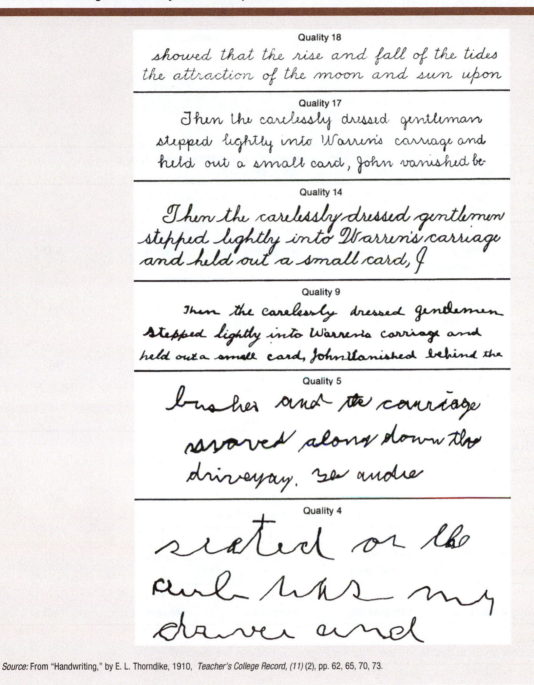

Source: From "Handwriting," by E. L. Thorndike, 1910, *Teacher's College Record, (11)* (2), pp. 62, 65, 70, 73.

with more behavioral descriptions makes your ratings much more consistent and meaningful.

Rating Scale Research

Most research on rating scales has focused on the kind of rating scales used in questionnaires, not rating scales for academic work. Several recent reviews of rating scale research done with adults (Shulruf, Hattie, & Dixon, 2008; Tourangeau, Couper, & Conrad, 2004) and children (Betts & Hartley, 2012; Borgers, Hox, & Sikkel, 2004) focused on questionnaire-type rating scales. This work has converged on some generalizations, although all of them represent conclusions over evidence that does not hold for at least some of the respondents, some of the time.

FIGURE 13.11   A simple graphic scale for assessing cooperative learning objectives with a group project.

Form for Rating Collaboration and Cooperation Learning Targets in a Group Project

Student being assessed: Date:

Other group members:

Project description:

Teacher or observer:

Directions: Place a check mark any place along the line to show judgment of the student's performance on that item. If you have not had sufficient opportunity to observe this student, circle N/O.

ACHIEVEMENT OF GROUP GOALS
1. Does the student attend the group meetings?

| Never | Seldom | Occasionally | Frequently | Always | N/O |

2. When attending is the student prepared?

| Never | Seldom | Occasionally | Frequently | Always | N/O |

3. Does the student work actively toward achieving the group's goals?

| Never | Seldom | Occasionally | Frequently | Always | N/O |

4. Does the student work outside of the group meetings on the group project?

| Never | Seldom | Occasionally | Frequently | Always | N/O |

INTERPERSONAL SKILLS
5. Does the student interact appropriately with the group's members?

| Never | Seldom | Occasionally | Frequently | Always | N/O |

6. Is the student sensitive to the others' feelings when expressing own ideas and views?

| Never | Seldom | Occasionally | Frequently | Always | N/O |

7. Is the student's behavior disruptive to others in the group?

| Never | Seldom | Occasionally | Frequently | Always | N/O |

GROUP MAINTENANCE
8. Does the student help the group to decide whether changes in group processes are needed?

| Never | Seldom | Occasionally | Frequently | Always | N/O |

9. Does the student work actively toward helping the group change its processes when necessary?

| Never | Seldom | Occasionally | Frequently | Always | N/O |

COMMENTS:

In general, the evidence does suggest that how you format and present rating scales may affect the results, at least on survey and attitude measures. Adults seems to interpret rating scales visually, starting with whatever is on the top or the left, and they expect response choices to be arranged in a progression (Tourangeau, Couper, & Conrad, 2004). A study with children (Betts & Hartley, 2012) found that presenting a positive label or a high score on the left, as opposed to the right, led to higher mean ratings. A study with children and adolescents (Borgers, Hox, & Sikkel, 2004) investigated the reliability of ratings using different numbers of options. Interpreting the results of several different analyses of the reliability and stability of the ratings, they recommended rating scales with four options.

The extent to which these findings about questionnaire rating scales generalize to rating scales about academic performance is not clear. Our advice, however, is clear. First, whenever possible, use rubrics instead of rating scales for academic work. One exception is for ratings of behavior, where a simple frequency scale (e.g., Always, Often, Sometimes, Never) is a sensible way to indicate academic behaviors like work habits. For academic learning, the descriptions used in the performance levels for rubrics will be helpful in focusing judgments of quality for both students and teachers. Second, construct rating scales with substance in mind first, and then consider the research results. For example, if there are five scale points that make sense for a particular rating scale, and reducing the options to four would eliminate a logical position, use the five that make conceptual sense.

Scoring Errors

Several common errors occur when teachers evaluate students with either ratings scales or rubrics. Teachers who do not use all of the points on a rating scale or rubric cause the following errors:

- **Leniency error** occurs when a teacher tends to make almost all ratings toward the high end of the scale, avoiding the low end.
- **Severity error** is the opposite of leniency error: A teacher tends to make almost all ratings toward the low end of the scale.
- **Central tendency error** occurs when a teacher hesitates to use extremes and uses only the middle part of the scale. Central tendency errors sometimes occur when a teacher has to make strong inferences about students (e.g., regarding "creativity" or "dedication"), and, in hesitation, the teacher tends to mark nearly everyone as average. Central tendency errors may occur when a teacher does not know the students very well.

Using only certain parts of the rating scale has two negative consequences. First, when you give only very high, very low, or "middle" ratings, you introduce your own quirks and biases into the ratings, thus lowering their validity for describing students' ability in performing the task. Second, when your ratings bunch up and do not distinguish one student's performance from another's, they become unreliable, which in turn reduces the validity of the scores.

There are other common rating scale errors. We mentioned these errors in Chapter 12, because they happen during essay scoring, as well.

- A **halo effect** occurs when teachers lets their general impressions of students affect how they rate the students on specific dimensions. For example, if you gave a student a higher rating for his project than the student deserves because you "just know" that the student is "really" very good, you would be committing the halo effect error. The halo effect may *work in reverse*, of course: Your general impression of a student as "not very good" may lead you to lower ratings on specific dimensions more than the student deserves.)
- **Personal bias** occurs when teachers tend to rate based on inappropriate or irrelevant stereotypes favoring boys over girls, Whites over Blacks, working families over welfare recipients, or particular families and individual students the teachers may dislike.
- A **logical error** occurs when teachers give similar ratings on two or more dimensions of performance that the teachers believe are logically related but that are in fact unrelated. For example, a teacher may falsely believe that students with exceptionally high scores on scholastic aptitude tests also should be the top students in all subject areas. The teacher then marks the high-scoring aptitude test students differently from the way the low scorers are marked.

Other errors occur when "outsiders" rate performance assessments. When states and large school districts implement performance assessments, individuals other than their teachers usually evaluate students' work. In these cases, the raters are trained in and practice using a particular scoring rubric.

■ **Rater drift** occurs when the raters, whose ratings originally agreed, begin to redefine the rubrics for themselves. As a result, the raters no longer produce ratings that agree with the original rubrics even though they were trained on the same rubrics. The remedy for this is to monitor the ratings and to retrain those raters who appear to have drifted away from agreed-on standards.

■ **Reliability decay** is a related error: Immediately after training, raters apply the rubrics consistently across students and mark consistently with one another. However, as time passes, the ratings become less consistent, both across students and across raters. Monitoring and retraining are remedies for this effect, too.

Evaluating Scoring Rubrics and Rating Scales

The checklist below provides guidance for evaluating scoring rubrics and other classroom rating scales. We have already provided checklists for evaluating the criteria and performance-level descriptions in rubrics separately. This checklist allows you to evaluate the overall properties of rubrics or rating scales.

Checklist

A Checklist for Evaluating the Quality of Scoring Rubrics and Rating Scales

Ask these questions of every rubric or rating scale you write. If you answer no to one or more questions, revise the rubric or rating scale accordingly.

1. Overall, does the rubric emphasize the most important content and processes of the learning objectives?

2. Will the scores you get from the parts of your rubric (i.e., the criteria or achievement dimensions) match the emphasis you gave them in your assessment plan?

3. Does the maximum possible total number of marks (points) obtained from the rubric match the emphasis you gave these learning objectives in your assessment plan?

4. Will your students understand the rubric?

5. Are the categories rated with the rubric suitable for giving students the guidance they need to improve their performance on the learning objectives?

6. Is the rubric for this particular task a faithful application of the general rubric or conceptual framework?

7. Are the performance levels for the scales (criteria or achievement dimensions) on the rubric described clearly in terms of performance you can observe students doing?

8. With regard to this particular task, does the rubric allow you to assess the students' use of the appropriate:

a. declarative and procedural content dimensions?

b. processes that are important to the learning objective(s)?

9. If the purpose of this task is to assess students' use of alternative correct answers/products or alternative correct processes/strategies, does the rubric clearly describe how each is to be rated and marked?

10. Does the rubric allow you to distinguish a wide range of students' achievement levels on this task, rather than putting all students into one or two achievement levels?

Improving Reliability of Rubrics and Ratings

The **reliability of ratings** is an important criterion for evaluating performance assessments. Many of the suggestions for improving the reliability of grading essays (Figure 12.6) apply to performance assessments, as well. The following reliability coefficients (discussed in Chapter 4) are among those appropriate to use with the more continuous scores awarded to students from performance assessments. For classroom performance assessments, scorer reliability (teacher consistency in marking) and alternate forms (differences due to students selecting a different task, if that was allowed) are usually the most problematic.

Estimating Reliability Over Time
■ Test-retest
■ Alternate forms on different occasions

Estimating Reliability on a Single Occasion
■ Alternate forms
■ Coefficient alpha
■ Split-halves coefficient

Estimating Scorer Reliability

- Correlation of two scorers' results
- Percentage of agreement
- Kappa coefficient

Appendix G shows how to calculate coefficient alpha, split-halves percentage agreement, and kappa coefficient. However, the appendix shows percent agreement and kappa calculations only for the special case in which pass-fail or mastery-nonmastery decisions are made. Although these two indices can be applied to scores in more than two categories, that is beyond the scope of this book.

Figure 4.8 in Chapter 4 discussed how to improve the reliability of assessment results. Here are additional suggestions that apply specifically to improving the reliability of ratings from scoring rubrics and rating scales:

1. Organize the achievement dimensions within a scoring rubric into logical groups that match the content and process framework of the curriculum.

2. For each achievement dimension, use behavioral descriptors to define each level of performance.

3. Provide specimens or examples of students' work to help define each level of an achievement dimension.

4. Have several teachers work together to develop a scoring rubric or rating scale.

5. Have several teachers review and critique the draft of a scoring rubric or rating scale.

6. Provide training and supervised practice for all persons who will use the scoring rubric or rating scale.

7. Have more than one rater rate each student's performance on the task.

8. Monitor raters by periodically sampling their ratings, checking on the accuracy and consistency with which they are applying the scoring rubrics and rating scales. Retrain those persons whose ratings are inaccurate or inconsistent.

MyLab Education Self-Check 13.2

MyLab Education Application Exercises 13.2:
Analyzing Performance Assessment
Tasks and Rubrics

PORTFOLIOS

Although some consider portfolios a type of performance assessment, they differ enough from other types that we will discuss them separately. For purposes of assessment, a **portfolio** is a limited collection of a student's work used either to present the student's best work(s) or to demonstrate the student's educational growth over a given time. A portfolio is not simply a scrapbook or collection of all of a student's work. The works put into a portfolio are carefully and deliberately selected, so the collection as a whole accomplishes its purpose. Portfolios were extremely popular in the 1980s and 1990s. They were seen as an antidote to "back to the basics" drill and as a way to teach lifelong learning skills like self-reflection and responsibility for one's own learning. Since that time, portfolios have proven themselves more valid and useful for classroom purposes than for large-scale purposes, and for formative purposes more than summative purposes (Brookhart, 2008b).

Many authors have lists of different types of portfolios. Most of them fall into one of two assessment purposes: demonstrating educational growth or presenting one's best work.

Growth Portfolios

A growth portfolio contains examples of a student's work, along with comments, that demonstrate how well the student's learning has progressed over a given period. For this reason, growth portfolios are sometimes called *progress portfolios* (Renwick, 2014). They do not focus on the final products a student produces. Instead, you and the student use the portfolio for formative purposes to monitor the student's learning and thinking progress, to diagnose learning and thinking difficulties, and to guide new learning and thinking. The student plays a significant role in deciding what should be included in this portfolio and learns to use the portfolio to understand and evaluate her own progress. Here are some examples:

Examples

Examples of Growth Portfolios
General purpose: Monitoring progress of individual students
Possible specific purposes
- Teachers and/or students want to review progress and change in achievement.

- Student needs to look over his or her work to see the "long view" or "whole picture" of what has been accomplished.

Contents of the portfolio
- A student's products or works that appear at intermediate stages in the course of the student's learning. These may include early drafts, records of thinking, and rewrites. The final product is placed into the portfolio, too.

General purpose: Daily instruction
Possible specific purposes
- A basis for discussing with the student individual ideas and work.
- Keep a record of changes in a student's thinking and conceptual explanations.
- A basis for diagnosing a student's learning difficulties in a subject.

Contents of the portfolio
- Examples of a student's recently completed work, data the student collected, recent findings from an ongoing investigation in the subject matter, a student's own explanations of the work that is under way, and so on.

The clearer you are about your portfolio learning objectives and purpose(s), the better you are able to design it. If the portfolio must serve more than one purpose, you will need to consider carefully the focus of each portfolio entry so that each entry serves at least one of your intended purposes.

Initial Planning for a Growth Portfolio   The purpose of a growth portfolio is to serve as a tool for you and students to monitor learning, diagnose difficulties, guide new learning, as well as show progress and development. For a growth portfolio to be effective, design it by using the following principles:

1. *Be very clear about the learning objectives or standards toward which you wish to monitor students' learning progress.* The clearer you are, the better your portfolio system will be.

2. *Have a firm understanding of a learning progress theory.* The theory you choose to follow will guide you to identify what you should look for when assessing changes in a student's conceptual development or in diagnosing a student's learning difficulties.

3. *If several teachers in a school are committed to using growth portfolios, collaborate and work cooperatively with them.* If teachers coordinate the general approach, contents to be included, and the portfolio organization, students will not be confused and will receive a consistent message about the nature and purposes of their portfolio activities.

4. *Use some type of rubric to define assessment criteria and to help you be consistent in how you apply these criteria, both across students and with the same student over time.*

Here is an example of an organizational structure for a writing process portfolio in high school.

Example

Standards to be addressed (Common Core Writing Standards Grades 9–10, #4 and #5)
- Produce clear and coherent writing in which the development, organization, and style are appropriate to task, purpose, and audience.
- Develop and strengthen writing as needed by planning, revising, editing, rewriting, or trying a new approach, focusing on addressing what is most significant for a specific purpose and audience.

Exhibits to be put in the portfolio (over the course of one year)
- At least one complete example of the writing process for an expository or informational piece, including brainstorming, outline, free writing, at least one draft with feedback, and final piece—to be chosen by the student
- At least one complete example of the writing process for a narrative piece, including brainstorming, outlining or diagramming, free writing, at least one draft with feedback, and final piece—to be chosen by the student
- Drafts with feedback of analytical, informational, and narrative work (one of each), and their accompanying revisions—to be chosen by the teacher
- Optional additional pieces that the student feels demonstrate specific progress on one of the standards, with annotation—to be chosen by the student
- Each entry is accompanied by a self-reflection
- Mid-year and end-of-year essay-length self-reflection

Students' Self-Evaluation Entries in Growth Portfolios   Notice that the example calls for students to reflect on and evaluate their own progress as writers. Teachers often design portfolio entry forms. These forms contain the questions students are to ask of themselves and a place for them to answer the questions. Structured self-reflection is one of the most important reasons to use a growth portfolio. The evidence—the student's writing—is right there. Here is an example of questions that might be used on an annotation form for one of the entries in the writing portfolio example above.

Example

- Describe one aspect of this piece of writing that shows you have improved as a writer. What is it (e.g., your ideas, development, organization, style), and how do you know this piece is an improvement in that area?

- How do you feel about yourself as a writer when you read this piece? Explain why you feel that way.

- What area of writing do you most want to work on next? Why? Write a specific goal and tell how you will work on it in your next writing pieces.

Growth portfolios, like other assessments, work best when integrated fully into your teaching. Some writers advocate making the portfolio the center of your instructional planning and teaching activities so you and your students will interact intensively with the portfolio contents. The following suggestions are consistent with their views:

1. *Include authentic work.* The work that students include in their portfolio must provide a direct opportunity for them to engage in the types of thinking and abilities typically used by those working in the field or discipline. For example, in a science portfolio, students should work on evaluating evidence, using scientific explanations to account for data, or collecting data to support or refute explanations.

2. *Record conceptual development.* Portfolio entries must record students' own explanations, understandings, and conceptual frameworks. This record must be frequently updated as the students progress through a project or a problem solution to show changes in the students' conceptual framework and thinking as the project develops. It is not enough to include only the finished work. For example, students should periodically record in a science portfolio their current scientific explanation of the events encountered, results observed, and concepts being studied.

3. *Engage in reflective activity.* The students should use the portfolio contents as a basis for discussions with the teacher about their understanding of concepts, principles, and theories that underlie the work. The teacher guides the discussion so that students use the same thinking strategies and abilities used by workers in the fields or discipline. For example, if students are working on a scientific problem, they should use the portfolio contents to engage in scientific thinking and activities. The students should record changes in their explanations as new evidence accumulates.

Best Works Portfolios

A best works portfolio contains a student's best final products. Best works portfolios are primarily for summative purposes, and are sometimes called *performance portfolios* (Renwick, 2014). Here are examples of some of the purposes that best works portfolios serve:

Examples

Examples of Best Works Portfolios
General purpose: Evaluation of individual students
Possible specific purposes
- Evidence of subject-matter mastery and learning
- Evidence of high-level accomplishment in an area such as art or writing
- Evidence of minimal competence in a subject for purposes of graduation
- Evidence of a school district's accomplishments

Contents of the portfolio
- A student's best works are selected to provide convincing evidence that the student has achieved specific learning objectives

General purpose: Communications
Possible specific purposes
- A student's showcase for his or her parents
- Pass on information about a student to the next teacher
- A school's showcase

Contents of the portfolio
- Examples of accomplishments that may be typical or may impress others

Very often the contents of the best works portfolio are prescribed. For example, to certify a student's accomplishment in art, educational authorities may require a drawing, a painting, a sculpture, a craft product, and one work in a medium of the student's choosing. Scoring rubrics for portfolios usually apply to the entire portfolio rather than to each piece separately, although there are exceptions.

Like growth portfolios, best works portfolios are organized around learning objectives or standards. For example, a portfolio may be designed to assess learning objectives in the areas of problem solving, mathematical reasoning, mathematical communication, and understanding the core curriculum concepts. Thus, each portfolio must contain examples of mathematics investigations, applications, solutions to nonroutine problems, projects, interdisciplinary problem solutions, and writing about mathematics. Here is a brief description of the contents of a mathematics best works portfolio intended for summative assessment at the end of a unit.

Example

Standards to be addressed (Common Core Mathematical Practices #1 and #2 and Grade 6 Standards 6.RP #1 and #3)

- Make sense of problems and persevere in solving them.
- Reason abstractly and quantitatively.
- Understand the concept of a ratio and use ratio language to describe a ratio relationship between two quantities.
- Use ratio and rate reasoning to solve real-world and mathematical problems.

Exhibits to be put in the portfolio (over the course of the unit)

- A copy of each returned, graded quiz or test. For each error or for each partially correct answer that could be improved, redo the problem correctly, showing your work and explaining your reasoning.
- Five ratio or rate word problems from other sources besides class assignments or your textbook (e.g., from other textbooks, from the Internet). For each, solve the problem, showing your work and explaining your reasoning, and explain how the problem you selected is related to the work on ratios and rates you have studied this report period. Make sure to use appropriate mathematical vocabulary in your explanations.
- Two original word problems. Write two original problems that use the concepts about ratio and rate that you studied this report period. Get a friend or relative to solve them. Add your own annotation

evaluating your friend or relative's solution and explaining why you evaluated it as you did. Again, use appropriate mathematical vocabulary.

- A self-reflection statement. After correcting your test errors, solving additional problems, and thinking about the solutions of others, what can you say about your understanding of ratios and rates? What are your particular strengths and weaknesses? How will you address those in the next report period?

To be effective, portfolios should emphasize the same standards, curriculum goals, and learning objectives emphasized in your daily instruction. The criteria used to evaluate students' portfolio entries should be the same as those used in daily instruction. If your teaching emphasizes students taking responsibility for their own learning, the portfolio procedure you use should be consistent with this approach (Arter & Spandel, 1992).

A portfolio can quickly become a mess of materials and papers that is difficult to assess. To improve the situation, each entry should have an appropriate portfolio entry sheet (or caption) containing the following information:

- Name of the student.
- Date of entry.
- Title or description of the entry. For example, "Comparison of the Population Growth of Canada and the United States."
- Some indication of the learning objective or purpose for including the entry. A student may write, "This entry shows that I can use numbers in real-world situations to draw conclusions about how populations grow. I can use growth rates and draw conclusions about when the two populations will be the same."
- Why this particular entry is important or valuable. For example, "I think this was a good piece to include because it shows an actual situation in which I had to use mathematics. Population growth is a social studies topic that I applied mathematics to solve. Also, I had to use a computer spreadsheet program to make the calculations many times in order to discover that the two countries will have the same population in about 59 years."

The size of a portfolio is no small matter. A portfolio that contains too many entries is difficult to understand and may be confusing to students who can get lost in the mass of materials. Also, evaluating long portfolios is difficult and time-consuming.

Portfolio size is related to validity and reliability. Does the portfolio represent the student's attainment? How many entries and what varieties of entries are needed to ensure a representative sample of the student's work? Will a long portfolio be scored less consistently than a short portfolio?

Self-Reflection on Portfolio Entries Effective self-reflection can enhance student learning. The reflection must be substantive (not simply comments like "I worked hard") because that requires students to reason with the subject matter. Reflection also develops metacognitive skills. Arter and Spandel (1992) suggest asking students the following types of questions to prompt self-reflective activities:

■ What is the process you went through to complete this assignment? Include where you got ideas, how you explored the subject, what problems you encountered, and what revision strategies you used.

■ What were the points made by the group as it reviewed your work? Describe your response to each point—did you agree or disagree? Why? What did you do as the result of their feedback?

■ What makes your most effective piece different from your least effective piece?

■ How does this activity relate to what you have learned before?

■ What are the strengths of your work? What still makes you uneasy?

Such questions prompt students to review and evaluate their work. When student thinking is made visible, it can be evidence that the student and teacher evaluate together to take stock of where a student is in regard to expected learning outcomes and plan next steps. Thus, even in the context of a best works portfolio intended for summative assessment, that is, intended for grading, the most powerful aspect of the portfolio may still be supporting formative assessment (Brookhart, 2008b).

Six Steps for Crafting a Portfolio System

Because portfolios are used for such a wide range of formative and summative purposes, a single set of design guidelines is difficult to devise. The

six steps that follow are general enough, however, to give you overall guidance in the portfolio-crafting process. Feel free to adapt the steps to suit your particular purposes.

Following each step is a set of portfolio-crafting questions to sharpen the focus of your development efforts. Notice that after answering the questions in Step 1, you may decide *not* to develop a portfolio system. Steps 2 through 5 assume that you have completed Step 1 and have decided to use a portfolio system. If you decide to develop a portfolio system, the answers to the questions in Step 1 will set the boundaries and context as you apply the last five steps.

Step 1. Identify Portfolio's Purpose and Focus

■ Why do I want a portfolio?

■ What learning objectives and curriculum goals will it serve?

■ Will other methods of assessment serve these learning objectives better?

■ Should the portfolio focus on best work, growth and learning progress, or both?

■ Will the portfolio be used for students' summative evaluation, formative evaluation, or both?

■ Who should be involved in defining the purpose, focus, and organization of the portfolio (e.g., students, teachers, parents)?

Step 2. Identify the General Achievement Dimensions to Be Assessed

■ Do I need to use the same content and thinking processes framework as I do for individual performance tasks?

■ Should I focus primarily on how well the students use the portfolio to reflect on their progress or growth?

■ What kinds of knowledge, skills, and abilities will be the major focus of the portfolio?

■ If I require a growth portfolio, what do I want to learn about students' self-reflections?

Step 3. Identify Appropriate Organization

■ What types of entries (student products and activity records) will provide assessment information about the content and process dimensions identified in Step 2?

■ What should the outline or table of contents for each portfolio contain?

■ Define each category or type of entry:
- Which content and process dimension does it assess?
- What will the teacher or the student "get out of" each entry?
- What is the time frame for each entry being put into the portfolio?
- When will the entries be evaluated?
- What are the minimum and maximum numbers of entries per category?
- How will the entries within students' portfolios be organized?
- Will this set of entries fully represent the students' attainment or growth and learning progress?
- What type of container will I need to hold all of the students' entries, and where will I keep them—or will the portfolio be electronic?

Step 4. Portfolio's Use in Practice

■ When will the students work on or use their portfolios (e.g., 15 minutes of every class period)?

■ How will the portfolio fit into the classroom routine?

■ Will the teacher, student, or both decide what to include in the portfolio?

■ Do I need to create a special climate in the classroom to promote the good use of portfolios?

■ When will the students and/or the teacher review and evaluate the portfolios?

■ How will the portfolios be weighted, if at all, when the time comes to assign letter grades for the marking period?

■ Will I schedule a conference to go over the portfolio with the students?

■ Will the portfolio be shared with parents? Other teachers? Other students?

Step 5. Evaluation of Portfolios and Entries

■ Are scoring rubrics already available for each type of entry?

■ Does an evaluation framework or general scoring rubric exist for evaluating the portfolio as a whole?

■ Will students, teachers, or both evaluate entries? Which ones?

■ Will evaluations of every entry count toward a marking-period grade?

■ Given its purpose, is it necessary to have an overall score for the portfolio?

■ Who will score the portfolio (e.g., student, teacher, outsider)?

■ How often will the whole portfolio need to be scored (e.g., each week or each marking period)?

Step 6. Evaluation of Rubrics

■ Are the scoring rubrics consistent with the purpose of the portfolio? Are they aligned with the state standards and school district's curriculum framework?

■ Has the scoring rubric been tried on portfolios from different students? From students with different teachers? With what results?

■ Does the scoring rubric give the same results for the same students when applied by different teachers?

Electronic Portfolios

Textbook publishers and software developers have created products that allow a portfolio to be presented digitally. These are called **electronic portfolios**. A digitized portfolio can reside on a local computer, a CD or DVD, or a website. The software provides an organization for the portfolio contents. Persons then add electronic documents and images in various categories.

Institutions have taken four basic routes to developing e-portfolio system software. At some institutions, the information technology department designs a system locally. Other institutions use open source e-portfolio software, commercially available software from a vendor, or common HTML editing tools like Microsoft Front Page or Adobe Dreamweaver (Lorenzo & Ittelson, 2005). These digital formats allow for a much wider range of portfolio entries than is possible for portfolios that are housed in folders or crates. In theory, this practice should enhance validity because more forms of evidence are possible. However, a digital format does not guarantee appropriate learning objectives or assignments and scoring schemes that reflect those objectives well. Assessment quality principles apply to electronic portfolios, too.

At the present time, electronic portfolios are more common in higher education than in K-12 education (Lorenzo & Ittelson, 2005; Reese & Levy, 2009). Primary purposes for e-portfolios in higher education include academic advising, institutional accreditation and departmental review, curricular development at the program level, career planning and development, and alumni development (Reese & Levy, 2009). The latter, a relatively new development, allows alumni to support their professional development while staying connected with the university and each other through social media like Facebook.

The American Association of Colleges and Universities (AACU) is working to develop an e-portfolio framework for assessing learning outcomes for college students. They intend their portfolios to measure a wider range of learning outcomes than those measured by tests. Their project it titled Valid Assessment of Learning in Undergraduate Education (VALUE). It includes research and development work to highlight commonalities of outcomes and expectation of achievement levels across institutions, as embodied in faculty rubrics and actual student work. Examples from several campuses are available as links on the AACU website (aacu.org).

However, the use of digital portfolios is increasing in K-12 education. Renwick (2014) describes the development of digital portfolios in the elementary school where he is principal and the insights into assessment and learning that are resulting from the use of these portfolios. One of the benefits his school discovered is that digital portfolios can increase access to student work, in two ways. First, digital portfolios can bring parents into the portfolio process more easily than paper portfolios. Paper portfolios require a special event to review with parents, while digital ones can be reviewed at home any time. Second, digital portfolios allow student work to be accessed at multiple times and in multiple locations. For example, many teachers in Renwick's building use Evernote (evernote.com), software that can handle different kinds of media and makes teacher and student notes, videos, and other materials available on any electronic device, using an app. It also supports sending e-mails to parents with specific pieces of student work, at any time.

Of course, just as we have described for paper portfolios, the existence of student work and access to it is not enough. Renwick's teachers discovered students need a purpose for using digital portfolios and a sense that an interested audience (e.g., teachers, parents) existed and would actively review their work and their insights on their work. He observed (Renwick, 2014, p.75), "Providing these tools [digital portfolio tools] for students allows them to draw closer to what they understand and are able to do. They become motivated to do their very best because they know someone is on the other end ready to see and listen, and that their work might benefit others." An important outcome of such cycles of review by parents and teachers is that, no matter what type of portfolio was intended, "summative becomes formative" (p. 77).

Renwick (2014) recommends a whole-school approach to taking up digital portfolios, and points out that a successful schoolwide move to digital portfolios requires teachers and principals have assessment literacy, digital literacy, and change literacy. He recommends starting small, involving staff and students, celebrating small successes and building up to a schoolwide action plan that includes helping educators continue to improve their assessment, digital, and change skills.

It seems clear that digital portfolios are changing in nature as software and apps, multimedia technology, and electronic devices become more and more flexible. One important result of these changes seems to be the possibility of connecting assessment and instruction more closely. As with any changes in assessment and instruction, new teacher competencies are required; digital portfolios must be used skillfully and effectively if they are to have a positive impact. Digital portfolio technologies are not developing in a vacuum, however; technology is infusing many aspects of modern life. Thus, it seems reasonable that these developments will continue in schools, as well, with more and more applications.

MyLab Education Self-Check 13.3

MyLab Education Application Exercise 13.3:
Using Portfolios to Communicate with Parents

CONCLUSION

This chapter has described a broad range of performance-assessment tasks and scoring schemes. We have presented examples and suggestions for each. This completes our description of how to design and construct or write various assessment methods. Next, we turn to how to prepare your students for assessment.

EXERCISES

1. Apply the ideas in Figure 13.1 to a subject you teach or plan to teach. For each category and sub-category, describe one performance assessment applicable to your subject. (Do not use the examples given in the text, but you can adapt them.) You do not have to actually create a workable task. Rather, in one or two sentences describe a task that could be created. Which types of tasks are not applicable to your teaching situation? Explain.

2. Make three columns on a sheet of paper. In the first column, list the task properties from Figure 13.5. Select two performance tasks from either your own experience or from this chapter. Identify the second column with one of these two tasks, the third column with the other. Then, in each cell of the table, describe the task with respect to each property.

3. For a subject you teach (or plan to teach), identify learning objectives that would be appropriately assessed with on-demand performance tasks using a paper-and-pencil format and with on-demand performance tasks not using paper and pencil.
   a. Using these results, create one on-demand performance task using paper and pencil and one on-demand performance task not using paper and pencil.
   b. Exchange your tasks with another student in the course. Evaluate each other's task by applying the checklist for judging the quality of performance tasks. If a task resulted in a no answer to one of the checklist items, explain why. Revise the tasks where necessary.
   c. Share your results with others in the course.

4. Select one performance task that you created in Exercise 1 or that you obtained from other sources. Following the procedures in this chapter, prepare scoring rubrics.
   a. Write a description of each step you used to craft the rubrics.
   b. Exchange your rubrics with another student in the course. Evaluate each other's rubrics using the checklist for judging the quality of scoring rubrics. Whenever your rubrics received a "no" answer to one of the checklist items, explain why. Revise the rubrics where necessary.
   c. Share your results with others in your course.

5. Select two or more learning objectives that can be assessed by one performance task and a corresponding scoring rubric (of your own or others' creation). Justify your selection by explaining how this task best assesses these learning objectives.
   a. Administer the performance task to at least five students. Score the task using the scoring rubric.
   b. Write a short essay describing your scoring experience. Was the scoring rubric adequate? Were there any reliability problems in using it? Why or why not? Make suggestions for improving the scoring rubric based on your experience.
   c. Prepare a summary of your students' results.

6. Design a best works portfolio system for assessing students in the subject you teach (or plan to teach). Follow the six-step procedure suggested in the chapter.
   a. Prepare a report describing the portfolio system you designed. Be sure your report addresses all of the questions listed under each step.
   b. Discuss your portfolio system in class with other students.

Preparing Your Students to Be Assessed and Using Students' Results to Improve Your Assessments

KEY CONCEPTS

1. To prepare students for an upcoming assessment, give students the information and skills they need to perform their best. Testwiseness is the ability to use test-taking strategies, clues from poorly written items, and experience to improve a score beyond that expected from mastery of the subject matter. Test anxiety is increased emotional tension based on a student's appraisal of a testing situation. Use strategies to mitigate both of these.

2. The following will help help you understand students' scores and response patterns. Improve multiple-choice item quality by editing items flagged by unacceptable difficulty or discrimination indices or by poorly functioning distractors.

   a. Correction for guessing formulas adjust scores for expected effects of random choices. They are not recommended for classroom use.

   b. Item-analysis results can be used to improve the quality of true-false, matching, and multiple-choice items. Analogous statistics can be examined for constructed-response (multi-point) tasks.

   c. Item difficulty shows students' average level of performance on a test item.

   d. Item discrimination shows how students' performance on an item is related to their total test performance.

IMPORTANT TERMS

ambiguous alternatives

complete versus partial ordering of students

content analysis of responses

correction for guessing formulas

dichotomous item scoring

homogeneous versus heterogeneous test

item analysis

item bank

item difficulty index (p and p^*)

item discrimination index (D and D^*)

maximum performance assessment

miskeyed items

negatively discriminating item

nondiscriminating item

poorly functioning distractor

positively discriminating item

relative versus absolute achievement

task-directed versus task-irrelevant thoughts

test anxiety

testwiseness

types of test-anxious students

typical performance assessment

upper-, middle-, and lower-scoring groups

PREPARING STUDENTS FOR ASSESSMENT

Assess Maximum, Not Typical, Performance in the Classroom

You assess **maximum performance** when you set the conditions so that students are able to earn the best score they can. You assess **typical performance** when you gather information about what a student would do under ordinary or typical conditions. Assess students' maximum performance rather than their typical performance (Cronbach, 1990).

For example, you may have taught students a practical skill such as balancing a checkbook, and your assessment procedure gathers information about whether each student is capable of doing so. This is maximum performance assessment. Some students may make errors later outside class when actually using checks, or they may never reconcile their checking account. Thus, such students may be *capable* of performing the skill you taught, but may *typically not perform* the skill to their maximum capacity. Because schooling usually attempts to teach learners new abilities at high levels, achievement assessments are carried out under conditions that encourage students to perform to the best of their abilities.

Give Students Enough Information Before Assessing Them

In Chapter 5, we called informing students about an upcoming assessment a professional responsibility. To assess students under the best conditions, you should provide at least the following information about your upcoming assessment:

1. When it will be given.
2. The conditions under which it will be given (timed, speeded, take-home).
3. The content areas it will cover.
4. The emphasis or weighting (point value) of content areas to be included on the assessment.
5. The types of performance the student will have to demonstrate (the kinds of items on the test, the degree to which memory will be required).
6. The way the assessment will be scored and graded (e.g., will partial credit be given?).
7. The importance of the particular assessment result in relation to decisions about the student (e.g., it will count for 20 percent of the marking period grade).

When an Assessment Will Be Given If you want students to perform at their best, you need to tell them when your test will be given, so they can prepare in advance. Students need to organize their study efforts and set their priorities. They can learn to do this planning when they know a test date in advance. Teachers of various subjects should coordinate their schedules of assessment, so they are spread out. However, the end of the marking period is often problematic.

Pop Quizzes Do Not Assess Maximum Performance Some teachers advocate "surprise" or "pop" quizzes. Their reasoning is often some vague notion that a good student should always be prepared to perform on command, which seems to be an unrealistic expectation of students. Some teachers use surprise quizzes to threaten or to punish a disobedient class. The authors consider this an unethical use of an assessment. Remember that the purpose of classroom assessment is to assess maximum performance and gather evidence of the degree of students' achievement of learning goals. Using quizzes as a disciplinary measure changes their purpose and often makes students' attitudes about all assessment more negative. Both of these circumstances undermine validity.

Assessment Conditions Tell students the conditions under which they are expected to perform: How many items will be on the test? How much time will the students have to complete the assessment? Will the assessment be speeded? Will it be open or closed book? Will there be a penalty for guessing? And at what time of day will it be given (if not during a regular period)?

Explain to Students What the Test Will Include Saying that the assessment will cover the first three chapters of the book doesn't help students much. To plan and study effectively, students need more detail. Some teachers prepare lists of study questions to help students focus their efforts. This process may be especially helpful for elementary students for whom almost everything in a book seems to be equally important. Study questions also help older students, especially when a large amount of material has been covered during the term. For high school and college students, an alternative to developing a set of study questions is to give them a copy of the assessment blueprint (see Chapter 6), a list of learning objectives, a copy of the scoring criteria or rubrics, or a detailed content outline indicating the number of items covering each element.

Explain What the Test Will Emphasize

Tell students how the content in an assessment is weighted, including how many items (and how many points) will be devoted to each objective, content element, or blueprint cell. Weight of the different parts of an assessment should match your teaching emphasis; otherwise, the results will have low validity. Students can waste hours studying a topic that will be of little or no importance on the assessment. Many teachers share their assessment plan with students, telling them at the beginning of the course or marking period the weight they assign to each assignment, quiz, test, and classroom performance activity. Students can then organize their efforts in terms of these priorities.

Give Opportunity to Practice Expected Performance

Give students the opportunity to practice the kind of performance for which you will hold them accountable, with feedback. Students should not have to guess at the nature or type of question that will appear on an assessment. For example, a teacher gave a sixth grader practice exercises that asked him to identify prepositional phrases in isolation using a given list of words and phrases. The next day, his assessment consisted of finding the subject, predicate, and prepositional phrase in the more authentic context of several paragraphs. Unfortunately, the student never had the opportunity to practice the task for which he was held accountable.

The best way to familiarize students with tasks that will appear on an assessment is to give them sample tasks, perhaps an old form of an assessment on which they can practice. This strategy may be particularly effective when the types of tasks to appear on the assessment are complex and/or unfamiliar to the students.

Tell Students How You Will Score the Test

Telling students how you will score the assessment helps them prepare, especially for answering open-ended tasks. If you will assign points for spelling important terms and proper names, then the students need to practice these spellings in addition to learning the main ideas and rehears-ing how to organize their answers. Students also need to know whether and how you will award marks for less-than-perfect answers and how much weight (i.e., marks) you will give for each question. Share scoring rubrics with students well in advance of giving a test.

Tell Students How the Test Results Will Be Used

Tell students the importance of the assessment score for any decisions you will make about them, including putting students into groups, placing them in another section of the course, assigning them to remedial instruction, giving them enrichment or advanced work, and assigning grades.

Minimum Assessment-Taking Skills

Skills You Need to Teach Students

Students need more than information about what an assessment is: They need to learn how to take tests. You may need to teach students the following minimum assessment-taking skills, perhaps through direct instruction in the classroom:

- Paying attention to oral and written directions and finding out the consequences of failing to follow them.
- Asking how the assessment will be scored, how the individual tasks will be weighted into the total, and how many points will be deducted for wrong answers, misspellings, or poor grammar.
- Writing their responses or marking answers neatly to avoid lowered scores because of poor penmanship or mismarked answers.
- Studying throughout the course and in paced reviewing to reduce cramming and fatigue.
- Using assessment time wisely so that all tasks are completed within the given time.
- Using their partial knowledge and guessing appropriately.
- Reflecting, outlining, and organizing answers to essays before writing; using an appropriate amount of time for each essay.
- Checking the marks they make on the separate answer sheets to avoid mismatching or losing one's place when an item is omitted.
- Reviewing their answers to the tasks and changing answers if they can make a better response.

Avoid Shortchanging Your Students   Some teachers have strong opinions about not giving multiple-choice items to students. Others give only short quizzes and tests lasting 15 to 20 minutes. Still others give almost no tests, relying on assignments and class work. We ask you to consider your own position on these matters. Students will almost always be required to take state assessments and/or standardized tests. Doing well on these tests will be important for your students because decisions about them and your school will depend on how well they do.

We are not advocates of using multiple-choice tests exclusively, nor even extensively. Neither do we advocate always giving long tests. But we must be fair to the students. If we are expecting them to do well on the state assessments and standardized tests, then they should experience these types of assessment during their normal classes as part of their normal instruction and assessment process. Prepping students for taking these longer multiple-choice tests a week or so before the tests does not seem right. It is a waste of instructional time and may well be an unethical teaching practice.

TESTWISENESS

A Testwiseness Quiz

Before reading further, take the following short test (adapted from Diamond & Evans, 1972, p. 147). Be sure to mark an answer for every item, even if you are unsure of the answer. There *is* a correct or best answer for every item.

1. The Augustine National Party has its headquarters in
   a. Camden, New Jersey.
   b. St. Augustine, Florida.
   c. Palo Alto, California.
   d. Dallas, Texas.
2. Hermann Klavermann is best known for
   a. developing all musical scales used in the Western world.
   b. composing every sonata during the Romantic era.
   c. translating all Russian classics into English.
   d. inventing the safety pin.
3. The Davis Act of the twentieth century
   a. provided more money for schools.
   b. struck down an earlier law.
   c. prohibited the manufacture, sale, transportation, or use of several specific drugs that were being used for illegal purposes.
   d. gave a raise to government employees.
4. Harold Stone's book *The Last Friendship* is an example of an
   a. political satire.
   b. autobiography.
   c. science fiction.
   d. biography.
5. The population of Franktown is more than
   a. 50 thousand.
   b. 60 thousand.
   c. 70 thousand.
   d. 80 thousand.

Each item's content is fictitious, but the right answer to each can be determined by using certain clues in the item:

Item 1. An obvious association between a word or phrase in the stem (*Augustine National Party*) and one in an alternative (*St. Augustine*).

Item 2. Specific determiners in the alternatives (*all, every*) result in these being eliminated from consideration.

Item 3. A longer, more qualified answer is keyed as the correct response.

Item 4. A grammatical clue (*an*) is contained in the stem.

Item 5. An alternative overlaps or includes the others.

A Taxonomy of Testwiseness Skills

The ability to correctly answer items like the preceding is often called testwiseness. **Testwiseness** is the ability to use assessment-taking strategies, clues from poorly written items, and experience in taking assessments to improve your score beyond what you would otherwise attain from mastery of the subject matter itself. When you write classroom assessments, be aware of how students may take advantage of your idiosyncrasies in item writing or flawed items to improve

FIGURE 14.1 Testwiseness skills.

I. General test-taking skills

1. Begin work as soon as possible. Work with "all deliberate speed," quickly enough to be efficient but slowly enough to avoid careless mistakes.
2. If a test item is too difficult, skip it and go on. Return to skipped items after completing the rest of the test.
3. If you do not know an answer to a multiple-choice item, guess. First, see if you can eliminate some options you know are incorrect and make your guess from the remaining options. This process increases your chances of guessing correctly. Make a random guess only if you cannot eliminate some options.
4. If you have time, go back and check your work.
5. Change an answer if, after thoughtful consideration, you believe the new answer is better.

II. Using clues from poorly designed tests or poorly written items

1. Take advantage of cues in poorly designed tests. For example, poorly designed tests provide clues for guessing when
   a. The stem of one item includes information that identifies the correct option in another item.
   b. The correct answer is more likely to be a particular option (e.g., B), or there are more Falses than Trues, etc.
2. Take advantage of cues in poorly written items. (The various guidelines for writing different types of items in Chapters 9, 10, and 11 were prepared to help you avoid these cues in your own tests.) Examples of cues include:
   a. Correct answer includes the same or similar vocabulary as the stem.
   b. Correct answer uses a specific determiner (e.g., "often, sometimes") that tends to make the option correct.
   c. Correct answer is longer and more detailed than other options.
   d. Correct answer is quoted from the textbook.
   e. Correct answer is the only one that fits the stem grammatically.

their scores without attaining the desired level of mastery. Figure 14.1 is an outline or taxonomy of testwiseness principles.

You should create good-quality assessments that minimize any advantage that testwise students have. It will be beneficial, however, if you teach all students many of the skills listed in Part I of Figure 14.1, so they are not at a disadvantage when being assessed with more testwise peers. And of course, you should work to make sure your own tests are well crafted, so the "skills" in Part II do not help with answers. Research has demonstrated that testwiseness is learned, and it improves with grade level, experience in being assessed, maturation, and motivation to do well on the assessment (Geiger, 1997; Sarnacki, 1979).

Advice About Changing Answers

Will students benefit if they change their answers once they have been marked on the answer sheet? Despite popular opinion, it *does* pay to change answers if changing them is based on a thoughtful reconsideration of the item. A summary of the research findings (Wise, 1996) on this issue follows.

■ Most test-takers and many educators believe it does not pay to change answers.

■ Most students, however, do in fact change their answers to about 4 percent of the items.

■ Research studies show that it does, in fact, pay to change answers. Typically two-thirds to three-quarters of answers changed will become correct (Bridgeman, 2012).

■ The payoff for changing answers diminishes as the items become more difficult for the student.

■ Lower-scoring students benefit less from changing answers than higher-scoring students do.

TEST ANXIETY

Nature of Test Anxiety

Task-Directed and Task-Irrelevant Thoughts How students perceive being evaluated varies widely, and those perceptions affect students' performance on assessments. Some students are motivated to perform well; others don't care. Among the students who are motivated to do well, assessments and evaluations are likely to lead to increased emotional tension: **test anxiety**. Students' perceptions of evaluation situations shape their reactions to them. Some well-motivated students may perceive these evaluation situations as challenges, whereas other equally well-motivated students perceive them as threats. A student who perceives an assessment as threatening may not have the ability to perform the task at hand, not have been taught how to perform the task, or not have properly studied or otherwise prepared for the assessment. Not all perceived threats are based upon poor preparation, however.

Students who accept assessments and evaluations as challenges have thoughts that are **task-directed**. Their thoughts and actions are focused on completing the tasks and thereby reduce any tensions that are associated with them. Schutz, Distefano, Benson, and Davis (2004) called these task-focusing processes. Students who perceive assessments and evaluations as threats have **task-irrelevant thoughts**: They are self-preoccupied, centering on what could happen if they fail, on their own helplessness, and sometimes on a desire to escape from the situation as quickly as possible. Schutz et al. (2004) called these emotion-focusing processes.

Cognitive appraisal—that is, students making judgments about the tests they take and about their ability to manage the situation—affects how students cope with text anxiety (Schutz et al., 2004). Emotional reactions to an assessment situation trigger worry, which in turn results in poor performance. That is, highly test-anxious students worry about doing poorly, which keeps them from focusing their attention on the task at hand. If students can change their appraisal of the situation, however, they can also change their emotional experience and focus.

Factors in Test Anxiety   Sarason (1984) conceptualized students' reactions to assessment situations as four related factors: tension, worry, test-irrelevant thinking, and bodily reactions. Tension is the feeling of unease or jitters before a test. Worry includes worrying about failure and what is going to happen. Test-irrelevant thinking, as discussed above, is thinking about things other than the test, which in turn interferes with performance. Bodily reactions include headaches, upset stomach, and rapid heartbeat.

Davis and Li (2008) suggest that it might be helpful to consider students' emotional reactions to tests more broadly than just anxiety reactions. Examples of students' potential beliefs or judgments about tests are listed below, according to what emotion they engender: anxiety, anger, or pride. Beliefs and judgments that lead to pride and self-confidence are more productive than beliefs that lead to anxiety or anger.

Example

Students' beliefs and judgments about tests

Anxiety	Anger	Pride
Tests are important	Tests are important	Tests are important
Tests are **not** helping my goals	Tests are **not** helping my goals	Tests are helping my goals
Tests scores are **not** under my control (my fault)	Tests scores are **not** under my control (someone else's fault)	Tests scores are under my control
I **cannot** cope with problems on tests	I **cannot** cope with problems on tests	I can cope with problems on tests

Source: Davis, H. A., & Li, J. (2008). *The relationship between high school students' cognitive appraisals of high stakes tests and their emotion regulation and achievement.* Paper presented at the annual meeting of the American Educational Research Association, New York. Used by permission.

Three Types of Test-Anxious Students

There are at least three **types of test-anxious students** (Mealey & Host, 1992). Your ability to recognize these differences among students will help you work with them so they perform their best on your assessments. First are students who do not have good study skills and do not understand how the main ideas of the subject you are teaching are related and organized. These students become anxious about an upcoming evaluation because they have not learned well. The second group contains students who do have a good grasp of the material and good study skills but have fears of failure associated with assessment and evaluation (Herman, 1990). Third are students who believe they have good study habits but who do not. They perform poorly on assessments and learn to be anxious about being assessed (Mealey & Host, 1992).

Helping Test-Anxious Students

The following eight factors have been shown to be related to test anxiety (Hembree, 1988) and may be under your control in classroom assessment situations:

1. When students perceive an assessment to be difficult, their test anxiety rises.

2. At-risk students have higher levels of test anxiety than passing students.

3. Students whose teachers gave them item-by-item feedback after the test have lower test anxiety than students who receive no feedback.

4. Tests whose items were arranged from easy to difficult raise test anxiety less than tests with other item arrangements.

5. More frequent testing of highly test-anxious students seems to improve their performance.

6. Highly test-anxious students are more easily distracted by auditory and visual activity than less test-anxious students.

7. Giving extremely test-anxious students instructions to concentrate their attention on the assessment tasks and not to let themselves be distracted from the tasks is more beneficial to their performance than simply reassuring them with "don't worry" or "you'll be fine" statements.

8. Students with low test-taking skills can lower their test anxiety with testwiseness training.

In addition, Mealey and Host (1992) suggest that you ask your students what you might do to help them feel more relaxed or less nervous before, during, and after you assess them. The researchers' own developmental reading college students reported these four suggestions:

1. The teacher should not talk or interrupt while students are working on an assessment.

2. The teacher should review the material with the entire class before the assessment is given.

3. The teacher should not walk around looking over students' shoulders while they are being assessed.

4. The teacher should convey a sense of confidence about students' performance on an upcoming assessment (and avoid such statements as "this is going to be a difficult test").

Further reviews of test anxiety and its treatment can be found in Ergene (2003), Hembree (1988), Huberty (2010), and Zeidner (1998).

> **MyLab Education** Self-Check 14.1
>
> **MyLab Education** Application Exercise 14.1:
> Helping a Test-Anxious Student

ASSESSMENT FORMAT AND APPEARANCE

The final appearance and arrangement of your test are important to the validity of the results. An illegible, poorly typed, or illogically arranged assessment annoys the well-prepared student, can cause unnecessary errors, and gives all students the impression that you have not taken your assessment responsibilities seriously. The organization and appearance of an assessment may be especially important for less able students.

As a rule, you should word process a test and duplicate it so that each student can have a copy. Obvious exceptions are dictated spelling assessments and similar assessments of aural abilities. Sometimes a teacher will write the items on the board or dictate them to the class. If you do this, it may cause problems for students, especially those with visual, listening comprehension, or hearing problems. If you dictate the questions, you use valuable time that your students could otherwise spend in responding to the items. Further, reading a question aloud and requiring students to write their responses places a demand on short-term memory that many students cannot meet.

Test Layout and Design

Experts usually recommend placing items in the order of difficulty with the easiest items first. If items are grouped by type of format, arrange them from easiest to most difficult within each format. Most students can go through the easiest items quickly and reserve the remaining test time for the difficult items. Another way to arrange items is according to the sequence in which the content was taught or appeared in the textbook. Students can then use this subject-matter organization as a kind of "cognitive map" through which they can retrieve stored information. If you use this sequential arrangement, you should tell students to skip over difficult items and go on to subsequent items, which may be easier. Always encourage students to return to the omitted items if they have time. Better yet, within content areas arrange the items from easiest to most difficult. This process minimizes test-created anxiety and, in turn, raises the validity of your assessment results.

Directions to Students Assessment directions should contain certain minimum information: the number and format of items, amount of time allowed for the assessment, where and how answers should be written, any correction or penalty for guessing, and the general strategy the student should follow when answering questions. For example, should students guess if they think they know the answer but are unsure? Should they answer all items or should they omit some? Which ones? Should they do each item in turn, or should they skip those they are uncertain about, returning to them later if they have time? If the student perceives that the answer to an item requires an opinion, whose opinion is being asked? Most written directions need not be elaborate.

Use side headings on the pages with the test questions to signal a change in the general directions that may occur within the test booklet. Some items may require specific, rather than general, directions. Here is an example:

Example

Example of side heading on a test page to signal changes in the general directions

> **Items 16, 17, and 18 refer to the data found in the table below.**
>
> [Table is put here]
>
> 16.   Question 16 goes here.
> 17.   Question 17 goes here.
> 18.   Question 18 goes here.

Make sure your test copies are clear and readable. Poor-quality copies may affect student performance. Test security may be a problem if the tests are sent to a central location for duplication and assembly, so check the security procedures in your school.

Preparations for Scoring the Assessment

Prepare for scoring an assessment before you administer it. Prepare and *verify* every answer on the scoring key in advance so that you can score students' assessments efficiently and accurately and report results to the students quickly for feedback and motivation. Advance preparation of the answer key will help you identify errors in the assessment items, too.

Separate answer sheets are not recommended for the first three grades. However, with older elementary and high school students, it may be advisable to use a separate answer sheet for objective items. Using separate answer sheets greatly facilitates scoring and permits the test booklet to be reused. It also gives students practice for the state assessment or other standardized tests they will have to take. An answer sheet for completion items might consist of columns with numbered blanks, each number corresponding to an item number. The student writes the answer to an item on the correspondingly numbered blank. If you have essays or extended responses, be sure to provide an answer sheet or examination booklet to record students' responses.

Scanning the Answer Sheets

Scannable answer sheets are available in most schools. These can be used for hand scoring as well as scanning. If you are planning to scan, check with the office in your school that does the scanning to be sure that you use the proper answer sheets. Also, be sure the students follow the correct answer-marking procedures. You can make your own scoring key by punching out the correct answers on an answer sheet. Lay the punched sheet on top of each student's answer sheet to score it.

CORRECTION FOR GUESSING
Correction for Guessing Formulas

With true-false and/or multiple-choice items, **correction for guessing formulas** are sometimes applied to scores by subtracting from the number of right answers a fraction of the number of wrong answers. An astute student may wonder how the machine can "get into my head" and figure out whether the student guessed. Assure your student no machine can do that. Correction for guessing formulas correct scores so that *on average* the effects of chance (and therefore the probability of getting a correct answer by guessing) are removed. Here is the usual formula:

$$\text{corrected score} = R - \frac{W}{(n-1)} \quad \text{[Eq. 14.1]}$$

where

R means the number of items answered correctly

W means the number of items marked wrong

n means the number of options in each item

If there are two choices per item (e.g., true-false), then

$$\text{corrected score} = R - W$$

If there are four options per item, then

$$\text{corrected score} = R - \frac{W}{3}$$

The correction formula is designed to eliminate the advantage a student might have as a result of guessing correctly. Here is an example of how to use the correction. You would apply the correction to every student.

Example

How to apply the correction for guessing correctly score formula

Suppose Juan took a 50-question multiple-choice test with four options per item. Further, suppose Juan's test results were 40 items marked correct, six items marked wrong, and four items omitted. Applying the formula, we find:

$$\text{corrected score} = R - \frac{W}{(n-1)}$$

$$\text{corrected score} = 40 - \frac{6}{(4-1)} = 40 - 2 = 38$$

Notice the number of omitted items is not used in this correction formula; only the number of answers marked wrong (W) and the number marked correct (R).

A complementary version of the preceding correction formula does use the number of omitted items: Instead of penalizing a student for responding wrongly, it rewards the student for omitting items (i.e., for refraining from guessing). This formula is

$$\text{adjusted score} = R + \frac{O}{n} \qquad \text{[Eq. 14.2]}$$

where

R means the number of items answered correctly

O means the number of items omitted

n means the number of options in each item

(The term *adjusted* instead of *corrected* distinguishes this formula from the previous one, which is not standard practice. The general term for such equations is formula scoring.) Here is an example of its use:

Example

How to apply the correction for guessing adjusted score formula

Suppose Juan took a 50-question multiple-choice test with four options per item. Further, suppose Juan's test results were 40 items marked correct, six items marked wrong, and four items omitted. Applying the formula, we find:

$$\text{adjusted score} = R + \frac{O}{n}$$

$$\text{adjusted score} = 40 + \frac{4}{4} = 41$$

This formula credits the student with the number of points to be expected if random responses were substituted for the omitted responses. If a student omitted every item, the score would be equal to the average score expected if the student guessed randomly on every item. Thus, the scores obtained by the adjusted score formula will be higher than the same students' scores if they had been obtained from the corrected score formula. However, the scores under the two methods are perfectly correlated; that is, the rank ordering of persons is the same regardless of which formula is used.

The uncorrected score (R) is simply the number of items marked correct. When every student marks every item, the uncorrected scores are perfectly correlated with the corrected or adjusted scores so that the rank ordering of persons is the same, whether or not the scores are corrected for guessing.

Figure 14.2 lists a few things to keep in mind when deciding whether to use a correction formula. On balance, we recommend that you do not use formula scoring for most classroom assessment purposes.

Current Practices Among Test Publishers

Most current commercial achievement tests use item response theory, whose mathematical models take guessing into account in scoring, without using Equations 14.1 and 14.2. If you hand-score a standardized test, follow the instructions in the manual exactly. If hand-scoring is required and you fail to apply a correction the publisher

FIGURE 14.2   Things to consider for correction for guessing.

1. A correction formula does not correct for good luck nor compensate for bad luck.
2. The relative ordering of pupils is usually the same for uncorrected as for corrected scores.
3. The chance of getting a good score by random guessing is very slim.
4. Pupils who want to do well on the test, and who are given enough time to attempt all items, will guess on only a few items.
5. Encouraging pupils to make the best choice they can, even if they are not completely confident in their choice, does not seem to be morally or educationally wrong.
6. Responding to an item on a rational basis, even when lacking complete certainty of the correctness of the answer, provides useful information on general educational achievement.
7. Using a correction-for-guessing penalty may discourage slower students from guessing blindly on items near the end of a test when time is short.
8. Correction-for-guessing directions do not seem to discourage the test-wise or risk-taking examinee from guessing, but do seem to discourage the reluctant, risk-avoiding, or non-test-wise examinee.
9. A formula score makes the scoring more complicated, offering additional opportunities for the teacher to commit scoring errors.

Source: From *Measuring Educational Achievement* (pp. 251–257), by R. L. Ebel, 1965, Englewood Cliffs, NJ: Prentice Hall. Reprinted by permission.

intended, apply it when the test publisher didn't intend it to be used, or otherwise alter the instructions to students at the time of testing, you will make the test's norms unusable because the alterations result in new unstandardized test conditions.

ITEM ANALYSIS FOR CLASSROOM ASSESSMENTS

Item analysis is the process of collecting, summarizing, and using information from students' responses to make decisions about each item. Standardized test developers, especially developers of norm-referenced tests, try out as many as five times more items than will appear on the final version of a test. Item-analysis data from these tryouts are used to help select items for the final form. The developers discard items that fail to display proper statistical properties. Your classroom assessments, being more closely linked to the daily teaching-learning process, serve purposes that are somewhat different from published standardized tests. Thus, you will use item-analysis data differently than a test publisher.

Classroom Uses for Item Analyses

For teacher-made assessments, the following are among the important uses of item analyses:

1. *Determining whether an item functions as you intended.* You can't expect to write perfectly functioning items. To decide whether an

item for a classroom assessment is functioning properly, you need to know whether it assesses the intended learning objectives, whether it is at the appropriate level of difficulty, whether it distinguishes those who have command of the learning objectives from those who do not, whether the keyed answer is correct, and (for response-choice items) whether the distractors are working. Procedures to help you decide whether an item seems to be assessing the intended learning objective were discussed in Chapter 6. The other four elements are discussed in this chapter.

2. *Feedback to students about their performance and as a basis for class discussion.* Students are entitled to know how their performance on each assessment task is marked and the correct answer to each task. Going over a test with students makes instructional common sense: You can correct students' errors, clarify for students the level of detail you expect of them, and reinforce good (and correct) responses. Also, students lacking test-taking skills may learn how a correct answer is formulated or why (in response-choice items) foils are incorrect, and you can alleviate some test anxiety if you teach your students to view your assessments rationally in the context of instruction.

3. *Feedback to the teacher about pupil difficulties.* A simple procedure such as tabulating the percentage of students answering an item correctly may provide you with information about

areas that need additional instruction and remediation. Many school systems have electronic equipment to scan answer sheets and a computer program that can provide an item analysis. Feedback from item analysis can help you focus your teaching on both group and individual needs. Note, however, that a subscore based on a cluster of several items measuring similar learning objectives provides more reliable information than does a single item, so use these results cautiously.

You will also find it helpful to identify the nature of students' errors on assessment tasks. With essay, short-answer, and completion items, a **content analysis of responses** will determine the major types of student errors and how often they occur.

4. *Areas for curriculum improvement.* If particular content is repeatedly difficult for students, or if certain kinds of errors occur often, perhaps the problem extends beyond you: A more extensive curriculum revision may be needed. Item-analysis data help to identify specific problems. But any assessment is likely to represent a school's curriculum objectives incompletely, so you should use caution when attempting to generalize item analysis to the whole of student learning.

5. *Revising the assessment tasks.* Use information about students' responses to and perceptions of an item to revise it. Items can be reused for future assessments and, if you revise a few each time, the overall quality of the assessment will eventually improve. Usually you will find it less time-consuming to revise an item than to write a new one. Some teachers, especially in middle and senior high schools and in colleges, develop an item file or **item bank**. They write and try new items, and through item analysis they keep the best items each time, revise some, and discard the rest. You can keep a copy of the item and information about it in a spreadsheet or database file for future use. Following is an example of the information for one entry in such a file:

Example

Example of item-analysis data for one item. Tabulations were made for Item 1 on the summary record form shown in Figure 14.3.

Course: English 10   **Date(s):** Fall 2007
  Spring 2008
  Fall 2008

Topic: Poetry

ITEM

The poet John Donne began the second verse of his poem "The Message" with this line: "Send home my harmless heart again." This is an example of what element of poetry?

  *a. Alliteration
  b. Assonance
  c. Irony
  d. Simile

ITEM DATA SUMMARY

	Upper Group	Lower Group	Middle Group
*a.	10	7	14
b.	0	0	0
c.	0	2	0
d.	0	1	0
Omits	0	0	0

Difficulty Index: 0.91   **Number of Students:** 34
Discrimination Index: 0.3

After several years, a file of good items accumulates. Once a file of items is established, equivalent versions of a test can be constructed relatively easily. You can construct equivalent versions of tests and use them for makeup tests when students are absent during the regularly scheduled administration, when you teach multiple sections of the same course, or when you use tests in an alternating pattern from year to year.

6. *Improving item-writing skills.* Probably the most effective way to improve your item-writing skills is to analyze the items and understand the ways in which students respond to them and then use this information to revise items and try them again with students.

Item Analysis of Response-Choice Tests

The basic bits of data you need to begin an analysis of response-choice items (true-false, matching, or multiple-choice) are the responses each student makes to each item. Although this information is easier to use if students have marked their answers on separate answer sheets, such sheets are not necessary. Here is a summary of the steps necessary for doing an item analysis.

Step 1. Score each student's test by marking the correct answers and putting the total number correct on the test (or answer sheet).

Step 2. Sort all the papers in numerical order according to the total score.

Step 3. Determine the upper, middle, and lower groups.

Step 4. Tabulate the number of students choosing each alternative in the upper and lower groups, and tabulate the number of students in the middle group who chose the correct answer.

Step 5. Calculate the difficulty index for each item.

Step 6. Calculate the discrimination index for each item.

Step 7. Using the results of Step 4, check each item to identify poor distractors, ambiguous alternatives, miskeying, and indications of random guessing.

Although this section is written primarily for analyses of response-choice items, you can use several of the techniques described with any assessment tasks that are **dichotomously scored** (correct/incorrect or pass/fail), such as completion or short-answer items. Item-analysis techniques do exist for analyzing tasks scored more continuously, such as essays or performance assessments, but we start with the simplest case, response-choice tests with right/wrong scoring.

Upper- and Lower-Scoring Groups (Step 3)

After you have scored the tests, arrange them in numerical order according to the students' total score. Next, divide the stack of tests into three groups: **upper-, middle-, and lower-scoring groups**. Then, contrast the responses of the upper- and lower-scoring groups in various ways (described later) to determine whether each item is functioning well.

How you form these groups is important. When the total number of students taking your test is between 20 and 40, select the 10 highest-scoring and the 10 lowest-scoring papers, but keep the middle-scoring group intact. (When there are 20 students, there will be no middle group.) If there are 20 students or fewer, the responses of only one or two students may greatly influence the results you will obtain from the procedure described here. If you use item analysis with too few students, you may come to quite incorrect conclusions about how a particular item would

function if you were to use it again. Nevertheless, if you want to go ahead with the analysis for groups with very few students, separate the test papers into two sets (upper and lower halves) and interpret the results cautiously. For groups larger than 40, testing experts frequently recommend using the upper- and lower-scoring 27 percent of the group on technical grounds (based on classic work by Kelly, 1939). For purposes of classroom assessment, however, when the group is almost always smaller than 40, any percentage between 25 and 33 seems appropriate.

Summarize Responses to Each Item (Step 4)

For each item, record the number of students in the (a) *upper group* choosing each alternative (and, separately, the number not responding [omitting]); (b) *lower group* choosing each alternative (and, separately, the number omitting the item); and (c) *middle-scoring group* choosing the correct alternative. The example we gave previously shows the results of such tabulation for one item. Many machine-scoring programs provide item-analysis printouts with some or all of this information.

Without a doubt, the most tedious part of an item analysis is tabulating the students' responses to items. Using an upper and lower group instead of the entire class makes the task easier. One simplifying procedure is to make a form such as in Figure 14.3. Or, you may find that, like many teachers, you would not do an item analysis by hand, but working through an example by hand helps you understand and interpret item-analysis printouts.

Compute the Item Difficulty Index (*p*) (Step 5)

The fraction of the total group answering the item correctly is called the **item difficulty index (*p*)**. To compute it, add together the number of students choosing the correct answer in the upper, middle, *and* lower groups, then divide this sum by the total number of students who took the test. Equation 14.3 summarizes this.

$$p = \left[\frac{\text{number of students choosing the correct answer}}{\text{number of students taking the test}} \right]$$

$$= \left[\frac{\substack{\text{number of students choosing the correct answer} \\ \text{for the upper} + \text{middle} + \text{lower groups}}}{\text{total number of students taking the test}} \right]$$

[Eq. 14.3]

FIGURE 14.3 Item responses to the first 10 items of a 59-item test taken by a group of 34 college students.

		Item number: 1	2	3	4	5	6	7	8	9	10
Upper group	Doris	A	C	B	B	C	C	B	A	B	D
	Jerry	A	C	B	B	C	C	B	A	B	D
	Robert	A	C	B	B	C	C	E	A	B	D
	Elazar	A	B	B	B	C	C	B	A	B	D
	Marya	A	C	B	B	C	C	B	A	B	D
	Anna	A	C	B	B	C	C	B	A	B	D
	Diana	A	C	B	B	C	C	B	A	B	D
	Harry	A	C	B	B	C	C	B	A	B	D
	Anthony	A	C	B	B	C	C	B	A	B	D
	Carolyn	A	C	B	B	B	C	B	A	B	D
	Key	A	C	B	B	C	C	B	A	B	D
Number choosing each option	A	10	0	0	10	0	0	0	10	0	0
	B	0	1	10	0	1	0	9	0	10	0
	C	0	9	0	—	9	10	0	0	0	0
	D	0	—	0	—	0	0	0	0	0	10
	E	—	—	—	—	—	—	1	—	—	—
	Omits	0	0	0	0	0	0	0	0	0	0
Middle group	No. right	14	12	12	13	12	13	11	11	12	12
	No. omits	0	0	0	0	0	0	0	0	0	0
Lower group	Anita	A	C	B	B	D	C	E	A	A	D
	Larry	A	C	B	B	D	C	D	A	B	D
	Charles	C	B	B	B	C	C	B	A	B	C
	Joel	A	C	B	B	C	C	E	A	B	D
	Leslie	A	C	B	B	C	C	E	A	B	B
	Alida	A	C	B	B	C	C	A	B	B	B
	Marilyn	A	C	D	B	C	C	D	C	D	A
	Wayne	A	B	A	A	C	C	B	B	C	A
	Ina	D	C	C	A	B	B	C	B	A	D
	Donald	C	B	B	B	D	C	E	C	D	D
	Key	A	C	B	B	C	C	B	A	B	D
Number choosing each option	A	7	0	1	2	0	0	1	5	2	2
	B	0	3	7	8	1	1	2	3	5	2
	C	2	7	1	—	6	9	1	2	1	1
	D	1	—	1	—	3	0	2	0	2	5
	E	—	—	—	—	—	—	4	—	—	—
	Omits	0	0	0	0	0	0	0	0	0	0

Note: This is an example of the basic data needed to do an item analysis. For the middle group, you record only the number choosing the right answer and the number of omits.

The next example shows how to apply Equation 14.3 with the data in the class summary form for Item 3:

$$p = \left[\frac{\text{number of students choosing the correct answer for the upper + middle + lower groups}}{\text{total number of students taking the test}}\right]$$

Example

How to calculate the item difficulty index for Item 3 from the data in the class summary using Equation 14.3

$$= \left[\frac{10 + 12 + 7}{34}\right] = 0.85$$

As we will discuss later, this value can range from 0.00 to 1.00.

Compute the Item Discrimination Index (*D*) (Step 6)

The **item discrimination index (*D*)** is the difference between the fraction of the upper group answering the item correctly and the fraction of the lower group answering it correctly. The discrimination index describes the extent to which a particular test item is able to differentiate the higher-scoring students from the lower-scoring students. The following equation is used to compute this index:

$$D = \left[\begin{array}{c} \text{fraction of the} \\ \text{upper group answering} \\ \text{the item correctly} \end{array} \right] - \left[\begin{array}{c} \text{fraction of the} \\ \text{lower group answering} \\ \text{the item correctly} \end{array} \right]$$

[Eq. 14.4]

Another way you will see this expressed is:

$$D = p_U - p_L$$

This index is sometimes referred to as the *net D index of discrimination*. Commercial test developers seldom use net *D* today; they now use a correlation coefficient as a discrimination index or other indices based on mathematical modeling of item responses. Net *D* is probably the most useful discrimination index available for use with teacher-made assessments, however.

Here is an example of how to calculate the discrimination index for one item:

Example

How to calculate the item discrimination index for Item 3 from the data in the class summary using Equation 14.4

$$D = \frac{10}{10} - \frac{7}{10} = 1.0 - 0.7 = 0.3$$

As we will discuss later, this index can range from −1.00 to +1.00.

Item Analysis of Constructed-Response and Performance Assessments

The *concepts* of item difficulty and item discrimination extend to tasks with multipoint scoring such as that obtained when you use rubrics and rating scales. Constructed-response items and performance assessment tasks often are scored on a scale from 0 to 3, 1 to 4, or some other range of scores, instead of scoring 0 or 1. The *difficulty* of an essay question or performance task scored by a rubric or rating scale is defined as the average score. The *discrimination* of an essay question or performance task scored by a rubric or rating scale is the difference between the upper and lower group averages. There are many other ways to compute difficulty and discrimination, but we shall limit our discussion to simple ways appropriate for classroom assessment. You should monitor these values, making sure that your tasks are at an appropriate level of difficulty and that they discriminate—that is, that students who are more accomplished do indeed score better on the tasks intended to demonstrate that accomplishment.

Compute the Item Difficulty Index (*p**)

The item difficulty for a constructed-response or performance item is simply the average score for that item. For example, if Item 1 was an essay item, scored on a scale of 1 to 6, and if the average score on this item was 4.2, then the difficulty of the item is 4.2.

To keep this item difficulty on the same scale as the *p*-value of Equation 13.3, we should adjust this average to give us a value that is between 0 and 1.00, the same as in Equation 14.3. The lowest possible score is subtracted from the average score then divided by the possible range of scores to make the minimum value of *p** be 0.00. This difficulty index is illustrated here:

$$p^* = \frac{\begin{array}{c} \text{average score} \\ \text{for} \\ \text{the item} \end{array} - \begin{array}{c} \text{minimum} \\ \text{possible} \\ \text{item score} \end{array}}{\begin{array}{c} \text{maximum} \\ \text{possible} \\ \text{item score} \end{array} - \begin{array}{c} \text{minimum} \\ \text{possible} \\ \text{item score} \end{array}}$$

[Eq. 14.5]

Here are examples of how to use this equation:

Example

Examples of applying Equation 14.5

1. Suppose the class average score on Item 1 (an essay item) was 4.2. Suppose further that the essay was scored on a scale from 1 to 6. Thus, lowest *possible* score was 1 and the highest *possible* score was 6. What is the *p** difficulty index?

$$p^* = \cfrac{\begin{array}{c}\text{average score} \\ \text{for} \\ \text{the item}\end{array} - \begin{array}{c}\text{minimum} \\ \text{possible} \\ \text{item score}\end{array}}{\begin{array}{c}\text{maximum} \\ \text{possible} \\ \text{item score}\end{array} - \begin{array}{c}\text{minimum} \\ \text{possible} \\ \text{item score}\end{array}}$$

$$= \frac{4.2 - 1}{6 - 1} = \frac{3.2}{5} = 0.64$$

2. Suppose on Item 2 (also an essay item) the class average was 4.2. Suppose further that it was scored on a scale from 0 to 10. Thus, the lowest *possible* score was 0 and the highest *possible* score was 10. What is the difficulty index?

$$p^* = \cfrac{\begin{array}{c}\text{average score} \\ \text{for} \\ \text{the item}\end{array} - \begin{array}{c}\text{minimum} \\ \text{possible} \\ \text{item score}\end{array}}{\begin{array}{c}\text{maximum} \\ \text{possible} \\ \text{item score}\end{array} - \begin{array}{c}\text{minimum} \\ \text{possible} \\ \text{item score}\end{array}}$$

$$= \frac{4.2 - 0}{10 - 0} = \frac{4.2}{10} = 0.42$$

You can see from these two examples that by taking into account the minimum possible score and the possible score range the interpretation of the average score becomes clear. In Item 1 the average score is 4.2 but the minimum possible score is 1 and possible range of marks is 1 through 6. Thus, $p^* = 0.64$ means that on average, students received 64 percent of the maximum possible score range for this item. Item 2, however, has a different interpretation. Item 2 has the same average score, 4.2. However, the minimum possible score is 0 and the possible score range for this item is from 0 to 10. The difficulty index then is 0.42, meaning that on average, students received only 42 percent of the maximum possible score range for this item. Thus, Item 2 is much harder for the students than is Item 1. So, as you see, *you cannot fully interpret the average score of a performance item unless you know the range of the possible marks.*

Incidentally, to distinguish Equation 14.5 from the earlier Equation 14.3, we used an asterisk (*) along with *p*, which is not standard.

Compute the Item Discrimination Index (*D**)

The discrimination index for items such as constructed-response and performance items that have multipoint scoring is simply the difference between the average score on the item for the upper group and the corresponding average for the lower group. The upper and lower groups are defined in the same way as described previously; that is, based on their ranking in the total assessment. Here is an example:

Example

Suppose the upper group's average for an item is 5.3, and the lower group's corresponding average is 2.8, and the item is scored from 1 to 6. The discrimination for the item is 5.3 −2.8 = 2.5.

To keep the item discrimination index on the same scale as the *D*-value of Equation 14.4, we adjust this difference by dividing it by the possible score range, which gives us a possible range for the discrimination index of between −1.00 and +1.00, just as with Equation 14.4. This is summarized in Equation 14.6.

$$D^* = \cfrac{\left[\begin{array}{c}\text{average score of} \\ \text{the upper group} \\ \text{on the item}\end{array} - \begin{array}{c}\text{average score of} \\ \text{the lower group} \\ \text{on the item}\end{array}\right]}{\left[\begin{array}{c}\text{maximum} \\ \text{possible} \\ \text{item score}\end{array} - \begin{array}{c}\text{minimum} \\ \text{possible} \\ \text{item score}\end{array}\right]}$$

$$= \frac{\left[\begin{array}{c}\text{different between the upper} \\ \text{and lower groups' average score}\end{array}\right]}{\left[\,\text{range of possible scores}\,\right]} \quad \text{[Eq. 14.6]}$$

The next example shows how to use this equation:

Example

Example of applying Equation 14.6

Suppose the upper group's average for an item is 5.3, and the lower group's corresponding average is 2.8, and the item is scored from 1 to 6. What is the discrimination index, *D**?

$$D^* = \frac{5.3 - 2.8}{6 - 1} = \frac{2.5}{5} = 0.5$$

Because we divide by the possible item score range, we can interpret this value to mean that the difference between the average scores of the upper and lower groups for this item is 50 percent of the possible item score range. (This item discriminates fairly well.) As with the previously discussed discrimination index for dichotomous items (Equation 14.4), the index here can show negative values, zero, or positive values. If the value is negative, the lower group scored higher on the average than the upper group. We would generally consider such a result to mean that the item is not good.

ITEM DIFFICULTY INDEX

Effect on Test Score Distribution

Shape of the Distribution   The difficulty of test items affects the shape of the distribution of total test scores. Very difficult tests, containing items with p-values < 0.25, will tend to be positively skewed, whereas easy tests, containing items with p-values > 0.80, will tend to be negatively skewed. (See Chapter F.7 in Appendix F for an explanation of distribution shapes.) The shapes of total score distributions for other kinds of assessments are not so easily deduced.

Average or Mean Test Score   The difficulty of items affects the average or mean test score: The average test score (M) is equal to the sum of the difficulties of the items. The relationship is given here:

$$M = \sum p \qquad \text{[Eq. 14.7]}$$

The mean (M) test score is equal to the sum of the difficulty values (that is, the p-values) of the items comprising the test. When the assessment contains only performance or constructed-response items, the mean is simply the sum of the item means, *not* the sum of the p^* values from Equation 14.5.

Spread of Scores   The spread of item difficulties and the spread of test scores are related. A test with all p-values clustered around 0.50 has the largest spread of test scores, whereas tests with difficulties distributed between 0.10 and 0.90 have smaller score spreads.

Item difficulties (p-values) are not the sole factor contributing to the spread of test scores. Another factor is the correlation (Appendix F) among the items: The higher these item intercorrelations, the larger the test's standard deviation. However, the correlations among items may be affected by the p-values: Items for which $p = 0.00$ or 1.00 have correlations of 0.00.

Uses of Item Difficulty Information

Figure 14.4 summarizes some of the ways in which teachers and school officials can use p-values and p^*-values in assessment and instruction. For the teacher, perhaps identifying concepts to be retaught and giving students feedback about their learning are the more important uses

FIGURE 14.4 Examples of ways in which item difficulty indexes can be used in testing and instruction.

Purpose	Procedure	Comments
Identifying concepts that need to be retaught	Find items with small p-values. These items may point to objectives needing to be retaught.	a. Poor test performance may not reflect poor teaching: Poor performance may reflect poorly written items, incorrect prior learning, or poor motivation on tests. b. A score based on several similar items is more reliable than performance on a single item.
Providing clues to possible strengths and weaknesses in school curricula	Calculate p-values for clusters of similar items for a school building or district. Compare these to p-values of the same items from the publisher's national norm group. Note areas of strength and weakness.	a. See a and b above. b. This procedure applies to standardized tests only. c. Items must correspond to local curriculum objectives and instruction. d. No published test will cover all the objectives of a school district.
Giving feedback to students	Report p-value of each item to student along with ID number of the items missed.	e. Such reporting is more useful for high school and college students.

of item difficulty data. Using item information to determine curriculum strengths or to identify suspected item bias requires districtwide cooperation. Such analyses tend to be employed only with state-mandated and standardized tests because test publishers make this information readily available to district offices. You may find yourself involved in interpreting state-mandated or standardized test data if you serve on school committees or if you serve in administrative positions.

ITEM DISCRIMINATION INDEX

The way you use item discrimination values should depend on the purpose of the assessment: Are you interested in absolute or relative achievement? The main purpose of **absolute achievement** assessment is to determine accurately the knowledge and skills each student has learned. The main purpose of **relative achievement** assessment, on the other hand, is to accurately determine the rank ordering among students with respect to the knowledge and skills learned. When you are gathering information mainly about the rank order of students, you should revise or remove from the test items that do not contribute information about ordering students or that provide inconsistent, thus confusing, information about this ordering.

Suppose you wanted to order a class of students from high to low using a 30-item unit test. Suppose, further, that when doing an item analysis, you divide the class in half based on the total test score (as usual, higher scorers in the upper group, lower scorers in the lower group). Finally, suppose that for one of the items, you discover that all of the lower-group students answered the item correctly, and the entire upper group answered it incorrectly. In this case, the item difficulty index is $p = 0.50$, but the item discrimination index is $D = 0 - 1.00 = -1.00$. This negatively discriminating item is poor because it works in the opposite way from most of the other items. That is, high-scoring students answer it incorrectly and low-scoring students answer it correctly. If you were to put such negatively discriminating items on a test, they would work to arrange students in an order inconsistent with the arrangement resulting from the positively discriminating items on the assessment.

Only the discrimination index is able to detect the type of malfunctioning item just described. The difficulty index gives the proportion of the class that answers an item correctly, but it does not indicate whether more higher- or lower-scoring students answered correctly. *For this reason, you should give more weight to an item's discrimination index than its difficulty index when deciding whether the item should appear on a test.*

Numerical Limits of D

For each item, the possible net D range is from -1 to $+1$. If all the discriminations made by an item were correct discriminations (everyone in the upper group answers the item right, whereas everyone in the lower group answers it wrong), net D would equal $+1$. Such an item is said to be a perfect **positively discriminating item**. If the number of correct discriminations equals the number of incorrect discriminations (an equal number of upper- and lower-group students answer the item right), then $D = 0$. Such an item is said to be a **nondiscriminating item**. Finally, if all discriminations were incorrect (everyone in the upper group answers the item wrong while everyone in the lower group answers it right), the D would equal -1. Such an item is said to be a perfect **negatively discriminating item**.

The values $+1$ and -1 are seldom obtained in practice. $D = 0$ is obtained most often for very easy or very hard items. The values 1, 0, and $+1$ serve as benchmarks when interpreting D.

Score Reliability and Item Discrimination Power

If none of the items discriminated ($D = 0$ for all items), everyone would be bunched together. If individual items can't distinguish students, then the collection of items comprising the test won't be able to do so, either. The larger the test's average level of item discrimination, the more diverse the scores will be. A more reliable assessment will be made up of tasks with high, positive discrimination indices. Thus, if the primary purpose of using an assessment is to interpret differences in achievement among students, the assessment procedure must include tasks with high discriminating power.

Interpret a negative value of D as a warning that you should carefully study the item and either revise or eliminate it. If you cannot find a technical flaw in the item, it might be that students in the upper-scoring group learned the material either incompletely or entirely incorrectly. Barring any rational explanation to the contrary, all of your assessment's items should be positively discriminating; otherwise, the total score on the assessment won't provide usable information.

IMPROVING MULTIPLE-CHOICE ITEM QUALITY

Poorly Functioning Distractors

Response Patterns for Distractors   The main purpose of the distractors or foils in a multiple-choice item is to appear plausible to those students lacking sufficient knowledge to choose the correct answer. Item-analysis data of the type summarized by the class record shown in Figure 14.3 can be used to find out which item distractors are not meeting this purpose and are therefore **poorly functioning distractors**. The general rule is this: *Every distractor should have at least one lower-group student choosing it, and more lower-group students than upper-group students should choose it.*

Because of fluctuations in responses from one small group of students to another, use the rules of thumb carefully. The following data, from the previous example item, illustrates these points. Each distractor (B, C, and D) was chosen by at least one lower-group person; no student in the upper group chose a distractor.

Example

Example of item-analysis data showing an appropriate pattern of responses to distractors

Alternative	Upper group	Lower group
*A	10	7
B	0	1
C	0	1
D	0	1

The rationale for the general rule is as follows: Students scoring lowest on the test are, on the whole, least able (in a relative, not absolute, sense) regarding the performance being assessed. If they are not, then the test on which they scored lowest must lack validity. For every item, it is among these lower-scoring students that you should

expect to find incorrect alternatives (distractors) chosen. Thus, if an item is working properly, one or more lower-scoring students should choose each distractor, and more lower-scoring than upper-scoring students should choose distractors.

Notice that not every lower-scoring person lacks knowledge about every item: In the preceding example, seven out of 10 lower-scoring persons knew the answer. Neither is it the case that every higher-scoring person always chooses the correct answer (see, for example, Items 2, 5, and 7 in Figure 14.3).

If no student in the lower group chooses a particular distractor, the distractor may be functioning poorly. Here is an example of a response pattern that shows that Distractor B may not be functioning properly. This example is for Item 1 of Figure 14.3.

Example

Example of item-analysis response pattern showing that Alternative B should be checked to see if it is functioning poorly

Alternative	Upper group	Lower group
*A	10	7
B	0	0
C	0	2
D	0	1

You should review the item and speculate why this occurred. Perhaps the particular alternative contains one of the technical flaws described in Chapter 10. If all students recognize a particular option as obviously incorrect, then you will want either to eliminate the alternative entirely (thus reducing the number of options in the item), substitute an entirely new alternative, or revise the existing alternative.

Subject Matter Has Precedence   It isn't always true that an alternative is flawed if no one in the lower group chooses it. Here's where your knowledge of the subject matter, of the students, and of the instruction students received prior to taking the assessment come into play: Perhaps in this year's group, even the lowest-scoring students have enough knowledge to eliminate a particular distractor, yet they do not have enough knowledge to select the correct answer. Perhaps in other groups a concept will not be learned as well, and this particular distractor will be plausible. Eliminating the alternative would prevent you from identifying those few individuals who lack this learning. In other words, use your own expertise along with the data to decide whether to eliminate a distractor that isn't working.

Finally, note that even though it seems reasonable to *expect* a larger number of lower-scoring students than higher-scoring students to choose a particular distractor, this result may not always happen. Technical flaws may cause higher-scoring students to be deceived, such as when they know a great deal about the subject and thus are able to give a plausible reason why an unkeyed alternative is at least as correct as the keyed one. In such cases, the alternative definitely should be revised. And sometimes there is neither a technical flaw nor a subject-matter deficiency in an incorrect alternative, yet higher-scoring students choose it in greater numbers than lower-scoring ones. In these cases, students may have incomplete or wrong learning.

Ambiguous Alternatives

Student responses can provide leads to **ambiguous alternatives**. In this context, alternatives are ambiguous if *upper-group students* are unable to distinguish between the keyed answer and one or more of the distractors. When this happens, the upper group tends to choose a distractor with about the same frequency as the keyed response, as illustrated in the following example:

Example

Example of an upper-group distractor response pattern showing ambiguous alternatives

On which river is the city of Pittsburgh, Pennsylvania, located?	Upper group	Lower group
A Delaware River	0	3
B Ohio River	5	3
C Monongahela River	4	1
D Susquehanna River	1	3

The confluence of the Allegheny and Monongahela Rivers forms the Ohio River at Pittsburgh. The upper group in the example chose B and C with approximately equal frequency, thus reflecting the students' ambiguity in selecting only one

of these two alternatives as a correct answer. This item should be rewritten so that only one answer is clearly correct or best.

You might notice that very often the lower group is equally divided among two or more alternatives, which is usually *not* an indication that you must revise the item. Rather, this result means that students with less knowledge will find many alternatives equally plausible, so the task becomes an ambiguous one for them. The cause of these students' ambiguity is likely to be insufficient knowledge.

Before concluding that you need to revise an item, however, study the item in relation to the students taking the test and judge whether the ambiguity stems from the students' lack of knowledge rather than from a poorly written item. Consider the next example, which shows how incomplete learning may produce a response pattern that gives the appearance of ambiguous alternatives.

Example

Example of how incomplete learning may result in a response pattern that gives the appearance of ambiguous alternatives

$$3 + 5 \times 2 = ?$$

	Upper group	Lower group
A 10	0	2
*B 13	5	3
C 16	5	3
D 30	0	2

This item requires applying arithmetic operations in a certain order: multiplication first, then addition. Option B reflects this order, whereas Option C is the answer obtained by adding first and then multiplying. Apparently, half the upper group followed this erroneous procedure and chose C. The item is not technically flawed, but the responses indicate to the teacher that a number of students need to learn this principle. The entire group's responses to this item should be checked, of course.

Miskeyed Items

You may have **miskeyed** an item if a larger number of upper-group students select a particular wrong response. When this happens, check to be sure that the answer key is correct. Look at this example:

Example

Example of an upper-group distractor response pattern showing a possible miskeyed item

Who was the fourth president of the United States?	Upper group	Lower group
A John Quincy Adams	0	3
B Thomas Jefferson	1	2
C James Madison	9	3
*D James Monroe	0	2

In the example, C is the correct answer, but the teacher inadvertently used Alternative D as the answer key. The response pattern in the figure is typical of such an item.

Again, be sure to check the item content. The numbers from the item analysis only warn of possible miskeying—perhaps there is no miskeying and the upper group simply lacks the required knowledge.

Random Guessing

Students may be guessing randomly if many of the alternatives are equally plausible to the upper-scoring group. If the upper-group students guess randomly, each option tends to be chosen an approximately equal number of times, as illustrated in this example:

Example

Example of an upper-group distractor response pattern showing possible random guess or confusion

In what year did the United States enter World War I?	Upper group	Lower group
A 1913	2	3
B 1915	2	2
C 1916	3	3
*D 1917	3	2

Remember to look at the pattern of responses of the upper group, *not* the lower group, to find items on which many students may be guessing. Guessing among the most knowledgeable students may signal widespread confusion in the class. Lower-scoring students may, in fact, be guessing on the more difficult items too, but this result indicates you need to reteach them rather

than simply revise the test item. Random guessing adds errors of measurement to the scores, thereby reducing reliability and validity.

SELECTING TEST ITEMS

Most teachers who use item-analysis procedures do so for one or more of the following reasons: (a) to check whether the items are functioning as intended, (b) to give students feedback on their assessment performance, (c) to acquire feedback for themselves about students' difficulties, (d) to identify areas of the curriculum that may need improvement, and (e) to obtain objective data that signal the need for revising their items. You can also use item analysis for selecting some items and culling others from a pool of items.

Purpose of Assessment Helps Select Items

No statistical item selection rule is helpful if it is inconsistent with your purpose for conducting assessments. Further, any procedure you use for selecting some items over others changes the definition of the domain of performance. Those performances represented by items you eliminate are never assessed.

Relative Versus Absolute Student Attainment   Careful selection of items results in shorter, more efficient, and more reliable assessments. In the classroom, *statistically based item selection* seems to apply most when you are concerned primarily with students' relative achievement rather than their absolute achievement, which is not a typical classroom purpose. You are focusing on assessing relative achievement when your priority is to rank students with respect to what they have learned. You are focus on assessing absolute achievement when your priority is to determine the precise content (or performance) each student has learned.

As an example, suppose you wanted to assess students' learning of the 100 simple addition facts typically taught in first and second grades. If you want to know only the relative achievement of the students (which student knows the most, next most, and so on), you could use a relatively short test, made up of only addition facts that best discriminate among the students. This test would probably contain mostly the middle and upper parts of the addition table. Addition facts that almost everyone knows (such as 1 + 1 = 2) would not be included on such a test because these items would not discriminate ($D = 0$) and thus would not provide information to rank the students. However, excluding certain addition facts from the assessment because they do not discriminate well means that you will be unable to observe a student's performance on all 100 addition facts.

On the other hand, suppose your purpose for assessment is to identify the particular addition combinations with which a student has difficulty. In this case, finding out the absolute level of achievement would be your main assessment focus. You may find it necessary to use a longer, less efficient test (or several shorter ones), perhaps assessing all 100 facts.

Absolute, rather than relative, achievement is more important for diagnostic assessments intended to identify such things as whether a student has acquired particular reading skills, learned a certain percentage of facts in some specified domain, or has the ability to solve certain types of problems. Relative achievement is more important when you are assessing a student's general educational development in a subject area.

Complete Versus Partial Ordering For some educational decisions, you may need to accurately rank all students using their test performance, called a **complete ordering of students**. On the other hand, you may only want to separate students into five ordered categories so you can assign grades (A, B, C, D, and F). In so doing, you may not wish to make precise distinctions among the students within each category. Similarly, you may wish to divide the class into two groups, such as mastery/nonmastery or faster/slower readers. We say there is **partial ordering** when the categories themselves are ordered, but there is *no ordering of individuals within a category*. Categorizing students by their grades, or into fail-pass groups, are examples of partial ordering.

When you focus your assessment on either partial or complete ordering, it is inefficient to include items that do not contribute to ordering and distinguishing students. Such items therefore are culled from the pool. To cull, you try out items with students before creating the final version of the test (or you use items from past administrations of the test for which you have data). Calculate item statistics (p and D). Select and assemble into the final test those items with high, positive discrimination indices. Select items with p-values (difficulty) at each level of performance where

you wish to have information (e.g., A through F). C students, for example, should not simply be C students because they got right, partly by chance, a portion of the items that A students are expected to get. C students should be in that category because they scored correctly on items at that level of difficulty.

Realities, Content Coverage, and Compromise

In practice, you must include test items with less than ideal statistical properties, so a test can match its blueprint. Actual assessment construction tends to be a compromise between considerations of subject-matter coverage and psychometric properties. The general principle is as follows: *Select the best available items that cover the important areas of content as defined by the blueprint, even though the discrimination and difficulty indices of these items have values that are less than ideal.*

Rules of Thumb for Selecting Test Items

Figure 14.5 summarizes guidelines for selecting items for classroom tests, keeping in mind our discussion of the differences between building a test to measure relative achievement and building one to measure absolute achievement. Note that coverage of content and learning objectives has primacy over statistical indexes when selecting test items by the procedures recommended here. The guidelines shown in Figure 14.5 require you to understand whether the prospective test should assess only one ability or a combination of several abilities. A **homogeneous test** will measure one ability, whereas a **heterogeneous test** will assess a combination of abilities. If your test contains some items for which students can get the right answer by random guessing (such as with multiple-choice items), then the items you select should be approximately 5% easier than shown in the figure.

In choosing between two items assessing the same learning objective for a test of relative achievement, good item discrimination takes precedence over obtaining the ideal item difficulty level. That is, if two items assess the same learning objective and are of approximately the same difficulty level, use the one that discriminates better.

When you design a criterion-referenced classroom test, item statistics play a lesser role for selecting and culling items. You should still calculate item statistics to obtain data on how the items

FIGURE 14.5 Guidelines for selecting items.

	Relative achievement is the focus		Absolute achievement is the focus
	Complete ordering	**Partial ordering (two groups)**	
General concerns	Ranking all the pupils in terms of their relative attainment in a subject area.	Dividing pupils into two groups on the basis of their relative attainment. Pupils within each group will be treated alike.	Assess the absolute status (achievement) of the pupil with respect to a well-defined domain of instructionally relevant tasks.
Specific focus of test	Seek to accurately describe differences in relative achievement between individual pupils.	Seek to accurately classify persons into two categories.	Seek to accurately estimate the percentage of the domain each pupil can perform successfully.
Attention to the test's blueprint	Be sure that items cover all important topics and objectives within the blueprint.	Be sure that items cover all important topics and objectives within the blueprint.	Be sure items are a representative, random sample from the defined domain that the blueprint operationalizes.
How the difficulty index (p) is used	Within each topical area of the blueprint, select those items with the following: (1) p between 0.16 and 0.84 if performance on the test represents a single ability. (2) p between 0.40 and 0.60 if performance on the test represents several different abilities. *Note:* Items should be easier than described above if guessing is a factor.	Within each topical area of the blueprint, select those items with p-values slightly larger than the percentage of persons to be classified in the upper group (e.g., if the class is to be divided in half [0.50] then items with p-value of about 0.60 should be selected; if the division is lower 75% vs. upper 25%, items should have $p = 0.35$ [approximately]). *Note:* The above suggestion assumes the test measures a single ability.	Don't select items on the basis of their p-values, but study each p to see if it is signaling a poorly written item. Make sure there is a sufficient number of items with p-values at each level of performance.
How the discrimination index (D) is used	Within each topical area of the blueprint, select items with D greater than or equal to +0.30.	Within each topical area of the blueprint, select items with D greater than or equal to +0.30.	All items should have D greater than or equal to 0.00. Unless there is a rational explanation to the contrary, revise those items not possessing this property.

might be improved, however. Items exhibiting zero or negative discrimination frequently contain technical flaws that you may not notice unless you do an item analysis. You should also make sure that the item difficulties cover the range of expected performance.

MyLab Education **Self-Check 14.2**

MyLab Education **Application Exercise 14.2:** Difficulty and Discrimination Indexes

CONCLUSION

In this chapter, we discussed preparing students for assessment. We also discussed how to use item analysis to assist you in maximizing the quality of your tests. Both of these are important aspects of handling assessments that sometimes do not get the thoughtful planning they deserve. We turn next to grading, which may

have the opposite problem: Teachers and students sometimes devote more time and energy to grades than is probably good for them. We hope the next chapter will help you approach grading thoughtfully, as the classroom-summative part of a balanced assessment system that also includes your classroom formative assessments and external summative assessments like state tests.

FIGURE 14.6 Item-analysis summary for use with Exercises 3 and 4.

Item number	Groups	Options				Faulty distractors	Miskeying	Ambiguous	Guessing
		A	B	C	D				
1.	Upper	0	2	*9	0	——	——	——	——
	Middle			*5					
	Lower	1	2	*4	4		$p =$ ——	$D =$ ——	
2.	Upper	2	*7	0	2	——	——	——	——
	Middle		*4						
	Lower	0	*9	1	1		$p =$ ——	$D =$ ——	
3.	Upper	9	*1	1	0	——	——	——	——
	Middle		*1						
	Lower	6	*2	2	1		$p =$ ——	$D =$ ——	
4.	Upper	*5	5	0	1	——	——	——	——
	Middle	*8							
	Lower	*3	3	3	2		$p =$ ——	$D =$ ——	
5.	Upper	3	2	3	*3	——	——	——	——
	Middle				*4				
	Lower	3	2	3	*3		$p =$ ——	$D =$ ——	

EXERCISES

1. The following statements are thoughts that students might have during an assessment situation. Read each statement and decide whether it is a task-relevant (TR) thought or a task-irrelevant (TI) thought.
   a. "I have to be very careful in answering this problem. My teacher takes points off for computational errors."
   b. "I am really dumb. I just can't do it!"
   c. "If I don't pass this test, Dad will kill me!"
   d. "I know I don't know the answer to this question. It's no use trying to fool Mr. Jones. He'll just think I'm dumber than I am."
   e. "Oops! I forgot to study the material this question is asking. Oh well, I'd better write something down. I usually am able to get a few points from Mr. Jones!"

2. Explain the meaning of each of the following values of D.
   a. +1.00
   b. +0.50
   c. 0.00
   d. –0.50
   e. –1.00

3. Figure 14.6 shows a summary of item-analysis data for five multiple-choice items for a class of 30 students. There are 11 students in the upper group and 11 students in the lower group. The keyed answer to each item is marked with an asterisk. For each item, calculate the difficulty index (p) and the discrimination index (D), then decide whether the item has poor distractors, is possibly miskeyed, the upper group is possibly guessing, or two options seem to be ambiguous.

4. The following questions refer to your analysis of the item data in Exercise 3.
   a. Which item is a negative discriminator?
   b. Which item is the easiest?
   c. Which item is the most difficult?
   d. For which items do more upper-group students than lower-group students choose a distractor?
   e. Which item has the highest discrimination index?
   f. Which item has the lowest discrimination index?
   g. What is the average (mean) score on this five-item test for the 30 students who took it?

Evaluating and Grading Student Achievement

KEY CONCEPTS

1. The main purpose of grading is to communicate information about student achievement. Report cards are one of several means of reporting student achievement.

2. There are norm- and criterion-referenced methods for combining scores into one summary achievement grade. You should choose the one appropriate to your situation. A criterion-referenced grading model matches the typical standards-based or objectives-based approach to teaching.

3. Choose and weight components for grading according to your assessment plan. Grading creates a measurement scale that—like any scale—should yield valid and reliable scores.

IMPORTANT TERMS

assessment variables (evaluation variables)

borderline cases

continuous assessment

criterion-referenced grading framework (absolute standards)

fixed-percentage method for grading

gradebook program

grading

grading on a curve

grading variables

logic rule method for grading

median score method

minimum attainment method

multiple marking system

narrative report

norm-referenced grading model

permanent record

quality-level method for grading (rubric method)

report card

reporting method (checklist, letter grades, letter to parents, narrative reports, numbers, parent-teacher conferences, percentages, pupil-teacher conferences, rating scale, two-category)

reporting variables

self-referenced grading framework (growth-based grading)

SS-score method for making composites

stakeholders

standard deviation method of grading

standards-based report card

total points method for grading

THE MEANINGS AND PURPOSES OF GRADES

What Are Your Attitudes Toward Grades?

Before starting this chapter, consider how you feel about assigning grades and marks. (In this chapter, we'll use the term "grades." The term "marks" was more common in the early twentieth century, though, and is still used today.) Read each of the statements in Figure 15.1. Next to each one, check A if you agree, D if you disagree, and U if you are undecided. Compare your answers with those of your classmates and your instructor. Keep these attitudes in mind as you study this chapter and think about how to apply the concepts to your own teaching. Revisit your answers after you study this chapter. How many answers did you change?

Continuous Assessment and Grading

Formative Assessment **Continuous assessment** is the daily process by which you gather information about students' progress in achieving the curriculum's learning objectives (Nitko, 1995). Continuous assessment has both formative and summative aspects. You use formative continuous assessment to make decisions about daily lesson planning and how well your day's lesson is going. You may not formally record such formative evaluations; most formative evaluations are reported directly to the student.

Summative Assessment This chapter emphasizes how to use grades to report your summative continuous assessments of students' achievement of the curriculum's major learning objectives. **Grading** (or marking) refers primarily to the process of using a system of symbols (usually letters, numbers, or proficiency levels) for reporting various types of student progress. Grading for summative purposes lets you provide yourself, other teachers, school officials, students, parents or guardians, postsecondary educational institutions, and potential employers with a report about how well students have achieved the curriculum learning objectives. You usually are required to report students' grades several times a year. The report covers several weeks of school, called a grading period; this is often a quarter of the academic year. In the later years of schooling, students' grades become part of their transcripts. The school reports grades to students and parents through various means such as a **report card**, conferences, or letters.

Validity Grades serving official summative evaluation purposes must be based on formal, continuous assessments that are aligned with your

FIGURE 15.1 **What are your feelings about grades (A = agree, U = undecided, D = disagree)?**

	A U D		A U D
1. There are justifiable reasons why the grades of some teachers, courses, and departments average consistently higher than others.	_ _ _	6. Absolute standards are more desirable than relative standards in evaluating and grading students in academic areas.	_ _ _
2. Academic grades should be based more on achievement status than on growth or progress.	_ _ _	7. In the absence of an institutional grading policy, grades should not be used in determining eligibility for athletics and other extraclass activities.	_ _ _
3. Students' academic grades should be determined solely by their academic achievements and not by attendance, citizenship, effort, or attitudes.	_ _ _	8. "Pass/fail" or "credit/no credit" are more desirable than grading systems with three or more categories for academic classes.	_ _ _
4. Schools should adopt and enforce a clearly defined institutional grading policy.	_ _ _	9. Allowing students to contract for their own grades is preferable to marking on a relative basis.	_ _ _
5. In the absence of an institutional grading policy, grades should not be used in determining students' eligibility for academic courses and programs.	_ _ _	10. Teachers should attempt to evaluate and grade students in such areas as interests, attitudes, and motivation.	_ _ _

school's standards, official curriculum's learning objectives, and educational psychology. As one fourth-grade teacher said:

> I don't know how other teachers feel, but anytime I send out an official report with my name on it, it is the equivalent of a legal document. The information in that report declares itself to be the best and latest educational information on a child. This may sound overly dramatic, but parents are expecting that report to tell them about an important chunk of their child's life. It is supposed to be true, and it is official. (Cited in Azwell & Schmar, 1995, pp. 7–9)

Because many **stakeholders** will use your summative grades for many different purposes, the grades must be validly prepared and based on high-quality assessments. Assessments contributing to grades come from several sources: curriculum materials, quizzes and tests, performance tasks you create, projects and other long-term tasks, portfolios you and your students assemble, and assessments set by groups of teachers working together.

It seems unfair to base a student's final grade on a single examination or assessment. This "big bang" approach to evaluation ignores several important factors about assessing students: (a) Only a limited amount of time is available during one teaching period for assessing; (b) in a limited time, only a small sample of tasks can be administered to students; (c) students may know much more than what appeared on the "one shot" assessment; (d) students' illness or family problems can interfere with their ability to demonstrate the required achievement; (e) students can demonstrate their achievement in several ways other than the one way you decided to assess it; and (f) some important learning objectives are best assessed through longer-term projects, papers, or out-of-school assignments.

On the other hand, we know teachers who record *too many* grades, most of which are really from practice work. Adding in practice grades does two things, and both of them are harmful to the validity of grades. One, it confuses students' achievement of learning objectives with their practice, and the final result is an "average" that doesn't represent either one. Two, it makes grades a mechanism for enforcing work habits or compliance. Grades should reflect achievement, not discipline.

Jennifer McDaniel, AP Calculus teacher
Clay County High School, Manchester, KY

MyLab Education

Video Example 15.1

The primary purpose of a grade is to communicate information about student achievement. The teachers and students in this video describe how effective grading systems do not grade practice work, and that this approach contributes to learning and motivation as well as to more accurate communication about achievement.

Why Teachers Dislike Grading   Grading for many teachers is one of the most difficult and troublesome aspects of teaching. Teachers are usually much more comfortable in their role as advocates for their students than as judges or evaluators. In spite of teachers' dislike of grading, it is a required part of the job, which is one reason why you need to learn how to grade students as validly as possible.

How People Perceive and Use Grades

Figure 15.2 gives examples of information frequently found on formal student progress reports and various kinds of decisions that may be based on such information. Different persons will use grades in different ways. Figure 15.3 shows several different types of stakeholders and the ways they use grades. This figure illustrates that grades have serious meaning beyond your classroom. The grades you assign must be clear to judge whether any of these uses are valid.

Although assessment specialists generally recommend that you keep the meaning of grades clear by basing them only on a student's achievement of your course's learning objectives, we know that many teachers do not follow this advice (Brookhart, 1991, 2013b; Stiggins, Frisbie, & Griswold, 1989; Waltman & Frisbie, 1994). It is part of the goal of this chapter to help you understand why grading on achievement is important and how to do it. We need to be clear here: Grades are not intended to be simply a mirror of tested achievement. Achievement tests are usually intended to be context-free measures of learning, and grades are measures of the learning that happens in the context of a particular classroom (Brookhart, 2015; Brookhart et al., 2016). Grades should, however, reflect student

FIGURE 15.2 Examples of the types of information found on report cards and the types of decisions made from that information.

Information in report	Decisions that can be made			
	Selection	Placement, remediation	Guidance, counseling	Course improvement
1. Content or objectives learned	Promotion, probation, graduation, admissions	Selecting courses to take, remedial help needed	Selecting next courses to take, additional schooling needed, career-related choices	Deciding where instruction can be improved
2. Comparison of performance in different subjects	Admission	Selecting advanced and/or remedial courses	Determining pattern of a pupil's strengths and weaknesses	Identifying areas that are strong points of school
3. Performance relative to other people	Scholarships, prizes, admission	Estimating likely success, eligibility for special programs	Estimating likely success in certain areas	
4. Social behavior		Matching personal characteristics to course and teacher placement	Determining need for adjustment, likes, dislikes, ability to get along with others	Identifying problems with a course or with a teacher

FIGURE 15.3 Various uses to which grades are put by different stakeholders.

Usage for grades	Stakeholder likely to use the grades in the way indicated						
	Student	Parents	Teacher	Guidance counselor	School administrators	Postsecondary educational institutions	Employers
1. Reaffirm what is already known about classroom achievement	✓		✓				
2. Document educational progress and course completion	✓	✓	✓	✓	✓	✓	✓
3. Obtain extrinsic rewards/punishments	✓	✓					
4. Obtain social attention or teacher attention	✓						
5. Request new educational placement		✓	✓	✓	✓		
6. Judge a teacher's competence or fairness		✓			✓		
7. Indicate school problems for a student		✓	✓	✓	✓		
8. Support vocational or career guidance explorations	✓	✓		✓			
9. Limit or exclude student's participation in extracurricular activities		✓	✓		✓		
10. Promote or retain			✓		✓		
11. Grant graduation/diploma					✓		
12. Determine whether student has necessary prerequisite for a higher-level course			✓	✓	✓		
13. Select for postsecondary education						✓	
14. Decide whether an individual has basic skills needed for a particular job							✓

achievement of your intended learning outcomes, linked to your curriculum and standards.

Communicating to parents is especially challenging. Some research shows that parents' and teachers' understanding of what report card grades mean are often far apart (Waltman & Frisbie, 1994). For example, parents may see grades as reflecting pure achievement. Or they may interpret the grading scale differently than teachers do, for example thinking of a C as "average" when most teachers' average grade is about a B.

For the teacher, grades communicate more than achievement information about a student. The grades you assign communicate your (and your school's) values. If obedience to your classroom rules is rewarded by an A or "performing satisfactorily" in *reading*, but "fooling around" during class means the *reading grade* is lowered, in spite of successful reading performance, you have communicated that obedience is valued more than reading well. The teacher who gives an unsatisfactory grade to the student whose academic performance is satisfactory and then says, "I warned you about passing notes during class!" is perhaps communicating vindictiveness. You may value both social behavior (e.g., conformity) and achievement, but if the grade you report intertwines the two, you are communicating poorly and are encouraging confusion. To clarify matters, you must separate your evaluations of achievement from your evaluations of noncognitive student characteristics.

Educators have voiced a number of criticisms of grades over the years. You need to be aware of these criticisms to explain the rationale for your own grading policy to parents and other educators. Many of these criticisms can be summarized under the four headings in Figure 15.4 (Ebel, 1974; Laska & Juarez, 1992).

REPORTING METHODS

Schools use several different **reporting methods** to communicate to students and parents and to keeping records of students' achievement. Figure 15.5 summarizes the advantages and disadvantages of different methods. Your school district may use more than one method of reporting student progress because different methods may serve different purposes and different audiences.

FIGURE 15.4 Commonly expressed criticisms of grades.

A. Grades are essentially meaningless.
1. There is great diversity among institutions and teachers in grading practices.
2. Many schools lack definite grading policies.
3. A single symbol cannot possibly report adequately the complex details of an educational achievement.
4. Teachers are often casual or even careless in grading.
5. Grades are frequently used to punish or to enforce discipline rather than to report achievement accurately.

B. Grades are educationally unimportant.
6. Grades are only symbols.
7. The most important outcomes are intangible and hence cannot be assessed or graded.
8. A teacher's grades are less important to pupils than their own self-evaluations.
9. Grades do not predict later achievement correctly.
10. What should be evaluated is the educational program, not the pupils.

C. Grades are unnecessary.
11. Grades are ineffective motivators of real achievement in education.
12. When students learn mastery, as they should, no differential levels of achievement remain to be graded.
13. Grades have persisted in schools mainly because teachers cling to traditional practices.

D. Grades are harmful.
14. Low grades may discourage the less able pupils from efforts to learn.
15. Grading makes failure inevitable for some pupils.
16. Parents sometimes punish pupils for low grades, and reward high grades inappropriately.
17. Grades set universal standards for all pupils despite their great individual differences.
18. Grading emphasizes common goals for all pupils and discourages individuality in learning.
19. Grading rewards conformity and penalizes creativity.
20. Grading fosters competition rather than cooperation.
21. Pressure to get high grades leads some pupils to cheat.
22. Grading is more compatible with subject-centered education than with humanistic, child-centered education.

FIGURE 15.5 Advantages and disadvantages of some commonly used methods of reporting student achievement.

Name	Type of code used	Advantages	Disadvantages
Letter grades	A, B, C, etc., also "+" and "−" may be added.	a. Administratively easy to use b. Believed to be easy to interpret c. Concisely summarize overall performance	a. Meaning of a grade varies widely with subject, teacher, school b. Do not describe strengths and weaknesses c. Kindergarten and primary schoolchildren may feel defeated by them
Number or percentage grade	Integers (5, 4, 3 …) or percentages (99, 98, …)	a. Same as points a, b, and c above b. More continuous than letter grades c. May be used along with letter grades	a. Same as points a, b, and c above b. Meaning not immediately apparent unless explanation accompanies them
Standards-based grade	Advanced, Proficient, Basic, Below Basic, or similar	a. Requires standards-referenced grading methods b. Often used with fine-grained reporting categories	a. May not match state test results b. "Advanced" grade requires assessments that go beyond many conventional assessments
Two-category grade	Pass-fail, satisfactory-unsatisfactory, credit-entry	a. Less devastating to younger students b. Can encourage older students to take courses normally neglected because of fear of lowered GPA	a. Less reliable than more continuous system b. Does not communicate enough information about pupil's performance for others to judge progress
Narrative report	None, but may refer to one or more of the above; however, usually does not refer to grades	a. Allows teacher the opportunity to describe a student's educational development b. Shows a student's progress in terms of standards, indicators of achievement, learning objectives, or a continuum of educational growth c. Provides opportunity to open dialogue and other types of communication with parents and students	a. Very time-consuming b. Requires excellent writing skill and effective communication skills on the teacher's part c. May require translation into language read by parents, with possible loss of meaning in the translation d. Parents who are not skilled readers may misunderstand it or may be put off e. Parents may be overwhelmed and not respond f. Often modified to include checklist-like list of indicators with short teacher comments
Pupil-teacher conference	Usually none, but any of the above may be discussed	a. Offers opportunity to discuss progress personally b. Can be an ongoing process that is integrated into instruction	a. Teacher needs skill in offering positive as well as negative comments b. Can be time-consuming c. Can be threatening to some pupils d. Doesn't offer the institution the kind of summary record desired
Parent-teacher conference	None, but often one or more of the above may be discussed	a. Allows parents and teachers to discuss concerns and clarify misunderstandings b. Teachers can show samples of students' work and explain basis for judgments made c. May lead to improved home-school relations	a. Time-consuming b. Requires teacher to prepare ahead of time c. May provoke too much anxiety for some teachers and parents d. Inadequate means of reporting large amounts of information e. May be inconvenient for parent to attend
Letter to parents	None, but may refer to one or more of the above	a. Useful supplement to other progress-reporting methods	a. Short letters inadequately communicate pupil progress b. Requires exceptional writing skill and much teacher time
Student-parent-teacher conferences	None	a. Students take ownership b. Students can show samples of their work and interpret them c. Typically generates family interest	a. Same points as a through e above. b. Students must learn how to lead conferences c. Requires class practice time

Traditional Report Cards

Traditional report cards typically use letters or numerical grades, or some combination of both. They are often coupled with other reporting methods, as for example when traditional report cards are used with parent-teacher conferences. Teachers use some methods of reporting student achievement more frequently at certain grade levels. Letter grades are used with high frequency in the upper elementary, junior high, and senior high school levels. Parent-teacher conferences do not occur often in junior and senior high schools.

Often schools use combinations of methods on the same report card. For example, letter grades may report students' subject-matter achievement; rating scales may report the students' attitudes and deportment. A parent-teacher conference may convey information on achievement, effort, attitudes, and behavior. Schools may use a combination of nearly all methods.

A **permanent record** is the official record of a student's school performance. Not all information needs to appear in a student's permanent record. Putting elementary students' letter grades in a permanent record is controversial. Many educators (and some professional associations) argue that reporting or recording grades at the elementary level is inappropriate. However, students and parents may become upset if, for the first time in middle school, a student receives a C (or lower) in a subject, when previously the student has received only "performing satisfactorily" checks on the elementary report card or a narrative report.

Some intermediate policy may help a student with this transition from the elementary school marking code to a new marking code at the junior high. A school may decide, for example, to have teachers prepare letter grades for fourth and fifth graders, but not to report them on report cards or in the permanent record. Parents, however, are apprised of these grades. Thus, a "performing satisfactorily" can mean a C for some students and a B for others. At the end of the year, the letter-grades records are destroyed.

Conflicts may arise between methods. School administrators need a concise summary of each student's progress for accountability and record keeping. Parents and teachers may need slightly more detailed explanations of the content taught, the standards mastered, and how a student's educational development compares with members of a peer group.

Narrative Reports

Narrative reports are detailed, written accounts of what each student has learned in relation to the school's curriculum framework and the student's effort in class. The hope is that narrative reports will replace the shortcomings of letter grades because the latter tend to condense too much information into a single symbol. Narratives also allow teachers to include unique information about students' learning or something unique the teacher has done for that student—things that would not appear on a standardized form (Power & Chandler, 1998). Bagley (2008) studied students' reactions to narrative report cards in a private school. Most students found narrative evaluations more stressful than letter grades, but ultimately they appreciated the usefulness of the personalized detail. Teachers said that writing evaluations was time-consuming, but realized it allowed the opportunity to provide highly personalized feedback to students. Bagley (2008) also noted that the private school, with its small student-teacher ratio, was not typical in its ability to use narrative reports as its main reporting method.

Advantages   The concept of providing a rich description of a student's learning and educational development is laudable. When done well, these descriptions can mean much more to parents and students than the simple summaries that grades provide. A rich description would be especially useful for describing elementary students' learning if a state or school has defined a continuum of learning objectives and performance standards over several grades, with benchmarks defined for each grade.

Limitations   Narrative reports can be poorly or insensitively written, of course. Even teachers with good intentions find them difficult to write well. They may confuse or overwhelm parents, who may be asked to read five to 10 pages of narrative to understand what their children are learning. Using narrative reports should not be undertaken without considerable teacher development. A mean teacher can be just as mean in narrative writing as in letter grading: "Johnny thinks like a chicken!" Sensitivity and constructive comments are necessary. Lots of guided practice in writing nonthreatening and nonblaming comments is needed.

Standards-Based Report Cards

Standards-based report cards are report cards where academic achievement is reported by standard, instead of by subject. Typically a proficiency scale (e.g., Advanced, Proficient, Basic, Below Basic) is used instead of letter or numerical grades. The standards on the report card are often reporting standards derived from state standards rather than the state standards in their original form (Guskey & Bailey, 2010). This derivation is because state standards are too many in number and too complex to be effective communication tools. Figure 15.6 gives an example of a standards-based report card from the Lincoln Public Schools, Grade 3. As you can see, it uses a **multiple marking system**, that is, there is more than one method used for reporting. The report card in Figure 15.6 has separate methods of reporting for academic achievement and work habits, plus a section in which to record attendance.

Districts develop reporting standards that are specific enough to communicate what students learned, but not so specific that they overwhelm parents and others. Some districts also develop brochures to further detail what students were expected to learn during the year or in each report period. When standards communicate specific learning outcomes, it is especially important to make the reported grades reflect achievement and not work habits, effort, citizenship, or behavior.

Typically, standards-based report cards have a work habits, citizenship, character development, or behavior scale in addition to the academic portion. The report card in Figure 15.6 has a scale called Character Development that serves this purpose. Having a separate place to report these important characteristics makes it easier to leave them out of the academic grades. Often, the work habits portion of a standards-based report card uses a frequency scale to rate students (e.g., Always, Frequently, Sometimes, Never). Sometimes a rubric is used instead.

Advantages The major advantage of standards-based report cards is the focus on learning that comes with spelling out in more detail the learn-

ing outcome on which the student is being evaluated. Traditional subject-matter grades have for a century been known to include nonachievement factors (Brookhart, 2009), and despite efforts to the contrary the practice of counting nonachievement factors in grades has been difficult to eradicate. Standards-based report cards, with their separate scales for nonachievement factors, may actually succeed where past efforts have failed.

A second advantage of standards-based report cards is that they make it easier to see grades as part of an assessment system. Standards-based report cards make it easier to see classroom summative assessment (grading) as consistent with large-scale summative assessment, especially state tests. Standards-based reporting when done well can be consistent with state test results; however, without attention to using learning-focused grading practices, standards-based reporting can also suffer from a mix of achievement and nonachievement factors that lower the grades' validity (Welsh & D'Agostino, 2009).

Disadvantages One disadvantage of standards-based report cards is the cultural weight of traditional grades and grading practices. "Everyone" knows—or thinks they know—what A, B, C, D, and F mean. Standards-based grading reform has to fight the public's tendency to want to "translate" standards-based grades as if they meant the same thing as traditional grades (e.g., "Advanced is just another name for A"). Given human nature, major changes in any cultural system are always difficult.

A second disadvantage of standards-based report cards is that when done properly, it requires truly advanced work to merit a grade of "Advanced." Well-behaved, dutiful students who are used to doing what is asked of them in ordinary assignments and receiving a grade of A— and their parents—may be disappointed and angry to find that sort of work merits a grade of "Proficient." There is also some concern that proficiency grades do not translate well into the grade-point averages that are currently expected for college admission. While there's no reason that expectation cannot ultimately change, at the present time many high schools are taking a compromise approach to standards-based grading (Brookhart, 2009). They maintain the traditional symbols for the academic grades (e.g., ABCDF),

FIGURE 15.6 **Example of standards-based report card for Grade 3.**

Source: Lincoln Public Schools, Lincoln, Nebraska. Used by permission.

Designing Report Card Grading Policies

Student _____

Student ID _____

School _____

Homeroom Teacher _____

REPORT CARD
3rd Grade
Lincoln Public Schools
Year_____

Rev. 7/10

	Q1	Q2	Q3	Q4
Absences				

	Q1	Q2	Q3	Q4
Tardies				

ACADEMIC ACHIEVEMENT

4=Exceeds district standards   3=Meets district standards   2=Approaches but does not meet district standards   1=Does not meet district standards   •=Not taught/assessed this quarter

WORK/STUDY HABITS

4=Exceeds expectations   3=Meets expectations   2=Approaches expectations   1=Does not meet expectations

Indicators: Listens, Follows oral and written directions, Is on task, Participates in class, Strives for quality work, Seeks help as necessary, Completes assignments on time.

The descriptions below reflect the Lincoln Public Schools standards for this grade level. The marks given reflect quarterly performance.

CHARACTER DEVELOPMENT

	Q1	Q2	Q3	Q4
Selects and Uses Age-Appropriate Behavior • Accepts consequences for actions taken • Demonstrates self-discipline/control • Follows school and classroom rules				
Selects and Uses Age-Appropriate Coping Skills • Demonstrates decision making skills • Demonstrates organizational skills • Acts on the need for help				
Demonstrates Confidence in Self • Recognizes and accepts own abilities • Demonstrates a positive attitude toward self • Expresses personal feelings and ideas				
Interacts with Others Appropriately • Develops and maintains friendships • Demonstrates respect for individual rights • Works cooperatively with others				

Teacher(s) _____

MATHEMATICS

MATHEMATICS CONTENT	Q1	Q2	Q3	Q4
Numeration and Number Sense • Reads, writes, and compares whole numbers through 10,000 • Writes fractions • Rounds numbers to nearest 10 or 100 • Compares and orders decimals to hundredths				
Computation and Estimation • Adds and subtracts 3-digit numbers • Knows multiplication and division facts to 10				
Measurement • Tells time • Finds elapsed time • Finds perimeter				
Geometry • Uses properties of lines and angles • Plots ordered pairs				
Data Analysis and Probability • Collects, organizes, and interprets data • Interprets graphs • Uses probability to make predictions				
Algebra • Writes addition and subtraction sentences • Solves addition and subtraction work problems				

LANGUAGE ARTS

READING	Q1	Q2	Q3	Q4
Word Analysis/Spelling • Uses knowledge of advanced phonics patterns and multi-syllable word structures to read, write, and spell words				
Fluency • Reads grade level text accurately with appropriate phrasing, expression, and rate				
Vocabulary • Builds knowledge of literary, content, and academic words • Applies context clues and text features to infer meanings • Identifies word relationships (e.g., synonyms, antonyms, multiple meanings)				
Comprehension • Identifies author's purpose • Retells information from narrative text including characters, setting, and plot • Summarizes main ideas from informational text • Uses prior knowledge to connect text to self, to other texts, and to the world • Monitors understanding and self-corrects when appropriate				
Multiple Literacies • Identifies, locates, and evaluates print and electronic resources to find and share information				
Work/Study Habits				

WRITING	Q1	Q2	Q3	Q4
Writing Process • Applies writing process to plan, draft, revise, and edit • Writes strong sentences using correct spelling, grammar, punctuation, and capitalization				
Writing Genres • Writes for a variety of purposes and audiences • Writes considering characteristics of a specific genre				
Handwriting/Publishing • Writes legibly and fluently • Publishes using electronic resources				
Work/Study Habits				

Copyright © 2010 by Lincoln Public Schools

FIGURE 15.6 *(Continued)*

Grading and Learning

MATHEMATICS

MATHEMATICAL PROCESSES	Q1	Q2	Q3	Q4
Problem Solving				
Develops Conceptual Understanding				
Work/Study Habits				

Teacher(s) _____

HEALTH

HEALTH CONTENT	Q1	Q2	Q3	Q4
Mental/Emotional Health				
Communicable/Chronic Diseases				
Family/Social Health				
Consumer/Community/Environmental Health				

HEALTH PROCESSES	Q1	Q2	Q3	Q4
Uses Health-Promoting Skills • Makes decisions, sets goals, and accesses information				
Work/Study Habits				

Teacher(s) _____

SCIENCE

SCIENCE CONTENT	Q1	Q2	Q3	Q4
Dinosaurs and Fossils				
Energy				
Embryology				
Simple Machines				

SCIENCE PROCESSES	Q1	Q2	Q3	Q4
Uses Scientific Method • Observes, measures, and predicts				
Work/Study Habits				

Teacher(s) _____

SOCIAL STUDIES

SOCIAL STUDIES CONTENT	Q1	Q2	Q3	Q4
Communities Have a Place				
Communities Have a History				
Communities Have Responsible Citizens				
Communities Provide Goods and Services				

SOCIAL STUDIES PROCESSES	Q1	Q2	Q3	Q4
Uses Social Studies Skills and Knowledge • Acquires and analyzes information, communicates, and develops a historical awareness				
Work/Study Habits				

Teacher(s) _____

ART

	Q1	Q2	Q3	Q4
Thinks with Art • Integrates the 5 steps of the Creative Process				
Connects with Art • Reflects upon art in relation to history, cultures, and careers				
Communicates with Art • Uses the elements and principles of design with a variety of materials to communicate ideas through art				
Talks about Art • Looks at and talks about their work and the work of others using the language of art				
Work/Study Habits				

Teacher(s) _____

LANGUAGE ARTS

SPEAKING/LISTENING	Q1	Q2	Q3	Q4
Conversations and Presentations • Communicates ideas in classroom activities • Demonstrates presentation techniques and conversation strategies				
Listening • Listens in formal and informal settings for a variety of purposes				
Work/Study Habits				

Teacher(s) _____

MUSIC

MUSIC CONTENT (Skills)	Q1	Q2	Q3	Q4
Sings				
Plays Instruments				
Improvises & Composes				
Reads & Notates				

MUSIC PROCESS (Musicianship)	Q1	Q2	Q3	Q4
Elements of Music • Applies melody, rhythm, harmony, form, tone color and expressive qualities				
Work/Study Habits				

Teacher(s) _____

PHYSICAL EDUCATION

	Q1	Q2	Q3	Q4
Physical Skills and Movement Patterns • Combine skills and sequences in game-like settings				
Movement and Fitness Concepts and Principles • Identifies concepts of skills, fitness, and activities				
Health-Related Physical Activity/Fitness • Demonstrates cardiorespiratory endurance, muscle fitness, and flexibility				
Work/Study Habits—Personal and Social Behavior • Demonstrates fair play, cooperation, sharing, and respect for others				

Teacher(s) _____

TECHNOLOGY

	Q1	Q2	Q3	Q4
Creativity & Innovation • Plans and develops original products using technology tools				
Communication & Collaboration • Uses digital media and technology tools to communicate and collaborate				
Research & Information Fluency • Uses digital tools to gather, evaluate, and process information				
Technology Operations & Concepts • Selects and uses applications effectively and productively				
Work/Study Habits & Digital Citizenship • Actively attends to instruction and contributes to a productive learning environment • Understands and practices responsible, safe, & ethical uses of information and technology				

Teacher(s) _____

Copyright © 2010 by Lincoln Public Schools

This report offers the best professional judgment about your child's performance in relation to school expectations. It is designed to convey a general view of your child's performance. A more specific report can be gained through a parent-teacher conference. Two conference days are scheduled each year. Additional conferences are welcome.

FIGURE 15.7 Suggestions for organizing and conducting parent-teacher conferences.

SET PURPOSE

■ Set goals for the conference.

■ Decide what information you need to communicate with parents.

■ Decide how, if at all, students will be involved, and what their role and tasks will be at the conference.

PLAN LOGISTICS

■ If possible, send home report cards or other information about a week before, so parents have time to prepare questions and talk with their child.

■ Schedule times and locations for each appointment. Include breaks for yourself at regular intervals.

■ Keep to the schedule to respect everyone's time.

■ Arrange for a waiting area where waiting parents cannot overhear your conference with other parents.

■ Arrange a comfortable setting (chairs, tables, etc.) where you can converse easily.

COLLECT EVIDENCE

■ Have grades, portfolios, student work samples, checklists, anecdotal records, etc., as appropriate, organized to share with parents. Work samples should illustrate the general level of student work and help parents understand their student's grades, current achievement level, and next steps.

■ Involve students in the collection of evidence whenever possible.

INTERPRET EVIDENCE

■ Prepare your main points ahead of time. Don't rely on spur-of-the-moment thinking to convey important information about students. Clear oral communication requires just as much preparation as written comments do.

■ Prepare questions you may have for parents about their child's work, interests, activities, etc.

■ If you are well prepared, you can communicate clearly and remain confident.

COMMUNICATE

■ Aim for clarity of expression; make your points clearly and brief and support them with evidence.

■ Listen carefully to what parents say. Respond to their concerns. Be open to learning more about the student than you know from the school setting.

■ Use interpersonal skills: communicate genuine care for the student, develop rapport, and reflect parents' feelings.

■ If the child is present, include him or her in the communication; if the child is not present, plan with parents how to share what went on, so the child does not experience the conference as "people talking behind my back."

■ Plan the next steps for the student jointly with parents.

■ Do not allow antagonistic parents to derail communication. Your job is to understand the child's work and behavior as best you can, not to become the family's counselor or to become afraid or anxious. Listen and try to understand.

Source: Based on ideas from Brookhart (2009); Newman (1997–1998); Perl (1995); and Swiderek (1997).

but try to make those grades truly reflect achievement and give separate work habits grades for each subject. The academic grades are then used to calculate grade-point averages.

Conferences

Parent-Teacher Conferences **Parent-teacher conferences** build strong connections with parents, provide them with an understanding of their children's learning strengths and needs, and help them be involved in their children's learning. However, you need to conduct them carefully and skillfully if they are to be successful. Figure 15.7 lists some of the things to do before, during, and after parent-teacher conferences.

Student-Led Parent Conferences **Student-led parent conferences** accomplish several good things. In addition to building strong connections with parents, student-led parent conferences develop students as agents of their own learning. With proper preparation, conferences help students build confidence, self-regulation skills, and communication skills (Bailey & Guskey, 2001;

FIGURE 15.8 Suggestions for organizing and conducting student-led parent conferences.

Before Student-Led Conferences

■ Maintain a student-focused assessment atmosphere in your classroom. Students should be used to self-assessment as part of their regular learning routine.

■ Meet parents before the conference—or at least call or e-mail. The student-led conference should not be the first time you meet parents.

■ Have students make portfolios to showcase their work, beginning at least several weeks before the conference. Organize the portfolios around learning outcomes you want students to be able to demonstrate. Design portfolios and student self-reflection sheets students can use for both the portfolio and the conference.

■ Role-play or practice conferences in class. Base conferences on claims and evidence. For example, "I can [learning outcome]. Let me show you how I know I can do this."

During Student-Led Conferences

■ Greet parents and make sure there is a comfortable, appropriate place for them and their child to talk. Make sure everyone is aware of the agenda, the time frame, and the ground rules.

■ Younger students can use demonstrations as part of their evidence, in addition to collected work. For example, "I can count to 100 by 5s. Let me show you. 5, 10, 15 …"

■ Older students can refer to evidence collected in their portfolio and interpret it to their parents. For example, "I can analyze how a novel and a movie based on the novel are alike and different, and tell why the authors of the novel and the screenplay probably made the choices they did. Let me show you this report …"

■ Ask students to reflect on their attitudes and dispositions toward their work, and their effort and work habits as well. Set this up with a self-reflection form in the portfolio (or simple questions for younger children) and practice ahead of time. For example, "This report period I tried extra hard to ___. I did this because ___."

After Student-Led Conferences

■ Thank parents for coming and students for their work.

■ Follow up on any particular questions or issues that arise with a phone call, e-mail, or additional conference as appropriate.

■ Evaluate the effectiveness of conferences. Ask students, for example, what they liked and didn't like, how they felt during the conference, what they might do differently next time.

■ Use the conference experience to support continued student self-regulation and self-assessment in the classroom.

Dawson, 2005). Figure 15.8 lists some of the things to do before, during, and after student-led parent conferences.

Limitations of Conferences Conferences are time-consuming for the teacher, both in preparation time and in actual contact time. Schools frequently schedule 1 or 2 days for holding conferences during school hours; some schedule evening hours for the convenience of working parents. Sometimes schools neglect to give teachers time to plan and prepare for the conferences, assuming that teachers either need little or no planning time or that they will do the necessary preparation after hours. Student-led conferences only work well when the students have developed the confidence that comes with lots of practice.

Attendance may also be a problem. Not all parents will come to conferences. Parents may be working, ill, embarrassed about their poor English or their poverty, unwilling to attend, or otherwise unable to come. Some parents are courteous and will notify you that they cannot attend, but you should not expect most parents to do this.

Finally, teachers and/or parents may have too much information, too many issues, or too many concerns to discuss in the brief time allotted to the conference. Often about 20 minutes is allotted for the conference. Also, some parents (and teachers) talk too much and use up more than their share of time. Scheduling another conference with the parents may be necessary.

Privacy Parent conferences and student-led parent-teacher conferences should be private. The school principal should provide facilities to allow confidential discussions. Avoid holding a conference where other teachers, other students, or other parents can overhear what is being said. This courtesy protects the rights of all involved. It may be difficult to limit the conference to one teacher and the parent(s), especially in schools where students have different teachers for different subjects.

In contrast, student-led parent conferences that happen simultaneously and without individual discussion with the teacher are often held in a classroom, sometimes at the student's desk. For this kind of conference, the teacher usually circulates around the room but does not provide official, individual information about student achievement. Rather, the purpose of this kind of conference is the student showcasing his or her work and sharing with parents.

MyLab Education **Self-Check 15.1**

MyLab Education **Application Exercise 15.1:**
Limitations to Letter Grading Systems

CHOOSING A GRADING MODEL

To make grades meaningful, adopt a framework for conceptualizing your grades and use that framework in a well-reasoned way consistent with your teaching approach. Grades must be consistent with the reasons why you want to assign them and with your school district's educational philosophy and policies. You must be able to explain your grading framework to students, parents, and school officials. In this section, we focus on making a decision about which grading framework to use.

Basic Approaches

Although there are many teaching methods and educational philosophies, most have a great deal in common. We can group teaching methods into two broad categories based on their major focus: learning focused or peer-comparison focused. If your teaching focuses on student attainment of standards and learning objectives, use a criterion-referenced grading model, which is the approach used in most schools today. If your teaching focuses on students' competition and out-performing their peers, use a **norm-referenced grading model**. Use self-referencing for formative feedback, but except in special cases do not use it as a grading model.

Criterion Referencing: Absolute Standards

Criterion-referenced grading is also referred to as **absolute standards grading**. You assign grades by comparing a student's performance to a defined set of standards to be achieved, objectives to be learned, or knowledge to be acquired. Students who meet the standards are given the better grades, regardless of how well other students perform or whether they have worked up to their potential. Thus, it is possible that you may give all students As and Bs if they all meet the absolute standards specified by the learning objectives. Similarly, when you use this framework you must be prepared to assign all students Fs and Ds if none of them meet the standards set by the learning objectives.

Criterion-referenced grading is most meaningful when you have a well-defined domain of performance for students to learn. This is the basic teaching approach that underlies the standards movement. State standards in all subjects, including the Common Core State Standards, function as the general goals for learning. Individual districts often are left to align the specific learning objectives with the standards. The aligned learning objectives serve as the well-defined domain of performance students are expected to learn. Achievement of these learning objectives becomes the basis for assigning grades. Arguments both for and against criterion-referencing, in general, center on whether it is of value to know exactly what the student has learned independently of the student's own capability and the learning of others.

Norm-Referencing: Relative Standards

Norm-referencing is also called **grading with relative standards**. In this approach, you assign grades based on how a student's performance compared with others in the class: Students performing better than most classmates receive the higher grades. Norm-referenced grading fits with a teaching philosophy that emphasizes having students attain high achievement by outperforming their peers. The philosophy is that education should make one competitive, that the "cream rises to the top," that all students are not capable of achieving high standards.

Advocates of norm-referencing base their arguments on the necessity of competition in life, the value of knowing one's standing in relation to peers, and the idea that relative achievement is more important than absolute achievement. Arguments against norm-referenced grading center on the ill effects of competition, that the knowledge of standing in a peer group does not describe what a student has learned, and that ascertaining the absolute level of achievement is more important than ascertaining relative achievement.

With norm-referenced grading, you must define the reference group against which you compare a student. Is the reference group the other students in this class or section of the course, in all sections taking the course this year, or all students taking the course during the past 5 years? Just as the criterion-referenced framework requires clearly defining learning objectives for grades to be meaningful, so too does a norm-referenced framework require clearly defining the reference group.

A grade based purely on a student's relative standing in a group does not convey to parents and school officials what the student is capable of doing relative to the curriculum's learning objectives. Further, to act consistently within this framework, you should give good grades to the "top" students, even though they may not possess the level of competence specified by standards or the curriculum's learning objectives. Similarly, you should give poor grades to the low-ranking students even though they may have met the minimum level of competence that the curriculum's learning objectives specify.

Don't waffle and retrofit. You may start out wanting to grade using criterion-referencing and standards, but then discover that your students have done poorly. Being afraid to give poor grades, you may then waffle and start to "grade on the curve" (i.e., use norm-referencing). This retrofitting of a norm-referenced framework simply does not fit either approach and is not good educational practice. If the standards you set are grade appropriate and if students performed poorly, then you should determine why. Perhaps your assessment instruments were poorly designed (e.g., you may have used poor-quality testing materials that came with your curriculum). If so, then your assessments are invalid and no amount of norm-referencing can make them more valid. Perhaps your teaching was inadequate. Then reteaching is in order. Or perhaps the standards are simply not appropriate for the educational development of the students you teach. This is a matter that needs to be addressed by your principal or by the curriculum coordinator. In this case you need to adjust the standards, and then reteach: Grading on the curve in this instance distorts the real educational problem.

Self-Referencing: Growth Standards   There are actually three possible conceptual frameworks for grades. The three basic frameworks are the two mentioned above—criterion-referencing (absolute standards) and norm-referencing (relative standards)—and a third, self-referencing (growth or improvement standards). Figure 15.9 illustrates how grades can reflect the quality of a student's performance in relation to (a) quality levels describing achievement of learning objectives or standards, (b) the performance of others in a specific group (such as classmates), or (c) the student's starting point or overall ability.

A **self-referenced grading framework** is also called **growth-based grading**. You assign grades by comparing students' performance with their own past performance or with your perceptions of their capability: Students performing at or above the level at which you believe them capable of performing receive the better grades, regardless of their absolute levels of attainment or their relative standing in the group. A student who came to the class with very little previous knowledge but who has made great strides may be given the same grade as a student who has learned more but who initially came to the class with a great deal more previous learning.

Arguments in favor of self-referenced grading center on the possibility of reducing competition among students and the idea that grades can be adjusted to motivate, to encourage, and to meet the students' needs. Arguments against the system center on the unreliable nature of teachers' judgments of capability, the need for parents and students to know standing relative to peers, the idea that this procedure tends to be applied mostly to lower-ability students, and the possibility that this system may eventually lead to grading based solely on effort. Additionally, students may not achieve the state's standards set for the grade.

Taken together, these arguments lead to a recommendation. Use self-referencing for some formative assessment purposes, especially for lower-achieving students. Students who hear that today's work is better than yesterday's, even if it is not yet up to expectations, have more

Grade	Absolute scale: task-referenced, criterion-referenced, standards-based *Relative to reporting standards and curriculum learning outcomes, the student has:*	Relative scale: group-referenced, norm-referenced *Relative to the other students in the class, the student is:*	Growth scale: self-referenced, change scale *Relative to the ability and knowledge this student brought to the learning situation, the student:*
A	■ High level of performance on the learning outcomes ■ Extended or advanced learning beyond expectations	■ Far above the class average	■ Made significant gains ■ Performed significantly above what the teacher expected
B	■ Solid performance on the learning outcomes ■ Prepared well for more advanced learning	■ Above the class average	■ Made very good gains ■ Performed somewhat better than what the teacher expected
C	■ Minimum performance on the learning outcomes ■ Deficiencies in a few prerequisites needed for later learning	■ At or very near the class average	■ Made good gains ■ Met the performance level the teacher expected
D	■ Lacking some essential knowledge or not able to perform some of the essential skills from the learning outcomes ■ Deficiencies in many, but not all, of the prerequisites needed for later learning	■ Below the class average	■ Made some good gains ■ Did not quite meet the level of performance the teacher expected
F	■ Lacking *most* of the essential knowledge and skills from the learning outcomes ■ Not acquired most of the prerequisites needed for later learning	■ Far below the class average	■ Made insignificant or no gains ■ Performed far below what the teacher expected

reason to continue to try than students who simply hear they have been compared with standards and found wanting. For grading, use criterion-referencing to report the standard of achievement the student has met after learning opportunities that included practice and formative assessment. That way, you reap both benefits: the motivational value of self-referencing and the interpretability of criterion-referenced grades.

Another argument against self-referenced grading is statistical. Grading purely on growth or change may result in a negative correlation between the students' initial level of achievement and their growth: Students coming into class with the highest levels of achievement tend to have the smallest amount of measurable improvement or change, even though their final absolute levels of achievement remain the highest. This presents an irony: Students knowing most when they come into the course will tend to get the lowest grades because, even though in an absolute sense they may know more than most other students at the end of the course, they have shown a smaller amount of growth or change.

Your school district's grading policy and a grading culture are important factors in selecting a grading framework. Not every school district has a clearly written grading policy, but if your school district has a grading policy, you will be required to work within its guidelines. If it is a poor or inconsistent policy, you may wish to suggest ways to improve it. If you are a new teacher, your suggestions may not be taken seriously until the administration has confidence in your ability to teach. Press on with your reforms after you have taught for a year or two: Begin by working out your ideas with your most valued teaching colleagues. Don't ever give up on improving education for your students.

MyLab Education **Self-Check 15.2**

MyLab Education **Application Exercise 15.2:**
Understanding Criterion-Referenced Grading

GRADING PRACTICES

This section focuses in more detail on using your assessment plan for summative grading. As you implement summative grading, you must address at least four issues so that your grades are valid:

1. Consider what types of student performance you should grade. We discuss three categories of student performances: those assessed, those reported, and those graded.

2. Once you have decided on the components of the report period grade, consider (a) how to make grading scales consistent across all of them and (b) the weight of each in the final grade.

3. Consider the standards or boundaries for each letter grade: How are they set and are they meaningful? What about borderline cases? What do you do with students who are just at the border between two letter grades?

4. Be concerned with the issue of failures (Fs). What does failure mean? Be concerned with the practice of assigning zero for a mark on one or more components going into a grade: What is the impact of this practice? When should a zero not be given?

What to Grade

In Chapter 6 we discussed how to craft an assessment plan. Your assessment plan describes what component assessments will make up the summative assessment for each instructional unit and for the marking period and the weights the components will carry in calculating the final grade for the marking period. Figure 6.2 showed an example of this type of assessment plan. The

assessment plan is critical for assigning grades. It enables you to integrate all the assessment components meaningfully into a valid grade and to explain your grading to students, parents, and school administrators.

Figure 15.10 will help you understand the relationships among types of assessment variables and how they are used. When you consider what to grade, it is important to distinguish among assessment, reporting, and grading variables, which are successively narrower terms.

Assessment Variables In Chapter 6 we discussed the types of student information you need when teaching, including sizing up the class, diagnosing students' needs, prerequisite student achievements, students' attitudes, students' work habits, students' study skills, and students' motivation and effort in school. The complete set of these characteristics for which you gather information are called **assessment variables** (sometimes called **evaluation variables**; Frisbie & Waltman, 1992). However, not all variables you assess need to be recorded and reported. Clearly, you will use some of the information to plan and guide your own teaching. This information is primarily formative and should not make its way into a grade. A grade is a summative evaluation of a student's achievement.

Reporting Variables Your school district will expect you to report a subset of the assessment variables to parents and for official purposes. These are called **reporting variables** (Frisbie & Waltman, 1992). They often include the students' achievement in the subject, study skills, social behavior and interpersonal skills, motivation and study efforts in class, leadership skills, and aesthetic talents. This is illustrated by the multiple-marking system report card example shown earlier in this chapter.

Grading Variables: Components of the Final Grade Reporting variables represent important school outcomes and therefore should be appropriately reported to parents and others, but not all of them go into the academic grade. From among the reporting variables, there is a more learning-focused subset on which you base your grades. The variables in this limited subset are called **grading variables** (Frisbie & Waltman, 1992). Grading variables describe a student's

FIGURE 15.10
Relationships among different types of assessment variables.

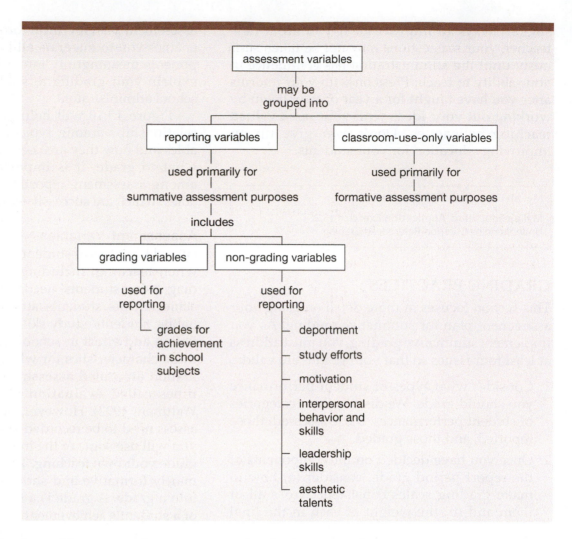

accomplishments in the subject or on the standards. These usually include assessments such as performance tasks, portfolios, projects, tests, and quizzes. They are the most valid and reasonable bases for assigning grades.

If you mix grading variables with other variables, you create grades that have confusing and invalid meanings. For example, if you punish a student by lowering his or her grade for failing to turn in an assignment or for turning it in late, then you have confused the student's achievement with the student's behavior. Similarly, if you lower a science or social studies grade because of poor language usage or poor appearance, your grade is a less valid assessment of the student's achievement of the science or social studies curriculum learning objectives.

This does not mean that language usage or turning in work on time is irrelevant to a student's school experience. Rather, the intention is clarity of meaning for grades so they become more valid indicators of achievement. Some

schools, for example, use a "writing across the curriculum" approach. This means that social studies, history, mathematics, and science work is evaluated for both the subject-matter correctness and language usage. Evaluations of the students' language usage are reported as part of the language grade, whereas evaluations of students' subject-matter achievement become part of the subject grade. Similarly, tardiness, failure to complete work, and other problems can be reported separately from achievement and may be used to explain a student's lack of school accomplishment.

Not all achievement variables should be included as grading variables. Many achievement variables are formative in nature. Homework, small quizzes, and oral responses to classroom activities, for example, may serve mostly formative purposes—to support student practice and feedback and to help you make instructional decisions. These formative assessments *should not* be included in the subject grade for the marking period. Not all out-of-class assignments are formative, of course. Most projects and research papers can be used for summative evaluation. The general rule, then, is to *include in the grade the assessments that you establish as useful for summative evaluation and exclude all assessments established primarily for formative evaluation.*

Valid Decisions About Component Grades' Scales and Weights

Make Scales Compatible   Think ahead to make your assessment scales compatible across all the components that go into the summative grade. The assessment plan for the weather unit in Figure 6.1, for example, shows three components entering into the summative grade for the unit: independent investigation, map drawing, and the end-of-unit test. Suppose each of these is graded on a different scale as follows:

Component	Scale
Independent investigation	1–20
Map drawing	1–4
End-of-unit test	0–100

If you simply add students' grades from each of these components using these scales, you will have difficulty because they are incompatible. The map-drawing scale, for example, may be based on a rubric with four levels of quality whereas the end-of-unit test is based on a percentage scale from 0% to 100%. Such incompatibilities make a *simple sum of the marks* an invalid basis for a grade. You will need to grade each assessment in a way that makes scales compatible.

The planning stage is the time to prevent this situation. You may use one of several options, which we shall discuss later in this chapter. Solving this problem is not that complicated, but it is best solved up front. The following anecdote illustrates this point:

> In a school district I work with, eighth-grade teachers were faced with the task of combining percentage-correct scores from conventional language arts tests and writing performances scored on a 4-point rubric into five levels for report card grades (A, B, C, D, F). Several of the teachers did not have the quantitative reasoning background to understand why or how scale conversions could be made, and it had not occurred to any one of the several people

who adopted the 4-point writing rubric that it would not be very helpful for assigning five levels of grades. This is a more complicated problem to solve after the fact than to solve at the design stage, when it would be appropriate to choose rubrics and construct decision rules. (Brookhart, 1999, p. 8)

Understand Precision   The most reliable scores are those that are able to distinguish small differences in the quality of students' learning. To allow reliable detection of small differences between students, a score scale needs many gradations or "points." For example, a scale that shows Sally at 89 and Johnny at 82 displays their relative learning better than a scale that shows them both receiving the same rating of B. More points mean more precision. For many assessments, however, tiny differences in points do not represent real differences in performance. Adding points without adding meaning leads to a false sense of precision.

You lose precision when you transform scores from a fine-grained scale (e.g., percentage correct scale) to a coarse-grained one (e.g., letter grades). If a B were defined to be a score from 80 to 89, then both Sally and Johnny would receive the same grade, B. Because they both receive the same grade, their true difference cannot be distinguished with the letter-grade scale. By transforming the 89 and 82 both to a B, you have lost reliability.

Not all percentage scales are, in fact, fine-grained. For example, if you have five quiz questions, each worth 1 point, then the only possible percentages are 0, 20, 40, 60, 80, and 100. Thus, only six possible percentage values are used, not the 100 values you may think of with a percentage scale. In this example, the percentage scale is just as coarse as the letter-grade scale. A test of 10 questions, each worth 1 point, is similarly not very fine-grained. *If you use only a few of the many possible values of a scale, then you lose precision.*

Although you lose precision when you move from a fine-grained scale to a coarse-grained scale, you *do not gain precision by moving from a coarse-grained to a fine one.* If we have only the coarse scores initially, no transformation will make them more precise. Suppose, for example, you had the following writing scale: 4 = advanced, 3 = proficient, 2 = basic, 1 = below basic. Suppose your scoring rubric evaluated a student's writing as a 3 on this 4-point scale.

If you transform the 3 to a percentage, 3 out of 4 points becomes 75%. You have not gained any precision, however, in distinguishing among students because all students who received 3s now receive 75%. The scale has only 4 points after the transformation (25%, 50%, 75%, and 100%), the same as before the transformation. Only the labels have changed. In addition, because the 100% scale implies there are other possible percentages between those reported (especially between 75% and 100%), you have changed the meaning of the scale from advanced, proficient, basic, below basic (if those were the rubric levels) to an implied (from the percents) scale of A = 100%, C = 75%, F = 50%, and F = 25%. You can see that these so-called grades have a corrupted meaning—they are not aligned with the original meaning intended by the verbal labels of the writing scale.

Choices about scoring scales and precision can support or undermine the effects of even well-designed assessment tasks. It is important, therefore, to design your scoring scales as carefully as you design your assessment instruments.

Weight the Components Decide how much weight to assign to the components of a grade—tests, quizzes, term papers, and other elements—by deciding their importance to the description of students' achievement of the report period learning objectives. Consider at least six factors when deciding how much to weight each component:

1. Components that assess more of the important learning objectives and content should be weighted more heavily than those that focus only on one or a few objectives.
2. Components that focus on what you spent the most time teaching the students should receive the most weight in determining the grade.
3. Components that require students to integrate and apply their learning should receive more weight than those that require students simply to recall what was taught.
4. When two components assess some of the same learning objectives, each should be given less weight individually than other components that assess an equal number of unique learning objectives.
5. If you know that one of the components you want to count toward the grade has some degree of unfairness to certain groups of students, be extremely cautious in using it for

grading. If you decide that on the whole it is still appropriate to use it, weight it less, especially for students for whom it is less fair. For example, you may find that a timed, written test does not adequately assess students with certain disabilities. In such cases, it would be appropriate to weight this procedure less for these students and to give other, more appropriate procedures more weight in determining their grades.
6. Components that are less reliable should be weighted less heavily than those that are more reliable and objective. We do not mean to say you should avoid using less objectively scored assessments such as essays and performance assessments for assigning grades. Instead, use scoring rubrics for marking them so the marks are more reliable.

Standards or Boundaries Between Grades
What constitutes an A, B, and so on? The answer will depend on the reference framework you are using and your school district's policy. The procedure for setting norm-referenced grading boundaries is quite different from the procedure for setting criterion-referenced grading boundaries.

Grade boundaries must have the same meaning across all assessments that will make up the grade, which doesn't mean that you need to use the same number of points for each assessment. It does mean, however, that an A on one assessment should be of approximately the same standard of quality across all assessments. For example, if each assessment is marked according to the percentage correct, then the same percentage range (e.g., 90%–100%) should be used for an A across all assessments, *and the quality of work represented by these percentages should be comparable across assessments.* The former is easier to arrange than the latter.

Borderline Cases You will always have **borderline cases**—students whose composite grades are very near or right on the boundary between two grades. Should you consider adjustments? How close to the grade boundary does a student have to be before you adjust a letter grade upward or downward? Many teachers are comfortable reviewing students' work and raising grades for those who are just under the borderline, but do not consider lowering the grades of those just above the borderline (Brookhart, 1993). Nevertheless, lowering borderline grades is just as valid as raising them when additional achievement evidence justifies it.

As you learned in Chapter 4, assessment results contain errors of measurement, so students whose scores are on or near the border are likely to have true scores that are *different* from their observed scores. This point argues against being hard-nosed and telling a student that he or she missed the next higher grade by 1 or 2 points. You can think of scores near the grade boundary as in an "uncertainty band" much like the one discussed in Chapter 4. Use additional achievement information about the student to help you decide whether the student's true score is above or below the boundary. Using additional *achievement* information to help make boundary decisions is more valid than using information about how much effort a student put forth in studying (Brookhart, 1999). If you are still in doubt, it is better pedagogy to give the next higher grade than to give the lower grade.

The Meaning of Failure

A failing grade carries a lot of emotion with it, and there are usually negative consequences for students who receive it. What should an F mean? Your answer should be consistent with your grading framework. The least confusing way to assign a failing grade (F) is to set reasonable minimum standards regarding performance on the curriculum learning objectives. Students who *consistently* perform below these minimum performance standards receive an F.

Consider two students. Darnell does not turn in an important assignment, even though he knew the deadline and you made several announcements in class. You decide to give Darnell a zero. James, on the other hand, turns in the assignment on time, but the work is so poor you must give it a 55, which is in the F range. Both James and Darnell receive Fs. The question is, do these Fs mean the same thing? If not, how meaningful (i.e., valid) is using an F?

One way to frame this issue is to consider two categories of student performance (Brookhart, 1999): (1) doing work that is of very poor quality, that is, failing work and (2) not doing the work at all, that is, failing to try. The first category describes the student's achievement: the student's status compared to the standards or learning

objectives. The meaning of failure marks or grades for such students is reasonably clear.

The second category reflects a student's motivation (and perhaps attitudes and personality characteristics, such as lack of self-confidence or rebelliousness). Darnell's failure to turn in an assignment might be a signal to you that he has not understood what you taught. Darnell may have failed to do the assignment because he didn't know how. This problem calls for working with Darnell and his parent(s) to see that he receives the help he needs. Darnell may be insecure and afraid to admit his failure to learn: Not every failure to try is malicious. Sometimes children who have an emotional crisis at home actually do the work in school but do not turn it in because they have given up being successful students. In "failure-to-try" cases, giving a failing grade (or lowering a grade) is always invalid because the resulting grade does not accurately describe achievement. This fact does not mean that you should avoid reporting failure to try; it does mean that describing these two types of student responses with the same grade (F or 0) is not valid.

A closely related question is, "Should I lower a student's grade when the assignment is turned in *late*?" Some teachers, for example, grade assignments that are turned in late, but deduct points or otherwise limit the highest grade possible for this assignment. Again, such a practice lowers the validity of the resulting grades because it mixes up their meaning: Do not use the same grade to describe for some students only achievement, but for other students a mixture of achievement, attitudes, and behavior.

Abhorrent grading practices like these are practiced because teachers face difficult teaching conditions. They seek to use grades (and student evaluations, in general) to control students' behavior. As we discussed in Chapter 5, it is poor practice to threaten, punish, or manipulate students by lowering achievement grades for behavior that is unrelated to achievement. The issue of what to do with missing and late assignments is a real one with which you and your colleagues must struggle, but it is not a measurement problem per se. It is a result of the conditions of teaching, school policies, and assumptions people make about the way one should educate (Brookhart, 1999).

A school district's policy needs to address how to handle students who do not turn in

FIGURE 15.11   Example of
the impact of substituting
zero or 59 for one
assignment a student did
not turn in.

Note: Substituted values are
shown in parentheses. (Assume
A = 90–100, B = 80–89,
C = 70–79, D = 60–69,
F = 0–59.)

		1	2	3	4	5	Avg	Grd
A.	True Performance	80	70	85	75	90	80	B
B.	Strategy 1—Substitute zero for the missing assessment							
	Case 1	(0)	70	85	75	90	64	D
	Case 2	80	(0)	85	75	90	66	D
	Case 3	80	70	(0)	75	90	63	D
	Case 4	80	70	85	(0)	90	65	D
	Case 5	80	70	85	75	(0)	62	D
C.	Strategy 2—Substitute the highest possible failing mark (i.e., 59) for the missing assessment							
	Case 1	(59)	70	85	75	90	76	C
	Case 2	80	(59)	85	75	90	76	C
	Case 3	80	70	(59)	75	90	75	C
	Case 4	80	70	85	(59)	90	75	C
	Case 5	80	70	85	75	(59)	74	C
D.	Strategy 3—Base the grade on only those assignments that were turned in							
	Case 1	—	70	85	75	90	80	B
	Case 2	80	—	85	75	90	83	B
	Case 3	80	70	—	75	90	79	C
	Case 4	80	70	85	—	90	81	B
	Case 5	80	70	85	75	—	76	C
E.	Strategy 4—Substitute zero for the missing assignment, and use the median to calculate the grade							
	Case 1 (0)	(0)	70	85	75	90	80	B
	Case 2	80	(0)	85	75	90	83	B
	Case 3	80	70	(0)	75	90	78	C
	Case 4	80	70	85	(0)	90	82	B
	Case 5	80	70	85	75	(0)	78	C

assignments or who turn them in late. A culture for punctuality and completing assigned work on time needs to be developed. For example, some schools institute ZAP policies (zeroes aren't permitted) and put in place various supports to ensure that students complete work like supervised after-school sessions. A policy needs to be legal, fair, and valid, and it needs to meet criteria for sound educational philosophy. Punishing, threatening, or manipulating students should be eliminated from any policy.

The Deadly Zero
If you use a percentage scale, a zero can have a huge effect on a composite grade. Suppose Ashley is capable of B work. What happens to her average grade if she fails to turn in one assignment and you give her a zero for it? You may be surprised to learn that her average grade could drop from a B to a D.

The impact of a zero, of course, depends on the component grades a student receives, how many components enter into the composite grade,

the weights assigned to the component, and the grade the student would have received had she turned in the assignment. Figure 15.11 illustrates the impact of zero on a student's grade.

In this example, there are five assignments. To keep things simple, let us assume they are equally weighted. As a point of reference, suppose Ashley's "true performance," what she would have received had she completed all her assignments, is shown in Panel A. Ashley is a B student.

Panel B shows what will happen to Ashley if she fails to turn in one assignment and if you were to give her zero for that assignment. The impact on her grades is dramatic: One missing assignment results in her dropping two whole grades, from a B to a D, which happens no matter which assignment she fails to turn in.

Using a zero means that you have given Ashley the lowest possible failing grade as a substitute for her missing assignment. Instead, you could give her the highest possible failing grade. In this example, the F range is from 0 to 59, so 59 is the highest possible failing mark. Panel C shows what happens to Ashley's grade if you follow this strategy. Ashley goes from a B average (Panel A) to a C average (Panel C). Still, one missing assignment has resulted in her average dropping one whole grade.

Panel D shows what happens when you simply ignore the missing assignment, basing your grade on the remaining four. As shown in Panel D, the impact on her grade depends on which assignment she failed to turn in. If she failed to turn in one of the two on which she could have scored the highest (Case 3, where Assignment 3 was 85, or Case 5, where Assignment 5 was 90), her grade would drop a whole grade; in the other cases, it would remain at B. Alternative strategies (not shown) could be used, such as using 50 instead of 59 or substituting the average of the four completed assignments for the missing assignment. In Ashley's case, these other approaches give the same letter-grade results as shown in Panel D.

Panel E shows what happens when you do give Ashley the zero for missing assignment, but instead of using the mean of the grades to calculate the average, you use the median. Appendix F shows how to calculate the median, which is a good measure of central tendency to use for distributions that include extreme scores, like the zeros here.

From the measurement perspective, Strategy 3 (basing the grade only on assignments turned in) would be the best of the three when (a) assignments are of approximately equal difficulty for the students, (b) assignments are weighted equally (or are worth the same number of points), and (c) there are several assignments and only one or two are missing. This recommendation does not consider other factors, such as whether (a) the "missing assignment" is the most important one to complete (e.g., a project or a final examination), (b) a student fails to turn in an assignment because of illness or personal tragedy, (c) a student fails to complete the assignment because she didn't understand how to do the work, and (d) a student has made a habit of not turning in work on time. As we stated previously, these are not measurement issues per se but matters of educational practice, classroom management, and school policy.

From a practical perspective, we recommend Strategy 4 if it is not possible for you to ignore a missing assignment. Sometimes grading policies or timelines require a set of work to be considered

at a certain time. If repeated efforts to help students turn in assigned work have not yielded results, using the median method of calculation allows you to take the zero into account but not give it undue weight. However, we recommend that you use the same calculation method for all students in the same class, so if you use the median for one student in a class you should use it for all of them.

TECHNIQUES FOR COMBINING GRADES TO SUMMARIZE ACHIEVEMENT

Assigning Norm-Referenced Letter Grades

We have recommended criterion-referenced grading (see next section) to match with standards-based instruction. We include this section on norm-referenced grading for the sake of completeness, because there may be occasions when norm-referenced grading methods are required. Your instructor may ask you to skip this section or to postpone studying this section until you have studied Chapter 17.

Several methods of assigning grades use relative or norm-referenced standards. One method, called **grading on the curve**, uses the rank order of students' marks: Grades are ordered from highest to lowest, and grades (A, B, C, etc.) are assigned on the basis of this ranking. A second, called the **standard deviation method**, uses the standard deviation (see Appendix F) as a unit: A teacher computes the standard deviation of the scores and uses this number to mark off segments on the number line that define the boundaries for grade assignment. The two methods do not necessarily give the same results. To use norm-referenced grading, both individual grades (the components) and the final grade (the composite) should be norm-referenced.

Grading a Single Test or Assessment There are several methods of grading a single test or assignment in a norm-referenced manner. Most of these were devised before criterion-referenced assessment became the method of choice and are now somewhat dated. We present only one such method here, known as grading on the curve. To use the grading on the curve method to assign letter grades, you decide on the percentage of As, Bs, Cs, and so on to award. For example, you may decide as follows:

Example

Example of one possible set of percentages to use for grading on the curve

Top 20% of the students get A

Next 30% get B

Next 30% get C

Next 15% get D

Lowest 5% get F

There are no rules on how you would select the percentages to use. They are chosen arbitrarily based on your experience as to what is realistic in your school for a distribution of letter grades. This approach does not require using a normal or bell curve.

Another way to set the percentages is to divide the range of a normal or bell curve (see Chapter 17) into five equal-length intervals. The example below shows the resulting percentages of students receiving each grade.

Example

Example of one possible set of percentages to use for grading using the normal curve with five equal intervals

Top 3.6% of the students get A

Next 23.8% get B

Next 45.2% get C

Next 23.8% get D

Lowest 3.6% get F

This set of percentages assumes that the true achievement in the group of students in your class is normally distributed, an assumption which, in the authors' view, is hard for you or any teacher to justify. Notice that (a) the width of the interval that determines the percentages is completely arbitrary, (b) the assessment scores must be valid measures of the desired achievement, and (c) there is no reference to learning objectives or standards (except that higher-ranked students have more competence than lower-ranked students). If you do decide to grade on a curve, you should provide a convincing and educationally sound argument to justify the validity of the particular percentages that you use.

Grading a Composite of Several Scores Usually a report card grade reflects a student's performance on several assessments such as assignments, quizzes, reports, and perhaps an examination. Here we discuss how to combine the scores from several grading components into a single (composite) grade in a manner consistent with the norm-referenced grading framework.

Weighting Guidelines With norm-referenced grading, the component that contributes the most to the final rankings of the students in the group carries the most weight. This principle is likely to be violated if you simply multiply the component scores by some arbitrary weights and then add the weighted scores to form a composite. The reason is that the rank of a composite score is influenced by the standard deviations of the components making up the composite (and by the intercorrelations among components). To illustrate this point, consider the next example:

Example

Example showing how a grading component can work in the opposite way the teacher intends when norm-referenced grading is used

Suppose that the final grades are based on the sum of the grades from one exam and one project. Suppose further that the project is intended to weigh twice as much as the exam. In an attempt to accomplish this goal, the teacher decides to give twice as many points to the project as to the exam: 100 points for the project and 50 points for the exam. Remember that in a norm-referenced grading framework, those who rank highest should receive the highest grades. Here are the marks and ranks of five students.

| Student | Exam (50 points) | | Project (100 points) | | | |
	Grade	Rank	Grade	Rank	Grade	Total Rank
Anthony	44	1	77	5	120	1
Ashley	33	2	78	4	111	2
Billy	26	3	79	3	105	3
Chad	22	4	80	2	102	4
Vanessa	15	5	81	1	96	5

Notice that the project ranks students exactly opposite from the exam. The final order is exactly the same as the exam, however, even though the teacher weighted the project more. This result is because the ranking of the students on the total grade depends on the spread of scores rather than on the teacher's intended weighting. The spread of scores is measured by the standard deviation (see Appendix F). The project scores are close to each other, so their standard deviation is small, whereas the exam scores are quite different from each other, so their standard deviation is large. Because of the exam score's larger standard deviation, the students' *exam ranking* dominates their final total ranking in spite of the teacher's intention to make the project the dominant component. In general, when using norm-referenced grading, the larger the standard deviation of one component's scores, the more that component influences the final ranking of students when a composite is formed.

Using SS-Score Method The **SS-score method** preserves the influence (weights) you want the components to have by first adjusting the values of the components' standard deviations. After adjusting, you may then apply the weights you desire. There are three steps: First, change all of the scores on each component into SS-scores (SS means linear standard score; see Chapter 17). This shift makes all of the standard deviations equal. Second, multiply the components' SS-scores by the weights you want. Finally, add these products to form the composite mark for each student. The following formula summarizes these steps.

$$\text{weighted composite score} = \Sigma(\text{weight} \times SS) \quad [\text{Eq. 15.1}]$$

where

weight = weight you want the component to have

SS = the linear SS-score for the component

$$= [10(X - M)/SD] + 50$$

The procedure is illustrated in Figure 15.12.

Note that these weighted composite scores are not themselves SS-scores. However, the weighted composite scores do provide a way to rank students so that the component weightings you specify will have the desired influence on the students' final standings.

To appreciate the influence of the SS-score method on the students' ranking in the final weighted composite, recall our earlier example in which the teacher's attempt to make the project dominate the ranking of the students failed. In the example below, we'll apply the SS-score method to those same marks.

Assigning Criterion-Referenced Letter Grades

There are several methods for grading using the criterion-referencing grading framework. In this book we shall discuss only three. One method is known as the **fixed-percentage method**: The scores on each component entering into the composite are first converted to percentage correct (or percent of total points); then the percentages are translated to grades. For each component, you must use the same percentage to define the letter-grade boundaries.

A second method is called the **total points method**: Each component included in the final composite grade is assigned a maximum point value (e.g., quizzes may count 10 points, exams may count a maximum of 50 points each, and projects may count a maximum of 40 points each);

Example

Hypothetical example showing using the SS-score method can help the teacher weigh the assignments as intended when norm-referenced grading is used

Student	Exam (Weight = 1) Grade	SS	Rank	Project (Weight = 2) Grade	SS	Rank	Total Composite	Rank
Anthony	44	66	1	77	36	5	138	5
Ashley	33	55	2	78	43	4	141	4
Billy	26	48	3	79	50	3	148	3
Chad	22	44	4	80	57	2	158	2
Vanessa	15	37	5	81	64	1	165	1

Compare the final rankings in this example with the final rankings in the earlier example. Now the project dominates the rankings based on the composite instead of the exam, as the teacher initially intended. Transforming the grades to SS-scores first made the exam grades' and project grades' standard deviations equal. Then when the weight of two was applied, the composite better matched the teacher's intent. You can use the standard deviation formula in Appendix F to work through this example yourself.

FIGURE 15.12   Example of calculating composite grades using the *SS*-scores method.

	Components entering into the grade			
	Quizzes	Homework	Term paper	Exam
Mean (*M*)	70	85	75	65
Standard deviation (*SD*)	5	8	15	20
Teacher's weight	20%	10%	20%	50%
Calculation for *SS*[a]	$SS = 10(\text{Mark} - 70)/5 + 50$	$SS = 10(\text{Mark} - 85)/8 + 50$	$SS = 10(\text{Mark} - 75)/15 + 50$	$SS = 10(\text{Mark} - 65)/20 + 50$

[a]*SS*-scores are calculated by subtracting the component mean from a student's raw score, dividing the difference by the standard deviation, multiplying by 10, and adding 50 to the product. The results for each student are shown below. For example:

    The quizzes *SS*-score for Bob   = 10(87 − 70)/5 + 50 = 84
    The quizzes *SS*-score for Chad   = 10(85 − 70)/5 + 50 = 80
    The quizzes *SS*-score for Susan   = 10(75 − 70)/5 + 50 = 60
    The quizzes *SS*-score for Theresa   = 10(70 − 70)/5 + 50 = 50

	Raw scores on components				SS-scores on components				
Students	Quizzes	Home-work	Term paper	Exam	Quizzes	Home-work	Term paper	Exam	Weighted composite
Bob	87	85	70	80	84	50	47	58	60
Chad	85	80	80	70	80	44	53	53	58
Susan	75	82	85	60	60	46	57	48	51
Theresa	70	78	75	65	50	41	50	50	49

Composite scores are calculated by multiplying the component *SS*-score by the corresponding teacher's component weights and summing the products. For example:

    Composite score for Bob   = .2(84) + .1(50) + .2(47) + .5(58) = 60
    Composite score for Chad   = .2(80) + .1(44) + .2(53) + .5(53) = 58
    Composite score for Susan   = .2(60) + .1(46) + .2(57) + .5(48) = 51
    Composite score for Theresa = .2(50) + .1(41) + .2(50) + .5(50) = 49

Source: From *Essentials of Educational Measurement* (3rd ed., pp. 248–251), by R. L. Ebel, 1979, Englewood Cliffs, NJ: Prentice Hall. Copyright 1979. Adapted by permission of the copyright holder.

the letter grades are assigned based on the number of total points a student accumulated over the marking period.

A third method is the **quality-level method** or the **rubric method**. In this method, you describe the quality level of performance a student must demonstrate for each grade—what types of performance will constitute an A, B, C, and so on (see column one in Figure 15.9) or what types of performance will constitute Advanced, Proficient, and so on. Given these definitions, you evaluate the student's work on each component, decide the quality level of work, and then assign the corresponding grade. This method is very similar to using scoring rubrics for performance tasks (see Chapter 13). It is appropriate for standards-based grading, using proficiency levels as the quality categories.

Below we discuss using each of the three methods for grading a single test or assessment, and then we discuss each of the three methods for combining grades. Whichever method you use, be consistent in using it for both grading individual assessments and combining those results for a report card grade.

Grading a Single Test or Assessment: Fixed-Percentage Method

Teachers frequently use percentages as bases for marking and grading papers. The relationship between percentage correct and letter grade is arbitrary. In some schools, 85% is an A; in others, 90% is an A. In still others, 93% is an A. Some school boards have a policy on this matter. The following is an example of one such set of percentages that defines letter grades:

Example

Example of one possible set of percentages for grading using the fixed-percentage method

90%–100% = A
80%–89% = B
70%–79% = C
60%–69% = D
0–59% = F

Note that a percentage begs the question, percentage of what? Often, the only answer that you can defend is that the score represents the percentage of the maximum points on the test or the performance assessment. This answer ignores the broader concern: The assessment should be a representative sample from a well-defined domain of performance implied by the curriculum learning objectives. If you have not built the assessment to sample the domain representatively, then you cannot use the percentage grade to estimate the student's status accurately on that broader domain. Scores on poorly designed tests or assessments cannot be considered criterion-referenced.

The percentage that defines each grade should take into account a teacher's experience with the kinds of students being taught and the difficulty of the assessments the teacher develops. Thus, norm-referenced information helps establish a criterion-referenced grading system.

One limitation of this fixed-percentage method stems from the fact that every assessment you create has a different level of difficulty, which you may not know in advance. This method, however, uses the same fixed percentages for A, B, and so on for every component. Thus, if you create a test that is too difficult for your class, you may end up giving too many low grades based on the percentages you fixed in advance. This result will be frustrating for students and may put you into a position where you have to change the grading system.

A second limitation is that this method encourages you to focus more strongly on the difficulty level of the assessment than on the learning objectives it should assess. For example, if you fix the percentages, you will be looking for ways to make the assessment easy enough or difficult enough so that you get a reasonable distribution of letter grades for your class. This process

seems to go against the principles of absolute or criterion-referenced grading.

Grading a Single Test or Assessment: Total Points Method To use this method, you must decide in advance all the components that will enter into the end-of-a-marking-period grade. Then, also in advance, you decide the maximum number of points for each component. Your assessment plan should do this. The maximum number of points each component is worth mirrors the weight you assign to each component. If you want the unit test(s) to count more toward the grade, for example, you would assign the unit tests more of the total points. Finally, you sum all the maximum points for components and use that maximum possible total to set letter-grade boundaries. Notice that, unlike for the fixed percentage method, you do not assign letter grades for each component, but only for the total summed over all components.

As an example, suppose you used the same four components that were used in one of our earlier examples: quizzes, essay, a term paper, and an exam.

Example

Example of one possible set of points to use with the total points method of grading

Component	Maximum points	"Weighting" expressed as a percentage
Quizzes	40	20%
Essay	20	10%
Term paper	40	20%
Exam	100	50%
Total Points	200	100%

Having decided on the components and their maximum point values, you then set the boundaries for assigning letter grades to the total points that students accumulate in the marking period. For example:

Total point grade boundaries	Grade
180–200	A
160–179	B
140–159	C
120–139	D
0–119	F

Notice that these total point grade *boundaries* correspond to percentages of 90%, 80%, 70%, and

60% of the 200 total points for A, B, C, and D, respectively. (For example, for an A, 180 ÷ 200 = 0.90 or 90%.) You may use other percentages to define the letter-grade boundaries. Adjust the total point boundaries accordingly.

One limitation of the total points method is that it makes it too easy for you to give "extra credit" assignments to boost the total points of low-scoring students. Extra credit assignments tend to distort the meaning of the grades, especially when these assignments do not properly assess the same learning objectives as the original set of components. For example, if a student does poorly on the term paper, you may be tempted to have the student read and summarize a current events magazine article to boost the student's score instead of writing another term paper. The meaning of the total points for this student would be distorted relative to other students. As a result, your grades are less valid.

Another limitation of this method is that by defining the maximum number of points before creating the assessments, you may be faced with an unacceptable choice when you do create an assessment tool. Consider this situation:

> Suppose I need a 50-point test to fit my [total points] grading scheme, but find that I need 32 multiple-choice items to sample the content domain thoroughly. I find this unsatisfactory (or inconvenient) because 32 does not divide into 50 very nicely. (It's 1.56!) To make life simpler, I could drop 7 items and use a 25-item test with 2 points per item. If I did that, my points total would be in fine shape, but my test would be an incomplete measure of the important unit objectives. The fact that I had to commit to 50 points prematurely dealt a serious blow to obtaining meaningful assessment results. (Frisbie & Waltman, 1992, p. 41)

Grading a Single Test or Assessment: Quality-Level Method
When you grade an individual assignment with a rubric or grading scale, you make a judgment based on the quality level of the work, overall or according to several criteria. In fact, as you saw in Chapter 13, performance levels for rubrics are specifically written to be descriptions of work at various quality levels. Whether the rubric scale is defined as 1, 2, 3, and 4 or as A, B, C, D, and F, or Advanced, Proficient, Basic, Below Basic, or some other scale, assigning a level to a piece of work in this manner is an example of the quality-level method.

Combining Grades: Fixed-Percentage Method
If you use a fixed-percentage grading method, you will have a percentage score for each student for each component. Then, you multiply each component percentage by its corresponding weight, add these products together, and divide the sum of products by the sum of the weights. This procedure may be summarized by the following formula:

composite percentage score

$$= \frac{\Sigma(\text{weight} \times \text{percentage score})}{\Sigma(\text{weight})}$$

[Eq. 15.2]

where
Σ = sum of
weight = weight you give to a component
percentage score = the percentage you gave the student on the component

Figure 15.13 illustrates this method.

If you did not use the weights, each component would count equally toward the composite—which actually is a form of weighting where each assignment gets a weight of one. This procedure should not be used with norm-referenced grading because the weights assigned here fail to reflect the standard deviations of the components.

Combining Grades: Total Points Method
The way we described the total points method in the previous section automatically grades composites. The composite score for a student is the total of the points the student accumulates. Therefore, make sure that the points you assign for each component reflect the weight you want each component to contribute to the total composite. For example, if the weights you want for the components are project 20%, quizzes 10%, term paper 20%, and exam 50%, then points for each component should reflect these percentages of the total maximum points. Thus, if the maximum total points is 200, then all of the quizzes are worth a maximum of 20 points (= 10% of 200), the project a maximum of 40 points, term paper 40 points, and exam 100 points.

Combining Grades: Quality-Level Methods
You can derive a grade from a set of rubric scores on various assignments in one of several ways: summing across components, using the median score, or using rules for minimum attainment. These methods may also be used when the components

FIGURE 15.13 Example of how to calculate composite grades using the fixed-percentage method.

Suppose you had four components (quizzes, essay, term paper, and exam) that you want to combine into a composite score for the end of a grading period. Suppose, further, that each component was originally marked as a percentage correct. Suppose, too, you did not want to weigh each component the same. Finally, suppose that the students' marks and weights for each component were as follows:

Student	Quizzes (wt. = 20%)	Essay (wt. = 10%)	Term paper (wt. = 20%)	Exam (wt. = 50%)	Weighted composite percentage
Bob	87	85	70	80	80
Chad	85	80	80	70	75
Susan	75	82	85	60	65
Theresa	70	78	75	65	69

Calculate the weighted composite (last column) and compare that score to the boundaries you set for the letter grades. Use Equation 15.2 to calculate the weighted composite score. Round your results to the nearest percentage.

weighted composite score for Bob = $[20 \times 87 + 10 \times 85 + 20 \times 70 + 50 \times 80] \div [100] = 80$
weighted composite score for Chad = $[20 \times 85 + 10 \times 80 + 20 \times 80 + 50 \times 70] \div [100] = 76$
weighted composite score for Susan = $[20 \times 75 + 10 \times 82 + 20 \times 85 + 50 \times 60] \div [100] = 70$
weighted composite score for Theresa = $[20 \times 70 + 10 \times 78 + 20 \times 75 + 50 \times 65] \div [100] = 69$

Suppose your grade boundaries were:

A = 90–100; B = 80–89; C = 70–79; D = 60–69; and F = 0–59

Then using the weighted composite percentages as calculated, the grades for these students are:

Bob = B; Chad = C; Susan = C; and Theresa = D

are a mixture of percentage scores on tests and quizzes and rubrics-based scores. As we pointed out in our discussions of the other methods, be careful to place all of the component grades on comparable scales before combining them into a composite for grade assignment. So, for instance, all components marks may be converted into an A, B, C, D, and F quality scale or an Advanced, Proficient, Basic, Below Basic scale before combining them to arrive at a final grade. These grades represent achievement scales on which students are *partially ordered*.

Using the Median Score This strategy works well for components that include a mixture of rubrics and percent-correct scores. The **median score method** approach treats all component marks as ordinal data (i.e., essentially as ranks) and uses the student's median mark to calculate the grade instead of using the sum of grades or the average grade. Before taking the median, convert all scores (rubrics, percents, and so on) to the same scale (for example, A, B, C, D, F). The median is discussed in Appendix F. See Brookhart (2009) for a more complete explanation of this method.

Combining Grades for Standards-Based Grading: Privileging Recent Evidence When a final grade is reported for one standard instead of a whole subject area, it is best to weigh more recent evidence more heavily. Students may improve their achievement of a standard as they work on it over a report period. In fact, that is the desired result. Standards-based grading aims to report the median proficiency level that the student finally achieves after work on the standard for the report period. Just using the very last grade on a standard would report "final" achievement, but one grade alone is not very reliable as an indicator of achievement. Therefore, it is better to take the median grade a student achieves on a standard after his performance "settles" into a reliable level of proficiency (Brookhart, 2013a). Here is an example.

EXAMPLE OF CALCULATING FINAL STANDARDS-BASED GRADES

	Standard: Uses Scientific Method					
Student	9/6	9/12	9/20	9/24	10/4	10/8
Brianna	2	1	2	3	3	3
Hailey	2	2	4	3	4	4
Troy	3	1	3	2	3	1

Scale: 4=Advanced, 3=Proficient, 2=Basic, 1=Below Basic

Brianna: Brianna's performance shows a beginning practice period followed by a leveling off of achievement. After beginning at the level of "basic," her performance leveled out at a reliable 3, or "proficient," level. The median of her performance after this leveling out is a 3 (median of 3, 3, and 3 = 3).

Hailey: Hailey's performance also shows the pattern of a learning curve. After beginning at the level of "basic," Bailey's performance leveled out at around 4, or "advanced." The median of her performance after this leveling out is a 4 (median of 4, 3, 4, and 4 = 4).

Troy: Troy's performance does not resemble a learning curve, but rather unsystematic fluctuations. There is no discernable change in his performance over time. The teacher should try to find out why this is so. Unless she finds some reason to revise the proficiency ratings, the best summary of Troy's performance is the median of what he has demonstrated, which is a 2 or the "basic" level (median of 3, 1, 2, 2, 3, 1 = 2).

Using Minimum Attainment The **minimum attainment method** bases the composite grades on whether students meet minimum standards on the most important assessments that comprise the final grade, while at the same time allowing somewhat lower performance on a few of the less important components. Although this method could be used in a variety of circumstances, it is suitable when you have marked the components using quality-level scores such as letter grades, rubric scores, or proficiency labels and you do not want to convert these quality-level grades to percentages. Sometimes this method of grading is referred to as the **logic rule method** (Arter & McTighe, 2001).

The minimum attainment rules method is a *noncompensatory approach to grading.* The methods whereby you add together scores from the components are called *compensatory* methods because a student's low score on one component can be compensated by a high grade on another.

In the minimum attainment method, a teacher sets the minimum grades on some important assessment components that the students must meet in order to receive a particular grade. If students fail to meet the minimum standards on these specified assessments, they cannot receive high grades, no matter how well they did on the other, less important, assessments. Students who *do* meet the minimum standards on the specified assessment also must meet some standards on the other, less important components. The minimum attainment rules method is only one such noncompensatory approach to grading.

To use this method, first determine what components will be included in students' final grades, and which of those are more important to demonstrating the students' achievement of the learning objectives. Second, for each of these "more important" components, specify the minimum level of performance you will accept for each of the final grade levels of A, B, C, D, and so on. Third, establish rules for what levels of performance you will accept, at each final grade level, on each of the "less important" components. These rules form a set of decision rules for how to assign grades. An example of how to use these rules follows:

Example

Example of the minimum attainment method for grading

Assume an English class with one test (graded in percentages that are then converted to letter grades), four small writing assignments (graded with rubrics as A, B, C, D, F), and one longer paper (also graded with rubrics as A, B, C, D, F). That is, six components go into the final grade. Assume, also, you want the combined test and paper marks to be worth twice as much as the four smaller assignments.

If a student scores	*Then the grade is*
As on at least three of the writing assignments, *and* As on the paper and test, or an A on one and a B on the other	A
As or Bs on at least three of the writing assignments, *and* at least Bs on the paper and test, or an A on one and a C on the other	B
C or better on at least three of the writing assignments, *and* at least Cs on the paper and test, or a B or better on one and a D or better on the other	C
D or better on at least three of the writing assignments, *and* at least Ds on the paper and test, or a C or better on one and an F on the other	D
A combination lower than the above	F

Below an example of how these rules would be applied for eight students.

Example

Example of applying the minimum attainment method for grading in the preceding example to eight students

	Writing 1	Writing 2	Writing 3	Writing 4	Long paper	Test	Final grade
Aiden	A	A	C	A	A	A	**A**
Anthony	A	B	A	A	A	B	**A**
Ashley	A	B	B	C	B	B	**B**
Billy	A	B	B	C	B	B	**B**
Blake	C	C	C	A	C	C	**C**
Chad	D	D	D	A	D	D	**D**
Jesse	D	D	D	A	F	C	**D**
Sophia	D	D	F	F	D	D	**F**

Of course, you may use other decision rules beside the ones we used in the example. Other decision rules might describe minimum attainment in the manner of a holistic rubric, for example.

Grading in Early Childhood

In kindergarten and early primary grades, report cards may use non-standard grading scales (e.g., Outstanding, Satisfactory, and Needs Improvement) and assessments may rely heavily on teacher observation. This is appropriate for early childhood. However, it is important to remember that the principles for effective grading from this chapter still apply. Principles for creating effective rubrics (Chapter 13) also will be helpful.

We once knew a kindergarten teacher who was also a graduate student in one of our university assessment classes. The report card she was expected to use included entries for qualities like "Listens attentively." The report card had a non-traditional scale that used three letters: O, G, and N (Outstanding, Good, and Needs Improvement). She based many of her grades on observation, waiting until report card time and assigning what she felt was the appropriate grade, based on her overall observations. She asked us what to do and said she was terrified that someday a parent would ask how she settled on a grade. She felt that if she said, "I just observe," the parent might consider her grading arbitrary. Her instinct was a good one. Some additional strategies would strengthen the validity of her grades.

We asked whether, for each of these observational grades, she could tell us what she usually looked for. Oh yes, she said. We then suggested that she write down the indicators she looked for each of the grading decisions she was expected to make. That way, she would have an answer, if anyone asked, to the question of how she settled on a grade. In addition, writing down the indicators she looked for would increase the likelihood that she would apply the same criteria to all students consistently. This would enhance the validity and reliability of her grades. Essentially, this approach turns the grade entries into rubrics. Our kindergarten teacher was very happy with this solution, and later reported that it worked well for her.

We recommend this method for observation-based early childhood grades. We also recommend that you keep records of multiple observations over time, and treat the pattern of your observations in the same manner as we recommended for combining grades for standards-based grading, weighting most recent observations more heavily in your grading decisions. This strategy documents multiple sources of evidence (multiple observations), analyzes the evidence for patterns, and thus further enhances validity and reliability for observation-based grading criteria.

Gradebook Computer Programs

Usually, the calculations for combining component grades into a final, composite grade are done by computer with a **gradebook program**. Most educational administration software has a gradebook module, and there are also stand-alone gradebook programs. These will allow you to choose from a variety of grading frameworks, keep a class roster, keep attendance, record comments about students' assignments, obtain class summaries, and print reports for the total class or for one student to take home.

School districts often provide—and require—teachers to use a particular gradebook program. These programs are sometimes linked to the district's administrative software so that report cards can be printed without the extra step of "turning in grades." Some of these programs are linked to a website where parents, with password and identification, can log in and check their students' grades at any time, and sometimes even compare their student's grade with the rest of the class. This technology opens up new opportunities for home-school communication. It also requires even clearer grading plans and policies so that students and parents who check incomplete records for a marking period correctly interpret the information in front of them. Smith and Walker (2002) recommend that before implementing a universal electronic gradebook system, principals should consider (a) teachers' technology comfort level, (b) computer availability, (c) network capability, (d) interface with student information management system, (e) staff development, (f) ongoing support, and (g) principal's commitment.

One disadvantage of some gradebook programs is that they limit the type of grading you may employ, or they may not permit you to use your own grading method to override the method(s) built into the program. We have seen a gradebook program advertised that claims to "think like an elementary school teacher" and includes ways to encode "effort" into students' grades! Be a careful and critical consumer of any program you choose. If your district chooses a gradebook program for you, you should still investigate what kind of framework it uses for its calculations and adjust default settings to what you intend for your grades whenever possible.

Software for delivering online courses also includes gradebook capability. If you are teaching online, use the same approach to these gradebooks as you would for a gradebook program you use for a face-to-face class. Find out what its capabilities are, what kinds of data it will accommodate, and how it will display summaries or print reports. Most important, find out what framework it uses for combining individual grades or scores into composite grades and check that the method is what you intend. If not, adjust the program's settings. Standards-based grading, in particular, may require adjustments, and one of the most common complaints of teachers trying to implement standards-based grading is making it compatible with the school's grading software (Brookhart, 2011).

MyLab Education **Self-Check 15.3**

MyLab Education **Application Exercise 15.3:** Choosing Weights for Grading

---

CONCLUSION

The main theme of this chapter is that in most situations, it is best to combine measures of classroom achievement to create a grading scale that will communicate achievement information to students and parents. Assess and report citizenship, behavior, and work habits separately. We demonstrated various grading methods. Base your choices on your teaching philosophy, district grading policy, and classroom context.

This ends our discussion of educational assessment in the classroom. The next section discusses standardized testing.

EXERCISES

1. Prepare a brief paper explaining the grading system you use (or plan to use). In a separate section explain the educational rationale for using this system, including an explanation of how your system has improved (or will improve) your students' educational development. Discuss your grading point of view with others in your class. Prepare at least one paragraph explaining each of the following:
   a. The meaning of your grade symbols.
   b. The meaning of failure in your class.
   c. How you distinguish between "failure" and "failure to try."
   d. How you handle late work or work not handed in.
   e. How you avoid the "deadly zero."
   f. What student performances count toward grades you assign your student.
   g. The number of each letter (or other symbol) grade you typically assign (or will assign) in your class.
   h. What components go (or will go) into the end-of-term grade for your students.

FIGURE 15.14 List of students and the grades they received on each component during one marking period. Use this table for Exercise 4.

Pupil	Last year's grade average	Teacher's judgment of ability	Deportment	Class problem sets 1	2	3	Project	Quizzes 1	2	Test score
A	B	Average	Very good	10	3	8	12	8	4	25
B	C	Average	Very good	9	2	7	15	7	4	20
C	A	Very high	Poor	10	0	9	15	10	5	29
D	A	Above average	Excellent	10	4	10	15	6	5	28
E	D	Average	Poor	0	2	5	0	5	3	10
F	B	Average	Good	10	1	2	10	5	3	18
G	C	Below average	Good	10	3	9	8	6	2	15
H	C	Above average	Poor	10	1	4	15	8	4	12
I	C	Above average	Excellent	10	1	3	13	8	3	21
J	C	Above average	Very good	10	1	5	10	8	2	23
Maximum possible score:				10	10	10	15	10	5	30
Mean				8.9	1.8	6.2	11.3	7.1	3.5	20.1
Standard deviation:				3.0	1.2	2.6	4.5	1.5	1.0	6.1
Teacher's weights:				5%	5%	5%	15%	10%	10%	50%

i. How much weight each component in Item h should receive.

j. What boundaries you use (or would use) for each grade.

k. How you handle students who are on the borderline between grades.

l. Any other factors you take into account.

2. Talk with school administrators and teachers at several grade levels in the school district in which you live or work. Take Figure 15.5 with you.

a. What method(s) of student progress reporting is (are) used?

b. Is the district satisfied with the method(s) it uses?

c. Which of the advantages and disadvantages listed in Figure 15.5 has the school district experienced? Explain.

d. Obtain copies of the district's report card(s). Share all your findings with the other members of your class.

e. Summarize the similarities and differences among the district represented in your class and offer suggestions for improving student progress reporting.

3. Identify a unit that you have taught or will teach.

a. In the context of your teaching situation and this unit, identify the assessment variables, the reporting variables, and the grading variables.

b. Prepare a three-column table listing these variables and describing how you have assessed (or will assess) each one.

c. Share your findings with the others in your class.

4. Figure 15.14 contains information about the performance of a class of 10 students. Use it to complete this exercise.

a. Determine an overall report card grade for each student using the following methods: (i) self-referencing; (ii) criterion-referencing, fixed-percentage; (iii) criterion-referencing, total points; and (iv) norm-referencing, SS-score (standard deviation) method.

b. Prepare a table with the students' names as the row headings and the four different methods as the column headings. Enter the students' grades under each method and compare the results.

c. Share your results with the others in your class. Where do you see the most agreement and most disagreement?

d. List the reasons for agreements and disagreements for each method.

5. Name several kinds of student performances (reflections, class discussion, performance tasks, tests, etc.) that you believe should be included in each of the following levels: primary, middle school, or high school.

a. State what weight should be assigned to each type of performance. Explain the reasons for these weights by discussing each of the six factors stated in the chapter in relation to each kind of performance.

b. Would the weights vary with different grade levels or with different subjects? Explain.

Standardized Achievement Tests

KEY CONCEPTS

1. Standardized tests are tests for which the procedures, administration, materials, and scoring rules are fixed so that as far as possible the assessment is the same at different times and places. Appropriate administration of standardized tests and appropriate use of results is key to their effectiveness. Inappropriate administration or use can lead to harmful consequences.

2. Standardized achievement tests include multilevel survey batteries, multilevel criterion-referenced tests, other multilevel tests for a single curricular area, and single-level tests for one course or subject area. State- or district-mandated tests include state achievement tests customized to state standards, interim or benchmark tests and services, Response to Intervention (RTI) assessments, early childhood assessments, and English language proficiency tests.

IMPORTANT TERMS

computer-adaptive tests

empirically documented tests

generalizability of assessment results

in-level versus out-of-level testing

interim or benchmark assessments

multilevel survey battery versus single-level test

special norms

state-mandated assessments

test levels

universal design

OVERVIEW OF STANDARDIZED TESTS

Standardized tests are tests for which the procedures, administration, materials, and scoring rules are fixed so that as far as possible the assessment is the same at different times and places. Because so much attention is paid to high-stakes tests, some people think that the terms "high-stakes tests" and "standardized tests" mean the same thing, which is not true. *Any* test for which the procedures, administration, materials, and scoring rules are fixed is a standardized test. Most high-stakes tests are standardized (e.g., a state-mandated test given for accountability purposes is both high-stakes and standardized). However, not all standardized tests are high-stakes (e.g., a multilevel survey battery given for program evaluation purposes is standardized but not high-stakes).

The focus of this chapter is limited to standardized tests that have empirical data to document their effectiveness. Standardizing is necessary if you want the results to be comparable from time to time, place to place, and person to person. If an assessment procedure is standardized, you are better able to properly interpret students' scores on it. The quality of any assessment procedure is demonstrated by using empirical data to document its validity and effectiveness. When you look for tests (see Chapter 18) do not assume that all commercially available tests have empirical documentation. Make sure to check that they do. These data provide the test developers with a basis for (a) improving and selecting tasks, (b) establishing reliability and validity, (c) describing how well the assessment works in the target population of students, (d) creating scales to measure growth, (e) equating scores (making scores comparable from grade to grade and from one form of the assessment to another), and (f) developing a variety of norm-referenced scores.

How a Standardized Test Is Developed

A standardized test should be the product of a carefully conducted program of research and development. The activities involved in each step are briefly described in this section. Such a well-run development program involves the work of many persons and includes the following steps (Robertson, 1990, pp. 62–63).

1. Assemble preliminary ideas.
2. Evaluate proposal (approve/reject).
3. Make formal arrangement (sign contract if publication is approved).
4. Prepare test specifications.
5. Write items.
6. Conduct item tryout.
   a. Prepare tryout sample specifications.
   b. Prepare participants.
   c. Prepare tryout materials.
   d. Administer tryout items.
   e. Analyze tryout data.
7. Assemble final test form(s).
8. Conduct national standardization.
   a. Prepare standardization sample specifications.
   b. Obtain participants.
   c. Prepare standardization materials.
   d. Administer tests.
   e. Analyze data.
   f. Develop norms tables.
9. Prepare final materials.
   a. Establish publication schedule.
   b. Write manual.
   c. Prepare test books and answer forms.
   d. Manufacture/produce/print materials.
10. Prepare marketing plan.
    a. Initiate direct-mail promotion.
    b. Initiate space advertising.
    c. Train sales staff.
    d. Attend professional meetings and conventions.
11. Publish.

More details about these steps and what test developers are expected to do at each stage of development are found in the *Standards for Educational and Psychological Testing* (AERA et al., 2014).

Note, however, that many assessments available in the marketplace do not follow all steps, because to do so is quite expensive and time-consuming. The steps most likely to be omitted are those concerned with collecting and analyzing data used to improve the quality of the test and/or to support the validity of the claims made for the test. Shortcutting assessment development steps usually means lowering validity, so beware of poorly developed assessments.

Universal Design Considerations

More and more, publishers of large-scale assessments try to incorporate principles of universal design into their test development. **Universal design** is a concept that began in the field of architecture and is intended to maximize access. So, for example, when the curb is cut to street level at intersections, people in wheelchairs don't need special assistance to navigate them. However, the curb design is also good for others: people with strollers, rolling briefcases, even the temporarily tired pedestrian. Universal design has rapidly spread to other fields, including educational assessment. The idea is to design tests that work for most test-takers and avoid as much as possible the need for special accommodations.

Applied to educational testing, universal design in assessment means developing tests from the beginning in order to allow the broadest possible range of students to participate. The National Center on Educational Outcomes (NCEO; Thompson, Johnstone, & Thurlow, 2002) lists the following elements of universally designed assessments:

1. Inclusive assessment population
2. Precisely defined constructs
3. Accessible, non-biased items
4. Amenable to accommodations
5. Simple, clear, and intuitive instructions and procedures
6. Maximum readability and comprehensibility
7. Maximum legibility

Readers who would like further details about these elements should consult the NCEO report, available at nceo.info.

Technology-Based Assessments and Accommodations

Developing technology-based assessments should follow the same basic development plan as is outlined above for paper-based tests. Technology-based assessments should also use principles of universal design as much as possible, again similar to paper-based tests. Technology-based assessments, however, offer some innovative ways to deal with accommodations for students with disabilities that were not possible for paper-and-pencil tests. Because they need to be designed into the technology delivery system, such accommodations need to be planned earlier in the test development process than they would for paper-and-pencil tests.

The National Center on Educational Outcomes (NCEO, 2011) prepared a brief intended for the those developing assessments of the Common Core State Standards. The points they raise apply more broadly to considering accommodations and universal design issues for any technology-based assessment. NCEO distinguishes between accommodations, which are available to students with disabilities, embedded features, tools that are part of the test platform (for example, being able to change the font size) for all students, and good testing practices that should be available to all students (for example, the use of scratch paper for some tests). Planning for technology-embedded features must include decisions about what features will be programmed into the assessment (e.g., a pop-up glossary, an audio file to read each question), about who may access the features (all students or only designated students), about whether the student turns on the feature (voluntarily) or whether the teacher does, and about whether the feature is available on test day or prior to testing.

Planning must address teacher training, so teachers are aware of accommodations and able to help students learn how to use them. Planning must also address student training so that an embedded feature like a pop-up glossary does not become a distraction or something to play with. Finally, planning should include building into the technology-based assessment platform the capability of tracking a student's use of accommodations. As technology opens up, a broader range of possibilities for accommodations and embedded test features than were possible for paper-and-pencil tests, it also requires more long-range planning in test development so that the features can be built in to the system.

Score Reports

Results of standardized tests are reported at many different levels. Individual student reports, class reports, building- and district-level reports are intended for different audiences and purposes. Goodman and Hambleton (2004, p. 150) distilled thirteen general principles for effective reporting of standardized test results. We summarize them here:

1. The report should be concise and readable.
2. The presentation should be simple and uncluttered.

3. Focus data displays on a few purposes, without too much information.

4. Written text should support the readers' interpretation of charts and tables.

5. Minimize the use of statistical jargon.

6. Include a glossary of key terms.

7. Use bar charts for comparisons.

8. Group data meaningfully.

9. Use boxes and other graphics to emphasize key findings.

10. Avoid decimals.

11. If color is used, it should be for communication purposes, not decoration.

12. Pilot test score report designs.

13. Design different reports for different audiences.

Goodman and Hambleton (2004) pointed out that students and parents, educators, and policy makers may have a difficult time interpreting score reports, and accurate interpretation is the first step toward using results in sound and meaningful ways. O'Leary, Hattie, and Griffin (2017) argued for including evidence of different audiences' *actual* (in addition to intended) interpretation and use of test scores in validation work. Such evidence, they reasoned is surely relevant and appropriate to validation. Many times, actual interpretation differs from the interpretation the score report designers intend.

Goodman and Hambleton (2004) sampled score reports from U.S. states, Canadian provinces, and testing companies. They analyzed the reports according to four categories: contextual information, design features, types of information and how presented in the reports, and types of information and how presented in the interpretive material provided with the reports. Their overall finding was that great variability exists in score reports. They saw this variability as a strength, because in all these examples of ways to present information about test results some promising ideas surfaced. They identified (Goodman & Hambleton, 2004, p. 208) five general areas of concern, which we summarize here:

1. Some score reports included too much information, while others omitted key information (e.g., the purpose of the test).

2. Many reports did not give information about the precision of scores (e.g., the score bands we discussed in Chapter 4).

3. Some reports used statistical jargon.

4. Interpretive guides did not always define key terms (e.g., performance levels).

5. Some reports and interpretive guides used fine print, were cluttered, and were difficult to read.

In the section below, we describe four general types of standardized tests. In the four following sections, we give examples of each of these types. Sample score reports for many of the tests mentioned are available by visiting the test's website. If you check several of these, we think you will agree with Goodman and Hambleton's analysis that score reports are exceedingly varied.

VARIETIES OF STANDARDIZED TESTS

Achievement tests vary in their purpose, usefulness, and quality. To appreciate their variety, you may find it helpful to classify them. Here is one classifying scheme (for a more comprehensive classification scheme, see Ferrara and DeMauro, 2006):

I. *Commercially Published Achievement Tests.* Standardized, **empirically documented tests** have a high degree of standardization and follow the development procedures just outlined, especially the steps that require using empirical data to document their effectiveness. The following types are in this group:

A. *Multilevel survey batteries* survey students' general educational growth or basic skill development in each of several curricular areas. *Multilevel* means that the test content spans several grade levels; *battery* means that several curricular areas are assessed by different subtests.

B. *Multilevel criterion-referenced tests, other multilevel tests,* and *single-level standardized tests* are less comprehensive in scope than multilevel survey batteries but are standardized and empirically documented.

1. *Multilevel criterion-referenced tests for a single curricular area* provide detailed information about students' status for a well-defined domain of performance in a single subject area (e.g., mathematics). The test spans several grade levels.

2. *Other multilevel tests for a single curricular area* are noncriterion-referenced tests that assess students in a broader way than do subtests in a survey battery.

3. *Single-level standardized tests for one course or subject* are developed for assessing achievement at only one educational level or for one course (e.g., Algebra I). Usually they are stand-alone tests, neither coordinated with tests from other courses nor normed on the same students as other tests. They are often called "end-of-course" tests or exams.

2. *Federally Mandated State Assessments.* The *No Child Left Behind Act of 2001* and the *Individuals with Disabilities Education Improvement Act (IDEA) of 2004* necessitated state compliance with testing and reporting requirements on a much larger scale than ever before. The *Every Student Succeeds Act of 2015*, which takes full effect in the 2017–2018 school year, continues to require achievement testing for accountability. Test publishers have created many assessments to address these requirements.

3. *Commercially Produced Interim and Benchmark Assessments and Services.* **Interim** or **benchmark assessments** provide information on groups of students and identify, usually in 6- to 9-week cycles, where students are with respect to achievement of state standards to date. Interim assessments can be customized, but many districts also use off-the-shelf interim tests. Some publishers market products they call "formative assessments," but if they are standardized tests intended for administration across classes, we would call them interim or benchmark assessments. Some companies also market item banks that districts, schools, or teachers can use to make their own tests.

4. *Other Commercially Available Tests.* Districts use a variety of other commercially available tests, often in response to state or district policy mandates. These tests include Response to Intervention (RTI) assessments, early childhood assessments, and English language proficiency tests.

COMMERCIALLY PUBLISHED ACHIEVEMENT TESTS
Multilevel Survey Batteries

Historically the workhorse of standardized achievement testing has been the **multilevel survey battery**. Currently, federally mandated state achievement tests are more commonly used, but the multilevel survey batteries are still what many people think of when they think of a "standardized test." Although each publisher's test battery emphasizes different details of content and skill, the batteries are organized similarly.

Common Features   Most group-administered survey batteries have the following features in common.

1. *Test development features.* Manuals and other materials describe for each subtest the (a) content and learning objectives covered, (b) types of norms and how they were developed, (c) type of criterion-referencing provided, (d) reliability data, and (e) techniques used to screen items for offensiveness and possible gender, ethnic, and racial bias.

2. *Test administration features.* Tests generally (a) have two equivalent forms; (b) require a total administration time of 2 to 3 hours, spread among several testing sessions over several school days (although length and administration time vary widely); (c) provide practice booklets for students to use before being tested; (d) have separate, machine-scorable answer sheets for upper grades (students in lower grades mark answers directly on the machine-scorable test booklets), and often computer-based administration forms; and (e) permit both **in-level and out-of-level testing**.[1] An important current issue in test administration is the equivalence of paper and online forms. Districts and schools should make sure tests that claim to be equivalent across these modalities supply empirical evidence of this equivalence.

3. *Test norming features.* Tests generally use broadly representative national sampling for norms development and provide both fall and spring individual student norms. Mid-year empirical norms are sometimes created, as

---

[1] Tests are organized by level; each level is designed for use with a few grades. A student is said to be tested *in-level* if the test level corresponds to the student's actual grade placement. If a student's level of academic functioning is either above or below the actual grade placement, the school may administer the test level that more nearly corresponds to the student's functioning level. This is called *out-of-level testing.* A student is measured best when a test is tailored to the student's functioning level.

well. Sometimes **special norms** such as the following are provided: (a) large-city norms, (b) norms for students in special government entitlement programs, (c) norms for high-income communities, (d) norms for nonpublic schools, (e) regional norms, and (f) norms for school-building averages.

4. *Test score features.* Tests provide raw scores for each subtest and the following norm-referenced scores: percentile ranks, normal curve equivalents, stanines, extended normalized standard scores, and grade equivalents (or some similar grade-level indicator score). Attitudes toward using grade equivalents vary. Some tests provide instructional reading-level scores that are keyed to commonly used basal readers. (We discuss these scores in the next chapter.)

5. *Test score reporting and interpretation features.* Tests generally have interpretive manuals for teachers, school administrators, and/or counselors. Most group tests provide computer-prepared narrative reports that contain summaries of district, school-building, and classroom test results. Some types of reports may be provided with the purchase of the test, and others may be sold separately.

Differences Although survey batteries share common features, they are definitely not interchangeable. Scores obtained from different publishers' batteries, even on subtests with similar-sounding titles, will be different and cannot be compared directly. Among the features that are different and that seriously affect comparability of scores are the following:

1. *Emphasis within content areas.* Subtest scores on batteries from different test publishers have different meanings. For example, a study of the mathematics subtests of four standardized survey batteries for the fourth-grade level indicated that the percentage of items covering a topic such as fractions varied widely among tests—from 5.4% to 14.4% (Freeman, Kuhs, Knappen, & Porter, 1982). This difference in coverage affects pupils' scores significantly. Because each test publisher chooses to emphasize each subtopic somewhat differently, there may be a serious mismatch between what a given battery calls "reading comprehension" or "social studies" and what a given school and/or teacher emphasizes in class. These mismatches result in subtest scores

that may not represent a student's current level of functioning. The overlap of a test and a school's instructional program is an extremely important consideration in choosing among test batteries.

2. *Quality of developmental scales' articulation between grade levels.* One use of a standardized test is to measure students' growth on a continuous scale. If the scale is constructed properly, it is possible to track students' educational growth over the various grade levels. But different test developers use different technical methods for creating developmental scales, even when the scales have the same name. A chief consideration in the practical use of test results concerns the amount of grade-to-grade overlap in the development scores (Kolen, 2006). For example, a fourth grader may have a grade equivalent of 6.0 on the fourth-grade mathematics subtest and a grade equivalent of 4.9 on the sixth-grade counterpart of the same subtest. Different techniques for constructing grade equivalents will create differing amounts of overlap. If this happens, the result will be scores that show a spuriously erratic pattern of growth for youngsters as they progress through the grades.

3. *Quality of services offered to schools.* Test publishers differ in the extent of their technical support and interpretative services for schools using their products. Some publishers sell the product and certain standard services (such as computer printouts summarizing test results for a school district) but do not provide knowledgeable consultants who can advise a school on particular problems or even on how to interpret their results in general. A school official who is planning to purchase a survey battery should explore fully with the publisher's sales representative the nature and cost of technical support services that will come with the test battery. Score reporting, in particular, can be a significant source of cost over time.

Organization of Batteries Each battery contains several subtests. A subtest assesses one area, such as reading, mathematics, listening skills, English usage (mechanics), writing, spelling (recognition), vocabulary (word meaning), or skills in using library and reference materials. Not all questions on these subtests are multiple-choice items: In recent years, publishers have added constructed-response items or performance tasks to several subtests or have offered them as separate subtests. Separate scores are given for each subtest. Usually, a battery has subtests for six to eight curriculum areas. Different publishers may have different subtest names for the same curriculum area.

Each subtest is made up of a coordinated series of **test levels** that span the grades. For example, a reading subtest may be organized into four levels: one level for Grades 1 and 2, another for Grades 3 and 4, another for 5 and 6, and a fourth for 7 and 8. It is not unusual for a publisher to have adjacent levels with overlapping grades (e.g., one level covering Grades 3–4–5 and the next level covering Grades 5–6–7).

Many achievement survey batteries are available in the marketplace. Here, in alphabetical order, are the most widely used batteries. The grade ranges they cover are noted in parentheses.

ACT Aspire (3–10)

Iowa Assessments (K–12)

Peabody Individual Achievement Test (K–adult)

Stanford Achievement Test Series, Tenth Edition (K–12)

TerraNova, Third Edition (K–12)

Wide Range Achievement Test 4 (K–adult)

These are all group-administered tests, except for the *Peabody* and the *Wide Range*, which are individually administered. Publishers are listed in Appendixes H and I. Details about each battery can be obtained from the publishers' catalogs and websites. Critical reviews are found in the *Mental Measurements Yearbooks*, *Test Critiques*, and other sources identified in Chapter 18. Figure 16.1 shows the curriculum areas, subtests, and grade levels covered by some of the more popular standardized achievement tests. As you look at Figure 16.1, remember that although different publishers' survey batteries may be similar in their surface features, they are not interchangeable, even though subtest names may sound similar.

Tests vary in how well they match any school district's curriculum or state's standards. In some curricula, such as reading and perhaps mathematics, the curricula differ very little from one school district to another within a state. The tests and these curricula may match closely. In other curricula such as science and social studies, especially among elementary schools, there are much larger variations between school districts. For a teacher, this disparity means that the different subtests in the battery have less value in assessing the specifics of what the teacher taught during the year. However, such subtests can assess general information and general ability to apply knowledge and skill.

These differences make it necessary for school officials to actually inspect the test items before they adopt a battery, matching their local curriculum to the battery's content and skills emphasis. If there is a wide gap between your local curriculum's learning objectives and the battery's tasks, do not adopt the survey battery.

Publishers think of each subtest (e.g., reading comprehension) as assessing a continuous dimension that grows or develops over a range of grades. Because each subtest is a graded series of assessments, the publisher can use empirical data to link the levels together and to place the scores of students from every grade on one numerical scale that spans all the grades. This process allows you to use a multilevel subtest to measure a student's year-to-year educational development and growth in a curricular area. Different types of educational development scales are explained in Chapter 17.

Each publisher norms and standardizes its tests on different samples of students, so the samples and the resulting norm-referenced scores are not comparable. However, all the subtests in one publisher's survey battery are administered to the same national sample of students. The major advantage of administering all subtests to the same students is that the different subtest results can be referenced to the same norm group, allowing you to compare a student's relative strengths and weaknesses across the different curricular areas. You can assess these strengths and weaknesses, however, only by comparing a student's percentile rank in one curricular area to that student's percentile rank in another. An example of the kind of comparison you make follows:

Example

Shanna is better in mathematics than she is in social studies because her score in mathematics is higher than 98 percent of the students at her grade level, whereas her score in social studies is higher than only 60 percent of students at her grade level.

FIGURE 16.1 Examples of curriculum areas and grade levels assessed by survey batteries.

Curriculum area/subarea[a]	Stanford Achievement (10th Test ed.)	Metropolitan Achievement Tests (8th ed.)	Iowa Tests of Basic Skills (Form C)	Iowa Tests of Educational Development (Form C)	TerraNova3 Complete Battery Plus
Reading multiple-choice					
Alphabet knowledge	K.0–1.5	K.0–K.5	K.1–1.9		
Word/sentence reading	K.0–2.5	1.5–4.5	K.8–3.5		1.0–4.2
Phonetic/structural analysis	1.5–3.5	K.0–4.5	K.1–3.9		1.0–4.2
Decoding skills	K.0–1.5	K.0–1.5	K.1-3.9		1.0–4.2
Vocabulary	2.5–12.9	1.5–12.9	K.1–9.9	9.0–12.9	K–12.9
Comprehension	1.5–12.9	1.5–12.9	K.8–9.9	9.0–12.9	K–12.9
Reading performance assessment	1.5–12.9[b]	1.5–12.9[b]			3.0–12.9[c]
Language multiple-choice					
Punctuation	1.5–12.9	1.5–12.9	1.7–9.9	9.0–12.9	1.6–12.9
Capitalization	1.5–12.9	1.5–12.9	1.7–9.9	9.0–12.9	1.6–12.9
Usage	1.5–12.9	1.5–12.9	1.7–9.9	9.0–12.9	1.6–12.9
Listening	K.0–9.9	K.0–3.5	K.1–9.9		K.6–2.6
Sentence/paragraph organization	1.5–12.9	3.0–8.9	3.0–9.9	9.0–12.9	1.6–12.9
Language/writing performance assessment	3.5–12.9[b]	1.5–12.9[b]	3.0–12.9[b]	3.0–12.9[b]	3.0–12.9[c]
Spelling multiple-choice	1.5–12.9	1.5–12.9	1.7–9.9	9.0–12.9	2.0–12.9
Mathematics multiple-choice					
Computation	K.0–12.9	K.5–9.5	1.7–9.9	9.0–12.9	K.6–12.9
Concepts	K.0–12.9	K.5–12.9	K.1–9.9	9.0–12.9	K.0–12.9
Problem solving	K.5–12.9	1.5–12.9	K.1–9.9	9.0–12.9	K.6–12.9
Mathematics performance assessment	1.5–12.9[b]	1.5–12.9[b]			3.0–12.9[c]
Study skills multiple-choice					
Maps, graphs, tables	4.5–12.9	3.5–12.9	1.7–9.9	9.0–12.9	1.6–12.9
Library/reference materials	4.5–12.9	3.5–12.9	1.7–9.9	9.0–12.9	1.6–12.9
Study skills performance assessment		K.0–8.9[b]			
Science multiple-choice	K.0–12.9	1.5–12.9	1.7–9.9	9.0–12.9	1.6–12.9
Science performance assessment	1.5–12.9[b]	1.5–12.9[b]			
Social studies multiple-choice	3.5–12.9	1.5–12.9	1.7–9.9	9.0–12.9	1.6–12.9
Social studies performance assessment	1.5–12.9[b]	1.5–12.9[b]			

Notes: [a]Publishers may have somewhat different names for these areas than those used here. Separate scores are not provided for every area.

[b]Assessments in these areas are available as supplements or additional purchase components that are not part of the battery itself.

[c]Part of the Multiple Assessments Edition.

Survey batteries report grade-equivalent scores and standard scores, too, but you should not use them to compare a student's achievement in two curricular areas. Percentile ranks, standard scores, and grade-equivalent scores are explained in Chapter 17.

Common Learning Outcomes Virtually all published standardized tests cover content and learning objectives judged to be common to many schools rather than one specific school district. Therefore, standardized achievement tests are not focused on the teaching emphasis of one teacher, one school, one textbook, or one set of curricular materials. This is an advantage because it gives you an "external" or "objective" view of what your students have learned. It is also a disadvantage because the cognitive skills and knowledge assessed by the test may not have been taught to the students before they were tested. Therefore, it is imperative that a school district carefully compares a test's content and *when* that content is taught in their schools, item by item, to the state's standards and the school district's curriculum framework before deciding to adopt it. Sometimes as few as three or four misaligned items can have a serious impact on the results. Some publishers provide tools to help you do this. For example, the Stanford 10 has a *Compendium of Instructional Standards* that describes the content and cognitive processes each item on each test measures. Also, a teacher must develop and use his or her own assessment procedures for day-to-day instructional decisions (e.g., whether a student has mastered a specific concept).

Auxiliary Materials   Most publishers of standardized, empirically documented tests provide auxiliary materials to help you interpret and use the assessment results. Teacher's manuals describe in considerable detail the intended purpose and uses of the results, often suggesting ways to improve students' skills by using assessment results for instructional planning. Some publishers provide separate manuals for curriculum coordinators and school administrators to help them use assessment results in curriculum evaluation and reports to the school board. Most publishers provide nicely printed score reports that the school district may use both within the school and with students and parents. Most publishers also provide score reports on compact disc.

Survey Achievement Battery Selection   Examine and review each test individually to judge its appropriateness for your purposes. Before selecting an elementary school survey battery, consider these four points:

1. Survey batteries measure only part of the outcomes desired for elementary schools. Use additional assessment procedures to evaluate the other outcomes.

2. Specific content in subjects such as social studies and science may quickly become dated. Tests designed to measure broad cognitive skills or levels of educational development become dated less quickly.

3. Tests measuring broad cognitive skills or levels of educational development need to be

supplemented by teacher-made or standardized tests of specific content.

4. Each battery has a different mix and emphasis of content and skills; each is accompanied by various kinds of interpretive aids. Examine a test battery carefully before deciding to purchase it.

Because high school curricula vary so much, choosing a survey battery for this educational level is difficult. School officials should keep the following six points in mind before selecting a high school test battery:

1. Survey batteries that emphasize basic skills (reading, mathematics, language) may be more useful as measures of high school readiness than as measures of high school outcomes (unless a high school program is especially directed toward basic skills development).

2. Some tests are more oriented toward testing specific content than educational development broadly defined. If you want a content-oriented test, review each item on the test carefully to see if the test measures what the school intends.

3. Tests stressing the measurement of levels of educational development that cut across several subject areas rather than knowledge of specific content tend to measure more complex skills and global processes.

4. The variety of course offerings at the high school level makes it more necessary than at the elementary level to examine the content of each survey battery carefully.

5. You may find it necessary to supplement a high school survey battery with assessments measuring content knowledge of specific subjects.

6. A practical consideration is the continuity of measurement from elementary to secondary levels, which often means purchasing a high school battery from the same company that published the elementary school battery.

Complementing Your State Assessment   Currently, all states mandate their own assessment. Take state assessment coverage into account before choosing a published standardized test. Most state assessments have school, district, and state accountability as their main purpose. This is not the case for a published standardized test, which is used primarily to measure individual students' educational growth. Keep the following four points in mind if you are trying to select a standardized multilevel achievement test when you are also faced with a state-mandated assessment:

1. All things being equal, choose a standardized test that requires students to demonstrate learning that is very consistent with your state's standards or curriculum framework.

2. If your community does not like the focus of your state-mandated assessment, choose a multilevel achievement test that reflects the community's concerns. For example, your community may not wish to limit assessment to the higher-order thinking and complex problem solving on which the state assessment focuses. The community may wish to know whether basic skills such as computation, reading comprehension, English writing mechanics, and spelling are being learned.

3. Plan to use the chosen test over a period of at least 5 years, so that you can track changes in your school district.

4. When possible, test at grade levels not tested by the state-mandated assessment to avoid overburdening students and teachers.

Individually Administered Surveys   Individually administered achievement batteries are commonly used for students with special needs, such as students with disabilities who otherwise would have difficulty taking assessments in group settings. Students who cannot be assessed in groups often can be validly assessed in individual sessions where the assessment administrator can provide the special accommodations they need and can establish greater rapport than is possible in a group. (See Chapter 5, Figure 5.2, for examples of test accommodations.)

Sometimes individual achievement batteries are used as "screening" tests to identify students with learning difficulties, or as part of a broader series of individual assessments when a school psychologist conducts a general psychological evaluation. A school district may use individual achievement survey batteries to assess the general educational development of a newly transferred student, or as a double check on a previously administered group survey test when the results are being questioned for a particular

student. Because both the content and norms of an individual assessment are different from the group test, you should proceed very cautiously when double-checking. You can expect a student's results from the two types of tests to correspond only very roughly.

Two commonly administered individual survey achievement tests are the *Wide Range Achievement Test, Fourth Edition (WRAT-4)* and the *Peabody Individual Achievement Test—Revised-Normative Update (PIAT-R/NU)*. These single instruments contain items that span many ages or grades (essentially ages 5 to adult). Thus, by their very nature, they contain few items specifically associated with a given age or grade level. Such tests do not have as much in-depth coverage as group survey tests that have separate levels for each age or grade level. This comment is not necessarily a criticism of these tests. These wide-range tests make a quick assessment of a student's strengths in several basic curricular areas. This quickly obtained assessment helps the teacher determine relatively weak areas needing more in-depth diagnostic follow-up.

The *PIAT-R/NU*'s items are printed on a small easel. Students do not write responses to the multiple-choice items; they must only say or point to the option. Within each subtest the items are arranged in order of difficulty. A student does not take each item; a starting point (called a basal level) and an ending point (called a ceiling level) are established, based on the student's pattern of correct answers and errors.

Multilevel Criterion-Referenced Tests

Multilevel criterion-referenced tests provide information about students' status with respect to the specific learning objectives in a domain. Although some survey batteries also provide this information, most surveys assess very broadly or globally defined educational development. Multilevel criterion-referenced tests tend to focus on a more narrowly defined set of learning objectives. Some publishers make efforts to align their tests with states' standards.

Other Multilevel Tests

Other types of multilevel tests are stand-alone products that cover one curricular area, such as reading or mathematics, across several grades. These assessments provide a deeper and broader sampling of content than a corresponding subtest of a survey battery. Thus, more time is devoted to assessing students in a single curricular area than when you use a survey battery subtest. However, if the same sample of students was not used to norm a stand-alone multilevel test concurrently with tests from other curricular areas, you cannot use the stand-alone tests to compare a student's relative strengths and weaknesses across curricular areas. For example, you could not say a student is better in reading than in mathematics.

Single-Level Standardized Tests

If you do not want to measure growth or development, a **single-level test** may be useful. Rather than cover several grade or age levels, such tests are directed toward one level or a particular course. Usually these assessments are built for high school and college courses. There are, for example, tests for Algebra I, first-year college chemistry, and first-year college French. The Advanced Placement (AP) and International Baccalaureate (IB) programs use single-level standardized tests tied to their specific courses.

Each test is a stand-alone product and is not coordinated with other tests. Thus, these test results cannot be used to compare a student's relative standing in several subjects. For some of these single-level standardized test, scores use norm-referencing schemes such as percentile ranks and standard scores. For others, for example the AP tests, cut scores are established for score groupings (e.g., 1 through 5 for the AP), and colleges can choose the level for which they will assign college credit, effectively establishing a "criterion" for the test scores.

For most purposes, a teacher-made test for a subject is most appropriate: It is closest to the course content and contains the emphasis you desire. Single-subject or course tests have been found most useful for such purposes as pretesting to determine the general background of students coming into a course; advanced placement in college courses; exemption from required or introductory courses; contests and scholarship programs that reward general knowledge of a particular subject; and granting college credit for knowledge acquired by independent study, work experience, or other types of nontraditional education.

The use of single-subject tests as end-of-course tests has recently increased. Some states have begun to use high school end-of-course tests

in their assessment systems in place of more general reading and mathematics tests (Ferrara & Way, 2016). Some have begun requiring their use in teacher evaluation systems, although that may change in the future. As of February 2015, twenty-seven states required high school students to take at least one end-of-course test. Thirteen of those required students to pass those tests in order to graduate (Ferrara & Way, 2016, p. 11). In some cases, end-of-course test scores are also a component of students' final course grades.

FEDERALLY MANDATED STATE ASSESSMENTS

Starting with the NCLB act of 2001 and now with the ESSA act of 2015, all students in grades 3 through 8 and high school must sit for official **state-mandated assessments**. State-mandated customized tests are developed by test developers, including some of the same companies that produce other kinds of standardized tests, for use only in a particular state. The tests are said to be *customized* because a publisher contracts with a state to prepare standardized tests that are aligned with the state's standards and are secure, so they can be used for accountability purposes. Since the NCLB Act, the grades typically covered are 3 through 12 and the subjects tested are reading, language arts, mathematics, and science. In this chapter, we discuss the tests themselves. Sometimes the public may view testing as an educational reform in itself. However, it is important to note that while tests can highlight areas of need, they do not in themselves contain information about what to do about those areas (Supovitz, 2009). This section discusses only the tests.

State-mandated tests vary greatly in their focus, makeup, and quality. Most state assessments have accountability as a focus. Accountability may be at the school district, school-building, or student level. The federal government required accountability at the school level in an attempt to ensure all students in the school receive quality instruction. At the district or school level, there may be consequences if scores do not improve over time. For example, ESSA requires states to intervene in the lowest-performing 5 percent of schools and in high schools where the graduation rate is 67 percent or less. Thus, the test may be a high-stakes test for a school, but a low-stakes test for a student.

State test results are not comparable from one state to another. State standards differ, and each state test is different and has its own standard setting. Therefore, for example, an eighth grader who scores "proficient" in mathematics in one state may or may not be at the proficient level in another state. The National Center for Education Statistics (NCES) has produced several studies comparing state test results using the National Assessment of Educational Progress (NAEP) as a common metric. Using the state percentage of students who scored at or above its proficiency cut point along with the state's distribution of performance on NAEP, researchers can estimate the stringency of each state's standards on the common NAEP scale. The most recent (as of this writing) such study, from the 2013 NAEP reading and mathematics assessments (Bandeira de Mello, Bohrnstedt, Blankenship, & Sherman, 2015) found that states continue to vary widely in their achievement standards. For example, in Grade 8 reading, the difference between the highest and lowest state proficiency standards in 2013 was 83 points on the 0 to 500 NAEP scale. This is a difference of about two standard deviations on the NAEP scale. Chapter 17 discusses standard deviations in more detail, but for now, just know this is a huge difference.

Some states require individual student accountability in addition to school accountability. This individual accountability usually takes the form of a graduation test. The test may cover basic skills or be more challenging, depending on the state. Often a basic skills graduation test is given in Grade 9 or Grade 10 so that students with low scores may be forewarned and placed into remedial programs to improve their skills. Graduation tests are high stakes for students.

State assessments are based on a state's curriculum framework and standards. The trend had been to make standards that are challenging to students rather than to limit them to minimum competencies or basic skills. The most recent compendium of state assessments we were able to find was for the 2009–2010 school year (Council of Chief State School Officers [CCSSO], 2010). All states except Iowa (which used the Iowa Assessments) reported using a criterion-referenced test. Some states, in addition, used norm-referenced tests or augmented norm-referenced tests. An augmented norm-referenced test is a norm-referenced test that is customized to state standards, usually by adding some additional items.

Customized state assessments are also built for states' alternate achievement standards, and sometimes for modified achievement standards. Alternate or modified standards are prepared for eligible students, typically by projecting downward from regular standards so that each alternate standard is related to a regular standard. ESSA allows that 1 percent of students may be given alternate assessments; however, this is only about 10 percent of all students in special education. You can usually find out about your state's assessment program through its education department's website. Websites for individual schools (if they exist) can be located by searching for the school name and location. See Chapter 18 for more about locating information about your state assessment program.

The consensus is that state assessment programs wanting to change classroom practices must place great emphasis on teacher development because assessment programs alone do not improve schools (Linn & Baker, 1997; McDonnell, 1997; Smith, 1997; Supovitz, 2009). In addition, compromises due to financial constraints, time pressures, technology limitations, and political pressures usually mean that the original plans for state assessment need to be scaled back. This reduction may result in failing to implement key components such as improving classroom assessment practices, using performance assessments, or failing to implement appropriate teacher development programs.

State testing programs have faced some community backlash. A movement called "opt-out" (Bennett, 2016) gained some momentum in some states and among some demographic groups, becoming especially notable in 2015. When students opt out, however, the validity of the resulting test information for its main uses (e.g., school and district accountability) is compromised. Sometimes those who opt out cite the amount of testing time as the rationale, and sometimes they voice concerns about students' perceived test anxiety. The use of tests for teacher evaluation, which has been mitigated somewhat with the ESSA legislation, also put pressure on teachers and students and appears to have been part of the opt-out movement in some states. According to Bennett (2016, p. 9), these concerns are as much about test use than about testing per se. Affected states and districts are meeting this complicated issue by clearer communication about the purposes and uses of test results and, sometimes, working to shorten testing time or change assessment system designs or policies.

Some states have joined partnerships for state assessment. As of this writing, the Partnership for Assessment of Readiness for College and Careers (PARCC, parcc-assessment.org, with 11 states) and the Smarter Balanced Assessment Consortium (smarterbalanced.org, with 17 states) are in the process of working with a wide variety of developers and contractors to create assessment systems for their states. There are also two consortia working on Alternative Assessments for the Common Core State Standards for students with significant cognitive disabilities. The National Center and State Collaborative Partnership (NCSC, ncscpartners.org) is a consortium of several states, the District of Columbia, and several territories, led by the National Center on Educational Outcomes at the University of Minnesota. The Dynamic Learning Maps Alternate Assessment System Consortium (DLM, dynamiclearningmaps.org) is a consortium of states led by the University of Kansas. A consortium of 35 states, called Assessment Services Supporting ELs through Technology Systems (ASSETS, assets.wceruw.org), was funded in 2011 to create a comprehensive assessment system for English language learners.

COMMERCIALLY PRODUCED INTERIM AND BENCHMARK ASSESSMENTS AND SERVICES

Because of the high stakes attached to annual state testing, local districts have been interested in predicting and shaping students' performance during the year, to maximize performance on the annual state test. Test publishers have rapidly developed many products to meet this need. These tests can be called "benchmark," "diagnostic," "formative," and/or "predictive." Perie, Marion, and Gong (2007) call these tests by the umbrella term "interim assessment," a term we think is appropriate, too, and that seems to be beginning to stick. When test publishers call these tests "formative assessments," we believe they are mislabeled. Standardized tests or banks of items intended as assessments to be administered across classes in a grade or subject area have a formative intent, namely to inform changes in instruction or curriculum. However, they are

formative evaluation tools. With other authors (e.g., Shepard, 2008; Black & Wiliam, 2009), we reserve the term "formative assessment" for assessment that includes students in envisioning a learning target, understanding where they are in relation to it, and deciding on learning strategies they will use to move closer to their target. We discussed this view of formative assessment in Chapters 7 and 8.

Claims are made that interim assessments will help schools and districts meet adequate yearly progress requirements or improve performance on high school exit exams. A good interim assessment can be part of a district's balanced assessment system if the information is used well. At the present time, there is little research documenting prediction of state test scores or positive effects on student achievement (Brown & Coughlin, 2007). However, we predict that such research is about to increase. Under the ESSA regulations, states may experiment with using information aggregated from interim tests to supplement or replace the summative state assessment. Dadey and Gong (2017, p. 1) observe, "There are many technical and practical challenges inherent to such systems, many of which currently lack clear solutions…. Current commercially available interim assessments, then, will likely need additional documentation, development, or both."

Following are some examples of products or suites of products marketed for interim or benchmark assessment. Some of these are administered online; others are paper-and-pencil tests or a combination. Some include item banks for creating customized interim assessments.

Acuity (Data Recognition Corporation)—Grades 3–8 and 10

Benchmark Tracker (Pearson)—Grades K–12

iReady (Curriculum Associates)—Grades K–12

eMPower (*Measured Progress*)—Grades 3–8

Measures of Academic Progress (*MAP*, Northwest Evaluation Association)—Grades 2–12

TerraNova Math and Reading Assessments (Data Recognition Corporation)—Grades K–12

We describe only one of these tests here, the *Measures of Academic Progress* (*MAP*). The *MAP* are computer-adaptive tests to measure achievement in Reading, Language Usage, Mathematics, General Science Topics, and Science Concepts and Processes in Grades 2 through 12. A

computer-adaptive test is a test administered by computer, in which the next item or item set presented to the student is selected based on the student's performance on a previous item or item set. Students who get items wrong are branched to easier items, while students who get items right are branched to more difficult items. Therefore, in computer-adaptive tests not all students take the same items. Computer-adaptive tests are more efficient than fixed-form tests, because they require fewer items to arrive at a reliable estimate of a student's score.

The *MAP* scores are reported on a scale called an RIT scale (short for Rasch Unit Scale) that ranges from approximately 140 to 300. They can be administered up to four times a year (Northwest Evaluation Association [NWEA], 2011). MAP tests can be administered as "survey with goals tests" of approximately 40 items, which are designed to measure achievement of students as they grow through the grades. The "survey" is the total score for the test, and the "goals" are subscores for more specific topics within these areas. Five goals under Reading include: Evaluative Reading Comprehension, Interpretive Reading Comprehension, Literal Reading Comprehension, Literary Response and Analysis, and Word Analysis and Vocabulary Development. Five goals under Language Usage include: Basic Grammar and Usage, Capitalization, Composing and Writing Process, Composition Structure, and Punctuation. Seven goals under Mathematics include: Algebraic Concepts; Computation; Geometry; Measurement; Number Sense and Numeration; Problem Solving; and Statistics, Probability and Graphing. Three goals under General Science Topics include: Earth and Space Sciences, Life Sciences, and Physical Sciences. Two goals under Science Concepts and Processes include: Develop Abilities Needed for Scientific Inquiry and Unifying Processes and Concepts of Science.

MAP tests can also be administered as shorter (approximately 30 items) survey tests, which yield overall subject test scores without the goals scores. Interpretation aids called RIT Charts are available that give sample problems students can solve according to their survey scores. Norms are provided for both status and growth from one testing administration to a subsequent administration (NWEA, 2012).

Some test publishers also market item banks so that schools or districts can make their own

interim or benchmark tests, or for other purposes. For example, "common formative assessments"—a term we believe is a misnomer—are sometimes constructed and administered across classes to help teachers plan instruction in certain content areas. Item banks are databases that contain test items, typically multiple-choice items, and identifying tags like grade level, content area, state standard, cognitive level (e.g., from the Bloom or Webb taxonomy), and other identifiers. Teachers or administrators can specify a certain number of items keyed to a given standard or standards, for example, and the item bank will return a test form built to those specifications. Some item banks also have the capability for local educators to add their own items, as well, so that an item bank may contain a mixture of purchased and locally written test items.

In our work with school districts over the years, we have seen several problems arise when teachers use district-purchased item banks. We describe here two such problems that may have serious consequences. First, we have seen teachers use item banks to construct tests that they will use for locally developed measures of achievement to be used in either common assessments or for teacher evaluation. Thus, students at several grades will be taking similarly constructed tests. Depending on the grade level of items requested, this can result in some of the same items—and for reading tests, some of the same reading passages—ending up on tests for different grades, for example, second and third grades. Without coordination, some students might see the same items two or more years in a row. This may compromise the meaning, and thus the validity, of the test results.

Second and even more dramatic—but we have seen this happen—is that unthinking use of item banks can lead to some ridiculous tests. Item banks are sorted by individual test item. Therefore, when a teacher calls up an item for a particular standard, the computer gives just that, one item. Reading passages in item banks may have several questions associated with them, but the questions may be keyed to different standards. When you ask for one item on a particular standard, you get the passage and the one item. As you know from our discussion of both context-dependent items and of assessment of reading (Chapter 11), if a student is going to have to read a relatively long passage, they should use the passage to answer several questions. It is not an effective use of student time to read a whole passage to answer one question. We have seen some drafts of first- and second-grade tests that ran to 20 pages because of this problem, with many passages having only one associated item.

The solution to these and similar problems is thoughtful use of item banks and considering their output only a first draft of a test. First, build the test blueprint (Chapter 6) for which you want the item bank to offer items. Then do the search, and review the draft. Make sure that the resulting test makes sense from the point of view of the student, that it does not repeat items students will have already seen, and that all items are appropriate given the instruction the students have had. Make sure any introductory material, including reading passages, is appropriate and well used. Revise the draft test until it meets all these conditions.

OTHER COMMERCIALLY AVAILABLE TESTS

Tests can be used for screening or readiness for a particular program and for monitoring student progress during a program. We discuss three of these types of assessments briefly here: Response to Intervention assessments, early childhood assessments, and English language proficiency assessments.

Response to Intervention (RTI) Assessments

As Chapter 6 described, Response to Intervention refers to a process that emphasizes how well students respond to changes in instruction. The essential elements of an RTI approach are the provision of scientific, research-based instruction and interventions in general education; monitoring and measurement of student progress in response to the instruction and interventions; and use of these measures of student progress to shape instruction and make educational decisions (Klotz & Canter, 2006).

Response to Intervention (RTI) *assessments* focus on early identification of struggling learners and the delivery of targeted interventions. Most RTI solutions from test publishers have a variety of assessment and intervention tools and employ a tiered approach, which progresses from universal screening to progress monitoring and

interventions. Universal screening happens during tier 1 and helps identify students who might benefit from intervention strategies that are more intense than regular instruction. Progress monitoring happens during tiers 2 and 3 where students receive instructional interventions of increasing intensity. Examples of RTI assessments include the following:

Acuity (McGraw-Hill Education)—Grades 1–12

Academic Intervention Monitoring System (*AIMSWeb*, Pearson)—Grades K–12

Early Childhood Assessments

Early childhood assessments are of several types. Some are designed to assess academic readiness of concepts (e.g., colors, letters, numbers, sizes) that are seen to be directly related to early childhood education or predict readiness for more formal education (Bracken, 2002). Others are designed to assess student performance like the interim or benchmark assessment described above, but with the focus on pre-K to Grade 2 students.

The impetus for early childhood assessments seems to be making certain that children are ready at a younger age for the demands of accountability testing when they are older. Both academic readiness (Bracken, 2002) assessments for early childhood and interim assessments for pre-K to Grade 2 students have this general purpose. Examples include the following.

Bracken School Readiness Assessment (*BSRA-3*, Pearson Assessments)—Measures academic readiness for ages 3.0 to 6.11

Children's Progress Academic Assessment (*CPAA*, NWEA)—An interim assessment system for pre-K to Grade 3 (available pre-K to Grade 2 for English language learners)

English Language Proficiency Tests

The purpose of *English language proficiency* assessments is to place English language learners (ELLs) at the appropriate proficiency level for bilingual or English as a second language programs, or determine if ELLs are ready to exit these programs. ELL testing was required under Title III of NCLB. With the advent of ESSA, ELL accountability moves to Title I, where all other students' accountability resides. During the first year that ELL students are in the United States, ELL students' scores on their state accountability test will not count toward a school's rating. By the third year of residency, the state assessment accountability scores of ELL students must be treated just like any other students' scores.

Meanwhile, schools may also test ELL students for English language proficiency. The purpose of English language proficiency tests is to place English language learners (ELLs) at the appropriate level for bilingual or English as a second language programs or to determine if ELLs are ready to exit these programs. English language proficiency tests assess the domains of reading, writing, speaking, and listening, and provide a comprehension score for English language learners from Grades K through 12. An additional feature is that the tests measure progress from year to year. This is typically accomplished by placing the test levels on a developmental or vertical scale.

Examples of English language proficiency tests include the following:

LAS Links K-12 Assessments (Data Recognition Corporation)—Grades K–12

Stanford English Language Proficiency Test 2 (SELP 2, Pearson)—Grades pre-K–12

ACCESS for ELLs (WIDA Consortium)—Grades pre-K–12

MyLab Education **Self-Check 16.1**

MyLab Education **Application Exercise 16.1:**
The Importance of Educator Understanding of Standardized Tests

---

APPROPRIATE USES OF STANDARDIZED TEST RESULTS
Within-Classroom Uses

How can you use standardized test results? Here are some suggestions for within-classroom uses of test results:

1. *Describe the educational developmental levels of each student.* Use this information about the differences among your students to modify or adapt teaching to accommodate individual students' needs.

2. *Describe specific qualitative strengths and weaknesses in students.* These strengths vary from one curriculum area to another. Use this

information to remediate deficiencies and capitalize on strengths.

3. *Describe the extent to which a student has achieved the prerequisites needed to go on to new or advanced learning.* Combine these results with a student's classroom performance to make recommendations for placement.

4. *Describe commonalities among students.* Use this information to group students for more efficient instruction. Figure 16.2 outlines suggestions for using survey battery information in planning classroom instruction.

5. *Describe students' achievement of specific learning objectives.* Use students' performance on clusters of items to make immediate teaching changes.

6. *Provide students and parents with feedback about students' progress toward learning goals.* Use this information to establish a plan for home and school to work together.

Survey tests measure broad, long-term educational goals rather than immediate learning outcomes. It may take all year for a student to learn to read well enough, for example, to show some sign of improvement on a survey test. Meanwhile, however, the student may learn many specific skills and reading strategies. The student may perform well on your classroom assessments of these immediate learning objectives.

Norm-referenced survey information is not likely to give you the fine-grained details you need to design an individual student's daily or weekly instructional plans. Classroom assessment procedures provide information about a student's performance in more specific areas. They are likely to be more useful to you for daily or weekly instructional planning than are ordinary survey tests. The results of survey tests can be used, however, to help you plan for a year or a term.

Standardized tests are often administered in the fall, after you have organized the class, and the answer sheets are sent away for scoring. By the time you receive students' results, several weeks of schooling have already passed. Such circumstances work against the possibility of using standardized tests for immediate instructional decisions. This is not to say, however, that you should disregard the results. Results from tests administered last spring will help you plan your teaching this fall.

FIGURE 16.2   A systematic procedure for using the results of a standardized achievement test to plan instruction for a class.

Step 1. Review the class report to determine weaknesses

Use a report that summarizes performance on clusters of items for all students in your class. Within each curriculum area, identify on which clusters your students most need improvement. Match the clusters to your state's standards and determine the class's weakness and strengths with respect to the standards. Use your knowledge of the subject and of your students to verify the areas of greatest need. Don't be afraid to contradict the picture given by the test if you have good evidence that supports the fact that the students know more than they have shown on the test.

Step 2. Establish instructional priorities

Review your list of instructional needs. Put them into an order for instruction. Be sure to teach prerequisite needs first. Concentrate on the most important areas—those that will help students in their further understanding of concepts and principles in the subject.

Step 3. Organize the class for instruction

The test information may help you form small groups of students who have similar instructional needs. Alternately, you could form small groups that have students at different levels of learning so that those who already know the material can help instruct those who have not yet mastered it. You will need to use your own resources to organize your class, as the test cannot do that directly.

Step 4. Plan your instruction before you begin

Be clear about your instructional objectives. Look at the test items to get an idea of the types of tasks you want students to learn to do, but remember that you are trying to teach generalizable skills and abilities. The tasks on the test are only a small sample of the domain of tasks implied by the curriculum.

Look to the curriculum to see where the areas of need fit into the larger scheme. Teach within this larger framework, rather than narrowing your teaching to the test items. Create your own assessment instrument for each of the areas of need, so you can clarify what you will expect students to do at the end of the lessons. Organize your teaching activities to accomplish these ends.

Step 5. Assess students' progress toward your instructional objectives and state's standards

Monitor students' progress through both informal and formal assessments. Observe students as they complete the assignments you give them to see if they are making progress toward your learning objectives and state standards. Use performance and paper-and-pencil assessments to monitor their progress in more formal ways. Adjust your teaching for those students who are not making appropriate progress. Give feedback to students by showing them what they are expected to do (i.e., the learning objective or state standard), explaining to them what their performance is like now, how it is different from the target performance, and what they have yet to learn to accomplish the target performance.

Step 6. Carry out summative assessment

Use a variety of assessment techniques to assess each student so that you are certain that the student has learned the objective and can apply the concepts and principles to appropriate realistic situations. Use performance assessments, extended responses, and objective items in appropriate combinations. Do not limit your assessment to only one format.

Another use of standardized test results is to confirm or corroborate your judgment about a student's general educational development. It is important to realize that no single source of information about a student is entirely valid—be that source your own observations, results from assessments you developed, or results on standardized tests. Nevertheless, standardized tests can provide additional information that may alert you to the need to consider a particular student further.

Extraclassroom Uses

Standardized survey tests are also useful for extraclassroom purposes. Among these external uses of test results are the following:

1. *The average scores of a group (class, building, or school system) help school officials make decisions about needed curriculum or instructional changes.* The results provide one important piece of information if school officials judge the tests to be relevant and important to the goals of the local community.

2. *Test results also help school superintendents describe to parents, school boards, and other stakeholders the relative effectiveness of the local educational enterprise.* However, school board members should realize that no single instrument can account for all the factors that affect the learning of students in a particular community.

3. *Results help educational evaluators compare the relative effectiveness of alternate methods of instruction and describe some of the factors mitigating their effectiveness.*

4. *Results help educational researchers describe the relative effectiveness of innovations or experiments in education.*

INAPPROPRIATE USES OF STANDARDIZED TEST RESULTS

Criticisms of Standardized Tests

Criticisms of norm-referenced standardized achievement tests are quite common. Of course, any assessment procedure—standardized or not, norm-referenced or criterion-referenced, formative or summative, external or teacher-made, qualitative and quantitative—can be misused. Much of this misuse, moreover, comes not from something inherent in a particular standardized test, but from the invalid claims that persons make for some assessments or the unscrupulous way(s) in which an assessment might be used. Throughout this text, we discuss appropriate uses and emphasize the need to validate claims made for assessments. Use professional judgment in administering and interpreting all assessment procedures. The *Code of Professional Responsibilities in Educational Measurement* (Appendix C) and the *Code of Fair Testing Practices in Education (Revised)* (Appendix B) describe your responsibilities with regard to standardized achievement tests.

Criticisms of standardized tests may focus on some intrinsic characteristic of a test, such as its content coverage; something that is not part of a test, such as its failure to test certain student characteristics; or the misuse of test results, such as inappropriately using a test to classify or label a student. Some criticize several of these aspects of standardized testing. For example, they may say that tests (a) measure only a small portion of what is taught in the classroom (intrinsic characteristic), (b) do not measure the real goals of an educational program (characteristics not measured), and (c) foster undesirable changes in school curricula or teacher emphasis (misuse of test results).

Some criticisms are contradictory, and many of the criticisms can be overcome. The same test may be criticized by some persons because its focus is too narrow and by others because its scores are influenced by too broad a range of human characteristics. You may overcome many problems by either using the test in the way the publisher intended it to be used or by choosing another, more appropriate test.

Misuses of Standardized Tests

Always strive to use the results of achievement assessments—survey batteries, performance assessments, or authentic tasks—in valid, professional ways. Never use a single assessment result to make an important decision about a student. Inappropriate uses of a survey achievement battery or state-mandated assessment include the following.

1. *Placing a student in a special instructional program solely on results from a standardized achievement test.* Special programs include remedial programs as well as programs for students who are gifted and talented. School officials should use many pieces of information when making these decisions, including students' daily classroom performance, teachers' assessments, and results from other assessments in addition to the survey achievement battery.

2. *Retaining a student in a grade solely on the results from a standardized test.* First, the wisdom of retaining students is very much an open educational question, and the common practice of retention in the early grades often does not help students (Jimerson, 2001). Second, your daily observation, teaching, and evaluation of students are the most relevant types of information that a school official should use when making this decision. Third, parents have information about a child that school officials and teachers do not. Although standardized achievement test scores may have some bearing on this type of decision, their importance should have little weight in the final decision.

3. *Judging an entire school program's quality solely on the basis of the results from a standardized achievement test.* School programs are complex. They teach many things other than those assessed by standardized tests. You know, too, that even within a curriculum area assessed by a test, there is no perfect match between what is assessed and all the instructional objectives in the curriculum framework. School officials can overcome misuse by aggressively placing program evaluation decisions in a broader context of the full curriculum framework and the full context of school and community factors.

4. *Using a survey achievement battery to prescribe the specific content teachers should teach at certain grade levels.* A test only samples the many tasks that students could be asked to perform. Although test tasks are important, each task is not an end in itself. If the tasks are a representative sample from this larger domain, they allow you to generalize

beyond them to estimate a student's performance on the domain. If school officials manipulate the sample or try to limit the curriculum domain primarily to the sample appearing on a test, they destroy the ability to generalize. School officials may overcome this misuse by developing curriculum frameworks using appropriate principles drawn from educational development, child development, learning, and the subject-matter disciplines. They should then select the test that best matches the important curriculum learning objectives, rather than vice versa.

5. *Attributing a student's poor assessment results to only one cause.* Sometimes a teacher or school administrator interprets a student's assessment result as though it was entirely the result of the student's own shortcomings rather than the result of several interacting conditions. A student's poor assessment result may very well reflect the quality of previous teaching as well as the student's personal environment and experiences.

6. *School officials or parents trying to blame the teacher if the class does poorly on a standardized test.* Before a person can attribute the rise (or fall) of a class's test scores solely to a particular teacher, that person would have to consider how each of several factors influences the scores: Did the content of the test match the breadth and emphasis of what was taught in the classroom? Did the students in this year's class have, on the whole, better or worse general school aptitude than classes in the past (or classes assigned to other teachers)? Were students in this (or another) class taught the answers to the items or otherwise given an unfair advantage? Did last year's teacher do an exceptionally good (or poor) job of teaching, and did this influence carry over to this year? What home factors influenced the students' successes (or lack thereof)? Did the school principal (or other instructional leader) facilitate or inhibit the teacher's teaching or the students' learning? You can probably name other factors to consider when trying to find the reasons for a class's test results.

HOW TO ADMINISTER STANDARDIZED TESTS

You will most likely be required to administer one or more standardized assessments per year. These may be standardized achievement tests, performance assessments, or assessments mandated by your state department of education. Part of the validity of your students' results will depend on how well you follow the standardization procedure specified in the teacher's administration manual.

The Right Way to Prepare Yourself and Students for a Standardized Test

There are two important areas of assessment administration that you directly control and that directly affect the validity of your students' results. One area is how you prepare yourself and the students for the assessment. Standardized assessments, regardless of whether they are performance or multiple-choice formats, require students to be aware of (a) the fact that they will be assessed, (b) what they will be assessed on, (c) the reasons for the assessment, and (d) how their results will be used. Students should be prepared to do their best. You must also be prepared to administer, and perhaps to mark, the assessments. That means you must be familiar with the assessment procedures and materials, prepare the assessment environment so that a valid assessment can be done, understand how to administer the assessment—including what you are permitted to say to the students—and know how to prepare the students for the assessment.

The Right Way to Administer a Standardized Test

A second area in which you need to perform well is in actually administering the assessment. Valid assessment results will depend on how well you carry out your responsibilities during the administration phase. You need to follow the procedures stated in the manual exactly: Otherwise, the assessment results will not be comparable across students and using the norms will be invalid. Also, you need to monitor students to be sure they are following directions, marking their answers in the proper manner, and otherwise attending to the tasks. Figure 16.3 is a checklist of what you must do to administer a standardized assessment without lowering its validity.

ETHICAL AND UNETHICAL STUDENT PRACTICE FOR STANDARDIZED TESTS

The question of what type of practice to give students before they take a standardized assessment is an important one for you to answer. Educators

FIGURE 16.3 **Checklist for administering a standardized assessment procedure to your students.**

Before the assessment

____ Receive information from the building principal, district assessment director, or whomever is responsible for the testing program. Ask any questions you have.

____ Eliminate any schedule conflicts between the testing schedule and your other teaching responsibilities.

____ Communicate with students. Explain the time, date, and purpose of the test. Explain how they will receive their results and how results will be used.

____ Familiarize yourself with the assessment materials and procedures. Participate in any necessary training sessions. Maintain test security as directed.

____ Schedule computer access if necessary. Obtain pencils, scratch paper, calculators, and any other necessary materials. Move desks if necessary.

____ Make a "Test in progress—Please do not disturb" sign for your classroom door.

During the assessment

____ Administer the test according to the directions in the test manual and/or according to the directions given during training.

____ Observe students. Make sure they are working on the correct pages or screens and are recording their responses as directed.

____ Note any problems that occur for individual students or for the class.

After the assessment

____ Return test materials and response sheets to the designated person. Maintain test security as directed during this process.

____ Answer any general questions students may have, but do not supply answers to the test questions.

do not agree about what is appropriate (Koretz & Hamilton, 2006; Mehrens & Kaminski, 1989). The controversy concerns ethical test preparation practices. If you prepare students in inappropriate ways, then the validity of their assessment results is questionable.

A Clearly Unethical Teaching Practice

One of the guiding principles for ensuring validity is the **generalizability of assessment results**. (See Figure 3.2.) When you assess students, you want to generalize from their performance to the larger and broader domain of abilities and knowledge that the curriculum framework is supposed to foster. Responses on a particular test or assessment are only signs or pointers to the students' possible performance in the larger domain implied by the learning objectives of the curriculum framework. However, if you give specific practice only on the questions or tasks on the assessment, you focus students' learning only on these few tasks. It is very unlikely that such narrowly focused instruction and learning can generalize to the broader learning objectives that are the real goals of education.

For example, suppose there are 100 key concepts in a particular area of social studies. Further, suppose that instead of teaching students strategies for organizing and understanding these concepts and principles, you picked only the four concepts that will appear on a standardized social studies test and taught answers only to the questions about those four concepts. Assuming you are a good teacher, your students would do very well on the test questions related to these concepts, and their test scores would be higher. However, your students would most likely not understand or integrate the broader social studies framework and the full set of concepts the course was supposed to teach. In other words, by narrowing your teaching to only those few tasks that appear on a specific test, you have failed to provide your students with empowering strategies to organize social studies concepts and principles. Further, you cannot interpret their test results as reflecting their general knowledge of the course concepts and principles. By teaching only those four concepts, you invalidated the students' test results and corrupted the students' education.

The Range of Ethical to Unethical Practices

You can provide a variety of practice activities to help students improve their performance on an assessment. Which of these is appropriate? The following list of assessment preparation activities is arranged in order from the most to the least legitimate (Haladyna, Nolen, & Haas, 1991; Mehrens & Kaminski, 1989):

1. Teaching the learning objectives in the curriculum without narrowing your teaching to those objectives that appear on a standardized assessment.

2. Teaching general test-taking strategies, such as those discussed in Chapter 14, and integrating a variety of test-taking formats into teaching, so students learn how to respond to them.

3. Teaching only those learning objectives that specifically match the objectives that will appear on the standardized assessment your students will take.

4. Teaching only those learning objectives that specifically match the objectives that will appear on the standardized assessment your students will take and giving practice on those objectives using only the same types of task formats that will appear on the assessment.

5. Giving your students practice on a published parallel form of the assessment they will take.

6. Giving your students practice on the same questions and tasks that they will take later.

Most educators would agree that the first activity is always ethical because it is the teacher's job to teach the official curriculum. Most educators would also agree that the second activity, teaching students how to take tests and do their best on them, is not unethical. The fifth and sixth activities would always be considered unethical because they narrow instruction to only the specific assessment tasks that your students will be administered and practically eliminate your ability to generalize from the assessment results to the performance domain specified by the curriculum.

Thus, the boundary between ethical and unethical test preparation practices falls somewhere between Activities 3 and 5. The deciding factor lies in the degree to which a school wishes to generalize the test results. The closer the activity is to the fifth one, the less able are school officials to generalize students' assessment results to the official curriculum—unless, of course, the official curriculum is identical to the assessment instrument.

Koretz and Hamilton (2006) summarize a somewhat broader set of test preparation steps that have been documented as responses to recent high-stakes testing: teaching more, working harder, working more effectively, reallocation, alignment, coaching, and cheating. Their criterion for positive or desirable preparation is the generalizability of test results, and thus test preparation is desirable if it produces "unambiguously meaningful increases in scores" (p. 548).

Teaching more, working harder, and working more effectively all therefore constitute positive test preparation, because increases in scores would mean increases in learning in the whole domain (reading, mathematics, etc.). Reallocation of instructional time and resources, coaching, and other practices, sometimes done in the name of "alignment," that narrow the domain to only what is covered by the sample of test items are negative consequences of high-stakes testing, because increases in scores would mean increases only in the sampled part of the domain. And Koretz and Hamilton's last category, cheating, never produces a valid increase in scores.

MyLab Education Self-Check 16.2

MyLab Education Application Exercise 16.2:
Differences Between Standardized and Classroom Tests

CONCLUSION

This chapter has explored the meaning of the term *standardized test*. What are standardized are the conditions of administration, procedures, and scoring so that possible scores are comparable across time and place. The chapter discussed the most common kinds of standardized achievement tests, along with their purposes and uses, and described how to follow directions for test administration. Finally, the chapter discussed ways to prepare students for standardized tests. The next chapter turns to interpreting the various kinds of norm-referenced scores that are provided in standardized test results.

EXERCISES

1. Using test publishers' catalogs, the *Mental Measurements Yearbooks*, and other resources, identify one published test that fits into each category of the authors' scheme for classifying published achievement tests. Share your findings with your classmates.

2. Describe the students, their community, and subject(s) that you teach (or plan to teach). Through self-reflection, give specific examples of how you may misuse achievement test results in this context in each of the following ways. Share your findings with the others in your course.
   a. Failing to consider measurement error when interpreting a student's scores.
   b. Using only the test results for making a decision about a student.
   c. Uncritically interpreting a student's score as measuring a pure trait.
   d. Failing to consider the complex nature of the causes for a particular student's test performance.

3. Evaluate the appropriateness of each of the following standardized test preparation practices.
   a. The school uses the latest version of a certain test. A teacher uses a version of the test that is no longer being administered in the school to give students special practice.
   b. A teacher copies items from a test that is currently being used in the school and gives these to students for practice.
   c. A teacher teaches students general rules and strategies for taking standardized tests, such as how to eliminate options and "guess" when they are not certain, and how to plan their testing time wisely.
   d. The curriculum framework calls for learning the grammar rules covered by the test the school uses. The teacher teaches the students how to use these rules to answer the same format of questions that will appear on the test, but does not provide practice in more natural contexts of writing sentences and paragraphs.
   e. The curriculum framework calls for learning the grammar rules covered by the test the school uses. The teacher teaches the students how to use these rules to answer the same format of question that will appear on the test, but

also teaches them how to apply the rules in their own writing of sentences and paragraphs.
   f. A deaf student who is mainstreamed in an inclusive program plans to go to a special post-secondary school for deaf students. For admission, the postsecondary school requires the student to submit results from standardized reading and mathematics tests. The teacher gives the upcoming tests to the student to take home to read a few days ahead of time, then answers any clarifying questions the student has about the vocabulary and the type of strategies that should be used when answering the questions. Later in the week, the teacher administers the tests to the student under standardized conditions but with the help of a sign language interpreter.

4. Using the Internet, locate three states' education departments and descriptions of their state assessment program. (A comprehensive list of state education department contact information is found on the U.S. Department of Education's Website: ed.gov.) If your state has an assessment program, be sure to include it as one of the three. Compare the assessment programs in terms of student versus school accountability; objective versus constructed-response assessment; use of standards, teacher development, and capacity building; and general objectives and purposes. Share your findings with others in this course.

5. Figure 16.4 lists various types of tests across the top and various characteristics as row headings. For each characteristic, describe the extent to which it is found in each type of test. In the cells in the body of the table, mark:
   a. ++ if most tests in that category exhibit this characteristic.
   b. + if a few tests in that category exhibit this characteristic.
   c. 0 if it is very rare that tests in that category exhibit this characteristic.

FIGURE 16.4 Comparisons of the characteristics of various kinds of published tests with teacher-made tests.

Characteristic		Survey batteries	Criterion-referenced tests	Other single-area tests	State-mandated accountability test	Single-course tests	Interim assessments	Criterion-referenced tests
Content/ objectives covered	1. Common to many schools 2. Specific to one teacher/school 3. Specific to one text or set of materials							
Intended to measure	1. Growth over time 2. Status on each specific objective in domain 3. Profile of strengths and weaknesses							
Norm referencing provided	1. Several types of scores 2. Several types of norm groups 3. Spans several grades							
Criterion-referencing provided	1. Many items per objective 2. Diagnosis possible							
Provides materials for interpreting scores to	1. Students 2. Parents 3. Teachers 4. Administrators							
Technical quality	1. Professionally written items 2. Empirical data on reliability and validity							

Interpreting Norm-Referenced Scores

KEY CONCEPTS

1. A referencing framework is a structure used to compare a student's performance to something external to the assessment in order to interpret performance. A norm-referencing framework interprets a student's assessment performance by comparing it to the performance of a well-defined group of other students who have taken the same assessment. A criterion-referencing framework interprets a student's performance according to the kinds of performances a student can do in a domain. A standards-referenced framework combines elements of both. Test publishers may provide norm-referenced scores based on information from several different norm groups. Use normative information to describe student strengths, weaknesses, and progress.

2. Different types of norm-referenced scores are constructed to serve different purposes. The percentile rank tells the percentage of the students in a norm group who have scored *lower* than the raw score in question. A linear standard score tells how far a raw score is from the mean of the norm group, expressing the distance in standard deviation units.

3. A normal distribution is a mathematical model (an equation) based on the mean and standard deviation of a set of scores. Normalized standard scores are based on transforming raw scores on an assessment to make them fit a normal distribution. Developmental and educational growth scales are norm-referenced scores that can be used to

chart educational development or progress. An extended normalized standard score tells the location of a raw score on a scale that is anchored to a lower grade reference group. A grade-equivalent score tells the grade level at which a raw score is average.

IMPORTANT TERMS

area under the normal curve

criterion-referencing

derived scores

empirical norming dates

extended normalized standard score

grade-equivalent scores (*GE*)

grade mean equivalent

growth modeling

interpolation versus extrapolation

IRT pattern score

item response theory (IRT)

linear standard scores (*z, SS*)

modal-age norms

normal curve equivalent (*NCE*)

normal distributions

normal growth (grade-equivalent view, percentile rank view)

normalized standard scores (z_n, *T, DIQ, NCE, SAT*)

normalizing a set of scores

norm groups (local, national, special)

norm-referencing

percentile ranks (local and national)

raw score

relevance, representativeness, and recency of norm data

SAT-score

school averages norms

standards-referencing framework

stanine scores (national stanine)

student growth percentiles

value-added modeling

THREE REFERENCING FRAMEWORKS

Suppose that you took a spelling test and your score was 45, found by giving one point for each correctly spelled word. How well have you performed? Knowing only that your task was "a spelling test" and that your score was 45 leaves you unable to interpret your performance.

Raw scores are the number of points (marks) you assign to a student's performance on an assessment. You may obtain these marks by adding the number of correct answers, the ratings for each task, or the number of points awarded to separate parts of the assessment. As in the preceding spelling score example, a raw score tells a student what he or she "got," but says very little about the *meaning of the score*.

Practically all educational and psychological assessments require you to use some type of referencing framework to interpret students' performance. A *referencing framework* is a structure you use to compare a student's performance to something external to the assessment itself. In Chapter 15, we discussed referencing frameworks in the context of grading.

Norm-Referencing Framework

Norm-Referencing   A **norm-referencing framework** interprets a student's assessment performance by comparing it to the performance of a well-defined group of other students who have taken the same assessment. The well-defined group of other students is called the **norm group**. To make valid norm-referenced interpretations, all persons in the norm group must have been given the same assessment as your students under the same conditions (same time limits, directions, equipment and materials, etc.). This is why you must follow administration instructions exactly when administering a standardized achievement test whose results you later will want to interpret through a norm-referenced framework.

To understand a norm-referenced interpretation, let's return to your score on the spelling test.

Suppose your raw score of 45 means that your percentile rank (*PR*) is 99—that is, 99% of the persons who took the spelling test have scored lower than 45. Before you congratulate yourself, however, you should determine who is in the norm group to which your raw score is being referenced. You would interpret your performance differently if you knew the norm group was composed of third graders than if the norm group comprised adults.

Validity of Norm-Referenced Interpretations   Your norm-referenced interpretations are less valid when the norm group is not well defined. The more you know about who is in the norm group, the better you can interpret a student's performance in a norm-referenced framework. Consider the difference in interpreting your performance on the spelling test, for example, when the norm group is adults in general versus a norm group composed of adults who have won prizes in national spelling contests.

Norm-Referenced Scores   **Derived scores** make norm-referenced interpretations easier. A more or less standard set of derived scores is now routinely reported for most published tests in education:

1. *Percentile ranks* tell the percentage of persons in a norm group scoring lower than a particular raw score.
2. *Linear standard scores* tell the location of a particular raw score in relation to the mean and standard deviation of a norm group.
3. *Normalized standard scores* tell the location of a particular raw score in relation to a normal distribution fitted to a norm group.
4. *Grade-equivalent scores* tell the grade placement for which a particular raw score is the average for a norm group.

Criterion-Referencing Framework

Beyond Norm-Referencing   Norm-referencing is not enough to interpret your score fully: You may be a better speller than other people—whoever they happen to be—but what can you spell? At a minimum, you would need to know the kinds of words in the pool from which those on the spelling test were selected, the number of words selected, and the process used to select the words. Were they really words, or were they nonsense syllables? Were they English words? Were they selected from a list of the most difficult (or easiest) English words? Did the test have 45 words or 500 words? Did the words on the test represent some larger class or domain? Did spelling the words require you to use certain mental processes or to apply certain spelling rules?

These questions are especially important when you need to make absolute interpretations of students' assessment performance—for example, when you need to know which specific learning objective your students are having trouble mastering. Norm-referencing provides information to help in your relative interpretations of scores, but frequently these are not enough. Scores that reflect relative achievement such as rank order, for example, may be helpful in picking the best readers, or in sectioning a class into better, good, and poor readers. However, to plan appropriate instruction, eventually you need to know each student's specific reading skills and the particular types of difficulties each student is experiencing. When your diagnosis and prescription are based on students' error patterns or on your analysis of their faulty reasoning or thinking processes, as described in Chapter 7, you must put aside the norm-referencing framework and use a criterion-referencing framework.

Criterion-Referencing You use a **criterion-referencing framework** to infer the kinds of performances a student can do in a domain, rather than the student's relative standing in a norm group. This domain of performance to which you reference a student's assessment results is called the *criterion*. When you teach, the criterion that is of most interest is the domain of performance implied by your state's standards, your curriculum framework, and your lessons' learning objectives.

Validity of Criterion-Referenced Interpretations Your criterion-referenced assessment interpretations lose validity when the domain of performances to which you wish to infer your students' status is poorly defined or when your assessment is a poor sample from that domain. The more you know about the domain from which the tasks on your assessment were sampled, the more validly you can interpret their results. For example, if you did not construct your assessment using clearly defined statements of learning objectives, or if your assessment inadequately represents the wide range of performance implied by a clearly defined set of learning objectives, then you have only a weak basis for making criterion-referenced interpretations.

You can easily see why by reviewing the spelling example again. Suppose you knew that the spelling domain was the 10,000 most frequently misspelled English words and that the assessment had been constructed as a sample of 100 words representative of the spelling patterns in this domain. In this case, you may interpret your score of 45 on a 100-word assessment as an estimate of the proportion of those 10,000 words you know how to spell. You can see that if there were only 50 words on the assessment, your estimate would be less accurate than when there are 100. A sample of 10 words is even less accurate. Further, if the 100 words did not sample the domain representatively, your estimate also would be less accurate, even though there were 100 words. For example, the 100 words may contain only regular spelling patterns and ignore others. Thus, both the number of items on the assessment and how well they represent the domain contribute to how valid your criterion-referenced interpretation is.

Criterion-Referenced Scores Criterion-referenced assessments do not have well-developed, derived score systems like norm-referenced assessments. Nevertheless, certain types of scores are often used with these assessments:

1. *Percentage*—a number telling the proportion of the maximum points earned by the student (percentage correct, percentage of objectives mastered, etc.).

2. *Speed of performance*—the time a student takes to complete a task, or the number of tasks completed in a fixed amount of time (keyboarding 40 words per minute, running a mile in 5 minutes, completing 25 number facts correctly in 1 minute, etc.).

3. *Quality ratings*—the quality level at which a student performs ("Excellent," rating of "5," "mastery," etc.).

4. *Precision of performance*—the degree of accuracy with which a student completes a task (measuring accurately to the nearest 10th of a meter, weighing accurately to the nearest gram, fewer than 10 typing errors, etc.).

Standards-Referencing Framework

Standards-Referencing   The NCLB Act of 2001 required states to report the percentage of students who have achieved at three levels—basic, proficient, and advanced—in meeting a state's Reading, Language Arts, Mathematics, and Science standards. The Every Student Succeeds Act of 2015 continues to require this type of accountability reporting. Students' scores on a test must be referenced to the standards-defined achievement levels. The immediate testing question that a state faces is deciding what range of test scores is to be called "basic," what range is "proficient," and what range is "advanced." Once these ranges of scores are defined, students' scores are referenced to those ranges and interpreted to mean basic, proficient, or advanced achievement in a subject. This is called a **standards-referencing framework** (Young & Zucker, 2004).

Combining Frameworks   The standards-referencing framework is accomplished by combining aspects of the criterion-referencing and the norm-referencing frameworks. On the criterion-referencing side, test items are selected to match or align with the state's standards. On the norm-referencing side, the state administers the test to the students and gathers information about the performance of students on each test item. A common procedure is then to order the items from easiest to most difficult. Panels of experts (including teachers) use this ordered list of test items, along with their knowledge of the subject area and students, to set the score that forms the boundary between each achievement level. If a student's score falls between the lower and upper boundaries of a category, the proficiency category, for example, then the student is classified into that category (e.g., proficient).

Reporting Methods   States use the standards-referencing framework for accountability purposes under ESSA. States report the status of English Language Arts (and/or Reading), Mathematics, and Science proficiency by school, based

on state test results. These reports are usually called School Profiles. The report about proficiency can take the form of an indicator of whether an adequate yearly progress target was met (Yes/No), the percentage of students scoring Proficient or above, or the percentage of students in each category (e.g., Advanced, Proficient, Needs Improvement, or whatever scale the state uses).

Many educators and the public have begun to believe that students' annual achievement status was the wrong thing for which to hold schools accountable. It seemed that, instead, schools should be held accountable for the growth or improvement students made during the year (Bushaw & Gallup, 2008). In addition, there are some statistical problems associated with using changes in percentages in standards-referenced categories from year to year as an indicator of improvement (Ho, 2008). Where a cut score for a proficiency category is located in the distribution of test scores makes a big difference in the percentage of students in the category. In 2005, the federal government launched a pilot program for states to propose using growth models and to evaluate their usefulness. Plans from the states, including descriptions of the different growth models they used, are available at ed.gov.

Reporting Growth   Several methods are used to report student growth instead of status on state achievement tests. A discussion of the statistical modeling behind these methods is beyond the scope of this text. Here we describe the methods conceptually. All of these methods have become possible only with the advent of statewide longitudinal databases, sometimes called data warehouses, to store student information.

Growth modeling is a general term for statistical models that investigate change over time. The simplest kind of growth model asks how far students have come from the beginning to the end of the year on a vertical scale (see Developmental and Educational Growth Scales, below). The simplest growth models simply report whether there was change over time and say nothing about how or why change occurred.

Value-added modeling is a special case of growth modeling, where the statistical model includes parameters (statistical estimates) for the effects of various factors expected to be related to student growth in achievement. The model can simply compare growth in a school with overall state growth, or it can include terms for various effects. Effects modeled statistically can include a variety of school and demographic variables as well as teacher effects. In many varieties of value-added modeling, effects of individual teachers (and sometimes schools) are calculated, based on the growth of their students after controlling for demographic and other effects. One of the first value-added models in use in a state was the Tennessee Value-Added Assessment System (TVAAS; Sanders & Horn, 1994).

As initiatives press to include teacher effects as part of teacher evaluation data, it is important to remember that there are many unresolved issues (Schafer, Lissitz, Zhu, Zhang, Hou, & Li, 2012). One of these issues is which variables are included in the value-added model. For example, including ethnicity might make a statistical model more precise, but at the price of statistically holding some ethnic groups to more stringent growth standards than others. Another issue is the weak evidence for stability of value-added estimates (and other reliability and validity evidence). Other issues include the reliance on vertical (across grades) scales, the selection of cut points for proficiency categories, and the distribution of scores. Different statistical models and different distributional properties of scores lead to different results regarding teacher effectiveness (Briggs & Domingue, 2011).

Student growth percentiles (not to be confused with student growth modeling, which usually means the kind of growth modeling we described above) describe the probability of a student attaining a certain level of growth, given their prior achievement (Betebenner, 2009). So, for example, what is the likelihood of a student who is on the border between not proficient and nearing proficient in grade 3 to become proficient by grade 10 in mathematics? Student growth percentiles estimate this kind of information, and it remains to the users of the information to decide on an acceptable level of likelihood. Betebenner (2009) provides an explanation using the analogy of the height and weight charts pediatricians use for infants and toddlers. Parents are interested not only in the amount of growth their children demonstrate but also how that growth compares with other children. For example, what is the likelihood that children at the 25th percentile in height, like my child, will be of average height by a certain age? Despite the complexities of this

approach, it shows promise, especially by mixing norm-referenced information (the percentiles) with criterion-referenced information (the proficiency categories). Some states (e.g., Colorado) use student growth percentiles as part of their state accountability system.

USING NORMS
Importance of Norms
Norm-referencing indicates how one student's performance compares to the performances of others. However, simply comparing students with one another is not a very good reason for assessing them (Hoover et al., 1993b). Here are the major reasons for assessing students:

1. To describe, within each subject area, the performances a student has achieved.
2. To describe, within each subject area, student deficiencies that need further improvement.
3. To describe, across the curriculum, which subjects are the student's strengths and weaknesses.
4. To describe, within each subject area, the amount of educational development (progress) a student has made over the course of one or more years.

The first two purposes are best served within a criterion-referencing framework. In essence, this requires you to look carefully at a student's performance, item by item, and compare it to your learning objectives.

The second two purposes are best served within a norm-referencing framework. A student's relative strength in reading and mathematics, for example, cannot be described on purely a criterion-referenced basis. You can describe what a student can do in each area, but you need a norm basis to conclude whether these are relative strengths or weaknesses. A teacher may say, for example, that a student is able to solve routine linear and quadratic equations in mathematics and is able to read with comprehension age-appropriate texts. However, which is the stronger area? Normative information can determine this.

Standardized tests describe students' relative strengths and weaknesses in different curricular areas because of the normative information they provide. The same group of students at the same grade level (the norm group) is administered tests covering several curricular areas. Thus, if fourth-grader Blake ranks at the top of the norm group in mathematics but in the middle of the norm group in reading, we know that of the two subjects, Blake is stronger in mathematics.

The fourth purpose mentioned earlier—measuring educational growth and development—also requires norm-referencing. Norm groups provide the basis for defining an educational development scale (such as the grade-equivalent scale) across different grade levels. We assess a student once every year or two, each time referencing the results to this developmental scale. We measure growth by the student's progress along this scale.

The remainder of this chapter discusses the various norm-referenced scores and scales used in educational assessment. As a teacher, you will not be required to create growth scales or calculate scale scores. However, you will be required to interpret and to use such scales and scores with your students. In addition, you will be expected to explain the meaning of reports of these scores to your students and their parents.

TYPES OF NORM GROUPS

Before you can understand and use norm-referenced scores you need to understand the meaning of norms and norm groups. As we've already stated, a norm group is the large representative sample of students for which test manuals report performance. The performance of a norm group on a particular assessment represents the present, average status of that group of students on that particular assessment. A group's current average does not represent a standard, however, nor does it establish what your school or your students should attain. Your state's content and performance standards and your curriculum's learning objectives tell you what students should achieve. Comparing your students and school to norm groups can help, however, decide the general range of performance to expect from your students, provided your students are similar to those in the norm group. As you will see, test publishers may provide information on several different groups when reporting norm-referenced scores.

Multiple Norm-Group Comparisons

Ordinarily, a student is a member of more than one group. For example, a 14-year-old, eighth-grade boy with a hearing impairment took a standardized mathematics concepts test and obtained a raw score of 32, which may represent a percentile rank of:

- 99 in a national group of hearing-impaired eighth graders.
- 94 in the test publisher's national eighth-grade standardization sample.
- 89 in the group of eighth graders in his local community.
- 80 in the group of eighth graders currently enrolled with him in an advanced mathematics course.

Depending on the decisions you must make, referencing a student's score to more than one norm group may be in order. Vocational counseling decisions, for example, may require that you compare a student's profile of abilities and achievements to each of several occupational or vocational groups about which the student is seeking career information. Comparing the person only to "students in general" may offer less information for career exploration.

Local Norms

For many of your norm-referenced interpretations, the most appropriate group with which you should compare a student is the **local norm group**: the group of students in the same grade in the same school district. It is this group with which you and the students will interact the most. Local percentile ranks or standard scores are easy to compile for a school's testing program, and your director of testing should provide them to you every time a standardized test is administered. Publishers also offer this service for their customers—frequently at extra cost, however.

National Norms

Most norm-referenced, standardized achievement and aptitude batteries have what are called **national norms**. In principle, the national norm groups are supposed to be representative of the students in the country, and some publishers expend a great deal of effort to ensure representativeness. But each publisher uses a somewhat different definition of what constitutes a truly representative national sample and conducts the sampling processes differently. The result is that the norms from different publishers are not comparable. You should note, however, that no publisher's norming sample exactly mirrors the nation's schools. A school's participation in a publisher's norming sample is voluntary. Sometimes this creates a self-selection bias in a given publisher's norms that may distort the norms in favor of schools that have used that publisher's tests in the past. A more detailed description of how publishers obtain norming samples is given in Chapter 18.

National norms need not be composed simply of students in general at a grade level. A publisher may provide separate male/female norms or may provide separate norms for students with certain disabilities. Sometimes modal-age norms are provided. **Modal-age norms** include, from among all students at a particular grade level, only those near the most typical chronological age for that grade.

Special Norm Groups

For some tests, **special norm groups** are formed. Examples include students with deafness or blindness, students with developmental disabilities, students enrolled in a certain course of study or curriculum, and students attending regional schools. A student may belong to more than one special group, of course.

School Averages Norms

School averages norms consist of a tabulation of the average (mean) score from each school building in a national sample of schools and provide information on the relative ordering of these averages (means). This distribution of averages is much less variable than the distribution of individual student scores. Figure 17.1 illustrates this difference in variability for one publisher's reading test.

If your school principal wants to know how the school's third-grade average score compares with that of other school buildings, then the principal needs to use school averages norms. For individual students' norms, a distribution of individual scores is made and used as the basis

FIGURE 17.1 Comparison of the distributions of students' scores and school averages for the Reading Comprehension subtest of the *Iowa Tests of Basic Skills*, Grade 5, spring norms.

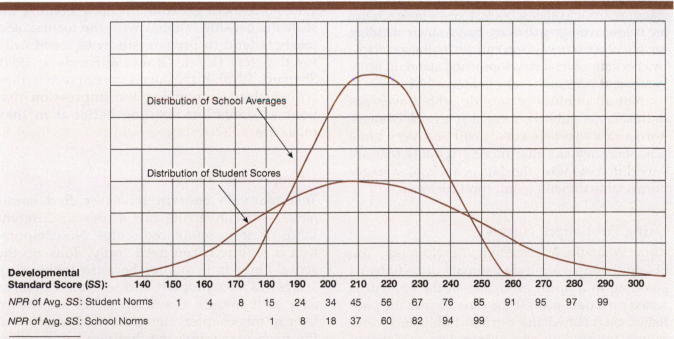

Developmental Standard Score (SS):	140	150	160	170	180	190	200	210	220	230	240	250	260	270	280	290	300
NPR of Avg. *SS*: Student Norms		1	4	8	15	24	34	45	56	67	76	85	91	95	97	99	
NPR of Avg. *SS*: School Norms					1	8	18	37	60	82	94	99					

Note: *NPR* = national percentile rank

for norm-referencing. But individual student scores vary widely, so much so that comparing a school's average to that group may lead to misinterpretations.

The following example should give you an idea of what your school district may gain from using school averages norms:

Example

Example of how using the wrong norms may lead to underestimating how well a school is doing

In Lincoln School, the average spring fifth-grade developmental standard score on the *Iowa Tests of Basic Skills* (Reading Comprehension subtest) is 250 (see Figure 17.1). The principal looked up this number in the individual student norms table and erroneously concluded that the school ranks higher than 85% (*PR* = 85 for individuals) of the schools. (In Figure 17.1, look at the row labeled "*NPR* of Avg. *SS*: Student Norms.") Actually, the school is much better, ranking at the top 1% (*PR* = 99 for school averages, "*NPR* of Avg. *SS*: School Norms").

In general, if someone uses individual score norms erroneously and the school is above average, the results will underestimate that school's standing among other schools; those whose schools are below average will overestimate their standing among other schools. You can verify this principle by checking several developmental standard score values and percentile ranks in Figure 17.1.

Not all publishers provide school averages norms. Some publishers say that school averages norms mix together very small and very large schools. They say that mixing schools that are very different makes the data in a school averages norms table difficult to interpret correctly.

Using Publishers' Norms

Know When the Assessment Was Normed
You obtain the most accurate estimate of a student's standing in a norm group when the student is tested on a date nearest the time of year the publisher established the norms. Publishers commonly interpolate and extrapolate to develop norm tables: They may provide spring norm tables, for example, even though no tests were actually administered to the norm group in the spring. Each publisher's empirical norming dates are different, but the publisher should state the dates in the test manual or technical report. To be

accurate, your school should administer a standardized test within 2 or 3 weeks before or after the midpoint date of the publisher's empirical norming period.

Criteria for Evaluating Norms
It is generally accepted (AERA et al., 2014) that published norms data should satisfy three Rs: relevance, representativeness, and recency. **Relevance** means that the norm group(s) a publisher provides should be the group(s) to which you will want to compare your students. **Representativeness** means that the norm sample must be based on a carefully planned sample. The test publisher should provide you with information about the subclassifications (gender, age, socioeconomic level, etc.) used to ensure representativeness. Remember that the sample size is not as crucial as its representativeness. Of course, if the population of students is very large, a representative sample should necessarily be large.

Recency means that the norms are based on current data. As the curriculum, schooling, and social and economic factors change, so too will students' performance on tests. Further, if your school uses the same form of a test year after year, scores will generally increase because the students become familiar with the format, and teachers tend to prepare students specifically for that test (Linn, Graue, & Sanders, 1990; Shepard, 1990). If the norms are not recent, they will mislead, conveying the impression that your students are learning better than they really are.

Using Norms Tables

Test manuals contain tables—called *norms tables*—for converting raw scores to different kinds of norm-referenced scores. No computation is required: You need "only" look up the score. Only is in quotes because looking up scores in a table properly and accurately is not as easy as it sounds. Specimen tables are shown later in this chapter, along with a discussion of the particular scores, so that you can practice using the tables.

MyLab Education   **Self-Check 17.1**

MyLab Education   **Application Exercise 17.1:**
Choosing Between Norm- and Criterion-Referenced Tests

FIGURE 17.2 Organization of major score-referencing schemes.

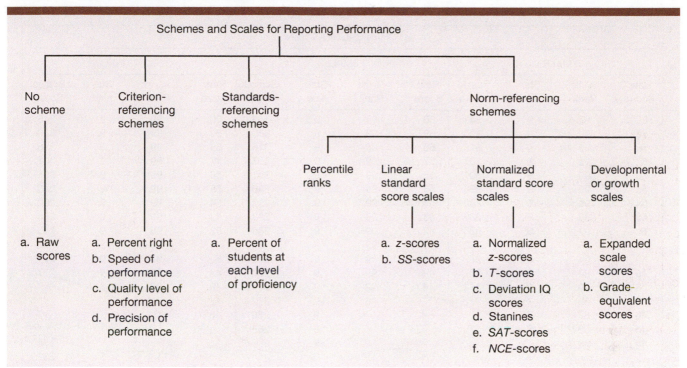

NORM-REFERENCED SCORES

Norm-referenced scores are derived from the raw scores of an assessment. You should be aware that many types of norm-referenced scores exist. Space permits discussion of only the ones you will most often encounter, which are represented in the concept map shown in Figure 17.2.

Norm-referenced tests use, on average, more difficult items than classroom tests. Contrast this fact with items used in testing when the purpose is to describe students along a standards-based continuum of achievement (e.g., Basic, Proficient, Advanced; or A, B, C). For such criterion-referenced testing, items should cover the range of difficulty levels to be described.

PERCENTILE RANKS

We begin at the leftmost branch of norm-referencing schemes in Figure 17.2. The **percentile rank** tells the percentage of the students in a norm group that have scored *lower* than the raw score in question. The percentile rank is perhaps the most useful and easily understood norm-referenced score. Figure 17.3 is an example of a publisher's norms table that gives percentile ranks for each raw score.

To read the norms table, locate the raw score obtained from the assessment in its correct column in the body of the table, and read out the

corresponding percentile rank. For example, suppose a seventh grader named Veronica takes the *Differential Aptitude Tests* (*DAT*) on October 23, and she scores 48 in Mechanical Reasoning. Her percentile rank from the norms table in the last example is 98. She is above average in the norm group of seventh-grade females in mathematics; her raw score exceeds 98 percent of the females in the standardization group.

Notice there are three sets of percentile ranks in the example table—one for the seventh-grade boys, one for the seventh-grade girls, and one for the combined group. This is common practice for norm-referenced assessments in which there are large differences between males and females.

A raw score of 48 has a percentile rank of 90 for boys. This lower percentile rank for boys for the same raw score reflects that seventh-grade boys do much better as a group on this Mechanical Reasoning test. As a result, 48 does not rank as high for boys as it does for girls. When the boys and girls are combined, the resulting distribution is shown in the Combined column of the table in the last example.

Which gender norms should teachers and counselors use? The answer depends on how they will use the test scores. Be sure to use the norms table that corresponds to the time of year during which the student takes the assessment. In our example, a raw score of 48 in the fall of the

FIGURE 17.3   Example of a percentile norms table: *Differential Aptitude Tests, Level 1, Form C.*

| MECHANICAL REASONING | | | | | | | | | | | |
| MALE | | | | FEMALE | | | | COMBINED | | | |
Raw Score	%-ile Rank	Sta-nine	Scaled Score	Raw Score	%-ile Rank	Sta-nine	Scaled Score	Raw Score	%-ile Rank	Sta-nine	Scaled Score
60	99	9	343	60	99	9	343	60	99	9	343
59	99	9	330	59	99	9	330	59	99	9	330
58	99	9	316	58	99	9	316	58	99	9	316
57	99	9	307	57	99	9	307	57	99	9	307
56	99	9	301	56	99	9	301	56	99	9	301
55	99	9	296	55	99	9	296	55	99	9	296
54	99	9	292	54	99	9	292	54	99	9	292
53	98	9	288	53	99	9	288	53	99	9	288
52	97	9	285	52	99	9	285	52	99	9	285
51	95	8	282	51	99	9	282	51	98	9	282
50	94	8	279	50	99	9	279	50	97	9	279
49	92	8	277	49	99	9	277	49	97	9	277
48	90	8	274	48	98	9	274	48	95	8	
47	88	7	272		98	9	272				
46	85	7				9	270	46			
45	82	7				9	268				
44	79					9	266				234
				23	15				14	3	232
				22	14				13	3	231
				21	13	2		21	10	2	229
			227	20	12	2		20	8	2	227
19	6	2	226	19	10	2	226	19	7	2	226
18	5	2	224	18	9	2	224	18	5	2	224
17	4	2	222	17	7	2	222	17	4	2	222
16	3	1	220	16	6	2	220	16	3	1	220
15	2	1	218	15	4	1	218	15	3	1	218
14	2	1	216	14	3	1	216	14	2	1	216
13	1	1	214	13	2	1	214	13	2	1	214
12	1	1	212	12	2	1	212	12	1	1	212
11	1	1	209	11	1	1	209	11	1	1	209
10	1	1	207	10	1	1	207	10	1	1	207
9	1	1	204	9	1	1	204	9	1	1	204
8	1	1	201	8	1	1	201	8	1	1	201
7	1	1	198	7	1	1	198	7	1	1	198
6	1	1	194	6	1	1	194	6	1	1	194
5	1	1	190	5	1	1	190	5	1	1	190
4	1	1	185	4	1	1	185	4	1	1	185
3	1	1	178	3	1	1	178	3	1	1	178
2	1	1	169	2	1	1	169	2	1	1	169
1	1	1	155	1	1	1	155	1	1	1	155

year corresponds to a percentile rank of 95 (combined). If you looked up a raw score of 48 in the spring norms table, it would have a slightly lower percentile rank. This lower percentile rank reflects that students learn or improve during the year.

As with all scores, you should not interpret percentile ranks too precisely. For example, a student with a percentile rank of 44 and a student with a percentile rank of 46 differ little. Therefore, for many educational decisions you should interpret these scores as essentially equivalent. Some publishers, to reflect that all scores contain measurement error, report percentile bands or uncertainty intervals instead of a single percentile rank. These percentile bands are based on the assessment's standard error of measurement (see Chapter 4).

Percentile ranks have some advantages. Percentile ranks:

- Are easily understood by pupils, parents, teachers, and others.
- Clearly reflect the norm-referenced character of the interpretation.
- Permit a person's performance to be compared to a variety of norm groups.
- Can be used to compare a student's relative standing in each of several achievement or ability areas.

They also have some limitations. Percentile ranks:

- Can be confused with percentage correct scores.
- Can be confused with some other types of two-digit derived scores.
- Do not form an equal-interval scale. Differences between PRs in the middle of the scale tend to be overinterpreted. Differences of the same magnitude near the tails of a distribution tend to be underinterpreted.

Because percentile ranks are easy to understand, your school district will most likely report them. Percentile ranks are also easy to calculate. Figure F.8 in Appendix F shows the procedure. The same procedure can be used for results from your classroom or for your entire district.

Remember that percentile ranks are specific to the group being referenced. After your students take a standardized test, the publisher will probably report both the **local percentile ranks** and the **national percentile ranks**. Your student Robert, for example, may have a national percentile rank of 40 and a local percentile rank of 30. Local percentile ranks are lower than national percentile ranks only when the population of students in a local school system scores higher, on the average, than the national standardization sample. Keep the reference group in mind when you interpret percentile ranks.

LINEAR STANDARD SCORES

The second branch of the norm-referencing schemes diagram in Figure 17.2 shows two types of linear standard scores. Both are discussed in this section. A **linear standard score** tells how far a raw score is from the mean of the norm group, the distance being expressed using standard deviation units. The standard deviation is an index that measures the spread of scores in a distribution. The standard deviation is denoted *SD* in this book and is explained in Appendix F.

In general, linear standard scores have the same-shaped distribution as the raw scores from which they are derived (this is not true of percentile ranks and nonlinear standard scores) and can be used to make two distributions more comparable by placing them on the same numerical scale. Linear standard scores are called linear because if you plot each raw score against its corresponding linear standard score in a graph and then connect these points, you will always have a straight line.

z-Scores

The fundamental linear standard score is the **z-score**, which tells the number of standard deviation units a raw score is above (or below) the mean of a given distribution. Other linear standard scores are computed from z-scores. Equation 17.1 explains.

$$z = \frac{X - M}{SD} \qquad \text{[Eq. 17.1]}$$

where

X represents the raw score

M represents the mean (average) raw score of the group

SD represents the standard deviation of the raw scores for that group

Here is an example of how to apply this equation:

Example

Example of calculating a linear z-score using Equation 17.1

Suppose Ashley's raw score was 38 on Test A. Suppose further that the test mean is 44 and the standard deviation is 4. The corresponding z-score is calculated as follows:

$$z = \frac{38 - 44}{4} = \frac{-6}{4} = -1.5$$

The z-score tells the number of standard deviations a raw score is above or below the mean. For example, if a student's raw score falls below the mean a distance equal to one and one half times the standard deviation of the group, the student's z-score equals −1.5. A z-score is negative when the raw score is below the mean, positive when the raw score is above the mean, and equal to zero when the raw score is exactly equal to the mean.

An advantage of using z-scores is that they communicate students' norm-referenced achievement expressed as a distance away from the mean. In many groups, the majority of students' scores cluster near the mean, usually within one standard deviation on either side of the mean. A distance of one standard deviation above the mean is $z = +1.0$; a distance of one standard deviation below the mean is $z = -1.0$. Thus, you would interpret a student whose z-score is between +1.0 and −1.0 as having typical or average attainment relative to others. Similarly, you would interpret a student with $z = -1.5$ or less as having atypically low attainment because few students have z-scores of −1.5 or less. You interpret a student with $z = +1.5$ or greater as having atypically high attainment because relatively few students attain z-scores of +1.5 or greater.

Another advantage of using z-scores is to put raw scores with different metrics on the same norm-referenced scale. Consider the following example, in which the same students are measured in both pounds and kilograms. Notice what happens when each student's measurements are transformed to z-scores.

Example

Example showing how a student's z-scores remain the same even though the measurement scale changes

Student	Weight in kilograms		Weight in pounds	
	X	z	X	z
A	48	−1.52	105.2	−1.52
B	52	−0.17	114.4	−0.17
C	54	0.51	118.8	0.51
D	56	1.18	123.2	1.18

Even though the pounds mean and standard deviation are different from the kilograms mean and standard deviation, the students' relative positions in the distributions are the same. This is expressed by the z-scores (which are identical for pounds and kilograms), not by the pounds and kilograms raw scores.

The z-score has several practical disadvantages. It is difficult to explain to students and parents, because understanding it requires an understanding of the mean and standard deviation. Another practical disadvantage is that plus and minus signs are used. Transcription errors, resulting in omitted or interchanged signs, are frequent. Further, you will find it difficult to explain to students (or parents) why assessment performances are reported as negative and/or fractional numbers. For example, a student may say, "I got 15 of the 45 questions right. How could my score be −1.34?" Likewise, the decimal point is subject to frequent transcription error.

These practical problems are easily overcome, however, by transforming the z-score to other types of scores. These additional transformations maintain the conceptual norm-referenced advantage of z-scores while overcoming their practical limitations.

SS-Scores

The second type of score under the linear standard score branch of Figure 17.2 is the SS-score. An SS-score tells the location of a raw score in a distribution having a mean of 50 and a standard deviation of 10. To remedy some of the disadvantages of z-scores, some publishers apply a modification (transformation) to eliminate both the negative scores and the fractional portion of the z-scores. Equation 17.2 for an SS-score shows how these two things are accomplished:

$$SS = 10z + 50$$
$$= (10 \text{ times the } z\text{-score}) + 50 \quad \text{[Eq. 17.2]}$$

First, z-scores are computed; then, each z-score is transformed to an SS-score: Each z is multiplied by 10, the product rounded to the nearest whole number, and finally 50 is added. Multiplying by 10 and rounding eliminates the z-score's decimal. Adding 50 eliminates the z-score's negative value. Here is an example of how to use the equation:

Example

Example showing how a student's z-score is transformed into an SS-score

Suppose Ashley's z-score was computed to be −1.5. (See the earlier example.) To convert this to an SS-score, multiply it by 10 and add 50 to the result. Thus,

$$SS = 10(-1.5) + 50$$
$$= -15 + 50 = 35$$

The result of applying this conversion to the z-scores is that the distribution of *SS*-scores will have a mean of 50 and a standard deviation of 10. Once you know this fact, you can interpret anyone's *SS*-score, essentially by doing a mental conversion back to a z-score.

Example

Example showing how to interpret a student's SS-score by converting it back to a z-score

Ashley's *SS*-score is 35; a score of 35 is 15 points or 1.5 standard deviations below 50, the mean. Thus, Ashley's z-score is −1.5.

SS-scores have the advantage of not changing the shape of the original raw score distribution. The distribution of *SS*-scores always has a mean of 50 and a standard deviation of 10. The *SS*-score is interpretable in terms of standard deviation units while avoiding negative numbers and decimal fractions. A disadvantage is that a person needs to understand the concepts of standard deviation and linear transformation to interpret them.

Comparison of Linear Standard Scores

It may help you understand these scores if we display the numerical relationship between them. Because all linear standard score systems reflect essentially the same information, interpreting their meaning is easy once you know the multiplier and the added constant. The next example shows how each type of score is related to the other and to the raw scores:

Example

Example comparing z-scores and SS-scores for the same raw score

Raw score in a group with M = 41 and SD = 3	Linear standard scores corresponding to each raw score	
	z-score	SS-score
32	−3.0	20
35	−2.0	30
38	−1.0	40
41	0.0	50
44	+1.0	60
47	+2.0	70
50	+3.0	80

MyLab Education Self-Check 17.2

MyLab Education Application Exercise 17.2:
Interpreting Percentile Ranks

NORMAL DISTRIBUTIONS

Shortly, we will discuss the normalized standard score branch of Figure 17.2. However, first we need to discuss normal distributions of scores.

Definition

Assessment developers have found it advantageous to transform the scores to a common distributional form: a normal distribution. A **normal distribution**, sometimes called a *normal curve*, is a mathematical model invented in 1733 by Abraham de Moivre (Pearson, 1924). It is defined by a particular equation that depends on two specific numbers: the mean and the standard deviation, signifying that many normal distributions exist and each has a different mean and/or standard deviation. Figure 17.4 shows several different normal curves. Each of these was obtained by using the normal curve equation and plotting points on a graph. In Figure 17.4 (A), each normal distribution has the same mean but a different standard deviation. Although each is centered on the same point on the X-scale, some appear flatter and more spread out because their standard deviation is larger. Figure 17.4 (B)

FIGURE 17.4 **Illustrations of different normal distributions.**

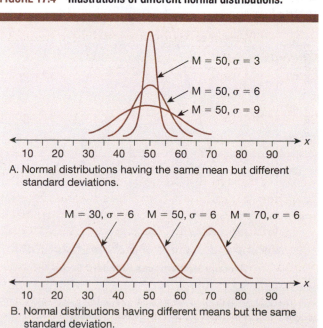

A. Normal distributions having the same mean but different standard deviations.

B. Normal distributions having different means but the same standard deviation.

shows three normal curves, each with the same standard deviation but each with a different mean. The degree of spread is the same for each, but each is centered on a different point on the score scale.

Every normal curve is smooth and continuous; each has a symmetrical, bell-shaped form. In theory, a normal curve never touches the baseline (horizontal axis) but is asymptotic to it, extending out to infinity in either direction from the mean. Graphs of actual raw-score distributions are nonsymmetrical and jagged. For actual raw-score distributions, the lowest possible score is 0 and the highest possible score equals the total number of items on the assessment. An idea of how an actual distribution compares to the mathematically defined normal curve may be obtained from Figure 17.5. Both distributions have the same mean and the same standard deviation. This normal curve approximates the actual distribution but does not match it exactly.

FIGURE 17.5 **Example of a mathematically defined normal curve (smooth curve) superimposed on an actual distribution (histogram) of average eighth-grade mathematics standard scores for 575 schools. Both distributions have the same mean and standard deviation.**

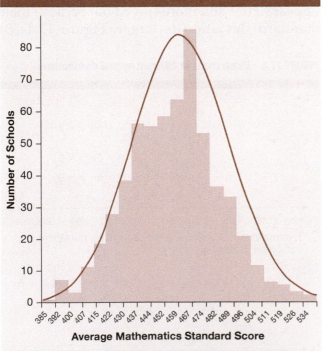

Source: Histogram drawn from 2004 eighth-grade school averages from the Arizona Department of Education, Accountability Division, Research and Evaluation Section, http://www.ade.state.az.us/profile/publicview/Download.asp. Used with permission.

Natural Law Versus Normal Distributions

Early users of normal curves believed that somehow natural laws dictated that nearly all human characteristics were distributed in a random or chance fashion around a mean or average value. This view of the normal curve's applicability was, perhaps, begun by de Moivre (1756), but it was adamantly held to be true for intellectual and moral qualities by Quetelet (1748) (Dudycha & Dudycha, 1972; Landau & Lazarsfeld, 1968).

This thought—that somehow the distributions of human characteristics are by nature normal distributions—has carried over to mental measurement. Some believe that a bell-shaped distribution means not only the scores but also the human abilities *underlying* the scores are normally distributed. This statement is, of course, not true. The assessment's score distribution depends not only on the underlying abilities of the persons tested but also on the properties of the assessment procedure itself. An assessment developer can, by judicious selection of tasks, make the score distribution have any shape: rectangular, skewed bimodal, symmetrical, and so on (Lord, 1953). (See Appendix F for shapes of distributions.) These nonnormal score distribution shapes could appear in the data, for example, even though the underlying ability of the group is normal in form. Similarly, score distributions could appear to be normal in shape even though the underlying ability of the group is nonnormal in form.

From your own experience, you know that you can control the shape of a test score distribution. For example, if all items on a test are easy, there will be a lot of high scores and few low scores. A very difficult test will have many low scores and few high scores. The point is, the normal distribution is a convenient model, but you should not believe it is a natural representation of educational achievement outcomes.

Percentile Ranks and z-Scores in a Normal Distribution

To understand the relationship between percentile ranks and normal curve z-scores, look at the graph at the top of Figure 17.6. If we cut up a normal distribution into sections one standard deviation wide, each section will have a fixed percentage of cases or **area under the normal curve**. For example, a section that is one standard deviation wide

FIGURE 17.6
Relationships among percentile ranks, *z*-scores, and *T*-scores in a normal distribution.

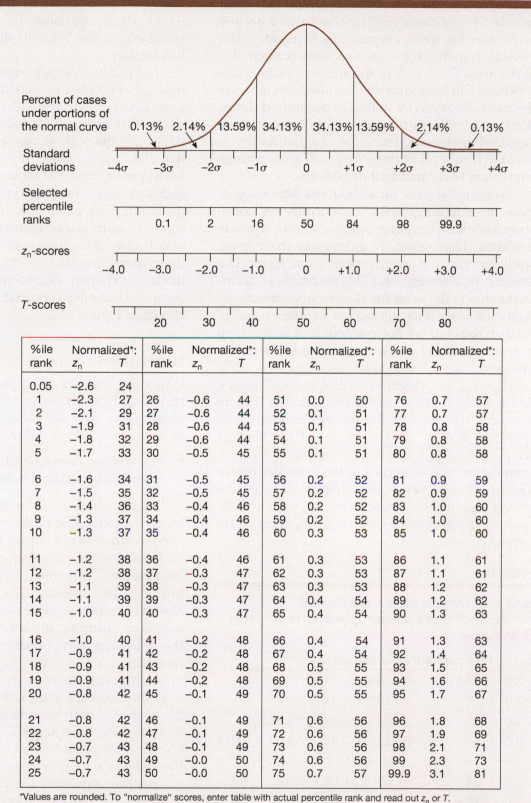

%ile rank	Normalized*: z_n	T	%ile rank	Normalized*: z_n	T	%ile rank	Normalized*: z_n	T	%ile rank	Normalized*: z_n	T
0.05	−2.6	24									
1	−2.3	27	26	−0.6	44	51	0.0	50	76	0.7	57
2	−2.1	29	27	−0.6	44	52	0.1	51	77	0.7	57
3	−1.9	31	28	−0.6	44	53	0.1	51	78	0.8	58
4	−1.8	32	29	−0.6	44	54	0.1	51	79	0.8	58
5	−1.7	33	30	−0.5	45	55	0.1	51	80	0.8	58
6	−1.6	34	31	−0.5	45	56	0.2	52	81	0.9	59
7	−1.5	35	32	−0.5	45	57	0.2	52	82	0.9	59
8	−1.4	36	33	−0.4	46	58	0.2	52	83	1.0	60
9	−1.3	37	34	−0.4	46	59	0.2	52	84	1.0	60
10	−1.3	37	35	−0.4	46	60	0.3	53	85	1.0	60
11	−1.2	38	36	−0.4	46	61	0.3	53	86	1.1	61
12	−1.2	38	37	−0.3	47	62	0.3	53	87	1.1	61
13	−1.1	39	38	−0.3	47	63	0.3	53	88	1.2	62
14	−1.1	39	39	−0.3	47	64	0.4	54	89	1.2	62
15	−1.0	40	40	−0.3	47	65	0.4	54	90	1.3	63
16	−1.0	40	41	−0.2	48	66	0.4	54	91	1.3	63
17	−0.9	41	42	−0.2	48	67	0.4	54	92	1.4	64
18	−0.9	41	43	−0.2	48	68	0.5	55	93	1.5	65
19	−0.9	41	44	−0.2	48	69	0.5	55	94	1.6	66
20	−0.8	42	45	−0.1	49	70	0.5	55	95	1.7	67
21	−0.8	42	46	−0.1	49	71	0.6	56	96	1.8	68
22	−0.8	42	47	−0.1	49	72	0.6	56	97	1.9	69
23	−0.7	43	48	−0.1	49	73	0.6	56	98	2.1	71
24	−0.7	43	49	−0.0	50	74	0.6	56	99	2.3	73
25	−0.7	43	50	−0.0	50	75	0.7	57	99.9	3.1	81

*Values are rounded. To "normalize" scores, enter table with actual percentile rank and read out z_n or T.

and located just above the mean contains approximately 34% of the area. The comparable section just below the mean contains, by symmetry, 34% as well. Together those two sections contain 68% of the area. Thus, 68% of the area in a normal distribution will be within one standard deviation of the mean; 95% will be within two standard deviations; and 99.7% of the area will fall within three standard deviations. Therefore, if a distribution is normal, nearly all of the scores will span a range equivalent to six standard deviations.

You can use these facts about the percentage of cases in various segments to determine the correspondence between percentile ranks and z-scores in a normal distribution. To emphasize that we are speaking only of a normal distribution, Figure 17.6 denotes the z-scores as z_n. This percentile rank correspondence, the same for all normal distributions, permits an easy interpretation of standard scores in normal distributions. For example, look at the graph in Figure 17.6 and the two scales below the graph. The percentage of cases below $z_n = -2.00$ is 2.27% ($= 0.13 + 2.14$). (Figure 17.6 also shows T-scores, which we will explain later in this chapter.) Thus, in a normal distribution the percentile rank corresponding to $z_n = -2.00$ is (rounded) 2. Other z_n-scores' percentile ranks can be computed similarly from Figure 17.6, as shown in the examples below. The chart under the drawing in Figure 17.6 provides more complete information on percentile rank correspondences between z_n-scores and normal curves.

Example

How to determine the percentile rank corresponding to selected z_n-scores in a normal distribution

z_n	PR (rounded)	How calculated
−3.0	0.1	= 0.13
−2.0	2	= 0.13 + 2.14
−1.0	16	= 0.13 + 2.14 + 13.59
0.0	50	= 0.13 + 2.14 + 13.59 + 34.13
1.0	84	= 50 + 34.13
2.0	98	= 50 + 34.13 + 13.59
3.0	99.9	= 50 + 34.13 + 13.59 + 2.14

NORMALIZED STANDARD SCORES

Now that you have a little background on the meaning of a normal curve, let's return to the third branch of Figure 17.2: normalized standard scores. The figure shows five types of normalized standard scores. We will discuss all of them in this section.

Test publishers may transform raw scores to a new set of scores that is distributed normally (or nearly so). Such transformation changes the shape of the original distribution, squeezing and stretching the scale to make it conform to a normal distribution. Once this is accomplished, various types of standard scores can be derived, and each can have an appropriate normal curve interpretation. The general name for these derived scores is **normalized standard scores**. These are also termed *area transformations*, as opposed to linear transformations, which we presented earlier in this chapter. This section reviews five of the common varieties reported in test manuals and shown in Figure 17.2.

Normalized z-Scores

When the z-scores have percentile ranks corresponding to what we would expect in a normal distribution, they are called normalized z-scores, or z_n**-scores**, and the following symbol is used:

z_n = the z-score corresponding to a given percentile rank in a normal distribution

If a distribution of raw scores is not normal in form, the percentile ranks of its z-scores will not correspond to what would be expected in a normal distribution. However, one can create a set of "normalized" z-scores for any nonnormal distribution. After making this transformation, the new set of scores is more nearly like a normal distribution. **Normalizing a set of scores** is done in the following way: (a) determine the percentile rank of each raw score in the norm group, (b) look up each percentile rank in a normal curve table (e.g., the chart in Figure 17.6), and (c) read out the z_n-value that corresponds to each. The resulting z_n-values are "normalized." That is, they are the z-scores that *would have been attained if the distribution had been normal in form.*

To show you how the process works, and to illustrate the difference between z and z_n, consider the scores in the next example. The scores and the percentile ranks came from our example of the class of 25 students that showed how percentile ranks were calculated (Figure F.8 in Appendix F).

Example

Illustration of normalized z-scores and (actual) linear z-scores corresponding to the distribution of 25 test scores shown in the previous example in Figure F.8

Raw score	Percentile rank	Normalized[a] standard scores (zn)	Linear[b] standard scores (z)
36	98	2.05	2.43
33	96	1.75	1.64
32	94	1.55	1.38
31	90	1.28	1.12
30	88	1.18	0.86
29	84	0.99	0.59
28	72	0.58	0.33
27	54	0.10	0.07
26	32	−0.47	−0.20
25	16	−0.99	−0.46
24	10	−1.28	−0.72
22	8	−1.41	−1.25
21	6	−1.55	−1.51
15	4	−1.75	−3.09
14	2	−2.05	−3.36

Notes: [a]z_n-values are obtained by looking up the percentile ranks in Figure 17.6 and reading out the corresponding z_n-values.
[b]z-values are obtained by using the actual distribution of scores in Table F.8 (Appendix F) and by applying the equation:

$$z = \frac{X - M}{SD}$$

where $M = 26.75$ and $SD = 3.80$.

Next, you look up each percentile rank in Figure 17.6, and read out the corresponding z_n. The results appear in the example. For the sake of comparison, the actual, linear z-scores are computed via Equation 17.1, using $M = 26.75$ and $SD = 3.8$. The difference between the normalized and linear z-scores represents the "stretching and squeezing" necessary to make the original distribution correspond more nearly to a normal distribution.

Normalized *T*-Scores (McCall's *T*)

The second type of score in the normalized standard score branch of Figure 17.2 is a ***T*-score**. A normalized *T*-score tells the location of a raw score in a normal distribution having a mean of 50 and a standard deviation of 10. The normalized *T*-score is the counterpart to the linear *SS*-score. Thus,

$$T = 10z_n + 50 \qquad \text{[Eq. 17.3]}$$

The difference between Equation 17.3 and Equation 17.2 ($SS = 10z + 50$) is that z_n is a normalized standard score instead of a linear standard score.

Normalized *T*-scores have the same advantages over normalized z-scores as *SS*-scores have over linear z-scores with the additional advantage that *T*-scores have the percentile rank interpretations of a normal curve. Here is an example:

Example

Examples of how to interpret T-scores using a normal curve like the one shown in Figure 17.6

1. Joey's *T*-score is 40, which means he is one standard deviation below the mean of the norm group, and his percentile rank is approximately 16.
2. Keisha's percentile rank is 84, which means her *T*-score is 60, and she is a distance of one standard deviation above the norm-group mean.

Figure 17.6 shows the correspondence between percentile ranks, *T*-scores, and z_n scores in a normal distribution. That figure can help you convert percentile ranks directly to *T*-scores without using Equation 17.3.

Deviation IQ Scores

The third type of normalized standard score shown in Figure 17.2 is the deviation IQ score used with certain assessments of mental ability. A **deviation IQ score**, or **DIQ-score**, tells the location of a raw score in a normal distribution having a mean of 100 and a standard deviation of 15 or 16. The norm group is usually made up of all those students with the same chronological age, regardless of grade placement. For example, if the test developer sets the standard deviation at 16, *DIQ*s are given by the following formula:

$$DIQ = 16z_n + 100 \qquad \text{[Eq. 17.4]}$$

These *DIQ*s are interpreted in a way similar to *T*-scores, but with reference to the normal distribution having a mean of 100 and a standard deviation of 16. Here is an example:

Example

The meaning of DIQ-scores

1. Meghan has *DIQ* = 116, which means she has scored one standard deviation above the mean of her age group and the percentile rank of her score is 84.

2. Sherry has *DIQ* = 100, which means she has scored at the mean of her age group and the percentile rank of her score is 50.

Usually, assessment manuals provide tables that permit you to convert raw scores directly to *DIQs*.

Stanines

The fourth normalized standard score shown in Figure 17.2 is the stanine. A **stanine score** tells the location of a raw score in a specific segment of a normal distribution. Publishers frequently recommend using **national stanines** for norm-referenced interpretation of achievement and aptitude assessments.

Figure 17.7 illustrates the meaning of a stanine score. A normal distribution is divided into nine segments, numbered from a low of one through a high of nine. Scores falling within the boundaries of these segments are assigned one of these nine numbers (hence, the term *stanine* from "standard nine"). Each segment is one half a

FIGURE 17.7   Illustration of a normal distribution showing stanines, percentile ranks, and percentage of cases having each stanine.

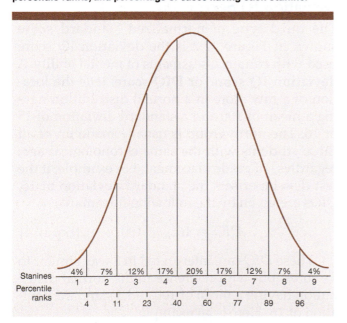

standard deviation wide, except for stanines one and nine. The percentage of the cases in a normal curve falling within each segment is shown in Figure 17.7, along with the range of percentile ranks associated with each.

All persons with scores falling within an interval are assigned the stanine of that interval. For example, all persons with scores having percentile ranks from 11 through 22 are assigned a stanine of three; all from 23 through 29 a stanine of four; and so on. Twelve percent of the persons in the norm group would be assigned a stanine of three and 17% a stanine of four. When raw scores from normal distributions are converted to stanines, the stanines have a mean of five and a standard deviation equal to two. Here is an example of how stanines are interpreted. As you read these examples, refer to Figure 17.7.

Example

How to interpret stanine scores

1. Sophia received a stanine of five on the mathematics subtest of a standardized test, which means her raw score on the test was in the middle 20% of the norm group.

2. Jesse received a stanine of nine in the reading subtest of a standardized test, which means his raw score on the test was in the top 4% of the norm group.

3. Blake's stanine on the spelling subtest of the standardized test was three, which means that his raw score was in the lower 20% of the norm group. Specifically, his percentile rank was between 11 and 22.

Among the advantages claimed for stanines: They are always single-digit numbers, have approximately equal units all along the score scale, and do not imply an exactness greater than that warranted by the assessment.

Not all assessment experts agree with using stanines for norm-referenced interpretations. Some hold that stanines present more difficult interpretative problems than percentile ranks, especially for reliable assessments, because stanines reflect coarse groupings of scores.

As with percentile ranks, stanines are specific to the reference group on which they are calculated. Some test publishers report both local and national stanines. For a specific student, these two stanines may be different, depending on how the student ranks in each reference group.

The example in Appendix F (Figure F.11) shows how you can transform any set of scores into stanines. The example uses the distribution of 25 scores we used in Figure F.8.

SAT-Scores

The fifth score in the normalized standard score branch of Figure 17.2 is the **SAT-score**. The *SAT Test (SAT)* results are reported using this type of score. Historically, the *SAT*-score was a normalized standard score from a distribution that has a mean of 500 and a standard deviation of 100. This is shown in Equation 17.5:

$$SAT\text{-score} = 100z_n + 500 \qquad [\text{Eq. 17.5}]$$

With this method of scoring the *SAT*, results depended in part on the ability level of the cohort of students with whom a person was tested. Beginning in 1941, scores were calculated in this manner, and then subsequent scores were equated to the 1941 reference group, to ensure that scores have the same meaning from year to year, but not the meaning within one test administration that Equation 17.5 conveys. The scores were recentered again (Dorans, 2002), using transformations that are beyond the scope of this book, for a reference group of 1,052,000 students who graduated from high school in 1990 and who took the *SAT* in either their junior or senior year. Similar to the equating after 1941, the 1990 recentered scores no longer reflect the historical equation (Dorans, 2002). However, the current *SAT*-scores do reflect performance on the historic 200–800 scale and preserve the intent to make scores comparable from one administration of the test to the next.

Normal Curve Equivalents

The sixth type of normalized standard score in Figure 17.2 is the normal curve equivalent. The **normal curve equivalent (NCE)** is a normalized standard score with a mean of 50 and a standard deviation of 21.06. It was developed primarily for use with federal program evaluation efforts (Tallmadge & Wood, 1976). Its primary value is evaluating gains from various educational programs that use different publishers' tests. *NCE*-values are found by the formula shown in Equation 17.6. Their highest possible value is 99 and their lowest possible value is 1.

$$NCE = 21.06z_n + 50 \qquad [\text{Eq. 17.6}]$$

As stated previously, *NCE*-scores have a mean of 50 and a standard deviation of 21.06. By comparison, *T*-scores have a mean of 50 and a standard deviation of 10. Why choose a standard deviation of 21.06? This choice of standard deviation was made so the *NCE*-scores would span the range one to 99.

The following example shows the relationship between selected percentile ranks, *NCE*-scores, and stanines:

Example

Correspondences between selected percentile ranks, NCE-scores, and stanines

Percentile rank	NCE	Stanine
1	1	1
5	15	2
10	23	2
20	32	3
25	36	4
30	39	4
35	42	4
40	45	5
45	47	5
50	50	5
55	53	5
60	55	6
65	58	6
70	61	6
75	64	6
80	68	7
85	72	7
90	77	8
95	85	8
99	99	9

As you can see in the table, percentile ranks of 1, 50, and 99 are identical in value to *NCE*-scores. At other points, however, percentile ranks and *NCE*-scores differ: *NCE*-scores are less spread out than percentile ranks in the middle of the distribution and more spread out than percentile ranks at the lower and upper extremes. Notice the *NCE*-scores look very similar to percentile ranks, which is why they are often confused with percentile ranks. Although some publishers present *NCE* norms tables in their standardized test manuals, we do not recommend *NCE*-scores for reporting individual student results because they are too easily confused with percentile ranks.

You may notice the relationship of the *NCE*-score to stanines. If you move the *NCE* decimal point to the left one digit and round to the nearest whole number, you will roughly have the stanine. For example, an *NCE* = 72 has a stanine equivalent of seven; *NCE* = 58 has a stanine equivalent of six; and so on. This rough correspondence stems from the fact that both *NCE*-scores and stanines are based on a normal distribution, and *NCE*-scores and percentile ranks have the same range.

DEVELOPMENTAL AND EDUCATIONAL GROWTH SCALES

We turn now to the fourth branch of the norm-referencing schemes in Figure 17.2. The normalized standard score scales discussed so far are specific to a particular grade level or age group. If a score scale is specific to a particular grade, you cannot use it to measure growth as a student moves from one grade to the next. For example, suppose Billy tested at the 84th percentile in Grades 5, 6, and 7. Although Billy would be growing in skills and knowledge, his percentile rank (84) has stayed the same. The number, 84, by reflecting only location in each grade's norm group, does not communicate Billy's growth. Similarly, suppose Ashley's *T*-score determined separately for each grade's norm group remained nearly the same from year to year, say about 60. Ashley in fact exhibited educational growth each year as she moved through the grades. The *T*-score, because it remains constant, does not communicate growth.

You would find it useful, however, if your students' educational growth were reported on one scale of numbers that spanned the school years. Survey achievement batteries, for example, usually span several grades—say second through eighth, or ninth through twelfth. If the score scale of such batteries linked the assessments from several grade levels to a single developmental score scale, you could measure your students' growth over those years. We now turn to a discussion of the two scales shown in the developmental or growth scales branch of Figure 17.2: the extended normalized standard score scale and the grade-equivalent score scale.

EXTENDED NORMALIZED STANDARD SCORE SCALES

Basic Idea of the Extended Normalized Score Scales

An **extended normalized standard score** tells the location of a raw score on a scale of numbers that is anchored to a lower grade reference group. Educators find that a "ruler" or achievement continuum on which a student's progress can be measured over a wide range of grades is very useful. On this continuum, low scores represent the lowest levels of educational development and high scores the highest level of educational development. Publishers refer to this type of scale with a variety of names, for example: *obtained scale score*, *scale score*, *extended standard score*, *developmental standard score*, or *growth-scale values*.

Development of Extended Score Scales

Although each publisher prepares expanded scales somewhat differently, and the numbers obtained are not comparable from publisher to publisher, extended scaled scores share the same goals and the same general method of development: (a) a base or anchor group is chosen and normalized *z*-scores are developed that extend beyond the range of scores for this anchor group; (b) a series of assessments are administered with common items given to adjoining groups (e.g., second and third graders take a common set of items, then third and fourth graders, and so on); (c) distributions of scores are tabulated and normalized for each grade; and (d) through these overlapping items, all of the groups are placed on the extended *z*-score scale of the anchor group. This extended *z*-scale becomes the ruler or growth scale spanning the several grades.

The extended *z*-scale is then transformed again to a scale that removes the unpleasant properties (such as negative numbers and decimals) of the *z*-scores. The new scale may range from 00 to 99, from 000 to 999, or any other set of positive integers, depending on the publisher; there are no standards for what this range should be.

Item Response Theory Method

Recent technical advances have given publishers two choices of how extended standard scores can be calculated. One is the method we described above, using the traditional raw score for students (i.e., number right score) as a beginning step for calculating. A second method uses **item response theory (IRT)** in which a mathematical equation is fit to the publisher's sample of students' item responses. The results are then used to derive a score scale. According to this method, students' scores depend on the pattern of their right or wrong answers. **IRT pattern scoring** considers whether students answered an easy or difficult item correctly, and how sharply that item distinguishes students of different achievement levels. This means, for example, that two students who answer correctly the same number of items may get different scaled scores if the pattern of correctly answered items is substantially different for the two students.

The advantage is that the resultant extended standard scores have lower measurement error and greater reliability than traditional number-right scores. The disadvantages are (a) the direct link between the number correct and the extended scale score is broken (when certain equations are used), and (b) the method does not work well for every type of test and every population of students.

A full explanation of item response theory is beyond the scope of this book. To learn more about item response theory you may consult echo.edres.org for links to different tutorials. On that site you will also find an introductory book, *The Basics of Item Response Theory* (Baker, 2001), that you may read online.

Recommendations

Although program evaluators and school researchers generally prefer to use extended standard scores, their meaning is not immediately apparent to teachers, parents, and students. To understand what they mean, you have to compare a student's score with the average score of students in that grade. Some educators consider this an advantage because it lessens the chance of overinterpreting scores. On the other hand, if no one knows what they mean, they will not be used, and therefore the scores will be underutilized.

Extended standard scores tend to show that, on the average, students exhibit less achievement growth in the upper elementary grades than in the lower grades. Note that extended standard scores show different standard deviations for school subjects and progressively increasing

standard deviations as grade levels increase. Thus, you cannot compare a student's extended assessment score from one subject area to another. In this respect, they share a common property with grade-equivalent scores, discussed next.

GRADE-EQUIVALENT SCORES

Basic Idea of Grade-Equivalent Scores

A **grade-equivalent score (GE)** tells the grade placement at which a raw score is average. *GE*s are the educational development scores most often used with achievement tests at the elementary school level. A grade-equivalent score is reported as a decimal fraction, such as 3.4 or 7.9. The whole number part of the score refers to a grade level, and the decimal part refers to a month of the school year within that grade level. For example, you read a grade-equivalent score of 3.4 as "third grade, fourth month"; similarly, you read 7.9 as "seventh grade, ninth month." Suppose 6.3 is the grade-equivalent score corresponding to the raw score 31. This means that the average in the norm group during the third month of sixth grade was 31. The example below shows how the grade-equivalent scale is laid out:

Example

The grade-equivalent score scale layout

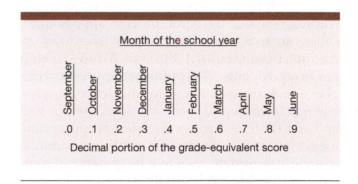

When using these scores, you assume that the time between June and September (i.e., the summer months) represents an increment of one tenth (or 1 month) on the grade-equivalent scale (see above). By defining the grade-equivalent scale this way, the average of the scores shows 10 months' growth every year. However, you should not expect every student to show 1 month's growth each summer.

Overall Usefulness of Grade-Equivalent Scores

Grade-equivalent scores are useful for reporting a pupil's educational development. If a standardized test is administered periodically throughout a student's school years, the resulting grade-equivalent scores can help monitor the student's educational progress using a grade-based educational development scale. To a lesser extent, grade equivalents can be used to evaluate a student's grade placement. The problem with grade placement interpretations of *GE*-scores is that they depend on how well the test content matches what was taught to the students up to the point at which the test was administered—the poorer this match, the less valid are grade placement interpretations.

Grade-equivalent scores (and extended standard scores) cannot be used to compare a student's strengths and weaknesses across different subject matters. Nor can they be used to determine a student's rank among his or her peers. An explanation of these limitations follows.

Development of Grade-Equivalent Scores

Understanding how the test publisher obtains grade equivalents will help you avoid misinterpretation. There is no need, of course, for you to compute them because test manuals provide the needed conversion tables.

The development process is illustrated with a reading test, but the same process applies to all subject areas. Suppose a publisher wishes to assess reading from Grades 1 through 8 and develop grade equivalents. The publisher creates a series of overlapping tests that spans the desired grades: one test for first and second grades, one for second and third, and so on. Each test is appropriate for specific grade levels. The publisher administers the appropriate tests to a large national sample at each grade level. Usually, the publisher does this once or twice during the year (fall and/or spring) because it is impossible to administer them continuously throughout the year. The dates on which tests are administered are called **empirical norming dates**. These overlapping tests are then linked using an expanded score scale, which allows the raw scores from the different tests to be placed on a grade-based reading ability scale. The process is called *vertical linking* or *vertical equating* because the links go up the grades.

On this common scale, large differences in reading ability exist in the norm group at each grade level. Therefore, at each grade level there is a spread of reading scores. These distributions of reading scores are shown in Figure 17.8. In this illustration, the publisher administered the assessments only once during the year—in February (Month = 0.5)—so the figure graphs the distributions directly above 1.5, 2.5, 3.5, and so forth.

The *GE* is the median score (the mean score is used sometimes instead) in each grade's norm group. Actual grade equivalents can be obtained only for those points in time when the publisher administered the tests. Grade equivalents for other points are obtained by **interpolation** or **extrapolation**. Interpolation means finding an unknown number between two known numbers (e.g., between the first and second graders' median performance at the norming month). Extrapolation means estimating an unknown number that lies outside the range of available data. Sometimes extrapolation leads to silly interpretations. We once had a parent who wondered why her seventh-grade son received a *GE*-score of 12.0 on a science test in an achievement battery. He had told his parents that he didn't need to pay attention in science class any more, which was definitely not a good interpretation! "How would you expect a twelfth grader to score on a seventh-grade science test?" we asked. "He just got all those seventh-grade science questions right."

An example of an actual conversion table from a published test is shown in Figure 17.9. You will use this type of conversion table when you consult a publisher's norms booklet to convert your students' raw scores to grade equivalents.

What to Keep in Mind When Interpreting Grade Equivalents

Spring-to-Fall Drops: Summer Losses
One special concern in the process of interpreting grade equivalents is the phenomenon of summer achievement losses. In some subject areas—arithmetic, for example—students' performance loses some of its edge over the summer months. A performance drop over the summer months has several meanings: (a) the assumption of an over-the-summer growth of one month is not true in every subject area, (b) educational growth is not regular and uniform for many children, and (c) using fall-to-spring gains in grade-equivalent

FIGURE 17.8 Hypothetical example of data used to obtain grade-equivalent scores.

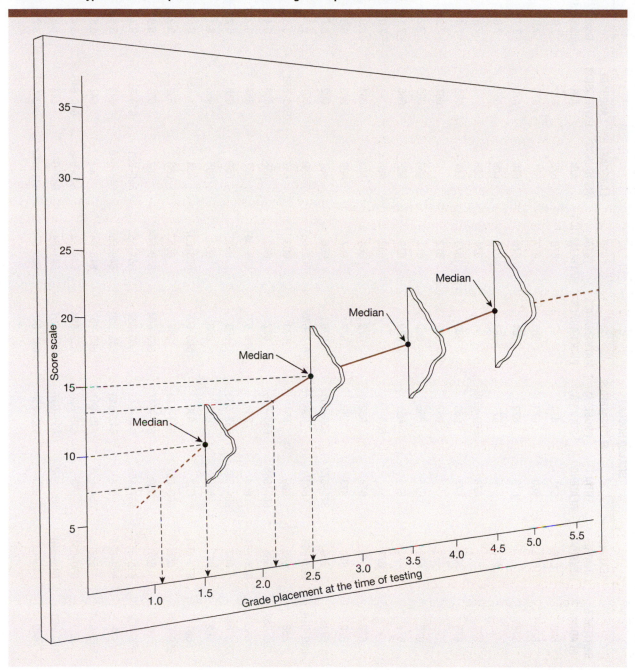

scores to evaluate an instructional program may lead to wrong conclusions. The third point is less problematic when the test publisher has separate fall and spring norms and when a school system tests on dates very close to the dates on which the publisher's norms were established.

Grade Equivalents and Curriculum Correspondence It would be a misconception to say that students ought to have the same placement as their grade-equivalent scores. To understand

why, recall that grade equivalents are based on the median. By definition, half the students in the norm groups at a particular grade placement will have scores above the median. Thus, half the students in the norm group have grade-equivalent scores higher than their actual grade placement. Second, recall that a publisher uses a series of tests, rather than a single test, to establish grade equivalents. You can't interpret a third grader's grade-equivalent score of, say, 5.7 on a mathematics test covering third-grade content to mean that

FIGURE 17.9 Part of grade-equivalent table for the *Stanford Achievement Tests* (10th Edition), *Forms S/T, Fall Norms*. Notice that you enter the table with the (expanded) scaled scores and read the grade-equivalent scores in the margins.

SCALED SCORES

Grade Equivalent	WORD STUDY SKILLS	WORD RDG/ READING VOCABULARY	SENTENCE READING	READING COMPRE-HENSION	TOTAL READING	MATHEMATICS PROBLEM SOLVING	MATHEMATICS PROCEDURES	TOTAL MATHEMATICS	LANGUAGE MECHANICS A/B	LANGUAGE EXPRESSION A/B	Grade Equivalent
7.9	684	692	680	676	681	674	-	678	672	672	7.9
7.8	683	691	679	675	680	673	685	677	671	671	7.8
7.7	682	690	678	-	679	672	684	676	670	670	7.7
7.6	-	689	-	674	-	671	683	675	669	669	7.6
7.5	681	688	677	-	678	669–670	-	674	668	-	7.5
7.4	680	687	676	673	677	668	682	673	667	668	7.4
7.3	-	685–686	-	-	-	667	681	672	-	667	7.3
7.2	679	684	675	672	676	666	680	671	666	666	7.2
7.1	678	683	674	-	675	665	679	670	665	665	7.1
7.0	-	682	-	671	-	663–664	-	669	664	-	7.0
6.9	677	681	673	-	674	662	678	668	663	664	6.9
6.8	676	680	672	670	673	661	677	667	662	663	6.8
6.7	674–675	678–679	671	669	671–672	659–660	676	666	661	662	6.7
6.6	673	677	669–670	667–668	670	658	674–675	664–665	660	661	6.6
6.5	672	676	668	666	669	657	673	663	659	659–660	6.5
6.4	670–671	674–675	666–667	665	667–668	655–656	672	662	658	658	6.4
6.3	669	673	665	663–664	666	654	670–671	660–661	657	657	6.3
6.2	667–668	671–672	663–664	662	664–665	652–653	669	659	656	656	6.2
6.1	666	670	662	661	663	651	668	658	655	655	6.1
6.0	665	669	661	659–660	662	650	666–667	656–657	654	653–654	6.0
5.9	663–664	667–668	659–660	658	660–661	648–649	665	655	653	652	5.9
5.8	661–662	666	658	657	659	646–647	663–664	653–654	652	651	5.8
5.7	660	664–665	656–657	655–656	657–658	644–645	660–662	651–652	650–651	649–650	5.7
5.6	659	662–663	655	653–654	656	642–643	658–659	649–650	648–649	648	5.6
5.5	657–658	661	653–654	652	654–655	640–641	655–657	646–648	647	647	5.5
5.4	656	659–660	652	650–651	653	638–639	652–654	644–645	645–646	645–646	5.4
5.3	655	658	650–651	648–649	651–652	635–637	650–651	641–643	643–644	644	5.3
5.2	654	656–657	649	646–647	650	633–634	647–649	639–640	641–642	642–643	5.2

FIGURE 17.9 *(continued)*

SCALED SCORES

Grade Equivalent	WORD STUDY SKILLS	WORD RDG/ READING VOCABULARY	SENTENCE READING	READING COMPRE-HENSION	TOTAL READING	MATHEMATICS PROBLEM SOLVING	MATHEMATICS PROCEDURES	TOTAL MATHEMATICS	LANGUAGE MECHANICS A/B	LANGUAGE EXPRESSION A/B	Grade Equivalent
5.1	653	654–655	647–648	645	648–649	631–632	644–646	637–638	640	641	5.1
5.0	651–652	653	646	643–644	647	629–630	642–643	634–636	638–639	640	5.0
4.9	650	651–652	644–645	641–642	645–646	627–628	639–641	632–633	636–637	638–639	4.9
4.8	649	650	643	640	644	625–626	637–638	630–631	635	637	4.8
4.7	648	648–649	642	-	643	624	636	629	634	636	4.7
4.6	-	646–647	641	639	642	623	634–635	628	-	635	4.6
4.5	647	644–645	640	638	641	-	633	627	-	634	4.5
4.4	646	642–643	639	-	640	622	632	626	633	-	4.4
4.3	-	641	638	637	639	621	630–631	625	-	633	4.3
4.2	645	639–640	637	-	638	620	629	624	-	632	4.2
4.1	644	637–638	636	636	637	619	628	623	632	-	4.1
4.0	-	635–636	635	635	636	-	626–627	622	-	631	4.0

this student ought to be placed in fifth-grade mathematics. The test shows that the student did very well on third-grade content, but the student was not assessed on fifth-grade mathematics. Many factors, of course, besides a single assessment result determine whether the student should receive an accelerated placement.

The meaning of grade-equivalent scores as describing a student's learning status in a subject depends very much on the subject matter. In reading, for example, students' educational growth may be less tied to the curriculum sequence than it is mathematics. In such cases, third-grade students with grade equivalents of 5.7 may well be reading much like a fifth grader, and a fifth grader with a grade equivalent of 3.7 may well be reading like a third grader.

Grade Equivalents and Mastery   Sometimes teachers, parents, and school administrators misinterpret grade equivalents as meaning mastery of a particular portion of a curricular area. For example, a parent may erroneously think that a student's grade equivalent of 3.5 in mathematics means the student has mastered 5/10ths of the local school's third-grade mathematics curriculum. The most that can be said, however, is that this student's test score equals the average score of the norm group when it was in the 5th month of third grade. This result is unlikely to mean mastery of third-grade mathematics because the test does not systematically sample the entire domain of third-grade mathematics in the student's local curriculum.

Grade Equivalents and What Was Covered in the Class   The more closely the test items match the material you emphasized in the classroom before the test was administered, the more likely your students are to score well above grade level on these nationally standardized tests. You may teach the content of some test items after the testing date. As a result, your students may perform poorly when tested but will learn the material before the end of the school year. Answering three or four items wrong will significantly lower a student's grade-equivalent score. If your teaching sequence and the testing sequence are not aligned, inferring mastery is problematic. This points out the norm-referenced character of grade-equivalent scores and illustrates that criterion-referenced interpretations are difficult to make from them.

Grade Equivalents from Different Tests Cannot Be Interchanged   Grade-equivalent (and other norm-referenced) scores depend on the particular items placed on the test and the particular norm group used. You would be misinterpreting grade equivalents, for example, if you said, "A grade equivalent of 3.7 on the *ABC Reading Assessment* means the same thing as a grade equivalent of 3.7 on the *DEF Reading Assessment*." The results from two different publishers' assessments are simply not comparable except under special conditions (Holland & Dorans, 2006).

Grade Equivalents for Different Subjects Cannot Be Compared   Another misinterpretation is to compare a student's mathematics grade equivalent with the student's reading grade equivalent, which is invalid. Consider the following hypothetical assessment results for three third-grade students.

Example

		Survey Subtest	
		Reading	**Mathematics**
Ian	*GE*	4.9	4.9
	PR	78	90
Santos	*GE*	4.9	4.3
	PR	78	78
Priya	*GE*	4.9	4.6
	PR	78	84

Notice that Ian has two identical grade equivalents, but their corresponding percentile ranks are *different*. Santos has two different grade equivalents but has *identical* percentile ranks. Finally, Priya has one grade equivalent higher than another, yet her higher grade equivalent has a lower percentile rank than her *lower* grade equivalent.

The reason for the phenomena is that scores for one subject area are more diverse than those of another, resulting in different patterns of interpolation when grade equivalents are prepared. Expanded standard scores cannot be used to compare a student's performance in different areas, either.

What should you use to describe a student's relative strengths and weaknesses in different subject areas? *Use percentile ranks to compare a student's scores from different subjects* if all students in the norm group took the same tests in all subjects. Thus, in the preceding illustration, Ian is somewhat better in mathematics and in reading, Santos is about the same in both subjects, and Priya is slightly better in mathematics than in reading. Because these are norm-referenced interpretations, "better" implies "compared with other persons."

"Normal" Growth   Sometimes teachers and school administrators use grade equivalents to answer questions of what educational growth they should expect of a student. This is not a good practice, and the results of doing it are unsatisfactory. One view of **normal growth** is the following: "A student ought to exhibit a growth of 1.0 grade-equivalent unit from one grade to the next." Under this view, a student taking the test in second grade and scoring 1.3, for example, would need to score 2.3 in third grade, 4.3 in fifth, and so on to show "normal" or expected growth.

This *grade-equivalent view of normal growth* cannot be supported at all percentile ranks. Figure 17.10 shows examples of what will happen to three hypothetical students on the mathematics subtests of two published tests if this view were adopted.

The students have these characteristics: Student A is one year behind in terms of grade

equivalents, Student B is at grade level, and Student C is one year ahead. Each year, the students' grade equivalents show a one-year "growth" over the preceding year. But look at the percentile ranks corresponding to their scores: Student A, who starts out one year behind, has to *exceed more persons* in the norm group to maintain a one-year-behind grade equivalent. Being one year behind in second grade means being at the 12th or 25th percentile. However, one year behind in Grade 8 means being around the 39th or 43rd percentile. One has to move from the bottom of the group toward the middle. An opposite phenomenon occurs for Student C, who begins one grade ahead at around the 86th or 93rd percentile. In this case, the student can fall behind more and more students and still be "one year ahead." Students who are at grade level (Student B) have raw scores equivalent to the average. By definition, the average at a grade is assigned one year's growth from the preceding year. Thus, only students who are exactly at the average each year will maintain their approximate percentile rank from year to year.

An alternate norm-referenced definition is the *percentile view of normal growth*: A student shows normal growth if that student maintains the same position (i.e., percentile rank) in the norm from

FIGURE 17.10   Examples of changes in the percentile ranks for three hypothetical students as each "gains" one year in grade-equivalent units from second through eighth grade.

Grade placement at the time of testing	Stanford Achievement Tests, Total Mathematics						Iowa Tests of Basic Skills, Total Mathematics					
	Student A: "Below grade level"		Student B: "On grade level"		Student C: "Above grade level"		Student A: "Below grade level"		Student B: "On grade level"		Student C: "Above grade level"	
	GE	PR	GE	PR	GE	PR	GE	PR	GE	PR	GE	PR
2.3	1.3	25	2.3	61	3.3	86	1.3	12	2.3	60	3.3	93
3.3	2.3	25	3.3	59	4.3	77	2.3	18	3.3	55	4.3	86
4.3	3.3	32	4.3	54	5.3	68	3.3	24	4.3	55	5.3	80
5.3	4.3	36	5.3	52	6.3	69	4.3	29	5.3	54	6.3	74
6.3	5.3	37	6.3	56	7.3	68	5.3	34	6.3	53	7.3	69
7.3	6.3	41	7.3	54	8.3	62	6.3	36	7.3	52	8.3	65
8.3	7.3	43	8.3	52	9.3	59	7.3	39	8.3	51	9.3	63

FIGURE 17.11   Examples of changes in the grade-equivalent score for four hypothetical students as each student's percentile rank remains the same from second through eighth grade.

| Grade placement at the time of testing | Stanford Achievement Tests, Total Mathematics | | | | Iowa Tests of Basic Skills, Total Mathematics | | | |
| | Student A: "Below grade level" (PR = 16 each year) | | Student B: "Above grade level" (PR = 84 each year) | | Student C: "Below grade level" (PR = 16 each year) | | Student D: "Above grade level" (PR = 4 each year) | |
	GE	"Grades behind"	GE	"Grades ahead"	GE	"Grades behind"	GE	"Grades ahead"
3.3	2.0	1.3	5.1	1.8	2.2	1.1	4.2	0.9
4.3	2.6	1.7	6.8	2.5	3.0	1.3	5.5	1.2
5.3	3.1	2.2	8.6	3.3	3.6	1.7	6.9	1.6
6.3	3.6	2.7	10.2	3.9	4.3	2.0	8.6	2.3
7.3	4.6	2.7	above 12.9		4.9	2.4	10.1	2.8
8.3	5.3	3.0	above 12.9		5.5	2.8	12.4	4.1

year to year. Figure 17.11 shows examples of what happens to a student's grade-equivalent score if that student's *percentile rank stays the same each year*.

Lower-scoring students (such as Students A and C)—even though they do not change their position in the norm group—have grade equivalents indicating they are further and further behind. An opposite trend occurs for initially high-scoring students. The exact magnitude of this falling-behind phenomenon will vary from one publisher's test to another's and depends on the student's percentile rank. The grade-equivalent scales of some tests are created to minimize the falling-behind effect. Students close to the 50th percentile will exhibit less of the falling-behind effect than will those further from the center of the distribution. The reasons for this effect are twofold: (1) the line connecting the medians of the distributions at each grade level tends to flatten out at higher grades rather than being a diagonal line (that is, the median gain decreases as grade increases), and (2) scores at upper grades become more spread out, spanning a larger range than scores at lower grades.

Unequal Units   The grade-equivalent score scale does not have a one-to-one correspondence with the number of questions a student answers correctly on a test. This means, for example, that students in the middle of the distribution who get one more item correct are likely to raise their grade-equivalent scores by only one tenth (i.e., one "month"). For students in the upper part of the distribution, however, one additional correct item may result in an increment of several tenths (several "months" of growth). As a result of these unequal units, calculating averages using grade equivalents becomes problematic.

Grade Mean Equivalents   Because it is problematic to average grade-equivalent scores, some publishers (e.g., CTB/McGraw-Hill) have tried other ways to give schools information on how well their students performed on the average. One technique is to report the **grade mean equivalent** that tells the grade placement of a group's average extended scale score. Instead of averaging grade-equivalent scores directly, you first average the extended scale scores. Second, you look up the grade-equivalent that corresponds to this average extended scale score (CTB/McGraw-Hill, 2008). This averaging of extended scores is also problematic, however. There is evidence to suggest that extended score scales do not have equal units of measurement either, even though some test developers claim they do (Hoover, 1984a, 1984b). If this is the case, then their averages and the grade mean equivalents on which they are based would be just as problematic as averaging grade equivalents.

Recommendations

In light of the problems with grade equivalents, you may wonder why they are used at all. Indeed, many assessment specialists believe they should be eliminated. Yet such scores are popular with teachers and administrators who are generally unaware of the complex criticisms. Teachers and school administrators have a real need for at least some crude measure of educational development or growth that they can relate to years of schooling. Despite the technical difficulties in doing so, grade equivalents seem intuitively to be a "natural metric." Some assessment specialists recommend extended standard scores as measures of growth, but they possess many of the same interpretive problems as grade equivalents, and because they cannot be easily referenced to grade levels, their interpretation can be confusing.

You should use grade-equivalent scores as coarse indicators of educational development or growth but do so only when you report them with their corresponding percentile ranks. Grade equivalents are norm-referenced growth indicators. If you want information about the content of a student's learning, you need to look carefully at the kinds of performances the student can do. To do that, you need to review for each student the kinds of test items the student answered correctly. When you do this, of course, you are making criterion-referenced interpretations.

Summary of Grade Equivalents

As a summary of grade-equivalent scores, consider the situation in which a school administered a published, norm-referenced achievement test to third graders in May. Further, assume that the school's teachers have judged the assessment to match the curriculum validly and to be an appropriate way to assess the students. Finally, assume that the publisher's norms are appropriate. Then, even with all these nice assumptions, each of the following statements—except the first—are *false*:

1. Pat's Reading subtest grade-equivalent score is 3.8, which suggests that she is an average third-grade reader.

2. Ramon's Arithmetic subtest grade equivalent is 4.6, which means that he knows arithmetic

as well as the typical fourth grader who is at the end of the 6th month of school.

3. Melba's Arithmetic subtest grade equivalent is 6.7, which suggests that next year she ought to take arithmetic with the sixth graders.

4. Debbie's Reading subtest grade equivalent is 2.3, which means she has mastered three tenths of the second-grade reading skills.

5. John's grade-equivalent profile is Vocabulary = 6.2, Reading = 7.1, Language = 7.1, Work-Study Skills = 7.2, Arithmetic = 6.7. These results mean that his weak areas are vocabulary and arithmetic.

6. Two of Sally's grade equivalents are Language = 4.5 and Arithmetic = 4.5. Because her language and arithmetic grade equivalents are the same, we conclude that her language and arithmetic ability are about equal.

7. Half of this school's second graders have grade equivalents below grade level, which means that instructional quality is generally poor.

8. This year one teacher was assigned all of the students whose assessment scores were in the bottom three stanines. The average of her class's grade equivalents this May was further below grade level than the class's average last year, which means that her instruction has been ineffective for the class as a whole.

GENERAL GUIDELINES FOR SCORE INTERPRETATION

Figure 17.12 summarizes the various norm-referenced scores discussed in this chapter. Although each type of score describes the student's location in a norm group, each does so differently. The easiest type of score to explain to parents and students is a percentile rank. Various types of linear standard scores require an understanding of the mean and standard deviation for their meaning to become clear. Usually, you will need to interpret normalized standard scores in conjunction with percentile ranks. From test to test, normalized standard scores will have the same percentage of cases associated with them. Consequently, their meaning remains fairly constant as long as a normal distribution can be assumed. Grade equivalents and extended standard scores provide scores along an educational growth continuum, but because of their inherent technical complexities, teachers and school

FIGURE 17.12   **How to interpret different types of norm-referenced scores.**

Type of score	Interpretation	Score	Examples of interpretations
Percentile rank linear standard score (z-score)	Percentage of scores in a distribution below this point. Number of standard deviation units a score is above (or below) the mean of a given distribution.	$PR = 60$ $z = +1.5$ $z = -1.2$	"60% of the raw scores are lower than this score." "This raw score is located 1.5 standard deviations *above* the mean." "This raw score is located 1.2 standard deviations *below* the mean."
Linear standard score (SS-score or 50 ± 10 system)	Location of score in a distribution having a mean of 50 and a standard deviation of 10. (Note: For other systems, substitute in these statements that system's mean and standard deviation.)	$SS = 65$ $SS = 38$	"This raw score is located 1.5 standard deviations *above* the mean in a distribution whose mean is 50 and whose standard deviation is 10." "This raw score is located 1.2 standard deviations *below* the mean in a distribution whose mean is 50 and whose standard deviation is 10."
Stanine	Location of a score in a specific segment of a normal distribution of scores.	Stanine = 5 Stanine = 9	"This raw score is located in the middle 20% of a normal distribution of scores." "This raw score is located in the top 4% of a normal distribution of scores."
Normalized standard score (T-score or normalized 50 ± 10 system)	Location of score in a normal distribution having a mean of 50 and a standard deviation of 10. (Note: For other systems, substitute in these statements that system's mean and standard deviation [e.g., *DIQs* have a mean of 100 and a standard deviation of 16: This is a 100 ± 16 system].)	$T = 65$ $T = 38$	"This raw score is located 1.5 standard deviations above the mean in a normal distribution whose mean is 50 and whose standard deviation is 10. This score has a percentile rank of 84." "This raw score is located 1.2 standard deviations below the mean in a normal distribution whose mean is 50 and whose standard deviation is 10. This score has a percentile rank of 12."
Extended standard score	Location of a score on an arbitrary scale of numbers that is anchored to some reference group.		(No interpretation is offered here because the systems are so arbitrary and unalike.)
Grade-equivalent score	The grade placement at which the raw score is average.	$GE = 4.5$	"This raw score is the obtained or estimated average for all pupils whose grade placement is at the 5th month of the fourth grade."

Source: Adapted from *Measuring Student Achievement and Aptitude* (2nd ed., p. 99), by C. M. Lindvall and A. J. Nitko, 1975, New York: Harcourt Brace Jovanovich. Reproduced by permission of the authors.

administrators may misinterpret them. Limit using grade equivalents to gross estimates of yearly student growth. Use them only when you accompany them with percentile ranks. Use percentile ranks to compare an individual student's performance in different curriculum areas.

Teachers and school administrators should consider the following points when interpreting student scores on norm-referenced standardized tests:

1. *Look for unexpected patterns of scores.* An assessment should confirm what a teacher knows from daily interactions with a student; unusually high or low scores for a student should be a signal for exploring instructional implications.

2. *Seek an explanation for patterns.* Ask why a student is higher in one subject than another. Check for motivation, special interests, special difficulties, and so on.

3. *Don't expect surprises for every student.* Most students' assessment results should be as you expect from their performance in class. A valid assessment should confirm your observations.

FIGURE 17.13 **Example of an individual performance profile report.**

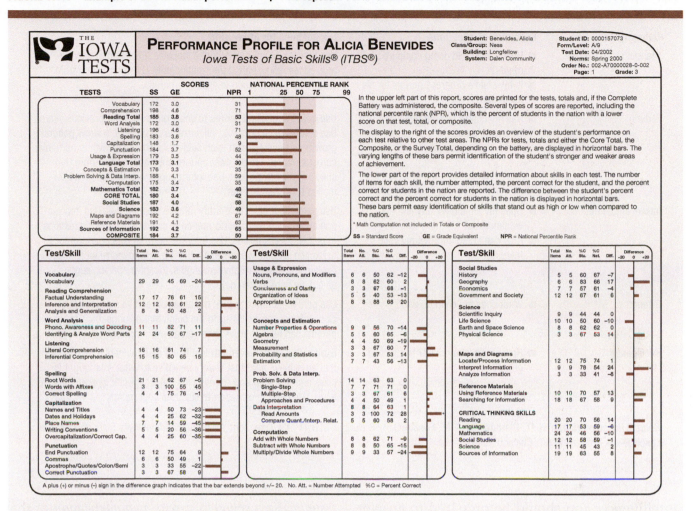

4. *Small differences in subtest scores should be viewed as chance fluctuations.* Use the standard error of measurement (Chapter 4) to help decide whether differences are large enough to have instructional significance.

5. *Use information from various assessments and observation to explain performance on other assessments.* Students low in reading comprehension may perform poorly on the social studies subtest, for example.

You may wish to try your hand at implementing these general guidelines by reviewing the case presented in Figure 17.13. Your interpretation of Alicia Benevides's report may be different from that of the computer.

Types of Questions Parents Ask and Suggested Ways of Answering Them

A teacher has the most direct contact with parents regarding norm-referenced score reports. Parents call the teacher first if they have questions about students' standardized test results. You must be prepared, therefore, to explain students' test results to their parents. Studying the concepts and principles in this chapter is a prerequisite for effectively communicating to parents.

Figure 17.14 contains examples of many of the questions parents ask when they receive standardized test results from a school. The questions are organized into five categories: standing, growth, improvement needed, strengths, and

FIGURE 17.14   How to answer parents' questions about standardized test results.

Category	Examples of questions	Suggestions for answering
Standing	■ How is my child doing compared to others? ■ Is my child's progress normal for his or her grade?	Use percentile ranks to describe standing. Explain that a standardized test gives partial information only. Use information from classroom performance to explain progress.
Growth	■ Has my child's growth been as much as it should be?	Use grade-equivalent scores to show progress from previous years. Use composite scores (i.e., all subjects combined) to show general growth; use scores from each subject to explain growth in particular curricular areas. Obtain past performance information from the child's cumulative folder. Use information from classroom performance to explain growth.
Improvement needed	■ Does my child have any learning weaknesses? ■ How can I help improve my child's learning?	Use percentile ranks to identify relative weaknesses. Use information about a student's performance to clusters of similar questions to pinpoint weaknesses. Use information from class performance to explain specific weaknesses. Don't overemphasize weaknesses. Explain a student's relative strengths, too; give specific suggestions as to how parents can help.
Strengths	■ What does my child do well?	Use percentile ranks to pick out areas of relative strengths. Use class information to illustrate the point. Make suggestions for how parents can help improve these areas even more.
Intelligence	■ How smart is my child? Is my child gifted?	Explain that an achievement test is not an intelligence test. Explain that an achievement test is very sensitive to what was taught in class and that high scores may only reflect specific opportunities to learn. Use class information to illustrate your points.

Source: Based on Hoover, H. D., Hieronymus, A. N., Frisbie, D. A., & Dunbar, S. B. (1993). Directions for administration: Iowa Tests of Basic Skills, Levels 9–14, Forms K and L. Chicago: Riverside.

intelligence. You should be prepared to answer questions in these categories. The table contains suggestions for answering each category of questions. Note that we indicate which type of norm-referenced score to use. Although other scores might be used, we believe the ones suggested will be most helpful to your explanation. Notice, too, that we suggest always using a student's classroom performance to complement and explain the student's standardized test results. Because in the majority of cases students' standardized test performance will be quite consistent with their classroom performance, using students' classroom performance to illustrate their standardized test performance will help you reinforce to the parents your assessment of the students.

Parent Misunderstandings

Parents also have misunderstandings about what norm-referenced test scores mean. We have already discussed many of the misconceptions and limitations in this chapter. The following list *summarizes common parent misunderstandings* that you need to be clear about before you can help parents correct them:

1. The grade-equivalent score tells which grade the student should be in.
2. The percentile rank and percent-correct scores mean the same thing.
3. The percentile rank norm group consists of only the students in a particular classroom.
4. "Average" is the standard to beat.
5. Small changes in percentile ranks over time are meaningful.
6. Percent-correct scores below 70 are failing.
7. If you get a perfect score, your percentile rank must be 99 (Hoover et al., 1993b, pp. 103–105).

MyLab Education Self-Check 17.3

MyLab Education Application Exercise 17.3:
Interpreting Grade-Equivalents and Percentile Ranks

CONCLUSION

We hope this chapter has given you enough detail about the most common norm-referenced scores that you can use them thoughtfully in making decisions about your students, class, and school. We hope, too, that this chapter has given you enough information about norm-referenced scores to communicate their meaning to students, parents, school board members, and other interested community members. A central point is that no matter which norm-referenced score you are using, the score derives its meaning from comparisons to other test-takers in a norm group, so it is important to know the nature of the norm group and how it is relevant to your purpose.

The next chapter presents information about finding and evaluating published tests. The next chapter also describes briefly how standardized tests are developed.

EXERCISES

1. A student takes a test during the middle of the school year. By mistake, the student's teacher uses the norms tables published for the end of school year to look up the student's percentile rank. What effect does this error have on the percentile ranks the teacher reports? What would be the effect in this case if the teacher used the norms tables from the beginning of the year?

2. Read each of these statements and decide to which norm-referenced score(s) each mainly refers. Justify your choice(s) to your classmates.
   a. In this skewed distribution, John's score places him one standard deviation below the mean.
   b. Roberto's test score is the same as the average score of students tested in the 4th month of fifth grade.
   c. Because Bill's score increased this year, I know that his general educational development has increased, even though his position in the norm group remained the same.
   d. Nancy's score is 5 because it is located in the middle 20% of a normal distribution.

3. Judge each of the following statements true or false. Explain the basis for your judgment in each case.
   a. A person's percentile rank is 45, which means that the person's raw score was the same as 45% of the group assessed.
   b. Kaiko's arithmetic assessment score is 40. The class's mean score is 45, and its standard deviation is 10. Therefore, Kaiko is located one standard deviation below the mean.

FIGURE 17.15 Use with Exercise 17.4.

Percentile rank	Stanine	z_n	DIQ (SD = 15)	T-score
99.9	9	+3.00		
98				
84				
50				
16				
2				
0.1				

   c. The norms tables show that the distribution of deviation IQ scores on a school ability test is approximately normal in form. For the people in the norm groups, the intellectual ability that naturally underlies the scores is normally distributed.

4. Figure 17.15 shows several types of normalized scores. Use the relationships between the scores to complete the table and thereby show how various scores are related to one another. The first two are completed for you. You may use Figure 17.6 for assistance.

5. Figure 17.16 shows part of a norms table that might appear in a manual of a standardized achievement test. The table shows selected raw scores, grade-equivalent scores, and percentile ranks for the publisher's standardization sample (i.e., norm group). Assume that (a) the local school system has judged the test's content to be a good match to its curriculum, (b) the norm data were collected during the 7th month of the fourth grade, (c) the norms are appropriate for use with the local school system, (d) the publisher has computed grade equivalents and percentile ranks in the usual way and with no errors, and (e) the school tested the students in April.

   Use the table and your knowledge of norm-referenced frameworks to judge each of the following statements as true or false. Explain and justify your position in each case.
   a. James is a fourth-grade student with a grade-equivalent profile of $V = 6.2$, $R = 5.6$, $L = 5.6$, $W = 5.6$, $A = 6.2$. Decide whether each of the following conclusions is true or false, and explain the basis for your judgment.
      i. James should be in fifth grade.
      ii. James is strongest in vocabulary and arithmetic.
      iii. James's scores are above average for his grade.

FIGURE 17.16   Use with Exercise 17.5.

Raw score	Vocabulary (*V*) GE	Vocabulary (*V*) PR	Reading (*R*) GE	Reading (*R*) PR	Language (*L*) GE	Language (*L*) PR	Work-study (*W*) GE	Work-study (*W*) PR	Arithmetic (*A*) GE	Arithmetic (*A*) PR
5	1.8	1	1.6	1	1.9	1	2.3	1	2.5	1
20	4.1	34	3.3	17	4.4	41	5.6	74	5.5	65
30	5.1	61	4.2	36	5.6	75	7.0	96	6.2	74
40	6.2	74	4.8	52	6.4	86	7.6	99	6.9	97
50	7.0	96	5.6	74	7.9	99	8.0	99	7.7	99
70			8.1	99						

b. Fourth-grader Jasmine's raw score on reading is 50, and on language it is 30. Decide whether each of the following conclusions is true or false, and explain your decision.

   i. Jasmine is more able in reading because her raw score in reading is higher.

   ii. Because Jasmine's grade-equivalent scores are equal, she is equally able in reading and vocabulary (relative to the norm group).

   iii. Jasmine is more able in language than reading (relative to the norm group) because her percentile rank in language is higher.

Finding and Evaluating Published Assessments

KEY CONCEPTS

1. You can search printed materials, online resources, and personal contacts to locate information about published assessments. After locating published tests, obtain and read evaluations or reviews of these tests. Internet searches and test publishers' websites will help you locate computerized testing materials. There are also print and online resources for locating unpublished test materials, which can be useful in research and evaluation projects. Some publishers restrict the sale of test materials. To evaluate and select a test or assessment, clarify your purpose, obtain and review assessment materials, and try them out in a pilot study.

IMPORTANT TERMS

ETS Test Collection

external assessment procedure

Mental Measurements Yearbooks (MMYs)

Pruebas Publicadas en Español

specimen set

Standards for Educational and Psychological Testing

technical manual

Test Critiques

Tests in Print

LOCATING A PUBLISHED TEST

Suppose you want to locate a test that you can use to diagnose students' reading problems, assess students' self-concept, or assess some other category of students' characteristics. How do you locate possible tests for such purposes if you do not even know the name(s) of the particular test(s)? You can begin your search in one of three ways: (a) search printed materials, (b) search online resources, or (c) make personal contacts with persons who may know what you are looking for. Figure 18.1 is an overview of the available sources for locating a test. We describe each of these resources in this section.

Locating Published Tests from Print Sources

Four print resources are available. Three of these resources are likely to be in your library: *Tests in*

Print, *Tests*, and textbooks on testing and measurement. You are not likely to find the fourth, test publishers' catalogs, in a library.

Tests in Print (TIP) IX   The ***Tests in Print*** (9th ed.; Anderson, Schlueter, Carlson, & Geisinger, 2016) is a test bibliography that contains information on more than 4,000 commercially available instruments. You can use this resource to identify appropriate tests, locate reviews of tests in the *Mental Measurements Yearbook*s (discussed later), and find publishers' addresses. To appear as an entry in *Tests in Print*, a test must be currently in print and must be published in English. Each entry includes the following information: a description of the test and its purpose, information on population and scoring, test editions available and their price, name of the publisher, and location of the test's review in the *Mental Measurements Yearbook* if there is one. See Figure 18.4 for an

FIGURE 18.1 **Where to look to locate an assessment tool.**

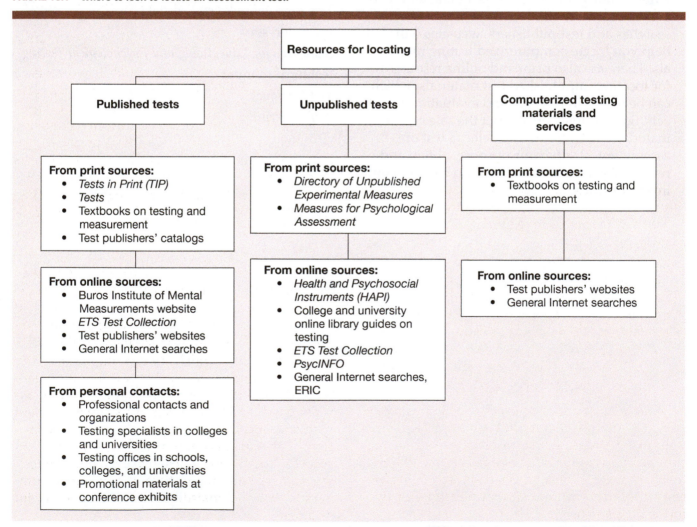

example of a *TIP* entry. The *TIP IX* also provides listing notations on out-of-print tests.

You locate a test by using one of the book's five indexes:

1. If you know or have some idea of the test's name, look in the Index of Titles. The index lists all of the tests in *TIP IX* plus all those that are out of print. Or, since tests are listed alphabetically by name, you can simply page through the book.

2. If you do not know the test name, but know the category or type of test, look in the Classified Subject Index. All tests in the book are grouped into categories (e.g., Social Studies, Speech & Hearing, etc.), with the individual tests listed alphabetically under the category.

3. If you know the name of the test author or person who has reviewed the test in one of the *Mental Measurements Yearbook*s, look in the Index of Names.

4. If you know the type of score a test may yield, look in the Score Index. For example, you may recall from your reading that a test contained an "aggression/hostility" score or an "enjoyment of mathematics" score, but do not know the names of the respective tests. The Score Index lists all such scores alphabetically for the tests included in *TIP IX*. The entries in this index are very specific to the tests that provide the scores. This means that your definition of the score may differ from a test publisher's or that different publishers may score the same student trait under different names. Thus, check all alternative or related score names before concluding that a test is not included in *TIP IX*.

5. If you know the acronym for a test but not its complete name, look in the Index of Acronyms. You may want to use this index, for example, if you recall that there is a test called the *DAT* that was used in counseling and want to locate it. The Index of Acronyms lists two *DATs*: *Dental Admissions Test* and *Differential Aptitude Tests*. Because you want the counseling test, it is likely the latter rather than the former.

Pruebas Publicadas en Español, a Spanish version of *Tests in Print*, has just been published. This volume includes descriptions of tests that are commercially available in Spanish. Some of these tests are written only in Spanish, and some are tests published in English that have one or two forms in Spanish.

Tests: A Comprehensive Reference for Assessments in Psychology, Education, and Business (6th ed.)   This reference (Maddox, 2008) lists and describes approximately 2,000 tests, but gives no evaluations of them. (The test evaluations are given in *Test Critiques*, a companion volume, described later.) *Tests* is divided into three primary groups—psychology, education, and business—and 90 subcategories. Each listing describes the test and its purpose, for whom it is intended, scoring procedures, costs, and publisher.

The organization of the indexes makes locating tests easy. *Tests* has several indexes: title, publisher, computer-scoring, hearing impaired, visually impaired, physically impaired, out of print, tests found in the fifth but not in the sixth edition, and foreign language availability. Publishers' websites are also listed.

Textbooks on Testing and Measurement   A number of textbooks list, describe, and (sometimes) review selected tests. If you are looking for a test in a specific area, looking in the index of a textbook in the area may be a useful way to see which tests are frequently used. (Appendix H in this book lists a selection of published tests in several areas.) A textbook, however, is not a comprehensive source for information about tests because (a) tests are often selected for inclusion primarily for their merits in illustrating an author's point, (b) space permits only a few tests being mentioned, (c) often only the most popular or easily available tests are mentioned or illustrated, and (d) no single author is aware of all available tests.

Test Publishers' Catalogs   An important way to get information about a test is directly from the test publisher. (See Appendix I for a partial list of publishers and their websites.) Most test publishers have catalogs that describe the tests they publish in detail. A publisher's catalog is especially helpful for finding out about current editions of tests along with information about scoring services, costs, and how to obtain specimen sets, test manuals, and technical reports. Current information of this sort is seldom found in other print sources. Your school's testing office and the testing and measurement office of a college or university usually maintain collections of recent catalogs.

Locating Published Tests Online

Buros Test Locator The home page of the Buros Institute of Mental Measurements (buros. org) may be navigated to locate its database of published tests. This site lists more than 4,000 commercially available tests.

ETS Test Collection The *ETS Test Collection* is a database of approximately 20,000 tests and other assessment instruments, both published and unpublished. Some of the instruments listed in the database are out of print, some are available from publishers, some are available from the test authors, and some can be purchased and downloaded from *ETS*. Some of the tests are even from outside the United States. You may search for a test type, an author, or a title. Click the "Find a Test" tab from the Test Collection home page for further assistance in searching. You can access the *ETS Test Collection* database directly at ets.org/test_link.

Test Publishers' Websites As we discussed earlier, an important way to get information about a test is directly from the test publisher. (See Appendix I for a partial list of publishers and their websites.) Most test publishers have websites that describe the tests they publish in detail. A publisher's website is especially helpful for finding out about current editions of tests along with information about scoring services, costs, and how to obtain specimen sets, test manuals, and technical reports. Current information of this sort is seldom found in other print sources. Remember, however, that publishers' websites are marketing tools, not objective sources of test information.

General Internet Searches If you are unable to locate a test through one of these online sources, you could try searching the Internet with the test title, author's name, or subject area. Including "test" or "assessment" with the subject-area key word helps to narrow the search. Usually, searching through eric.ed.gov will yield more relevant hits for educational tests than a general search, say on Google. You may also want to try searching on *PsycINFO* in your library.

Locating Published Tests Through Personal Contacts

Professional Contacts and Organizations

Figure 18.2 lists organizations that may help you locate published tests. Larger testing companies

FIGURE 18.2 **Examples of organizations that provide information on educational assessment.**

Professional associations prepare periodicals and other publications related to educational assessment, work toward improved assessment usage, and may be contacted to identify members who are experts in certain areas of educational assessment.
1. American Educational Research Association (Washington, DC) [aera.net]
2. Association for Assessment and Research in Counseling (Arlington,VA) [aac.ncat.edu]
3. International Reading Association (IRA) (Newark, DE) [reading.org]
4. National Association of Test Directors (NATD) [natd.org]
5. National Council on Measurement in Education (NCME) (Washington, DC) [ncme.org]

Educational Research Information Center (ERIC). Online services are provided.
1. Search ERIC [eric.ed.gov]

Research centers and regional laboratories invest in research on technical or policy issues in educational assessment. They have catalogs of these publications and sometimes answer inquiries about specific assessment issues.
1. Buros Institute of Mental Measurements (University of Nebraska) [buros.org]
2. Center for the Study of Testing, Evaluation, and Educational Policy (Boston College) [bc.edu/research/csteep]
3. Center for Research on Evaluations, Standards, and Student Testing (CRESST) (UCLA) [cse.ucla.edu]
4. National Center on Educational Outcomes (University of Minnesota) [cehd.umn.edu/nceo/]
5. West Ed [wested.org]
6. Mid-continent Research for Education and Learning (Mcrel) (Aurora, CO) [mcrel.org]

Nonprofit testing corporations offer a wide range of assessment services, conduct assessment research, and disseminate assessment information.
1. American College Testing Program (ACT) (Iowa City, IA) [act.org]
2. Educational Testing Service (ETS) (Princeton, NJ) [ets.org]

Nonprofit advocacy and public interest groups research matters of legality, individual rights, and public policy related to assessment.
1. National Center for Fair and Open Testing (Fair Test) (Cambridge, MA) [fairtest.org]

and agencies usually have an information and/ or advisory office to answer questions that you can reach via toll-free telephone numbers. Professional organizations, such as the National Council on Measurement in Education, can sometimes help by referring you to a member in your local area who can be of assistance. Some professional associations whose focus is not on assessment per se may have special interest

FIGURE 18.3 **Where to locate published reviews of tests.**

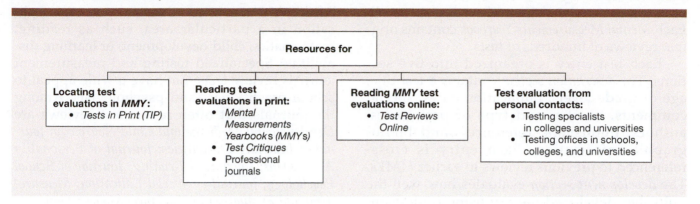

groups that are interested in specific issues such as performance, critical thinking, or classroom assessment. In some areas, federally funded research and development centers and regional laboratories have technical assistance offices that can help with testing problems. In some states, county-based school agencies, state-related school agencies, or technical assistance centers are specially organized to offer assistance in reviewing and using tests.

Testing Specialists in Colleges and Universities Testing and measurement professors at colleges and universities usually work in departments of educational research, educational psychology, measurement and statistics, counseling and guidance, or psychology. Ask the department chairperson for recommendations of persons to call.

Testing Offices in Schools, Colleges, and Universities The director of your school's testing office or the school's psychologist is frequently a useful resource. Many larger colleges and universities have testing offices designed to help their faculties and students with testing problems, and such offices are usually available to answer questions from the public as well.

Promotional Exhibits at Conferences If you attend a professional conference you may go to the exhibit area. The exhibits will have books and instructional materials, and may also have exhibits by test publishers. The exhibitor may have a test you are seeking or may put you in contact with a sales representative in your area who has the information you seek.

LOCATING EVALUATIONS OF PUBLISHED TESTS

In the preceding section we discussed how to find a test. But finding a test is only one part of the information you need to evaluate a published test. You will also need to locate published reviews of the test, preferably by reviewers who are competent assessment specialists and who are not associated with the test publisher. In this section, we discuss three places to look for reviews of the test you have located: (a) printed materials, (b) online resources, or (c) direct contacts with persons who may know about the test. Figure 18.3 gives an overview of the resources that are available for locating test reviews.

Locating Evaluations of Published Tests from Print Sources

Three print resources are likely to be in your academic library: *Mental Measurements Yearbooks*, *Test Critiques*, and professional journals.

Mental Measurements Yearbooks (MMYs) Among the most useful resources for locating information on tests are the publications of the Buros Institute of Mental Measurements (located at the University of Nebraska). The late Oscar K. Buros founded the institute and began a series of test bibliographies and *Mental Measurements Yearbooks* (**MMYs**). The *Mental Measurements Yearbooks* (Buros, 1938 through present) are a series of volumes that critically evaluate many of the currently available published tests in English. Each volume supplements rather than replaces the earlier editions, so it is occasionally necessary to consult earlier volumes to obtain complete coverage of a test. One or more experts review each test especially for the *MMY*s, and each volume gives excerpted journal reviews as well. Each *Mental Measurements Yearbook* contains original reviews of hundreds of tests.

Each test entry is organized into five sections. The *description section* contains a test title, age or grade levels, publication dates, special comments, number and type of part scores, authors, publishers, references, and bibliographic information. Each entry is cross-referenced to previous reviews in earlier *MMY*s. The *development section* evaluates how well the publisher developed the test using professionally accepted standards, including the use of empirical data in the development process (recall our discussion of empirically developed tests in Chapter 17). The *technical section* evaluates the test's standardization procedure, reliability, and validity. The *commentary section* contains the reviewer's overall evaluation of the test. The *summary section* is a concise wrap-up of the reviewer's opinion of the test. Names and addresses of hundreds of test publishers are listed in each *MMY*. A disadvantage of the printed *MMY*s is that because of the publication lag, editions of tests reviewed may not correspond to publishers' newest editions.

To locate a test evaluation, you need to know the *MMY* volume in which the test appears. If your test title appears in *Tests in Print IX*, that publication will tell you the review's *MMY* volume and entry number. You may also use the *Test Reviews Online* described in the last section by accessing it on the Internet through the Buros Institute home page. Figure 18.4 shows how a page in the *MMY* is laid out. This example will give you a better sense of what to expect from this resource. For online guides to using the MMY, see buros.org.

Test Critiques (Volumes I–XI)   *Test Critiques* (Keyser & Sweetland, 2005) is a series of volumes that reviews the most frequently used tests in business, education, and psychology. A testing specialist reviews each test. Entries cover an introduction to the test, practical uses and applications, technical aspects, and an overall evaluation of the test. You may use *Tests: A Comprehensive Reference for Assessments in Psychology, Education, and Business,* described earlier, to locate the *Test Critiques* volume in which the test is found.

Professional Journals   Professional journals in a field often review tests that have potential application in a particular area, such as reading, mathematics, child development, or learning disabilities. Specialized testing and measurement journals review tests that have a wide appeal to school practitioners and psychologists. Among the journals that often report test reviews are *Developmental Medicine and Child Neurology; Journal of Learning Disabilities; Journal of Personality Assessment; Journal of Reading; Journal of School Psychology; Journal of Special Education; Measurement and Evaluation in Guidance; Modern Language Journal; Psychological Reports; Psychology in the Schools;* and *Reading Teacher.*

Bibliographic information about these and other journals (including those that review testing books) appears at the back of some *Mental Measurements Yearbook*s. Journal references are indexed in such sources as *PsycINFO* and *Research in Education* (ERIC).

Locating Evaluations of Published Tests Online

One source for obtaining test reviews online is *Test Reviews Online* from the Buros Center for Testing (buros.org). Test reviews from *MMY*s nine through 20 are available. More than 2,000 test reviews are available, and they can be seen and downloaded for a fee. Your university library may have a subscription to *MMY* that allows its members to use this resource.

Locating Evaluations of Published Tests Through Personal Contacts

Testing Specialists in Colleges and Universities   Just as your professional contacts may help you locate a test, these same people may help you evaluate a test. Testing and measurement professors at colleges and universities usually work in departments of educational research, educational psychology, measurement and statistics, counseling and guidance, or psychology. Call the department chairperson for recommendations of persons to call. A testing specialist may have personal experience with a particular test and be willing to share that experience with you.

Testing Offices in Schools, Colleges, and Universities   The director of your school testing

FIGURE 18.4 Layout of a *Mental Measurements Yearbook* review entry for a hypothetical test.

Entry Number: The number cited in all indexes when referring to this test.

Title: Test titles are printed in boldface type; secondary or series titles are set off from main titles by colon.

Population: A description of the groups for which the test is intended.

Administration: Individual or group administration is indicated.

Distribution: This is noted only for tests that are put on a special market by the publisher.

Special Editions: Various types of special editions are listed here.

Author: All test authors' names are reported, exactly as printed on the test materials.

Cross References: For tests that have been previously listed in a Buros publication, cross references to the reviews, excerpts, and references will be noted here. "9:1410," for example, refers to test 1410 in the *Ninth Mental Measurements Yearbook*; "T4:3010" refers to test 3010 in *Tests in Print IV*.

[420]
The Hypothetical Test: Reading.
Purpose: Designed to "measure achievement in reading."
Population: Grades 9–12.
Publication Dates: 1989–1994.
Acronym: HYPE.
Scores, 3: Vocabulary, Comprehension, and Total.
Administration: Individual or group.
Forms, 3: Survey, Abbreviated, Complete Battery.
Restricted Distribution: Distribution of Survey Form restricted to school principals.
Price Data, 1995: $70 per complete kit including 100 tests, scoring key, and manual ('94, 120 pages); $9 per scoring key; $32 per manual.
Special Editions: Braille edition available.
Time: 50 (60) minutes.
Comments: May be self-scored.
Author: Jane J. Doe.
Publisher: Hypothetical Tests, Inc.
Cross References: See T4:3010 (2 references); for reviews by John Roe and Robert Smith of an earlier edition, see 9:1410 (6 references).

Review of the Hypothetical Test: Reading by JOHN J. SMITH, Associate Professor of Instruction and Learning, State University, Jonestown, Any State:

The actual text of the test review would be here. Space does not permit including a review.

Purpose: A brief, clear statement describing the purpose of the test; often these are quotations from the test manual.

Publication Date: The inclusive range of publication dates.

Acronym: Acronym by which the test may be commonly known.

Scores: The number and names of explicit scores are presented.

Forms: All available forms, parts, and levels are listed.

Price Data: Price information is reported for test packages, answer sheets, accessories, and specimen sets.

Time: This is the amount of time to take, and administer, the test. The first number is the actual working time examinees are allowed, and the second (parenthesized) number is the total time needed to administer the test.

Comments: Special notations and comments.

Publisher: The publisher's full address can be found in the Publishers Directory and Index.

Source: Entry information is from "*Mental Measurements Yearbook* and *Tests in Print: A Guide to the Descriptive Entries*," Lincoln, NE: Buros Center for Testing (www.buros.org). Used with Permission.

Source: Entry information is from *Mental Measurements Yearbook and Tests in Print* and *Tests in Print: A Guide to the Descriptive Entries*. Lincoln, NE: Buros Center for Testing. (www.buros.org) Used with permission.

office or the school psychologist may be a useful resource. Many larger colleges and universities have testing offices designed to help their faculties and students with testing problems. Such offices are usually available to answer questions from the public as well.

LOCATING COMPUTERIZED TESTING MATERIALS

General Internet Searches

You may have some luck searching for computerized testing products using Google or another search engine. Be sure to use "computer testing + education" as the search term; otherwise, you will get lots of false links. Most sites you find will be selling computerized testing products, so you cannot find objective expert evaluations of products at these sites.

Test Publishers' Websites

Test publishers may have several computerized testing products, which will be listed on their websites. Again, these sites are marketing tools, so you will not find objective evaluations of the products at the sites. A list of test publishers and their URLs is given in Appendix I of this book.

LOCATING UNPUBLISHED TEST MATERIALS

Not all test materials are published. Many tests have been used in research and evaluation projects. Some of these are available, if you can find them. We describe some sources for locating these types of tests in this section.

Locating Unpublished Tests from Print Sources

ETS Test Collection   Earlier we discussed the online *ETS Test Collection* as an online database of tests. Many of the tests in this database are unpublished. Look for the term *unpublished* in the description. The *ETS Test Collection* has incorporated the former Tests in Microfiche collection, which contains more than 800 unpublished tests used in education, business, and psychology. These tests are now downloadable from the *ETS Test Collection* database.

Directory of Unpublished Experimental Mental Measures   This directory edited by Goldman and Mitchell (2008) lists unpublished tests and surveys in a variety of educational and psychological areas. The listings are arranged in 24 categories and include tests' availability, purpose, content, format, and related research. Each volume has a cumulative index that lists all the approximately 5,000 tests across the earlier volumes.

Locating Unpublished Tests Online

Health and Psychosocial Instruments (HAPI)
This resource is available online through Ovid Technologies (a vendor of databases) at ovid.com.

It includes instruments from journal articles in health sciences, nursing, psychology, and social sciences.

ETS Test Collection   We discussed earlier this database of approximately 20,000 tests and other assessment instruments. It contains information on both published and unpublished instruments. You can access the *ETS Test Collection* database directly at ets.org/testcoll.

General Internet Searches   If you are unable to locate a test through one of the preceding sources, you could try searching the Internet with the test title, author's name, or subject area. As we mentioned earlier, including "test" or "assessment" with the subject-area key word helps to narrow your search. Usually, searching through ERIC will yield more relevant hits for educational tests than conventional search engines. You may also try searching on *PsycINFO*.

RESTRICTIONS ON PURCHASING AND USING TESTS

Purchasing Restrictions

Although you may find the name of a test you want to use, its availability may be restricted. To guard against assessment abuse, some publishers restrict the sale of test materials. The publisher's catalog will list any restrictions on test purchasing: The sale of certain tests, especially individually administered intelligence and personality tests, is restricted to qualified psychologists. Typically, publishers label the tests according to the severity of the restrictions in purchasing:

Level A—may be ordered on official letterhead by an agency or organization in which qualified persons will administer and interpret the results. The agency or institution would employ persons who meet the recommendations of the **Standards for Educational and Psychological Testing** (AERA et al., 2014). An individual who is ordering would have to verify completion of sufficient training and a course in test interpretation and use from a recognized program.

Level B—individuals will need to verify that they have had sufficient graduate-level training (typically a master's degree) and supervised experience to administer and interpret the test being ordered. Membership in an appropriate professional association may be required. The recommendations of the *Standards* would be followed.

Level C—individuals need to verify that they have a PhD or related degree in psychology or education as well as appropriate coursework and supervised training in administration and interpretation of the test being ordered.

Sales restrictions vary with the publisher, each implementing a somewhat different policy on establishing a purchaser's qualifications and selling tests. The test user must be sure to acquire the requisite training and experience before purchasing a test. A form needs to be completed, signed, and submitted to the publisher for approval before a test can be purchased.

If you are a practicing teacher and want to review the achievement tests your school district uses, then you should contact the district's testing director. If you are taking a course in which you are expected to write an evaluation of a test, you should ask your instructor how to proceed. Your university may have a testing office that contains specimen sets of tests for this purpose. If you must order a test, your instructor will likely need to prepare a letter for you to include with the order explaining the assignment and how the test will be used. Start your search for a test early. Last-minute searches will likely result in problems completing your assignment.

Guidelines for Proper Test Development and Use

Test Standards   A useful publication for evaluating educational and psychological tests is the *Standards for Educational and Psychological Testing* (AERA et al., 2014). Prepared jointly by the American Educational Research Association, the American Psychological Association, and the National Council on Measurement in Education, the *Standards* describe various kinds of information that a publisher should provide in a test manual and accompanying materials. It includes suggestions for how a test should be developed as well as guidelines for how a test should be used. Further information can be obtained by calling the National Council on Measurement in Education.

The Code   The ideas and concepts in the *Standards* are directed to the professional tester rather than to measurement students and the public.

However, the Joint Committee on Testing Practices (2004) prepared a set of major obligations for professionals (like yourself) who use tests in formal educational testing programs. These obligations, described in the *Code of Fair Testing Practices in Education* (*Revised*), are included in Appendix B. The code will be especially useful to you as you evaluate a test or your school's testing program. The code lists separate obligations for test users and for test developers. The *Code of Professional Responsibilities in Educational Measurement* (NCME, 1995) also describes professional obligations and is reproduced in Appendix C. (See also Chapter 5.)

EVALUATING AND SELECTING A TEST

Because tests play important roles in the educational system, school officials should select them carefully. Before your district adopts a test, a committee of parents, teachers, and administrators should carefully examine and evaluate it. This section describes a systematic procedure for conducting such a review and evaluation. Part of your professional responsibility as a teacher is to participate and offer informed judgments when serving on such test selection committees. School administrators who select tests without the informed judgment of teachers run the risk of egregious errors. Because no test can perfectly match a school district's needs, comparing the merits of one test with another is an important step in choosing the better product.

Clarify Your Purpose

The first step in reviewing a test is to pinpoint the specific purpose(s) for obtaining student information and to find out who will be using the information to make decisions. The more specific you are about the purposes and conditions under which assessment information will be used, the better you will be able to select the appropriate procedure. Information from Chapter 3, which discusses test score validity, will be especially helpful.

Things you need to keep clearly in mind as you begin your selection include:

■ *The school setting in which the assessment will be used*—type of community, ages or grades of students, persons who will be helped by an appropriate assessment, and persons who will be in charge of using the assessment results.

■ *The specific decisions, purposes, and/or uses intended for the assessment results*—for example, identifying specific reading skills needing remediation, appraising students' emotional needs or areas of anxiety as a prelude to counseling, appraising students' aptitude for mechanical activities that a counselor will discuss during guidance sessions, or surveying general levels of reading and mathematics achievement to report curriculum evaluation information to the school board.

■ *The way you believe that using test scores or other assessment information will help improve the decision, serve the purpose, or solve the problem*—the better you can articulate, from the outset, what you expect an assessment procedure to accomplish, the better you will be able to evaluate the many options open to you and to choose the most satisfactory one.

■ *The need to strike a balance between the strengths and limitations of performance tasks relative to multiple-choice tests*—such factors as time, cost, in-depth assessment of narrow curricular areas, and less in-depth assessment of broad areas of the curriculum. The assessment procedure you select will be the result of compromises on several dimensions, so it is helpful to think about these early in the process.

Put the New Assessment Plans into Local Context

Before you set out to select a new assessment procedure, you should take stock of the assessments already being used in the district. For example, what type of assessments do teachers already do, of what quality are these assessments, and do they serve the perceived need?

External Assessments Versus Teacher-Made Assessments

You will need a perspective on what an external assessment contributes beyond the school-based assessments currently used by teachers. Externally imposed assessments do not match a local curriculum framework exactly. You may decide, for example, that it will be wiser and instructionally more effective to spend the district's money in professional development for improving teacher-made assessment procedures rather than purchasing an **external assessment procedure** such as a standardized test. *In general, a school district should rely on teacher-made assessments for 90% to 95% of its assessment needs.* Principals, because they are responsible for the quality of the instruction in their schools, bear a special responsibility to evaluate teacher-made assessments to ensure they are of high quality and should be aware of how high-quality, teacher-made assessments impact students' learning.

State-Mandated Assessments Versus Standardized Tests

States have mandated standardized assessment programs. These programs may be basic skills assessments, accountability programs, or more complex assessments, including the new assessments of the Common Core State Standards. To reduce redundancy, the assessment a school district purchases should supplement the mandated assessment and serve other, nonduplicating purposes. Chapter 16 gave a set of guidelines for selecting a standardized achievement test that is compatible with state-mandated assessment requirements.

Instructional Value of Standardized Tests

As discussed in Chapter 16, standardized assessments with norms and educational development scales are most helpful to (a) assess students' relative strengths and weaknesses across curricular areas, (b) assess students' growth within a specific curricular area, and (c) provide an "independent, external" assessment of students' accomplishments relative to a standardization sample. You should weigh these purposes against teacher-based assessments; use instructional benefit to students as a criterion.

Evaluating a School District

Sometimes a school district wishes to use an external assessment, such as a standardized test, to evaluate itself. School officials should be aware that not only do single tests provide an especially poor foundation on which to evaluate teachers and curricula, but also that program evaluation itself is a technical area requiring well-prepared professional evaluators. Very often, qualified program evaluation personnel are not on a district's payroll. Being unaware of the need for a professional program evaluator, school officials often assign the task to persons professionally trained in other areas, such as school psychologists or guidance counselors. Superintendents wanting to use assessments for program evaluation may wish to consult curriculum evaluation experts before

FIGURE 18.5 Facts to be reported in addition to standardized test results when evaluating school effectiveness.

Attendance Includes absences of staff and students from school and parents from participation in parent-teacher organizations.

Holding power Includes graduation and dropout rates.

Parent involvement Includes parent-teacher organizations, volunteers, and parent-staffed programs.

Diversity Includes staff and student gender, ethnicity, home language, and staff responsibilities.

Economic conditions Includes parent income levels and students receiving free or reduced-cost lunches.

Stability Includes percent of staff and students new to a school district.

Experience Includes years of teaching experience and years of education beyond the initial qualifications.

Staff development Includes in-service programs, peer mentoring, collaboration with businesses or colleges, and courses taken.

Programs for students Includes study skills, counseling, dropout and at-risk prevention, reentry, cross-age tutoring, extracurricular, and summer school.

Achievement Includes performance of students at the next higher educational level; longitudinal patterns of achievement test results, student awards and honors, per student library loans, National Merit scholars, college entrance test results, and out-of-class student accomplishments.

School environment Includes incidents of vandalism and violence, gang-related activities, types of disciplinary actions, special services, extracurricular activities, and library facilities.

Instructional variables Includes length of day, year, and class periods; amount of time per subject per week; number of students using extended day academic program; homework actually assigned; and percent of school days devoted exclusively to academic learning.

Fiscal Includes average teacher, staff, and administrator salaries; expenditures per student.

Source: Based on "Putting Test Scores in Perspective: Communicating a Complete Report Card for Your Schools," by K. K. Matter, in *Understanding Achievement Tests: A Guide for School Administrators* (pp. 121–129) by L. M. Rudner, J. C. Conoley, and B. S. Plake (Eds.), 1989. Washington, DC: ERIC Clearinghouse on Tests, Measurement, and Evaluation.

designing these evaluation strategies. One suggestion is to contact the American Educational Research Association (aera.net) and ask about contacting a member of Division H who lives near your school district. Another organization you might contact is the American Evaluation Association (eval.org).

Figure 18.5 summarizes some factors affecting the difficulty of the school's educational task. Information about these factors should be used along with test results to help interpret a school's effectiveness.

Qualifications of the Staff Another consideration is the qualifications of a school district's staff in relation to the assessment procedure proposed. For example, specially trained professionals are needed to administer and interpret individual intelligence and personality tests as well as group-administered scholastic ability tests. If such professionals are in short supply in a district, you will want to use other assessment procedures. Similarly, using performance assessments and portfolios requires educating teachers about scoring and interpreting these procedures. This process will cost time and money that a district may not have. Sometimes partial implementation may be helpful, such as assessing students at some grades and not others.

Review the Actual Assessment Materials

Obtain Copies of the Test to Review After locating potential assessment instruments and reading reviews if available, narrow your choices to a few assessment procedures that appear to suit your needs. Obtain copies of the assessment materials and tasks; detailed descriptions of the assessment content and rationale behind its selection; materials related to scoring, reporting, and interpreting assessment results; information about the cost of the assessment materials and scoring service; and technical information about the assessment. (See our earlier discussion about restrictions when ordering tests.)

Much of this material may be bundled together in a **specimen set**, which is designed as a marketing tool as well as for critical review of materials. As a result, not all materials you will need to review a test intelligently are included. For example, some publishers' specimen sets do not include complete copies of the assessment booklets or scoring guidelines. You will need to order these separately.

Technical Information About a Test's Quality Technical information about a test's quality is not found in a publisher's catalog. A test's **technical manual** gives information about how the test was developed, reliability coefficients, standard errors of measurement, correlational and validity studies, equating methods, item-analysis procedures, and norming-sample data. Technical manuals are not typically included in specimen sets and must be ordered separately from the tests. Often the publisher prepares several technical reports for a standardized test. Although school testing directors should have copies of the technical manuals for the tests the school uses, often they do not. Some colleges and universities that maintain test collections for their faculty and students may have technical manuals. Usually, you will need to order the technical manual directly from the test's publisher.

The Committee Should Review All Materials

Once you obtain the materials, the committee can review them. Be sure to compare similar assessments against the purposes you had in mind for using the assessments. It might be helpful for the committee to obtain input from noncommittee members for certain parts of the assessment: for example, mathematics teachers for the mathematics section, reading teachers for the reading assessment, and so forth. You could also call on a college or university faculty member to help: For example, a testing and measurement faculty member may be better qualified to review and/or explain technical material. Contact the National Council on Measurement in Education (ncme. org) for the names of specialists who live near your school district.

Achievement Tests Must Match the Curriculum

It is important to match each test item with your state's standards and state or local curriculum. You do this by obtaining the complete list of standards or learning objectives, organized by grade level. Two persons independently read each test item and record which standard or learning objective it matches. When all items have been matched, the persons compare their results and reconcile the differences. The findings are summarized in a table that lists each standard and the ID number of the test items matching each. The number of nonmatching items is also recorded. This procedure should be done separately for each grade, because a test's items may appear at a grade level that is different than the grade at which the corresponding learning objective is taught. If there are a lot of these grade-sequence mismatches, the test will not be

suitable for your school district. Be sure to note especially the match between the kinds of thinking and performance activities implied by the standards and the test items. Often the content matches, but the thinking processes and performances required do not. An example of how to do this is found in Nitko et al. (1998). As we discussed in Chapter 3, one should examine whether a test and the standards are aligned with respect to content span, depth of understanding required, topical emphasis, expected student performance, and applicability of the test for all students (La Marca et al., 2000).

Finally, find out the month during which the district plans to administer the test. Then, determine what proportion of the test's items assess content that will have been taught before testing begins. When a test assesses content that students have not yet been taught, scores are lowered. (See Chapter 17 for further discussion of this point in connection with grade-equivalent scores.)

Pilot the Test   If possible, you should administer the assessment to a few students to get a feel for how students might respond. This tryout would be especially important with writing tasks or performance tasks. You may find that for some otherwise appealing performance tasks, student time limits or instructions are not sufficient and confusion results. This uncertainty is less likely if the assessment was professionally developed and standardized on a national sample.

A Sample Outline for Your Test Review

It will help your review if you systematically organize relevant information in one or two pages. Using a form is a concise way of sharing information among committee members or with others who may help make decisions about the choice. Figure 18.6 suggests what information to record for your review in such a form.

LOCATING INFORMATION ABOUT YOUR STATE TESTS

State accountability tests are not available for review in the same way as commercially produced tests or unpublished tests used for research purposes. However, you can and should find out as much information as you can about the tests

FIGURE 18.6 Suggested outline for recording relevant information for reviewing and evaluating an assessment procedure.

Identifying information
1. Title, publisher, copyright date
2. Purpose of the test as described by the publisher
3. Grade level(s), subject(s), administrative time
4. Cost per student, service costs
5. Types of scores and norms provided

Content and curricular evaluation
1. Publisher's description and rationale for specific types of tasks
2. Quality and clarity of the tasks themselves
3. Currency of the content and match to recent curricular trends
4. Match of the tasks to each of the school district's curricula
5. Inclusion of ethnic and gender diversity in the task content

Instructional use evaluation
1. Publisher's description and rationale for how the assessment results may be used by teachers to improve instruction
2. Local teachers' evaluations of how the assessment results could be used for improving their instruction
3. Overlap of assessment with the existing teacher-based assessment procedures

Technical evaluation
1. Representativeness, recency, and local relevance of the national norms
2. Types of reliability coefficients and their values (use average values if necessary)
3. Summary of the evidence regarding the validity of the assessment for the purpose(s) you have in mind for using it
4. Quality of the criterion-referenced information the assessment provides
5. Likelihood that the assessment will have adverse effects on students with disabilities, minority students, and female students

Practical evaluation
1. Quality of the manual and teacher-oriented materials
2. Ease of administration and scoring
3. Cost and usefulness of the scoring services
4. Estimated annual costs (time and money) if the assessment procedure is adopted for the district
5. Likely public reaction to using the assessment procedure

Overall evaluation
1. Comments of reviewers (e.g., *MMY* or *Test Critiques*)
2. Conclusions about the positive aspects of the assessment
3. Conclusions about the negative aspects of the assessment
4. Summary and recommendation about adoption

List of references and sources used

you are required to give as part of your state accountability process. State test information can usually be found on the website of the state's department of education. States vary in how much information is available.

To locate information about your state's testing program, go to the website of your state's education department. Depending on the state, this might be called the Department of Education, Office of Public Instruction, or some other name. Use the menus on the department's home page to locate information about its assessment program. The link may be called Assessment, or Assessment and Accountability, or something similar. Sometimes assessment information will be placed under Standards, and sometimes it will be a link on its own.

A variety of information will be available, again depending on the state. You may find all or most of the following:

- Names of all the tests used in the state's accountability program, with a description of each and the grade level(s) with which they are used.
- Dates for administration of tests in the school's accountability program.
- A description of the standards each test is intended to measure, performance level descriptions, and cut scores.
- Guides for how to administer a particular test.
- Guides for administrators, teachers, parents, and students on how to prepare for a particular test, sometimes with practice questions or tasks and sample rubrics.
- Guides for administrators, teachers, parents, and students on interpreting score reports.
- Description of policies associated with the test(s) and testing program.
- Results of the assessments, aggregated by district and school. Often these are available as spreadsheets which you can download and use to make graphs or charts. Sometimes they are in written reports combined with other data about a school, in a school profile.
- The technical manual for the state test, if it is provided on the website, will give you information about test development, reliability and validity, scaling and equating, and the results of other technical analyses. While all states should have a technical manual for their test (the test developer with whom they contract should provide this as part of their services), not all states make these available on their website.

For example, at the time of this writing, the Pennsylvania Department of Education has an Assessment and Accountability page on their website (http://www.education.pa.gov/K-12/ Assessment%20and%20Accountability/Pages/ default.aspx#tab-1) that describes a variety of different tests. They write: "The assessment system includes the Pennsylvania System of School Assessment (PSSA), the Pennsylvania Alternate System of Assessment (PASA), the Pennsylvania

Accountability System (PAS), the Pennsylvania Value-Added Assessment System (PVAAS), the Keystone Exams (end-of-course), Classroom Diagnostic Tools (CDT), and the National Assessment of Educational Progress (NAEP)." The home page describes each of these assessments and contains links to more detail for each one.

Following these links yields all of the kinds of information listed above.

CONCLUSION

In this chapter, we presented a brief overview of resources for locating, evaluating, and selecting published and unpublished tests. These overviews should be sufficient to get you started when the occasion arises that you need to find and evaluate an assessment.

In the next chapter, we conclude our consideration of standardized tests with a tour of some of the kinds of tests, in addition to achievement tests, that you may find used in your school. These include scholastic aptitude, career interest, attitude, and personality tests.

EXERCISES

1. Describe the types of assessment information you would find in each of the following sources:
   a. *Mental Measurements Yearbook*
   b. *Tests in Print*
   c. *Tests*
   d. *Test Critiques*
   e. *ETS Test Collection*
   f. *Standards for Educational and Psychological Testing*
   g. a test publisher's catalog
   h. ncme.org
2. Describe how each of the following professional organizations may help you obtain test information:
   a. Association for Assessment in Counseling and Education
   b. International Reading Association
   c. National Association of Test Directors
   d. National Council on Measurement in Education
3. Read each of these statements and identify the one source that would most likely contain the information the speaker is requesting.

   a. "I want to know what kinds of instruments are available to assess attitudes of female students toward work, home, marriage, and family life."
   b. "I want to know what professionals in the field think of this criterion-referenced test."
   c. "What services does a publisher provide for interpreting assessment results, and what are the charges?"
   d. "I want to know the newest instruments developed for assessing perceptual-motor development of primary school students."
4. Suppose you have already located a particular test and you want the specific information about it implied by the following statements. What source would you consult first for each statement?
   a. "What are the reliability coefficients for their test?"
   b. "What kind of norms does the publisher provide?"
   c. "How do test specialists view the quality of the procedures the publisher followed when developing the test?"
   d. "What research studies and reports have used this assessment instrument?"
5. Using the procedures described in this chapter, locate a specific standardized assessment instrument you believe can serve a purpose you have identified.
   a. Then, following the procedures described in this chapter, review and evaluate this assessment instrument in relation to your stated purpose. Write your review and evaluation using the outline given in Figure 18.6, using headings and subheadings appropriately.
   b. Share your evaluation with others in this course.

CHAPTER
19

Scholastic Aptitude, Career Interests, Attitudes, and Personality Tests

KEY CONCEPTS

1. Scholastic aptitude assessments describe a learner's general intellectual skills, rather than specific school achievements. However, intellectual skills are also learned, largely at school, and do not represent innate intellectual "capacity." There are several different types of group-administered scholastic aptitude tests. Individually administered tests of general school aptitude include the *Stanford-Binet Intelligence Scale*, the *Wechsler Intelligence Scales*, and the *Kaufman Assessment Battery for Children*.

2. Assessment of adaptive behavior focuses on how independently students can care for themselves and cope with the demands of everyday life. Vocational and career interests are preferences for specific kinds of activities and can be assessed with a questionnaire. Attitudes can also be assessed with a questionnaire. A variety of techniques have been developed to measure various aspects of personality.

IMPORTANT TERMS

adaptive behavior

affective saliency

age-based scores versus grade-based scores

aptitude (versus achievement)

attitudes

completion test of personality

direction and intensity of attitude

empirically keyed scales

expressed interests

inventoried interests, manifested interests, tested interests

figural reasoning

general versus specific intellectual skills

interests

mental age

multiple-aptitude tests

nonverbal tests

omnibus test

people-similarity rationale versus activity-similarity rationale

pictorial reasoning

projective hypothesis

projective personality test techniques

quantitative reasoning

readiness test

spiral format

standard age score (*SAS*)

structured (self-report) personality assessment techniques

two-score test

values

verbal comprehension tests

verbal reasoning tests

vocational interest inventories

APTITUDES FOR LEARNING

General Versus Specific Intellectual Skills

Assessments of the kind discussed in this chapter describe a learner's **general intellectual skills**, rather than describing the **specific intellectual skills** a learner needs in, say, next week's geometry lessons. When the knowledge or skills students need for an upcoming lesson are specific and narrow, the students' present level of knowledge and skills are the best predictor of their learning success. For most of these specific, day-to-day instructional decisions, you will have to develop your own assessment procedures.

General Intellectual Skills and Aptitudes Measurement

A student's past performance in a specific course is not very helpful in establishing expectations for learning new material whenever (a) the student must learn to perform in ways that are quite different from those learned in the past, (b) the student's past performance has been very erratic, (c) previous test scores or school grades are known to be very unreliable or invalid, or (d) the student's record of past performance is not available.

Consider a ninth grader, for example, who wants to study Spanish for the first time, having had no previous foreign language training or experience. A test of Spanish language knowledge provides no information about this student's chances of succeeding in an upcoming Spanish course. In such cases, an assessment of more general intellectual skills and abilities *related to language learning* will better predict success. Usually, such tests assess English language skills and concepts, acquired auditory learning skills, and applied memory skills. Similarly, a student transferring from another school system or moving from one educational level to the next may have complete records, but the meaning of these records may be unclear. To clarify them, a school may test the student with an instrument assessing broad intellectual skills or scholastic aptitude.

School officials can use a number of ways to predict a student's likely success in an educational program. Three examples are the student's (a) level of past achievement for the same specific type of performance as the new performance the student needs to learn, (b) level of general scholastic ability, and (c) ability in several specific aptitudes related to the new performance to be learned. The validity

of these predictors is related to the specificity of the performance the school wants to predict. If a school wants to predict a very specific performance (for example, solving quadratic equations), then (a) a student's prior achievement of a very similar kind is the best predictor, (b) a student's general scholastic aptitude is the next best predictor, and (c) assessment of specific aptitudes is least preferred. If the school wants to predict a very general performance (such as overall school performance as measured by first-year-student grade point average), then the preferred order of predictors is (a) general scholastic aptitude assessment, (b) assessments of prior specific achievement, and (c) assessments of specific abilities (Snow, 1980).

Aptitude Tests Measure Learned Behavior

Capacity Is Not Fixed   Tests assessing aptitude or intellectual skills reflect only past learning. They do not directly assess innate ability or "capacity." Further, because we cannot obtain a sample of performance from the future, they cannot directly assess future ability. We have to be content to use past and present learning to predict future learning. It is important to recognize that a student's "aptitude for learning" implies learning through a specific type of instructional approach. If you change the instructional approach drastically, the student's aptitude for learning changes as well. A student's aptitude is influenced also by a number of facts of development (including biological makeup), experience in the environment (including interactions with other persons), and a complex interaction of the two.

The very idea of "capacity" implies some upper limit on a student's ability to learn. This limitation is likely to be untrue in general. For example, a student's capacity to do algebra may depend on the way a teacher currently teaches it, on the mathematics concepts the student learned previously, and on the motivational level a teacher stimulates in the student, as well as on some kind of native endowment. It seems reasonable to conclude that both developmental (life history) and instructional conditions affect one's particular potentials.

Aptitude-Achievement Distinctions   It sometimes troubles teachers to see assessment instruments bearing titles such as *readiness, intelligence, general mental ability,* and *"aptitude for X,"* but containing items closely resembling those found on achievement tests. It is important to distinguish between the abstract concepts of **aptitude** and **achievement** and the observations we make to infer the state of a person's aptitude and achievement. We can define an aptitude for X as the present state of a person that indicates the person's expected future performance in X if the conditions of the past and present continue into the future. A student's present aptitude (or state) could be indicated in many ways. An aptitude test is only one possible indicator of aptitude. Prior achievement, motivation, and interest are also possible indicators of aptitude.

Scholastic aptitude tests deliberately set out to assess a student's reasoning rather than the student's recall of factual knowledge or ability to use well-learned rules on problems practiced in school. These tests differ from traditional standardized achievement tests in at least three ways:

> First, tests of reasoning ability, especially mathematical reasoning, require a relatively small declarative knowledge base. The … amount of mathematical knowledge required by the typical SAT [for example] is rarely beyond that taught in a first year high school algebra course and an introductory semester of geometry … . [The SAT places heavy demands, however, on] procedural knowledge or, more precisely, the procedural use of declarative knowledge.
>
> A second way in which reasoning tests differ from subject matter tests is in the quite deliberate way in which they were constructed to not depend upon specific subject matter content. The verbal reasoning skills measured by the SAT-V, for example, have no specific secondary school course sequence on which they can be referred. A final way in which verbal and mathematical reason tests differ from at least some achievement tests is in degree of problem-solving and reasoning, as distinct from simple memory. Tests in subject matters such as geography, foreign languages, and history make primary demands on memory but minimal demands on problem-solving skills and reasoning (Bond, 1989, pp. 429–430).

Teaching Conditions for Aptitude Development

Nonadaptive Teaching An important part of the definition of aptitude given earlier was the continuance of past learning conditions into the future. One thing that made aptitude tests useful predictors of future school success is that schools have generally not been very adaptive to individual learners. Thus, the conditions under which students learn this year are usually quite similar to last year's learning conditions. In the current climate of standards-based reform, more and more emphasis is placed on maintaining standards for all (or most) learners and adapting instruction. Technology is particularly useful for these purposes, for example, allowing students to review web-based materials at home (e.g., "the flipped classroom"), to easily revise their work, and to search for information. It remains to be seen whether this will render aptitude tests less effective predictors of future school success. At the present time, it is safe to say classroom instruction has not changed dramatically (Cuban, 2009), and the assumptions underlying the use of aptitude tests still hold.

Underemphasizing Adaptive Teaching When a student must learn under the same conditions from year to year, there is a danger that teachers will believe that the results of the student's scholastic aptitude testing determine what the student is able to accomplish. That is, once they see a student's present aptitude level, they may do little to modify learning conditions to improve the student's aptitude. Past psychological conceptions of the learner have led some educators to overemphasize the (a) consistency of the general scholastic ability of learners, (b) passivity of learners as receivers of information, and (c) categorical placement of learners into educational tracks with narrow ranges of instructional options. They have *underemphasized* the (a) adaptivity and plasticity of learners, (b) learners' ability to actively construct information during problem solving, and (c) responsibility of educational systems to adapt to learners' initial performance levels (Glaser, 1977).

Invalidity for Instructional Placement Unfortunately, the aptitude tests described in this chapter have not been validated for use in assigning students to different kinds of instructional methods. Despite that fact, one can find districts that use scholastic aptitude tests, for example, for placement in gifted and talented programs. This amounts to using tests for purposes they have not been built to serve—and for which there is no evidence of validity. Rather, these tests have been built to predict how well students will perform when they must adapt to the fixed type of instruction. You should view the tests' helpfulness for decision making in that light.

Scholastic Aptitude Test Score Stability

Importance of Score Stability An important school concern is whether a student's scholastic aptitude remains constant or stable over time. If a student's scholastic aptitude test score changed erratically every year, you would have no confidence that it assessed a useful characteristic. Although on a student-by-student basis scores may systematically rise or decline, a definite tendency exists for students to maintain similar, but not identical, ranking in their age group throughout their school years. On balance, changes in students' rankings on general scholastic aptitude tests tend to be greater (a) as the time interval between the two testings grows and (b) the younger the students were at the time of the initial testing. Although groups of students tend to maintain their relative position in the distribution of aptitude scores, important changes in individual students do occur. Therefore, if a school wants to use a student's scholastic aptitude score for guidance or placement decisions, it should bear in mind that there are sufficient differences in individual students' patterns of score change to justify reassessment each time a decision is made.

Factors for Score Stability Among the factors that work to keep students' rankings on aptitude tests about the same over time are as follows:

1. The genetic makeup of students remains the same.

2. If a student's socioeconomic level, family configuration, and sociocultural influences remain stable over a long period, these contribute to aptitude stability.

3. Development and prerequisite learning is rarely reversible, so earlier development and learning continues to exert similar impact on new development and learning.

4. If the content assessment by different scholastic aptitude tests is similar, students' scores will be similar from one testing to the next.

Reasons for Score Changes Among factors that work to change students' rankings on aptitude tests from one testing to another are the following:

1. *Errors of measurement*—Even if the person's "true score" were to stay the same, the obtained score is likely to be different due to a test's unreliability (see Chapter 4).

2. *Test differences*—The content of tests produced by different publishers will vary. For example, the Otis-Lennon School Ability Test (OLSAT) uses verbal and nonverbal test items, while the Naglieri Non-verbal Ability Test (NNAT) uses nonverbal matrix completion items. Also, the content of the same publisher's test may vary with the age level of the student taking the test. Tests designed for young children are more concrete and perceptual; those designed for older children are more abstract and verbal.

3. *Norm-group differences*—The norms of different publishers' tests are not comparable. Because mental ability scores are norm-referenced, differences in scores may be due to differences in norms. Also, many of these tests use age-based rather than grade-based norms.

4. *Special interventions and enriched environments*—If a person's environment dramatically and persistently becomes more intellectually nurturing, that person's scores on a scholastic aptitude test are likely to increase. Conversely, if the person becomes physically or emotionally ill or deprived in a way that interferes with intellectual development, then aptitude scores may decrease.

GROUP TESTS OF SCHOLASTIC APTITUDES

Types of Group Aptitude Tests

Advantage The principal advantage of group testing over individual testing is the efficiency and cost savings gained by testing many persons at the same time. The ease with which group tests can be administered and scored has contributed greatly to schools adopting them.

Number of Aptitudes Reported There are different types of group aptitude tests. The **omnibus test** contains items assessing different abilities that comprise general scholastic aptitude, but it provides only a single score. A **two-score test** also assesses several different kinds of specific abilities, but reports only two scores, usually verbal/quantitative or verbal/nonverbal. The items on the verbal section of the test, for example, may assess several kinds of specific verbal abilities, but only one verbal ability score is reported.

Some school ability tests report three scores, such as verbal, quantitative, and nonverbal. **Nonverbal tests** assess how well students process symbols and content that have no specific verbal labels, such as discerning spatial patterns and relations or classifying patterns and figures. **Multiple-aptitude tests** assess several different abilities separately and provide an ability score for each. Multiple-aptitude tests, for example, may provide separate scores for verbal reasoning, verbal comprehension, numerical reasoning, and **figural reasoning**.

Type of Test to Use

The type of group scholastic aptitude test a school should use depends on how the staff will use the scores. Multiple-aptitude tests are most useful for providing information that profiles students' strengths and weaknesses to make better decisions about further schooling or planning a career. Omnibus tests are most useful when a school wants an estimate of their students' general level of school ability for purposes of predicting future success under standard classroom conditions. Examples of two-score and multiple-score aptitude tests are given in the following sections. Others are listed in Appendix H.

Two-Score Test: *Otis-Lennon School Ability Test*

Test Content The *Otis-Lennon School Ability Test (OLSAT)* provides verbal and nonverbal part scores as well as a total score. The identification of a test item as verbal versus nonverbal depends on whether students must understand English to answer the item. For example, Numeric Inference is classified as quantitative reasoning because English language is not necessary to succeed on the items. Once the directions for the subtest are understood, an examinee could answer the questions without knowing English. Arithmetic Reasoning, on the other hand, is classified as verbal reasoning because it "is made up of verbal problems, does not depend on computation, and depends on understanding English" (Pearson, 2003). Figure 19.1 describes the clusters and types of items the *OLSAT* contains.

Test Organization The *OLSAT* is organized into seven levels: Level A (kindergarten), Level B (Grade 1), Level C (Grade 2), Level D (Grade 3),

FIGURE 19.1 Description of the kinds of items on the *OLSAT*.

	Cluster description	Types of items
Verbal clusters	**Verbal comprehension** depends on the ability to perceive the relational aspects of words and word combinations, to derive meaning from types of words, to understand subtle differences among similar words and phrases, and to manipulate words to produce meaning.	Following Directions Antonyms Sentence Completion Sentence Arrangement
	Verbal reasoning depends on the ability to infer relationships among words, to apply inferences to new situations, to evaluate conditions in order to determine necessary versus optional, and to perceive similarities and differences.	Aural Reasoning Arithmetic Reasoning Logical Selection Word/Letter Matrix Verbal Analogies Verbal Classification Inference
Nonverbal clusters	**Pictorial reasoning** assesses the ability in young children to reason using pictorial representations. These items assess the ability to infer relationships among objects, to evaluate objects for similarities and differences, and to determine progressions and predict the next step in those progressions.	Picture Classification Picture Analogies Picture Series
	Figural reasoning items assess the ability to use geometric figures to infer relationships, to perceive progressions and predict the next step in those progressions, to generalize from one set of figures to another and from dissimilar sets of figures, and to manipulate spatially.	Figural Classification Figural Analogies Pattern Matrix Figural Series
	Quantitative reasoning items assess the ability to use numbers to infer relationships, derive computational rules, and predict outcomes according to computational rules.	Number Series Numerical Inference Number Matrix

Source: Adapted from *Otis-Lennon School Ability Test: Eighth Edition, Assessing the Abilities That Relate to Success in School.* Copyright © 2009 by Pearson Education, Inc. and/or its affiliates. Reproduced with permission. All rights reserved.

Level E (Grades 4 and 5), Level F (Grades 6, 7, and 8), and Level G (Grades 9, 10, 11, and 12). Not all of the different types of items are given at every grade. In Grades K through 2, the test items are organized into three sections, each section containing distinct item types. The three-part format places pictorial items together and items with dictated stems together, separated from other teacher-paced but not dictated items. The Grade K through 2 tests also group types of tasks (e.g., classifying) together. In Grades 4 through 12, similar types of items are not grouped together into subtests, but are arranged into a **spiral format**, similar to that shown in Figure 19.2. One item of each type is presented; then the sequence is repeated, but with more difficult items. Items at the upper levels are entirely self-administered: Students read the directions and answer the items without teacher pacing. The Grade 3 test has two sections, a classification section with figural and verbal items spiraled according to the easy-hard format, and then a section with all the rest of the items arranged in the same spiral format as that for Grades 4 through 12. The *OLSAT* 8 is also available for online administration.

Norm-Referencing Scheme The publisher of the *OLSAT* uses several norm-referencing schemes to report the verbal, nonverbal, and total test results. These are illustrated on the individual student report shown in Figure 19.3. These types of scores are described in the following list. The letters in this description correspond to the letters in Figure 19.3. The *OLSAT* 8 also has an online reporting capability.

FIGURE 19.2 Examples of the type of items on the *Otis-Lennon School Ability Test* (8th ed.).

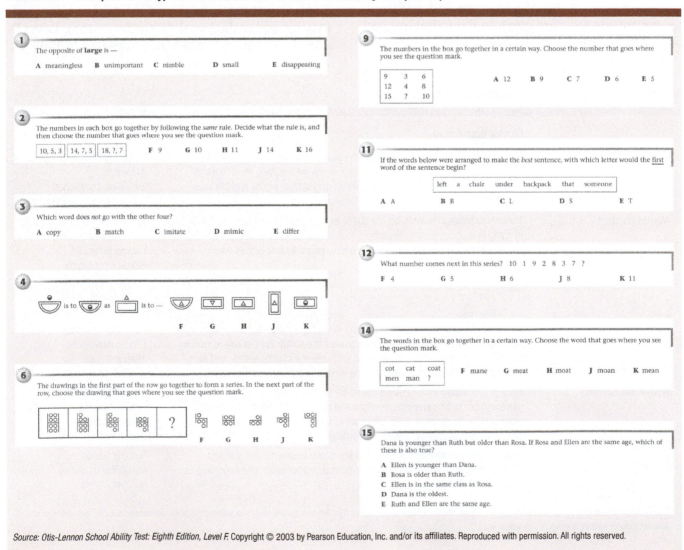

FIGURE 19.3 An individual student's report showing the type of scores reported for the *Otis-Lennon School Ability Test.*

OLSAT® *Otis-Lennon School Ability Test*
Eighth Edition

TEACHER: SAMPLE TEACHER - 0000000000
SCHOOL: SAMPLE SCHOOL - 0000000000
DISTRICT: SAMPLE DISTRICT - 0000000000

GRADE: 04
TEST DATE: 04/09

AGE-BASED SCORES	No. of Items	Number Correct	SAI	Age PR-S	Age NCE
Total	72	28	90	27-4	37.1
Verbal	36	14	92	27-4	39.6
Nonverbal	36	14	89	25-4	35.6

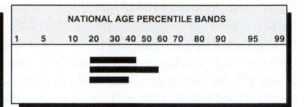

NATIONAL AGE PERCENTILE BANDS

GRADE-BASED SCORES	Scaled Score	National Grade PR-S	National Grade NCE
Total	581	31-4	39.6
Verbal	584	35-4	41.9
Nonverbal	578	27-4	37.1

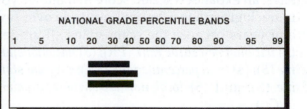

NATIONAL GRADE PERCENTILE BANDS

CLUSTERS	Number Correct/ Number of Items	Below Average	Average	Above Average
VERBAL	14/36		✓	
Verbal Comprehension	7/12		✓	
Verbal Reasoning	7/24	✓		
NONVERBAL	14/36		✓	
Figural Reasoning	8/18		✓	
Quantitative Reasoning	6/18		✓	
TOTAL	26/72		✓	

Recently this student took the *Otis-Lennon School Ability Test* (OLSAT). OLSAT measures those reasoning skills that are related to school-learning ability. The following is an interpretation of the student's performance on OLSAT.

The student's total OLSAT score is slightly below average, both in comparison with students of the same age and in comparison with students in the same grade. The verbal and nonverbal part scores are also in the slightly-below-average range.

The cluster analysis presents performance indicators for this student on each of the clusters in OLSAT. These indicators, which are expressed as above average, average, and below average, describe the student's performance relative to that of other students in the same grade.

Verbal Comprehension refers to the understanding of the structure of language, of relationships among words, and of subtle differences among similar words. Verbal Reasoning refers to the ability to use language for such reasoning tasks as inference, application, and classification. Figural Reasoning involves geometric shapes rather than words. This skill is independent of language. Quantitative Reasoning, which is also independent of language, refers to the ability to reason with numbers and mathematical concepts.

It should be kept in mind that OLSAT scores give only one piece of information about a student. Other factors such as school achievement and interest should also be taken into account.

OLSAT LEVEL/FORM: E/5
2002 NORMS: Spring National

COPY 01

PROCESS NO. 18904271-000O8SR-0000-03250-9

Note: Scores are simulated results.

1. **Age-based scores** compare this student with norm-group students who are the same age, regardless of grade placement. In addition to raw scores, *OLSAT* reports (1) *School Ability Index (SAI)*, a normalized standard score with mean 100 and standard deviation of 16; (2) *national percentile rank (PR)*; (3) *national stanine (S)*; and (4) *normal curve equivalent (NCE)*.

2. **Grade-based scores** compare this student with norm-group students who have the same grade placement, regardless of their age. The scores reported in this section are (1) *scaled score*, an expanded scaled score that allows you to track growth in scholastic aptitude over several years because the scale spans all grades; (2) *national percentile rank (PR)*; (3) *national stanine (S)*; (4) *local percentile rank (PR)*; (5) *local stanine (S)*; and (5) *local normal curve equivalent (NCE)*.

3. *Percentile bands* show the uncertainty interval for the student's scores that are reported in Sections A and B of Figure 19.3. Uncertainty bands are formed by adding and subtracting one *SEM* to the student's score. (See the discussion of *SEM* in Chapter 4.)

4. *Cluster scores* are the raw scores for each of the five clusters at a particular grade level (see Figure 19.1). Below average, average, and above average describe cluster performance in terms of stanines: below average includes stanines 1, 2, 3; average scores fall into stanines 4, 5, 6; and above-average stanines are 7, 8, 9. Stanines are different for the spring and fall standardization groups.

5. *Computer-generated narrative* explains the results in simplified language.

Interpretation of Results   Although the *OLSAT* is a two-score test, its authors encourage you to use the total test results as the main interpretive piece of information. They believe that because verbal and nonverbal abilities are needed to succeed in school, the total score is the best overall indicator. They recognize, however, that much of what you teach students relates to verbal learning. Thus, if a student is very much higher in nonverbal than in verbal ability, you might be alerted that the student may have good scholastic ability but may have difficulty in highly verbal subjects. Students with higher verbal than nonverbal ability may experience more difficulty

with quantitative subjects. The authors recommend that you consider score differences larger than two stanines as meaningful. You should interpret smaller differences much more cautiously because they may represent only measurement error.

Other possible causes for a verbal-nonverbal difference include bilingualism, reading problems, learning disability, hearing impairment, visual impairment, anxiety, illness, or irregularities in test administration. You should request a readministration of the *OLSAT* if a student has a large verbal-nonverbal difference. If retesting verifies a difference and you want further diagnostic information, then you should request assessment with an individual test such as the *Wechsler Intelligence Scale for Children* (described later in this chapter).

Achievement/Ability Comparisons   If you administer the *OLSAT* along with the *Stanford Achievement Test Series*, a score called the Achievement/Ability Comparison (AAC) is part of a student's test report. The AAC describes, for each achievement survey battery subtest, how this student's achievement compares to norm-group students who have the same *OLSAT* total score.

To do this, students in the grade-based *OLSAT* norm group are first sorted into stanines. Second, the students within each *OLSAT* stanine are then sorted into stanines for the achievement test subtest (e.g., reading comprehension stanines for all students whose *OLSAT* stanine is 5). Third, within each achievement subtest group from Step 2, students are clustered into high (stanines 7, 8, 9), middle (stanines 4, 5, 6), and low (stanines 1, 2, 3) groups. The student's *OLSAT* stanine is reported along with his achievement subtest stanines.

For example, Don's *OLSAT* stanine is 5. Don also took the *Stanford Achievement Test* and scored stanines of 4, 5, and 6 in Total Reading, Total Mathematics, and Spelling, respectively. Compared to the entire norm group for the achievement test, these stanines fall in the middle of the distribution. However, if we look only at those students who attained an *OLSAT* stanine of 5, Don will be in the low AAC range in Total Reading, in the middle AAC range in Total Mathematics, and in the high AAC range in Spelling. These AAC results tell us that compared to other students with the same scholastic aptitude as Don, he is below average in Total Reading, average in Total Mathematics, and above average in Spelling.

Multiple-Aptitude Test: *Differential Aptitude Tests*

Purpose The battery of *Differential Aptitude Tests (DAT)* was originally developed in 1947 to satisfy the needs of guidance counselors and consulting psychologists working in schools, social agencies, and industry (Bennett, Seashore, & Wesman, 1974). The tests were revised in 1962, 1972, 1982, and 1990. There is also an online version.

The primary purpose of the tests is to provide information about a student's profiles with respect to different cognitive abilities. This information is used for guiding and counseling students in junior and senior high schools (Grades 7 through 12) as they prepare for career decisions. There are two levels: Level 1 (Grades 7 through 9) and Level 2 (Grades 10 through 12). The *DAT* are also used with adults for vocational and educational counseling and as part of a battery of tests for job selection.

Test Content The *Differential Aptitude Tests* report scores for each of the eight subtests shown in Figure 19.4. (The online version has six subtests: Abstract Reasoning, Language Usage, Mechanical Reasoning, Numerical Ability, Space Relations, and Verbal Reasoning.) An additional ninth score, Scholastic Aptitude, which is a combination of the Verbal Reasoning and Numerical Reasoning scores, is reported: This score is used to assess general scholastic aptitude. Figure 19.4 also shows examples of items from each subtest.

Gender-Specific Norms The *DAT* have separate male and female norms, as well as combined norms. Separate norms allow comparisons of a student with his or her own gender, as well as with members of the opposite gender. Cross-gender comparisons may help students consider occupations or educational programs that they would have overlooked. This process may surprise you and may seem like a form of gender discrimination. However, because the tests are used for guidance and counseling, this purpose is better served by these separate norms, given the realities of the current job market.

Advantage of the *DAT* An advantage of using a multiple-aptitude battery such as the *DAT* instead of an omnibus or two-score aptitude test is the opportunity it provides for finding some aptitude for which a student has a relative strength. For example, a student may have low general scholastic ability (Verbal Reasoning and Numerical Reasoning) but have high Perceptual Speed and Accuracy or high Mechanical Reasoning. These results provide counselors with information on aptitude that they can use to encourage students.

Combining Aptitude with Interest Assessment The *DAT* comes with an optional *Career Interest Inventory*. Using the results of this instrument along with aptitude scores, achievement scores, and school grades can help a student make realistic career or further education decisions. The interest inventory presents sentences describing activities in various types of work and school situations. Students indicate their degree of agreement with the sentences. (Interest inventories are described in greater detail later in this chapter.)

GROUP TESTS OF SPECIFIC APTITUDES

The kinds of general scholastic aptitude tests illustrated earlier are widely used in schools, but other types used for special decisions should be mentioned, too. Among these are readiness tests, high school and college admissions tests, and tests of aptitude for specific subjects.

Readiness Testing

Schools often use **readiness tests** as supplemental information to make instructional decisions for first-grade pupils. Often such tests are used to supplement a kindergarten teacher's judgment about a youngster's general developmental and readiness level for first-grade work, especially reading, where grouping by readiness level is a common practice. Because readiness tests measure a child's acquired learning skills, they are frequently classified as achievement tests rather than aptitude tests.

Teachers frequently use readiness tests to help form instructional groups (for example, for reading instruction). When used in this way, they should be considered placement tests. Because teachers use readiness tests to predict implicitly a pupil's likely success in instruction, we discuss them as aptitude tests in this book. We also mentioned them in Chapter 16 as examples of a type of early childhood achievement test that has been experiencing expanded growth in the current NCLB accountability climate.

FIGURE 19.4 Brief descriptions, time limits, number of items, and a sample item from each subtest of the *Differential Aptitude Tests* (5th ed.).

Verbal Reasoning (25 min., 40 items)

Measures the ability to see relationships among words; may be useful in predicting success in business, law, education, journalism, and the sciences.

SAMPLE ITEM

Which answer contains the missing words to complete this sentence?

. . . . . is to fin as bird is to . . . . .

    A water — — feather
    B shark — — nest
 *C fish — — wing
    D flipper — — fly
    E fish — — sky

Numerical Reasoning (30 min., 40 items)

Measures the ability to perform mathematical reasoning tasks; important in jobs such as bookkeeping, lab work, carpentry, and toolmaking.

SAMPLE ITEM

What number should replace R in this correct addition example?

  7R   *A 9
 + R   B 6
 ——   C 4
  88   D 3
           E None of these

Abstract Reasoning (20 min., 40 items)

A nonverbal measure of the ability to reason using geometric shapes or designs; important in fields such as computer programming, drafting, and vehicle repair.

SAMPLE ITEM

Choose the Answer Figure that should be the next figure (or fifth one) in the series.

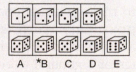

   A *B C D E

Perceptual Speed and Accuracy (6 min., 200 items)

Measures the ability to compare and mark written lists quickly and accurately; helps predict success in performing routine clerical tasks.

SAMPLE ITEM

Look at the underlined combination of letters or numbers and find the same one on the answer sheet. Then fill in the circle under it.

1 XY Xy XX <u>YX</u> Yy   Xy Yy YX XX XY   nn mn nv nm mm
2 6g <u>6G</u> G6 Gg g6   ○ ○ ● ○ ○   ○ ○ ○ ● ○
3 <u>nm</u> mn mm nn nv   g6 Gg 6g G6 6G   BD BB Bd Db Bb
4 Db <u>BD</u> Bd Bb BB   ○ ○ ○ ○ ●   ● ○ ○ ○ ○

Mechanical Reasoning (25 min., 60 items)

Understanding basic mechanical principles of machinery, tools, and motion is important for occupations such as carpentry, mechanics, engineering, and machine operation.

SAMPLE ITEM

Which load will be easier to pull through soft sand?

    A   B   C

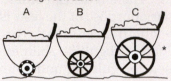

Space Relations (25 min., 50 items)

Measures the ability to visualize a three-dimensional object from a two-dimensional pattern, and to visualize how this object would look if rotated in space; important in drafting, architecture, design, carpentry, and dentistry.

SAMPLE ITEM

Choose the one figure that can be made from the pattern.

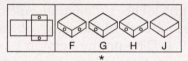

       F   G   H   J

Spelling (10 min., 40 items)

Measures one's ability to spell common English words; a useful skill in many academic and vocational pursuits.

SAMPLE ITEM

Decide which word is not spelled correctly in the group below.

 *A paragraf
   B dramatic
   C circular
   D audience

Language Usage (15 min., 40 items)

Measures the ability to detect errors in grammar, punctuation, and capitalization; needed in most jobs requiring a college degree.

SAMPLE ITEM

Decide which of the four parts of the sentence below contains an error. If there is no error, mark the space on your answer sheet for the letter next to No Error.

Jane and Tom/ is going/ to the office/ this morning.

    A   *B   C   D

E No Error

You should keep in mind the test author's point of view when selecting a readiness test. The author's viewpoint of what constitutes "readiness to learn" will determine the test content (as does an author's viewpoint for every test, of course). If you want to use the scores on a readiness test to make a statement about whether a student has mastered specific prerequisites, you must carefully examine the actual test items to see if they measure the kinds of skills and abilities you expect each student to have acquired before entering the new instruction.

Admissions Testing

Multiple-Assessment for Admission Test scores, previous grades, letters of recommendation, interviews, and biographical information on out-of-school accomplishments are among kinds of information colleges and selective high schools use to make admissions decisions. Some private and parochial high schools, for example, use a battery of achievement and aptitude tests to screen applicants. Testing sessions are usually held at the local high school, and its staff generally administers the tests.

College Admissions Tests Two widely used college admissions testing programs are the College Board's *SAT* and the *ACT Test* published ACT. Both programs administer secure tests. Both administer the tests through local testing centers (usually high schools and colleges) on preestablished dates several times during the year. For both programs, test booklets and answer sheets are returned to their respective publishers for scoring, recording, and processing results to the colleges the students designate.

SAT The College Board, currently located in New York City, was formed around 1899 to help select colleges in the northeastern United States coordinate their admissions testing requirements. The tests developed out of that effort around 1926 and were created by Carl Brigham, associate secretary for the College Board (Donlon & Angoff, 1971). More than 2 million college candidates take the test each year.

The program includes the *SAT* and *SAT Subject Tests*. Students generally take one or both types during their junior or senior year of high school. Only the *SAT* is discussed in this chapter. It has three parts: the Evidence-Based Reading and Writing section, the Mathematics section, and an Essay section. The Evidence-Based Reading and Writing section emphasizes reading comprehension. It includes reading passages and sentence completions, with questions based on reading passages. (Analogy questions, a feature of past *SATs*, have been eliminated.) In the essay, candidates are asked to develop a point of view on an issue, and they are evaluated on their ability to reason and use evidence to support their ideas. The test booklets and answer sheets are sent to the Educational Testing Service (ETS) for scoring, recording, and processing scores to the colleges the student designates. A student's essay responses are posted on a website that college admission officers can access and read. The Mathematics section includes questions on arithmetic operations, algebra, geometry, statistics, and probability. Two types of items are used: standard multiple-choice and gridded response.

The Evidence-Based Reading and Writing and Mathematics SAT sections are scored on a 200- to 800-point scale, for a possible total of 400 to 1600 points. The Essay scores are reported separately and are divided into three dimensions: Reading, Analysis, and Writing. Each dimension is scored on a 2- to 8-point scale.

ACT Program The *ACT Assessment Program* was formed in 1959, with the ideas and help of E. F. Lindquist, among others. This admissions-testing program was originally conceived to be of a different character than the *SAT* program. Whereas initially the College Board was concerned primarily with the private select colleges of the Northeast, the ACT program initially sought to serve midwestern public colleges and universities. What these colleges needed was help in (a) eliminating the few incapable students who were applying, (b) providing guidance services for those admitted, and (c) measuring broad educational development rather than narrower verbal and quantitative aptitudes (Lindquist as cited in Feister & Whitney, 1968). Today ACT in Iowa City is as active a research and test development enterprise as is the Educational Testing Service. More than 1.6 million college candidates take the test each year.

The ACT consists of four multiple-choice tests—English, Mathematics, Reading, and Science—plus an optional Writing Test. The English test measures standard written English and rhetorical skills: punctuation, grammar and usage, sentence structure, writing strategy, organization, and style. Two subscores are reported: Usage/mechanics and Rhetorical skills.

The Mathematics test measures mathematical skills students have typically acquired in courses taken up to the beginning of Grade 12. There are three subscores: pre-algebra/elementary algebra, intermediate algebra/coordinate geometry, and plane geometry/trigonometry.

The Reading test measures reading comprehension. There are four types of reading selections: social studies, natural sciences, prose fiction, and humanities. A Social Studies/Sciences subscore is based on the questions on the social studies and natural sciences passages, and an Arts/Literature subscore is based on the questions on the prose fiction and humanities passages.

The Science test measures interpretation, analysis, evaluation, reasoning, and problem-solving skills required in the natural sciences: biology, chemistry, physics, and Earth/space science. The test emphasizes scientific reasoning skills over recall of scientific content, skill in mathematics, or reading ability. It presents scientific information in three different formats: data representation (e.g., tables and graphs), research summaries, and expressions of conflicting viewpoints presented for analysis.

The optional Writing test measures writing skills emphasized in high school English classes and in entry-level college composition courses. It consists of one, 40-minute essay. The writing prompt defines an issue and describes two points of view on that issue. Examinees are asked to respond to a question about their position on the issue.

An ACT Composite score and a test score for each of the four multiple-choice tests (English, Mathematics, Reading, Science) are reported on a scale from 1 to 36. The Composite Score is the average of the four test scores. The seven subscores for the multiple-choice tests are reported on a scale from 1 to 18. For examinees who take the optional Writing test, a Writing subscore is reported on a scale of 2 to 12 and a Composite English/Writing score is reported on a scale of 1 to 36.

INDIVIDUALLY ADMINISTERED TESTS OF GENERAL SCHOLASTIC APTITUDES

Stanford-Binet Intelligence Scale

History   The *Stanford-Binet Intelligence Scale* is a widely used, individually administered test of general scholastic aptitude. First prepared in 1916 by Lewis M. Terman as a translation and revision of the *Binet-Simon Scale*, the test was revised in 1937 (with Maud A. Merrill), revised again in 1960, renormed in 1972, revised and renormed in 1986, and revised and renormed for the 2003 (fifth edition by Gale Roid). See Becker's (2003) *History of the Stanford-Binet Intelligence Scales*.

Content   The *Stanford-Binet V* is used with a wide range of ages, from 2 years old through adults age 85+. You can gain an idea of the nature and content of this assessment instrument by studying the diagram that follows, which shows that the subtests are clustered into five nonverbal areas (factors) and five verbal areas (factors). The scores from the five nonverbal factors are combined to obtain the Nonverbal IQ; the scores from the five verbal factors are combined to obtain the Verbal IQ.

Structure of the Stanford-Binet V

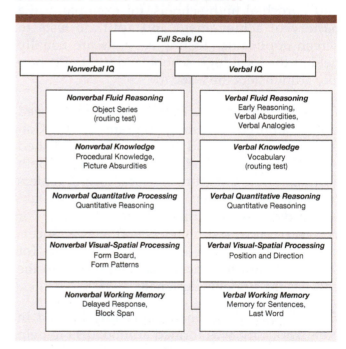

Not all items in each subtest are administered because within each subtest items are arranged in order of increasing difficulty. The object series and vocabulary subtest is given first and is used as a routing test. The student's performance on this test, along with the student's age or estimated ability, tells the psychologist the difficulty level on the other tests at which he or she should begin testing the student. If a quick (and less reliable) estimate of the Full-Scale IQ is desired, the psychologist can stop after administering the verbal and nonverbal routing tests. The standard scores on these two tests are combined to obtain an Abbreviated Full-Scale IQ score.

Scores A student's raw score on each subtest is converted to a normalized standard score called a **standard age score (SAS)** for the subtest. The *SAS*s for each of the 10 subtests have a mean of 10 and standard deviation of three in the norm group having the same age as the student being tested. The 10 *SAS*-scores from the subtests are combined in different ways to make nine different composite scores. There are four kinds of composite scores: Factor Index Scores, Domain Scores, Abbreviated Score, and Full-Scale Score. All the composite scores are deviation IQs (*DIQ*s) with a mean of 100 and a standard deviation of 15, as explained in Chapter 17, Equation 17.4. Within each composite score type, there are from one to five different *DIQ*-scores. The diagram below shows how these four composite scores are formed.

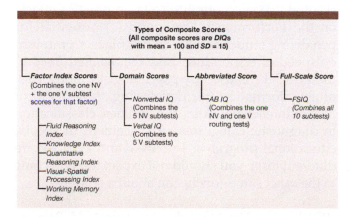

The subtest scores and the different composite scores are used by school psychologists or counseling psychologists along with other information (e.g., school records, other test results, interviews, and reports from teachers and parents) for (a) describing a profile of a student's intellectual skills and abilities, (b) classifying a student into a diagnostic category (e.g., attention-deficit/ hyperactivity disorder), or (c) placing a student into a special educational program (e.g., a gifted program).

The concepts of **mental age** and intelligence quotient (IQ) are no longer used with tests such as the *Stanford-Binet V* (or any other modern intelligence test). Thus, the ratio IQ (= 100 times mental age divided by chronological age) has been replaced by the *DIQ*.

Norm-Referenced Character Tests of scholastic aptitude describe a student's ability as the student's location in a norm group having the same age as the student. If the student's intellectual development does not keep pace with others in the norm group, the student will receive a lower *DIQ*. Norms become outdated and from time to time a test will have to be renormed.

Wechsler Intelligence Scales

Another widely used set of individual tests is the *Wechsler Intelligence Scales*. This set consists of three different intelligence tests, each designed for use with a different age level: (a) *Wechsler Preschool and Primary Scale of Intelligence–IV (WPPSI–IV)*, 2 years, 6 months to 7 years, 7 months; (b) *Wechsler Intelligence Scale for Children–V (WISC–V)*, 6 to 16 years, 11 months; and (c) *Wechsler Adult Intelligence Scale–IV (WAIS–IV)*, 16 to 90 years.

General Design All the Wechsler tests have a similar general design, although the items are not identical. The items are organized into subtests. The items within a subtest are similar in content but differ in difficulty. (The subtests on the different scales—*WPPSI*, *WISC*, and *WAIS*—contain different types of items, however.) Subtests are clustered into groups to represent different factors or aspects of general ability. These form a hierarchical pattern of abilities as shown below, but with some slight differences for the different age-level tests:

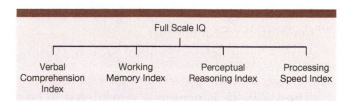

The four factors at the lowest level of the hierarchy are described as follows (Pearson, 2008):

Verbal Comprehension: One's ability to listen to, understand, and give spoken responses to verbal questions. It includes skills in understanding information presented verbally, using words to think and reason, and using words to express thoughts.

Working Memory: One's ability to learn new information and retain it in memory as one completes a task. It includes skills in paying attention, in concentrating, and in mental reasoning.

Perceptual Reasoning: One's ability to examine and think about pictures and designs as well as solve problems without using words. It involves skills working quickly with visual information to solve nonverbal problems.

Processing Speed: One's ability to scan symbols and make judgments about them quickly. It involves skills in paying attention, hand-eye coordination, and mental problem solving.

Scores All the Wechsler scales report subtest results as normalized, standard scores (mean = 10, standard deviation = 3). All of the scales report the total or Full-Scale IQ as *DIQ*-scores (mean = 100, standard deviation = 15). The four factor indexes are also *DIQ*-scores with a mean of 100 and a standard deviation of 15. The norm group to which a student is referenced is the group of students with the same age.

WAIS–IV The *Wechsler Adult Intelligence Scale–IV* is used with ages 16 to 90 years. It overlaps with the *WISC–IV* for age 16. It contains 15 subtests, but only 10 are used to calculate the four indexes as follows (supplemental subtests are in parentheses):

Verbal Comprehension Index: Vocabulary, Similarities, Information, (Comprehension)

Perceptual Reasoning Index: Block Design, Matrix Reasoning, Visual Puzzles, (Figure Weights), (Picture Completion)

Working Memory Index: Digit Span, Arithmetic, (Letter-Number Sequencing)

Processing Speed Index: Symbol Search, Coding, (Cancellation)

The *WAIS–IV* is generally considered to be a reasonably valid and reliable tool for assessing general cognitive ability. Following are some of its limitations (Sattler, 1992): (a) It does not provide low enough scores for persons with severe intellectual disabilities, (b) it does not provide high enough scores for persons with extremely gifted mental ability, and (c) the range of subtest scaled scores is restricted for some age groups.

WISC–V The *Wechsler Intelligence Scale for Children–V* is used with children ages 6 years through 16 years, 11 months. It contains 10 core and six supplemental subtests. In the Verbal Comprehension category are Similarities and Vocabulary (Informa-

tion and Comprehension are supplemental subtests). In the Visual Spatial category are Block Design and Visual Puzzles. In the Fluid Reasoning category are Matrix Reasoning and Figure Weights (Picture Concepts and Arithmetic are supplemental subtests). In the Working Memory category are Digit Span and Picture Span (Letter-Number Sequencing is a supplemental subtest). In the Processing Speed category is Coding and Symbol Search (Cancellation is a supplemental subtest).

The *WISC–V* is generally considered to be a good test of overall mental ability. Among its strengths (Sattler, 1992) are its (a) high-quality norms; (b) good reliability and validity; (c) usefulness in diagnosing cognitive abilities of most students; (d) good features of the materials, administration, and scoring; and (e) extensive research literature. Among its limitations (Sattler, 1992) are its (a) lack of usefulness for extremely low- and high-ability children, (b) restriction of the range of scores for certain subtests and age levels, (c) lack of appropriate norms when a subtest is substituted, (d) susceptibility to large practice effects on the Performance Scale, and (e) potential for penalizing students who do not place a premium on speed of responding. Like the *Stanford-Binet V*, the *WISC–IV* is used by psychologists, along with other information, for developing students' profiles of intellectual skills and abilities, classification in diagnostic categories, or placement in special educational programs. The *SB–V* and *WISC–V* are different tests; you should not expect them to come to the exact same conclusion about a student.

WPPSI–IV The *Wechsler Preschool and Primary Scale of Intelligence–IV* is used with children ages 2 years, 6 months years through 7 years, 3 months. It overlaps with the *WISC–V* for ages 6 years through 7 years, 7 months. For this overlapping age range, the *WISC–V* is recommended (Sattler, 1992). The *WPPSI–IV* contains 15 subtests (only some of which are used in the tests for ages 2 years, 6 months through 3 years, 11 months). For ages 4 years, 0 months through 7 years, 7 months, the Full-Scale IQ uses scores from 13 of the subtests, and there are five Primary Index Scales. The Verbal Comprehension Index uses the Information and Similarities subtests. The Visual Spatial Index uses the Block Design and Object Assembly subtests. The Fluid Reasoning Index uses the Matrix Reasoning and Picture Concepts subtests. The Working Memory Index uses the Picture Memory and Zoo

Location subtests. The Processing Speed Index uses the Bug Search and Cancellation subtests.

Kaufman Assessment Battery for Children

General Description The *Kaufman Assessment Battery for Children–II* (*KABC–II*) is an individually administered test of general intelligence (Kaufman & Kaufman, 2004). It is used with children ages 3 through 18. The *KABC–II* differs in several ways from other approaches to measuring scholastic aptitude described thus far: (a) The subtests were derived from a differential psychological model (Cattell-Horn-Carroll [CHC] model; see Alfonso, Flanagan, & Radwan, 2005) and neuropsychological theory (Luria model; see Das, 2002); (b) a psychologist must decide before testing which one of the two interpretive models to use with a particular child and base the overall score only on the chosen model; and (c) there is a deliberate attempt to organize the testing to make it "fairer" to students not in the mainstream culture and for certain students with language-affected disabilities. In the norming sample, nonmainstream ethnic groups had average scores that were slightly higher when the Luria model was used than when the CHC model was used. The use of different models for defining cognitive ability is helpful, too, when professionals are developing IEPs for students.

Content The *KABC–II* is organized into five scales. The scales and their subtests are organized as follows. The names in brackets are the scale names when the CHC model is used.

- *Sequential Processing Scale* [*Short-Term Memory*] $(G_{sm})^1$—One's ability to remember an ordered series of images or ideas and use this memory to do a task. Requires repeating a sequence of numbers or identifying a sequence of pictures that the examiner says. Includes two subtests (and one supplemental subtest): Number Recall and Word Order (Hand Movements).

- *Simultaneous Processing Scale* [*Visual Processing*] (G_v)—One's ability to consider an array of information and process the parts of the array simultaneously to do the task. This form of thinking requires the student to visualize and

integrate the elements in the array presented, so it is called visual processing ability. Consists of six subtests (and one supplemental subtest): Face Recognition, Triangles, Conceptual Thinking, Pattern Recognition, Rover, and Block Counting (Gestalt Closure), plus Pattern Reasoning and Story Completion for ages 5 and 6.

- *Planning Ability Scale* [*Fluid Reasoning*] (G_f)—One's ability to understand a nonverbal problem, generate a hypothesis about how to solve it, test that solution, and revise it if necessary. Students must use verbal reasoning to solve the nonverbal problems. Includes two subtests: Pattern Reasoning and Story Completion, for ages 7 to 18.

- *Learning Ability Scale* [*Long-Term Storage and Retrieval*] (G_{lr})—One's ability to successfully complete different types of tasks that require learning something new. Some tasks require immediate recall of the newly learned information and others require using that information after a period of delay. Includes two subtests: Atlantis and Rebus.

- *Knowledge Scale* [*Crystallized Ability*] (G_c)—One's ability to express knowledge and understanding of objects and events in the mainstream culture. Students are asked to express their knowledge of words and facts, when questions are asked verbally and through pictorial stimuli. They respond either verbally or by pointing. Consists of three subtests: Riddles, Expressive Vocabulary, and Verbal Knowledge.

A readable explanation of the Luria model and the CHC model, a full description of the *KABC–II*, and the history of the *KABC–II* are found in Kaufman, Lichtenberger, Fletcher-Janzen, and Kaufman (2005).

Scores The *KABC–II* provides *DIQ*-scores (mean = 100, standard deviation = 15) for each of the five scales: Sequential Processing, Simultaneous Processing, Planning Ability, Learning Ability, and Knowledge. Each of the subtests within these scales is reported as a normalized standard score (mean = 10, standard deviation = 3). In addition, there are three *DIQ* composite scores: the *Mental Processing Index* (*MPI*), the *Fluid-Crystallized Index* (*FCI*), and the *Non-Verbal Index* (*NVI*). Any one student can be assigned only *MPI* and *NVI* or *FCI* and *NVI*.

---

1 The notation used is *G* with a subscript. The *G* represents "general ability factor," first postulated by Spearman (1927). This factor can be decomposed into subfactors like the ones defined here for the CHC model. The subscript on the *G* denotes the subfactor.

You will recall that the examiner must choose to use either the Luria model or the CHC model before testing a student. If the examiner chooses the Luria model, then the student can receive the *MPI* composite but not the *FCI* composite; if the examiner chooses the CHC model, the student receives the *FCI* composite, not the *MPI*. The difference is that the *MPI* does not include the Knowledge/Crystallized Ability (*Gc*) subtest because it is not administered under the Luria model. Here is the structure:

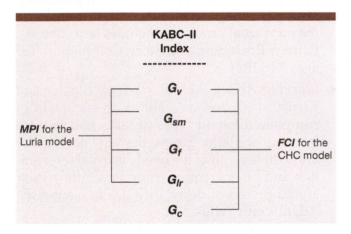

Usefulness of the *KABC–II* Approach The authors suggest the following uses for the *FCI* and *MPI* (Kaufman et al., 2005):

■ The *FCI* (i.e., all five areas) should be used for the majority of students; when there is a suspicion of a reading, written expression, or mathematics disability; for a child with mental retardation; for a child with attention-deficit/hyperactivity disorder (ADHD); for a child with an emotional or behavioral disorder; and with a child who is gifted.

■ The *MPI* (i.e., exclude administration of the Knowledge component) should be used with children from bilingual backgrounds; children from nonmainstream cultural backgrounds whose verbal development is problematic; and with children who have language disorders, autism, or deafness/hearing loss.

Until the research on the *KABC–II* has been completed, we cannot properly evaluate these proposed uses.

MyLab Education **Self-Check 19.1**

MyLab Education **Application Exercise 19.1:**
Interpreting Scholastic Aptitude Test Results

ASSESSING ADAPTIVE BEHAVIOR
Meaning of Adaptive Behavior

Tests such as the *Stanford-Binet*, the *WISC*, and the *KABC* measure general scholastic ability. A school setting, of course, is not the only environment in which persons are expected to cope. Some students may appear to teachers and other school personnel to suffer from intellectual disabilities, but their families, neighbors, and peers accept the students and consider the students normal in all other facets of life. It is recommended, therefore, that before labeling a student as having intellectual disabilities, the student's ability to cope with the demands of his or her environment outside classroom learning be assessed. According to the American Association on Intellectual and Developmental Disabilities (2002), "*Intellectual disability* is a disability characterized by significant limitations both in intellectual functioning and in *adaptive behavior,* which covers many everyday social and practical skills. This disability originates before the age of 18" [emphasis added].

Adaptive behavior assessment focuses on how independently students can care for themselves and how well they can cope with the demands placed on them by the immediate culture in which they are living. Thus, these types of assessments focus on a student's success as a family member, consumer, wage earner, member of a nonacademic peer group, person interacting with adults, and person caring for his or her health and physical needs—that is, skills in the three domains of conceptual, social, and practical adaptive skills. A psychological report for a student often includes assessment of the student's adaptive behavior as well as his or her general scholastic aptitude. This section presents one example.

Vineland Adaptive Behavior Scales, 3rd Edition (Vineland-3)

The *Vineland Adaptive Behavior Scales, 3rd Edition* (*Vineland-3*; revised and renormed by Sparrow, Cicchetti, & Balla, 2005) is a developmental checklist that assesses adaptive behavior in five areas: Communication (expressive, receptive, and written); Daily Living Skills (personal, domestic, community); Socialization (interpersonal relationships, play and leisure, coping skills); Motor Skills (gross motor and fine motor, optional); and Maladaptive Behavior (internalizing and externalizing, optional). The first three areas are assessed for persons from birth through 90 years (and low-functioning adults). Motor Skills assessment is limited to children younger than 9 years. A trained interviewer completes the assessment by interviewing a child's parent or caregiver.

The *Vineland-3* is available in digital or paper format. It has three forms: (1) Interview (ages birth to 90); (2) Parent/Caregiver (ages birth to 90); and (3) Teacher, for ages 3 to 22. Each form is available in two versions: Comprehensive (full-length) and Domain-level (abbreviated). The parent and caregiver forms are also available in Spanish. A qualified professional is needed to interpret the scores. The *Vineland-3* provides national norms for all editions. For the two interview editions, special supplemental norms are available for adults with intellectual disabilities (residential and nonresidential), children with hearing impairments, children with visual impairments, and children with emotional disturbances (the latter three groups in residential settings).

According to the authors, the *Vineland-3* may be used for diagnosing adaptive behavior deficits, determining eligibility for special services, planning intervention programs, and tracking progress in development. The authors have planned for its use with populations of individuals with intellectual disabilities, autism spectrum disorders (ASDs), Asperger syndrome, ADHD, posttraumatic brain injury, hearing impairment, and dementia/Alzheimer's disease.

ASSESSING VOCATIONAL AND CAREER INTERESTS

What Are Interests?

Attitudes, Interests, and Values Three characteristics of students are closely related: attitudes, interests, and values. Questionnaires very often assess these characteristics. The questionnaires appear similar because, when responding to the questionnaire, a student reads several statements and expresses his or her degree of agreement with the statements.

In spite of their similarity, the three concepts are not identical. To interpret assessment results properly, you must distinguish among these three concepts. An **attitude** is a positive or negative feeling about a physical object, a type of people, a particular person, a government or other social institution's policy, ideas, or the like. For example, when a student expresses agreement with the statement, "My mathematics class helps me become a better person," the student is expressing his attitude toward the mathematics class.

Interests, on the other hand, are preferences for specific types of activities when a person is not under external pressure. For example, when a student expresses agreement with the statement, "I enjoy working on the mathematics problems my teacher assigns," the student is expressing her interest in a mathematics activity.

Values, unlike attitudes and interests, are long-lasting beliefs of the importance of certain life goals, a lifestyle, a way of acting, or a way of life. For example, when a student expresses agreement with the statement, "I consider it more important to be one of the best students in mathematics than to be one of the best players in a football game," the student is expressing his valuing of mathematics success over football success.

When studying ways of assessing attitudes, interests, and values, keep in mind that the methods you use for assessing them are highly susceptible to students' providing socially desirable responses, as opposed to frank personal responses. Therefore, questionnaires can assess only what an individual wishes to reveal.

Focus on Career Interests This cluster of interests is important as students begin to prepare themselves for further schooling and for the world of work. No single piece of information is sufficient for a student to use in making vocational decisions, of course. However, the student's interest in various activities associated with specific types of work or work environments is an important consideration. Besides knowing the duty requirements of the job market, and his own abilities and aptitudes, a student should also understand his own interests regarding work-related activities. Thus, the types of career interest inventories described next can provide one source of information to help a student make educational and vocational choices.

Expressed, Manifested, Tested, and Inventoried Interests

Interest inventories of the type described in this section are limited to only vocational interests or career interests; and career interests are narrowed even further. You may find it useful to distinguish among expressed, manifested, tested, and inventoried interests.

Expressed interests are obtained when you ask students directly about their interests. The interests a student verbally professes when you ask the student directly may not express her true preferences: A youngster may express an interest in being a doctor, for example, because she perceives it as something parents expect. Or a teenager may say she wants to be a musician just to see the reaction of her parents.

Manifested interests are inferred from what a student actually does or the activities in which the student actually participates. When you attempt to infer students' interests from their activities, you may misjudge. For example, you may conclude a boy is interested in athletics because he participates in the junior high track team, but you later find out he only wants to be with his friends after school.

Tested interests are those you infer from the results of assessing a student's information and knowledge of a particular subject matter. For example, you may hypothesize that a student who has a lot of scientific knowledge and information has more interest in science than a student who knows little about science. Such knowledge assessments are not used very often in current vocational counseling practice.

Inventoried interests are identified through various paper-and-pencil tests or interest inventories. A limitation here is that the interests you discover through a particular interest inventory do not represent all interests or even all career interests. Further, as with other forms of educational and psychological assessment, the interest patterns identified with one publisher's interest inventory may not be the same ones that could be identified with others. When counseling students, you should use all three interests—expressed, manifested, and inventoried—to assess a student's interest patterns.

Vocational Interest Inventories

Vocational interest inventories are formal paper-and-pencil—or digital—questionnaires that help students express their likes and dislikes about a very wide range of work and other activities. A student's pattern of interests is then determined from these responses. This profile or pattern of interests becomes one source of information a student can use for career exploration, counseling, and decision making.

Building Interest Inventories The traditional rationale for describing a person's inventoried interests has been called the **people-similarity rationale** (Cole & Hanson, 1975, p. 6): "If a person likes the same things that people in a particular job like, the person will be satisfied with the job."

Certain parts of the *Kuder Career Interests Assessment* (*KCIA*) and the *Strong Interest Inventory* (*SII*) follow this rationale. Both the *KCIA* and the Occupational Scales of the *SII*, for example, are **empirically keyed scales**, made up of items especially selected because research has shown that responses to these items clearly differentiate between the persons who are currently and happily employed in a particular occupation and people in general.

A second rationale has been called the **activity-similarity rationale** (Cole & Hanson, 1975, p. 6): "If people like activities similar to the activities required by a job, they will like those job activities and consequently be satisfied with their job."

Inventories built using this rationale present the students with lists of activities that are similar to those required of persons working in certain jobs or studying certain subjects. The developers assume that if a person has an identifiable pattern of likes and dislikes common to a particular job, that person will be satisfied with that job. The *Ohio Vocational Interest Survey, Second Edition* (*OVIS–II*) was developed using this rationale.

The pioneers of the interest inventory technique used a variety of content to survey interests, including asking examinees likes and dislikes of job titles, school subject matter, hobbies, leisure activities, work activities, types of persons, and type of reading material, and assessing examinees' personal characteristics (Davis, 1980). Over time, however, the concept of interests narrowed to the world of work and careers. Today, the content of most inventories is limited exclusively to lists of activities, and most are concerned with work activities. An exception is the *SII*, which uses a large variety of content to measure a person's interest in relation to persons working in a wide range of careers.

A number of vocational interest inventories are listed in Appendix H. Two of the inventories, the *Strong Interest Inventory* (*SII*) and the *Kuder*® *Career Interests Assessment*™ (*KCIA*), are briefly described here.

Strong Interest Inventory The 2004 revision of the *SII*, which is used with persons 14-years-old and older, is composed of 291 items. A person is presented with occupations, subject areas, activities, leisure activities, and people and rates each item on a 5-point scale: strongly like, like, indifferent, dislike, or strongly dislike. The responses are then scored via a computer (tests cannot be scored locally) and reported as standard scores on various scales. The *SII* results are reported to the examinee in four ways: (1) Six General Occupational Themes, which describe a person's overall pattern of occupational interests; (2) 30 Basic Interest Scales, which describe the somewhat narrower categories of interest areas a person likes within the Six General Occupational Themes; (3) 211 Occupational Scales, which describe the extent to which a person's likes and dislikes are similar to persons working in specific occupations; and (4) Five Personal Style Scales.

The student receives a score on each of six areas, which were adapted from Holland (1973). These are Realistic, Conventional, Investigative, Enterprising, Artistic, and Social. A counselor can use the student's profile regarding these areas to help her understand her overall or general pattern of interests, work activities, personal values, and how she appears to be oriented to the world of work. A normalized standard score (*T*-score) is reported for each of the six themes.

The 30 scales are grouped in clusters under each of the six themes. For example, six of the Basic Interest Scales—Teaching and Education, Social Sciences, Human Resources and Training, Healthcare Services, Religion and Spirituality, and Counseling and Helping—are clustered under the general occupational theme of Social. The Basic Interest Scales are intermediate between the General Occupational Themes and the more specific Occupational Scales (described next). The Basic Interest Scales describe the clusters of interests a student has. These activity areas may be common to several specific occupations (for example, there are many types of teachers).

Paralegal, respiratory specialist, florist, artist, and social science teacher are some of the occupational scales. The occupational scales are organized under each of the six general occupation themes. A person receives a standard score for each occupation based on the combined male and female norms. This score describes how similar the student's pattern of likes and dislikes is to

persons who are experienced and satisfied in each occupation. In the report to the student within each General Occupational Theme, occupations are ordered according to the student's similarity to persons of their own gender. Occupations listed first are those for which the students' *SII* responses are most similar to persons of their own gender who are working in that occupation.

There are five Personal Style Scales describing how the student approaches learning, people, and the workplace: Work Style, Learning Environment, Leadership Style, Risk Taking, and Team Orientation. In addition to these scales, there is a special administrative index, the Typicality Index. This index is used to assess the consistency of a student's responses to items that are very highly correlated in the norm group in an attempt to detect random and atypical response patterns. A counselor uses this index to help decide whether a student responded well enough to make the results meaningful. If not, the counselor will need to explore with the student individually why he did not respond consistently to very similar items.

Although the *SII* has a single booklet for both males and females, there are 122 Occupational Scales for men and 122 Occupational Scales for women for a total of 244 Occupational Scales. The authors have kept scale reporting separate for each gender because (a) there are large differences in the strength of interests in the two genders in many areas and (b) combined-sex (unisex) scales appear less valid for many occupations. Students may understand their interests better if they can compare them to both like-gender and opposite-gender norms. This comparison may be especially helpful to students who are thinking of entering occupations dominated by the gender opposite of their own.

Kuder® Career Interests Assessment™ The 2012 version of the *KCIA*, which like the *SII* is for secondary school students and adults, includes 96 items arranged in sets of three. Each triad lists three different activities (e.g., "visit an art gallery"). Respondents select which activity, out of the three choices in the set, that they would most enjoy and which they would least enjoy. Final item selection was based on the responses of a national sample of 958 workers from a large variety of occupations and from a sample of 142 ninth and twelfth graders.

The student receives a score on each of the six Holland areas: Realistic, Investigative, Artistic, Social, Enterprising, and Conventional. Based on these six interest scores, O*NET occupations and 16 National career clusters and pathways are identified for students (Suen, 2012). O*NET (onetcenter.org) is a repository of occupational information. The O*NET database contains information on hundreds of standardized and occupation-specific descriptors. The database is available to the public at no cost and is constantly updated with survey results from workers in a broad range of occupations.

ASSESSING ATTITUDES
Attitudes and Their Characteristics

Attitudes are characteristics of persons that describe their positive and negative feelings toward particular objects, situations, institutions, persons, or ideas. Keep in mind that attitudes are learned, and once learned they direct or guide the students' actions. The attitudes of older students and adults are changeable, but it is much easier to change the attitudes of younger students. You cannot observe students' attitudes directly; you must infer them from the students' actions or from responses to an attitude questionnaire. Because students can fake their responses to attitude questionnaires, you should interpret the results very cautiously. Attitude surveys are more commonly used in research than in classroom practice. Sometimes, however, teachers use attitude questions as part of student self-reflection exercises to help understand students' work in class.

Attitudes differ in both **direction** and **intensity**. Two students may hold the same positive attitude (direction), but the students may differ greatly regarding the strength of feeling (intensity) they attach to that attitude. Students' attitudes will also differ in **affective saliency** or emotionality. Two students may have the same positive attitude, but one may become much more emotional than the other regarding it.

ASSESSING PERSONALITY DIMENSIONS

A variety of techniques have been developed to measure various aspects of personality. A person using a personality test must be trained in psychological interpretation of the results. This training usually requires extensive graduate work in counseling or school psychology and a lengthy supervised internship. School psychologists sometimes use personality tests as well as other measures (e.g., aptitude, achievement, interest) to help understand students who are having difficulties in school. Teachers will encounter the results of such tests, however, if they are part of a child study team or if they read psychological reports of students. Thus, some familiarity with a few basic concepts of personality measurement is in order.

Assessment Approaches

The kind of personality tests a counselor or psychologist uses depends primarily on the psychological orientation of the particular professional. Currently, there is no standard model or conception of personality, nor do counselors and psychologists agree on which particular aspects of personality are most important to assess. The kinds of personality tests used in psychological reports a teacher may encounter depend on the background and training of the psychologist assigned to a given student's case. Two broad methods for assessing personality dimensions are projective techniques and structured techniques.

Projective Techniques

Projective personality test techniques present the examinee with ambiguous stimuli and ask the examinee to respond to them. The proponents of this technique assume that an examinee's interpretations of these vague stimuli will reveal the examinee's innermost needs, feelings, and conflicts, even though the examinee is unaware of what he or she is revealing. This assumption is known as the **projective hypothesis** (Frank, 1939). A trained examiner is needed to interpret an examinee's responses. Examples of projective personality tests are the *Rorschach Test*, the *Thematic Apperception Test* (*TAT*), word association tests, various sentence completion tests, certain picture arrangement tests, and various figure drawing tests. School psychologists use projective tests less often now than in the past.

Sentence **completion tests of personality** ask the examinee to complete sentences related to various aspects of self and interpersonal relations (e.g., "Compared with most families, mine..."). The results of content analyses are used similarly to generate hypotheses about a subject's personality.

Structured Techniques

Structured personality assessment techniques follow very specific rules for administering, scoring, and interpreting the tests. Usually they follow a response-choice format: yes-no, true-false, or multiple-choice. Examples of structured personality tests are the *Guilford-Zimmerman Temperament Survey*, the *Minnesota Multiphasic Personality Inventory—Second Edition*, the *California Psychological Inventory*, and the *Personality Inventory for Children—Second Edition*. Each test is sometimes referred to as a **self-report personality inventory** because it requires examinees to respond to the items in a way that describes personal feelings. For instance, examinees may be asked whether the statement, "I usually express my personal opinions to others," is true of themselves.

Another characteristic of structured personality inventories is that the items are related to various scales or personality dimensions. The *Guilford-Zimmerman Temperament Survey*, for example, reports an examinee's profile with respect to 10 scales: general activity, restraint, ascendance (leadership), sociability, emotional stability, objectivity, friendliness, thoughtfulness, personal relations, and masculinity.

Usefulness of Tests for the Teacher

Self-report personality inventories require persons to (Thorndike, Cunningham, Thorndike, & Hagen, 1991) (a) read and comprehend each item, (b) be able to understand their own actions enough to know whether a given statement is true of them, and (c) be willing to respond honestly and frankly. Reading in the context of personality testing requires that students understand the items well enough to be able to decide the degree to which the statements apply to their own lives. To decide whether a statement applies, a student must view that behavior objectively, which may not be within the repertoire of a poorly adjusted student. Finally, if a student is neither able nor willing to respond frankly to the items, a distorted personality description may result. This lack of frankness may occur more often when testing children who feel vulnerable or threatened if they reveal their feelings to the teacher or, more generally, to the school. Considering the shortcomings of self-report personality and adjustment inventories, some measurement experts conclude they have a limited role in education.

> **MyLab Education Self-Check 19.2**
>
> **MyLab Education Application Exercise 19.2:** Interpreting Career Interests with a Student

CONCLUSION

There is a lot more to say about scholastic aptitude, career interests, attitudes, and personality tests than we have been able to fit into one chapter. We hope, however, that this chapter has been a useful introduction to some types of tests you will encounter as you work in schools.

This textbook has been about educational assessment of all sorts. Returning to the theme that began in Chapter 1, the goal of good educational assessment is to provide valid—and you now know in some detail what that means—information to support sound educational decisions. Educational assessment happens in individual sessions (as for some of the aptitude tests described in this chapter), in classrooms, and at the school, district, state, national, and international levels. Education-related decisions are made at all these levels, as well. We hope that, armed with understandings from this textbook and experience from your course- and schoolwork, you are prepared to participate in sound assessment of students and in the resulting educational decisions.

EXERCISES

1. Describe several school situations in which it is less helpful to know a student's level of specific skill development than to know a student's general intellectual skill development in setting expectations for learning new material.
2. Read each of the following statements of educational needs. For each statement, choose a test that possibly could meet the stated need. Choose from among the tests in this set to respond to this exercise: *OLSAT, DAT*, readiness tests, *SAT, ACT*, aptitude tests for a specific subject, *SB–V, WISC–IV, KABC–II*.
   a. "In addition to finding out a student's verbal and quantitative aptitudes, I would like to know how well the student processes symbols and other nonverbal material."
   b. "I'd like to give all ninth graders a test that would provide information helpful to them in making career decisions."
   c. "I would like to know which of my fifth-grade students could learn computer programming quickly and well."

d. "I need a general ability test for a student who recently arrived from Cuba."

e. "I need a college admissions test that gives me information that I can use in guidance and counseling activities as well as in admissions."

3. Both the *DAT* and *Strong Interest Inventory* report results on separate gender norms. Explain why they do so, and discuss whether this practice is helpful to the career and further schooling planning of females.

4. Read the following statements. Each statement expresses a student's status with respect to achievement, aptitude, attitude, interest, or values. Classify each statement into one of the five categories.

a. "I am in control of my learning in this class at all times."

b. "I like science fiction stories better than biographies."

c. "I think my math class is boring."

d. "It is more important for me to be in personal control of my working hours than to earn a high salary."

e. "I am constantly striving to be the best student in this school."

5. Visit your school's guidance department and determine how its counselors use interest inventories. Share your findings with your classmates.

Educational Assessment Knowledge and Skills for Teachers

FIGURE A.1

I. Teachers should understand learning in the content area they teach.

II. Teachers should be able to articulate clear learning intentions that are congruent with both the content and depth of thinking implied by standards and curriculum goals, in such a way that they are attainable and assessable.

III. Teachers should have a repertoire of strategies for communicating to students what achievement of a learning intention looks like.

IV. Teachers should understand the purposes and uses of the range of available assessment options and be skilled in using them.

V. Teachers should have the skills to analyze classroom questions, test items, and performance assessment tasks to ascertain the specific knowledge and thinking skills required for students to do them.

VI. Teachers should have the skills to provide effective, useful feedback on student work.

VII. Teachers should be able to construct scoring schemes that quantify student performance on classroom assessments into useful information for decisions about students, classrooms, schools, and districts. These decisions should lead to improved student learning, growth, or development.

VIII. Teachers should be able to administer external assessments and interpret their results for decisions about students, classrooms, schools, and districts.

IX. Teachers should be able to articulate their interpretations of assessment results and their reasoning about the educational decisions based on assessment results to the educational populations they serve (student and his/her family, class, school, community).

X. Teachers should be able to help students use assessment information to make sound educational decisions.

XI. Teachers should understand and carry out their legal and ethical responsibilities in assessment as they conduct their work.

Source: From Brookhart, S. M. (2011). Educational assessment knowledge and skills for teachers. *Educational Measurement: Issues and Practice, 30*(1), Table 1, p. 7. Used by permission.

Code of Fair Testing Practices in Education (Revised)

Prepared by the Joint Committee on Testing Practices

The *Code of Fair Testing Practices in Education* (*Code*) is a guide for professionals in fulfilling their obligation to provide and use tests that are fair to all test-takers regardless of age, gender, disability, race, ethnicity, national origin, religion, sexual orientation, linguistic background, or other personal characteristics. Fairness is a primary consideration in all aspects of testing. Careful standardization of tests and administration conditions helps to ensure that all test-takers are given a comparable opportunity to demonstrate what they know and how they can perform in the area being tested. Fairness implies that every test-taker has the opportunity to prepare for the test and is informed about the general nature and content of the test, as appropriate to the purpose of the test. Fairness also extends to the accurate reporting of individual and group test results. Fairness is not an isolated concept, but must be considered in all aspects of the testing process.

The *Code* applies broadly to testing in education (admissions, educational assessment, educational diagnosis, and student placement) regardless of the mode of presentation, so it is relevant to conventional paper-and-pencil tests, computer-based tests, and performance tests. It is not designed to cover employment testing, licensure or certification testing, or other types of testing outside the field of education. The *Code* is directed primarily at professionally developed tests used in formally administered testing programs.

Although the *Code* is not intended to cover tests made by teachers for use in their own classrooms, teachers are encouraged to use the guidelines to help improve their testing practices.

The *Code* addresses the roles of test developers and test users separately. Test developers are people and organizations that construct tests, as well as those that set policies for testing programs. Test users are people and agencies that select tests, administer tests, commission test development services, or make decisions on the basis of test scores. Test developer and test user roles may overlap, for example, when a state or local education agency commissions test development services, sets policies that control the test development process, and makes decisions on the basis of the test scores.

Many of the statements in the *Code* refer to the selection and use of existing tests. When a new test is developed, when an existing test is modified, or when the administration of a test is modified, the *Code* is intended to provide guidance for this process.

The *Code* is not intended to be mandatory, exhaustive, or definitive, and may not be applicable to every situation. Instead, the *Code* is intended to be aspirational, but and it is not intended to take precedence over the judgment of those who have competence in the subjects addressed.

The *Code* provides guidance separately for test developers and test users in four critical areas:

A. Developing and Selecting Appropriate Tests

B. Administering and Scoring Tests

C. Reporting and Interpreting Test Results

D. Informing Test-Takers

The *Code* is intended to be consistent with the relevant parts of the Standards for Educational and Psychological Testing (American Educational Research

Association [AERA], American Psychological Association [APA], and National Council on Measurement in Education [NCME], 1999). The *Code* is not meant to add new principles over and above those in the Standards or to change their meaning. Rather, the *Code* is intended to represent the spirit of selected portions of the Standards in a way that is relevant and meaningful to developers and users of tests, as well as to test-takers and/or their parents or guardians. States, districts, schools, organizations, and individual professionals are encouraged to commit themselves to fairness in testing and safeguarding the rights of test-takers. The *Code* is intended to assist in carrying out such commitments.

The *Code* has been prepared by the Joint Committee on Testing Practices, a cooperative effort among several professional organizations. The aim of the Joint Committee is to act, in the public interest, to advance the quality of testing practices. Members of the Joint Committee include the American Counseling Association (ACA), the American Educational Research Association (AERA), the American Psychological Association (APA), the American Speech-Language-Hearing Association (ASHA), the National Association of School Psychologists (NASP), the National Association of Test Directors (NATD), and the National Council on Measurement in Education (NCME).

A. DEVELOPING AND SELECTING APPROPRIATE TESTS*

Test Developers

Test developers should provide the information and supporting evidence that test users need to select appropriate tests.

1. Provide evidence of what the test measures, the recommended uses, the intended test-takers, and the strengths and limitations of the test, including the level of precision of the test scores.

2. Describe how the content and skills to be tested were selected and how the tests were developed.

3. Communicate information about a test's characteristics at a level of detail appropriate to the intended test users.

4. Provide guidance on the levels of skills, knowledge, and training necessary for appropriate review, selection, and administration of tests.

---

* Many of the statements in the *Code* refer to the selection of existing tests. However, in customized testing programs test developers are engaged to construct new tests. In those situations, the test development process should be designed to help ensure that the completed tests will be in compliance with the *Code*.

5. Provide evidence that the technical quality, including reliability and validity, of the test meets its intended purposes.

6. Provide to qualified test users representative samples of test questions or practice tests, directions, answer sheets, manuals, and score reports.

7. Avoid potentially offensive content or language when developing test questions and related materials.

8. Make appropriately modified forms of tests or administration procedures available for test-takers with disabilities who need special accommodations.

9. Obtain and provide evidence on the performance of test-takers of diverse subgroups, making significant efforts to obtain sample sizes that are adequate for subgroup analyses. Evaluate the evidence to ensure that differences in performance are related to the skills being assessed.

Test Users

Test users should select tests that meet the intended purpose and that are appropriate for the intended test-takers.

1. Define the purpose for testing, the content and skills to be tested, and the intended test-takers. Select and use the most appropriate test based on a thorough review of available information.

2. Review and select tests based on the appropriateness of test content, skills tested, and content coverage for the intended purpose of testing.

3. Review materials provided by test developers and select tests for which clear, accurate, and complete information is provided.

4. Select tests through a process that includes persons with appropriate knowledge, skills, and training.

5. Evaluate evidence of the technical quality of the test provided by the test developer and any independent reviewers.

6. Evaluate representative samples of test questions or practice tests, directions, answer sheets, manuals, and score reports before selecting a test.

7. Evaluate procedures and materials used by test developers, as well as the resulting test, to ensure that potentially offensive content or language is avoided.

8. Select tests with appropriately modified forms or administration procedures for test-takers with disabilities who need special accommodations.

9. Evaluate the available evidence on the performance of test-takers of diverse subgroups. Determine to the extent feasible which performance differences may have been caused by factors unrelated to the skills being assessed.

B. ADMINISTERING AND SCORING TESTS

Test Developers

Test developers should explain how to administer and score tests correctly and fairly.

1. Provide clear descriptions of detailed procedures for administering tests in a standardized manner.
2. Provide guidelines on reasonable procedures for assessing persons with disabilities who need special accommodations or those with diverse linguistic backgrounds.
3. Provide information to test-takers or test users on test question formats and procedures for answering test questions, including information on the use of any needed materials and equipment.
4. Establish and implement procedures to ensure the security of testing materials during all phases of test development, administration, scoring, and reporting.
5. Provide procedures, materials, and guidelines for scoring the tests as well as, and for monitoring the accuracy of the scoring process. If scoring the test is the responsibility of the test developer, provide adequate training for scorers.
6. Correct errors that affect the interpretation of the scores and communicate the corrected results promptly.
7. Develop and implement procedures for ensuring the confidentiality of scores.

Test Users

Test users should administer and score tests correctly and fairly.

1. Follow established procedures for administering tests in a standardized manner.
2. Provide and document appropriate procedures for test-takers with disabilities who need special accommodations or those with diverse linguistic backgrounds. Some accommodations may be required by law or regulation.
3. Provide test-takers with an opportunity to become familiar with test question formats and any materials or equipment that may be used during testing.
4. Protect the security of test materials, including respecting copyrights and eliminating opportunities for test-takers to obtain scores by fraudulent means.
5. If test scoring is the responsibility of the test user, provide adequate training to scorers and ensure and monitor the accuracy of the scoring process.
6. Correct errors that affect the interpretation of the scores and communicate the corrected results promptly.
7. Develop and implement procedures for ensuring the confidentiality of scores.

C. REPORTING AND INTERPRETING TEST RESULTS

Test Developers

Test developers should report test results accurately and provide information to help test users interpret test results correctly.

1. Provide information to support recommended interpretations of the results, including the nature of the content, norms or comparison groups, and other technical evidence. Advise test users of the benefits and limitations of test results and their interpretation. Warn against assigning greater precision than is warranted.
2. Provide guidance regarding the interpretations of results for tests administered with modifications. Inform test users of potential problems in interpreting test results when tests or test administration procedures are modified.
3. Specify appropriate uses of test results and warn test users of potential misuses.
4. When test developers set standards, provide the rationale, procedures, and evidence for setting performance standards or passing scores. Avoid using stigmatizing labels.
5. Encourage test users to base decisions about test-takers on multiple sources of appropriate information, not on a single test score.
6. Provide information to enable test users to accurately interpret and report test results for groups of test-takers, including information about who were and who were not included in the different groups being compared, and information about factors that might influence the interpretation of results.
7. Provide test results in a timely fashion and in a manner that is understood by the test-taker.
8. Provide guidance to test users about how to monitor the extent to which the test is fulfilling its intended purposes.

Test Users

Test users should report and interpret test results accurately and clearly.

1. Interpret the meaning of the test results, taking into account the nature of the content, norms or comparison groups, other technical evidence, and benefits and limitations of test results.
2. Interpret test results from modified test or test administration procedures in view of the impact those modifications may have had on test results.
3. Avoid using tests for purposes other than those recommended by the test developer unless there is evidence to support the intended use or interpretation.

4. Review the procedures for setting performance standards or passing scores. Avoid using stigmatizing labels.

5. Avoid using a single test score as the sole determinant of decisions about test-takers. Interpret test scores in conjunction with other information about individuals.

6. State the intended interpretation and use of test results for groups of test-takers. Avoid grouping test results for purposes not specifically recommended by the test developer unless evidence is obtained to support the intended use. Report procedures that were followed in determining who were and who were not included in the groups being compared and describe factors that might influence the interpretation of results.

7. Communicate test results in a timely fashion and in a manner that is understood by the test-taker.

8. Develop and implement procedures for monitoring test use, including consistency with the intended purposes of the test.

D. INFORMING TEST-TAKERS

Test Developers or Test Users

Under some circumstances, test developers have direct communication with the test-takers and/or control of the tests, testing process, and test results. In other circumstances, the test users have these responsibilities.

Test developers or test users should inform test-takers about the nature of the test, test-taker rights and responsibilities, the appropriate use of scores, and procedures for resolving challenges to scores.

1. Inform test-takers in advance of the test administration about the coverage of the test, the types of question formats, the directions, and appropriate test-taking strategies. Make such information available to all test-takers.

2. When a test is optional, provide test-takers or their parents/guardians with information to help them judge whether a test should be taken—including indications of any consequences that may result from not taking the test (e.g., not being eligible to compete for a particular scholarship)—and whether there is an available alternative to the test.

3. Provide test-takers or their parents/guardians with information about rights test-takers may have to obtain copies of tests and completed answer sheets, to retake tests, to have tests rescored, or to have scores declared invalid.

4. Provide test-takers or their parents/guardians with information about responsibilities test-takers have, such as being aware of the intended purpose and uses of the test, performing at capacity, following directions, and not disclosing test items or interfering with other test-takers.

5. Inform test-takers or their parents/guardians how long scores will be kept on file and indicate to whom, under what circumstances, and in what manner test scores and related information will or will not be released. Protect test scores from unauthorized release and access.

6. Describe procedures for investigating and resolving circumstances that might result in canceling or withholding scores, such as failure to adhere to specified testing procedures.

7. Describe procedures that test-takers, parents/guardians, and other interested parties may use to obtain more information about the test, register complaints, and have problems resolved.

Note: The membership of the working group that developed the *Code of Fair Testing Practices in Education* and of the Joint Committee on Testing Practices that guided the working group is as follows: Peter Behuniak, PhD; Lloyd Bond, PhD; Gwyneth M. Boodoo, PhD; Wayne Camara, PhD; Ray Fenton, PhD; John J. Fremer, PhD (Co-chair); Sharon M. Goldsmith, PhD; Bert F. Green, PhD; William G. Harris, PhD; Janet E. Helms, PhD; Stephanie H. McConaughy, PhD; Julie P. Noble, PhD; Wayne M. Patience, PhD; Carole L. Perlman, PhD; Douglas K. Smith, PhD; Janet E. Wall, EdD (Co-chair); Pat Nellor Wickwire, PhD; Mary Yakimowski, PhD. Lara Frumkin, PhD, of the APA served as staff liaison. The Joint Committee intends that the *Code* be consistent with and supportive of existing codes of conduct and standards of other professional groups who use tests in educational contexts. Of particular note are the *Responsibilities of Users of Standardized Tests* (Association for Assessment in Counseling, 1989), APA Test User Qualifications (2000), ASHA Code of Ethics (2001), *Ethical Principles of Psychologists and Code of Conduct* (1992), NASP Professional Conduct Manual (2000), NCME *Code of Professional Responsibility* (1995), and *Rights and Responsibilities of Test Takers: Guidelines and Expectations* (Joint Committee on Testing Practices, 2000).

Code of Professional Responsibilities in Educational Measurement

Prepared by the NCME Ad Hoc Committee on the Development of a Code of Ethics: Cynthia B. Schmeiser, ACT—Chair; Kurt F. Geisinger, State University of New York; Sharon Johnson-Lewis, Detroit Public Schools; Edward D. Roeber, Council of Chief State School Officers; William D. Schafer, University of Maryland

PREAMBLE AND GENERAL RESPONSIBILITIES

As an organization dedicated to the improvement of measurement and evaluation practice in education, the National Council on Measurement in Education (NCME) has adopted this Code to promote professionally responsible practice in educational measurement. Professionally responsible practice is conduct that arises from either the professional standards of the field, general ethical principles, or both.

The purpose of the Code of Professional Responsibilities in Educational Measurement, hereinafter referred to as the Code, is to guide the conduct of NCME members who are involved in any type of assessment activity in education. NCME is also providing this Code as a public service for all individuals who are engaged in educational assessment activities in the hope that these activities will be conducted in a professionally responsible manner. Persons who engage in these activities include local educators such as classroom teachers, principals, and superintendents; professionals such as school psychologists and counselors; state and national technical, legislative, and policy staff in education; staff of research, evaluation, and testing organizations; providers of test preparation services; college and university faculty and administrators; and professionals in business and industry who design and implement educational and training programs.

This Code applies to any type of assessment that occurs as part of the educational process, including formal and informal, traditional and alternative techniques for gathering information used in making educational decisions at all levels. These techniques include, but are not limited to, large-scale assessments at the school, district, state, national, and international levels; standardized tests; observational measures; teacher-conducted assessments; assessment support materials; and other achievement, aptitude, interest, and personality measures used in and for education.

Although NCME is promulgating this Code for its members, it strongly encourages other organizations and individuals who engage in educational assessment activities to endorse and abide by the responsibilities relevant to their professions. Because the Code pertains only to uses of assessment in education, it is recognized that uses of assessments outside of educational contexts, such as for employment, certification, or licensure, may involve additional professional responsibilities beyond those detailed in this Code.

The Code is intended to serve an educational function: to inform and remind those involved in educational assessment of their obligations to uphold the integrity of the manner in which assessments are developed, used, evaluated, and marketed. Moreover, it is expected that the Code will stimulate thoughtful discussion of what constitutes professionally responsible assessment practice at all levels in education.

SECTION 1: RESPONSIBILITIES OF THOSE WHO DEVELOP ASSESSMENT PRODUCTS AND SERVICES

Those who develop assessment products and services, such as classroom teachers and other assessment specialists, have a professional responsibility to strive to produce assessments that are of the highest quality. Persons who develop assessments have a professional responsibility to:

1.1 ensure that assessment products and services are developed to meet applicable professional, technical, and legal standards.

Source: © 1995 by the National Council on Measurement in Education. Reprinted by permission of the publisher. Available: ncme.org

1.2 develop assessment products and services that are as free as possible from bias due to characteristics irrelevant to the construct being measured, such as gender, ethnicity, race, socioeconomic status, disability, religion, age, or national origin.

1.3 plan accommodations for groups of test takers with disabilities and other special needs when developing assessments.

1.4 disclose to appropriate parties any actual or potential conflicts of interest that might influence the developers' judgment or performance.

1.5 use copyrighted materials in assessment products and services in accordance with state and federal law.

1.6 make information available to appropriate persons about the steps taken to develop and score the assessment, including up-to-date information used to support the reliability, validity, scoring and reporting processes, and other relevant characteristics of the assessment.

1.7 protect the rights to privacy of those who are assessed as part of the assessment development process.

1.8 caution users, in clear and prominent language, against the most likely misinterpretations and misuses of data that arise out of the assessment development process.

1.9 avoid false or unsubstantiated claims in test preparation and program support materials and services about an assessment or its use and interpretation.

1.10 correct any substantive inaccuracies in assessments or their support materials as soon as feasible.

1.11 develop score reports and support materials that promote the understanding of assessment results.

SECTION 2: RESPONSIBILITIES OF THOSE WHO MARKET AND SELL ASSESSMENT PRODUCTS AND SERVICES

The marketing of assessment products and services, such as tests and other instruments, scoring services, test preparation services, consulting, and test interpretive services, should be based on information that is accurate, complete, and relevant to those considering their use. Persons who market and sell assessment products and services have a professional responsibility to:

2.1 provide accurate information to potential purchasers about assessment products and services and their recommended uses and limitations.

2.2 not knowingly withhold relevant information about assessment products and services that might affect an appropriate selection decision.

2.3 base all claims about assessment products and services on valid interpretations of publicly available information.

2.4 allow qualified users equal opportunity to purchase assessment products and services.

2.5 establish reasonable fees for assessment products and services.

2.6 communicate to potential users, in advance of any purchase or use, all applicable fees associated with assessment products and services.

2.7 strive to ensure that no individuals are denied access to opportunities because of their inability to pay the fees for assessment products and services.

2.8 establish criteria for the sale of assessment products and services, such as limiting the sale of assessment products and services to those individuals who are qualified for recommended uses and from whom proper uses and interpretations are anticipated.

2.9 inform potential users of known inappropriate uses of assessment products and services and provide recommendations about how to avoid such misuses.

2.10 maintain a current understanding about assessment products and services and their appropriate uses in education.

2.11 release information implying endorsement by users of assessment products and services only with the users' permission.

2.12 avoid making claims that assessment products and services have been endorsed by another organization unless an official endorsement has been obtained.

2.13 avoid marketing test preparation products and services that may cause individuals to receive scores that misrepresent their actual levels of attainment.

SECTION 3: RESPONSIBILITIES OF THOSE WHO SELECT ASSESSMENT PRODUCTS AND SERVICES

Those who select assessment products and services for use in educational settings, or help others do so, have important professional responsibilities to make sure that the assessments are appropriate for their intended use. Persons who select assessment products and services have a professional responsibility to:

3.1 conduct a thorough review and evaluation of available assessment strategies and instruments that might be valid for the intended uses.

3.2 recommend and/or select assessments based on publicly available documented evidence of their technical quality and utility rather than on unsubstantiated claims or statements.

3.3 disclose any associations or affiliations that they have with the authors, test publishers, or others involved with the assessments under consideration for purchase and refrain from participation if such associations might affect the objectivity of the selection process.

3.4 inform decision makers and prospective users of the appropriateness of the assessment for the intended uses, likely consequences of use, protection of examinee rights, relative costs, materials and services needed to conduct or use the assessment, and known limitations of the assessment, including potential misuses and misinterpretations of assessment information.

3.5 recommend against the use of any prospective assessment that is likely to be administered, scored, and used in an invalid manner for members of various groups in our society for reasons of race, ethnicity, gender, age, disability, language background, socioeconomic status, religion, or national origin.

3.6 comply with all security precautions that may accompany assessments being reviewed.

3.7 immediately disclose any attempts by others to exert undue influence on the assessment selection process.

3.8 avoid recommending, purchasing, or using test preparation products and services that may cause individuals to receive scores that misrepresent their actual levels of attainment.

SECTION 4: RESPONSIBILITIES OF THOSE WHO ADMINISTER ASSESSMENTS

Those who prepare individuals to take assessments and those who are directly or indirectly involved in the administration of assessments as part of the educational process, including teachers, administrators, and assessment personnel, have an important role in making sure that the assessments are administered in a fair and accurate manner. Persons who prepare others for, and those who administer, assessments have a professional responsibility to:

4.1 inform the examinees about the assessment prior to its administration, including its purposes, uses, and consequences; how the assessment information will be judged or scored; how the results will be kept on file; who will have access to the results; how the results will be distributed; and examinees' rights before, during, and after the assessment.

4.2 administer only those assessments for which they are qualified by education, training, licensure, or certification.

4.3 take appropriate security precautions before, during, and after the administration of the assessment.

4.4 understand the procedures needed to administer the assessment prior to administration.

4.5 administer standardized assessments according to prescribed procedures and conditions and notify appropriate persons if any nonstandard or delimiting conditions occur.

4.6 not exclude any eligible student from the assessment.

4.7 avoid any conditions in the conduct of the assessment that might invalidate the results.

4.8 provide for and document all reasonable and allowable accommodations for the administration of the assessment to persons with disabilities or special needs.

4.9 provide reasonable opportunities for individuals to ask questions about the assessment procedures or directions prior to and at prescribed times during the administration of the assessment.

4.10 protect the rights to privacy and due process of those who are assessed.

4.11 avoid actions or conditions that would permit or encourage individuals or groups to receive scores that misrepresent their actual levels of attainment.

SECTION 5: RESPONSIBILITIES OF THOSE WHO SCORE ASSESSMENTS

The scoring of educational assessments should be conducted properly and efficiently so that the results are reported accurately and in a timely manner. Persons who score and prepare reports of assessments have a professional responsibility to:

5.1 provide complete and accurate information to users about how the assessment is scored, such as the reporting schedule, scoring process to be used, rationale for the scoring approach, technical characteristics, quality control procedures, reporting formats, and the fees, if any, for these services.

5.2 ensure the accuracy of the assessment results by conducting reasonable quality control procedures before, during, and after scoring.

5.3 minimize the effect on scoring of factors irrelevant to the purposes of the assessment.

5.4 inform users promptly of any deviation in the planned scoring and reporting service or schedule and negotiate a solution with users.

5.5 provide corrected score results to the examinee or the client as quickly as practicable should errors be found that may affect the inferences made on the basis of the scores.

5.6 protect the confidentiality of information that identifies individuals as prescribed by state and federal law.

5.7 release summary results of the assessment only to those persons entitled to such information by state or federal law or those who are designated by the party contracting for the scoring services.

5.8 establish, where feasible, a fair and reasonable process for appeal and rescoring the assessment.

SECTION 6: RESPONSIBILITIES OF THOSE WHO INTERPRET, USE, AND COMMUNICATE ASSESSMENT RESULTS

The interpretation, use, and communication of assessment results should promote valid inferences and minimize invalid ones. Persons who interpret, use, and communicate assessment results have a professional responsibility to:

6.1 conduct these activities in an informed, objective, and fair manner within the context of the assessment's limitations and with an understanding of the potential consequences of use.

6.2 provide to those who receive assessment results information about the assessment, its purposes, its limitations, and its uses necessary for the proper interpretation of the results.

6.3 provide to those who receive score reports an understandable written description of all reported scores, including proper interpretations and likely misinterpretations.

6.4 communicate to appropriate audiences the results of the assessment in an understandable and timely manner, including proper interpretations and likely misinterpretations.

6.5 evaluate and communicate the adequacy and appropriateness of any norms or standards used in the interpretation of assessment results.

6.6 inform parties involved in the assessment process how assessment results may affect them.

6.7 use multiple sources and types of relevant information about persons or programs whenever possible in making educational decisions.

6.8 avoid making, and actively discourage others from making, inaccurate reports, unsubstantiated claims, inappropriate interpretations, or otherwise false and misleading statements about assessment results.

6.9 disclose to examinees and others whether and how long the results of the assessment will be kept on file, procedures for appeal and rescoring, rights examinees and others have to the assessment information, and how those rights may be exercised.

6.10 report any apparent misuses of assessment information to those responsible for the assessment process.

6.11 protect the rights to privacy of individuals and institutions involved in the assessment process.

SECTION 7: RESPONSIBILITIES OF THOSE WHO EDUCATE OTHERS ABOUT ASSESSMENT

The process of educating others about educational assessment, whether as part of higher education, professional development, public policy discussions, or job training, should prepare individuals to understand and engage in sound measurement practice and to become discerning users of tests and test results. Persons who educate or inform others about assessment have a professional responsibility to:

7.1 remain competent and current in the areas in which they teach and reflect that in their instruction.

7.2 provide fair and balanced perspectives when teaching about assessment.

7.3 differentiate clearly between expressions of opinion and substantiated knowledge when educating others about any specific assessment method, product, or service.

7.4 disclose any financial interests that might be perceived to influence the evaluation of a particular assessment product or service that is the subject of instruction.

7.5 avoid administering any assessment that is not part of the evaluation of student performance in a course if the administration of that assessment is likely to harm any student.

7.6 avoid using or reporting the results of any assessment that is not part of the evaluation of student performance in a course if the use or reporting of results is likely to harm any student.

7.7 protect all secure assessments and materials used in the instructional process.

7.8 model responsible assessment practice and help those receiving instruction to learn about their professional responsibilities in educational measurement.

7.9 provide fair and balanced perspectives on assessment issues being discussed by policymakers, parents, and other citizens.

SECTION 8: RESPONSIBILITIES OF THOSE WHO EVALUATE EDUCATIONAL PROGRAMS AND CONDUCT RESEARCH ON ASSESSMENTS

Conducting research on or about assessments or educational programs is a key activity in helping to improve the understanding and use of assessments and educational programs. Persons who engage in the evaluation of educational programs or conduct research on assessments have a professional responsibility to:

8.1 conduct evaluation and research activities in an informed, objective, and fair manner.

8.2 disclose any associations that they have with authors, test publishers, or others involved with the assessment and refrain from participation if such associations might affect the objectivity of the research or evaluation.

8.3   preserve the security of all assessments throughout the research process as appropriate.

8.4   take appropriate steps to minimize potential sources of invalidity in the research and disclose known factors that may bias the results of the study.

8.5   present the results of research, both intended and unintended, in a fair, complete, and objective manner.

8.6   attribute completely and appropriately the work and ideas of others.

8.7   qualify the conclusions of the research within the limitations of the study.

8.8   use multiple sources of relevant information in conducting evaluation and research activities whenever possible.

8.9   comply with applicable standards for protecting the rights of participants in an evaluation or research study, including the rights to privacy and informed consent.

AFTERWORD

As stated at the outset, the purpose of the *Code of Professional Responsibilities in Educational Measurement* is to serve as a guide to the conduct of NCME members who are engaged in any type of assessment activity in education. Given the broad scope of the field of educational assessment as well as the variety of activities in which professionals may engage, it is unlikely that any code will cover the professional responsibilities involved in every situation or activity in which assessment is used in education. Ultimately, it is hoped that this Code will serve as the basis for ongoing discussions about what constitutes professionally responsible practice. Moreover, these discussions will undoubtedly identify areas of practice that need further analysis and clarification in subsequent editions of the Code. To the extent that these discussions occur, the Code will have served its purpose.

Summaries of Taxonomies of Educational Objectives: Cognitive, Affective, and Psychomotor Domains

FIGURE D.1 Categories and subcategories of the Bloom et al. taxonomy of cognitive objectives.

1.00 **Knowledge**
- 1.10 **Knowledge of Specifics**
- 1.11 **Knowledge of Terminology** Knowledge of the referents for specific symbols (verbal and nonverbal)
- 1.12 **Knowledge of Specific Facts** Knowledge of dates, events, persons, places, etc.
- 1.20 **Knowledge of Ways and Means of Dealing with Specifics**
- 1.21 **Knowledge of Conventions** Knowledge of characteristic ways of treating and presenting ideas and phenomena.
- 1.22 **Knowledge of Trends and Sequences** Knowledge of the processes, directions, and movements of phenomena with respect to time.
- 1.23 **Knowledge of Classifications and Categories** Knowledge of the classes, sets, divisions, and arrangements that are regarded as fundamental for a given subject field, purpose, argument, or problem.
- 1.24 **Knowledge of Criteria** Knowledge of the criteria by which facts, principles, and conduct are tested or judged.
- 1.25 **Knowledge of Methodology** Knowledge of the methods of inquiry, techniques, and procedures employed in a particular subject field as well as those employed in investigating particular problems and phenomena.

2.00 **Comprehension**
- 2.10 **Translation** Comprehension as evidenced by the care and accuracy with which the communication is paraphrased or rendered from one language or form of communication to another.
- 2.20 **Interpretation** The explanation or summarization of a communication.
- 2.30 **Extrapolation** The extension of trends or tendencies beyond the given data to determine implications, consequences, corollaries, effects, etc., that are in accordance with the conditions described in the original communication.

3.00 **Application** The use of abstractions in particular and concrete situations. The abstractions may be in the form of general ideas, rules of procedures, or generalized methods.

4.00 **Analysis**
- 4.10 **Analysis of Elements** Identification of the elements included in a communication.
- 4.20 **Analysis of Relationships** The connections and interactions between elements and parts of a communication.
- 4.30 **Analysis of Organized Principles** The organization, systematic arrangement, and structure that hold the communication together.

5.00 **Synthesis**
- 5.10 **Production of a Unique Communication** The development of a communication in which the writer or speaker attempts to convey ideas, feelings, and/or experiences to others.
- 5.20 **Production of a Plan or Proposed Set of Operations** The development of a plan of work or the proposal of a plan of operations.
- 5.30 **Derivation of a Set of Abstract Relations** The development of a set of abstract relations either to classify or to explain particular data or phenomena, or the deduction of propositions and relations from a set of basic propositions or symbolic representations.

6.00 **Evaluation**
- 6.10 **Judgments in Terms of Internal Evidence** Evaluation of the accuracy of a communication from such evidence as logical accuracy, consistency, and other internal criteria.
- 6.20 **Judgments in Terms of External Criteria** Evaluation of material with reference to selected or remembered criteria.

FIGURE D.2 Webb's Depth-of-Knowledge by subject descriptors.

Subject	Depth of Knowledge			
	Level 1 **Recall**	**Level 2** **Skill/Concept**	**Level 3** **Strategic Thinking**	**Level 4** **Extended Thinking**
English Language Arts	Requires students to recall, observe, question, or represent facts or simple skills or abilities. Requires only surface understanding of text, often verbatim recall. Examples: • Support ideas by reference to details in text • Use dictionary to find meaning • Identify figurative language in passage • Identify correct spelling or meaning of words	Requires processing beyond recall and observation. Requires both comprehension and subsequent processing of text. Involves ordering, classifying text as well as identifying patterns, relationships, and main points. Examples: • Use context to identify unfamiliar words • Predict logical outcome • Identify and summarize main points • Apply knowledge of conventions of standard American English • Compose accurate summaries	Requires students to go beyond text. Requires students to explain, generalize, and connect ideas. Involves inferencing, prediction, elaboration, and summary. Requires students to support positions using prior knowledge and to manipulate themes across passages. Examples: • Determine effect of author's purpose on text elements • Summarize information from multiple sources • Critically analyze literature • Compose focused, organized, coherent, purposeful prose	Requires extended higher order processing. Typically requires extended time to complete task, but time spent not on repetitive tasks. Involves taking information from one text/passage and applying this information to a new task. May require generating hypotheses and performing complex analyses and connections among texts. Examples: • Analyze and synthesize information from multiple sources • Examine and explain alternative perspectives across sources • Describe and illustrate common themes across a variety of texts • Create compositions that synthesize, analyze, and evaluate
Mathematics	Requires students to recall or observe facts, definitions, terms. Involves simple one-step procedures. Involves computing simple algorithms (e.g., sum, quotient) Examples: • Recall or recognize a fact, term, or property. • Represent in words, pictures, or symbols a math object or relationship • Perform routine procedure, such as measuring	Requires students to make decisions on how to approach a problem. Requires students to compare, classify, organize, estimate, or order data. Typically involves two-step procedures. Examples: • Specify and explain relationships between facts, terms, properties, or operations • Select procedure according to criteria and perform it • Solve routine multiple-step problems	Requires reasoning, planning, or use of evidence to solve problem or algorithm. May involve activity with more than one possible answer. Requires conjecture or restructuring of problems. Involves drawing conclusions from observations, citing evidence and developing logical arguments for concepts. Uses concepts to solve nonroutine problems. Examples: • Analyze similarities and differences • Formulate original problem given situation • Formulate mathematical model for complex situation	Requires complex reasoning, planning, developing, and thinking. Typically requires extended time to complete problem, but time spent not on repetitive tasks. Requires students to make several connections and apply one approach among many to solve the problem. Involves complex restructuring of data, establishing and evaluating criteria to solve problems. Examples: • Apply mathematical model to illuminate a problem, situation • Conduct a project that specifies a problem, identifies solution paths, solves the problem, and reports results • Design a mathematical model to inform and solve a practical or abstract situation

FIGURE D.2 (*continued*)

Subject	Depth of Knowledge			
	Level 1 **Recall**	**Level 2** **Skill/Concept**	**Level 3** **Strategic Thinking**	**Level 4** **Extended Thinking**
Science	Requires students to recall facts, definitions, or simple procedures or processes. Involves rote responses, use of well-known formulae, or following a set of clearly defined one-step procedures. Examples: • Recall or recognize a fact, term, or property • Represent in words or diagrams a scientific concept or relationship • Provide or recognize a standard scientific representation or simple phenomenon	Requires students to make some decisions as to how to approach the question or problem. Involves comparing, classifying, organizing, estimating, ordering, or displaying data (e.g., tables, graphs, charts). Typically involves multiple-step procedures. Examples: • Specify and explain the relationship between facts, terms, properties, or variables • Describe and explain examples and non-examples of science concepts • Select a procedure according to specified criteria and perform it	Requires students to solve problems with more than one possible answer and justify responses. Experimental design involves more than one dependent variable. Requires drawing conclusions from observations, citing evidence, and developing logical argument for concepts; explaining phenomena in terms of concepts, and using concepts to solve nonroutine problems. Examples: • Identify research questions and design investigations for a scientific problem • Develop a scientific model for a complex situation • Form conclusions from experimental data	Requires students to make several connections and apply one approach among many to solve problems. Involves developing generalizations from obtained results and formulating strategies to solve new problems in a variety of situations. Requires extended time to complete problem, but time spent not on repetitive tasks. Examples: • Based on provided data from a complex experiment that is novel to the student, deduce the fundamental relationship between several controlled variables • Conduct an investigation, from specifying a problem to designing and carrying out an experiment, to analyzing its data and formulating conclusions
Social Studies	Requires students to recall facts (who, what, when, and where), terms, concepts, trends, generalizations, and theories or to recognize or identify specific information contained in maps, charts, tables, graphs, or drawings. Examples: • Recall or recognize an event, map, or document • Describe the features of a place or people • Identify key figures in a particular context	Requires students to compare or contrast people, places, events, and concepts; give examples, classify or sort items into meaningful categories; describe, interpret or explain issues and problems, patterns, reasons, causes, effects, significance or impact, relationships, and points of view or processes. Examples: • Describe the causes/effects of particular events • Identify patterns in events or behavior • Categorize events or figures into meaningful groupings	Requires students to draw conclusions, cite evidence, apply concepts to new situations; use concepts to solve problems, analyze similarities and differences in issues and problems; propose and evaluate solutions; recognize and explain misconceptions; make connections and explain main concepts. Examples: • Analyze how changes have affected people or places • Apply concepts in other contexts • Form alternate conclusions	Requires students to connect and relate ideas and concepts within and among content areas. Involves analyzing and synthesizing information from multiple sources; examining and explaining alternative perspectives across a variety of sources; making predictions with evidence as support; planning and developing solutions to problems. Examples: • Given a situation/problem research, define and describe the situation/problem and provide alternative solutions • Describe, define and illustrate common social, historical, or geographical themes and how they interrelate

Source: Webb, N. L. (2002). *Alignment study in language arts, mathematics, science and social studies of state standards and assessments for four states.* Washington, DC: Council of Chief State School Officers. Adapted with permission from Figure 1, pp. 9–12.

FIGURE D.3 Categories and subcategories of the Krathwohl et al. taxonomy of affective objectives with illustrative statements of objectives.

Category	Definition	Learning Targets
1.0 Receiving (attending)		
1.1 Awareness	Be conscious of something … take into account a situation, phenomenon, object, or state of affairs.	Develops awareness of aesthetic factors in dress, furnishings, architecture, city design, good art, and the like.
1.2 Willingness to receive	Being willing to tolerate a given stimulus, not to avoid it … . Willing to take notice of the phenomenon and give it … attention.	Appreciation (tolerance) of cultural patterns exhibited by individuals from other groups—religious, social, economic, national, etc.
1.3 Controlled or selected attention	The control of attention so that when certain stimuli are presented they will be attended to … . The favored stimulus is selected and attended to despite competing and detracting stimuli.	Alertness toward human values and judgments on life as they are recorded in literature.
2.0 Responding		
2.1 Acquiescence in responding	"Obedience" or "compliance" … . There is a passiveness so far as the initiation of behavior is concerned.	Follows school rules on the playground.
2.2 Willingness to respond	The learner is sufficiently committed to exhibiting the behavior that he does so not just because of fear … but "on his own" or voluntarily.	Volunteers to help classmates who are having difficulty with the science project.
2.3 Satisfaction in response	The behavior is accompanied by a feeling of satisfaction, an emotional response, generally of pleasure, zest, or enjoyment.	Finds pleasure in reading for recreation.
3.0 Valuing		
3.1 Acceptance of a value	The emotional acceptance of a proposition or doctrine on what one considers adequate ground.	Continuing desire to develop the ability to speak and write effectively.
3.2 Preference for a value	The individual is sufficiently committed to a value to pursue it, to seek it out, to want it.	Assumes responsibility for drawing reticent members of a group into conversation.
3.3 Commitment	"Conviction" and "certainty beyond a doubt" … . Acts to further the thing valued, … to extend the possibility of … developing it, to deepen … involvement with it.	Devotion to those ideas and ideals that are the foundation of democracy.
4.0 Organization		
4.1 Conceptualization of a value	The quality of abstraction or conceptualization is added (to the value or belief which permits seeing) … how the value relates to those he already holds or to new ones.	Forms judgments as to the responsibility of society for conserving human and material resources.
4.2 Organization of a value system	To bring together a complex of values … into an ordered relationship with one another.	Weighs alternative social policies and practices against the standards of the public welfare rather than the advantage of … narrow interest groups.
5.0 Characterization by a value or value complex		
5.1 Generalized set	Gives an internal consistency to the system of attitudes and values … . Enables the individual to reduce and order the complex world … and to act consistently and effectively in it.	Judges problems and issues in terms of situations, issues, purposes, and consequences involved rather than in terms of fixed, dogmatic precepts or emotional wishful thinking.
5.2 Characterization	One's view of the universe, one's philosophy of life, one's weltanschauung.	Develops for regulation of one's personal and civic life a code of behavior based on ethical principles consistent with democratic ideals.

Source: Krathwohl, David R.; Bloom, Benjamin S.; Masia, Bertram B., *Taxonomy of Educational Objectives: Book 2: Affective Domain, 1st Ed.*, © 1964, pp. 176–185. Adapted and Electronically reproduced by permission of, Pearson Education, Inc., Upper Saddle River, New Jersey.

FIGURE D.4 Categories and subcategories of the Harrow taxonomy of psychomotor and perceptual objectives.

Classification Levels and Subcategories	Definitions	Learning Targets
1.00 Reflex Movements **1.10 Segmental Reflexes** **1.20 Intersegmental Reflexes** **1.30 Suprasegmental Reflexes**	Actions elicited without conscious volition in response to some stimuli.	Flexion, extension, stretch, postural adjustments.
2.00 Basic-Fundamental Movements **2.10 Locomotor Movements** **2.20 Non-Locomotor Movements** **2.30 Manipulative Movements**	Inherent movement patterns which are formed from a combining of reflex movements and are the basis for complex skilled movement.	Walking, running, jumping, sliding, hopping, rolling, climbing, pushing, pulling, swaying, swinging, stooping, stretching, bending, twisting, handling, manipulating, gripping, grasping finger movements.
3.00 Perceptual Abilities **3.10 Kinesthetic Discrimination** **3.20 Visual Discrimination** **3.30 Auditory Discrimination** **3.40 Tactile Discrimination** **3.50 Coordinated Abilities**	Interpretation of stimuli from various modalities providing data for the learner to make adjustments to his environment.	The *outcomes* of perceptual abilities are observable in *all purposeful* movement. Examples: Auditory—following verbal instructions. Coordinated—jumping rope, punting, catching.
4.00 Physical Abilities **4.10 Endurance** **4.20 Strength** **4.30 Flexibility** **4.40 Agility**	Functional characteristics of organic vigor, which are essential to the development of highly skilled movement.	Distance running, distance swimming, weight lifting, wrestling, touching toes, back bend, ballet exercises, shuttle run, typing, dodgeball.
5.00 Skilled Movements **5.10 Simple Adaptive Skill** **5.20 Compound Adaptive Skill** **5.30 Complex Adaptive Skill**	A degree of efficiency when performing complex movement tasks, which are based upon inherent movement patterns.	All skilled activities, which build upon the inherent locomotor and manipulative movement patterns of classification level two.
6.00 Non-Discursive Communication **6.10 Expressive Movement** **6.20 Interpretive Movement**	Communication through bodily movements ranging from facial expressions through sophisticated choreographies.	Body postures, gestures, facial expressions, all efficiently executed skilled dance movements and choreographies.

Source: A. J. Harrow, *A Taxonomy of the Psychomotor Domain: A Guide for Developing Behavioral Objectives, 1st Ed.,* © 1972, pp. 104–106. Adapted and Electronically reproduced by permission of Pearson Education, Inc., Upper Saddle River, New Jersey.

FIGURE D.5A The knowledge dimension of a revision of Bloom's *Taxonomy of Educational Objectives.*

Major types and subtypes	Examples
A. Factual knowledge—The basic elements students must know to be acquainted with a discipline or solve problems in it	
Aᴀ. Knowledge of terminology	Technical vocabulary; musical symbols
Aʙ. Knowledge of specific details and elements	Major national resources, reliable sources of information
B. Conceptual knowledge—The interrelationships among the basic elements within a larger structure that enable them to function together	
Bᴀ. Knowledge of classifications and categories	Periods of geological time; forms of business ownership
Bʙ. Knowledge of principles and generalizations	Pythagorean theorem; law of supply and demand
Bᴄ. Knowledge of theories, models, and structures	Theory of evolution; structure of Congress
C. Procedural knowledge—How to do something; methods of inquiry; and criteria for using skills, algorithms, techniques, and methods	
Cᴀ. Knowledge of subject-specific skills and algorithms	Skills used in painting with watercolors; whole-number division algorithm
Cʙ. Knowledge of subject-specific techniques and methods	Interviewing techniques; scientific method
Cᴄ. Knowledge of criteria for determining when to use appropriate procedures	Criteria used to determine when to apply a procedure involving Newton's second law; criteria used to judge the feasibility of using a particular method to estimate business costs

FIGURE D.5A   *(continued)*

Major types and subtypes	Examples
D. Metacognitive knowledge—Knowledge of cognition in general as well as awareness and knowledge of one's own cognition	
DA. Strategic knowledge	Knowledge of outlining as a means of capturing the structure of a unit of subject matter in a textbook; knowledge of the use of heuristics
DB. Knowledge about cognitive tasks, including appropriate contextual and conditional knowledge	Knowledge of the types of tests particular teachers administer; knowledge of the cognitive demands of different tasks
DC. Self-knowledge	Knowledge that critiquing essays is a personal strength, whereas writing essays is a personal weakness; awareness of one's own knowledge level business costs

Source: Anderson, Lorin W.; Krathwohl, David R.; Airasian, Peter W.; Cruikshank, Kathleen A.; Mayer, Richard E.; Pintrich, Paul R.; Raths, James; Wittrock, Merlin C., *A Taxonomy for Learning, Teaching, and Assessing: A Revision of Bloom's Taxonomy of Educational Objectives, Complete Edition, 1st Ed.,* © 2001, pp. 46, 67–68. Reprinted and Electronically reproduced by permission of Pearson Education, Inc., Upper Saddle River, New Jersey.

FIGURE D.5B   The cognitive process dimension of a revision of Bloom's *Taxonomy of Educational Objectives.*

Categories & cognitive processes	Alternative names	Definitions and examples
1. Remember—Retrieve relevant knowledge from long-term memory		
1.1 Recognizing	Identifying	Locating knowledge in long-term memory that is consistent with presented material (e.g., recognize the dates of important events in U.S. history)
1.2 Recalling	Retrieving	Retrieving relevant knowledge from long-term memory (e.g., recall the dates of important events in U.S. history)
2. Understand—Construct meaning from instructional messages, including oral, written, and graphic communication		
2.1 Interpreting	Clarifying, paraphrasing, representing, translating	Changing from one form of representation (e.g., numerical) to another (e.g., verbal) (e.g., paraphrase important speeches and documents)
2.2 Exemplifying	Illustrating, instantiating	Finding a specific example or illustration of a concept or principle (e.g., give examples of various artistic painting styles)
2.3 Classifying	Categorizing, subsuming	Determining that something belongs to a category (e.g., concept or principle) (e.g., classify observed or described cases of mental disorders)
2.4 Summarizing	Abstracting, generalizing	Abstracting a general theme or major point(s) (e.g., write a short summary of the events portrayed on a videotape)
2.5 Inferring	Concluding, extrapolating, interpolating, predicting	Drawing a logical conclusion from presented information (e.g., when learning a foreign language, infer grammatical principles from examples)
2.6 Comparing	Contrasting, mapping, matching	Detecting correspondences between two ideas, objects, and the like (e.g., compare historical events to contemporary situations)
2.7 Explaining	Constructing models	Constructing a cause-and-effect model of a system (e.g., explain the causes of important eighteenth-century events in France)
3. Apply—Carry out or use a procedure in a given situation		
3.1 Executing	Carrying out	Applying a procedure to a familiar task (e.g., divide one whole number by another whole number, both with multiple digits)
3.2 Implementing	Using	Applying a procedure to an unfamiliar task (e.g., use Newton's second law in situations in which it is appropriate)
4. Analyze—Break material into its constituent parts and determine how the parts relate to one another and to an overall structure or purpose		
4.1 Differentiating	Discriminating, distinguishing, focusing, selecting	Distinguishing relevant from irrelevant parts or important from unimportant parts of presented material (e.g., distinguish between relevant and irrelevant numbers in a mathematical word problem)
4.2 Organizing	Finding coherence, integrating, outlining, parsing, structuring	Determining how elements fit or function within a structure (e.g., structure evidence in a historical description into evidence for and against a particular historical explanation)

FIGURE D.5B (*continued*)

Categories & cognitive processes	Alternative names	Definitions and examples
4.3 Attributing	Deconstructing	Determine a point of view, bias, values, or intent underlying presented material (e.g., determine the point of view of the author of an essay in terms of his or her political perspective)
5. Evaluate—Make judgments based on criteria and standards		
5.1 Checking	Coordinating, detecting, monitoring, testing	Detecting inconsistencies or fallacies within a process or product; determining whether a process or product has internal consistency; detecting the effectiveness of a procedure as it is being implemented (e.g., determine if a scientist's conclusions follow from observed data)
5.2 Critiquing	Judging	Detecting inconsistencies between a product and external criteria, determining whether a product has external consistency; detecting the appropriateness of a procedure for a given problem (e.g., judge which of two methods is the best way to solve a given problem)
6. Create—Put elements together to form a coherent or functional whole; reorganize elements into a new pattern or structure		
6.1 Generating	Hypothesizing	Coming up with alternative hypotheses based on criteria (e.g., generate hypotheses to account for an observed phenomenon)
6.2 Planning	Designing	Devising a procedure for accomplishing some task (e.g., plan a research paper on a given historical topic)
6.3 Producing	Constructing	Inventing a product (e.g., build habitats for a specific purpose)

Source: Anderson, Lorin W.; Krathwohl, David R.; Airasian, Peter W.; Cruikshank, Kathleen A.; Mayer, Richard E.; Pintrich, Paul R.; Raths, James; Wittrock, Merlin C., *A Taxonomy for Learning, Teaching, and Assessing: A Revision of Bloom's Taxonomy of Educational Objectives, Complete Edition, 1st Ed.,* © 2001, pp. 46, 67–68. Reprinted and Electronically reproduced by permission of Pearson Education, Inc., Upper Saddle River, New Jersey.

Implementing the Principles of Universal Design via Technology-Based Testing

FIGURE E.1

What are the principles of universal design?	What does the principle mean for testing?	How can the principle be implemented?
Principle 1: Equitable Use	Testing materials, strategies, and environments are designed so that they are useful, appealing, and safe for *all* to use. They are respectful of individual differences and are used by *all* learners in similar or equivalent ways and In different contexts.	• Use the principles of typographic and visual design. • Pair text with culturally and age appropriate visuals. • Provide instructional feedback to students.
Principle 2: Flexible Use	Testing materials, strategies, and environments are designed so that they accommodate individual preferences and abilities. They are flexible in terms of providing choices of the methods and pace of use.	• Offer options to students about the technology they use to take tests. • Give students choices about pace, location, and sequence of the test administration. • Allow students to take tests/quizzes multiple times.
Principle 3: Simple and Intuitive	Testing materials, strategies, and environments are designed so that they are easy for *all* to use and understand. Their use is not dependent on one's experience, prior knowledge, language and literacy skills, and other learning preferences and abilities.	• Use software/websites to check and enhance the readability of tests. • Provide second language learners with access to bilingual resources. • Embed varied visual supports that are current, age appropriate, and culturally sensitive.
Principle 4: Perceptible Information	Testing materials, strategies, and environments are designed so that they communicate essential information to *all* using multiple formats, backgrounds with sufficient contrasts, legible text guidelines, compatible teaching and testing techniques, and assistive technology devices.	• Use the principles of typographic and visual design to prepare legible and readable testing materials. • Use technology to present test directions and items (e.g., screen/text-reading programs). • Provide visual supports. • Offer prompts and cues to help students understand test directions and items.
Principle 5: Tolerance for Error	Testing materials, strategies, and environments are designed to minimize errors, adverse consequences, and unintentional actions. They provide safeguards and warnings to assist *all* in using them safely and efficiently.	• Provide learning strategy access and reminders. • Embed feedback and error minimization techniques into tests. • Allow students to use word processors, spellcheckers, word cueing and prediction, dictionaries and thesauri, and grammar checkers. • Teach technology-based test-taking skills.

FIGURE E.1 *(continued)*

What are the principles of universal design?	What does the principle mean for testing?	How can the principle be implemented?
Principle 6: Low Physical Effort	Testing materials, strategies, and environments are designed to be used comfortably and without much physical effort by *all*. They allow all to use them with a range of reasonable physical actions and do not require repetitive actions or sustained physical effort.	• Provide students with the technology they need to take tests (e.g., voice-activation, augmentative communication, and low-tech devices, etc.).
Principle 7: Size and Space Approach and Use	Testing materials, strategies, and environments are designed for use by *all* regardless of one's body size, posture, and mobility. They allow all users to see, reach, and activate important features and information and offer sufficient space for assistive technology devices and personal assistance.	• Provide students with ergonomic and alternative keyboards, an adapted mouse, keyguards, on-screen keyboarding, visual and auditory warnings, and highlighted mouse visibility and movement. • Format tests appropriately.
Principle 8: Community of Learners	Testing materials, strategies, and environments promote socialization and communication.	• Present tests/quizzes using technology-based and collaborative game formats.
Principle 9: Inclusive Environment	Testing materials, strategies, and environments foster acceptance and belonging.	• Use branching to tailor tests to students' skill levels. • Motivate students by providing choices regarding the frequency and type of feedback they receive.

Source: From "Using Technology to Create and Administer Accessible Tests," by S. Salend, 2009, *TEACHING Exceptional Children, 41*(3), p. 42. Copyright © 2009 by the Council for Exceptional Children, Inc. http://www.cec.sped.org. All rights reserved. Reproduced with permission.

Basic Statistical Concepts

Understanding a few basic statistical concepts will help you interpret the results of your classroom assessments, summarize assessment results, interpret your students' norm-referenced test scores, understand basic data in published test manuals, and understand assessment summary reports provided by your school district or state. This appendix focuses on concepts rather than on computations. However, we illustrate the computations of certain statistics, so you will understand the origin of their numerical values. We encourage you not to shy away from learning the few techniques shown in this appendix. With the availability of inexpensive calculators, computations become simple and accurate with only a little practice.

Statistical methods are techniques to summarize scores so that you may better understand how a group of students has performed and how well an individual student has performed relative to others in the group. A **statistical index** (or **statistic**) is a summary number that concisely captures a specific feature of a group of scores. For example, measures of central tendency focus on an average or typical score for a group. Measures of variability focus on quantifying the extent to which students' scores differ from one another. This appendix presents four categories of statistical methods that you will find most useful in understanding test scores and other assessment results: (1) distribution of scores, (2) typical or average score, (3) variability of scores, and (4) degree to which two sets of scores are correlated.

DESCRIBING DISTRIBUTIONS OF TEST SCORES

Suppose the scores shown in Figure F.1 are scores of our students on two tests you gave. The arrangement of the scores in the table is similar to how they might be arranged in your gradebook program: Students' names are arranged alphabetically with their mark next to their names. This arrangement does not make it easy to answer such questions as the following:

- How many students in the class have similar scores?
- What scores do most students obtain?
- Are the scores widely scattered along the score scale, or do they bunch together?
- Does the pattern of scores in the class appear unusual in some way? Or are they as expected?
- Does any student score unusually higher or lower than his or her classmates?

Ranking Scores

One simple way to begin answering questions such as these is to rank the scores. Most people know how to do this already. To rank the scores, *order them from largest to smallest*. The largest score is assigned a rank of 1; the next largest, a rank of 2; and so on, down to the smallest score. In this way, all of the raw scores (marks) are transformed into ranks.

Figure F.2 demonstrates the procedure for scores from Test 1. Notice what is done when students have the same score. In this case, they are tied for the ranks. The tie is resolved by awarding each of the persons whose scores are tied the average of the ranks for which they are tied. For example, four students have a score of 75 and thus are tied for ranks 9, 10, 11, and 12. Rather than arbitrarily awarding one person a rank of 9, and another a rank of 10, and so on, each person is awarded the average of the tied ranks, that is:

$$\frac{9 + 10 + 11 + 12}{4} = 10.5$$

A simple ranked list of scores helps you answer some basic questions about how well your class performed on a test. The list shows quickly the highest

FIGURE F.1   List of students in a class and their scores on two tests.

Name	Test 1	Test 2
1. Anthony	89	94
2. Ashley	75	68
3. Blake	74	72
4. Chad	84	77
5. Donald	56	66
6. Edward	80	68
7. Festina	66	68
8. George	86	73
9. Harriet	68	73
10. Irene	98	86
11. Jesse	65	78
12. Katherine	44	60
13. Lorraine	45	53
14. Marya	61	75
15. Nancy	75	76
16. Oprah	68	54
17. Peter	55	53
18. Quincy	70	68
19. Robert	69	65
20. Sally	60	47
21. Tina	73	74
22. Ula	75	88
23. Veronica	71	73
24. Wallace	43	61
25. William	83	87
26. Xavier	95	83
27. Yvonne	96	85
28. ZENA	75	70

FIGURE F.2   Rank order of students from Figure F.1 according to their scores on Test 1.

Name	Test 1	Rank	
Irene	98	1	
Yvonne	96	2	
Xavier	95	3	
Anthony	89	4	
George	86	5	
Chad	84	6	
William	83	7	
Edward	80	8	
Zena	75	10.5	Four scores
Ula	75	10.5	tied for ranks
Nancy	75	10.5	9, 10, 11, and 12
Ashley	75	10.5	
Blake	74	13	
Tina	73	14	
Veronica	71	15	
Quincy	70	16	
Robert	69	17	
Oprah	68	18.5	Two scores tied for
Harriet	68	18.5	ranks 18 and 19
Festina	66	20	
Jesse	65	21	
Marya	61	22	
Sally	60	23	
Donald	56	24	
Peter	55	25	
Lorraine	45	26	
Katherine	44	27	
Wallace	43	28	

and lowest scores. It shows how the scores are spread out and which scores occur most often. This ranked list may be all you need to understand how your students performed on a test. However, ranked lists are not easily understood if the number of students is very large: for example, the score of all fourth graders in the school district or in the state. A better way to organize the scores in such cases is discussed later.

Interpretations of simple ranks of this sort depend on the number of students in the group. For example, suppose I told you that of all the classes in testing and measurement I have taught, your class ranked second. You might be proud as a group until I also told you that I have taught only one other class. Adding another 13 classes might result in your class's rank dropping, say, from second to 15th: Although the class's rank has changed from second to 15th, its relative position—dead last—has not changed. The point is that a student's rank cannot be fully interpreted without knowing the number of other students being ranked. This problem is largely overcome by using *percentile ranks* (see Chapter 17). We show you how to calculate percentile ranks in Figure F.8.

Stem-and-Leaf Displays

A simple way to organize a large group of scores is to prepare a stem-and-leaf display. Figure F.3 illustrates the procedure for the scores of the 28 students in Figure F.1 for each of the two tests. The "stem" is the tens' digit and the "leaves" are the ones' digits of the score. For example, consider the scores 80, 83, 84, 86, and 89 from Test 1. The tens' digit is 8 and is written in the stem column. The ones' digits 0, 3, 4, 6, and 9 are the leaves and are written in the row to the right of the 8.

The stem-and-leaf display has the advantage of showing how the entire group of scores is distributed along the score scale when they are grouped together by intervals of 10. That is, it organizes the scores into the groupings of 40s, 50s, 60s, 70s, 80s, and 90s. With the ones' digits displayed, you can easily "reconstitute" individual values of the scores. This is useful if

FIGURE F.3 Stem-and-leaf display of the distribution of the students' scores from Figure F.1

	Test 1			Test 2	
Stem	**Leaves**	**Frequency**	**Stem**	**Leaves**	**Frequency**
0			0		
1			1		
2			2		
3			3		
4	3 4 5	3	4	7	1
5	5 6	2	5	3 3 4	3
6	0 1 5 6 8 8 9	7	6	0 1 5 6 8 8 8 8	8
7	0 1 3 4 5 5 5 5	8	7	0 2 3 3 3 4 5 5 6 7 8	10
8	0 3 4 6 9	5	8	3 5 6 7 8	5
9	5 6 8	3	9	4	1
		$N = 28$			$N = 28$

you need to make future calculations. In the Frequency column, the number of scores is written in each row.

Notice that tens' digits in the stem column (0, 1, 2, etc.) are ordered from lowest to highest. When you turn the page on its side, the display is a type of graph: The length of the "leaves" row is proportional to the frequency of the scores.

The scores in Figure F.3 are grouped into interval widths of 10. You could also group the scores into narrower intervals, say five digits wide, as shown in Figure F.4. The stem 4 represents the scores 40, 41, 42, 43, and 44; the stem 4* represents the scores 45, 46, 47, 48, and 49. Figures F.3 and F.4 contain the same information, but are organized slightly differently. Notice, too, that you can easily construct a ranked list from a stem-and-leaf display, because the individual score values are easily recovered from the display.

FIGURE F.4 Stem-and-leaf display of the scores from Figure F.1 when the internal width equals 5.

	Test 1			Test 2	
Stem	**Leaves**	**Frequency**	**Stem**	**Leaves**	**Frequency**
0			0		
0*			0*		
1			1		
1*			1*		
2			2		
2*			2*		
3			3		
3*			3*		
4	3 4	2	4		
4*	5	1	4*	7	1
5		0	5	3 3 4	3
5*	5 6	2	5*		0
6	0 1	2	6	0 1	2
6*	5 6 8 8 9	5	6*	5 6 8 8 8 8	6
7	0 1 3 4	4	7	0 2 3 3 3 4	6
7*	5 5 5 5	4	7*	5 6 7 8	4
8	0 3 4	3	8	3	1
8*	6 9	2	8*	5 6 7 8	4
9		0	9	4	1
9*	5 6 8	3	9*		0
		$N = 28$			$N = 28$

Frequency Distributions

When the number of scores to be organized is large, ranked lists and stem-and-leaf displays are cumbersome. In such cases, the collection of scores is organized into a figure called a **frequency distribution**. This figure shows the number of persons obtaining various scores. Figure F.5 shows frequency distributions for the two tests.

Notice that the figure shows scores grouped into intervals of 5 points on the score scale: 95–99, 90–94, 85–89, and so on. Grouping scores into intervals is a common practice when the students' scores span a wide range of values. The advantage is that the table shows the distribution of scores in a more compact space. The number of intervals is set at some convenient value, say 10 or 12. A common practice is to make the width of the interval an odd number, because then the midpoint of the interval is a whole number. Whole-number midpoints are desirable when the information in the table is to be used to construct a graph or for later calculations. The midpoints of each interval are shown in Figure F.5. Often the midpoints are not presented when the table can be interpreted without that information. Similarly, the Tally column is seldom shown in a finished table. Its only purpose is to make it easier and more accurate to count the scores in each interval. At the bottom of the frequency column you should record the sum of the frequencies. This is N, the total number of scores in the collection.

You can calculate the width of the interval to use as follows. Subtract the lowest score in the group from the highest score. Divide this difference by 12. The interval width to use is the nearest odd number to this quotient. For example, for Test 1, the highest score is 98 and the lowest is 43. Thus, $(98 - 43) \div 12$ is 4.56, and the nearest odd number is 5. For Test 2, this calculation is 3.91 and the nearest odd number is 3. However, if you want to compare the distributions of Tests 1 and 2, it is best to use the same interval width. Thus, we have used a width of 5 for each test distribution. This illustrates that there are no hard and fast rules for fixing interval widths.

To make the table, it is best to make the lower limit of the interval a multiple of the interval width. This makes it easier to construct the table. Thus, the lower limit of the highest interval in Figure F.5 is 95, the next is 90, next is 85, and so on. Be sure that the highest interval contains the highest score. You need not continue the intervals below the interval containing the lowest score. Thus, the lowest interval in Figure F.5 is 40–44.

The **grouped frequency distribution**, as Figure F.5 is called, provides the same convenient summary of the distribution of scores as the stem-and-leaf display. However, unlike the stem-and-leaf display, information about the specific numerical values of the scores in each interval is lost: Only the frequency of the scores falling into the interval is recorded. Unlike the stem-and-leaf display, however, the frequency distribution table can summarize large collections of scores in a compact, easy-to-interpret format.

Frequency Polygons and Histograms

Frequency distributions are often graphed because graphs permit an increased understanding of the distribution of scores. Two common types of graphs of frequency distribution are the histogram and frequency polygon. For both, a scale of score values is marked off on a horizontal axis. The **histogram** (sometimes called a *bar graph*) represents the frequency of each score by a rectangle. The height of each rectangle is made equal to (or proportional to) the frequency of

FIGURE F.5 Frequency distributions of the scores in Figure F.1. (Interval widths equal 5.)

	Test 1				Test 2		
Interval	Tally	Midpoint	Frequency	Interval	Tally	Midpoint	Frequency
95–99	III	97	3	95–99		97	0
90–94		92	0	90–94	I	92	1
85–89	II	87	2	85–89	III	87	4
80–84	III	82	3	80–84	I	82	1
75–79	IIII	77	4	75–79	IIII	77	4
70–74	IIII	72	4	70–74	NN I	72	6
65–69	NN	67	5	65–69	NN I	67	6
60–64	II	62	2	60–64	II	62	2
55–59	II	57	2	55–59		57	0
50–54		52	0	50–54	III	52	3
45–49	I	47	1	45–49	I	47	1
40–44	II	42	2	40–44		42	0
			28				28

FIGURE F.6 Histogram and frequency polygon for the scores of Test 1 from Figure F.5.

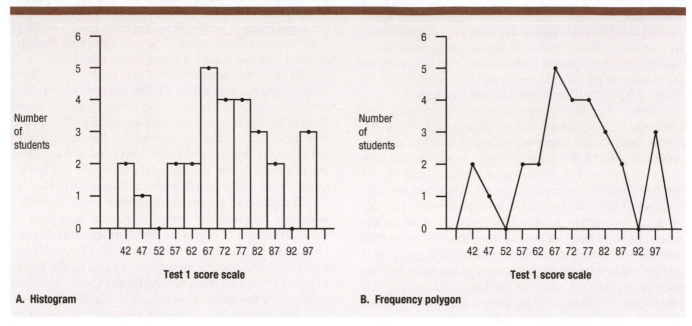

A. Histogram

B. Frequency polygon

the corresponding score. Figure F.6A shows a histogram for the Test 1 scores of Figure F.5. A **frequency polygon** for these same scores is shown in Figure F.6B. A dot is made directly above the score-value to indicate the frequency. (If no one has obtained a particular score-value, the dot is made at 0.) The dots are then connected with straight lines to make the polygon.

A graph communicates in an easy manner the shape or form of a frequency distribution. Using the names of these shapes is a compact way of describing how the scores are distributed.

Figure F.7 shows a variety of distributional forms, their corresponding names, and examples of measurement situations that might give rise to them. The illustrations of Figure F.7 are idealized and do not represent actual distributions. Nevertheless, it is helpful to have a mental picture of these distributional forms because, in practice, actual test score distributions resemble the ideal forms at least roughly. Test manuals and school and state reports often describe score distributions using the terms.

Score Distribution Shape Depends on Both the Test-Taker and the Test

The shape of a score distribution reflects the characteristics of the test as well as the ability of the group being tested. There is no single "natural" or "normal" shape toward which the test scores of a given group of students tends. A test composed of items that are not too difficult and not too easy for a particular group is likely to result in distributions of scores similar to those illustrated by A, B, or C of Figure F.7. This same group, with the same ability, could take a test in the same subject made up of items that few persons could answer correctly or a test made up of "easy" items. In these latter

cases, skewed distributions (F or G) might result. It is not accurate, therefore, to come to a conclusion about the *underlying ability* distribution of a group of students by examining only the shape of the distribution of observed test scores. The characteristics of the test the group took also need to be made a part of the decision.

Choice Between Histogram or Polygon

For many classroom purposes, you could use either a polygon or a histogram; the choice between them is rather arbitrary. The polygon emphasizes the continuous nature of the attribute that underlies the scores you see on the test; the histogram emphasizes the discrete nature. Although observed test *scores* usually are discrete whole numbers (0, 1, 2, …), the underlying characteristic a test is designed to measure is often thought of as continuous rather than discrete.

Comparing Two Distributions

It is sometimes useful to compare two or more frequency distributions by graphing on the same axes using polygons, rather than histograms. A graph could compare, for example, a class of students before and after instruction, or it could compare two different classes of students. Such a graph would display the forms of the distributions, the variability or disbursement of scores, and the place(s) along the score scale where the scores tend to cluster.

Calculating Percentile Ranks

Percentile ranks tell the percentage of the scores in a distribution that are below a particular point on the score scale. We explained the concept of percentile ranks in Chapter 17. We show how to calculate percentile ranks in Figure F.8.

FIGURE F.7 Histograms showing various forms of frequency distributions.

Histogram	Description of distribution form	Examples of when such shapes might occur
A	A. Unimodal, symmetrical but relatively peaked.	A distribution of scores on an arithmetic test of medium difficulty.
B	B. Unimodal, symmetrical with moderate degree of peakedness.	A distribution of scores on an arithmetic test of medium difficulty.
C	C. Unimodal, symmetrical but relatively flat.	A distribution of scores on an arithmetic test of medium difficulty.
D	D. Rectangular or uniform.	A distribution of monthly incidence of infant mortality in a large modern hospital.
E	E. Bimodal and symmetrical or U-shaped.	A distribution of ages at time of death of pedestrians killed by automobiles.
F	F. Positively skewed or skewed to right.	A distribution of scores on a "hard" arithmetic test.
G	G. Negatively skewed or skewed to left.	A distribution of scores on an "easy" arithmetic test.

FIGURE F.8 Example of how to calculate percentile ranks for a class of 25 students.

Raw	Tally	Frequency	Cumulative frequency	Percentile rank $PR = \dfrac{\frac{1}{2}\left[\text{number of persons having the score}\right] + \left[\text{number of persons below the score}\right]}{\text{total number of persons}} \times 100$
36	/	1	25	$98 = \dfrac{.5 + 24}{25} \times 100$
35		0	24	96
34		0	24	96
33		0	24	$96 = \dfrac{0 + 24}{25} \times 100$
32	/	1	24	$94 = \dfrac{.5 + 23}{25} \times 100$
31	/	1	23	$90 = \dfrac{.5 + 22}{25} \times 100$
30		0	22	$88 = \dfrac{0 + 22}{25} \times 100$
29	//	2	22	$84 = \dfrac{1 + 20}{25} \times 100$
28	////	4	20	$72 = \dfrac{2 + 16}{25} \times 100$
27	₥	5	16	$54 = \dfrac{2.5 + 11}{25} \times 100$
26	₥ /	6	11	$32 = \dfrac{3 + 5}{25} \times 100$
25	//	2	5	$16 = \dfrac{1 + 3}{25} \times 100$
24	/	1	3	$10 = \dfrac{.5 + 2}{25} \times 100$
23		0	2	8
22		0	2	$8 = \dfrac{0 + 2}{25} \times 100$
21	/	1	2	$6 = \dfrac{.5 + 1}{25} \times 100$
20		0	1	4
19		0	1	4
18		0	1	4
17		0	1	4
16		0	1	4
15		0	1	$4 = \dfrac{0 + 1}{25} \times 100$
14	/	1	1	$2 = \dfrac{.5 + 0}{25} \times 100$
		$N = 25$		

Step-By-Step

1. List the possible scores in descending order (Column 1). (You may group the scores into intervals if you wish.)
2. Tally the number of students attaining each score (Column 2).
3. Sum the number of students attaining each score (Column 3).
4. Add the frequencies consecutively, starting at the bottom of the column with the lowest score. Place each consecutive sum in the cumulative frequency column (Column 4). E.g., $0 + 1 = 1, \ldots, 2 + 1 = 3, 3 + 2 = 5$, etc.
5. Calculate the percentile rank of each score (Column 5). Below is an example for the score 27.
    (a) Calculate one-half of the frequency of the score $(1/2 \times 5 = 2.5)$.
    (b) Add the result in (a) to the cumulative frequency just below the score $(2.5 + 11 = 13.5)$.
    (c) Divide the result in (b) by the total number of scores $(13.5 \div 25 = .54)$.
    (d) Multiply the result in (c) by 100 $(.54 \times 100 = 54)$.

MEASURES OF CENTRAL TENDENCY

It is quite common when interpreting assessment results to speak of the "average score," as we speak of the "average student," "being above average in spelling," or "of average intelligence."

There are many ways to define averages, but we describe only three: mode, mean, and median. The **mode** is the score that occurs most frequently in relation to other scores in the collection. Thus, the modal score is average in the sense of being most popular or most probable in the group. The **mean**, or more precisely the *arithmetic mean*, is found by summing the scores and dividing by their number. Thus, the mean is the average that takes into account all of the scores and is the "center of gravity" of the collection. The **median** is the score point that divides the score scale so 50% of the scores in the collection are above it and 50% are below it. This makes the median a typical score in the sense of coming nearest in the aggregate to all the scores.

Mode

You find the mode by listing the scores and identifying the most frequently occurring. In Figure F.9, the mode of the Test 1 distribution is 75, and the mode of the Test 2 distribution is 68. You could identify the mode from either a stem-and-leaf display or a frequency distribution. If in one distribution two scores occur with approximately equal frequency, there are two modes. Such a distribution is said to be **bimodal**. A distribution with one mode is **unimodal**.

The mode is the point on the score scale where a large number of scores in a distribution are located. If there is more than one mode, there are concentrations of scores at more than one score level. You should note that a distribution may not have a mode. For example, the uniform distribution in Figure F.7D does not have a mode.

Mean

To calculate the mean, add the scores and divide by their number. The formula is

$$M = \frac{Sum\ of\ all\ the\ scores}{Total\ number\ of\ scores}$$

$$= \frac{\sum X}{N}$$

where M represents the mean, N represents the total number of scores involved, and Σ represents "sum of." The means of the Test 1 and Test 2 scores in Figure F.9 are 71.4 and 71.3, respectively.

An important property of the mean is that its value is affected by every one of the scores in the collection, because the sum on which it is based includes every score. When you want an average that focuses on the total rather than the typical or most frequent, choose the mean. The mean reflects the highest and lowest scores,

FIGURE F.9   Scores on Test 1 and Test 2 ranked separately and showing measures of central tendency.

Test 1		Test 2	
98		94	
96		88	
95		87	
89		86	
86		85	
84		83	
83		78	
80		77	
75		76	
75	Mode = 75	75	
75		74	
75		73	
74		73	
73	← Median = 72	73	← Median = 72.5
71		72	
70		70	
69		68	
68		68	Mode = 68
68		68	
66		68	
65		66	
61		65	
60		61	
56		60	
55		54	
45		53	
44		53	
43		47	
$\sum X = 1{,}999$		$\sum X = 1{,}995$	
$M = (1{,}999) \div 28 = 71.4$		$M = (1{,}995) \div 28 = 71.3$	

whereas the mode reflects only the most frequent. This influence of extremely high or low scores may be undesirable because such scores are not typical scores for the distribution. The median is preferred when you want an average to focus on typical performance and to be uninfluenced by extremely high or extremely low scores.

Median

A simple way to calculate the median is to arrange the scores by rank, and then count to the point on the score scale that has the same number of scores above it as below it. If there is an even number of scores in the collection, the median is halfway between the two middle scores. If there is an odd number of scores, the median is the middle score.

In Figure F.9, the median for Test 1 is 72; the median for Test 2 is 72.5. Notice that the median does not have to be a score that any person has attained. This is so because the median is a point on the score scale that divides the distribution into halves. The mean also need not be a score anyone attained; however, the mode must be a score that many persons attained.

Because the median separates the distribution into two halves, it is also the *50th percentile*. Further, it does not sum up all of the scores. As a result, its value is not affected by extremely high or low scores, as the mean is. The median is the average to use when you do not want an average that is sensitive to such extreme scores.

MEASURES OF VARIABILITY

Although averages summarize the central tendency of a group of scores, they do not summarize how the scores spread out over the score scale. For example, the mean reading test scores of two seventh-grade classes may be 75. However, in one class the scores may range widely from 55 to 95, while in the other the scores may range only from 70 to 80. Obviously, the students in the latter class are more nearly alike in their reading achievement than the students in the former class. You will need to address more widely different reading levels when teaching the former class than when teaching the latter.

This section describes three measures of the spread or variability of a set of scores: the range, the interquartile range, and the standard deviation.

Range (R)

The **range** is a simple index of spread. It is the difference between the highest and lowest scores in the set. For the two tests in Figure F.9, the range is 55 for Test 1 (98 – 43 = 55) and 47 for Test 2 (94 – 47 = 47). Although for either test the range is relatively large, it is smaller for Test 2, showing the scores are spread over a smaller part of the score scale. The procedure may be summarized as follows:

$$R = highest\ score - lowest\ score$$

A weakness of the range as an index of variability is that it is based on only two scores. It ignores the scores between the highest and lowest scores. Another problem with the range is that a change in either the highest or lowest score in the set can radically alter its value.

Interquartile Range (IR)

The **interquartile range** describes the spread of the middle 50% of the scores. It is the difference between the third and the first quartiles. **Quartiles** are points that divide the group of scores into quarters. The first quartile (Q_1) is the point *below which* the lowest 25% of the students score. The third quartile (Q_3) is the point *above which* the highest 25% of the students score. The second quartile (Q_2) is the median.

To obtain the interquartile range, you first order the scores and proceed similarly to calculating the median. That is, count down from the highest score 25% of the scores to locate Q_3 and up from the lowest

score 25% to calculate Q_1. The interquartile range is the difference between these two values:[1]

$$IR = Q_3 - Q_1$$

In Figure F.9, $Q_1 = 83$ and $Q_1 = 61$ for Test 1. That is, for Test 1 the 75th percentile is 83 and the 25th percentile is 61. The $IR = [83 - 61] = 22$ for this test. Thus, the middle 50% of the scores on Test 1 have a 22-point spread. For Test 2, $Q_3 = 73$, $Q_1 = 65$, and $IR = [73 - 65] = 8$. The middle 50% of the students have only an 8-point spread on Test 2.

Standard Deviation (SD)

The most frequently used index of variability is the **standard deviation**. Large numerical values of this index indicate that the scores are spread out away from the mean. Small values indicate that the scores tend to cluster near the mean. The standard deviation is the average amount by which the scores differ from the mean score.[2] In some test reports the squared standard deviation (SD^2), or *variance*, is used.

The definitional formula for the standard deviation is:

$$SD = \sqrt{\frac{\sum(X - M)^2}{N}}$$
$$= \sqrt{\frac{Sum\ of\ the\ Squared\ deviations\ from\ the\ mean}{total\ number\ of\ scores}}$$

Many inexpensive scientific calculators and computer programs have procedures for calculating the standard deviation. You should use one of these to calculate SD. If you want to calculate the standard deviation using a calculator that does not have this procedure built in, follow these steps:

1. First arrange the scores into a frequency distribution, as in Figure F.5 and reproduced in Figure F.10.

2. Apply a computational formula such as the one shown here. (You can find other computational formulas in an applied statistics text.)

$$SD = \sqrt{\frac{\sum f(X^2)}{N} - M^2}$$
$$= \sqrt{\frac{\begin{array}{c}sum\ of\ the\ product\ of\ the\ square\\ of\ each\ score\ and\ its\ frequency\end{array}}{total\ number} - [square\ of\ the\ mean]}$$

---

1 Some books divide the interquartile range by 2 to obtain the *semi-interquartile range* (*SIR*). This value indicates the approximate distance you would need to move on the score scale above and below the median to encompass the middle 50% of the scores.

2 This is not strictly correct, but as a practical matter little interpretive harm regarding assessment results is done by thinking of the standard deviation in this way.

FIGURE F.10 Computing the standard deviation of Test 1 scores after they are organized into a frequency distribution.

Score Interval	Midpoint	Frequency (f)	Step 1 (X^2)	Step 2 $f(X^2)$
95–99	97	3	9,409	28,227
90–94	92	0	8,464	0
85–89	87	2	7,569	15,138
80–84	82	3	6,724	20,172
75–79	77	4	5,929	23,716
70–74	72	4	5,184	20,736
65–69	67	5	4,489	22,445
60–64	62	2	3,844	7,688
55–59	57	2	3,249	6,498
50–54	52	0	2,704	0
45–49	47	1	2,209	2,209
40–44	42	2	1,764	3,528
		$n = 28$		150,357

The formula is:

$$SD = \sqrt{\frac{\sum f(X^2)}{N} - M^2} \text{ (Note that using the grouped data above, } M = 71.8)$$

Putting the numbers into the formula:

$$SD = \sqrt{\frac{150,357}{28} - (71.8)^2}$$

After Steps 4 and 5:

$$SD = \sqrt{5,369,89 - 5,155,24}$$

Then Step 6:

$$SD = \sqrt{214.65}$$

Step 7 gives the final result: $SD = 14.65$

This is not as hard to compute as it looks:

Steps

1. Square each interval midpoint.
2. Multiply each square by its frequency.
3. Add together all of these products.
4. Divide by the total number.

5. Square the mean. (If the mean has not been computed already, you need to compute it.)
6. Subtract the square of the mean from the result found in Step 4. (Stop here if you want only the variance.)
7. Take the square root of the difference. This is the standard deviation.

Symbols

1. X^2
2. $f(X^2)$
3. $\sum f(X^2)$

4. $\dfrac{\sum f(X^2)}{N}$

5. M^2

6. $\dfrac{\sum f(X^2)}{N} - M^2$

7. $\sqrt{\dfrac{\sum f(X^2)}{N} - M^2}$

Figure F.10 illustrates these calculations for Test 1. (Note that in this example, the result obtained from Figure F.10 is not the same result you would obtain if you did not group the scores into intervals. Grouping scores results in some error. However, the result is still useful.)

Calculating Stanines

Stanines are normalized standard scores that tell the location of a raw score in one of nine specific segments of a normal distribution. Stanines were explained in Chapter 17. We show how to calculate stanines in Figure F.11.

THE CORRELATION COEFFICIENT

Calculating the correlation coefficient requires using a calculator or a computer. Some scientific calculators have this capability already built in as a statistical function, so all you need to do is enter the paired scores of students. However, this section illustrates the calculation for those with calculators that do not have the correlation coefficient function built in.

FIGURE F.11   How to transform raw scores into stanines.

You may transform any set of scores to stanines by applying the normal curve percentage relationship implied by Figure 17.7. These theoretical percentages are:

Stanine	Percent of scores	Stanine	Percent of scores
9	top 4%	4	next 17%
8	next 7%	3	next 12%
7	next 12%	2	next 7%
6	next 17%	1	bottom 4%
5	middle 20%		

The preferred procedure is to begin assigning stanines at the middle of the score distribution (i.e., assigning stanine = 5 first) and then work toward each end. This procedure helps to make the resulting distribution of stanines more symmetric than if you started at the top or bottom. I illustrate the procedure below using the 25 students' scores shown in percentile rank calibration example given earlier (Figure F.8).

Step-by-step	Results from percentile ranks example	Comments
1. Make a frequency distribution or list the scores in order from high to low.	See PR example, first and third columns.	
2. Locate the median or middle score.	25 scores × ½ = 12.5 scores. Therefore, the middle score is 27.	Round the median to a whole number.
3. Use the theoretical percentages to determine how many scores should be assigned a stanine of 5.	20% of 25 = 5 scores.	
4. Assign stanines of 5 to the number of scores calculated in Step 3. (You should include scores just above and below the median if necessary to come as close as possible to the desired number.)	It so happens that in the PR example exactly 5 persons had a score of 27, so that we do not need to look to adjacent values. (See below.)	Remember that *all* equal scores must have the same stanine assigned to them.
5. Working up from the scores assigned stanine 5, use the theoretical percentages to assign scores to stanine categories of 6, 7, 8, and 9. Come as near to the theoretical percentages as possible.		
6. Repeat the procedure for the scores that are below those assigned stanine 5.		
7. It is important that you assign all equal scores the same stanine.		

Scores	Stanines	Actual number	Theoretical number
36	9	1	1
32–35	8	1	2
29–31	7	3	3
28	6	4	4
27	5	5	5
26	4	6	4
24–25	3	3	3
15–23	2	1	2
14	1	1	1

For practical work, you can use the following computational formula:

$$r = \frac{N(\sum XY) - (\sum X)(\sum Y)}{\sqrt{[N(\sum X^2) - (\sum X)^2][N(\sum Y^2) - (\sum Y)^2]}}$$

This formula is illustrated in Figure F.12 with the scores from the two tests in Figure F.1. In this example, Test 1 is symbolized X and Test 2 is symbolized Y. Figure F.13 shows the calculation.

If you have already computed the standard deviations and means of each variable, then the following formula (which is equivalent to the previous equation) will save you some computational labor.

$$r_{xy} = \frac{\dfrac{\sum XY}{N} - M_x M_y}{(SD_x)(SD_y)}$$

To illustrate with the data in Figure F.13, for which

$$M_x = 71.39, M_y = 71.25$$
$$SD_x = 14.81, SD_y = 11.57$$

we have:

$$r = \frac{\dfrac{145,902}{28} - (71.39)(71.25)}{(14.81)(11.57)}$$

The slight difference you obtain from these two equations is due to rounding error.

CALCULATING BASIC STATISTICS WITH THE EXCEL SPREAD SHEET

Many of the statistics in this appendix can be calculated very easily using the Microsoft Excel spreadsheet program. The first figure in this appendix (Figure F.1) shows the scores on two tests for a class of 28 students. We use the scores in this table to illustrate how to use the Excel program. You need to type students' names and scores into the spreadsheet as shown in the example in Figure F.14. Notice that the rows are labeled with numbers and the columns are labeled with letters. These column letters and row numbers appear automatically and cannot be changed.

FIGURE F.12 Example calculating a correlation coefficient.

Steps	Symbols	Examples
1. List everyone's pair of scores.	1. X, Y	1. *Blake: $X = 74$, $Y = 72$*
2. Square each score.	2. X^2, Y^2	2. *Blake: $X^2 = (74)^2 = 5,476$* *$Y^2 = (72)^2 = 5,184$*
3. Multiply the scores in each pair.	3. XY	3. *Blake: $XY = 74 \times 72$* *$= 5,328$*
4. Sum the X, Y, X^2, Y^2, and XY columns.	4. $\Sigma X, \Sigma Y$ $\Sigma X^2 \ \Sigma Y^2$ ΣXY	4. $\Sigma X = 1,999$, $\Sigma X^2 = 148,635$ $\Sigma Y = 1,995$, $\Sigma Y^2 = 145,761$ $\Sigma XY = 145,902$

5. Put the sums into equation.

$$r = \frac{28\,(145,902) - (1,999)(1,995)}{\sqrt{[28(148,635) - (1,999)^2]\,[28(145,761) - (1995)^2]}}$$

$$= \frac{4,085,256 - 3,988,005}{\sqrt{(4,161,780 - 3,996,001)(4,081,308 - 3,980,025)}}$$

$$= \frac{97,251}{\sqrt{(165,779)(101,283)}} = \frac{97,251}{129,578,53} = .75$$

FIGURE F.13 Computing a correlation coefficient between the scores in Figure F.1.

Names	Test 1		Test 2		Cross Products
	X	X²	Y	Y²	XY
Anthony	89	7,921	94	8,836	8,366
Ashley	75	7,625	68	4,624	5,100
Blake	74	5,476	72	5,184	5,328
Chad	84	7,056	77	5,929	6,468
Donald	56	3,136	66	4,356	3,696
Edward	80	6,400	68	4,624	5,440
Festina	66	4,356	68	4,624	4,488
George	86	7,396	73	5,329	6,278
Harriet	68	4,624	73	5,329	4,964
Irene	98	9,604	86	7,396	8,428
Jesse	65	4,225	78	6,084	5,070
Katherine	44	1,936	60	3,600	2,640
Lorraine	45	2,025	53	2,809	2,385
Marya	61	3,721	75	5,625	4,575
Nancy	75	5,625	76	5,776	5,700
Oprah	68	4,624	54	2,916	3,672
Peter	55	3,025	53	2,809	2,915
Quincy	70	4,900	68	4,624	4,760
Robert	69	4,761	65	4,225	4,485
Sally	60	3,600	47	2,209	2,820
Tina	73	5,329	74	5,476	5,402
Ula	75	5,625	88	7,744	6,600
Veronica	71	5,041	73	5,329	5,183
Wallace	43	1,849	61	3,721	2,623
William	83	6,889	87	7,569	7,221
Xavier	95	9,025	83	6,889	7,885
Yvonne	96	9,216	85	7,225	8,160
Zena	75	7,625	70	4,900	5,250
	1,999	148,635	1,995	145,761	145,902

To calculate the mean (*M*) of the scores for Test 1, click on cell B31. Then type =AVERAGE(B2:B29) and press the return key. (Be sure to include the equal sign and no space before the word AVERAGE.) This tells the program to calculate the average of the scores that are in cells B2 through B29. The value of the mean (71.39) will appear in the B31 cell. To calculate the standard deviation (*SD*) of scores for Test 1, click on cell B32. Then type =STDEV.P(B2:B29) and press the return key. The *SD* (14.54) of the scores in cells B2 through B29 will appear in cell B32. Similarly, if you type

=AVERAGE(C2:C29) into cell C31 and press return, the mean of Test 2 (71.25) will appear in cell C31. If you type =STDEV.P(C2:C29) into cell C32, the *SD* (11.37) will appear in cell C32.

To calculate the correlation coefficient, you need to tell the program the two columns of scores that are involved. Click on cell B33, then type =CORREL(B2:B29, C2:C29). This code tells the program to correlate the Test 1 scores in cells B2 through B29 with the Test 2 scores in cells C2 through C29. Press the return key and the correlation, *r* = .75, appears in cell B33.

FIGURE F.14 Computing basic statistics with the Excel spreadsheet.

	A	B	C	
1	Names	Test 1	Test 2	
2	Anthony	89	94	
3	Ashley	75	68	
4	Blake	74	72	
5	Chad	84	77	
6	Donald	56	66	
7	Edward	80	68	
8	Festina	66	68	
9	George	86	73	
10	Harriet	68	73	
11	Irene	98	86	
12	Jesse	65	78	
13	Katherine	44	60	Enter
14	Lorraine	45	53	students'
15	Marya	61	75	names and
16	Nancy	75	76	scores into
17	Oprah	68	54	these rows
18	Peter	55	53	and columns
19	Quincy	70	68	
20	Robert	69	65	
21	Sally	60	47	
22	Tina	73	74	
23	Ula	75	88	
24	Veronica	71	73	
25	Wallace	43	61	
26	William	83	87	
27	Xavier	95	83	
28	Yvonne	96	85	
29	Zena	75	70	
30				
31	Mean	71.39	71.25	Type =STDEV.P (B2:B29) into this cell
32	Std Dev	14.54	11.37	
33	Correlation	.75		

Type =AVERAGE(B2:B29) into this cell

Type =CORREL(B2:B29,C2:C29) into this cell

APPENDIX G

Computational Procedures for Various Reliability Coefficients

FIGURE G.1 Example of how to compute the Spearman-Brown double length and the Rulon split-halves reliability estimates.

A. Pupil's item scores and total test scores[a]

Pupils	Items on test				Total score
	1	2	3	4	(X)
Alan	1	0	0	0	1
Isaac	1	1	0	0	2
Leslie	0	0	1	1	2
Miriam	0	0	0	0	0
Rebecca	1	1	0	1	3
Robert	1	1	1	1	4

$$M = \frac{\Sigma X}{N} = \frac{12}{6} = 2; \quad (SD_X)^2 = \frac{(X - M)^2}{N} = \frac{10}{6} = 1.67$$

[a]An item is scored 1 if it is answered correctly; 0 otherwise.

B. Computation for Spearman-Brown formula

Pupils	Half-test scores		Computing correlation between halves[b]		
	odd items (1 + 3)	even items (2 + 4)	z-scores for: odd	even	Product ($z_0 \times z_e$)
Alan	1	0	0	−1.22	0
Isaac	1	1	0	0	0
Leslie	1	1	0	0	0
Miriam	0	0	−1.72	−1.22	2.10
Rebecca	1	2	0	+1.22	0
Robert	2	2	+1.72	+1.22	2.10
Means	1.00	1.00			
SDs	0.58	0.82	$r_{nn} = \dfrac{\Sigma z_0 z_e}{N} = \dfrac{4.6}{6} = 0.70$		

Spearman-Brown
 double length

$$\text{reliability estimates} = \frac{2r_{nn}}{1 + r_{nn}} = \frac{(2)(.70)}{1 + .70} = 0.82$$

[b]Other procedures may be used for computing the correlation coefficient (see Figure F.12).

FIGURE G.1 *(continued)*

C. Computation for Rulon formula

Pupils	Half-test scores[c] odd items (1 + 3)	even items (2 + 4)	Difference between half-test scores
Alan	1	0	1
Isaac	1	1	0
Leslie	1	1	0
Miriam	0	0	0
Rebecca	1	2	−1
Robert	2	2	0

Variance of differences $= (SD_{diff})^2 = 0.33$
Variance of total scores $= (SD_x)^2 = 1.67$
Rulon split-halves reliability estimate

$$= 1 - \frac{(SD_{diff})^2}{(SD_x)^2}$$

$$= 1 - \frac{0.33}{1.67} = 0.80$$

[c]Neither the Spearman-Brown nor the Rulon formula is restricted to an odd-even split. Other splits may be used (see text).

FIGURE G.2 Example of how to compute the Kuder-Richardson formula 20 (KR20) and the Kuder-Richardson formula 21 (KR21) reliability estimates.

A. Computing KR20

Pupils	Items on test[a] 1	2	3	4	Total score[b] (X)
Alan	1	0	0	0	1
Isaac	1	1	0	0	2
Leslie	0	0	1	1	2
Miriam	0	0	0	0	0
Rebecca	1	1	0	1	3
Robert	1	1	1	1	4
Fraction passing each item					$M = 2.0$ $(SD_x)^2 = 1.667$
(p-values)	.67	.50	.33	.50	
(1 − p)	.33	.50	.67	.50	
p(1 − p)	.222	.250	.222	.250	$\sum p(1 - p) = 0.944$

$$KR20 = \left[\frac{k}{k-1}\right]\left[1 - \frac{\Sigma p(1-p)}{(SD_x)^2}\right] = \left[\frac{4}{(4-1)}\right]\left[1 - \frac{0.944}{1.667}\right]$$

$$= (1.333)(1 - .566) = (1.333)(.434) = .58$$

[a]An item is scored 1 if it is answered correctly; 0 otherwise.
[b]The mean and variance are computed in Appendix F.

FIGURE G.2 (*continued*)

B. Computing KR21

Pupils	Total score[a] (*X*)
Alan	1
Isaac	2
Leslie	2
Miriam	0
Rebecca	3
Robert	4

$M = 2.0; (SD_x)^2 = 1.667$

$$\text{KR21} = \left[\frac{k}{k-1}\right]\left[1 - \frac{M(k-M)}{k(SD_x)^2}\right]$$

$$= \left[\frac{4}{4-1}\right]\left[1 - \frac{2(4-2)}{4(1.667)}\right]$$

$$= (1.333)\left[1 - \frac{4}{6.668}\right]$$

$$= (1.333)(1 - .600)$$

$$= .53$$

[a]The mean and variance are computed in Appendix F.

C. Comparing the values of various reliability estimates for the same test[a]

Estimating procedure	Numerical value
Spearman-Brown	.82[b]
Rulon	.80[b]
KR20	.58
KR21	.53

[a]See Appendix F also.
[b]Based on an odd-even split.

FIGURE G.3 Example of how to compute a coefficient alpha reliability estimate for a set of essay questions or judges' ratings.

	Questions or judges				
Persons	I	II	III	IV	Total score (*X*)
Aaron	4	3	4	4	15
Dorcas	2	5	5	5	17
Katherine	3	5	5	3	16
Kenneth	1	3	1	1	6
Lee	5	5	5	4	19
Peter	4	3	4	4	15
$(SD_i)^2$ values	1.81	1.00	2.00	1.58	$(SD_x)^2 = 16.89$

$\sum (SD_i)^2 = 1.81 + 1.00 + 2.00 + 1.58 = 6.39$

$$\alpha = \left[\frac{k}{k-1}\right]\left[1 - \frac{\sum (SD_i)^2}{(SD_x)^2}\right] = \left[\frac{4}{4-1}\right]\left[1 - \frac{6.39}{16.89}\right] = (1.33)(1 - .38) = (1.33)(.62) = .82$$

FIGURE G.4   Example of computing the general Spearman-Brown reliability estimate.

A. Formula

$$r_{nn} = \frac{nr_{11}}{1 + (n - 1)r_{11}}$$

B. Example

Q. A teacher has a 10-item test with reliability coefficient equal to 0.40. What would be the reliability if the teacher added 15 new items similar to those currently on the test?

A. Here $r_{11} = 0.40$ and $n = \dfrac{25}{10} = 2.5$. (The new test would be 25 items long, hence, 2.5 times as long as the original test.) Thus, the new test reliability is:

$$r_m = \frac{(2.5)(0.40)}{1 + (2.5 - 1)(0.40)}$$

$$= \frac{1.00}{1 + 0.6} = \frac{1.0}{1.6} = .625$$

C. Results of applying the formula to various values of r_{11} and n

Original reliability	Number of times original test is lengthened (n)				
	2	3	4	5	6
.10	.18	.25	.31	.36	.40
.20	.33	.43	.50	.56	.60
.30	.46	.56	.63	.68	.72
.40	.57	.67	.73	.77	.80
.50	.67	.75	.80	.83	.86
.60	.75	.82	.86	.88	.90
.70	.82	.88	.90	.92	.93
.80	.89	.92	.94	.95	.96
.90	.95	.96	.97	.98	.98

FIGURE G.5   Example of how to compute percentage agreement and the kappa coefficient. The kappa coefficient adjusts the percent agreement for chance agreement that is not related to the assessment procedure.

A. General layout of the data

		Results from Test 1		
		Mastery	Nonmastery	Marginal totals
Results from Test 2	Mastery	a	b	a + b
	Nonmastery	c	d	c + d
	Marginal totals	a + c	b + d	N = a + b + c + d

B. Formulas

P_A = total percentage agreement in figure

$$= \frac{a}{N} + \frac{d}{N} = \frac{a + d}{N}$$

P_C = percent agreement expected because of the composition of the goup

$$= \left(\frac{a + b}{N} \times \frac{a + c}{N}\right) + \left(\frac{c + d}{N} \times \frac{b + d}{N}\right)$$

$$\kappa = \frac{P_A - P_C}{1 - P_C}$$

FIGURE G.5   (*continued*)

C. Numerical example

		Results from Test 1		
		Mastery	**Nonmastery**	**Marginal totals**
Results from Test 2	**Mastery**	11	4	15
	Nonmastery	1	9	10
	Marginal totals	12	13	25

$$P_A = \frac{11}{25} + \frac{9}{25} = \frac{11 + 9}{25} = \frac{20}{25} = 0.80$$

$$P_C = \left(\frac{15}{25} \times \frac{12}{25}\right) + \left(\frac{10}{25} \times \frac{13}{25}\right) = \frac{180}{625} + \frac{130}{625} = \frac{310}{625} = 0.50$$

$$\kappa = \frac{0.8 - 0.50}{1 - 0.50} = \frac{0.30}{0.50} = 0.60$$

A Limited List of Published Tests

FIGURE H.1 Selected published tests.

Title	Age/Grade Level	Publisher[1]	Review[2]
Multilevel survey achievement batteries (group)			
• Iowa Tests of Basic Skills, Forms A, B, C	K–8	RP	**14**:159, **17**:93
• Iowa Tests of Educational Development, Forms A, B, C	Gr. 9–12	RP	**14**:160, **16**:116
• Measures of Academic Progress	Gr. 2-12	NWEA	**18**:73
• Metropolitan Achievement Tests, 8th ed.	K–12	PA	**12**:232, **16**:146
• Stanford Achievement Test, 10th ed.	K–12	PA	**13**:292, **16**:232
• TerraNova, 3rd ed.	K–12	DRC	**16**:245, **18**:125
Multilevel survey achievement batteries (individual)			
• Peabody Individual Achievement Test–R	K–12	PA	**11**:280, **14**:279
• Kaufman Test of Educational Achievement–2nd ed.	1–Adult	PA	**14**:191, **16**:124
• Wide Range Achievement Test–4	K–Adult	PAR	**16**:272, **18**:157
Multilevel criterion-referenced achievement tests			
• Degrees of Reading Power	1–12	QA	**14**:111, **16**:69
• Key Math–3	K–12	PA	**14**:194, **18**:63
Reading survey tests			
• Gates–MacGinite Reading Tests, 4th ed.	K–Adult	RP	**11**:146, **16**:94
Reading diagnostic tests			
• Woodcock-Johnson III Diagnostic Reading Battery	2–Adult	RP	**14**:422, **17**:201
Adaptive behavior inventories			
• Vineland Adaptive Behavior Scales–3rd ed.	0–90 yrs.	PA	**10**:381, **18**:150
Individual general ability/scholastic aptitude tests			
• Bayley Scales of Infant and Toddler Development, 3rd ed.	1–42 mo.	PA	**13**:29, **17**:17
• Draw a Person: A Quantitative Scoring System	5–17 yrs.	PA	**11**:114, **17**:59
• Kaufman Assessment Battery for Children, 2nd ed.	3–18 yrs.	PA	**9**:562, **16**:123
• Peabody Picture Vocabulary Test–IV	2–Adult	PA	**14**:280, **18**:88
• Stanford-Binet Intelligence Scale, 5th ed.	2–Adult	RP	**10**:342, **16**:233
• Wechsler Adult Intelligence Scale, 4th ed.	16–90 yrs.	PA	**14**:415, **18**:151
• Wechsler Intelligence Scale for Children, 5th ed.	6–16 yrs.	PA	**16**:262, **17**:197
• Wechsler Preschool and Primary Scale of Intelligence, 4th ed.	2–11 yrs.	PA	**16**:267, **19**:176

FIGURE H.1 (*continued*)

Title	Age/Grade Level	Publisher[1]	Review[2]
Group-administered tests of scholastic aptitude			
• ACT Test	Gr. 10–12	ACT	**12**:139
• Closed High School Placement Test	Gr. 8–9	STS	**8**:26, **14**:80
• Cognitive Abilities Test–Form 6	K–12	RP	**13**:71, **16**:55
• Otis-Lennon School Ability Test, 8th ed.	K–12	PA	**11**:274, **18**:82
• College Board SAT	Gr. 11–12	ETS	**9**:244
Multiple aptitude batteries			
• Differential Aptitude Test, 5th ed.	Gr. 7–adult	PA	**12**:118
Vocational interest inventories			
• Hall Occupational Orientation Inventories	Gr. 3–Adult	STS	**12**:175, **16**:100
• Jackson Vocational Interest Survey–Revised	Gr. 9–Adult	SAS	**14**:187, **15**:129
• Self-Directed Search, online	Gr. 7–Adult	PAR	**14**:345
• Strong Interest Inventory, 4th ed.	16 yrs.–Adult	CPP	**15**:248, **18**:129

[1]See Appendix I for names and addresses of publishers.

[2] The boldface number is the number of the *Mental Measurements Yearbook* volume; the number after the colon is the entry number. Reviews of previous editions are listed in some cases.

List of Test Publishers and Their Websites

See the current *Mental Measurements Yearbook*, or *MMY*, the Buros Institute of Mental Measurements (buros.org), or the Association of Test Publishers (testpublishers .org) for additional names and addresses.

16pf Questionnaire
16pf.com/

ACT (formerly American College Testing Program)
act.org/

Center for Applied Linguistics (CAL)
cal.org/

The College Board (CEEB)
collegeboard.org/

CPP (formerly Consulting Psychologist Press)
cpp.com/

Data Recognition Corporation (DRC)
datarecognitioncorp.com/

Educational and Industrial Testing Service (EDITS Online)
edits.net/

Educational Records Bureau, Inc. (ERB)
erblearn.org/

Educational Testing Service (ETS)
ets.org/

HMH Assessments
hmhco.com/

Measured Progress
measuredprogress.org/

Northwest Evaluation Association (NWEA)
nwea.org/

Partnership for Assessment of Readiness for College and Careers (PARCC)
parcconline.org/

Pearson Assessment (PA)
pearsonassessments.com/

PRO-ED (PE)
proedinc.com/

Questar Assessment, Inc. (QA)
questarai.com/

Scholastic Testing Service, Inc. (STS)
ststesting.com/

Sigma Assessment Systems (SAS)
sigmaassessmentsystems.com/

Slosson Educational Publishers, Inc.
slosson.com/

Smarter Balanced Assessment Consortium (SBAC)
smarterbalanced.org/

Western Psychological Services (WPS)
wpspublish.com/

Answers to Even-Numbered Exercises

Chapter 1

2. a. F
    b. F
    c. F
    d. F
    e. F
    f. F
4. a. Placement decision
    b. Classification decision
    c. Placement decision
    d. Certification decision

Chapter 2

2. a. Mastery learning objective
    b. Developmental learning objective
    c. Mastery learning objective
4. a. Psychomotor, because it requires perception and judgment of color (some cognitive—need to know how to use the remote, the on-screen programming, and so on)
    b. Cognitive, because the main requirement is understanding of parliamentary procedures (some affective—need to use some interpersonal skills to conduct the meeting successfully)
    c. Affective, because group maintenance requires interpersonal skills (some cognitive—operating without working on the science would not contribute to group maintenance)
    d. Psychomotor, because eye-hand coordination and skill at throwing is the primary objective (some cognitive—need to understand what a foul line is)

Chapter 3

2. a. Reliability evidence
    b. Reliability evidence
    c. Reliability evidence
    d. Relationship to other variables (external structure evidence), in this case science course-taking

    e. Content representativeness and relevance (content evidence)
4. a. Content representativeness and relevance (content evidence)
    b. Relationships of assessment results to the results of other variables (external structure evidence)
    c. Reliability over assessors (reliability evidence)
    d. Content representativeness and relevance (content evidence) and types of thinking skills required (substantive evidence)
    e. Content representativeness and relevance (content evidence); secondarily substantive evidence

Chapter 4

2. No, the teacher's claim is not justifiable. The split-halves reliability coefficient, using the Spearman-Brown double length formula, would be 0.57. This is too low a reliability coefficient to expect consistent performance.

$$\frac{2 \times .40}{1 + .40} = \frac{.80}{1.40} = .57$$

4   a. Harry's science grade equivalent is probably between 7.6 and 8.0.
    b. Harry's math and science performance still do not differ. The interval is 7.2–7.6 for math and 7.6–8.0 for science. These intervals still overlap, at one point (7.6).
    c. Jane's (6.8–7.2) and Sally's (8.0–8.4) performance still differ.

Chapter 5

2. a. Mr. Smith scenario—violation of professional responsibility
    Sound—testing at the end of a unit of instruction
    Unsound—not planning assessment to match

classroom learning outcomes; counting in official assessment points for material not related to learning outcomes for which the students were responsible

b. Ms. Williams scenario—violation of professional responsibility
Sound—testing at the end of a unit of instruction
Unsound—not reviewing the test or key for quality; unquestioning reliance on the "authority" of a publisher; unwillingness to discuss assessment with student and parent

4. a. Ms. Appleton scenario—violation of professional responsibility
Sound—using appropriate accommodations
Unsound—changing students' answers

b. Mr. Pennel scenario—violation of professional responsibility
Sound—using essays and performance assessment (assuming they are used for assessing appropriate learning objectives)
Unsound—not matching scoring schemes (whether rubrics, checklists, rating scales, or point schemes) to the learning objectives means student performance on the essays or performance assessments may not be interpreted appropriately as indicators of achievement

c. Ms. Dingle scenario—violation of professional responsibility
Sound—being willing to adjust borderline grades
Unsound—not using additional *achievement* information to make the adjustment; using her perceptions/opinions to make the adjustment (causing a "halo effect"); not having a sound rationale to give the students about their grades; making comments about the students that could be perceived as personal rather than as about their achievement; and, if the scenario is read to imply that the students indeed are at the same achievement level, giving two different grades for the same achievement level

Chapter 6

2. Answers will vary. Good answers will categorize and evaluate materials accurately and draw appropriate conclusions.

4. Answers will vary. Good answers will have coherent plans that support sound learning objectives with appropriate formative and summative assessment information.

Chapter 7

2. a. Prerequisite knowledge and skills deficits
b. Identifying student errors
c. Identifying student errors
d. Prerequisite knowledge and skills deficits

4. a. Sharing learning targets and criteria for success
b. Student self-assessment
c. Asking effective questions
d. Helping students ask effective questions

Chapter 8

2. a. Evaluative feedback, judgmental tone
b. Descriptive feedback, specifying improvement
c. Descriptive feedback, first-person response
d. Evaluative feedback, external reward

4. a. Example prompt
b. Reminder prompt
c. Scaffold prompt
d. Reminder prompt

Chapter 9

2. a. Have the blank toward the end of the sentence.
b. Be written as a question (with only one answer).
c. Have only one or two blanks. Have the blank toward the end of the sentence.
d. Be written as a question (with only one answer).
e. Be written as a question (with only one answer). Have directions for amount of precision required.
f. Population of what? Without that, it is impossible to know whether the question assesses an important aspect of the learning objectives.

4. a. Avoid verbal clues.
b. Assess important ideas (not trivia or common sense). Be definitely true or definitely false.
c. Assess important ideas (not trivia or common sense).
d. State the source of the opinion, if your item presents an opinion.
e. Focus on only one important idea or on one relationship between ideas.

Chapter 10

2. Answers will vary. Evaluations and revisions of items should be consistent with the Checklist for Reviewing the Quality of Multiple-Choice Items.

4. Flaws include the following: Premises and responses are not homogeneous. All responses are not plausible for each premise. Longer statements go in premises, not responses. Directions should clearly state the basis for matching. Avoid "perfect matching." Explanations should be logical. Revisions should address the flaws.

Chapter 11

2. Flaws are listed below. Revisions should address these flaws.
a. Match the assessment plan (which probably required higher-order thinking regarding students' understanding of prejudice). Require students to apply knowledge to a new situation. Require the students to demonstrate more than recall. Make clear length, purpose, amount of time, and evaluation criteria.
b. Define a task with specific directions (this is too broad—one appropriate answer might be, "It's horrible!"). Word the question in a way that leads all students to interpret the item as intended. Make clear length, purpose, amount of time, and evaluation criteria.

4. a Regarding the maximum marks (points) for each question, students should realize they have trouble allocating 50 points for these four questions, which probably can only support 10 or 15 points.

   b. Because there are no rubrics or point schemes associated with the maximum marks, there should be disagreement on how to score Jane's responses. Most likely, there will be more disagreement on the items that have more points. Discussion may point to the fact that there are no descriptions of performance required for each point level. Discussion may also highlight the difference between points for varying degrees of correctness of short-answer questions (#1, #2, #4) and the points for varying degrees of quality on the paragraph (#3). Discussion may also note that the essay question (#3) does not follow the checklist for evaluating the quality of essays; lack of definition of the task contributes to its being difficult to score.

Chapter 12

2. Answers will vary. There should be 17 well-designed tasks and scoring schemes.
4. Answers will vary. There should be 13 well-designed tasks and scoring schemes.

Chapter 13

2. Answers will vary. Analyses of the tasks should be accurate and thoughtful.
4. Answers will vary. Self- and peer-evaluations should use the checklist for judging the quality of rubrics and rating scales.
6. Answers will vary. The portfolio design should follow the six-step procedure suggested in the chapter.

Chapter 14

2. a. Perfect positive discrimination—all upper-group students got the item right, and no lower-group students did.

   b. Positive discrimination—50% more of the upper-group students than lower-group students got the item right.

   c. No discrimination—the same proportion of upper-group students and lower-group students got the item right.

   d. Negative discrimination—50% more of the lower-group students than upper-group students got the item right.

   e. Perfect negative discrimination—all lower-group students got the item right, and no upper-group students did.

3. See chart below.
4. a. Item 2 (and Item 3 as it stands, although it wouldn't discriminate negatively if it were keyed properly)

   b. Item 2
   c. Item 3
   d. Items 2 and 4 (and 3 as miskeyed)
   e. Item 1
   f. Item 2
   g. 45%

Chapter 15

2. Answers will vary.
4. a. Note that the fixed-percentage and total-points criterion-referenced methods are exact. The norm-reference rankings are also exact, although the letter grades arising from them are a matter of judgment. Self-referenced grades are also a matter of judgment.

		Options							
Item number	Groups	A	B	C	D	Faulty distractors	Miskeying	Ambiguous	Guessing
1.	Upper	0	2	*9	0	no	no	no	no
	Middle			*5					
	Lower	1	2	*4	4		$p = .60$	$D = .45$	
2.	Upper	2	*7	0	2	Possibly A	no	no	no
	Middle		*4						
	Lower	0	*9	1	1		$p = .67$	$D = -.18$	
3.	Upper	9	*1	1	0	no	A	no	no
	Middle		*1						
	Lower	6	*2	2	1		$p = .13$	$D = -.09$	
4.	Upper	*5	5	0	1	no	no	B	no
	Middle	*8							
	Lower	*3	3	3	2		$p = .53$	$D = .18$	
5.	Upper	3	2	3	*3	no	no	no	Yes
	Middle				*4				
	Lower	3	2	3	*3		$p = .33$	$D = .00$	

b.

Pupil	Self-referencing	CR, fixed-percentage	CR, total points	NR, SS score method
A	A	80%, B	78% of total points, C	Rank 3, B
B	B	72%, C	71% of total points, C	Rank 4, C
C	A	93%, A	87% of total points, B	Rank 1, A
D	A	90%, A	87% of total points, B	Rank 2, B
E	F	31%, F	28% of total points, F	Rank 10, F
F	D	58%, F	54% of total points, F	Rank 8, D
G	C	54%, F	59% of total points, F	Rank 9, F
H	F	59%, F	60% of total points, D	Rank 7, D
I	F	69%, D	66% of total points, D	Rank 6, C
J	F	68%, D	66% of total points, D	Rank 5, C

c. Most disagreement should be with self-referenced grading, and the next most disagreement with norm-referenced grading. Criterion-referenced grades should agree. Note that some might have given Pupil D a B for the fixed-percentage method, because his average is 89.6667. Typically, one would round to the nearest percent (90, or an A on the scale we're using).

d. Self-referenced grading requires the most subjective judgment. Norm-referenced ranking is mathematical, but how many of each grade to give is a judgment call. Criterion-referenced methods are objective once the individual assessments' scores and weights have been set.

Chapter 16

2. Answers will vary.
4. Answers will vary. Analyses should be complete, accurate, logical, and well-supported.

Chapter 17

2. a. Linear standard score (z- or SS-score)
   b. Grade-equivalent score
   c. Developmental or growth scale score (expanded scale score or grade equivalent)
   d. Stanine

4.

Percentile rank	Stanine	z_n	DIQ (SD = 15)	T-score
99.9	9	+3.00	145	80
98	9	+2.00	130	70
84	7	+1.00	115	60
50	5	0.00	100	50
16	3	−1.00	85	40
2	1	−2.00	70	30
0.1	1	−3.00	55	20

Chapter 18

2. These professional organizations have websites and journals that may lead you to test information. Also, contacting the organization may lead you to experts whom you might contact.
4. a. The test's technical manual
   b. The test's technical manual
   c. Test reviews, for example in the *Mental Measurements Yearbook*
   d. Professional journals (accessed by searching ERIC, PsycINFO, or other databases using the test's name)

Chapter 19

2. a. *OLSAT*
   b. *DAT*
   c. Aptitude test for a specific subject
   d. *KABC-II*
   e. *ACT*
4. a. Attitude
   b. Interest
   c. Attitude
   d. Values
   e. Values

Glossary

absolute achievement: The achievement of specific learning objectives and content without regard to what other students have achieved. See also **criterion-referencing** and **relative achievement**.

absolute standards grading: Evaluating student progress by comparing the student's achievement against content standards, performance standards, or learning objectives rather than against the achievement of other students. See also **criterion-referencing**.

abstract/visual reasoning subtests: A subtest of a scholastic aptitude battery that contains items in which the examinee is expected to reason using geometric shapes, sequences, and patterns.

accommodations: Changes in either the conditions or materials of assessment that allow students with disabilities to be assessed in the same areas as regular students (e.g., additional time, reading questions aloud), when such changes are not expected to change the construct being measured.

accountability testing: Assessment that is used to hold individual students or school officials responsible for ensuring that students meet state standards.

achievement: Knowledge, skills, and abilities that students have developed as a result of instruction.

activity-similarity rationale for assessing interests: Interest inventories built using this rationale present the students with lists of activities that are similar to those required of persons working in certain jobs or studying certain subjects.

adaptive assessment task: A computer-assisted assessment in which a student's response to one task will determine what the next presentation will be.

adaptive behavior: Behaviors indicating a child can cope with the normal social and physical environment that is appropriate for his or her age, especially outside the school context.

affective domain: A collection of educational outcomes and learning objectives that focus on feelings, interests, attitudes, dispositions, and emotional states.

affective saliency: The degree of emotionality with which students hold particular attitudes.

age-based scores versus grade-based scores: *Age-based scores* use as a norm group only those students with the chronological age that is typical for a particular grade placement. *Grade-based scores* include all students at a particular grade placement, regardless of their chronological age.

alignment studies: Empirical studies involving the collection of ratings from trained judges and summaries of students' responses to testing. Their aim is to describe, as objectively as possible, the degree to which the actual test items on a state's assessment instrument(s) are matched to the educational content and performance standards set by that state.

"all of the above": A possible alternative or option for a multiple-choice item; all of the preceding alternatives are correct answers to this multiple-choice question.

alternate-forms reliability coefficient [delayed]: A procedure for estimating reliability that is used when one wants to study how scores are influenced by differences in both content and testing occasion. The procedure is to administer to the same group of students one form of an assessment on one occasion and an alternate form on another occasion.

alternate-forms reliability coefficient [same occasion]: A procedure for estimating reliability that is used when one wants to study the consistency of scores from two different, but comparable, samples of test items that were administered on the same occasion. The procedure is to administer two forms of an assessment to the same group of students on the same (or nearly the same) occasion and to correlate the scores.

Also known as the *equivalent-forms reliability coefficient* or the *parallel-forms coefficient*.

alternate solution strategies: Different, but equally correct, procedures or methods for obtaining a correct solution to a problem or for producing the correct product.

alternative assessment: Generally refers to performance assessment. The "alternative" in alternative assessment usually means in opposition to standardized achievement tests and to multiple-choice (true-false, matching, completion) item formats. See also **performance assessment**.

alternatives: The list of choices from which an examinee answering a multiple-choice item must select the correct or best answer. Also known as *choices*, *options*, and *response choices*.

ambiguous alternatives: A type of multiple-choice and matching exercise item-writing flaw that results in *upper group students* being unable to distinguish between the correct answer and one or more of the distractors in a multiple-choice item.

analysis: A category in the Bloom et al. (1956) *Taxonomy of Educational Objectives*. Learning objectives in this category ask students to identify the parts of a piece of information, explain the interconnections and relationships among the parts, or explain the organization or structure of the piece of information. See also **application, comprehension, evaluation, knowledge,** and **synthesis**.

analytic rubric, analytic scoring rubric: A rule that you use to rate or score the separate parts or traits (dimensions) of a student's product or process first, then sum these part scores to obtain a total score. See also **holistic rubric** and **rubrics**.

application: A category in the Bloom et al. (1956) *Taxonomy of Educational Objectives*. Learning targets in this category ask students to use their knowledge and skills to solve new problems or to work effectively in new situations. See also **analysis, comprehension, evaluation, knowledge,** and **synthesis**.

aptitude: An aptitude for *X* is the present state of a person that indicates the person's expected future performance in *X* if the conditions of the past and present continue into the future.

area under the normal curve: The area in a segment of a normal curve between the graph of the curve and the horizontal axis.

argument-based approach to validation: Organizing the information used to demonstrate the validity of your assessment practices in the form of a persuasive argument. In other words, using a combination of logic and data to convince others that your interpretations and uses of the assessment results are valid. See also **assessment practice** and **validity**.

assessment: The process for obtaining information that is used for making decisions about students, curricula and programs, and educational policy. See also **evaluation, measurement,** and **test**.

assessment literacy: Teacher knowledge and skills in educational assessment, and the disposition and practice of using these skills in one's teaching, especially regarding assessment of student learning and achievement.

assessment variables: Characteristics about which you gather information needed for teaching, including sizing up the class and diagnosing students' needs, prerequisite achievements, attitudes, work habits, study skills, and their motivation and effort in school.

association test of personality: Examinees are presented with vague pictures as stimulus materials and asked to tell what their meaning is.

association variety of short answer: This format consists of a list of terms or a picture for which students have to recall numbers, labels, symbols, or other terms and write them next to the listed terms or given picture in the spaces indicated.

attitudes: A person's positive or negative feelings toward particular objects, situations, institutions, persons, or ideas. See also **interests** and **values**.

authentic assessment: A type of performance assessment in which students are presented with educational tasks that are directly meaningful instead of indirectly meaningful.

behavior checklist: A list of discrete behaviors related to a specific area of a student's performance that is used by observing a student and marking the behaviors on the list that were observed. See also **checklist**.

bell-shaped distribution: A distribution of scores that is unimodal, symmetrical, and the graph of which has the appearance of the cross section of a bell.

best answer item: A type of multiple-choice item where all the distractors contain degrees of correctness, but one is best.

best works portfolio: A portfolio containing only a student's best final products or work in a subject. See also **portfolio**.

bias (assessment or test): A general term to describe a test or an assessment used unfairly against a particular group of persons for a particular purpose or decision.

bias as content/experience differential: According to this approach, an assessment usage is biased if the content of the assessment tasks is radically different from a particular subgroup of students' life experiences, but the assessment results are interpreted without taking such differences into proper consideration.

bias as differential validity: According to this approach, an assessment would be biased if it predicted criterion scores better for one group of persons (e.g., Whites) than for another (e.g., African Americans) (Cole & Moss, 1989).

bias as mean differences: According to this approach, an assessment usage is biased against a particular group when the average (mean) score of that group is lower than the average score of another group.

bias as misinterpretation of scores: According to this approach, an assessment usage is biased if someone who uses the results tries to make inappropriate inferences about students' performances that go beyond the content domain of the assessment (Cole & Moss, 1989).

bias as the statistical model: According to this approach, an assessment usage is biased if the statistical procedure used for selection is unfair to persons who are members of a particular group.

bias as the wrong criterion: According to this approach, an assessment usage is biased if the criterion measure that the test tries to predict is biased, making the selection process biased, even if the test is unbiased.

bias stemming from testing conditions: According to this approach, an assessment usage is biased if the scores are interpreted without considering that the basic stresses of test taking, such as test anxiety, feeling unwelcome, or being tested by a member of the opposite gender or another race, can adversely affect the performance of some groups.

bimodal distribution: A frequency distribution of scores in which there are two pileups of scores in two separate intervals. Sometimes referred to as a *U-shaped distribution*. See also **unimodal distribution**.

blueprint: See **table of specifications**.

borderline cases: Students whose marks place them at or very near the border between two letter grades.

carryover effect: A type of scoring error that occurs when your judgment of a student's response to Question 1 affects your judgment of the student's response to Question 2.

central tendency error: A type of error in rating students that occurs when a teacher fails to use extreme ratings and uses ratings in the middle part of the scale only.

checklist: A list of specific behaviors, characteristics of a product or activities, and a place for marking whether each is present or absent.

checklist method of reporting student progress: A student progress report that contains a list of many specific behaviors, which a teacher checks off or rates as a student achieves each during the year.

choices: See **alternatives**.

clang association: A word in the stem of a multiple-choice or matching item that sounds very much like a word in the correct alternative.

classification decision: A decision that results in a person being assigned to one of several different but unordered categories, jobs, or programs. For example, children with disabilities may be classified into one (or more) of a few designated categories. See also **placement decision** and **selection decision**.

classification variety of multiple choice items: See **masterlist variety of matching exercise items**.

classroom activity versus assessments tasks: A performance activity used primarily as a teaching aid and without criteria for evaluating students' achievement is a *classroom activity* rather than an assessment task. *Assessments* must include achievement criteria and scoring guides in addition to a performance activity.

Classroom Assessment Standards **(2015):** Guidelines and recommendations prepared by the Joint Committee on Standards for Educational Evaluation to ensure ethical, useful, feasible, and accurate assessment of students in classrooms.

closed-response task: An assessment task allowing only a single correct answer. See also **open-response task**.

cloze reading exercise: A reading comprehension assessment method crafted by replacing every fifth word (excluding verbs, conjunctions, and articles) with blanks of equal length. The students' task is to read the passage and put in the missing words.

clueing: An item-writing flaw in which hints to the correct answer to one item are found in the contents of another item in the test.

Code of Fair Testing Practices in Education (*Revised*): A document based on the *Standards for Educational and Psychological Testing* that describes in nontechnical terms the obligations of test developers and test users to ensure that tests are used properly. See Appendix B.

Code of Professional Responsibilities in Educational Measurement (*CPR*): A document that describes the professional and ethical behaviors of test users regarding the interpretation, handling, and usage of test scores and materials. See Appendix C.

coefficient alpha reliability: A general version of the Kuder-Richardson formula 20 reliability coefficient. It is primarily used with tests and questionnaires that contain items that are scored more continuously.

cognitive domain: A collection of educational outcomes and learning objectives that focus on a student's knowledge and abilities requiring memory, thinking, and reasoning processes.

cognitive feedback: Feedback that describes the connections between aspects of the task (or the process students used to do the task) and the student's achievement.

complete ordering of students: Ranking all students in the class on their test performance. See also **partial ordering of students**.

completion test of personality: A type of personality test that asks the examinee to complete sentences related to various aspects of self and of interpersonal relations (e.g., "Compared with most families, mine…").

completion variety of short answer: A format of achievement assessment that presents a student with incomplete sentences and asks the student to add one or more words to complete them correctly.

comprehension: A category in the Bloom et al. (1956) *Taxonomy of Educational Objectives*. Learning objectives in this category ask students to paraphrase or explain concepts in their own words. See also **application, analysis, evaluation, knowledge**, and **synthesis**. [ch. 2]

computer-adaptive test: A test administered via computer, in which the next item or set of items selected to be administered depends on the correctness of the test taker's responses to the most recent items.

concept: A name that represents a category of things such as persons, objects, events, or relationships.

concept mapping: A graphical way to represent how a student understands relationships among the major concepts in a subject.

conceptual knowledge: One of four categories in the Knowledge Dimension of the revised Bloom's taxonomy, signifying a student's awareness and understanding of concepts. See also **factual knowledge, procedural knowledge**, and **metacognitive knowledge**.

concrete concept: A class, whose members have in common one or more physical, tangible qualities that can be heard, seen, tasted, felt, or smelled.

concurrent validity evidence: The extent to which individuals' current status on a criterion can be estimated from their current performance on an assessment instrument. See also **predictive validity evidence**.

confidence interval: See **uncertainty interval**.

confidentiality: The right of students to have their test results kept private, known only to authorized persons, and not released to those outside the school except by student-approved release.

construct: The trait or characteristic that an assessment instrument has been designed to measure.

content analysis of responses: An analysis of students' responses to written open-ended items. Responses are organized into meaningful categories to identify in the class common errors and misconceptions.

content-based method for grading: See **quality-level method for grading**.

content centered: A criterion for a well-stated learning objective. A learning objective should describe the specific subject-matter content to which a student should apply the performance learned. See also **performance centered** and **student centered**.

content relevance: Validity evidence that focuses on whether the assessment tasks belong in the user's definition of what the assessment should include.

content representativeness: Validity evidence that focuses on whether the assessment tasks are representative of a larger domain of performance.

content standards: Statements about the subject-matter facts, concepts, principles, and so on that students are expected to learn.

context-dependent item sets: See **interpretive exercises**.

context-dependent tasks: See **interpretive exercises**.

continuous assessment: The daily process by which you gather information about students' progress in achieving the curriculum's learning outcomes (Nitko, 1995).

correct-answer variety: A multiple-choice item format in which one of the alternatives is unarguably the correct answer to the question or problem posed by the stem.

correction for guessing formulas: An algebraic formula used with response-choice items for adjusting each student's raw score by estimating how many items on which the examinee guessed. See also **response-choice items**.

correction variety of true-false items: An item format that requires students to judge a proposition, as does the true-false variety, but students are also required to correct any false statement to make it true.

correlation coefficient: A statistical index that quantifies, on a scale of -1 to $+1$, the degree of relationship between the scores from one assessment and the scores from another.

credentialing: Decision processes in which persons who meet specified requirements (usually involving passing a test or other assessment) are awarded a certain status and given a credential.

criterion-referenced grading framework: The assignment of grades by comparing a student's performance to a defined set of standards to be achieved, targets to be learned, or knowledge to be acquired.

criterion-referencing: A score-interpreting framework that compares a student's test performance against the domain of performances that the assessment samples to answer the question, "How much of the targeted learning did this student achieve?"

critical thinking: This is "reasonable, reflective thinking that is focused on deciding what to believe or do"

(Ennis, 1985, p. 54). Critical-thinking educational goals focus on developing students who are fair-minded, are objective, reach sound conclusions, and are disposed toward seeking clarity and accuracy.

curricular relevance: Validity evidence that focuses on the degree of overlap between a specific curriculum and the specific tasks on a particular assessment.

deadwood alternative: An alternative of a multiple-choice or matching item that no examinee chooses and, hence, is nonfunctional.

decision consistency index: A statistical index used to describe the consistency of decisions made from scores rather than the consistency of the scores themselves.

decontextualized knowledge: The use of knowledge without its real-world context or application.

defined concept: The name of a class, the members of which can be defined in the same way by attributes that are not tangible and which frequently involve relationships among other concepts. Sometimes called *abstract* or *relational concepts*. See also **concept** and **concrete concept**.

derived score: A score obtained by statistically transforming a raw score in a way that increases its norm-referenced meaning. See also **percentile rank**, **raw score**, and **standard score**.

descriptive feedback: Feedback that gives information about characteristics of the work (as opposed to **evaluative feedback**).

developmental learning objectives: Skills and abilities that are continuously developed throughout life. Learning objectives such as these are more aptly stated at a somewhat higher level of abstraction than mastery learning objectives. See also **mastery learning objectives**.

diagnostic assessment: Assessment of a student's learning difficulties that serves two related purposes: (a) to identify which learning objectives a student has not mastered and (b) to suggest possible causes or reasons why the student has not mastered the learning objectives.

dichotomous item scoring: Scoring an item in such a way that there are only two possible scores.

differential item functioning (DIF): An approach to studying item fairness at the level of individual test items rather than looking simply at average differences in an item's performance. The approach studies whether persons of the same ability, but from two different groups, performed differently on the item.

differentiated instruction: Using different instructional practices to meet the needs, abilities, interests, motivations of students, regardless of differences in ability. Characterized by clearly focused learning goals, pre-assessment and responses, flexible grouping, appropriate student choice during instruction, and ongoing formative assessment; differentiated instruction gives all students avenues to learning.

DIQ-score: A type of normalized standard score, called a deviation IQ score. The distribution of such scores has a mean of 100 and a standard deviation of 15 (or 16 in some tests).

direct assessment: An assessment procedure that allows a student's learning target achievement to be expressed directly as it is intended by the learning objective.

direction and intensity of attitude: Two of the ways students' attitudes may differ. Direction means that the attitude may be positive or negative. Intensity refers to the strength of feeling of a student's attitude. See also **attitudes**.

disaggregation of test results: Separation of test results for the total population of students in order to report on individual subgroups of students such as students who are poor or minorities, students with limited English proficiency, and students with disabilities, in addition to reporting on the total population.

dispositions toward critical thinking: The tendencies or habitual uses of critical thinking abilities.

distractor rationale taxonomy: A way to categorize the developmental level represented by an incorrect response choice in order to obtain diagnostic information from students' wrong answers to multiple-choice items (King, Gardner, Zucker, & Jorgensen, 2004).

distractors: Alternatives in a multiple-choice item that are not the correct or best answer to the question or problem posed by the stem, but that appear to be correct or plausible answers to less knowledgeable examinees.

domain of achievement: A description of all possible tasks that might be appropriate for assessing achievement for a particular set of learning targets.

due process: Whether a person was treated fairly before a judgment was made against the person. *Substantive due process* concerns the appropriateness of the requirement (e.g., passing the test) and the purpose (e.g., maintaining high-quality teaching). *Procedural due process* focuses on the fairness with which the examinee was treated in the proceeding that led to a judgment.

educational goals: Statements of "those human activities which contribute to the functioning of a society (including the functioning of an individual *in* society), and which can be acquired through learning" (Gagné, Briggs, & Wager, 1988, p. 39).

empirically documented tests: Refers to standardized tests that have data to support the development of the test, the selection of items, claims to reliability, and claims to validity.

empirically keyed scales: Interest inventory scales made up of items especially selected because research has shown that persons' responses to these items clearly differentiate between those who are currently and happily employed in a particular occupation and people in general.

empirical norming dates: Refers to the dates during the school year when tests were actually administered to students during the process of developing the grade-equivalent scores.

enhanced multiple-choice items: Multiple-choice items that assess combinations of skills and knowledge in ways that require students to apply what they know.

equivalence: In the context of classroom assessment, the degree to which past and present students are required to know and perform tasks of similar (but not identical) complexity and difficulty to get the same grade on the same content of the units. See also **table of specifications**.

error score: The score an examinee would obtain if you could quantify the amount of error in the examinee's obtained score. See also **obtained score** and **true score**.

ethnic and gender stereotyping: Depiction of races or genders in assessment material that is subtly or blatantly offensive to any subgroup of students or depicts races or genders in oversimplified inappropriate ways. See also **role stereotype**.

ETS Test Collection: Educational Testing Service database of approximately 20,000 tests and other assessment instruments. It contains information on both published and unpublished instruments.

evaluation: The process of making value judgments about the worth of a student's product or performance. Also, a category in the Bloom et al. (1956) *Taxonomy of Educational Objectives*. See also **application, analysis, comprehension, knowledge,** and **synthesis**.

evaluative feedback: Feedback that passes judgment on the work (e.g., "Excellent," "Good job").

evaluation variables: See **assessment variables**.

example prompts: Feedback to students that includes examples of how they might improve their work.

exemplar: Examples of student work that illustrate or exemplify different levels on a scoring rubric.

expectancy table: A grid or two-way table that shows how criterion scores are related to test scores. It describes how likely it is for a person with a specific score to attain each criterion score level.

experiment-interpretation items: A type of context-dependent exercise in which an experiment and its results are presented to the examinee and the examinee must explain the results or choose the correct explanation from among several explanations presented.

expository writing: A type of writing that has as its purpose to give an explanation to and information for the reader.

expressed interests: What students will tell you their career or occupational interests are when you ask them directly. See also **interests, inventoried interests, manifested interests,** and **tested interests**.

extended normalized standard score: A type of normalized standard score that tells the location of a raw score on an achievement scale that spans multiple grades anchored to a lower grade reference group.

extended-response essay item: A type of essay question that requires students to write essays in which they are free to express their own ideas, to show interrelationships among their ideas, and to organize their own answers. Usually no single answer is considered correct.

external assessment procedure: An assessment procedure that comes from outside the local school district and was not crafted by teachers in the district. A state's assessment and a standardized test are two examples.

external structure: Validity evidence that focuses on the pattern of relationships between assessment scores and external variables or criteria. See also **internal structure**.

extrapolation: The process of estimating an unknown number that lies outside the range of available data. Used extensively with standardized achievement tests to estimate the grade-equivalent scores of examinees whose raw scores lie well below or above the available data.

facial bias: According to this approach, an assessment is biased if it contains offensive stereotypes in its use of language or in pictures in the assessment tasks and materials (Cole & Nitko, 1981).

factual knowledge: One of four categories in the Knowledge Dimension of the revised Bloom's taxonomy, signifying a student's awareness and understanding of facts. See also **conceptual knowledge, procedural knowledge,** and **metacognitive knowledge**.

fair assessment or test: An assessment or test that provides scores that (a) are interpreted and used appropriately for specific purposes, (b) do not have negative or adverse consequences as a result of the way they are interpreted or used, and (c) promote appropriate values.

feedback to students: Information about how a student can improve his or her work, usually given by a teacher to a student on the basis of observation and diagnosis of performance on *formative assessments* or *classroom activities*. See also **formative uses of assessments**.

figural reasoning: The ability to reason using geometric figures: to infer relationships among the figures, to identify the similarities and differences among figures, and to identify progressions and predict the next figure in the progression.

filler alternative: A type of multiple-choice item-writing flaw in which a nonplausible alternative is added to an item primarily for the purpose of increasing the number of alternatives rather than as a useful functioning distractor.

fill-in-the-blank items: This item format requires a student to respond with a word, short phrase, number, or symbol.

fixed-percentage method for grading: Assigning grades by using percentages as bases for marking and grading papers. The relationship between percentage correct and letter grade is arbitrary.

foils: See **distractors**.

forced-choice item format: A technique used by interest inventories that presents activities in items in sets of three (triads). These items ask the student to mark the one activity in the triad that the student most ("M") likes and the one activity the student least ("L") likes. This is equivalent to asking a student to rank the three activities from most liked to least liked.

formative assessment of students' achievement: Judgment about the quality of students' achievement made while the students are still in the process of learning. Such judgments help you and the students guide their next learning steps. See also **summative assessment of students' achievement**.

formative evaluation of schools, programs, or materials: Judgment about the worth of curricula, materials, and programs made while they are under development leading to suggestions for ways to redesign, refine, or improve them. See also **summative evaluation of schools**, **programs**, or **materials**.

four principles for validation: Rules about interpretations, uses, values, and consequences that help you judge whether your assessment results have sufficient validity for their intended purposes.

frequency distribution: A table that shows the number of persons in a group having each possible score.

frequency polygon: A line graph of a frequency distribution.

functional alternatives: Response choices in a multiple-choice item that work effectively as distractors or correct answers. If no examinee in the lower scoring group chooses a particular alternative, it is considered nonfunctional. See also **distractors**.

gender representation: The number and ways that males and females are discussed or pictured in test items. See **role stereotype**.

gender stereotype: See **role stereotype**.

generalizability of assessment results: Validity evidence that focuses on the extent to which students' scores on a test can be generalized to their performance on the broader curriculum of the school district or state.

general learning goals: Statements of expected learning outcomes derived from educational goals that are more specific than the goals but not specific enough to be useful as classroom learning targets. See also **educational goals** and **specific learning objectives**.

general scoring rubric: Guideline for scoring that applies across many different tasks, not just to one specific task. It may be used in its generic format or serve as a general framework for developing more specific rubrics. Also called *generic scoring rubric*.

general versus specific intellectual skills: *General intellectual skills* are a student's overall abilities to engage successfully in academic learning in general or on the average. *Specific intellectual skills* are the student's abilities to engage successfully in learning one subject or one academic area.

gradebook program: A computer program combining a spreadsheet and database that allows you to enter students' names and grades and then automatically calculates averages and letter grades.

grade-equivalent score (*GE*): A norm-referenced growth scale score that tells the grade placement at which a raw score is average. A grade-equivalent score is reported as a decimal fraction, such as 3.4. The whole number part of the score refers to a grade level, and the decimal part refers to a month of the school year within that grade level.

grade mean equivalent: A norm-referenced score that tells the grade placement of a group's average expanded scale score.

grading: The process of summing up students' achievement in a subject through the use of letters such as A, B, C, D, and F.

grading on a curve: A method for assigning grades that ranks students' marks from highest to lowest, and assigns grades (A, B, C, etc.) on the basis of this ranking.

grading variables: The subset of variables, selected from among all the reporting variables, on which you may base your grades (Frisbie & Waltman, 1992). You use the grading variables to describe a student's accomplishments in the subject. See also **reporting variables**.

grammatical clue: A type of multiple-choice and matching item flaw in which the correct grammatical relationship between words in the stem and words in the correct alternate clue the examinee as to which alternative is correct. Similarly, incorrect grammatical relationships between words in the stem and distractors clue the examinee that those distractors can be eliminated from consideration.

graphic rating scale: A rating scale that contains an unbroken line to represent the particular achievement dimension and on which you rate a student's performance or product. See also **rating scale** and **descriptive graphic rating scale**.

greater-less-same items: A multiple-choice-item format that presents an examinee with a pair of concepts, phrases, quantities, and so on that have a greater-than, same-as, or less-than relationship and requires the examinee to identify what that relationship is.

grouped frequency distribution: A table showing the number of persons having specified intervals of scores. Unlike a frequency distribution, a grouped frequency distribution organizes the score scale into intervals, and then displays the number of persons with scores in each interval. See also **frequency distribution**.

growth modeling: The use of statistical models that investigate change in test scores over time.

growth portfolio: A portfolio containing a selection of a sequence of a student's work that demonstrates progress or development toward achieving the learning target(s). See also **portfolio** and **best works portfolio**.

halo effect: A type of error that occurs when a teacher's general impression of the student affects how the teacher rates the student on specific dimensions.

heterogeneous alternatives: A type of item-writing flaw in which one or more alternatives of a multiple-choice item or matching exercise do not belong to the same set of things. See also **homogeneous alternatives**.

heuristic: Any one of several general strategies that may help solve a given problem.

high-stakes assessments (tests): Assessments (or tests) of which the results are used for decisions that result in serious consequences for school administrators, teachers, or students.

histogram: A bar graph of a frequency distribution in which each frequency is represented by a rectangle. See also **frequency distribution**.

holistic rubric, holistic scoring rubric: Rubric that requires a teacher to rate or score a student's product or process as a whole without first scoring parts or components separately. See also **analytic rubric** and **rubrics**.

homogeneous alternatives; homogeneous premises and responses: A desirable item-writing practice in which each alternative of a multiple-choice or matching exercise is a member of the same set of "things," *and* each alternative is appropriate to the question asked or problem posed by the stem or premises.

homogeneous tasks: All of those tasks in one assessment that measure the same trait or ability.

homogeneous versus heterogeneous test: All items on a *homogeneous* test will measure one ability, whereas the items on a *heterogeneous* test will assess a combination of abilities.

IDEAL problem solver: A way of organizing general problem-solving skills into a five-stage process (Bransford & Stein, 1984):

I	Identify the problem
D	Define and represent the problem
E	Explore possible strategies
A	Act on the strategies
L	Look back and evaluate the effects of your activities

ill-structured problem: A type of problem in which the problem-solver must (a) organize the information to understand it; (b) clarify the problem itself; (c) obtain all the information needed, which may not be immediately available; and (d) recognize that there may be several equally correct answers.

imaginative writing: A type of writing in which the writer describes something that did not, often could not, happen.

incomplete stem: A type of multiple-choice item-writing flaw in which the stem does not contain enough information for the examinee to know what question or problem the item poses.

independent scoring of essays: When two or more raters score the same student's essay responses without consulting or collaborating with each other.

indirect assessment: A type of assessment that assesses part of the entire learning objective or assesses the learning objectives in a context that is not intended by the learning objective. See also **direct assessment**.

individualized education program (IEP): An educational plan designed by a child study team (including a teacher) and agreed to by the student's parents or guardians describing what learning objectives the student should attain, the time frame for attaining them, the proposed methods for attaining them, and the methods of evaluating the student's progress in achieving the learning objectives.

informal assessment techniques: Impromptu methods you use to gather information that guides and fine-tunes your thinking while you are teaching, to plan your next teaching activities, and to diagnose the causes of students' learning difficulties.

informed consent: Giving approval to release information or participate in an activity after understanding (1) the extent to which personal information will remain anonymous, (2) the extent participation is voluntary, (3) who (or what agency) is requesting the information and for what purpose, and (4) what will happen to the information after it is collected.

in-level versus out-of-level testing: *Out-of-level testing* is using a standardized test designed for a certain grade level with students above or below that level;

in-level testing is using a standardized test designed for students at that grade level.

intensity of attitude: See **direction and intensity of attitude**.

interacting with others: A criticalthinking strategy requiring the use of rhetorical devices to persuade, explain, or argue.

interests: A person's preferences for specific types of activities when he or she is not under external pressure. See also **attitudes** and **values**.

interim or benchmark assessments: Assessments administered periodically during the school year to evaluate students' knowledge and skills relative to academic standards in order to inform policy makers or educators at the classroom, school, or district level.

internal structure: Validity evidence that focuses on the interrelationships among the individual tasks (items) on an assessment, and the relationship between the individual tasks and the total scores. See also **external structure**.

interpolation: The process of finding an unknown number that is between two known numbers. Used extensively in estimating the grade-equivalent scores of students who are not tested on the empirical norming dates of a standardized achievement test.

interpretive argument: In assessment validation, the network of inferences and assumptions that lead from observed performance to interpretations, conclusions, and decisions based on performance. See **validity argument**.

interpretive exercises: A set of items or assessment tasks that require the student to use reading material, graphs, tables, pictures, or other material to answer the items. See also **interpretive materials**.

interpretive materials: The reading material, graphs, pictures, tables, or other material that accompany a set of items and that the examinee must use to answer the questions or problems posed by the item.

interquartile range: The difference between the third and fourth quartiles. It is the range spanned by the middle 50% of the scores. See also **quartiles**.

inter-rater reliability: A procedure for estimating reliability used when you want to study the extent to which a student would obtain the same score if a different teacher had scored the paper or rated the performance.

inventoried interests: Career and vocational interests that are identified through various paper-and-pencil tests or interest inventories. See also **interests, expressed interests, manifested interests,** and **tested interests**.

IRT pattern score: A norm-referenced expanded-scale score derived from a mathematical equation that is fit to the publisher's sample of students' item responses. *IRT* stands for *item response theory*.

item analysis: The process of collecting, summarizing, and using information from students' item responses to make decisions about how each item is functioning.

item bank: A file of previously used items, usually along with the statistics about each item, that can be drawn upon to create new tests.

item difficulty index (*p* and *p**): The fraction of the total group answering a dichotomously scored item correctly. The item difficulty for a constructed-response and performance item, denoted *p**, is simply the average score for the group for that item.

item difficulty level: See **item difficulty index (*p* and *p**)**.

item discrimination index (*D* and *D**): For dichotomously scored items, *D* is the difference between the fraction of the upper group answering the item correctly and the fraction of the lower group answering it correctly. The discrimination index describes the extent to which a particular test item is able to differentiate the higher scoring students from the lower scoring students. See also **upper-, middle-, and lower-scoring groups**.

item response theory (IRT) score: See **IRT pattern score**.

key: The correct answer to any type of item or assessment task.

keyed alternative: The alternative in a multiple-choice or true-false item that is correct.

keyed answer: See **keyed alternative**.

keylist variety of matching exercise items: See **masterlist variety of matching exercise items**.

knowledge: A category in the Bloom et al. (1956) *Taxonomy of Educational Objectives*. Learning objectives in this category ask students to recall information about facts, generalizations, processes and methods of doing things, theories, and so on. See also **application, analysis, comprehension, evaluation,** and **synthesis**.

Kuder-Richardson formula 20 reliability (KR20): A procedure for studying reliability when the focus is on consistency of scores on the same occasion and similar content, but when repeated testing or alternate forms testing are not possible. See also **coefficient alpha reliability**.

Kuder-Richardson formula 21 reliability (KR21): A procedure for studying reliability for the same purposes as Kuder-Richardson formula 20, except that this formula is used when the dichotomously scored test items are equally difficult, thus allowing for a simplified calculation procedure. See also **Kuder-Richardson formula 20 reliability (KR20)**.

learning objective: See **specific learning targets**.

learning progression: A description of development in a domain of knowledge along a continuum, usually with descriptions of what students at each level know or are able to do, often including misconceptions held at levels when knowledge is incomplete or not fully developed.

learning target: Student-friendly descriptions—via words, pictures, actions, and closely matching learning activities—of what you intend students to learn in a given lesson.

leniency error: A type of rating error that occurs when a teacher tends to rate almost all students toward the high end of the scale and avoids using the low end. It is the opposite of a severity error. See also **severity error**.

letter grades method of reporting student progress: A summative evaluation of student achievement that uses letters (e.g., A, B, C, D, F) to describe achievement in each subject area.

letter to parents method of reporting student progress: A summative evaluation letter written by a teacher to describe a student's achievement in each subject area.

linear standard scores (z, SS): Norm-referenced scores that tell the location of the raw scores in relation to the mean and standard deviation of the distribution of all scores.

linked items: An item-writing flaw in which the answer to one or more items depends on obtaining the correct answer to a previous item.

linking: See **linked items**.

local norm group: See **norm group (local, national, special)**.

local percentile rank: The percentile rank of a student in the distribution of scores for the school district the student attends.

logical error: A type of rating error that occurs when a teacher gives similar ratings on two or more dimensions of performance that the teacher believes are logically related but that are in fact unrelated.

logic rule method for grading: The use of a set of decision rules, based on student performance during a marking period, to assign grades. See also **quality-level method for grading** and **rubrics**.

mandated tests: Tests that students must take because the law says they are required to do so. State assessment programs are usually mandated.

manifested interests: Students' vocational and career interests that are deduced from what a student actually does, or the activities in which the student actually participates. See also **interests, expressed interests, inventoried interests,** and **tested interests**.

map-reading abilities: The abilities needed to obtain and use information from maps.

marking period: The period over which a teacher's summative evaluation of each student's achievement in each subject area is reported to the student, parents, and school officials.

masterlist variety of matching exercise items: A matching exercise that has three parts: (a) directions to students, (b) the masterlist of options, and (c) a list or set of stems.

mastery learning objectives: Statements of what students can do at the end of instruction. Sometimes these are called "can do" statements, specific learning outcomes, or behavioral objectives. See also **developmental learning objectives**.

matching exercise (basic): This format presents a student with three things: (a) directions for matching, (b) a list of premises, and (c) a list of responses. The student's task is to match each premise with one of the responses, using the criteria described in the directions as a basis for matching.

maximum performance assessment: Assessment of students when you set the conditions so that students are able to earn the best score they can. See also **typical performance assessment**.

MAZE item type: Reading comprehension assessment that is a multiple-choice adaptation of the cloze reading exercise. See also **cloze reading exercise**.

mean: An average score found by summing all of the scores and dividing by their number. Also known as the *arithmetic mean*.

measurement: A procedure for assigning numbers (usually called *scores*) to a specified attribute or characteristic of a person in such a way that the numbers describe the degree to which the person possesses the attribute. See also **assessment, evaluation,** and **test**.

measurement error: See **error score**.

median: The point on the score scale at which 50% of the scores are below and 50% are above.

median score method: A procedure for combining several component grades into a composite report card grade. All scores are converted to the same scale, usually a rubric or grade (A, B, C, D, F) scale, and the median mark is used as the composite grade.

mental age: The age at which the student's score on a scholastic aptitude test is average. This concept is no longer used in modern scholastic aptitude testing.

***Mental Measurements Yearbooks* (MMYs):** A set of volumes published by the Buros Institute of Mental Measurement that contains reviews of tests published in the English language.

mental model: The way a person mentally represents or characterizes a problem before attempting to solve it.

metacognition: Knowledge of one's cognitive processes, including monitoring and regulating one's own learning.

metacognitive knowledge: One of four categories in the Knowledge Dimension of the revised Bloom's taxonomy, signifying a student's awareness and understanding of one's own learning processes. See also **factual knowledge**, **conceptual knowledge**, and **procedural knowledge**.

minimum attainment method: A procedure for combining several component grades into a composite report card grade by the following process: determine which components of students' final grades are more important to demonstrating the students' achievement of the learning targets; specify, for each of these "more important" components, the minimum level of performance you will accept for each of the final grade levels; and establish rules for what levels of performance you will accept, at each final grade level, on each of the "less important" components. These rules form a set of decision rules for how to assign grades.

miskeyed items: Items for which the answer designated as correct in the answer key is wrong. An item may be miskeyed if a larger number of upper group students selects a particular wrong response.

modal-age norms: Norms that include, from among all students at a particular grade level, only those near the most typical chronological age for that grade.

mode: The most frequently occurring score in a distribution.

modifications: Changes in either the conditions or materials of assessment that allow students with disabilities to be assessed in the same areas as students who are assessed with unmodified assessments, although the meaning of the scores is altered.

multilevel survey battery: A survey battery of standardized tests that spans a wide range of grades in each school subject. See also **single-level test**.

multiple-aptitude tests: Tests that assess several different abilities separately and provide an ability score for each. See also **omnibus test** and **two-score test**.

multiple-assessment strategy: Combining the results from several different types of assessments (such as homework, class performance, quizzes, projects, and tests) to improve the validity of your decisions about a student's attainments.

multiple-choice item: This item format consists of a stem that poses a question or sets a problem and a set of two or more response choices for answering the question or solving the problem. Only one of the response choices is the correct or best answer.

multiple marking system: A system of reporting summative evaluation of educational progress to students and parents using several kinds of symbols and marks. Multiple marking systems usually take the form of a report card and report on academic achievement, attendance, deportment, and nonacademic achievement.

multiple true-false variety of true-false items: This format looks similar to a multiple-choice item. However, instead of selecting one option as correct, the student treats every option as a separate true-false statement.

narrative report method of reporting student progress: A detailed, written report describing what each student has learned in relation to the school's curriculum framework and the student's effort in class.

narrative writing: A type of writing in which the author describes something that really happened, usually a personal experience of the writer.

national norm groups: See **norm group (local, national, special)**.

national percentile rank: A student's percentile rank in the national sample of students who took the test.

national stanines: Stanines are scores derived from a test publisher's national norm sample. See also **stanine scores**.

NCE-score: See **normal curve equivalent (*NCE*)**.

negative correlation: A type of relationship between two sets of scores that occurs when high scores on one assessment are associated with low scores on the other; low scores on one are associated with high scores on the other. See also **correlation coefficient** and **positive correlation**.

negatively discriminating item: An item that high-scoring students tend to answer incorrectly and low-scoring students tend to answer correctly.

negatively skewed distribution: A frequency distribution of scores in which the scores are piled up at the upper end of the score scale and spread thinly toward the lower end of the score scale. See also **positively skewed distribution**.

nondiscriminating item: An item for which the number of correct discriminations equals the number of incorrect discriminations (so that an equal number of upper and lower group students answers the item correctly).

"none of the above": A multiple-choice alternative that means that none of the preceding alternatives is the correct answer to the question or problem posed by the stem.

nonverbal tests: Tests that elicit and assess nonverbal responses such as assembling objects, completing experiments, performing a psychomotor activity, and so on. See also **performance assessment**.

normal curve equivalent (*NCE*): A normalized standard score with a mean of 50 and a standard deviation of 21.06. This choice of standard deviation was made so the *NCE*-scores would span the range 1 to 99. It was developed primarily for use with federal program evaluation efforts (Tallmadge & Wood, 1976).

normal distributions: A set of theoretical distributions that takes on a bell-shaped and unimodal form through the use of a special mathematical formula.

normal growth (grade-equivalent view, percentile rank view): The *grade-equivalent view* of normal growth is that a student ought to exhibit a growth of 1.0 grade-equivalent unit from one grade to the next. Under this view, a student taking the test in second grade and scoring 1.3, for example, would need to score 2.3 in third grade, 4.3 in fifth, and so on to show "normal" or expected growth. The *percentile rank view* of normal growth is that a student shows normal growth if that student maintains the same position (i.e., percentile rank) in the norm from year to year.

normalized standard scores (z_n, T, DIQ, NCE, SAT): A category of scores in which the raw scores have been changed or transformed into other scores that are distributed more like a normal distribution.

normalizing a set of scores: The process used to transform the original raw scores in a distribution into a new set of scores that are distributed more like a normal distribution.

norm group (local, national, special): A well-defined group of students who have been given the same assessment under the same conditions (same time limits, directions, equipment and materials, etc.). See also **special norms**.

norm-referenced grading model: A framework for assigning grades on the basis of how a student's performance (achievement) compares with other students in the class: Students performing better than most classmates receive the higher grades.

norm-referencing: A framework for interpreting a student's score by comparing his or her test performance with the performance of other students in a well-defined group who took the same test.

novel material: A new situation, problem, or context for applying previously learned knowledge or skills.

numbers method of reporting student progress: A summative evaluation of a student's achievement in each subject that is reported using either numbers (e.g., 5, 4, 3, 2, 1) or percentages.

numerical rating scale: A scale for which you must mentally translate judgments of quality or degree of achievement into numerical ratings.

objectivity: The degree to which two or more qualified evaluators of a student's performance will agree on what quality rating or score to assign to it.

obtained score: The scores students actually receive when you assess them. These scores include ratings from open-ended tasks such as essays, number-right scores from multiple-choice or short-answer tests, and standard scores or grade-equivalent scores from norm-referenced standardized tests. See also **error score** and **true score**.

odd-even split-halves reliability coefficient: A procedure for estimating reliability when the focus is on consistency of scores on different samples of content on the same occasion, but when alternate forms have not been built. The items from one test are divided into two groups—the odd-numbered items in one group and the even-numbered in another. The full-test reliability is estimated from these two groups. See also **Spearman-Brown double length reliability formula** and **split-halves reliability coefficient**.

omnibus test: A type of test containing items assessing several different abilities that comprise general scholastic aptitude, but that reports only a single score. See also **multiple-aptitude tests** and **two-score test**.

on-demand task: An assessment in which the teacher or other authority decides what and when materials should be used, specifies the instructions for performance, describes the kinds of outcomes toward which students should work, tells the students they are being assessed, and gives students opportunities to prepare themselves for the assessment.

open-response task: An assessment task allowing multiple correct answers. See also **closed-response task**.

optional essay questions: Presenting students with several different essays and allowing them to select which one(s) to answer.

options: See **alternatives**.

outcome feedback: Feedback that presents the results (typically a score or grade) of an assessment.

overinterpreting score differences: Placing too much emphasis on small differences of students' obtained scores on a test or small differences in the obtained scores of one student on two different tests. See also **underinterpreting score differences**.

overlapping alternatives: A type of multiple-choice item-writing flaw in which the meaning of one alternative overlaps with or includes the meaning of another alternative.

parallel forms: Two forms (versions) of an assessment that are made up of tasks carefully matched to the same blueprint so the tests are as nearly alike as possible, even though they do not have any items in common.

parallel-forms reliability coefficient: See **alternate-forms reliability coefficient [same occasion]**.

paper-and-pencil assessments: Assessments administered using paper and pencil, typically used as a synonym for classroom tests.

parent-teacher conferences method of reporting student progress: A personal meeting between the parent(s) and the teacher that involves a summative report of a student's achievement in each subject.

partial credit: Giving the student some portion of an item's maximum possible points because the student's response is partially correct.

partial ordering of students: Placing students into two or more categories; the categories themselves are ordered, but there is *no ordering of individuals within a category*.

passage dependency: The degree to which correct answers to questions on a reading comprehension test depend on the students actually reading and comprehending the passage.

passing score: The score that identifies students who have attained the minimum level of knowledge needed to benefit from further instruction on the topic. This may vary from one learning target to the next.

Pearson product-moment correlation coefficient: A type of correlation coefficient that is the average product of the linear z-scores corresponding to the paired scores in the set being correlated. It is denoted by r or *r*. See also **correlation coefficient**.

people-similarity rationale for assessing interests: The traditional view of describing a person's inventoried interests based on the rationale that "if a person likes the same things that people in a particular job like, the person will be satisfied with the job" (Cole & Hanson, 1975, p. 6).

percentage of agreement: An index of the consistency of decisions made by two independent judges. It is the percentage of students for whom the two judges reached the same decision.

percentages method of reporting student progress: A summative evaluation of a student's achievement in each subject that uses the average percentage of schoolwork marked correct.

percentile rank: A norm-referenced score that tells the percentage of persons in a norm group scoring lower than a particular raw score. See also **local percentile rank** and **national percentile rank**.

perfect matching: When a matching exercise has an equal number of premise statements and response statements.

performance assessment: Any assessment technique that requires students physically to carry out a complex, extended *process* (e.g., present an argument orally, play a musical piece, or climb a knotted rope), or produce an important *product* (e.g., write a poem, report on an experiment, or create a painting). The complexity of the task distinguishes performance assessments from the short answers, decontextualized math problems, or brief (one class period) essay tasks found on typical paper-and-pencil assessments.

performance centered: A criterion for a well-stated learning objective: A learning objective should describe what a student is able to do (or to perform) after completing instruction. See also **content centered** and **student centered**.

performance standards: Statements about the things students can perform or do once the content standards are learned. See also **content standards** and **standards**.

performance task: One activity or item in a performance assessment. See also **performance assessment**.

permanent record: The official summative record by grade level of a student's achievement in each subject and his or her attendance in a particular school.

personal bias: A type of rating error that occurs when a teacher has a general tendency to use inappropriate or irrelevant stereotypes favoring boys over girls, Whites over Blacks, working families over welfare recipients, or particular families and individual students a teacher likes over others the teacher may dislike.

persuasive writing: A type of writing in which the writer attempts to convince the reader of the writer's point of view. The writer may want the reader to accept his or her idea or to take some actions that the writer supports.

pictorial reasoning: The ability to reason using pictures. For example, to infer relationships among the pictured objects, to identify the similarities and differences among pictures, and to identify progressions and predict the next picture in the progression.

placement decision: A decision in which persons are assigned to different levels of the same general type of instruction, education, or work; no one is rejected, but all remain within the institution to be assigned to some level (Cronbach, 1990). See also **classification decision** and **selection decision**.

plausible distractor: An incorrect alternative of a multiple-choice or matching exercise that seems correct to less knowledgeable students.

poorly functioning distractor: A distractor in a multiple-choice item that virtually no one in the lower scoring group chooses.

portfolio: A limited collection of a student's work used for assessment purposes either to present the student's best work(s) or demonstrate the student's educational growth over a given time span.

positive correlation: A type of relationship between two sets of scores that occurs when high scores on one assessment are associated with high scores on the other; low scores on one are associated with low scores on the other. See also **correlation coefficient** and **negative correlation**.

positively discriminating item: An item for which the proportion of upper scoring students getting high scores is larger than the proportion of lower scoring students getting high scores on it.

positively skewed distribution: A frequency distribution of scores in which the scores are piled up at the lower end of the score scale and spread thinly toward the upper end of the score scale. See also **negatively skewed distribution**.

predictive validity evidence: A type of external structure validity evidence showing the extent to which individuals' future performance on a criterion can be predicted from their prior performance on an assessment instrument. See also **concurrent validity evidence** and **external structure**.

preinstruction unit assessment framework: A plan to help assess cognitive and affective learning targets of an upcoming unit.

premises, premise list: The leftmost list of statements or elements in a matching exercise.

prewriting activities: Before writing, a writer clarifies the purpose for writing, begins to organize thoughts, brainstorms, and tries out new ideas. The writer discusses the ideas with others, decides what the format and approach to writing will take, and determines the primary audience. A plan for the piece develops.

principle: A rule that describes what to do or the relationships between two concepts.

principle-governed thinking: Thinking that is manifested when a person consistently uses appropriate rules to identify how two or more concepts are related.

privacy: Keeping a student's assessment results closed to those who are unauthorized to have access to them. See also **confidentiality**.

problem: The presence of obstacles to attaining a desired outcome so that immediate attainment of a goal is not possible without further mental processing.

procedural knowledge: One of four categories in the Knowledge Dimension of the revised Bloom's taxonomy, signifying a student's awareness and understanding of procedures. See also **factual knowledge, conceptual knowledge,** and **metacognitive knowledge**.

procedure checklist: A checklist of the steps necessary to complete a process correctly. See also **checklist**.

process: In performance assessment, a task where students engage in some sort of procedure or method (e.g., playing an instrument, engaging in discussion), and where their work during the procedure itself is what is assessed.

product: In performance assessment, a task where the end result or output from student work (e.g., a paper, a display) is what is assessed.

product checklist: A checklist of the necessary and important characteristics of the product a student is required to produce that is used to evaluate the quality of the work.

product versus process: The tangible thing a student produces is called a *product*. The procedure a student follows to complete a task or to produce the product is called a *process*.

professional responsibility: Acting toward students in a way that is ethical and consistent with one's role as a professional person.

progress monitoring: A method associated with Response to Intervention, using curriculum-based assessments to track and evaluate progress of students identified as at risk.

projective hypothesis: The assumption that an examinee's interpretations of vague stimuli (such as ink-blots) will reveal the examinee's innermost needs, feelings, and conflicts, even though the examinee is unaware of what he or she is revealing (Frank, 1939).

projective personality test techniques: Assessment techniques that present the examinee with ambiguous stimuli (such as inkblots) and ask the examinee to respond to them.

prompt (or writing prompt): A brief statement that suggests a topic or question for students to write about, provides general guidance, motivates students to write, and elicits students' best writing performance.

proposition: Any sentence that can be said to be true or false. See also **true-false variety**.

Pruebas Publicadas en Español: Tests in Print in Spanish

psychometric issues: Issues about assessment, especially bias in assessment, that concern the technical or statistical properties of the assessment in question.

psychomotor domain: A collection of educational outcomes and learning targets that focus on motor skills and perceptual processes.

pupil-teacher conferences method of reporting student progress: A method of reporting a student's summative achievement evaluation by means of a direct meeting between the teacher and student.

quality-level method for grading: A method for assigning letter grades in which the type of student performance required for each letter grade is specified beforehand. See also **logic rule method for grading** and **rubrics**.

quantitative reasoning: Reasoning with numerical quantities. For example, to infer relationships among the numbers, to identify the similarities and differences among numbers and patterns, and to identify progressions and predict the next number in the progression.

quartiles: Points on the score scale that divide the group of scores into quarters.

question: A prompt for student responses or discussion, typically oral. The most effective questions are designed so that student responses provide a window on students' thinking, not just a correct answer.

random guessing: Responding to an item using chance rather than using your knowledge.

range: The difference between the highest and lowest scores in a set. It is used as a simple index of the spread of the scores in the set.

rater drift: A type of rating error that occurs when the raters, whose ratings originally agreed, begin to redefine the rubrics for themselves. As a result, the raters no longer produce ratings that agree.

rating scale: A scoring rubric that helps a teacher assess the degree to which students have attained the achievement dimensions in the performance task. See also **checklist**.

rating scale method of reporting student progress: A summative evaluation of a student's achievement that uses a rating scale to describe the degree of mastery. See also **rating scale**.

raw score: The number of points (marks) you assign to a student's performance on an assessment. Points may be assigned based on each task, or points awarded on separate parts of the assessment.

readiness test: An assessment of a student's general developmental skills needed for first-grade work, especially reading, where grouping by readiness level is a common practice.

recency of norm data: How current the norm data are. As the curriculum, schooling, and social and economic factors change, so will the currency of the data.

relational concepts: See **defined concept**.

relative achievement: The level of a student's achievement expressed in terms of comparisons to peers rather than by describing the specific learning objectives the student has achieved. See also **absolute achievement** and **criterion-referencing**.

relative standards grading: See **norm-referenced grading framework**.

relevance of norm data: The extent to which the norm group a publisher provides is the appropriate group to which you want to compare your students' performance on the test.

reliability: The amount of consistency of assessment results (scores). Reliability is a limiting factor for validity.

reliability coefficient: Any of several statistical indices that quantifies the amount of consistency in assessment scores. See also **reliability**.

reliability decay: A rating error that results in the scores from multiple raters becoming less consistent over time.

reminder prompts: Feedback to students that focuses on reminding them what they are trying to learn.

report card: The document that reports the summative achievement grades to students and parents.

reporting method: Any one of several ways in which schools and teachers report each student's achievement to parents and for the official school records. These include letter grades, number grades, percentage grades, standards-based grades, checklists, rating scales, narrative reports, parent-teacher conferences, student-led parent conferences, and letters to parents.

reporting standards: The categories on which student achievement is reported on a standards-based report card. These may be the same as state standards, but typically are a prioritized and simplified set of standards for reporting in order to facilitate communication.

reporting variables: A subset, from among all the assessment variables, that a school district will expect a teacher to report to parents and for official purposes (Frisbie & Waltman, 1992).

representativeness of norm data: The extent to which the norm sample is based on a carefully planned sample that represents the target population. The test publisher should provide you with information about the subclassifications (gender, age, socioeconomic level, etc.) used to ensure representativeness.

response-choice items: Test items that provide students with alternatives from which to choose to answer the question or solve the problem posed.

response list: The list of plausible response alternatives in a matching exercise. This list is placed to the right of the premise list when crafting exercises. See also **premises**.

Response to Intervention (RTI): An initiative that many states are using to identify students in need of special assistance and to provide tiers of assistance in order to minimize the number of students identified for special education services. RTI defines students who do not progress in otherwise effective instruction as not responsive to that instruction.

restricted-response essay items: Essay prompts or instructions that restrict or limit both the substantive content and the form of the written response.

right-wrong variety of true-false items: This item format presents a computation, equation, or language sentence that the student judges as correct or incorrect (right or wrong).

role stereotype: Depiction in assessment materials of races or genders in oversimplified activities or work roles that convey the impression that such persons' capacities are limited in some way.

rubric method for grading: See **logic rule method for grading** and **quality-level method for grading**.

rubrics: A coherent set of rules you use to evaluate the quality of a student's performance: They guide your judgments and ensure that you apply the rules consistently from one student to the next. See also **checklist** and **rating scale**.

SAT-score: A normalized standard score from a distribution that has a mean of 500 and a standard deviation of 100.

scaffolding: The degree of support, guidance, and direction you provide students when they set out to complete the task.

scaffold prompts: Feedback to students that breaks down their work into small steps, usually using detailed questions to do so.

scatter diagram (scattergram): A graph on which paired scores are plotted to show their relationship.

schema (schemata): The way knowledge is represented in a person's mind through networks of connected concepts, information, rules, problem-solving strategies, and conditions for actions.

schema-driven problem solving: When a person recognizes a particular problem as part of or very similar to an existing schema and applies the solution strategy stored in that schema to solve the new problem (Gick, 1986). See also **schema (schemata)**.

school averages norms: A tabulation of the average (mean) score from each school building in a national sample of schools that provides information on the relative ordering of these averages (means).

score band: See **uncertainty interval**.

scorer reliability: See **inter-rater reliability** and **decision consistency index**.

scoring key: A rubric or list of rules that shows the correct answer and the kinds of partially correct answers that are to receive various amounts of credit.

selection decision: A decision in which an institution or organization decides that some persons are acceptable whereas others are not; those unacceptable are rejected and are no longer the concern of the institution or organization. See also **classification decision** and **placement decision**.

self-evaluation checklist: A checklist that students use to evaluate their own performance.

self-referenced grading framework: The assignment of grades by comparing a student's performance with his or her own past performance or your perceptions of his or her capability.

severity error: A rating error that occurs when a teacher tends to assign almost all ratings toward the low end of the scale. It is the opposite of a leniency error. See also **leniency error**.

short-term memory subtests: Assessments of a person's ability to remember patterns, objects, words, and numbers immediately after they are heard, seen, or read.

simulation: On-demand event that happens under controlled conditions and that attempts to mimic naturally occurring events.

single-level test: A standardized survey battery that is used only at one grade level or one narrow range of grade levels. See also **multilevel survey battery**.

Six + 1 Traits® of Writing: A framework and scoring rubrics for assessing general writing ability that focuses on evaluating a student on seven writing traits for each essay: ideas, organization, voice, word choice, sentence fluency, conventions, and presentation.

sizing up: Using assessment information to form a general impression of a student's strengths, weaknesses, learning characteristics, and personality at the beginning of a course or of the year.

skewed distribution: A description of a frequency distribution in which the scores are piled up on one end of the score scale and thinly spread out toward the other. See also **negatively**.

SOAP: An acronym for the following elements that should appear in the prompt to stimulate good writing on the part of the student (Albertson, 1998):

  S *Subject*—inform the student who or what the piece is supposed to be about.

  O *Occasion*—inform the student what is the occasion or situation that requires that the piece be written.

  A *Audience*—inform the student who the intended audience is.

  P *Purpose*—inform the student what the purpose is supposed to be: Is it to inform or narrate? To be imaginative? To be persuasive?

Spearman-Brown double length reliability formula: A procedure for estimating reliability when the focus of the study is on consistency of students' scores from one sample of items to another equivalent sample of items from the same content domain, but when only one form of the test exists. See also **odd-even split halves reliability procedure** and **split-halves reliability coefficient**.

special norms: Percentile rank or standard-score norms developed for specific subpopulations of students such as students with hearing impairments, Catholic school students, and so on.

specific determiner: A word or phrase (e.g., *always*, *never*, *often*, *usually*, and so on) in a true-false or multiple-choice item that "overqualifies" a given statement and gives the student an unintended clue to the correct answer (Sarnacki, 1979).

specific learning objective: A clear statement about what students are to achieve by the end of a unit of instruction. See also also **educational goals** and **general learning goals**.

specimen set: A packet of materials from a test publisher containing a sample of the test, sample computer reports, promotional materials, and (occasionally) a technical report of the test's quality.

speeded assessment: Any assessment that focuses on how quickly a student can perform.

spiral format: An arrangement of items in a test whereby similar types of items are not grouped together into subtests, but are arranged in a pattern so that one item of each type is presented; then the sequence is repeated, but with more difficult items.

split-halves reliability coefficient: Any method for estimating reliability on a single occasion by studying the relationship between students' scores on each half of the full-length test. See also **domain of achievement, Spearman-Brown double length formula,** and **odd-even split-halves reliability procedure**.

SS-score: A type of linear standard score that tells the location of a raw score in a distribution having a mean of 50 and a standard deviation of 10. See also **linear standard scores** and **raw score**.

SS-score method for making composites: A method for preparing students' composite marks for purposes of norm-referenced grading that preserves the influence (weights) you want the components of the composite to have.

stability coefficient: Any of several methods for estimating reliability that study the consistency of students' scores from one occasion to the next. See also **alternate forms reliability coefficient [delayed], alternate forms reliability coefficient [same occasion],** and **test-retest reliability coefficient**.

stages in crafting performance tasks: Three stages of developing a performance task are: (a) being very clear about the performance you want to assess, (b) crafting the task, and (c) crafting a way to score and record the results.

stakeholders: Persons or groups with an interest in the results of an assessment, usually because they will be affected by decisions made about them using the test results.

standard age score (SAS): Normalized standard score with a mean of 50 and standard deviation of eight in the norm group having the same age as the student being tested.

standard deviation: An index of the spread of the scores in a distribution calculated by taking the square root of the mean squared deviation of the scores from the arithmetic mean of the scores.

standard deviation method of grading: A norm-referenced grading method that uses the standard deviation of the class's scores as a unit of measure on the grading scale: A teacher computes the standard deviation of the scores and uses this number to mark off segments on the number line that define the boundaries for grade assignment. See also **standard deviation**.

standard error of measurement (SEM): An estimate of the standard deviation or the spread of a hypothetical obtained-score distribution resulting from repeated testing of the same person with the same assessment. See also **obtained score** and **standard deviation**.

standardized patient format: Originally used to assess the clinical skills of medical candidates and practicing doctors, an actor is trained to display the symptoms of a particular disorder. Each medical candidate meets and interviews this standardized patient to diagnose the illness and to prescribe treatment.

standardized test: A test for which the procedures, administration, materials, and scoring rules are fixed so that as far as possible the assessment is the same at different times and places.

standards: Statements about what students are expected to learn. Some states call these statements *essential skills, learning expectations, learning outcomes, achievement expectations,* or other names. Often there are two sets of standards: content and performance. See also **content standards** and **performance standards**.

standards-based report cards: A type of report card in which academic grades are assigned for standards of learning, rather than by subject or course. Work habits and citizenship are reported in a separate section of the report card from academic achievement.

standard score: A category of transformed scores that changes the mean, standard deviation, and sometimes the shape of the distribution of the original scores so they are more easily interpreted. See also **linear standard scores (z, SS)** and **normalized standard scores (z_n, T, DIQ, NCE, SAT)**.

Standards for Educational and Psychological Testing: Guidelines and recommendations prepared by the American Educational Research Association, the American Psychological Association, and the National Council on Measurement in Education for the development and use of educational and psychological assessments.

standards-referencing framework: A score-interpreting framework that compares a student's test performance to clearly defined levels of achievement of proficiency. These levels are established using both criterion-referencing and norm-referencing techniques. See also **criterion-referencing** and **norm-referencing**.

stanine scores: A type of normalized standard score that tells the location of a raw score in one of nine specific segments of a normal distribution. Thus, stanine is derived from standard nine.

state-mandated assessments: Tests and other assessments that the law requires to be administered to all students at designated grade levels.

statement-and-comment items: Items used to assess students' ability to evaluate a given set of interpretations of quoted comments using learned criteria.

statistic (statistical index): A summary number that concisely captures a specific feature of a group of scores.

stem: The part of a multiple-choice item that asks a question or poses a problem to be solved.

strip key: A strip of paper on which the correct answers to completion items are written in a column in such a manner that when the strip is put on a student's test paper, the correct answers line up with the locations of the student's responses.

structured (self-report) personality assessment techniques: These assessment procedures have a specific set of response-choice items; follow very specific rules for administering, scoring, and interpreting the tests; and require examinees to respond to the items in a way that describes their personal feelings (e.g., examinees may be asked whether the statement, "I usually express my personal opinions to others," is true of themselves).

student centered: A criterion for a well-stated learning target: A learning target should describe what a student is to learn. See also **performance centered** and **content centered**.

student growth percentiles: Values that describe the probability of a student attaining a certain level of growth, given their prior achievement.

student self-assessment: Involving students in judging the quality of their own work against learning targets and in deciding what actions they need to take to improve. See also **formative uses of assessments**.

subtest: A short test that is scored separately but is part of a longer battery of tests. The longer battery is comprised of two or more subtests.

summative assessment of students' achievement: Judgments about the quality or worth of students' achievement after the instructional process is completed. See also **formative assessment of students' achievement**.

summative evaluation of schools, programs, or materials: Judgments about the worth of programs, curricula, or materials after they are completed with the idea of suggesting whether they should be adopted or used. See also **formative evaluation of schools, programs, or materials**.

surface feature: A diagnostic assessment approach that uses the immediate external feature of the content of a test or test item to describe a student's achievement. This is contrasted with the deeper features of how a student perceives the structure or organization of that content, and processes information and knowledge to solve problems using that content knowledge. See also **knowledge structure assessment**.

symmetrical distribution: A frequency distribution of scores in which it is possible for the graph of the distribution to be folded along a vertical line so that the two halves of the figure coincide.

synthesis: A category in the Bloom et al. (1956) *Taxonomy of Educational Objectives*. Learning objectives in this

category ask students to combine parts into a whole that was not there before.

table of specifications: This chart describes the major content categories and skills that a test assesses. It describes the percentage of tasks (items) for each content-skills combination included on the test.

tabular (matrix) items: A type of matching exercise in which the student matches elements from several lists of *responses* (e.g., presidents, political parties, famous firsts, and important events) with elements from a common list of *premises*.

tandem arrangement of alternatives: A type of multiple-choice item-writing flaw in which the alternatives are arranged in a paragraph-like continuous stream of text instead of the more desirable list arrangement of one alternative placed beneath the other.

task-directed thoughts: Thoughts and test-taking actions that focus on completing the assessment tasks and thereby reduce any tensions that are associated with them (Mandler & Sarason, 1952). See also **task-irrelevant thoughts**.

task format: The way a task or item appears on an assessment. Typical formats include multiple-choice, true-false, matching, short-answer, and essays, among others.

task-irrelevant thoughts: Thoughts and test-taking actions that are self-preoccupied, centering on what could happen if a student fails a test or on a student's own helplessness, and sometimes on a desire to escape from the test situation as quickly as possible (Mandler & Sarason, 1952). One of the four test anxiety factors. See also **task-directed thoughts**.

task-specific rubrics: Scoring rubrics in which the description of quality levels refers to the specific task and expected responses. See also **general scoring rubric** and **rubrics**. [ch. 13]

taxonomies of instructional objectives: Highly organized schemes for classifying learning objectives into various levels of complexity. See also **cognitive domain**, **affective domain**, and **psychomotor domain**.

technical manual: A publication prepared by a test developer that explains the technical details of how the test was developed, how the norms were created, the procedures for selecting test items, the procedures for equating different forms of the test, and reliability and validity studies that have been completed for the test.

test: An instrument or systematic procedure for observing and describing one or more characteristics of a student using either a numerical scale or a classification scheme. See also **assessment**, **evaluation**, and **measurement**.

test anxiety: Increased emotional tension among students who want to do well on a test that results in bodily and autonomic arousal and thoughts about the negative consequences of failure and how a student's performance will compare to others.

Test Critiques: A series of volumes that reviews the most frequently used tests in business, education, and psychology. Published by the Test Corporation of America.

tested interests: Students' vocational and career interests inferred from the results of an assessment of a student's information and knowledge of a particular subject matter. See also **interests, expressed interests, inventoried interests**, and **manifested interests**.

test level: The grade level or narrow range of grade levels for which a standardized test is targeted.

test-retest reliability coefficient: A procedure for estimating reliability when the focus of the study is the consistency of the students' scores from one occasion to the next on the same test items.

Tests in Print: A test bibliography that contains information on more than 2,900 commercially available instruments. Published by the Buros Institute of Mental Measurements.

test-takers' rights: The rights of those who take tests to information from and fair treatment by those who administer tests and use the results.

testwiseness: A student's ability to use the characteristics of both the assessment materials and the assessment situation to attain a higher score than the student's knowledge would otherwise warrant.

total points method for grading: A criterion-referenced method of assigning grades in which each component included in the final composite grade is given maximum point value (e.g., quizzes may count 10 points, exams may count a maximum of 50 points each, and projects may count a maximum of 40 points each); letter grades are assigned on the basis of the number of total points a student accumulated over the marking period.

true-false variety: An item format consisting of a statement or proposition that the student must judge as true or false. See also **proposition**.

true score: The hypothetical score you would obtain if you subtracted the examinee's error score from the examinee's obtained score. See also **error score** and **obtained score**.

T-score: A type of normalized standard score that tells the location of a raw score in a normal distribution having a mean of 50 and a standard deviation of 10. The normalized *T*-score is the counterpart to the linear *SS*-score.

two-category method of reporting student progress: A method for reporting summative evaluations of student achievement that uses only two levels of achievement such as pass-fail.

two-score test: A type of test that assesses several kinds of specific abilities, but reports only two scores, usually verbal/quantitative or verbal/nonverbal. See also **omnibus test** and **multiple-aptitude tests**.

types of test-anxious students: There are three types of test-anxious students: those who do not have good study skills and fail to understand how the main ideas of the subject you are teaching are related and organized; those who do have a good grasp of the material and good study skills but have built up fears of failure associated with assessment and evaluation; and those who believe they have good study habits but who do not.

typical performance assessment: Gathering information about what a student would do under ordinary or everyday conditions. See also **maximum performance assessment**.

uncertainty interval: The score interval within which an examinee's true score is likely to be. The endpoints of this interval are calculated by (a) subtracting the standard error of measurement from an examinee's obtained score (lower endpoint) and (b) adding the standard error of measurement to the examinee's obtained score (upper endpoint). Also referred to as the score band. See also **obtained score, standard error of measurement (SEM),** and **true score**.

underinterpreting score differences: A type of score-interpretation error that occurs when differences in scores between two students or differences in scores of one student on two tests are ignored even though the differences are not due simply to error of measurement. Some action should be taken. See also **overinterpreting score differences**. [ch. 4]

unimodal distribution: A frequency distribution of scores in which there is one pileup of scores (i.e., one mode). See also **bimodal distribution**.

unit of instruction: A teaching sequence covering from 1 to 7 weeks of lessons, depending on the students and topics you are teaching.

universal design: A concept that originated in the field of architecture. In assessment, it means designing assessments to be accessible to as many students as possible, to the greatest extent possible, without the need for accommodations or modifications.

upper-, middle-, and lower-scoring groups: The three groups into which you divide the class before conducting an item analysis. The groups are formed after ranking students on the basis of their total score on the test that includes the items you will be analyzing.

validity: The soundness of your interpretations and uses of students' assessment results.

validity argument: In assessment validation, an evaluation of the interpretive argument as to whether it is coherent, clear, reasonable, and supported. See **interpretive argument**.

validity coefficient: A predictive or concurrent correlation that is used as one piece of external structure evidence to support the validity of an assessment. See also **correlation coefficient**, **concurrent validity evidence**, **external structure**, and **predictive validity evidence**.

value-added modeling: Use of statistical model that includes parameters (statistical estimates) for the effects of various factors (e.g., demographic factors, teacher and school effects) expected to be related to student growth in achievement.

values: A person's long-lasting beliefs of the importance of certain life goals, a lifestyle, a way of acting, or a way of life. See also **attitudes** and **interests**.

verbal clues: See **grammatical clue** and **specific determiner**.

verbal comprehension tests: Tests that assess the students' ability to understand verbal material and to use language to express themselves.

verbal reasoning tests: Tests that assess students' ability to see relationships among words, read critically, and reason with words.

vocational interest inventories: Formal paper-and-pencil questionnaires that help students express their likes and dislikes about a wide range of work and other activities. A pattern of vocational and career interests is then determined from the students' responses.

well-structured problems: Problems are presented as assessment tasks that are clearly laid out: All the information students need is given, the situations are very much the same as students were taught in class, and there is usually one correct answer that students can attain by applying a procedure that was taught.

window dressing: The use of words that tend to "dress up" an item stem to make it sound as though it is testing something of practical importance, when it does not (Ebel, 1965).

writing process: Most writing results from an orderly process that includes drafting, feedback, revisions, and polishing.

writing traits (writing dimensions): The several characteristics or qualities that can be used to evaluate writing quality. Each characteristic is expressed as a continuum of quality. See also **Six + 1 Traits® of Writing**.

yes-no variety of true-false items: An item format that asks a direct question, to which a student's answer is limited to yes or no.

yes-no with explanation variety of true-false items: An item format that asks a direct question and requires the student to respond yes or no and explain why his or her choice is correct.

z-score: A type of linear standard score that tells the number of standard deviation units a raw score is above or below the mean of a given distribution. The mean and standard deviation of the distribution of z-scores are always zero and one, respectively. See also **linear standard scores** and **raw score.**

z_n-score: A type of normalized standard score: z_n-scores have percentile ranks corresponding to what would be expected in a normal distribution. See also **normalized standard scores.**

References

Achieve. (2004). *Measuring up 2004: A report on language arts literacy and mathematics standards and assessments for New Jersey*. Washington, DC: Author.

Airasian, P. W. (2001). *Classroom assessment* (4th ed.). New York: McGraw-Hill.

Albertson, B. (1998). *Creating effective writing prompts*. Newark: Delaware Reading and Writing Project, Delaware Center for Teacher Education, University of Delaware.

Alfonso, V. C., Flanagan, D. P., & Radwan, S. (2005). The impact of the Cattell-Horn-Carroll theory on test development and interpretation of cognitive and academic abilities. In D. P. Flanagan & P. L. Harrison (Eds.), *Contemporary intellectual assessment: Theories, tests, and issues* (2nd ed., pp. 185–202). New York: Guilford Press.

Allen, R., Bettis, N., Kurfman, D., MacDonald, W., Mullis, I. V. S., & Salter, C. (1990). *The geography learning of high school seniors*. Princeton, NJ: National Assessment of Educational Progress, Educational Testing Service.

American Association on Intellectual and Developmental Disabilities. (2002). *Definition of intellectual disability*. Retrieved October 12, 2009, from http://www.aaidd.org/content_96.cfm?navID=20

American Counseling Association. (2005). ACA code of ethics. Alexandria, VA: Author. Available from http://www.counseling.org/resources/codeofethics/TP/home/ct2.aspx

American Educational Research Association. (2011). *Code of ethics*. Retrieved from http://www.aera.net/Portals/38/docs/About_AERA/CodeOfEthics%281%29.pdf

American Educational Research Association (AERA), American Psychological Association (APA), & National Council on Measurement in Education (NCME). (2014). *Standards for educational and psychological testing*. Washington, DC: AERA.

American Federation of Teachers et al. (1990). *Standards for teacher competence in educational assessment of students*. Available from http://buros.org/standards-teacher-competence-educational-assessment-students

American Federation of Teachers, National Council on Measurement in Education, & National Education Association. (1990). *Standards for teacher competence in educational assessment of students*. Washington, DC: National Council

on Measurement in Education. Available from http://www.unl.edu/buros/bimm/html/subarts.html

American Psychological Association. (1998). *Rights and responsibilities of test takers*. Washington, DC: Author. Available from http://www.apa.org/science/programs/testing/rights.aspx

American Psychological Association. (2010). *Ethical principles of psychologists and code of conduct*. Available from http://www.apa.org/ethics/code/index.aspx

Anderson, L. W., Krathwohl, D. R., Airasian, P. W., Cruikshank, K. A., Mayer, R. E., Pintrich, P. R., et al. (Eds.). (2001). *A taxonomy for learning, teaching, and assessing: A revision of Bloom's Taxonomy of Educational Objectives* (Complete ed.). New York: Longman.

Anderson, N., Schlueter, J. E., Carlson, J. F., & Geisinger, K. F. (Eds.) (2016). *Tests in Print IX*. Lincoln, NE: Buros Institute of Mental Measurements.

Arter, J. A. (1998, April). *Teaching about performance assessment*. Paper presented at the annual meeting of the National Council on Measurement in Education, San Diego, CA.

Arter, J., & McTighe, J. (2001). *Scoring rubrics in the classroom*. Thousand Oaks, CA: Corwin Press.

Arter, J. A., & Spandel, V. (1992). NCME instructional module: Using portfolios of student work in instruction and assessment. *Educational Measurement: Issues and Practice*, 11(1), 36–44.

Ascalon, M. E., Meyers, L. S., Davis, B. W., & Smits, N. (2007). Distractor similarity and item-stem structure: Effects on item difficulty. *Applied Measurement in Education*, 20, 153–170.

Assessment Reform Group. (2002). *Assessment is for learning: 10 principles*. Downloadable from http://www.assessment-reform-group.org

Association for Assessment in Counseling and Education. (2003). *Responsibilities of users of standardized tests (RUST)* (3rd ed.). Available from http://aac.ncat.edu/Resources/documents/RUST2003%20VII%20Final.pdf

Azwell, T., & Schmar, E. (Eds.). (1995). *Report on report cards: Alternatives to consider*. Portsmouth, NH: Heinemann.

Bagley, S. S. (2008). High school students' perceptions of narrative evaluations as summative assessment. *American Secondary Education*, 36(3), 15–32.

Bailey, J., & Guskey, T. R. (2001). *Implementing student-led conferences*. Thousand Oaks, CA: Corwin Press.

Baker, E. L. (1992). Issues in policy, assessment, and equity. In *Proceedings of the National Research Symposium on Limited English Proficiency Student Issues: Vol. 1 and 2: Focus on Evaluation and Measurement*. Washington, DC.

Baker, F. (2001). *The basics of item response theory*. College Park: ERIC Clearinghouse on Assessment and Evaluation, University of Maryland. Available from http://edres.org/irt

Bandeira de Mello, V., Bohrnstedt, G., Blankenship, C., & Sherman, D. (2015). *Mapping State Proficiency Standards onto NAEP Scales: Results From the 2013 NAEP Reading and Mathematics Assessments* (NCES 2015-046). U.S. Department of Education, Washington, DC: National Center for Education Statistics. Retrieved July 29, 2017 from http://nces.ed.gov/pubsearch

Barker, K., & Ebel, R. L. (1981). A comparison of difficulty and discrimination values of selected true-false item types. *Contemporary Educational Psychology, 7*, 35–40.

Becker, K. A. (2003). *History of the Stanford-Binet Intelligence Scales: Content and psychometrics*. Retrieved July 28, 2005, from http://www.assess.nelson.com/pdf/sb5-asb1.pdf

Bennett, G. K., Seashore, H. G., & Wesman, A. G. (1974). *Fifth edition manual for the Differential Aptitude Tests (Forms S and T)*. New York: Psychological Corporation.

Bennett, R. E. (2016). *Opt out: An examination of issues* (Research Report No. RR-16-13). Princeton, NJ: Educational Testing Service.

Betebenner, D. (2009). Norm- and criterion-referenced student growth. *Educational Measurement: Issues and Practice, 28*(4), 42–51.

Betts, L., & Hartley, J. (2012). The effects of changes in the order of verbal labels and numerical values on children's scores on attitude and rating scales. *British Educational Research Journal, 38*, 319–331.

Black, P., & Wiliam, D. (1998a). Assessment and classroom learning. *Assessment in Education, 5*, 7–74.

Black, P., & Wiliam, D. (1998b). Inside the black box: Raising standards through classroom assessment. *Phi Delta Kappan, 80*, 139–144.

Black, P., & Wiliam, D. (2009). Developing the theory of formative assessment. *Educational Assessment, Evaluation, and Accountability, 21*, 5–31.

Blommers, P. J., & Forsyth, R. A. (1977). *Elementary statistical methods in psychology and education* (2nd ed.). Boston: Houghton Mifflin.

Bloom, B. S. (1968). Learning for mastery. *Evaluation Comment, 1*, 1–12.

Bloom, B. S., Englehart, M. D., Furst, E. J., Hill, W. H., & Krathwohl, D. R. (1956). *Taxonomy of educational objectives: The classification of educational goals, Handbook I: Cognitive domain*. White Plains, NY: Longman.

Bloom, B. S., Englehart, M. D., Furst, E. J., Hill, W. H., & Krathwohl, D. R. (1984). *Taxonomy of educational objectives book I: Cognitive domain*. Boston: Allyn & Bacon.

Bloom, B. S., Hastings, J. T., & Madaus, G. F. (1971). *Handbook on formative and summative evaluation of student learning*. New York: McGraw-Hill.

Boekaerts, M. (2011). Emotions, emotional regulation, and self-regulation of learning. In Zimmerman, B. J., & Schunk, D. H. (Eds.) *Handbook of self-regulation of learning and performance* (pp. 408–425). New York: Routledge.

Bond, L. (1989). The effects of special preparation on measures of scholastic ability. In R. L. Linn (Ed.), *Educational measurement* (3rd ed., pp. 429–444). Upper Saddle River, NJ: Merrill/Prentice Hall.

Borgers, N., Hox, J., & Sikkel, D. (2004). Response effects in surveys on children and adolescents: The effect of number of response options, negative wording, and neutral midpoint. *Quality and Quantity, 38*, 17–33.

Boudett, K. P., City, E. A., & Murnane, R. J. (Eds.) (2005). *Data wise: A step-by-step guide to using assessment results to improve teaching and learning*. Cambridge, MA: Harvard University Press.

Bracken, B. A. (2002). *Bracken School Readiness Assessment: Administration manual*. San Antonio, TX: The Psychological Corporation.

Bransford, J. D., & Stein, B. S. (1984). *The IDEAL problem solver*. New York: W. H. Freeman.

Brelend, H. M., Camp, R., Jones, R. J., Morris, M. M., & Rock, D. A. (1987). *Assessing writing skill*. (Research Monograph No. 11.). New York: College Entrance Examination Board.

Brennan, R. L. (2001). An essay on the history and future of reliability from the perspective of replications. *Journal of Educational Measurement, 38*, 295–317.

Bridgeman, B. (2012). A simple answer to a simple question on changing answers. *Journal of Educational Measurement, 49*, 467–468.

Bridgeman, B., Trapani, C., & Attali, Y. (2012). Comparison of human and machine scoring of essays: Differences by gender, ethnicity, and country. *Applied Measurement in Education, 25*, 27–40.

Briggs, D., & Domingue, B. (2011). *Due diligence and the evaluation of teachers: A review of the value-added analysis underlying the effectiveness rankings of Los Angeles Unified School District teachers by the Los Angeles Times*. Boulder, CO: National Education Policy Center. Retrieved February 11, 2013, from http://nepc.colorado.edu/publication/due-diligence

British Educational Communications and Technology Agency (BECTA). (2010). *Messages from the evidence: Assessment using technology*. Retrieved September 29, 2012, from http://www.e-learningcentre.co.uk/

Brookhart, S. M. (1991). Letter: Grading practices and validity. *Educational Measurement: Issues and Practice, 10*(1), 35–36.

Brookhart, S. M. (1993). Teachers' grading practices: Meaning and values. *Journal of Educational Measurement, 30*, 123–142.

Brookhart, S. M. (1999). Teaching about communicating assessment results and grading. *Educational Measurement: Issues and Practice, 18*(1), 5–13.

Brookhart, S. M. (2001). Successful students' formative and summative uses of assessment information. *Assessment in Education, 8*, 153–169.

Brookhart S. M. (2008a). *How to give effective feedback to your students*. Alexandria, VA: ASCD.

Brookhart, S. M. (2008b). Portfolio assessment. In T. L. Good (Ed.), *21st century education: A reference handbook* (Vol. 1, pp. 443–450). Thousand Oaks, CA: Sage.

Brookhart, S. M. (2009). *Grading* (2nd ed.). Upper Saddle River, NJ: Prentice Hall/Merrill Education.

Brookhart, S. M. (2011). *Grading and learning: Practices that support student achievement*. Bloomington, IN: Solution Tree.

Brookhart, S. M. (2012). Preventing feedback fizzle. *Educational Leadership, 70*(1), 24–29.

Brookhart, S. M. (2013a). *How to create and use rubrics for formative assessment and grading.* Alexandria, VA: ASCD.

Brookhart, S. M. (2013b). Grading. In J. H. McMillan (Ed.), *SAGE handbook of research on classroom assessment* (pp. 257–271). Thousand Oaks, CA: SAGE.

Brookhart, S. M. (2013c). The public understanding of assessment in educational reform in the United States. *Oxford Review of Education, 39,* 52–71.

Brookhart, S. M. (2013d). *Grading and group work.* Alexandria, VA: ASCD.

Brookhart, S. M. (2015). Graded achievement, tested achievement, and validity. *Educational Assessment, 20*(4), 268–296.

Brookhart, S. M., Guskey, T. R., Bowers, A. J., McMillan, J. H., Smith, J. K., Smith, L. F., Stevens, M. T., & Welsh, M. E. (2016). A century of grading research: Meaning and value in the most common educational measure. *Review of Educational Research, 68,* 803–848.

Brown, R. S., & E. Coughlin. (2007, November). *The predictive validity of selected benchmark assessments used in the Mid-Atlantic Region* (Issues & Answers Report, REL 2007–No. 017). Washington, DC: U.S. Department of Education, Institute of Education Sciences, National Center for Education Evaluation and Regional Assistance, Regional Educational Laboratory Mid-Atlantic. Available from http://ies.ed.gov/ncee/edlabs

Brown, W. (1910). Some experimental results in the correlation of mental abilities. *British Journal of Psychology, 3,* 296–322.

Buros, O. K. (Ed.). (1938). *The nineteen thirty-eight mental measurements yearbook.* New Brunswick, NJ: Rutgers University Press.

Bushaw, W. J., & Gallup, A. M. (2008). Americans speak out— Are educators and policy makers listening? The 40th annual Phi Delta Kappa/Gallup Poll of the Public's Attitudes Toward the Public Schools. *Phi Delta Kappan, 90*(1), 8–20.

Butler, D. L., & Winne, P. H. (1995). Feedback and self-regulated learning: A theoretical synthesis. *Review of Educational Research, 65,* 245–281.

Cabrera, N. L., & Cabrera, G. A. (2008). Counterbalance assessment: The chorizo test. *Phi Delta Kappan, 89*(9), 677–678.

Camilli, G. (2006). Test fairness. In R. L. Brennan (Ed.), *Educational measurement* (4th ed., pp. 221–256). Westport, CT: Praeger.

Campbell, C. (2013). Research on teacher competency in classroom assessment. In J. H. McMillan (Ed.), *SAGE handbook of research on classroom assessment* (pp. 71–84). Thousand Oaks, CA: SAGE.

Carroll, J. B. (1963). A model of school learning. *Teachers College Record, 64,* 723–733.

Center for the Study of Testing, Evaluation, and Educational Policy. (1992, October). *The influence of testing on teaching math and science in grades 4–12.* Boston: Boston College.

Chetwynd, F., & Dobbyn, C. (2011): Assessment, feedback and marking guides in distance education. *Open Learning: The Journal of Open, Distance and e-Learning, 26*(1), 67–78.

Christiansen, L. L., Lazarus, S. S., Crone, M., & Thurlow, M. L. (2008). *2007 state policies on assessment participation and accommodations for students with disabilities* (Synthesis Report 69). Minneapolis: University of Minnesota, National Center on Educational Outcomes.

Cizek, G. J. (2001). *Setting performance standards.* Mahwah, NJ: Erlbaum.

Clarke, S. (2003). *Enriching feedback in the primary classroom.* London: Hodder Murray.

Coe, M., Hanita, M., Nishioka, V., & Smiley, R. (2011, December). *An investigation of the impact of the 6+1 Trait Writing Model on grade 5 student writing achievement: Final report.* NCEE Report 2012-4010. Washington, DC: U.S. Department of Education.

Coffman, W. E. (1971). Essay examinations. In R. L. Thorndike (Ed.), *Educational measurement* (2nd ed.). Washington, DC: American Council on Education.

Cohen, J. (1960). A coefficient of agreement for nominal scales. *Educational and Psychological Measurement, 20,* 37–46.

Cole, N. S., & Hanson, G. R. (1975). Impact of interest inventories on career choice. In E. E. Diamond (Ed.), *Issues of sex bias and sex fairness in career interest measurement.* Washington, DC: Career Education Program, National Institute of Education, Department of Health, Education, and Welfare.

Cole, N. S., & Moss, P. A. (1989). Bias in test use. In R. L. Linn (Ed.), *Educational measurement* (3rd ed., pp. 201–219). Upper Saddle River, NJ: Merrill/Prentice Hall.

Cole, N. S., & Nitko, A. J. (1981). Instrumentation and bias: Issues in selecting measures for educational evaluations. In R. A. Berk (Ed.), *Educational evaluation methodology: The state of the art.* Baltimore: Johns Hopkins University Press.

Cole, N. S., & Zieky, M. J. (2001). The new faces of fairness. *Journal of Educational Measurement, 38,* 369–382.

Committee on Education and the Workforce. (2005). *Full history of the ESEA effort: Press releases, summaries, and information related to H.R. 1, the Reauthorization of the Elementary and Secondary Education Act.* Available from http://edworkforce.house.gov/democrats/eseainfo.html

Connolly, A. J. (2007). *KeyMath™–3 Diagnostic Assessment.* Pearson.

Corby, K. (2002). *Tests and testing information.* East Lansing: Michigan State University, University Library.

Council of Chief State School Officers (CCSSO). (2006). *Aligning assessment to guide the learning of all students: Six reports.* Washington, DC: Author.

Council of Chief State School Officers (CCSSO). (2010). *Statewide student assessment: 2009–10.* Washington, DC: Author.

Covington, M. V. (1992). *Making the grade: A self-worth perspective on motivation and school reform.* Cambridge: Cambridge University Press.

Cronbach, L. J. (1951). Coefficient alpha and the internal structure of tests. *Psychometrika, 16,* 297–334.

Cronbach, L. J. (1963). Course improvement through evaluation. *Teachers College Record, 64,* 672–683.

Cronbach, L. J. (1971). Test validation. In R. L. Thorndike (Ed.), *Educational measurement* (2nd ed.). Washington, DC: American Council on Education.

Cronbach, L. J. (1988). Five perspectives on validity argument. In H. Wainer (Ed.), *Test validity* (pp. 3–17). Hillsdale, NJ: Erlbaum.

Cronbach, L. J. (1989). Construct validation after thirty years. In R. L. Linn (Ed.), *Intelligence: Measurement, theory, and public policy* (pp. 147–171). Urbana: University of Illinois Press.

Cronbach, L. J. (1990). *Essentials of psychological testing* (5th ed.). New York: Harper & Row.

CTB/McGraw-Hill. (2008). *TerraNova, third edition, technical report.* Monterey, CA: Author.

Cuban, Larry. (2009). *Hugging the middle: How teachers teach in an era of testing and accountability.* New York: Teachers College Press.

Dadey, N., & Gong, B. (2017, April). *Using interim assessments in place of summative assessments? Consideration of an ESSA option.* Washington, DC: Council of Chief State School Officers.

Dalton, S. S. (1998). *Pedagogy matters: Standards for effective teaching practice.* Research Report No. 4, Center for Research on Education, Diversity, and Excellence, University of California, Santa Cruz.

Darden, A. D. (2000). Thoughtful conversations: Student-teacher writing conferences. *Trade Secrets: Teaching Tips for Elementary, Middle, and High School Teachers, 20*(1), 3–5.

Das, J. P. (2002). A better look at intelligence. *Current Directions in Psychological Science, 11*(1), 28–33.

Davidson, J. E., & Sternberg, R. J. (Eds.) (2003). *The psychology of problem solving.* New York: Cambridge University Press.

Davis, H. A., & Li, J. (2008). *The relationship between high school students' cognitive appraisals of high stakes tests and their emotion regulation and achievement.* Paper presented at the annual meeting of the American Educational Research Association, New York.

Davis, R. V. (1980). Measuring interests. In D. A. Payne (Ed.), *New directions for testing and measurement: Recent developments in affective measurement* (No. 7). San Francisco: Jossey-Bass.

Dawson, O. (2005). Where students lead, achievement follows. *Education Update, 47*(1).

Debra P. v. Turlington, 474 F. Supp. 244 (M.D.Fla.1979)

Debra P. v. Turlington, 644 F.2d 397, 408 (5th Cir. 1981) (Unit B)

Debra P. v. Turlington, 730 F.2d 1405 (11th Cir. 1984)

DeLuca, C. (2012). Preparing teachers for the age of accountability: Toward a framework for assessment education. *Action in Teacher Education, 34*(5/6), 576–591.

Deussen, T., Autio, E., Miller, B. Lockwood, A.T., & Stewart, V. (2008). *What teachers should know about instruction for ELLs.* Education Northwest.

De Wever, B, Van Keer, H., Schellens, T., & Valke, M. (2011). Assessing collaboration in a wiki; The reliability of university students' peer assessment. *Internet and Higher Education, 14,* 201–206.

Diamond, J. J., & Evans, W. J. (1972). An investigation of the cognitive correlates of test-wiseness. *Journal of Educational Measurement, 2,* 145–150.

Dikli, S. (2006). An overview of automated scoring of essays. *Journal of Technology, Learning, and Assessment, 5*(1). Retrieved November 20, 2012, from http://www.jtla.org.

Doran, H. C., & Fleischman, S. (2005). Challenges of value-added assessment. *Educational Leadership, 63*(3), 85–87.

Deussen, T., Autio, E., Miller, B., Lockwood, A. T., & Stewart, V. (2008, November). *What teachers should know about instruction for English Language Learners: A report to Washington state.* Portland, OR: Northwest Regional Educational Laboratory. Retrieved October 30, 2012, from http://educationnorthwest.org/webfm_send/217

Donlon, T. F., & Angoff, W. H. (1971). The Scholastic Aptitude Test. In W. H. Angoff (Ed.), *The College Board Admissions Testing Program: A technical report on research and development activities relating to the Scholastic Aptitude Test and achievement tests.* New York: College Entrance Examination Board.

Dorans, N. J. (2002). *The recentering of SAT scales and its effects on score distributions and score interpretations.* Research Report No. 2002-11. New York: College Entrance Examination Board.

Downing, S. M., Baranowski, R. A., Grosso, L. J., & Norcini, J. J. (1995). Stem type and cognitive ability measured: The validity evidence for multiple true-false items in medical specialty certification. *Applied Measurement in Education, 8,* 187–197.

Dreyfus, L. R. (2002). *Setting reading standards, measuring progress, and informing instruction.* Brewster, NY: Questar Assessment, Inc. Retrieved November 24, 2012, from http://www.questarai.com/Resources/Documents/Testing_Brief_Setting_Reading_Standards_Measuring_Progress_and_Informing_Instruction.pdf

Dudycha, A. L., & Dudycha, L. W. (1972). Behavioral statistics: An historical perspective. In R. E. Kirk (Ed.), *Statistical issues: A reader for the behavioral sciences.* Monterey, CA: Brooks/Cole.

Dunbar, S., Hoover, H. D., Frisbie, D. A., & Mengeling, M. A. (2008). *Iowa Tests of Basic Skills complete and core batteries, Form C: 2005 norms and score conversions.* Chicago: Riverside.

Dunbar, S., Hoover, H. D., Frisbie, D. A., & Oberley, K. R. (2008). *Interpretive guide for school administrators: Iowa Tests of Basic Skills, Levels 5–14, Forms A, B, and C.* Chicago: Riverside.

Dweck, C. S. (2000). *Self-theories: Their role in motivation, personality, and development.* New York: Psychology Press.

Ebel, R. L. (1965). *Measuring educational achievement.* Englewood Cliffs, NJ: Prentice Hall.

Ebel, R. L. (1972). *Essentials of educational measurement* (2nd ed.). Upper Saddle River, NJ: Prentice Hall.

Ebel, R. L. (1974). Shall we get rid of grades? *Measurement in Education, 5*(4), 1–2.

Ebel, R. L. (1979). *Essentials of educational measurement* (3rd ed.). Upper Saddle River, NJ: Prentice Hall.

Ebel, R. L., & Frisbie, D. A. (1991). *Essentials of educational measurement* (5th ed.). Upper Saddle River, NJ: Prentice Hall.

Editorial Projects in Education Research Center. (2016, March). Issues A-Z: The Every Student Succeeds Act: An ESSA overview. *Education Week.* Retrieved February 4, 2017 from http://www.edweek.org/ew/issues/every-student-succeeds-act/

Educational Testing Service. (2009). *Guidelines for the assessment of English Language Learners.* Retrieved September 29, 2012, from http://www.ets.org

Education Week. (2016, October 27). Map: Tracking the Common Core State Standards. Retrieved March 13, 2017, from http://www.edweek.org/ew/section/multimedia/map-states-academic-standards-common-core-or.html

Egawa, K., & Azwell, T. (1995). Telling the story: Narrative reports. In T. Azwell & E. Schmar (Eds.), *Report on report cards: Alternatives to consider.* Portsmouth, NH: Heinemann.

Ennis, R. H. (1985). Goals for a critical thinking curriculum. In A. Costa (Ed.), *Developing minds: A resource book for teaching thinking.* Alexandria, VA: Association for Supervision and Curriculum Development.

Ennis, R. H. (1996). *Critical thinking.* Upper Saddle River, NJ: Prentice Hall.

Equal Employment Opportunity Commission, Civil Service Commission, Department of Justice, Department of Labor, & Department of the Treasury. (1979). Adoption of questions and answers to clarify and provide a common interpretation of the uniform guidelines on employee section procedures. *Federal Register, 44* (Publication Number: 11996–12006).

Equal Employment Opportunity Commission, Civil Service Commission, Department of Labor, & Department of Justice (1978, August 25). Uniform guidelines on employee selection procedures. *Federal Register, 43* (Publication Number: 38290–38315).

Ergene, T. (2003). Effective interventions on test anxiety reduction: A meta-analysis. *School Psychology International, 24,* 313–328.

Ericsson, K. A. (2003). The acquisition of expert performance as problem solving. In Davidson, J. E., & Sternberg, R. J. (Eds.). *The psychology of problem solving* (pp. 31–83). New York: Cambridge University Press.

Ericsson, K. A., & Simon, H. A. (1999). *Protocol analysis: Verbal reports as data.* Cambridge: Massachusetts Institute of Technology.

Evaluation Center. (1995). *An independent evaluation of the Kentucky Instructional Results Information System (KIRIS).* Frankfort: Kentucky Institute for Education Research.

Feister, W. J., & Whitney, D. R. (1968). An interview with D. E. F. Linquist. *Epsilon Bulletin, 42,* 17–28.

Feldt, L. S., & Brennan, R. L. (1989). Reliability. In R. L. Linn (Ed.), *Educational measurement* (3rd ed.). New York: Macmillan.

Ferrara, S., & DeMauro, G. E. (2006). Standardized assessment of individual achievement in K-12. In R. L. Brennan (Ed.), *Educational measurement* (4th ed., pp. 579–621). Westport, CT: Praeger.

Ferrara, S., & Way, D. (2016). Design and development of end-of-course tests for student assessment and teacher evaluation. In H. Braun (Ed.), *Meeting the challenges to measurement in an era of accountability* (pp. 11–48). New York: Routledge.

Fisher, D., & Frey, N. (2009). Feed up, back, forward. *Educational Leadership, 67*(3), 20–25.

Fisher, T. H. (1980). The courts and your minimum competency testing program—A guide to survival. *NCME Measurement in Education, 11*(1), 1–12.

Flavell, J. H. (1976). Metacognitive aspects of problem solving. In L. B. Resnick (Ed.), *The nature of intelligence* (pp. 231–235). Hillsdale, NJ: Erlbaum.

Forster, M., & Masters, G. (2004). Bridging the conceptual gap between classroom assessment and system accountability. In M. Wilson (ed.), *Towards coherence between classroom assessment and accountability.* Chicago, IL: University of Chicago Press.

Frank, L. K. (1939). Projective methods for the study of personality. *Journal of Psychology, 8,* 389–413.

Freeman, D. J., Kuhs, T. M., Knappen, L. B., & Porter, A. C. (1982). A closer look at standardized tests. *Arithmetic Teacher, 29*(7), 50–54.

Frey, N., Fisher, D., & Gonzalez, A. (2010). *Literacy 2.0: Reading and writing in the 21st century classroom.* Bloomington, IN: Solution Tree.

Frisbie, D. A. (1992). The multiple true-false format: A status review. *Educational Measurement: Issues and Practice, 11*(4), 21–26.

Frisbie, D. A., & Becker, D. F. (1990). An analysis of textbook advice about true-false tests. *Applied Measurement in Education, 4,* 67–83.

Frisbie, D. A., & Waltman, K. K. (1992). Developing a personal grading plan. *Educational Measurement: Issues and Practice, 11*(3), 35–42.

Fuchs, L. S., & Fuchs, D. (1999). Fair and unfair testing accommodations. *School Administrator, 56*(10), 24–29.

Fuchs, L. S., & Fuchs, D. (2007). *Progress monitoring in the context of responsiveness-to-intervention.* Retrieved January 15, 2009, from http://www.studentprogress.org/summer_institute/2007/RTI/RTIManual_2007.pdf

Gagné, R. M., Briggs, L. J., & Wager, W. W. (1988). *Principles of instructional design* (3rd ed.). New York: Holt, Rinehart & Winston.

Geiger, M. A. (1997). An examination of the relationships between answer changing, testwiseness, and examination performance. *Journal of Experimental Education, 66,* 49–60.

GI Forum, et al. v. Texas Education Agency, et al. (January 7, 2000). U.S. District Court (Civil Action SA–97-CA-1278-EP).

Gick, M. L. (1986). Problem-solving strategies. *Educational Psychologist, 21,* 99–120.

Glaser, R. (1963). Instructional technology and the measurement of learning outcomes. *American Psychologist, 18,* 519–521.

Glaser, R. (1977). *Adaptive education: Individual diversity and learning.* New York: Holt, Rinehart & Winston.

Glaser, R., & Nitko, A. J. (1971). Measurement in learning and instruction. In R. L. Thorndike (Ed.), *Educational measurement* (2nd ed., pp. 625–670). Washington, DC: American Council on Education.

Goldman, B. A., & Mitchell, D. F. (Eds.). (2008). *Directory of unpublished experimental measures, Volume 9.* Washington, DC: American Psychological Association.

Gong, B. (2008, February). *Developing better learning progressions: Some issues and suggestions for research and policy.* Dover, NH: Center for Assessment.

Gong, B., Venezky, R., & Mioduser, D. (1992). Instructional assessments: Level for systemic change in science education classrooms. *Journal of Science Education and Technology, 1,* 157–175.

Good, T. L., & Brophy, J. E. (2002). *Looking in classrooms* (9th ed.). Boston: Allyn & Bacon.

Goodman, D. P., & Hambleton, R. K. (2004). Student test score reports and interpretive guides: Review of current practices and suggestions for future research. *Applied Measurement in Education, 17,* 145–220.

Graham, S., Hebert, M., & Harris, K. R. (2015). Formative assessment and writing: A meta-analysis. *The Elementary School Journal, 115,* 523–547.

Gregg, N., & Nelson, J. N. (2012). Meta-analysis on the effectiveness of extra time as a test accommodation for transitioning adolescents with learning disabilities: More questions than answers. *Journal of Learning Disabilities, 45,* 128–138.

Gronlund, N. E., & Brookhart, S. M. (2009). *Gronlund's writing instructional objectives* (8th ed.). Upper Saddle River, NJ: Pearson.

Gulliksen, H. (1986). Perspective on educational measurement. *Applied Psychological Measurement, 10,* 109–132.

Guskey, T. R., & Bailey, J. M. (2010). *Developing standards-based report cards.* Thousand Oaks, CA: Corwin.

Guskey, T. R., & McTighe, J. (2016). Pre-assessment promises and cautions. *Educational Leadership, 73*(7), 38–43.

Haertel, E. H. (2006). Reliability. In R. L. Brennan (Ed.), *Educational measurement* (4th ed., pp. 65–110). Westport, CT: Praeger.

Haladyna, T. M. (2004). *Developing and validating multiple-choice test items* (3rd ed.). Mahwah, NJ: Lawrence Erlbaum Associates.

Haladyna, T. M., Downing, S. M., & Rodriguez, M. C. (2002). A review of multiple-choice item writing guidelines for classroom assessment. *Applied Measurement in Education, 15,* 309–334.

Haladyna, T. M., Nolen, S. B., & Haas, N. (1991). Raising standardized achievement test scores and the origins of test score pollution. *Educational Researcher, 20*(5), 2–7.

Hambleton, R. K., & Murphy, E. (1992). A psychometric perspective on authentic measurement. *Applied Measurement in Education, 5,* 1–16.

Harrow, A. J. (1972). *A taxonomy of the psychomotor domain: A guide for developing behavioral objectives.* White Plains, NY: Longman.

Hattie, J. A. C. (2009). *Visible learning.* London: Routledge.

Hattie, J., & Timperley, H. (2007). The power of feedback. *Review of Educational Research, 77,* 81–112.

Hawkes, H. E., Lindquist, E. F., & Mann, C. R. (Eds.) (1936). *The construction and use of achievement examinations: A manual for secondary school teachers.* Boston: Houghton Mifflin.

Hembree, R. (1988). Correlates, causes, effects and treatment of test anxiety. *Review of Educational Research, 58,* 47–77.

Heritage, M. (2008). *Learning progressions: Supporting instruction and formative assessment.* Washington, DC: Council of Chief State School Officers.

Herman, J. L., Aschbacher, P. R., & Winters, L. (1992). *A practical guide to alternative assessment.* Alexandria, VA: Association for Supervision and Curriculum Development.

Herman, J., & Linn, R. (2013). On the road to assessing deeper learning: *The status of Smarter Balanced and PARCC assessment consortia* (CRESST Report 823). Los Angeles, CA: National Center for Research on Evaluation, Standards, and Student Testing, UCLA.

Herman, W. E. (1990). Fear of failure as a distinctive personality trait measure of test anxiety. *Journal of Research and Development in Education, 23,* 180–185.

Hess, K. (2007). *Developing and using learning progressions as a schema for measuring progress.* Dover, NH: National Center for Assessment.

Higgins, K. M., Harris, N. A., & Kuehn, L. L. (1994). Placing assessment into the hands of young children: A study of self-generated criteria and self-assessment. *Educational Assessment, 2,* 309–324.

Hill, J. D., & Flynn, K. M. (2006). *Classroom instruction that works with English language learners.* Alexandria, VA: ASCD.

Ho, A. D. (2008). The poblem with "Proficiency": Limitations of statistics and policy under No Child Left Behind. *Educational Researcher, 37,* 351–360.

Hogan, T. P., & Murphy, G. (2007). Recommendations for preparing and scoring constructed-response items: What the experts say. *Applied Measurement in Education, 20,* 427–441.

Holland, P. W., & Dorans, N. J. (2006). Linking and equating. In R. L. Brennan (Ed.), *Educational Measurement* (4th ed., pp. 187–220). Westport, CT: Praeger.

Hoover, H. D. (1984a). The most appropriate scores for measuring educational development in the elementary schools: GE. *Educational Measurement: Issues and Practice, 3*(4), 8–14.

Hoover, H. D. (1984b). Rejoinder to Burket. *Educational Measurement: Issues and Practice, 3*(4), 16–18.

Hoover, H. D., Hieronymus, A. N., Frisbie, D. A., & Dunbar, S. B. (1993). *Directions for administration: Iowa Tests of Basic Skills, Levels 9–14, Forms K and L.* Chicago: Riverside.

Hough, H. (2005). *Tests and measures in social science: Tests available in compilation volumes.* University of Texas at Arlington, Central Library, Health Sciences. Available from http://libraries.uta.edu/helen/test&meas/testmainframe.htm

Huberty, T. J. (2010). Test and performance anxiety. *Education Digest, 75*(9), 34–38.

Huynh, H. (1976). On the reliability of decisions in domain-referenced testing. *Journal of Educational Measurement, 13,* 253–264.

Jakwerth, P. R., Stancavage, F. B., & Reed, E. D. (1999). *An investigation of why students do not respond to questions* (NAEP validity studies). Palo Alto, CA: American Institutes for Research.

Jimerson, S. R. (2001). Meta-analysis of grade retention research: Implications for practice in the 21st century. *School Psychology Review, 30,* 420–437.

Joint Advisory Committee. (1993). *Principles for fair student assessment practices for education in Canada.* Edmonton, Alberta: Author, Centre for Research in Applied Measurement and Evaluation, University of Alberta.

Joint Committee on Standards for Educational Evaluation. (2015). *The classroom assessment standards for preK-12 teachers.* Kindle Direct Press.

Joint Committee on Standards for Educational Evaluation. (2009). *Personnel evaluation standards* (2nd ed.). Thousand Oaks, CA: Sage.

Joint Committee on Standards for Educational Evaluation. (2011). *The program evaluation standards: A guide for evaluators and evaluation users* (3rd ed.). Thousand Oaks, CA: Sage.

Joint Committee on Testing Practices. (1999). *Rights and responsibilities of test takers: Guidelines and expectations.* Retrieved January 23, 2006, from http://www.apa.org/science/ttrr.html

Joint Committee on Testing Practices. (2004). *Code of fair testing practices in education (revised).* Washington, DC: Science Directorate, American Psychological Association. Available from http://www.apa.org/science/programs/testing/faircode.aspx

Jones, R. W. (1994). *Performance and alternative assessment techniques: Meeting the challenges of alternative evaluation strategies.* Paper presented at the Second International Conference on Educational Evaluation and Assessment, Pretoria, Republic of South Africa.

Kane, M. T. (1992). An argument-based approach to validity. *Psychological Bulletin, 112,* 527–535.

Kane, M. T. (2001). Current concerns in validity theory. *Journal of Educational Measurement, 38,* 319–342.

Kane, M. T. (2002). Validating high-stakes testing programs. *Educational Measurement: Issues and Practice, 21*(1), 31–41.

Kane, M. T. (2006). Validation. In R. L. Brennan (Ed.), *Educational measurement* (4th ed., pp. 17–64). Westport, CT: Praeger.

Kane, M. T. (2013). Validating the interpretation and uses of test scores. *Journal of Educational Measurement, 50,* 1–73.

Karweit, N. L., & Wasik, B. A. (1992). *A review of the effects of extra-year kindergarten programs and transitional first grades* (CDS Report 41). Baltimore: Center for Research on Effective Schooling for Disadvantaged Students, Johns Hopkins University.

Kaufman, A. S., & Kaufman, N. L. (2004). *Kaufman Assessment Battery for Children, Second Edition*. Circle Pines, MN: American Guidance Service.

Kaufman, A. S., Lichtenberger, E. O., Fletcher-Janzen, E., & Kaufman, N. L. (2005). *Essentials of KABC-II Assessment*. San Francisco: Jossey-Bass.

Kelly, T. L. (1939). The selection of upper and lower groups for the validation of test items. *Journal of Educational Psychology, 30*, 17–24.

Keyser, D. J., & Sweetland, R. C. (Eds.) (2005). *Test critiques: Volume 11*. Austin, TX: PRO-ED.

Kieffer, M. J., Lesaux, N. K., Rivera, M., & Francis, D. J. (2009). Accommodations for English Language Learners taking large-scale assessments: A meta-analysis on effectiveness and validity. *Review of Educational Research, 79*, 1168–1201.

King, K. V., Gardner, D. A., Zucker, S., & Jorgensen, M. A. (2004, July). *The distractor rationale taxonomy: Enhancing multiple-choice items in reading and mathematics* (Pearson Assessment Report). Retrieved January 21, 2009, from http://pearsonassess.com/NR/rdonlyres/D7E62EC6-CC3F-47B6-B1CB-A83F341AD768/0/Distractor_Rationales.pdf

Kingston, N., & Nash, B. (2011). Formative assessment: A meta-analysis and call for research. *Educational Measurment: Issues and Practice, 30*(4), 28–37.

Klopfer, L. E. (1969). *An operational definition of "understand."* Unpublished manuscript, Learning Research and Development Center, University of Pittsburgh, Pittsburgh, PA.

Klopfer, L. E. (1971). Evaluation of learning in science. In B. S. Bloom, J. T. Hastings, & G. F. Madaus (Eds.), *Handbook on formative and summative evaluation of student learning*. New York: McGraw-Hill.

Klotz, M. B., & Canter, A. (2006). *Response to Intervention (RTI): A primer for parents*. Retrieved February 5, 2009, from http://www.nasponline.org/resources/factsheets/rtiprimer.aspx

Kluger, A. N., & DeNisi, A. (1996). The effects of feedback interventions on performance: A historical review, a meta-analysis, and a preliminary feedback intervention theory. *Psychological Bulletin, 119*, 254–284.

Kolen, M. J. (2006). Scaling and norming. In R. L. Brennan (Ed.), *Educational measurement* (4th ed., pp. 155–186). Westport, CT: Praeger.

Kolencik, P. L., & Hillwig, S. A. (2011). *Encouraging metacognition: Supporting learners through metacognitive teaching strategies*. New York: Peter Lang.

Koretz, D. M., & Hamilton, L. S. (2006). Testing for accountability in K–12. In R. L. Brennan (Ed.), *Educational measurement* (4th ed., pp. 531–578). Westport, CT: Praeger.

Koretz, D., Stecher, B., Klein, S., & McCaffrey, D. (1994). The Vermont Portfolio Assessment Program: Findings and implications. *Educational Measurement: Issues and Practice, 13*(3), 5–16.

Krathwohl, D. R. (2002). A revision of Bloom's taxonomy: An overview. *Theory into Practice, 41*(4), 212–218.

Krathwohl, D. R., Bloom, B. S., & Masia, B. B. (1964). *Taxonomy of educational objectives: Book 2. Affective domain*. White Plains, NY: Longman.

Kroog, H. I., Ruiz-Primo, M. A., & Sands, D. (2014). *Understanding the interplay between the cultural context of classrooms and formative assessment*. Paper presented at the annual meeting of the American Educational Research Association, Philadelphia.

Kuder, G. F., & Richardson, M. W. (1937). The theory of the estimation of test reliability. *Psychometrika, 2*, 151–160.

Kuder, Inc. (2012). Kuder Career Interests Assessment (KCIA). Adel, IA: Author.

Kuhn, D. (1999). A developmental model of critical thinking. *Educational Researcher, 28*(2), 16–25, 46.

La Marca, P. M., Redfield, D., Winter, P. C., Bailey, A., & Despriet, L. H. (2000). *State standards and state assessment systems: A guide to alignment*. Washington, DC: Council of State School Officers.

Landau, D., & Lazarsfeld, P. F. (1968). Quetelet, Adolphe. *International Encyclopedia of the Social Sciences, 13*, 247–257.

Lane, S. (1992). The conceptual framework for the development of a mathematics performance assessment instrument. *Educational Measurement: Issues and Practice, 12*(2), 16–23.

Lane, S., Parke, C., & Moskal, B. (1992). *Principles for developing performance assessments*. Paper presented at the annual meeting of the American Educational Research Association, San Francisco, CA.

Lane, S., & Stone, C. A. (2002). Strategies for examining the consequences of assessment and accountability programs. *Educational Measurement: Issues and Practice, 21*(1), 23–30.

Langenfeld, T. E., & Crocker, L. M. (1994). The evaluation of validity theory: Public school testing, the courts, and incompatible interpretations. *Educational Assessment, 2*, 149–165.

Laska, J. A., & Juarez, T. (Eds.) (1992). *Grading and marking in American schools: Two centuries of debate*. Springfield, IL: Charles C. Thomas.

Lazarus, S. S., Kincaid, A., Thurlow, M. L., Rieke, R. L., & Dominguez, L. M. (2014). *2013 state policies for selected response accommodations on statewide assessments* (Synthesis Report 93). Minneapolis, MN: University of Minnesota, National Center on Educational Outcomes.

Lee, W-C, Hanson, B. A., & Brennan, R. L. (2002). Estimating consistency and accuracy indices for multiple classifications. *Applied Psychological Measurement, 26*, 412–432.

Leighton, J. P., Chu, M-W., & Seitz, P. (2012). Errors in student learning and assessment: The Learning Errors and Formative Feedback (LEAFF) model. In R. W. Lissitz (Ed.), *Informing the practice of teaching using formative and interim assessment: A systems approach*. Charlotte, NC: Information Age Publishing.

Leighton, J. P., & Gierl, M. J. (2007). Defining and evaluating models of cognition used in educational measurement to make inferences about examinees' thinking processes. *Educational Measurement: Issues and Practice, 26*(2), 3–16.

Li, H., & Suen, H. K. (2012). The effects of test accommodations for English Language Learners: A meta-analysis. *Applied Measurement in Education, 25*, 327–346.

Lindvall, C. M. (1976). Criteria for stating IPI objectives. In D. T. Gow (Ed.), *Design and development of curricular materials: Instructional design articles* (Vol. 2). Pittsburgh, PA: University Center for International Studies, University of Pittsburgh.

Lindvall, C. M., & Nitko, A. J. (1975). *Measuring pupil achievement and aptitude* (2nd ed.). New York: Harcourt Brace Jovanovich.

Linn, R. L. (1993). Educational assessment: Expanded expectations and challenges. *Educational Evaluation and Policy Analysis, 15*, 1–16.

Linn, R. L. (1994). Performance assessment: Policy, promises, and technical measurement standards. *Educational Researcher, 23*(4), 4–14.

Linn, R. L., & Baker, E. (1997, Summer). CRESST conceptual model for assessment. *Evaluation Comment, 7*(1), 1–22.

Linn, R. L., Baker, E. L., & Dunbar, S. B. (1991). Complex, performance-based assessment: Expectations and validation criteria. *Educational Researcher, 20*(8), 5–21.

Linn, R. L., Graue, M. E., & Sanders, N. M. (1990). Comparing state and district test results to national norms: The validity of claims that "everyone is above average." *Educational Measurement: Issues and Practice, 9*(3), 5–14.

Linn, R. L., & Gronlund, N. E. (1995). *Measurement and assessment in teaching* (7th ed.). Upper Saddle River, NJ: Prentice Hall.

Lord, F. M. (1953). The relation of test scores to the trait underlying the test. *Educational and Psychological Measurement, 13,* 517–549.

Lord, F. M., & Novick, M. R. (1968). *Statistical theories of mental test scores.* Reading, MA: Addison-Wesley.

Lorenzo, G., & Ittelson, J. (2005). *An overview of E-Portfolios.* Boulder, CO: Educause. Retrieved January 21, 2013, from http://www.educause.com.

Lovett, B. J. (2010). Extended time testing accommodations for students with disabilities: Answers to five fundamental questions. *Review of Educational Research, 80,* 611–638.

Maddox, T. (Ed.). (2008). *Tests: A comprehensive reference for assessments in psychology, education, and business* (6th ed.). Austin, TX: PRO-ED.

Mandler, G., & Sarason, S. B. (1952). A study of anxiety and learning. *Journal of Abnormal and Social Psychology, 47,* 166–173.

Marshall, J. C. (1967). Composition errors and essay examinations grades reexamined. *American Educational Research Journal, 4,* 375–385.

Marzano, R. J., Pickering, D., & McTighe, J. (1993). *Assessing student outcomes: Performance assessment using the Dimensions of Learning Model.* Alexandria, VA: Association for Supervision and Curriculum Development.

Mason, B. J., & Bruning, R. (2001). *Providing feedback in computer-based instruction: What the research tells us.* University of Nebraska-Lincoln. Retrieved February 2, 2012, from http://dwb.unl.edu/Edit/MB/MasonBruning.html

Matter, K. K. (1989). Putting test scores in perspective: Communicating a complete report card for your schools. In L. M. Rudner, J. C. Conoley, & B. S. Plake (Eds.), *Understanding achievement tests: A guide for school administrators* (pp. 121–129). Washington, DC: ERIC Clearinghouse on Tests, Measurement, and Evaluation.

Mayer, R. E., Larkin, J. H., & Kadane, J. B. (1984). A cognitive analysis of mathematical problem-solving ability. In R. J. Sternberg (Ed.), *Advances in the psychology of human intelligence.* Hillsdale, NJ: Erlbaum.

McCurry, D. (2010). Can machine scoring deal with broad and open writing tests as well as human readers? *Assessing Writing, 15,* 118–129.

McDonnell, L. (1997). *The politics of state testing: Implementing new student assessments. CSE Technical Report 424.* Los Angeles: National Center for Research on Evaluation, Standards, and Student Testing, UCLA.

Mealey, D. L., & Host, T. R. (1992). Coping with test anxiety. *College Teaching, 40,* 147–150.

Mehrens, W. A., & Kaminski, J. (1989). Methods for improving standardized test scores: Fruitful, fruitless, or fraudulent? *Educational Measurement: Issues and Practice, 8*(1), 14–22.

Messick, S. (1989a). Meaning and values in test validation: The science and ethics of assessment. *Educational Researcher, 18*(2), 5–11.

Messick, S. (1989b). Validity. In R. L. Linn (Ed.), *Educational measurement* (3rd ed., pp. 13–103). Upper Saddle River, NJ: Prentice Hall.

Messick, S. (1994). The interplay of evidence and consequences in the validation of performance assessments. *Educational Researcher, 23*(2), 13–23.

Miller, M. D., & Seraphine, A. E. (1993). Can test scores remain authentic when teaching to the test? *Educational Assessment, 1,* 119–129.

Millman, J., Bishop, C. H., & Ebel, R. L. (1965). An analysis of test-wiseness. *Educational and Psychological Measurement, 25,* 707–726.

Minstrell, J., Anderson, R., & Li, M. (2009). *Assessing teacher competency in formative assessment.* Annual Report to the National Science Foundation.

Mislevy, R. J. (2016). How developments in psychology and technology change validity argumentation. *Journal of Educational Measurement, 53,* 265–292.

Mislevy, R. J., & Haertel, G. (2006). Implications of evidence-centered design for educational testing. *Educational Measurement: Issues and Practice, 25*(4), 6–20.

Mo, W. (2007). "Can you listen faster?" Assessment of students who are culturally and linguistically diverse learners. In P. Jones, J. F. Carr, & R. L. Ataya (Eds.), *A pig don't get fatter the more you weigh it: Classroom assessments that work* (pp. 39–50). New York: Teachers College Press.

Mory, E. H. (2004). Feedback research revisited. In Jonassen, D. H., (Ed.), *Handbook of research on educational communications and technology* (2nd ed., pp. 745–784). Mahwah, NJ: Lawrence Erlbaum.

Moss, C. M., & Brookhart, S. M. (2009). *Advancing formative assessment in every classroom: A guide for instructional leaders.* Alexandria, VA: ASCD.

Moss, C. M., & Brookhart, S. M. (2012). *Learning targets: Helping students aim for understanding in today's lesson.* Alexandria, VA: ASCD.

Moss, P. A. (1992). Shifting conceptions of validity in educational measurement: Implications for performance assessment. *Review of Educational Research, 62,* 229–258.

Moss., P. A., Beck, J. S., Ebbs, C., Matson, B., Muchmore, J., Steele, D., Taylor, C., & Herter, R. (1992). Portfolios, accountability, and an interpretive approach to validity. *Educational Measurement: Issues and Practice, 11*(3), 12–21.

Murphy, S. (1998). *Fragile evidence: A critique of reading assessment.* Mahwah, NJ: Lawrence Erlbaum.

National Assessment of Educational Progress (NAEP). (2009). *Here comes the sun.* Released item, Grade 4. Available from http://nationsreportcard.gov/science_2009/ict_tasks.asp

National Association for the Education of Young Children (NAEYC). (2003). *Early childhood curriculum, assessment, and program evaluation.* Available from http://www.naeyc.org/

National Center on Educational Outcomes. (2011). *2009 state policies on assessment participation and accommodations for students with disabilities.* Available from http://cehd.umn.edu/NCEO

National Center on Educational Outcomes. (2011, March). Don't forget accommodations! Five questions to ask when moving to technology-based assessments (NCEO Brief #1). Minneapolis, MN: University of Minnesota, National Center on Educational Outcomes.

National Council on Measurement in Education (NCME). (1995). *Code of professional responsibilities in educational measurement (CPR)*. Available from http://ncme.org/resource-center/code-of-professional-responsibilities-in-educational-measurement/

National Governors Association Center for Best Practices & Council of Chief State School Officers. (2010). *Common Core State Standards*. Washington D.C.: Author.

Neal, M. R. (2011). *Writing assessment and the revolution in digital texts and technologies*. New York: Teachers College Press.

Newman, R. (1997–1998). Parent conferences: A conversation between you and your child's teacher. *Childhood Education, 74*, 100–101.

Ng, E. M. W., & Lai, Y. C. (2012). An exploratory study on using wiki to foster student teachers' learner-centered learning and self and peer assessment. *Journal of Information Technology Education: Innovations in Practice, 11*, 71–84.

Nichols, S. L., & Berliner, D. C. (2008). Why has high-stakes testing so easily slipped into contemporary American life? *Phi Delta Kappan, 89*(9), 672–676.

Nitko, A. J. (1989). Designing tests that are integrated with instruction. In R. L. Linn (Ed.), *Educational measurement* (3rd ed., pp. 447–474). New York: Macmillan.

Nitko, A. J. (1995). Curriculum-based continuous assessment: A framework for concepts, politics, and procedures. *Assessment in Education: Principles, Policy, and Practice, 2*, 321–337.

Nitko, A. J., & Hsu, T-C. (1987). *Teacher's guide to better classroom testing: A judgmental approach*. Pittsburgh, PA: Institute for Practice and Research in Education, School of Education, University of Pittsburgh.

No Child Left Behind Act of 2001. Pub. L. No. 107–110, 115 Stat. 1425 (2002).

Norris, S. P., & Ennis, R. H. (1989). *Evaluating critical thinking*. Pacific Grove, CA: Midwest Publications, Critical Thinking Press.

Northwest Evaluation Association (NWEA). (2011, February). *Technical manual for Measures of Academic Progress® (MAP®) and Measures of Academic Progress for Primary Grades (MPG)*. Portland, OR: Author.

Northwest Evaluation Association. (2012, January). *RIT Scale Norms Study: For use with Northwest Evaluation Association Measures of Academic Progress® (MAP®) and MAP for Primary Grades*. Portland, OR: Author.

Northwest Regional Educational Laboratory. (1998). *Improving classroom assessment: A toolkit for professional developers* (2nd ed.). Portland, OR: Author.

O'Leary, T. M., Hattic, J. A. C., & Griffin, P. (2017). Actual interpretations and use of scores as aspects of validity. *Educational Measurement: Issues and Practice, 36*(2), 16–23.

Parkes, J. (2007). Reliability as argument. *Educational Measurement: Issues and Practice, 26*(4), 2–10.

Parkes, J., & Stevens, J. J. (2003). Legal issues in school accountability systems. *Applied Measurement in Education, 16*, 141–158.

Partnership for 21st Century Skills. (2009). *Framework for 21st century learning*. Retrieved November 24, 2012, from http://www.p21.org/

Pearson. (1992). *Integrated Assessment System: Science Performance Assessment*. San Antonio, TX: Author.

Pearson. (2003). *Otis-Lennon School Ability Test (8th ed.) Levels E/F/G. Directions for administering*. San Antonio, TX: Author.

Pearson. (2007). *Stanford Achievement Test Series (10th ed.): 2007 fall supplemental multilevel norms book*. San Antonio, TX: Author.

Pearson. (2008). *WISC-IV and WIAT-II test scores. Report to parents/guardians*.

Pearson. (2009). *Otis-Lennon School Ability Test (8th ed.) Assessing the Abilities That Relate to Success in School*. Retrieved April 10, 2009, from http://pearsonassess.com/hai/images/dotCom/olsat8/OLSAT_Brochure.pdf

Pearson Education. (1991). *The Differential Aptitude Tests* (5th ed., Fall norms booklet). San Antonio, TX: Author.

Pearson, K. (1924). Historical note on the origin of the normal curve of errors. *Biometrika, 16*, 402–404.

Pellegrino, J. W., Chudowsky, N., & Glaser, R. (2001). *Knowing what students know*. Washington, DC: National Academy Press.

Pennock-Roman, M., & Rivera, C. (2011). Mean effects of test accommodations for ELLs and Non-ELLs: A meta-analysis of experimental studies. *Educational Measurement: Issues and Practice, 30*(3), 10–28.

Penuel, W. R., & Shepard, L. A. (2016). Assessment and teaching. In D. H. Gitomer & C. A. Bell (Eds.), *Handbook of research on teaching* (5th ed.) (pp. 787–850). Washington, DC: American Educational Research Association.

Perie, M., Marion, S., & Gong, B. (2007). *A framework for considering interim assessments*. National Center for the Improvement of Educational Assessment. Dover, NH: NCIEA. Available from *http://www.nciea.org*

Perl, J. (1995). *Improving relationship skills for parent conferences. Teaching Exceptional Children, 28*(1), 29–31.

Phillips, S. E. (1994). High-stakes testing accommodations: Validity versus disabled rights. *Applied Measurement in Education, 7*, 93–120.

Phillips, S. E. (2005, June). Legal corner: Reconciling IDEA and NCLB. *NCME Newsletter, 13*(2). Available from http://www.ncme.org/pubs/vol13_2_June2005.pdf

Popham, W. J. (2005, March). Wyoming's instructionally supportive NCLB Tests. *NCME Newsletter, 13*(1). Available from http://www.ncme.org/pubs/vol13_1_Mar2005.pdf

Porter, A. C., McMaken, J., Hwang, J., & Yang, R. (2011). Common Core Standards: The new U.S. intended curriculum. *Educational Researcher, 40*, 103–116.

Porter, A. C., & Smithson, J. L. (2001). Are content standards being implemented in the classroom? A methodology and some tentative answers. In S. H. Fuhrman (Ed.), *From the capitol to the classroom: Standards-based reform in the states—One hundredth yearbook of the National Society for the Study of Education, Part II* (pp. 60–80). Chicago: University of Chicago Press.

Porter, T. M. (1995). *Trust in numbers: The pursuit of objectivity in science and public life*. Princeton, NJ: Princeton University Press.

Power, B. M., & Chandler, K. (1998). *Well-chosen words*. York, ME: Stenhouse.

Pretz, M. E., Naples, A. J., & Sternberg, R. J. (2003). Recognizing, defining, and representing problems. In Davidson, J. E., & Sternberg, R. J. (Eds.). *The psychology of problem solving* (pp. 3–30). New York: Cambridge University Press.

Purves, A. C. (1971). Evaluation of learning in literature. In B. S. Bloom, J. T. Hastings, & G. F. Madaus (Eds.), *Handbook on formative and summative evaluation of student learning* (pp. 697–766). New York: McGraw-Hill.

Quellmalz, E. S. (1991). Developing criteria for performance assessments: The missing link. *Applied Measurement in Education, 4,* 319–331.

Rabinowitz, S., Roeber, E., Schroeder, C., & Sheinker, J. (2006). *Creating aligned standards and assessment systems.* Washington, DC: Council of Chief State School Officers. Retrieved July 31, 2012, from http://ccsso.org/Documents/2006/Creating_Aligned_Standards_2006.pdf

Raphael, T. E., & Au, K. H. (2005). QAR: Enhancing comprehension and test taking across grades and content areas. *Reading Teacher, 59,* 206–221.

Reardon, S. F., Greenberg, E., Kalogrides, D., Shores, K. A., & Valentino, R. A. (2012). *Trends in academic achievement gaps in the era of No Child Left Behind.* Presented at the Spring Conference of the Society for Research on Educational Effectiveness. ERIC Document No. ED 530 121

Reed, B., & Railsback, J. (2003, May). *Strategies and resources for mainstream teachers of English language learners.* Portland, OR: Northwest Regional Educational Laboratory.

Reese, M., & Levy, R. (2009). *Assessing the future: E-portfolio trends, uses, and options in higher education.* Boulder, CO: Educause. Retrieved January 21, 2013, from http://www.educause.com

Renwick, M. (2014). *Digital student portfolios: A whole school approach to connected learning and continuous assessment.* Virginia Beach, VA: Powerful Learning Press.

Robertson, G. J. (1990). A practical model for test development. In C. R. Reynolds & R. W. Kamphaus (Eds.), *Handbook of psychological and educational assessment of children: Intelligence and achievement* (pp. 62–85). New York: Guilford Press.

Rodriguez, M. C. (2005). Three options are optimal for multiple-choice items: A meta-analysis of 80 years of research. *Educational Measurement: Issues and Practice, 24*(2), 3–13.

Ross, J. A., Rolheiser, C., & Hogaboam-Gray, A. (2002). Influences on student cognitions about evaluation. *Assessment in Education, 9,* 81–95.

Rotheram, B. (2009, March). *Sounds Good final report.* Leeds, UK: Leeds Metropolitan University. Retrieved October 30, 2012, from http://sites.google.com/site/soundsgooduk/

Rozeboom, W. W. (1966). Scaling theory and the nature of measurement. *Synthese, 16,* 170–233.

Rudner, L. M., & Boston, C. (1994). Performance assessment. *The ERIC Review, 3*(1), 2–12.

Rulon, P. J. (1939). A simplified procedure for determining the reliability of a test by split halves. *Harvard Educational Review, 9,* 99–103.

Ryan, R. M., & Deci, E. L. (2000). Self-determination theory and the facilitation of intrinsic motivation, social development, and well-being. *American Psychologist, 55,* 68–78.

Sadler, D. R. (1983). Evaluation and the improvement of academic learning. *Journal of Higher Education, 54,* 60–79.

Sadler, D. R. (1989). Formative assessment and the design of instructional systems. *Instructional Science, 18,* 119–144.

Sadler, P. M., & Good, E. (2006). The impact of self- and peer-grading on student learning. *Educational Assessment, 11,* 1–31.

Salend, S. (2009). Using technology to create and administer accessible tests. *TEACHING Exceptional Children, 41*(3), 40–51.

Salvia, J., & Ysseldyke, J. E. (2004). *Assessment in special and inclusive education* (9th ed.). Boston: Houghton Mifflin.

Sanders, N. M. (1966). *Classroom questions: What kinds?* New York: Harper & Row.

Sanders, W. L., & Horn, S, P. (1994). The Tennessee Value-Added Assessment System (TVAAS): Mixed-model methodology in educational assessment. *Journal of Personnel Evaluation in Education, 12,* 247–256.

Sarason, I. G. (1984). Stress, anxiety, and cognitive inference: Reactions to tests. *Journal of Personality and Social Psychology, 46,* 929–938.

Sarnacki, R. E. (1979). An examination of test-wiseness in the cognitive test domain. *Review of Educational Research, 49,* 252–279.

Sattler, J. M. (1992). *Assessment of children: WSC-III and WPPSI-R supplement.* San Diego, CA: Author.

Schafer, W. D., Lissitz, R. W., Zhu, X., Zhang, Y., Hou, X., & Li, Y. (2012). Evaluating teachers and schools using student growth models. *Practical Assessment, Research and Evaluation, 17*(17).

Schraw, G., & Robinson, D. R. (Eds.) (2011). *Assessment of higher order thinking skills.* Charlotte, NC: Information Age Publishing.

Schutz, P. A., Distefano, C., Benson, J., & Davis, H. A. (2004). The Emotional Regulation During Test-taking scale. *Anxiety, Stress, and Coping, 17,* 253–269.

Scriven, M. (1967). *The methodology of evaluation.* AERA monograph series on curriculum evaluation (Publication No. 1). Chicago: Rand McNally.

Shavelson, R. J., & Baxter, G. P. (1991). Performance assessment in science. *Applied Measurement in Education, 4,* 347–362.

Shavelson, R. J., & Stern, P. (1981). Research on teachers' pedagogical thoughts, judgments, decisions, and behavior. *Review of Educational Research, 51,* 455–498.

Shepard, L. A. (1990). Inflated test score gains: Is the problem old norms or teaching the test? *Educational Measurement: Issues and Practice, 9*(3), 15–22.

Shepard, L. A. (2006). Classroom assessment. In R. L. Brennan (Ed.), *Educational measurement* (4th ed., pp. 623–646). Westport, CT: Praeger.

Shepard, L. A. (2008). Formative assessment: Caveat emptor. In C. A. Dwyer (Ed.), *The future of assessment: Shaping teaching and learning.* New York: Lawrence Erlbaum.

Shulruf, B., Hattie, J., & Dixon, R. (2008). Factors affecting responses to Likert type questionnaires: Introduction of the ImpExp, a new comprehensive model. *Social Psychology of Education, 11,* 59–78.

Shute, V. J. (2008). Focus on formative feedback. *Review of Educational Research, 78,* 153–189.

Sireci, S. G. (2005). Unlabeling the disabled: A perspective on flagging scores from accommodated test administrations. *Educational Researcher, 34*(1), 3–12.

Sireci, S. G., Scarpati, S. E., & Li, S. (2005). Test accommodations for students with disabilities: An analysis of the interaction hypothesis. *Review of Educational Research, 75,* 457–490.

Slavin, R. E. (1988). Cooperative learning and student achievement. *Educational Leadership, 46*(2), 31–33.

Smith, J., & Walker, J. (2002). Using electronic gradebooks. *Principal, 82*(2), 64–65.

Smith, M. L. (1997). *Reforming schools by reforming assessment: Consequences of the Arizona Student Assessment Program*

(ASAP): Equity and teacher capacity building (CSE Technical Report 425). Los Angeles: National Center for Research on Evaluation, Standards, and Student Testing, UCLA.

Snow, R. E. (1980). Aptitudes and achievement. In W. B. Schrader (Ed.), *Measuring achievement: Progress over a decade. Proceedings of the 1979 ETS Invitational Conference. New Directions for Testing and Measurement* (No. 5). San Francisco: Jossey-Bass.

Sparrow, S. S., Cicchetti, D. V., & Balla, D., (2016). *Vineland Adaptive Behavior Scales: Third Edition*. Pearson.

Spearman, C. (1910). Correlation calculated from faulty data. *British Journal of Psychology, 3*, 271–295.

Spearman, C. E. (1927). *The abilities of man, their nature and measurement*. New York: Macmillan.

Stiggins, R. J. (1991). Assessment literacy. *Phi Delta Kappan, 72*, 534–539.

Stiggins, R. J., Conklin, N. F., & Associates. (1992). *In teachers' hands: Investigating the practice of classroom assessment*. Albany: SUNY Press.

Stiggins, R. J., Frisbie, D. A., & Griswold, P. A. (1989). Inside high school grading practices: Building a research agenda. *Educational Measurement: Issues and Practice, 8*(2), 5–14.

Stiggins, R. J., Rubel, E., & Quellmalz, E. (1986). *Measuring thinking skills in the classroom*. Washington, DC: National Educational Association.

Struyven, K., Dochy, F., & Janssens, S. (2005). Student perceptions about evaluation and assessment in higher education: A review. *Assessment and Evaluation in Higher Education, 30*, 325–341.

Subkoviak, M. J. (1976). Estimating reliability from a single administration of a criterion-referenced test. *Journal of Educational Measurement, 13*, 265–276.

Subkoviak, M. J. (1980). Decision consistency approaches. In R. A. Berk (Ed.), *Criterion-referenced measurement: The state of the art*. Baltimore: Johns Hopkins University Press.

Sudweeks, R. R., Reeve, S., & Bradshaw, W. S. (2004). A comparison of generalizability theory and many-facet Rasch measurement in an analysis of college sophomore writing. *Assessing Writing, 9*, 239–261.

Suen, H. K. (2012). *Kuder® Career Interests Assessment™ 2012 (KCIA-32 2012) technical brief*. Adel, IA: Kuder Inc.

Supovitz, J. (2009). Can high stakes testing leverage educational improvement? Prospects from the last decade of testing and accountability reform. *Journal of Educational Change, 10*, 211–227.

Swaminathan, H., Hambleton, R. K., & Algina, J. (1974). Reliability of criterion-referenced tests: A decision-theoretic formulation. *Journal of Educational Measurement, 11*, 263–267.

Swiderek, B. (1997). Parent conferences. *Journal of Adolescent and Adult Literacy, 40*, 580–581.

Tallmadge, G. K., & Wood, C. T. (1976). *User's guide* (ESEA Title I Evaluation and Reporting System). Mountain View, CA: RMC Research Corporation.

Taylor, C. S. (1998). An investigation of scoring methods for mathematics performance-based assessments. *Educational Assessment, 5*, 195–224.

Thompson, S. J., Johnstone, C. J., & Thurlow, M. L. (2002). *Universal design applied to large scale assessments* (Synthesis Report 44). Minneapolis: University of Minnesota, National Center on Educational Outcomes. Retrieved January 9, 2009, from http://education.umn.edu/NCEO/OnlinePubs/Synthesis44.html

Thorndike, E. L. (1910). Handwriting. *Teachers College Record, 11*, 1–93.

Thorndike, R. L. (1951). Reliability. In E. F. Lindquist (Ed.), *Educational measurement*. Washington, DC: American Council on Education.

Thorndike, R. M., Cunningham, G. K., Thorndike, R. L., & Hagen, E. P. (1991). *Measurement and evaluation in psychology and education* (5th ed.). New York: Macmillan.

Tourangeau, R., Couper, M. P., & Conrad, F. (2004). Spacing, position, and order: Interpretive heuristics for visual features of survey questions. *Public Opinion Quarterly, 68*, 368–393.

Tunstall, P., & Gipps, C. (1996). Teacher feedback to young children in formative assessment: A typology. *British Educational Research Journal, 22*, 389–404.

Turner, J. C., Thorpe, P. K., & Meyer, D. K. (1998). Students' reports of motivation and negative affect: A theoretical and empirical analysis. *Journal of Educational Psychology, 90*, 758–771.

Ujifusa, A. (2012, June 6). New tests put states on hot seat as scores plunge. *Education Week, 31*(33), 1, 24.

United States Supreme Court. (1971). *Griggs et al., Petitioners v. Duke Power Company* (Publication No. 125, 401 U.S. 424, decided March 8, 1971).

U.S. Department of Education. (2005, May 10). *New flexibility for states raising achievement for students with disabilities*. No Child Left Behind. Available from http://www.ed.gov/policy/elsec/guid/raising/disab-factsheet.pdf

U.S. Department of Education. (2012, June 7). *ESEA flexibility*. Retrieved July 24, 2012, from http://www.ed.gov/esea/flexibility

U.S. Department of Education. (n.d.). *Accountability*. Available from http://www.ed.gov/nclb/accountability/index.html

U.S. Department of Health and Human Services (USDHHS). (2005, June). *Protection of Human Subjects* (CFR 45, Part 46). Available from http://www.hhs.gov/ohrp/humansubjects/guidance/45cfr46.htm

Valencia, S. W., & Place, N. A. (1994). Literacy portfolios for teaching, learning, and accountability: The Bellevue Literacy Assessment Project. In S. W. Valencia, E. H. Hiebert, & P. P. Afferbach (Eds.), *Authentic reading assessment: Practices and possibilities*. Newark, DE: International Reading Association.

Van der Kleij, F. M., Feskens, R. C. W., & Eggen, T. J. H. M. (2015). Effects of feedback in a computer-based learning environment on students' learning outcomes: A meta-analysis. *Review of Educational Research, 85*, 475–511.

Viadero, D. (1995). New assessments have little effect on contract, study finds. *Education Week, 14*(40), 6.

Wainer, H., & Thissen, D. (1994). On examinee choice in educational testing. *Review of Educational Research, 64*, 159–195.

Waltman, K. K., & Frisbie, D. A. (1994). Parents understanding of their children's report cards. *Applied Measurement in Education, 2*, 223–240.

Wang, X., Wainer, H., & Thissen, D. (1995). On the viability of some untestable assumptions in equating exams that allow examinee choice. *Applied Measurement in Education, 8*, 211–225.

Webb, N. L. (1997). *Criteria for alignment of expectations and assessments in mathematics and science education*. Council of Chief State School Officers and National Institute for

ScienceEducation. Madison, WI: Wisconsin Center for Education Research, University of Wisconsin.

Webb, N. M. , Herman, J. L., & Webb, N. L. (2007). Alignment of mathematics state-level standards and assessments: The role of reviewer agreement. *Educational Measurement: Issues and Practice, 26*(2), 17–29.

Welsh, M. E., & D'Agostino, J. V. (2009). Fostering consistency between standards-based grades and large-scale assessment results. In T. R. Guskey (Ed.), *Practical solutions for serious problems in standards-based grading* (pp. 75–104). Thousand Oaks, CA: Corwin Press.

Wesman, A. G. (1971). Writing the test item. In R. L. Thorndike (Ed.), *Educational measurement* (2nd ed.). Washington, DC: American Council on Education.

Wiliam, D. (2007). Content *then* process: Teacher learning communities in the service of formative assessment. In D. Reeves (Ed.), *Ahead of the curve: The power of assessment to transform teaching and learning* (pp. 183–204). Bloomington, IN: Solution Tree.

Wiliam, D. (2010). An integrative summary of the research literature and implications for a new theory of formative assessment. In Andrade, H. L., & Cizek, G. J. (Eds.), *Handbook of formative assessment* (pp. 18–40).

Wiliam, D. (2011). *Embedded formative assessment*. Bloominton, IN: Solution Tree.

Willingham, W. W., & Cole, N. S. (1997). *Gender and fair assessment*. Mahwah, NJ: Erlbaum.

Wilson, M., & Draney, K. (2004). Some links between large-scale and classroom assessments: The case of the BEAR assessment system. In M. Wilson (Ed.), *Towards coherence between classroom assessment and accountability* (pp. 132–154). Chicago, IL: 103rd Yearbook of the National Society for the Study of Education, Volume II.

Wise, S. L. (1996, April). *A critical analysis of the arguments for and against item review in computerized adaptive testing*. Paper presented at the annual meeting of the National Council on Measurement in Education, New York.

Woolfolk, A. (2005). *Educational psychology* (9th ed.). Boston: Allyn & Bacon.

Wormeli, R. (2006). *Fair isn't always equal: Assessing and grading in the differentiated classroom*. Portland, ME: Stenhouse, and Westerville, OH: National Middle School Association.

Xu, Y., & Brown, G. T. L. (2016). Teacher assessment literacy in practice: A reconceptualization. *Teaching and Teacher Education, 58*, 149–162.

Young, M. J., & Zucker, S. (2004). *The standards-referenced interpretive framework: Using assessments for multiple purposes* (Pearson Assessment Report). San Antonio, TX: Pearson. Available from http://pearsonassess.com/NR/rdonlyres/1AD36406-3B2A-491C-A280-D4A47D3121E8/0/InterpretiveFrameworks.pdf

Zeidner, M. (1998). *Test anxiety: The state of the art*. New York: Plenum Press.

Zimmerman, B. J., & Schunk, D. H. (Eds.) (2011). *Handbook of self-regulation of learning and performance*. New York: Routledge.

Zucker, S., Sassman, C., & Case, B. J. (2004). *Cognitive labs (Pearson Technical Report)*. San Antonio, TX: Pearson. Available from http://pearsonassess.com/NR/rdonlyres/E5CD33E6-D234-46F3-885A-9358575372FB/0/CognitiveLabs_Final.pdf

Name Index

Subject Index